Reuben A. Giuld

History of Brown University

With Illustrative Documents

Reuben A. Giuld

History of Brown University
With Illustrative Documents

ISBN/EAN: 9783743399242

Manufactured in Europe, USA, Canada, Australia, Japa

Cover: Foto ©ninafisch / pixelio.de

Manufactured and distributed by brebook publishing software (www.brebook.com)

Reuben A. Giuld

History of Brown University

HISTORY

OF

BROWN UNIVERSITY,

WITH

ILLUSTRATIVE DOCUMENTS.

BY

REUBEN ALDRIDGE GUILD,

LIBRARIAN OF THE UNIVERSITY,

Author of "Life, Times and Correspondence of James Manning," etc.

<blockquote>
HIC LOCUS ÆTATIS NOSTRÆ PRIMORDIA NOVIT,
ANNOS FELICES, LÆTITIÆQUE DIES.
HIC LOCUS INGENUIS PUERILES IMBUIT ANNOS
ARTIBUS, ET NOSTRÆ LAUDIS ORIGO FUIT.
HIC LOCUS INSIGNES MAGNOSQUE CREAVIT ALUMNOS.
Neckham.
</blockquote>

PROVIDENCE, R. I.
1867.

Published by Subscription.
THREE HUNDRED COPIES, LARGE PAPER, TEN COPIES.

Entered according to an Act of Congress, in the year 1867,

BY REUBEN ALDRIDGE GUILD,

In the Clerk's Office of the District Court of the United States for the District of Rhode Island.

PROVIDENCE PRESS COMPANY, PRINTERS.

TO

THE ALUMNI

OF

Brown University

THIS WORK IS RESPECTFULLY DEDICATED

BY

THE AUTHOR.

ENGRAVINGS.

1. VIEW OF THE COLLEGE GREEN AND HALLS IN 1840.   Frontispiece.
2. PORTRAIT OF PRESIDENT MANNING. - - - - - - Page 7
3. PORTRAIT OF NICHOLAS BROWN. - - - - - - " 28
4. PORTRAIT OF PRESIDENT WAYLAND. - - - - - " 43
5. SEAL OF THE UNIVERSITY. - - - - - - - " 62
6. UNIVERSITY HALL. - - - - - - - - - " 229
7. FIRST BAPTIST CHURCH. - - - - - - - " 247
8. HOPE COLLEGE. - - - - - - - - - " 261
9. MANNING HALL. - - - - - - - - - " 265
10. RHODE ISLAND HALL. - - - - - - - - " 271
11. PRESIDENT'S HOUSE. - - - - - - - " 277
12. NEW LABORATORY. - - - - - - - - - " 279

PREFACE.

In my former work* I have endeavored to present a full and accurate account of the origin and early progress of Brown University, in connection with the life, times and correspondence of him whose personal history is thoroughly identified with the history of the Institution over which he presided for more than a quarter of a century;—and of which he may, in a certain sense, be justly regarded as the founder.

A desire to continue this account down to the present time, and thus preserve, in the form of documentary history, some of the interesting manuscripts and rare printed sheets, which I have been enabled to collect during the nineteen years of my official connection with the University, has led to the publication of this work. A prominent object with me has been to gather up from documents and files of papers long since forgotten, as well as from those of a more recent date, the names of all persons, who, by their benefactions, have aided the College, and to place them on

---

*MANNING AND BROWN UNIVERSITY; or, LIFE, TIMES AND CORRESPONDENCE OF JAMES MANNING, AND THE EARLY HISTORY OF BROWN UNIVERSITY. 12mo. Boston: Gould & Lincoln. 1864. pp. 523.

permanent record, that so they may be transmitted to posterity. In accordance with this plan a careful index of such names has been added to the work.

The indulgent reader will pardon an occasional reference to my life of Manning, instead of a needless repetition of what is already in print. The preface to this work, I may add, contains an account of the acquisition of the Manning Papers, together with the various pamphlets, sheets and manuscript documents from which, in addition to the files and records of the Corporation, the present history has been mainly compiled. In some of the documents now for the first time published, I have ventured to change slightly the orthography and grammatical form of expression, but in no case have I made material alterations, or given any other than the real meaning and sense.

Several errors, partly typographical, have been discovered while the sheets were passing though the press, reminding me of what a modern bibliographer has said: " If you are troubled with a pride of accuracy and would have it completely taken out of you, print a catalogue."

The undertaking, like my former one, has been entered upon with diffidence, and continued from year to year, under all the disadvantages of numerous and exacting public and professional duties, and amidst frequent interruptions. In the confident hope that it may stimulate the graduates and friends of the Institution to renewed exertions on its behalf, the HISTORY OF BROWN UNIVERSITY, with all its faults of omission and commission, is now submitted to a generous and discerning public.

R. A. G.

Brown University, May 4, 1867.

CONTENTS.

HISTORICAL SKETCH
PAGES 1-62.

ORIGIN of Brown University—Isaac Eaton and the Hopewell Academy—Philadelphia Association—Morgan Edwards—First movement to establish a College in Rhode Island—James Manning selected as leader—Arrival at Newport—Charter granted by the General Assembly—Warren selected for the Location of the College—Manning begins a Latin School and founds a Church—Appointed President by the Corporation—David Howell—First Commencement—William Rogers—College removed to Providence—College Edifice—Interruptions during the War—Manning's Matriculation Roll of Students—Appointed Representative to Congress—Death—Howell's account of Manning—Goddard's account—Manning's history of the College in 1773—Jones's letter to Howell respecting Manning's Successor—Jonathan Maxcy appointed President—His administration—Resignation—Death—Elton's account of Maxcy—Succeeded by Asa Messer—His administration—College named Brown University—Nicholas Brown—Messer's resignation and death—Sears's account of Messer—Park's account—Succeeded by Francis Wayland—His administration—Adoption of the New System—Resignation—Tobey's remarks thereon to the Corporation—Resolutions of the Alumni—Thomas's remarks at the Commencement Dinner—Wayland's Death—Caswell's remarks at the funeral—Extracts from Bartol's sermon on Wayland—Succeeded by Barnas Sears—His administration—Extract from Sears's Centennial Discourse—Tabular view of the Graduates under the different Presidents—Review of the Triennial Catalogue—Justices of the Supreme Court—Governors and Lieutenant Governors—Senators and Representatives to Congress—Doctors of Divinity—Doctors of Law—Diplomatists, Orators and Statesmen—Presidents of Colleges—Trustees and Fellows—Roll of Honor, or List of Students who were in the recent War—Seal of the Corporation.

HISTORY OF THE LIBRARY.

PAGES 63-116.

Library in 1770—Manning's Account of two years later—Books presented by Jos. D. Russell—Donations from John Gill and Benj. Wallin, of London—Library removed to Wrentham during the Revolutionary War—Asher Robbins appointed Librarian in 1782—Library at this time contained five hundred volumes—Fourteen hundred volumes presented in 1784, by John Brown—List of books presented by Moses Brown—Books presented by John Tanner, of Newport, and Granville Sharp, of London—Donation from the Bristol Education Society—By-laws adopted by the Corporation in 1785—Extracts from the records, 1787-93—Law Library presented in 1792, by Nicholas Brown—Extracts from the records, 1794-6—Letter from George Benson—Extracts from the records, 1805-7—Books bequeathed by Isaac Backus—Donation from Thomas Carlile, of Salem—Legacy of William Richards, of Lynn, England—Subscription of 1825—Metcalf Collection of Pamphlets—Account of the Library Fund, with names of subscribers—Manning Hall erected in 1834—Catalogue published in 1843—Gammell's account of the Library in 1844—Subscription for the purchase of English books—Jewett's account of the French, German, Italian and English books purchased by him in Europe in 1844-5—Shakspeariana—Moses B. Ives—Donations of John Carter Brown—Donation from the Class of 1821—Patristic works added to the Library in 1847—Lincoln's account of purchases made in 1851, at the Jarvis sale—Tallmadge bequest of one thousand dollars—New Library building needed—Books presented by Geronimo Urmeneta, of Chili—Donation from the late Dr. Crocker—List of Architectural works belonging to the Library—Libraries of College Professors—Library of John Carter Brown—Librarians and Assistant Librarians—Regulations and By-laws.

HISTORY OF THE CHARTER.

PAGES 117-146.

Early history of the Charter one of struggle against opposing influences—Manning's narrative—Arrives at Newport in 1763 and unfolds his plans for a Baptist College—Committee appointed to draw up a Charter, and Dr. Stiles requested to assist them—The Charter so drawn as to throw the governing power into the hands of the Presbyterians or Congregationalists—Kingsley's statements respecting Dr. Stiles and Wm. Ellery—Petition for a Charter submitted to the General Assembly in August, 1763—Action upon the Charter deferred and a new Charter drawn by a Committee sent to Newport from Philadelphia—Alterations made by this Committee enumerated—Judge Jenckes's history of the Charter—Original Charter lost—Found, and presented to the University by Dr. Sprague, in 1864—Summary of the main points involved in

CONTENTS. ix

the history of the Charter—Extract from a letter of Morgan Edwards to President Manning—Charter given in full—Provision exempting from taxation the estates, persons and families of the President and Professors—Early controversy respecting—Of late years revived—Resolution of the City Council of Newport in 1862—Action thereon by the General Assembly—Joint action of the General Assembly and the Corporation of the University—President and Professors now exempted from taxation to the amount of ten thousand dollars—Names and residences of the Corporation in 1770 and 1867, classified according to the four religious denominations specified in the Charter.

SUBSCRIPTIONS OBTAINED BY MORGAN EDWARDS.
PAGES 147-171.

Measures taken at the first meeting of the Corporation to endow the infant College—Morgan Edwards requested to solicit subscriptions—Resolves to go on a mission to Great Britain and Ireland—Authorization by President Manning and Vice-Chancellor Ward—Letter to the General Assembly of the Church of Scotland, commending Mr. Edwards and his mission—He sets out for Europe in February, 1767—Well received in England—Letter to President Manning reporting progress in obtaining subscriptions—Names of subscribers in Ireland—Ditto in England—Returns to America in the latter part of 1768—Reports to the Corporation in 1769—Amount raised about forty-five hundred dollars—Original subscription book now among the archives of the University—Name of Morgan Edwards prominent in the early history of the College—Particulars respecting his early life and professional career—Extracts respecting, from letters of Francis Pelot and Oliver Hart—Extract from his funeral sermon by Dr. Rogers, published in Rippon's BAPTIST ANNUAL REGISTER.

FINAL LOCATION.
PAGES 172-210.

Important question, soon after the founding of the College, in regard to the most desirable place for its Location—Edwards's narrative of the struggle respecting Location—First mention of Location in the records of the Corporation—Vote in September, 1769, that the College be in some part of the County of Bristol—Special meeting of the Corporation called on account of subscriptions having been opened for placing the College in the County of Kent—Struggle thus far confined to Warren and East Greenwich—Moses Brown first suggests that the College be at Providence—Governor Sessions's views respecting Location—Meeting of the Corporation held at Newport, November 14, 1769, and continued three days—Memorial from Providence, presented on the second day of the meeting—Memorial from East Greenwich, presented on the last day of the meeting—Article published in the NEWPORT MERCURY, showing why the College should be located in Newport—Redwood Library—Extract from the Diary of Dr. Stiles—Main contest henceforward between Providence and Newport—Preamble to the Newport subscription book—Letter from a Judge in Kent County declaring his preference for Providence—Communication from Governor Hopkins and the Browns addressed to the town councils of Glocester and Scituate—Letter from Nicholas Brown & Co. to Joseph Brown at Newport—Extract from the PROVIDENCE GAZETTE—Call for another meeting of the Corporation—Printed handbills circulated in Providence—Meeting of the inhabitants at the Court House—Anonymous letter from President Manning addressed to Nicholas Brown—Final meeting of the Corporation on the question of Location, held at Warren, February 7, 1770—Manning's account of the meeting—Memorial presented from East Greenwich—Ditto from Providence—Gov. Hopkins's statement of the rival claims of Providence and Newport—Ward and Hopkins controversy—Moses Brown's account of the final meeting at Warren—Movement on part of the defeated contestants to establish a second college at Newport—Remonstrance from the Corporation to the Legislature respecting—Movement defeated—Letter from Moses Brown respecting file of papers relating to the Location of the College, and also respecting Roger Williams and the First Baptist Church.

SUBSCRIPTIONS OBTAINED BY HEZEKIAH SMITH.
PAGES 211—226.

Hezekiah Smith requested by the Corporation to solicit benefactions for the College in the South—Credentials from Chancellor Hopkins and President Manning—Biographical sketch of Smith—Leaves home on his mission October 2, 1769, and returns June 8, 1770—Collects about twenty-five hundred dollars in South Carolina and Georgia—Diary during his absence from home—Letter from Oliver Hart to President Manning—Names of Subscribers—Extracts from Southern newspapers—Smith's report to the Corporation—Money obtained mostly expended upon the College buildings.

ACCOUNT OF THE COLLEGE BUILDINGS.
1. University Hall.
PAGES 227–246.

First mention of a College building in Smith's diary for 1765—Committee on a building appointed in 1768—Report to the Corporation in 1769—Plan of a building adopted February 9, 1770—Home-lot of Chad Brown purchased for the location—Extracts from the Record of Deeds—Plan of the building adopted by the Committee, and approved by the Corporation, that of NASSAU HALL, Princeton—Corner Stone

CONTENTS. xi

laid May 14, 1770—Manning's description of the building—Extracts from the records of the Corporation—Account of Nicholas Brown & Co., submitted to the Corporation September 5, 1771—Extracts from the original account of "sundry supplies," illustrating the progress of the building, and the customs of our ancestors—Cost of the original College lands ninety dollars per acre—Names of Subscribers for the College buildings—Extracts from the records—Building occupied for barracks and a hospital during the War—Petition to the General Assembly in 1780, to have the building restored to the Corporation for the uses to which it was dedicated—Letter to Doct. Franklin respecting the Hall, and also giving the history of the College—Remuneration by Congress for damages and loss of rent—Named University Hall in 1823—Recent changes and improvements.

2. Baptist Meeting-House.

PAGES 247-253.

Church founded by Roger Williams in 1639—For more than sixty years without a house of worship—First house built by Pardon Tillinghast in 1700—Second house erected in 1726—Description of this house, and of the mode of worship, at the time of Manning's removal to Providence—Church and Society under the pastoral care of Manning increase in numbers and efficiency—Resolve, in 1774, to build a "meeting-house for the public worship of Almighty God, and also for holding Commencements in"—Old house and lot sold at auction—Mr. John Brown appointed "the committee man for carrying on the building"—John Angell's orchard purchased by Mr. Russell for a lot—Additional expense of purchasing a large lot and building a house sufficiently large to accommodate the College, defrayed by a lottery—Dedication of the house May 28, 1775—Dimensions—Historical discourse by Dr. Caldwell, preached May 28, 1865—Extract from.

3. University Grammar School.

PAGES 254-260.

Latin School opened by Manning in Warren—This School the germ of the College— Removed to Providence in 1770—First carried on in the Brick School House on Meeting street—In 1772 removed to a room on the lower floor of the College edifice—History of the School from this time—Corporation resolve in 1809 to erect a suitable building for the School, and appoint a Committee for this purpose, and to raise by subscription the necessary funds—List of the subscribers' names—Names of teachers—Building enlarged in 1852 by Messrs. Lyon and Frieze—Present condition of the School.

4. Hope College.
PAGES 261-264.

First mention of this building on the records—Corporation resolve in 1821 to erect another College building—Erected in 1822 at the expense of the Hon. Nicholas Brown, and by him presented to the Corporation—Dimensions, master mason, and master builder—Named Hope College in honor of Mrs. Hope Ives, the only surviving sister of the donor—Account of Mrs. Ives—Estimated cost of the building—Came near being destroyed by fire in 1866.

5. Manning Hall.
PAGES 265-270.

This building erected at the expense of the Hon. Nicholas Brown, and by him presented to the Corporation—Named Manning Hall in honor of his distinguished instructor and revered friend President Manning—Dedicated February 4, 1835—Ode by Albert G. Greene—Ode by George Burgess—Estimated cost of the building—Dimensions, architect, master mason, and master builders—Embellished and improved in 1857—Mural tablet in honor of Nicholas Brown—Latin inscription—Tablet in memory of the students and graduates of the University, who have fallen in the recent war—Latin inscription—Names reported by the Committee at the dedication in 1866.

6. Rhode Island Hall.
PAGES 271-276.

Corporation in 1836 appoint a Committee to devise means for the erection of another College building—Committee continued in 1838 and Dr. Wayland added to it—Letter from the Hon. Nicholas Brown, pledging ten thousand dollars towards the object, on condition that an equal amount be obtained by subscription on or before May 1, 1839—Names of subscribers—Most of the amount subscribed by citizens of Providence—Dedicated September 3, 1840—Address by Professor Goddard—Description of the building—Account of the Philosophical and Chemical Apparatus—Recent additions made to this department by Messrs. J. C. Brown and R. H. Ives.

7. President's House.
PAGES 277-278.

Dimensions, and names of builders—Occupied by President Wayland in 1840—Old house opposite removed—College grounds graded and adorned—Brick barn for the accommodation of the President erected in 1854.

8. Chemical Laboratory.

PAGES 279-282.

Advances made in the science of Chemistry create a demand for improved facilities for instruction—This demand met by the Corporation of the University—New Laboratory erected in 1862-3, mainly through the exertions of Professor Hill—Names of subscribers—Description of the building—Appointments of the Laboratory—Extract from the Annual Catalogue.

COLLECTION OF PORTRAITS IN RHODE ISLAND HALL.

PAGES 283—296.

Collection now comprises thirty-one, many of them painted from life—Obtained mainly through the exertions of John R. Bartlett—Descriptive account—Names of subscribers and donors—Communication respecting the portrait of Dr. Crocker, extracted from the records of the Corporation—Communication respecting the marble bust of Dr. Wayland.

FINANCIAL HISTORY OF THE COLLEGE.

1. College Lands.

PAGES 297-302.

First purchase of land in 1770 comprised eight acres—Cost ninety dollars per acre—First addition to the College estate made in 1815—Additions made in 1822, 1826, 1839, 1840, 1843, 1851, and 1860—Boundaries of the College enclosure proper—Entire College lands comprise about fifteen acres—Planting of trees in the "College Park."

2. Agricultural Lands.

PAGES 303-307.

Act passed by Congress in 1862, donating public lands for Agricultural Colleges—Resolutions adopted by the General Assembly accepting the grant of land made to Rhode Island—This land the Legislature propose to transfer to Brown University—Action of a special meeting of the Corporation held January 21, 1863—Matter referred to the Executive Board—Board accept of the transfer—Agreement between the Corporation and the Legislature respecting said transfer—Resolution adopted by the General Assembly, providing for the nomination of State Scholarships at the University—University thus comes into possession of one hundred and twenty thousand acres of land—These lands sold in January, 1865, for fifty thousand dollars.

3. Scholarships.

PAGES 308-313.

Bequest of Nicholas Brown in 1841—Income to be appropriated in the language of the will, "to the charitable purpose of aiding deserving young men in obtaining their education while members of the University"—A portion of this income appropriated in 1842 to be awarded in premiums—Statutes regulating the award of the "University Premiums," adopted by the Corporation in 1850—Corporation vote in 1858 to apply the bequest of Mr. Brown, to Scholarships of one thousand dollars each, the income thereof to be appropriated, "to the charitable purpose of aiding deserving young men in obtaining their education while members of the University"—Recommendation of the Rhode Island Baptist Education Society substituted for that of the late Warren Education Society—President Sears's views in regard to scholarships—List of forty-seven scholarships, and also of five from which no income has yet been received.

4. Aid Fund.

PAGES 314-316.

Letter from William S. Patten, read to the Corporation in September, 1860, stating conditions on which five thousand dollars is donated to the University by Miss Lydia Carpenter, of Pawtucket, as a fund to aid deserving students—Votes of the Corporation respecting—Account of Miss Carpenter—Donation from Seth Padelford.

5. Funds and Treasurers.

PAGES 317-339.

Early subscriptions for the College—John Tillinghast, the first Treasurer—Col. Job Bennet, the second Treasurer—Extracts from Col. Bennet's reports—Names of early benefactors—Resignation of Col. Bennet—Succeeded by John Brown—Character as Treasurer—Resignation in 1796—Letter resigning his place as Trustee to the Corporation in 1803—Names of benefactors taken from Mr. Brown's reports—Benjamin Wallin and Hannah Ward—Mr. Brown succeeded in the Treasurership by his nephew, Nicholas Brown—College named Brown University in 1804—Fund for the establishment of a Professorship of Oratory and Belles-Lettres—In 1825 Mr. Brown elected a Fellow of the University—Succeeded by his nephew, Moses B. Ives—Permanent funds of the University in 1826—Lotteries—Changes in the System of Collegiate instruction in 1850—Property and funds at that time—President Wayland—Subscribers to the fund of one hundred and twenty-five thousand dollars—Bequest of ten thousand dollars from Hon. Nicholas Brown—President's premium fund of one thousand dollars—Abstract from the Treasurer's annual report for September, 1854—Death of Mr. Ives in 1857—Succeeded by his brother, Robert H. Ives—Income of the University insufficient for its current expenses—Accumulation of a debt—Efforts to raise one hundred and fifty thousand dollars—Scholarships—Horace T. Love appointed

CONTENTS. XV

Agent for Brown and Waterville—List of Subscriptions—Bequest of two thousand dollars from William Baylies—Another vigorous effort to raise funds for the University—President Sears—Subscription still in progress—Names of subscribers—Subscription to raise funds to provide for military instruction—Names of subscribers—Resignation of Mr. Ives in 1866—Abstract from the Treasurer's last annual report to the Corporation—Succeeded by Marshall Woods—Statement of the invested funds of the University April 12, 1867—Summary of all the legacies and bequests made to the College during the first century of its existence—Summary of the various subscriptions undertaken in behalf of the College—Extracts from the last will and testament of the Hon. Nicholas Brown.

COMMENCEMENT EXERCISES.
PAGES 340–426.

First Commencement held in Warren in 1769—Names and residences of graduates—Brief sketch of—Order of Exercises of first Commencement—Wearing of gowns and caps begun in 1786—Valedictory and Intermediate Orations formerly assigned by the classes—Tristam Burges—Resolution of the Corporation in 1790 in regard to disorderly practices on Commencement days—Commencement in early days compared with the Commencements of later times—Earliest printed Order of Exercises—Second Commencement held in Providence in 1770—Order of Exercises—"Billy Edwards"—1771, 1772, 1773—Doct. Solomon Drowne—President Manning's Baccalaureate Address—1774—No Commencement in 1775—Order of Exercises for 1776—No Commencement from 1776 until 1783—Order of Exercises for 1783 not preserved—No Commencement in 1784 and 1785—1786, 1787—President Maxcy—1788 to 1791—Judge Howell's Baccalaureate Address—1792 to 1796—Tristam Burges—1797 to 1803—President Messer's Baccalaureate Address—1804 to 1825—President Sears—1826—President Messer—1827—President Wayland—1828 to 1851—New System—1852 to 1855—Resignation of President Wayland—1856—President Sears—1857 to 1866.

APPENDIX.
Resignation of President Sears.
PAGES 427–430.

Dr. Sears appointed General Agent of the Board of Trustees of the PEABODY EDUCATIONAL FUND—Resigns the Presidency of the University—Special meeting of the Corporation—Resignation accepted—Resolutions adopted—President M. B. Anderson, of Rochester University, elected as Dr. Sears's successor—Remarks upon the retiring President.

INDEX OF BENEFACTORS, - - - - - PAGES 431–440.
NAMES OF SUBSCRIBERS, - - - - - " 441–443.

HISTORICAL SKETCH

OF

BROWN UNIVERSITY.

1762–1866.

HISTORICAL SKETCH.

BROWN UNIVERSITY owes its origin to a desire, on the part of members of the Philadelphia Baptist Association, to secure for their churches an educated ministry, without the restrictions of denominational influence and sectarian tests. The distinguishing sentiments of the Baptists, it may be observed, were at variance with the religious opinions that prevailed throughout the American colonies a century ago. They advocated liberty of conscience, the entire separation of church and state, believer's baptism by immersion, and a converted church membership;—principles for which they have earnestly contended from the beginning. The student of history will readily perceive how they thus came into collision with the ruling powers. They were fined in Massachusetts and Connecticut, for resistance to oppressive ecclesiastical laws, they were imprisoned in Virginia, and throughout the land were subjected to contumely and reproach. This dislike to the Baptists as a denomination, or rather to their principles, was very naturally shared by the higher institutions of learning then in existence.*

* Brown University, which was founded in 1764, is the seventh American college, in the order of date. Harvard College was founded in 1638; William and Mary, in 1692; Yale, in 1701; College of New Jersey, in 1746; University of Pennsylvania, in 1753; and Columbia College, in 1754.

In the year 1756, the Rev. Isaac Eaton, under the auspices of the Philadelphia and Charleston Associations, founded at Hopewell, New Jersey, an academy "for the education of youth for the ministry." To him, therefore, belongs the distinguished honor of being the first American Baptist to establish a seminary for the literary and theological training of young men. The Hopewell Academy, which was committed to the general supervision of a board of trustees, appointed by the two above mentioned associations, and supported mainly by funds which they contributed, was continued eleven years. During this period, many, who afterwards became eminent in the ministry, received within its quiet shades the rudiments of an education. Among them may be mentioned the names of James Manning, Hezekiah Smith, Samuel Stillman, Samuel Jones, John Gano, Oliver Hart, Charles Thompson, William Williams, Isaac Skillman, John Davis, Robert Keith, David Jones, David Thomas, John Sutton, David Sutton, John Blackwell, Joseph Powell, William Worth and Levi Bonnel. Not a few of Mr. Eaton's students distinguished themselves in the professions of medicine and of law. Of this latter class was the late Hon. Judge Howell, a name familiar to the early students of Rhode Island College, and to the statesmen and politicians of that day. Benjamin Stelle, who graduated at the College of New Jersey, and who afterwards, in the year 1766, established a Latin school in Providence, was also a student at Hopewell. His daughter Mary, it may be added, was the second wife of the late Hon. Nicholas Brown, from whom the University derives its name.

The success of the Hopewell Academy inspired the friends of learning with renewed confidence, and incited them to establish a college. "Many of the churches," says the Rev. Morgan Edwards, "being supplied with able pastors from Mr. Eaton's Academy, and being thus convinced, from experience, of the great usefulness of human literature to more thoroughly furnish the man of God for the most important work of the gospel ministry, the hands of the Philadelphia Association were strengthened, and their hearts encouraged to extend their designs of promoting literature in the society, by erecting, on some suitable part of this continent, a college or university, which should be principally under the direction and government of the Baptists. At first, some of the southern colonies seemed to bid fairest to answer their purpose, there not being so many colleges in those colonies as the northerly; but the northern colonies, having been visited by some of the Association, who informed them of the great increase of the Baptist societies of late, in those parts, and that Rhode Island Government had no public school or college in it, and was originally settled by persons of the Baptist persuasion, and a greater part of the Government remained so still, there was no longer any doubt but that was the most suitable place to carry the design into execution." *

Mr. Edwards, to whom reference is made in the foregoing, was the pastor of the Baptist church of Philadelphia, to which he had been recommended by the Rev. Dr. Gill, and others, of London. He was a native of Wales, and had been educated in his early youth as an Episcopalian. He received his academical training at Bristol, under the Rev. Dr. Foskett, and, upon the completion of his studies, entered upon the work of the Christian ministry. He arrived in this country on the 23d of May, 1761. Possessing superior abilities, united with uncommon perseverance and zeal, he became a leader in various literary and benevolent undertakings, freely devoting to them his talents and his time, and thereby rendering essential service to the denomination to which he was attached. He was the prime mover in the enterprise of establishing a "Baptist college":—and to him, with the Rev. Samuel Jones, of

* Appendix to President Sears's Centennial Discourse, page 63.

Lower Dublin, Pennsylvania, the details of the plan, it appears, were mainly intrusted. His labors to advance this object he always deemed the most important of his life. In the prosecution of the enterprise, he received hearty coöperation and substantial aid from men like Oliver Hart and Francis Pelot, of the Charleston Association; John Hart of New Jersey, the signer of the Declaration of Independence; John Stites, the mayor of Elizabethtown, and father-in-law of Dr. Manning; and from others of kindred zeal and spirit. The final success of the movement, it should be added, is justly ascribed to the life-long labors of him who was appointed the first President of the College.

On the 12th of October, 1762, the Philadelphia Association, then comprising twenty-nine churches, met at the Lutheran Church, in Fifth street, "where," says the record, "the sound of the organ was heard in the Baptist worship." Mr. Edwards was chosen moderator, and the Rev. Abel Morgan, clerk. At this meeting, says the historian Backus,* the delegates and friends "obtained such an acquaintance with our affairs, as to bring them to an apprehension that it was practical and expedient to erect a college in the Colony of Rhode Island, under the chief direction of the Baptists; wherein education might be promoted, and superior learning obtained, free of any sectarian religious tests." The leader selected for this most important work was James Manning, who, on the 29th of the previous month, had graduated at the College of New Jersey, with the second honors of his class; and who had been formerly both a pupil and an assistant at the Hopewell Academy. He was only twenty-four years of age, but his extraordinary mental and physical powers were well matured, and gave ample promise of that success in his chosen vocation and calling to which he afterwards attained.

* Church History of New England, volume 2, page 235.

The accompanying likeness, engraved for our former work from an original portrait, exhibits him at a later period in life, when President of the Rhode Island College in Providence. His person, says a contemporary, was graceful, his countenance was stately and majestic, his manner enchanting, his voice harmonious, and his eloquence almost irresistible. He possessed, moreover, genuine piety, and a benevolence which beamed in every feature. And when to these varied gifts and accomplishments we add sterling good sense, for which he was preëminently distinguished, and superior learning, the wisdom of that choice which selected him as a leader and pioneer, in founding and establishing a college or university, will readily be seen and acknowledged.

In the month of July, 1763, Mr. Manning, accompanied by his friend, the Rev. John Sutton, a member with him of Mr. Miller's church in Elizabethtown, New Jersey, and also an early pupil of the Academy, stopped at Newport, on their way to Halifax, to arrange the preliminaries for establishing in Rhode Island a "seminary of polite literature, subject to the government of the Baptists." Newport was at this time the most flourishing town in the Colony, and the centre of opulence, refinement and learning. Immediately upon their arrival they "made a motion," quoting the words of Manning in his narrative,* "to several gentlemen of the Baptist denomination, whereof Col. Gardner, the deputy governor was one, relative to a seminary," etc. The project was received with favor, and, at a meeting of its friends held at Mr. Gardner's house on the following day, Mr. Manning presented a rough outline or sketch of the design, "the tenor of which was, that the institution was to be a Baptist one, but that as many of other denominations should be taken in as was consistent with the said design." A committee was accordingly appointed, consisting of the Hon. Josias Lyndon and Col. Job Bennet, to draw up a charter

* MANNING AND BROWN UNIVERSITY, page 46.

agreeably to the proposed plan, and present it to "the next General Assembly, with a petition that they would pass it into a law." These gentlemen pleading unskillfulness in a matter of this kind, solicited the assistance of the Rev. Dr. Stiles, afterwards the distinguished President of Yale College. The manner in which this eminent scholar and divine nearly succeeded in defeating the project, by drafting a charter at variance with the original design, is fully related in MANNING AND BROWN UNIVERSITY;—to which work, as also to a subsequent chapter on the College charter, the reader is referred for details and illustrations. After various difficulties and delays, in consequence of the determined opposition of those who were unfriendly to the movement, the Legislature, or "General Assembly," held by adjournment in East Greenwich, the last week in February, 1764, granted a charter, which has secured to the College or University, for a century, ample privileges; and which is "undoubtedly," says Prof. Kingsley, in his Life of Dr. Stiles, "in many respects, one of the best college charters in New England." Its chief provisions were: The exclusion of all religious tests for applicants for admission, and of all sectarian teachings in the College course; equality of privileges for all Protestant denominations; the choice of Professors without regard to denominational views; and government by a President of Baptist sentiments, and by a Board of Fellows and a Board of Trustees, in which, though the Baptists were to have the predominance, other denominations in the Colony were to be fairly represented. Of the twelve Fellows, eight, including the President, were to be Baptists; and of the thirty-six Trustees, twenty-two were to be Baptists; five, Friends; four, Congregationalists; and five, Episcopalians. The corporate name of the Institution was to be, " The College or University in the English Colony of Rhode Island and Providence Plantations in New England, in America," until it should be honored with that of some eminent benefactor—an anticipation in due time happily fulfilled.

But though the Colony of Rhode Island had been selected for the College, and a charter had been secured, no town stood prepared to welcome it in its infant state, without students, without funds, and with no certain means of support. To the friends and projectors of the enterprise it seemed therefore desirable, that it should be located where the President might have an opportunity to preach, in connection with the work of instruction, and thus secure for the time being a maintenance for himself and family. The two churches at Newport were already provided with competent pastors;—the Rev. Edward Upham, a graduate of Harvard College, and the Rev. Gardner Thurston, whose meeting-house and congregation were at this early period the largest, according to Edwards, of any connected with the Baptist denomination in New England. The church at Providence, although the oldest Baptist church in America, had never been accustomed to contribute liberally towards the support of a pastor. With only one hundred and eighteen members living widely apart, with a small and uncomfortable house, opposed to singing in public worship, and clinging to many prejudices and customs, which it afterwards threw off under the enlightened teachings of Manning, it offered but feeble encouragement to a seat of learning. Besides, the church was already provided with a pastor, the Rev. Samuel Winsor, who had been settled over them since 1759. Warren, a thriving town on the Narragansett Bay, ten miles from Providence, seemed to meet all the requirements of the case. Here were ample materials for the formation of a church;—and here the leader in the great educational movement of the Philadelphia Association would receive a cordial welcome.

Mr. Manning, therefore, shortly after the granting of the charter, or about the middle of April, 1764, removed with his family to Warren, where he immediately opened a Latin school, as a step preparatory to the beginning of College instruction. This school, which soon became flourishing, he continued to teach or superintend for many years, in connection with his professional duties and calling. In 1770, it was removed to Providence, and, upon the completion of what is now called "University Hall," was kept in the lower story of that building. Under the name of the "University Grammar School," it continues at the present day to render most efficient service, as an auxiliary to the Institution which called it into being.

At the time of Manning's arrival in Warren, there were nearly sixty Baptist communicants residing in the place, the majority of whom were members of the venerable church in Swanzey. The population of the village was increasing, and the time seemed to have come for carrying out their long cherished plans and wishes in regard to the formation of a church. The zeal and eloquence of Manning as a preacher had attracted a large congregation, and not a few persons had become believers in Christ, as the fruits of his ministry. Accordingly, on the 15th of November, 1764, a church of fifty-eight members was organized, over which Manning was duly installed as pastor. The relations thus assumed proved pleasant alike to minister and people. During the six years of their continuance the church greatly increased in numbers and strength, while the College flourished under its fostering care.

At the second annual meeting of the Corporation, held in Newport, on the first Wednesday in September, 1765, Mr. Manning was formally appointed "President of the College, Professor of Languages, and other branches of learning, with full power to act in these capacities at Warren, or elsewhere." This is the language of the record, which, as has been playfully remarked, "though not obnoxious to the charge of legal precision, seems to imply, on the part of the Corporation, no want of confidence in the variety of the President's attainments." In the following year, Mr. David Howell,* a graduate of the College of New Jersey, who was afterwards honored with high political and judicial trusts in the State of his adoption, became his assistant. As funds were needed for the support of the instructors, Mr. Edwards, in 1767, visited England and Ireland, for the purpose of soliciting aid; in which undertaking, considering the times, he was very successful. The original subscription book, containing among others, the honored signatures of Benjamin Franklin, Benjamin West, Thomas Llewelyn, Thomas Penn, Thomas Hollis, Rev. Dr. Stennett, Rev. Dr. Gifford, Rev. Dr. Gibbons, and the commentator, Rev. Dr. Gill, constitutes one of the most precious documents in the College archives. Collections were also made in South Carolina and Georgia, through the agency of the Rev. Hezekiah Smith, and also in the churches connected with the various Baptist associations.

The first Commencement of the College, was held in the meeting-house at Warren, on the 7th day of September, 1769. Four

* Hon. Judge Howell LL. D. He was born in New Jersey, January 1, 1747, and graduated at Princeton, in 1766. In 1770 he removed to Providence, where he continued to reside until his death, in 1824, at the age of seventy-seven years. In 1769 he was appointed a Professor in the College, and in 1773, he was elected to a Fellowship in the Corporation, retaining this latter position upwards of fifty-one years. He practised law a great while, and was among the most eminent members of the Rhode Island Bar. Under the Confederation he was a member of Congress, and he subsequently filled, with great ability, various high offices. In 1812 he was appointed United States Judge for the District of Rhode Island, and this office he sustained until his death. He was endowed, says Prof. Goddard, with extraordinary talents, and he superadded to his endowments extensive and accurate learning. He was a brilliant wit, and as a pungent and effective political writer he was unrivalled. Judge Howell, it may be added, was a man of enormous physical development, weighing, it is said, upwards of three hundred pounds. He married Mary, daughter of Jeremiah and Waitstill Brown, and granddaughter of the Rev. James Brown, one of the early pastors of the Baptist Church in Providence. One of his daughters, Waitstill, was married to Ebenezer Knight Dexter, Esq., who, dying without issue, bequeathed to the City of Providence, the "Dexter Asylum" lands, the "Dexter Training Ground," and a large portion of his ample estate. Another daughter, Sarah, married for her first husband, Gamaliel Lyman Dwight of Boston. Their grandson, Gamaliel Lyman Dwight, has recently founded the "David Howell Scholarship," to perpetuate in the University the name and memory of his distinguished ancestor.

years had elapsed since the President, with a solitary pupil,* began his Collegiate work as an instructor. Amid severe toils, and difficulties, and opposition even, he had quietly persevered, until the infant Seminary under his care had won its way to public favor. And now seven students were to take their first degree, and go forth to the duties of life. They were young men of unusual promise. Some of them were destined to fill conspicuous places in the approaching struggle for independence; others were to be leaders in the church, and distinguished educators of youth. Probably no class that has gone forth from the University, in her palmiest days of prosperity, has exerted so widely extended and beneficial an influence, the times and circumstances taken into account, as this first class† that graduated at Warren. The occasion drew together a large concourse of people from all parts of the Colony, inaugurating the earliest State holiday in the history of Rhode Island. A contemporary account preserves the interesting facts, that both the President and the candidates for degrees were dressed in clothing of American manufacture, and that the audience, composed of many of the first ladies and gentlemen of the Colony, behaved with great decorum.

Up to this date, 1769, the "Seminary," says Morgan Edwards, " was for the most part friendless and moneyless, and therefore, forlorn, insomuch that a College edifice was hardly thought of." But the interest manifested in the exercises of Commencement, and the frequent remittances from England, led some "to hope,

---

* Rev. Wm. Rogers, D. D., for many years Professor of Oratory and Belles Lettres in the University of Pennsylvania. He was matriculated by President Manning on the 3d of September, 1765. The next student of the College was Richard Stites, a nephew of the President, who was matriculated June 20, 1766. Mr. Rogers was therefore the first student of Brown University, and for nine months and seventeen days the only student. A fine portrait of him, painted by his daughter, forms a part of the Collection of Portraits in Rhode Island Hall.

†Biographical sketches of Varnum, Rogers, Williams, and Thompson, prominent members of this class, are given in MANNING AND BROWN UNIVERSITY, pp. 91-106.

and many to fear, that the Institution would come to something and stand. Then a building and the place of it were talked of, which opened a new scene of troubles and contentions, that had well nigh ruined all. Warren was at first agreed on as a proper situation, where a small wing was to be erected in the spring of 1770, and about £800 (lawful money) was raised toward effecting it. But soon afterwards, some who were unwilling it should be there, and some who were unwilling it should be anywhere, did so far agree, as to lay aside the said location, and propose that the county which should raise the most money should have the College." Subscriptions were immediately set on foot in several counties, but the claimants for the honor were finally reduced to two, viz: Providence and Newport. The contested question was finally settled, at a special meeting of the Corporation held in Warren, February 7, 1770. "The people had raised," says Manning, in his account of this meeting, " £4.000, lawful money, taking in their unconditional subscription. But Providence presented £4,280, lawful, and advantages superior to Newport in other respects." The dispute, he adds lasted from 10 o'clock Wednesday morning until the same hour Thursday night, and was decided in the presence of a large congregation, in favor of Providence, by a vote of twenty-one to fourteen.

Soon after this decision, the President and Prof. Howell, with their pupils, removed to Providence, occupying for a time the upper part of the Brick School House on Meeting street, for prayers and recitations. On the 14th of May, 1770, the foundations of the first College building were laid. The spot selected for it was the crest of a hill which then commanded a view of the bay, the river, with the town on its banks, and a broad reach of country on all sides. The land comprised about eight acres, and included a portion of the original " home lot" of Chad Brown, the associate and friend of Roger Williams, and the "first Baptist Elder in

Rhode Island." Now that the buildings of the city have crept up the hill, and, gathering round the College grounds, have stretched out far beyond them, thus shutting out the nearer prospect, the eye can still take in, from the top of "University Hall," the same varied and beautiful landscape which once constituted one of the chief attractions of the site.

During a portion of the revolutionary period, from December 6, 1776, until May 27, 1782, the College was disbanded; and a gap therefore occurs in its history. Up to this time the number of students had steadily increased from year to year. In 1765, there was, as we have already stated, but a single pupil pursuing a course of study under President Manning. In the year following there were six; in 1767 ten; in 1770 twenty-one; in 1773 thirty-five, and in 1775 forty-one. These facts we learn from a paper preserved on file by Judge Howell, and also from an interesting paper in the hand-writing of Manning. The latter is entitled "A Matriculation Roll of the number of students in Rhode Island College, with the time of their admission, up to 1769," and reads as follows, the several classes being separated by intervening lines: —

William Rogers,	entered	September 3, 1765,	from	Newport, R. I.
Richard Stites,	"	June 20, 1766,	"	Elizabethtown, N. J.
Joseph Belton,	"	November 4, 1766,	"	Groton, Ct.
Joseph Eaton,	"	" 10, 1766,	"	Hopewell, N. J.
William Williams,	"	" 10, 1766,	"	Hilton, Penn.
Charles Thompson,	"	" 10, 1766,	"	Amwell, N. J.
James M. Varnum,	"	May 23, 1768,	"	Dracut, Mass.

John Dennis,	entered	September, 1767,	from	Newport, R. I.
Theodore Foster,	"	" 1767,	"	Brookfield, Mass.
Samuel Nash,	"	" 1767,	"	Massachusetts.
Seth Read,	"	" 1767,	"	Uxbridge, Mass.

| Thomas Arnold, | entered | September, 1768, | from | Smithfield, R. I. |
| Thomas Ustick, | " | " 1768, | " | City of New York. |

HISTORICAL SKETCH.

Samuel Ward,	entered September,	1768,	from	Westerly, R. I.
Ranne Cossit,	"	"	1768,	"	Connecticut.
Benjamin Farnum,	"	"	1768,	"	Connecticut.
Micah Brown,	"	"	1768,	"	Barrington, R. I.
William Nelson,	"	"	1768,	"	Middleborough, Mass.

Joseph Appleton,	entered September,	1769,	from	Ipswich, Mass.
Ebenezer David,	"	"	1769,	"	City of Philadelphia.
Benjamin Greene,	"	"	1769,	"	Bristol, R. I.
Joseph Harris,	"	"	1769,	"	Smithfield, R I.
Elias Howell,	"	"	1769,	"	Egg Harbor, N. J.
Joseph D. Russell,	"	"	1769,	"	Providence, R. I.

Solomon Drown,	entered September,	1769,	from	Providence, R. I.
Joseph Litchfield,	"	"	1769,	"	Massachusetts
Jacob Nash,	"	"	1769,	"	Providence. R. I.
Philip Paddleford,	"	"	1769,	"	Middleborough, Mass.
Henry H. Tillinghast,	"	"	1769,	"	Providence. R. I.

On Saturday, December 7, 1776, Sir Peter Parker, the British commander, with seventy sail of men-of-war, anchored in Newport harbor, landed a body of troops, and took possession of the place. Providence was at once thrown into confusion and alarm. Forces hastily collected were massed throughout the town, martial law was proclaimed, College studies were interrupted, and the students were dismissed to their respective homes. The seat of the Muses now became the habitation of Mars. The dormitories and recitation-rooms were occupied as barracks by the State militia, and afterwards as a hospital by our French allies.

In the Spring of 1786, President Manning, whose graceful deportment, thorough scholarship, and wise and Christian character had commended him to all his fellow-citizens, was unanimously appointed by the General Assembly of Rhode Island to represent the State in the Congress of the Confederation. This was during a crisis of depression and alarm, when the whole political fabric was threatened with destruction. He, however, returned to his

College duties at the close of the year, being unwilling to remain longer away from the scenes of his chosen labors. With the momentous questions of the day he was thoroughly familiar, and he afterwards, by his voice and by his pen, contributed very materially to the adoption of the Federal Constitution by the State, in 1790.

On the morning of July 24, 1791, while uttering the voice of prayer around the domestic altar, Dr. Manning was seized with a fit of apoplexy, in which he remained, but with imperfect consciousness, till the ensuing Friday, when he expired, in the 54th year of his age. The sudden death of a man who was universally esteemed and loved, and who had filled for so many years, such various and responsible stations of usefulness and trust, produced throughout the entire community the most profound sorrow, reaching to every part of the city in which he lived. The College, with which he had been identified from its infancy; the Warren Association, which had been founded mainly through his instrumentality; the venerable Baptist church, over which he for twenty years had been pastor; the State, whose counsels and deliberations he had often guided; and especially the religious denomination, far and near, to which he was sincerely attached. all lamented the loss of a great and good man. A vast concourse of people attended his funeral, and followed with weeping eyes his remains to the grave. That the death of a Christian minister, and a teacher of science and letters, who possessed none of the advantages of wealth, but whose later years, on the contrary. had been oppressed by economic solicitude and care, should produce a regret so universal and so deep, "is a pleasing homage"— adopting the language of Robert Hall on the occasion of the death of Dr. Ryland—"to the majesty of moral power and intellectual greatness."

The following particulars relating to Dr. Manning's personal appearance, habits, character and influence, are from the pen of his early associate and friend, the Hon. David Howell, who wrote his obituary notice, and who also penned the inscription upon the marble tablet erected to his memory by the Trustees and Fellows of the College:—

In his youth he was remarkable for his dexterity in athletic exercises, for the symmetry of his body, and gracefulness of his person. His countenance was stately and majestic, full of dignity, goodness, and gravity; and the temper of his mind was a counterpart to it. He was formed for enterprise. His address was pleasing, his manner enchanting, his voice harmonious, and his eloquence almost irresistible.

Having deeply imbibed the spirit of truth himself, as a preacher of the gospel, he was faithful in declaring the whole counsel of God. He studied plainness of speech, and to be useful more than to be celebrated. The good order, learning, and respectability of the Baptist churches in the eastern states, are much owing to his assiduous attention to their welfare. The credit of his name and his personal influence among them, have never, perhaps, been exceeded by any other character.

Of the College he must be considered, in one sense, as the founder. He presided with the singular advantage of a superior personal appearance, added to all his shining talents for governing and instructing youth. From the first beginning of his Latin school at Warren, through many discouragements, he has, by constant care and labor, raised this seat of learning to notice, to credit, and to respectability in the United States. Perhaps the history of no other college will disclose a more rapid progress or greater maturity, in the course of about twenty-five years.

Although he seemed to be consigned to a sedentary life, yet he was capable of more active scenes. He had paid much attention to the government of his country, and had been honored by this State with a seat in the Old Congress. In state affairs he discovered an uncommon degree of sagacity, and he might have made a figure as a politician.

In classical learning he was fully competent to the business of teaching, although he devoted less time than some others in his station to the study of the more abtruse sciences. In short, nature seemed to have furnished him so completely, that little remained for art to accomplish. The resources of his genius were great. In conversation he was at all times pleasant and entertaining. He had as many friends as acquaintances, and he took no less pains to serve his friends than to acquire them.

His death is a loss, not to the College or church only, but to the world. He is lamented by the youth under his care, by the churches, by his fellow-citizens; and wherever his name has been heard, in whatever quarter of the civilized earth, the friends of science, of virtue and humanity will drop a tender tear on the news of his death.

We may be allowed to add further particulars respecting his voice, manners and discipline, from the pen of his accomplished biographer, the late Professor Goddard:—

The voice of Dr. Manning was not among the least of his attractions. To its extraordinary compass and harmony may, in no small degree, be ascribed the vivid impression which he made upon minds. How potent is the fascination of a musical and expressive voice! How sad to think, that, in these days of almost universal accomplishment, this mighty instrument for touching the heart of man should be comparatively neglected! When in connection with a more careful culture of our moral being, the voice shall be trained to a more perfect manifestation of its powers, a charm, hitherto unfelt, will be lent to the graceful pleasures of life, and an influence of almost untried efficacy to its serious occasions.

The manners of Dr. Manning were not less prepossessing than his personal appearance. They seemed to be the expression of that dignity and grace for which he was so remarkable, and of which he appeared to be entirely unconscious—a dignity and grace, not artificial or studied in the least, but the gift of pure nature. He was easy without negligence, and polite without affectation. Unlike many of the distinguished men in our country, he was too well bred to adopt an air of patronage and condescension towards his inferiors either in talent or in station. As a Christian, also, he felt the importance of cultivated manners, and he acknowledged no necessary connection between the sternest fidelity to principle and the precision and austerity with which it is sometimes found associated. Like the venerable Wheelock, the founder of Dartmouth College, he abhorred all religious profession which was not marked with good manners.

In the discipline and instruction of the College, Dr. Manning was eminently successful. He secured the obedience of his pupils, rather by the gentleness of parental persuasion than by the sternness of official authority. His instructions, which were always oral, never failed to command their attention, and to leave upon their minds a distinct impression. Classical learning was his forte, and to the classics and their cognate branches, he principally confined himself.

Dr. Manning, in his correspondence with friends in England, frequently alludes to a "Narrative" or sketch of the College, which he was preparing to publish in a pamphlet form, for general circulation. The breaking out of the war and the consequent interruption of College exercises, probably prevented the carrying out of his original plans. Among his manuscript papers we find a rough draft of the following sketch, which is interesting as a production from his pen, and as an exhibition of the condition of the College in 1773. It is entitled, "RHODE ISLAND COLLEGE. BY PRESIDENT MANNING."

The charter was granted by the Governor and Company of the Colony of Rhode Island, in the year 1764, incorporating a number of gentlemen therein mentioned by the name of "'The Trustees and Fellows of the College in her Majesty's English Colony of Rhode Island and Providence Plantations in New England in America," whereby they are "authorized to admit to and confer any and all the learned degrees which can or ought to be given, or conferred in any of the colleges in America." And it is likewise expressed in the charter, that "into this liberal and catholic Institution shall never be admitted any religious tests; but on the contrary, all the members hereof shall forever enjoy full, free, absolute and uninterrupted liberty of conscience;" and "that youth of all religious denominations shall and may be admitted to the equal advantages, emoluments and honors of the College, and shall receive a like fair, generous and equal treatment during their residence therein;" and "that the sectarian differences in opinion shall not make any part of the public and classical instruction;" and "that the places of Professors, tutors, and all other officers, the President alone excepted, (who shall forever be of the denomination called Baptists, or Antipœdobaptists) shall be free and open for all denominations of Protestants."

The number of Trustees is thirty-six, as follows: The Hon. Stephen Hopkins, Esq., Chancellor of the College, Hon. Samuel Ward, Esq., Vice Chancellor, Hon. Job Bennet, Esq, 'Treasurer, Hon Messrs. Josias Lyndon, Joseph Wanton, Jr, Nicholas Cook, Darius Sessions, James Helme and Thomas Greene, Esqrs., Rev. Mourra, John Gano, Gardner Thurston, Russel Mason, Joshua Clarke, John Maxon, Isaac Backus and Samuel Winsor. Messrs. Daniel Jonckes, James Honeyman, John Tillinghast, Henry Ward, Nicholas Brown, John Tanner, George Hazard and Sylvester Child, Esqrs., Dr. Ephraim Bowen, Messrs. Joseph Russel, Joseph Brown, John G. Wanton, Simon Pease, John Warren, William Brown, Peleg Barker, Edward Thurston, Jr, and Nathan Spear. Two places vacant.

The number of Fellows is twelve, as follows: Rev. James Manning, Dr. Thomas Eyres, Rev. Edward Upham, Rev. Morgan Edwards, Rev. George Bisset, Rev. Samuel Stillman, Rev. Hezekiah Smith. Dr. Joshua Babcock, Dr. Jabez Bowen, and Dr. Jonathan Easton. Two places vacant.

President of the College, Rev. James Manning, who also teaches Moral Philosophy, English and Oratory. Professor of Mathematics and Natural Philosophy, David Hoell, (Howell,) who also teaches the Hebrew and French Languages; Tutor, (vacant.) Supplied by the Professor. Master of the Grammar school, Ebenezer David. Librarian, John Dorrance. Steward, Josias Arnold.

The students are divided into four classes, viz.: Freshman, Sophomore, Junior and Senior. The three lower classes are examined quarterly, when graduates of any college have liberty to attend; and those students who appear to have merited it, are advanced to the next class; and on the contrary delinquents are degraded, or their standing is left conditional for another quarter's trial. Young gentlemen who produce certificates of a good moral character are admitted to such standing in the College, as their proficiency in knowledge will entitle them to, upon examination.

The annual meeting of the Corporation, and Commencement, is on the first Wednesday in September. The first Commencement was held at Warren in the year 1769, when seven alumni of the College were graduated. Present members of College, 35; members of the Grammar school, 18; in all, 53.

The College edifice, an elegant brick building, four stories high, 150 by 46 feet, besides a projection on each side of 33 by 10 feet, is situated on rising ground, adjoining the town of Providence, commanding an agreeable and extensive prospect, and enjoying a serene and salutary air.

The whole expense of the College edifice was defrayed by the voluntary contributions of particular gentlemen in this Colony. Collections have also been made for the College fund in this Colony and elsewhere, particularly in Great Britain and Ireland, by the application of the Rev. Morgan Edwards, and in some of the southern colonies on this continent by the Rev. Hezekiah Smith.

Tuition, twelve dollars per year. Boarding, one dollar per week.

Immediately upon the death of Dr. Manning, measures were adopted to secure a successor in the Presidency of the College. At an informal meeting of the Corporation held in Providence, the Hon. David Howell was requested to write on the subject to the Rev. Dr. Samuel Jones, of Lower Dublin, Pennsylvania. His interesting letter may be found in MANNING AND BROWN UNIVERSITY, pp. 454–5. The following is the reply, which we publish as a part of the history of this period. Mr. Jones, it will be remembered, was one of the original founders of the College.

LOWER DUBLIN, August 15, 1791.

DEAR SIR:—I received yours of the 3d instant the day before yesterday. The melancholy tidings of the decease of your worthy President had reached me six days before; on which sorrowful occasion, I am not ashamed to own, I shed many a tear. Our acquaintance commenced at the Grammar school, where we were classmates, thirty-five years ago, since which time an unusual intimacy and friendship, in various connections, transactions of business, consultations for advice, discussion of points, theological and political, respecting church and state, etc., have subsisted without a single disquieting jar. He was the dearest to me of all men on earth. But now he is no more! O Manning! Alas my brother! O irreparable loss!—But heaven had so decreed. It is our duty to submit.

As for what you have so handsomely said, respecting some thought of me as the late Doctor's successor in the Presidentship, waving the compliments paid me, I must beg leave to come forward, and totally decline it at once. The appointment would be so far above my abilities and other qualifications; it would be so unsuitable for a man so far advanced in years (fifty-six) to enter on a new scene of life, etc., etc , that my very acceptance would bear witness against you for the appointment, and me for accepting.

You will, however, suffer me to declare, that I am, and ever have been, warmly attached to the interests of the College ; and deem it of the utmost consequence, that the vacancy should be suitably filled, without any more loss of time than circumstances will render unavoidable. If I thought I could be indulged with the liberty of mentioning names, without giving offence, I would lay before the Corporation the names of the Hon. David Howell, and the Rev. Jonathan Maxcy, both of Providence. Should it be decided that the clause in the charter respecting a President militates against the one, and want of years against the other, (for a man may be too young as well as too old,) I would then suggest the expediency of casting an eye over the Atlantic In this case, I would just hint the expediency of deputing a person, in whose fidelity, prudence, discretion and judgment you could confide, to go over and negotiate the business We know that interest, connections, friendship, etc., do often so bias, as to make it unsafe to trust any man, or set of men where the application is made. I knew, some years ago, an application to a venerable board, whose conduct on the occasion was such as I thought they could not justify. I have only to add, that should you determine to send one over, and could not find one willing to go that would answer the end better than myself, I would not decline the service. I mention this with a view to save time.

As I have been a little particular, and mentioned the chief of what now occurs, I do not see that my attendance at your Commencement would be of much consequence. But I will consider of it. You will be so kind as to make my most respectful compliments to the Honorable Corporation. Remember me in a very particular and affectionate manner to Mrs. Manning, as also to Mrs. Howell, and in general to all my friends at Providence, or elsewhere, whom you may have an opportunity of seeing at your Commencement, and be assured

I remain, with sentiments of high esteem, your most obedient, most humble servant,

SAMUEL JONES.

A new era in the history of the College now opens to view. Agreeably to the suggestions contained in this friendly letter to Judge Howell, President Manning was succeeded, in 1792, by the Rev. Jonathan Maxcy, who, during the previous year, had held the temporary appointment of Professor of Divinity. The career of this remarkable man indicates a high order of genius. At the early age of fifteen he entered the Institution as a pupil, graduating in 1787, with the highest honors of his class. He was immediately appointed tutor, which position he held four years. It was during this period that he became the subject of renewing grace, and was baptized by his venerated President and pastor, Dr. Manning. In 1791, he was chosen pastor of the Baptist church, of which he was already a member, and the year following he was elected President of the College *pro tempore*, as appears from the records of the Corporation. In 1797, he was formally elected President. As a man of practical judgment, and safe views on all subjects, inspiring universal and unlimited confidence, he was undoubtedly far inferior to his distinguished predecessor; and this, with his extreme youth, may have been the reason why he was at first elected President *pro tempore*, or in other words, Vice-President. His great genius and learning, nevertheless, attracted public attention, and drew students to the College, adding materially to its literary reputation.

During his brilliant career of ten years, men were educated and sent out into all the professions, who, for learning, skill, and success in life, will not suffer in comparison with the graduates of any other period. It may be sufficient to mention, in illustration, the names of Samuel W. Bridgham, the first Mayor of Providence; Hon. William Baylies, LL. D., who has so recently died at Bridgewater, Massachusetts, and also his classmate, Hon. Ezekiel Whitman, LL. D.; Hon. Tristam Burges, LL. D., the orator and statesman of whom Rhode Island is so justly proud; Hon. John Holmes a member of Congress, and Senator from Maine; Rev. Dr. John M. Roberts, of South Carolina; Prof. Calvin Park; Hon. James Tallmadge, LL. D., a member of Congress from New York, and also Lieutenant-Governor; Jeremiah Chaplin, D. D., President of Waterville College; Hon. John Pitman, LL. D., of Providence; Hon. Nathan Fellows Dixon, Senator from Rhode Island; Rev. Dr. James Thompson; Rev. Dr. John M. Bradford; Rev. Dr. Lucius Bolles; Hon. Andrew Pickens, Governor of South Carolina; and Hon. Henry Wheaton, LL. D., the distinguished author of "Elements of International Law."

"The splendor of Dr. Maxcy's genius," says the American biographer Blake, "and his brilliant talents as an orator and divine, had become widely known; and under his administration the College acquired a reputation for belles-lettres and eloquence inferior to no seminary of learning in the United States." "His voice," says Tristam Burges, "seemed not to have reached the deep tone of full age; but most of all to resemble that of those concerning whom the Savior of the world said, 'of such is the kingdom of heaven.' The eloquence of Maxcy was mental. You seemed to hear the soul of the man; and each one of the largest assembly, in the most extended place of worship, received the slightest impulse of his silver voice as if he stood at his very ear. So intensely would he enchain attention, that in the most thronged audience you heard nothing but him and the pulsations of your own heart. His utterance was not more perfect than his whole discourse was instructive and enchanting."

In the month of September, 1802, Dr. Maxcy resigned the Presidency of the College, in the following letter addressed to the "Honorable Corporation":—

GENTLEMEN:—Agreeable to the information which I have communicated to you, I now resign my office, as President of this College. Nothing but necessity induces me to adopt this measure. My attachment to the College still remains, and I trust long will remain. I beg the gentlemen of the Corporation to accept the assurances of my respect and friendship, and my grateful acknowledgments of the honors to which you have promoted me.

I am, Gentlemen, your friend and humble servant,

JONATHAN MAXCY.

The reply is creditable to both parties:—

SIR:—Your resignation has this morning (September 2) been laid before us by the Honorable Chancellor, and in compliance with your wishes, we have, though with much reluctance, accepted it. The connection which has so long and so happily subsisted between you and this Institution; its increasing prosperity during the time which you have presided, together with our attachment to your person and family, are circumstances which exceedingly heighten our regret at the thought of a separation. We are persuaded, however, that nothing but a sense of duty could have induced you to remove your relation from this College, and you may be assured that nothing less could have prevailed on us to accept your resignation.

But, Sir, we are happy in the reflection, that your talents are still to be employed in the promotion of science and literature; that you are to preside over another institution, where we hope the sphere of your usefulness may be increased.

Our best wishes, dear Sir, for your prosperity and happiness will accompany you, and we most earnestly pray that the smiles of an indulgent Providence may attend you, that your life and health may be preserved, and that you may long be continued the friend of science, of virtue, and religion.

Submitted by

THOMAS BALDWIN,
ROBERT ROGERS, } *Committee*.
SAMUEL EDDY,

Immediately upon his resignation, Dr. Maxcy was appointed President of Union College, Schenectady, New York, as successor of the Rev. Dr. Jonathan Edwards, deceased. Previous to this event, when only thirty-three years of age, Harvard University had conferred on him the degree of Doctor in Divinity, such was his celebrity as a scholar and divine. He officiated at Schenectady with increasing reputation until 1804, when he accepted the unsolicited appointment of President of South Carolina College, with the fond anticipation of finding a warmer climate more congenial to his physical constitution. Over this institution he presided, with almost unprecedented popularity, during the remainder of his life. He died at Columbia, South Carolina, June 4, 1820, in the 53d year of his age.* His writings, or "Literary Remains," edited by the Rev. Dr. Romeo Elton, were published in 1844, in an octavo volume. Eight years later, a selection from his "Remains," consisting of collegiate addresses, was published in London, making a pleasant little duodecimo volume of one hundred and ninety-one pages. From the biographical introduction to these addresses, by Dr. Elton, a few extracts are made:—

In his person he was rather small of stature, yet of a fine and well-proportioned figure. His features were regular and manly, indicating intelligence and benevolence; and, especially in conversation and public speaking, they were strongly expressive. Grace and dignity were also combined in his movements.

As a scholar, Dr. Maxcy held a very high rank. His stores of knowledge were varied and profound, and he had at all times the command over them. Like the celebrated Robert Hall, he appears to have evinced an early taste for metaphysical studies, and to have thoroughly understood the various systems of philosophy. To this circumstance was probably owing much of that clearness, precision and facility, which enabled him at once to separate truth from error, and to wield his arguments with irresistible effect.

As an instructor, Dr. Maxcy possessed unusual ability, and, perhaps, no President of any college in the United States ever enjoyed a higher reputation. The precision and perspicuity with which he could develop his ideas in the most appropriate language, rendered him peculiarly qualified for this office. His numerous pupils all unite in pronouncing him, as a teacher, one of the most perfect models.

As a preacher, Dr. Maxcy's reputation did not depend so much on any one striking excellence, as on the union of many. These were so happily combined, that it would be difficult to say which was the most prominent. His conceptions were vigorous, and were expressed in a pure, terse and eloquent style. A profound and breathless silence, and intense feeling, and a spirit of holy elevation, were the almost invariable attendants of his preaching.

In the character of Dr. Maxcy, mental and moral worth were happily combined. And so long as genius, hallowed and sublimed by piety, shall command veneration, he will be remembered in his country as a star of the first magnitude.

* Dr. Maxcy was born in Attleboro, Massachusetts, September 2, 1768. He married Susan Hopkins, of Providence, a daughter of Commodore Esek Hopkins. They had several daughters and four sons, all of whom were liberally educated. It is to be regretted that no painted canvas or sculptured marble exists to perpetuate the likeness of the second President of the College.

4

The Rev. Asa Messer succeeded Dr. Maxcy in the Presidency of the College, and held this office until 1826, a period of twenty-four years. At the age of nineteen he entered the Sophomore class, graduating under Manning in 1790. Soon afterwards he became interested in religious truth, and was baptized by Maxcy. He was elected a tutor of the College in 1791, and continued in this relation until 1796, when he was elected Professor of the Learned Languages. In 1799 he was appointed Professor of Mathematics and Natural Philosophy. He was thus connected with the Institution as student, tutor, Professor and President, thirty-nine years. Under his wise and skillful management the College prospered;—its finances were improved; its means of instruction were extended; and the number of students was greatly augmented.

It was soon after the beginning of Dr. Messer's administration that the College received its present name, in honor of its distinguished benefactor, Nicholas Brown. Mr. Brown graduated in the class of 1786, being at the time but seventeen years of age. He commenced his benefactions in February, 1792, by presenting to the Trustees and Fellows of the College the sum of five hundred dollars, to be expended in the purchase of law books for the library. This he did, in the language of the letter announcing the donation, under a deep impression of the generous intentions of his honored father, deceased, towards the College, as well as from his own personal feelings towards the Institution in which he had received his education. In 1804, he presented to the Corporation the sum of five thousand dollars, as a foundation for a professorship of oratory and belles-lettres. It was on this occasion, in consideration of this donation, and of others that had been received from him and his kindred, that the name of the Institution was changed, in accordance with a provision in its charter, from Rhode Island College to Brown University.

The following is his letter to the Corporation:—

PROVIDENCE, September 6, 1804.

GENTLEMEN:—It is not unknown to you that I have long had an attachment to this Institution, as the place where my deceased brother Moses and myself received our education. This attachment derives additional strength, from the recollection that my late honored father was among the earliest and most zealous patrons of the College; and is confirmed by my regard for the cause of literature in general. Under these impressions I hereby make a donation of five thousand dollars to Rhode Island College, to remain in perpetuity as a fund for the establishment of a Professorship of Oratory and Belles-Lettres. The money will be paid next Commencement, and is to be vested in such funds as the Corporation shall direct for its augmentation to a sufficiency, in your judgment, to produce a competent annual salary for the within mentioned Professorship.

I am, very respectfully, Gentlemen, with my best wishes for the prosperity of the College,

Your obedient friend,

NICHOLAS BROWN.

In 1822, Mr. Brown erected at his own expense the second College building, which he presented to the Corporation, in a letter bearing date January 13, 1823. At his suggestion it was named "Hope College," in honor of his only surviving sister, Mrs. Hope Ives. In 1835 he erected the third building, which he also presented to the Corporation, with a request that it might be named "Manning Hall," in honor of the memory of his own distinguished instructor and revered friend, President Manning. Mr. Brown died September 27, 1841, at the age of seventy-two. A discourse commemorative of his character and life was delivered by President Wayland, in the University chapel, which discourse was afterwards published. The entire sum of his recorded benefactions and bequests to the University amounts to one hundred and sixty thousand dollars, assigning to the donations of lands and buildings the valuation which was put upon them at the time they were made. "Many years," says Prof. Gammell, "have now elapsed since he descended to the tomb, but the monuments of his wise and pious benefactions are all around us,—in the University with which his name is associated; in the Butler Hospital for the Insane, and the Providence Athenæum, to whose founding he so largely contributed; and in the churches, and colleges, and institutions of philanthropy over the whole land, to which he so often lent his liberal and most timely aid. So long as learning and religion shall have a place in the affections of men, these enduring memorials will proclaim his character, and speak his eulogy. *Hi sanctissimi testes, hi maximi laudatores.*" A few years before his death, at the annual meeting of the Corporation in 1835, Mr. Brown was formally requested to sit for his likeness, which was taken, at full length, by Harding, one of the most celebrated of American artists. It now graces the collection of portraits in Rhode Island Hall. The visitor will gaze upon it with renewed interest as successive years roll on. It is a matter of regret that the portraits of his worthy sire and ancestors cannot be placed by his side.* The accompanying likeness was engraved, it may be added, from a photograph taken from Harding's portrait.

In 1826, Dr. Messer resigned the Presidency of Brown University, in the following characteristic letter, addressed to the Hon. Samuel Eddy, Secretary of the Corporation:—

SEPTEMBER, 23, 1826.

DEAR SIR:—I take the liberty to request you to inform the Honorable Corporation of Brown University, that I resign my office in that Institution. On leaving an office which I have held twenty-four years, and a College of which I have been either an officer or a pupil thirty-nine years, I, though inclined to make many reflections, shall now make only this one; that probably I feel somewhat like one who is breaking up

---

*Mr. Brown's great ancestor was the Rev. Chad Brown, the friend and associate of Roger Williams, and the pastor of the first and only Baptist church in the infant settlement. A full account of him, and of his descendants, including the "Four Brothers," Nicholas, Joseph, John, and Moses Brown, to whom the College is so much indebted for its early prosperity and success, is given in MANNING AND BROWN UNIVERSITY, pages 143-176.

long dear friendships, and bidding the world farewell. I pray that, when the time for doing this shall actually arrive, and it may arrive in a day, or an hour, I may be enabled to think that I have served my God with as much faithfulness as I have served Brown University; and I also pray that He, who was the God of Abraham, and, if I may be allowed to utter a little heresy, the God of Jesus Christ, may have that seat of literature, and all its patrons, as well as you and me, in His holy keeping.

ASA MESSER.

Possessing, says his biographer, a handsome competence, the fruit in part of his habitual frugality, Dr. Messer was enabled to pass the remainder of his life in the enjoyment of independent leisure. After his retirement from collegiate toils, his fellow-citizens of Providence elected him, for several years, to responsible municipal trusts; and these trusts he discharged with his customary punctuality and uprightness. He died October 11, 1836, in the sixty-eighth year of his age.*

Of my old President, says Dr. Sears, in his recent Centennial Discourse, I cannot speak but with respect and affection. He had a vigorous and manly style of thought, and was a genial, pleasant teacher. In discipline, in his best days, he was adroit, having a keen insight into human nature, and touching at will, skillfully, all the chords of the student's heart. Rarely was he mistaken in the character of a young man, or in the motive to which he appealed, in order to influence him. Foibles and weaknesses, he treated with some degree of indulgence; but vice and willful wrong, he treated with unsparing severity.

In government, he followed no abstract principles,—which so often mislead the theorist,—but depended on his good sense in each case, giving considerable scope to views of expediency. The student who attempted to circumvent him, was sure to be outwitted in the end. On account of his great shrewdness, he was sometimes called "the cunning President." One of the many anecdotes related of him is, that he kept in his room a bottle of picra for sick students; and that every one who came to

---

* Dr. Messer was born in Methuen, Massachusetts, in the year 1769. He married Deborah Angell, by whom he had a son that died in infancy, and three daughters. The youngest daughter was married to the late Hon. Horace Mann, and the second to Sidney Williams, Esq., who now resides on the paternal estate. The oldest daughter was never married. The remains of Dr. Messer lie interred in the North Burial Ground, and over them a handsome monument has been erected to his memory. It is a subject of regret that no portrait or engraving exists to perpetuate his likeness.

him to be excused from duty on account of headaches, found it necessary to swallow a dose before leaving the room. * * * * *

His individuality, both in body and mind, was strongly marked. He was altogether unpoetical in his nature. His language had no coloring of the fancy; but was naked, plain and strong. His economy, which was proverbial, extended even to his words. His tendencies were rather to science than literature, and in the latter part of his life, as is often the case, more to practical wisdom and prudence, than to either. * *

His was not a mind to leave its own impress on that of his pupils. As he was independent himself, so he wished his pupils to be. He had no imitators, he wished to have none. The many eminent men educated under him had no other resemblance to each other, than freedom from authority. There is among them no uniform style of thought, resulting from its being run in the same mould. Even among the undergraduates, there was a personal independence of character and thought, and a manliness of deportment and self-respect that gave a certain air of dignity to the two upper classes. Each man was expected to develop and retain his own individuality, without being schooled down to tameness, either by the Faculty or by the collective will of his fellow-students. If he did right, it was his own act; if he did wrong, he would scorn to say that it was because he did not dare to do right.

Another portraiture is from the pen of the Rev. Dr. E. A. Park, of Andover, who was also one of his pupils:—

No one who has ever seen him can ever forget him. His individuality was made unmistakable by his physical frame. This, while it was above the average height, was also in breadth an emblem of the expansiveness of his mental capacity. A "long head" was vulgarly ascribed to him, but it was breadth that marked his forehead; there was an expressive breadth in his maxillary bones; his broad shoulders were a sign of the weight which he was able to bear; his manner of walking was a noticeable symbol of the reach of his mind; he swung his cane far and wide as he walked, and no observer would doubt that he was an independent man; he gesticulated broadly as he preached; his enunciation was forcible, and now and then overwhelming, sometimes shrill, but was characterized by a breadth of tone and a prolonged emphasis which added to its momentum, and made an indelible impress on the memory. His pupils, when they had been unfaithful, trembled before his expansive frown, as it portended a rebuke which would well-nigh devour them; and they felt a dilating of the whole soul, when they were greeted with his good and honest and broad smile. * * * * * As a son, brother, husband, father, he was the central object of attraction, and the beams of joy and love uniformly radiated from him over all the inmates of his happy home.

Dr. Messer was succeeded in the Presidency by the Rev. Francis Wayland, who was unanimously elected to this office on the 13th of December, 1826. Mr. Wayland was born in the city of New York, March 11, 1796, entered the Sophomore class of Union College in 1811, and was graduated in 1813, at the early age of seventeen. He then entered the office of Dr. Eli Burritt, of Troy, and studied medicine three years. As he was about to engage in the practice of his profession, he became convinced that it was his duty to prepare himself for the Christian ministry, and accordingly, in 1816, he repaired to the Andover Theological Seminary. Here he remained one year, receiving instruction from that eminent teacher, Moses Stuart, whom he ever afterwards regarded with filial respect and love. Having been appointed a tutor in Union College, he returned to his Alma Mater, and gave instruction in several departments, retaining the office to which he had been appointed, four years. Associated with him as tutor was the late Bishop Potter, of Pennsylvania, to whom through life he remained sincerely attached. His residence at Union College brought him into intimate relations with his esteemed President, Dr. Nott, for whom he always cherished feelings of gratitude and profound veneration. In 1821, he accepted a call to the pastorate of the First Baptist Church, Boston, over which he was ordained August 21. In the month of February, 1827, he entered upon his duties as President of Brown University.

Dr. Wayland was now in the fullness of his vigor and strength, being about to enter upon his thirty-second year. Few men possessed such a capacity for labor, and fewer still labored with such untiring energy and zeal. The circumstances in which he found the College were by no means favorable. It was scantily endowed, had no philosophical or chemical apparatus worthy of the name, its library was small, and it had no adequate means of enlarging the facilities for instruction. Its morale, too, needed elevating. From causes which we may not now stay to explain, the last two or three years of Dr. Messer's administration had been marked by idleness and dissipation on the part of many of the students. Influences beyond the reach of the President rendered salutary discipline almost impossible, and the results were disastrous alike to the moral and intellectual character of the young men under his care. Dr. Wayland at once instituted the most rigid and healthful discipline. His reputation as a scholar and a divine had preceded his entrance upon his appointed work. "The Moral Dignity of the Missionary Enterprise" had gained for him a wide celebrity, and prepared the way for all his subsequent influence and success. The students were fired with his spirit of industry and earnestness, and rejoiced in the beneficial results of the new administration. In 1835, the "Elements of Moral Science" was published, and gave to the author, and to the University over which he presided, a greatly increased reputation. It was at once introduced into most of our American colleges, and became the standard text-book in its department. Dr. Wayland now sought to supply some of the deficiencies of the Institution. Its generous patrons and friends nobly responded to the appeals which he and his associate Professors sent out. Large additions were made to the philosophical and chemical apparatus; a library fund of twenty-five thousand dollars was established, and one of the choicest collections of books in the country was secured; Manning Hall, containing the spacious chapel and the fine library room, and Rhode Island Hall, with its convenient lecture rooms, were erected; the College grounds were tastefully laid out and planted with elms, and the President's mansion was built.

But favored as Brown University was by the munificence of its friends and patrons; strict as was its discipline; and thorough as was the instruction its Professors gave, it did not realize the ideal formed by the earnest and practical mind of the President. The number of its students did not increase; and with its enlarged expenditure, it was not self-supporting. Despairing of improvement so long as the existing system was perpetuated. Dr. Wayland, in 1849, resigned the Presidency. He, however, consented to reconsider his purpose. His views of the needs of the College, and of the times, were presented to the Corporation, and adopted by them; and it was resolved to attempt to raise a fund for the purpose of realizing his theory of education. One hundred and twenty-five thousand dollars were cheerfully subscribed; and what is called "the New System" commenced. Its main features were, the provision of such new courses of study in science as the practical spirit of the age demanded; the abandonment of a fixed term of four years of study for students, and in place of it the pursuit of any selected course for such a length of time as the student's circumstances required; the privilege of selecting such studies as the student desired, and of pursuing such, and as many studies, as, under the guidance of his guardians, he might wish; the adjustment of the Bachelor's and the Master's degree, so as to represent a difference of attainment, such degrees being conferred on candidates producing certificates of proficiency in certain prescribed and sometimes interchangeable studies, and passing a special examination on some additional study; and the guaranty of a fixed salary to each Professor, to which should be added such sums as resulted from the sale of tickets to his lectures, the relative amount being thus determined somewhat by the attractiveness of his department. From 1850 to 1855, the College was carried on under this system, with but slight modifications. The degree of A. B. was conferred on students who had pursued prescribed studies, which represented a course of three years. The degree of A. M. was conferred, not in course, but on those whose prescribed studies represented a four years course. The degree of Bachelor of Philosophy was given to proficients in certain appointed scientific studies. Instruction was given in practical sciences. The number of students greatly increased, and a new impulse was given to the College.

In 1855, Dr. Wayland, wearied with the cares of a long and honored Presidency, extending over a period of twenty-eight and a half years, having inaugurated his cherished plan of collegiate instruction, resigned his office. The following letter announcing his resignation was presented to the Corporation at a special meeting held on the 21st of August:—

BROWN UNIVERSITY, August 20th, 1855.

To THE CORPORATION OF BROWN UNIVERSITY:

GENTLEMEN:—After more than twenty-eight years service, the conviction is pressed upon me that relaxation and change of labor have become to me a matter of indispensable necessity. These, I am persuaded, cannot be secured while I hold the office with which you have so long honored me. I therefore believe it to be my duty to resign the offices of President of Brown University and Professor of Moral and Intellectual Philosophy. If it be agreeable to you, I desire that this resignation may take place at the close of the present Collegiate year.

In sundering the ties which have so long bound us officially together, I shall not attempt to express the sentiment of gratitude and respect which I entertain towards the gentlemen of the Corporation of Brown University. For more than a quarter of a century we have labored together in promoting the cause of good learning, and especially in advancing the interests of this Institution. Those who, like myself, were young men when I entered upon office, are with me beginning to feel the approaches of age. Yet during this long period no spirit of dissension has either divided our counsels or enfeebled our exertions. We have beheld this University year after year advancing in reputation and usefulness, and diffusing more and more widely the blessings of education. Let us thank God for giving us this opportunity of conferring benefits on mankind, and for crowning our labors with so large a measure of success.

Permit me, Gentlemen, to tender to each one of you the assurances of my grateful regard, and believe me to be

With the highest respect, your obedient servant.

F. WAYLAND.

The feelings of the Corporation at this announcement, found fit expression in eloquent and forcible remarks on the part of the Chancellor, Dr. Samuel Boyd Tobey:—

GENTLEMEN OF THE CORPORATION :—

We all feel sadness at this hour. Our present official connection with President Wayland is soon to terminate. The important services he has rendered this University for nearly twenty-nine years press upon our memory. His unwearied exertions — his zeal — his power in promoting the interests of this Institution of learning, are vividly before us. His name has been a tower of strength. But with these convictions we are bound also to remember that this resignation is with him no sudden movement. For several years he has apprehended that the time was near when it would be right for him to ask to be released from his present position, that he might devote a portion of the days yet allotted him to the fulfillment of other duties, which he feels himself called upon to perform for the advancement of literature, the promotion of religion, and the good of his fellow-citizens. He has been admonished that continued persistence in one field of labor may interrupt the vigorous and healthy action of the best balanced physical and mental powers. He believes that the time has now fully come for him to retire from the Presidency of this University. We will not attempt to detain him. Let us rather thank him for the sacrifice he has made in giving so many of the best years of his life to the interests of the University, not doubting he will find a rich reward in the consciousness that he has been eminently useful. Let us invoke for him the blessing of Heaven, and pray that his life may long be spared, that his pen may continue to record his well-considered and instructive thoughts, that his voice may still be often heard, fearless in condemning error — eloquent in the support of truth

The foregoing remarks were accompanied by suitable resolutions, which were presented to the President by the Chancellor on the day of Commencement, and duly recorded by the Secretary of the Corporation. At a meeting of the alumni, held in Manning Hall, on Tuesday, September 4, 1855, it having been announced that Dr. Wayland had resigned his office, the following resolutions, presented by Hon. Benjamin F. Thomas, and seconded by Hon. John H. Clifford, were unanimously adopted:—

Resolved, That the alumni of this University have heard with profound regret that Francis Wayland has retired from the office of its President.

Resolved, That his clear, strong mind, his accurate learning, his vigorous common sense, his energetic will, his thorough knowledge of the interests and wants of the country and of the age, and his endowment, in so large a measure, with that rarest of all faculties, the power to teach, to cast other minds in the mould of his own, admirably fitted him for the duties of his great office. And that we review to-day with pleasure and pride, his long, rich and successful administration, gratefully recalling his generous, unwearied self-devotion to the welfare of the University, the new and lasting impulse he gave to all her interests, the enlargement of her sphere and capacities of usefulness, the impression of his own mind and character he made upon so many of his pupils, the respect and honor he has acquired in the world of letters and reflected upon the University.

Resolved, That those of us whose great privilege it was to have been his pupils, bring to him the offering of filial love and gratitude. We thank him for the thorough fidelity with which he discharged his trust, for the vigorous discipline of mind and heart he sought to give us, for his affectionate interest in our progress, for his words of wisdom, counsel and reproof, and for the beautiful illustration of a true life given to God and duty, which his own example furnished us.

Resolved, That Dr. Wayland carries with him to his retirement, our earnest wish that there may be a long and happy evening to a manly and useful life, that he may be yet spared to render eminent service to the cause of religion and letters, and that the day may be far distant when the voice of affectionate greeting shall be changed to that of eulogy.

In presenting these resolutions to President Wayland, at the Commencement dinner, September 5th, Judge Thomas addressed him substantially as follows:—

I rise, Mr. President, for the discharge of a painful and yet a grateful duty. The alumni of the University, having heard of your resignation of the office you have so long held with signal honor to yourself and signal advantage to her, met yesterday to give utterance to the feelings which that event naturally awakened. They passed resolutions (would they were worthier) expressing their sense of the value of your services to the College and of the loss she has sustained by your retirement. They instructed their committee (Gov. Clifford, of New Bedford, Hon. Mr. Bradley of this city, and myself) to present these resolutions to you to-day, the last time we shall have the pleasure of meeting you in this near and interesting relation.

It is but little to say, that these resolutions were passed unanimously — there was but one mind and one heart in the assembly, and that mind and heart were but one — for the calmest result of the judgment was in harmony with the warmest feelings of the heart. We did not, however, forget that we were speaking of and to the living, and in avoiding what may be said to be the natural warmth of eulogy — that, we trust, far distant service to come from the trembling lips of some later pupils — we may have assumed a tone too subdued.

One of these resolutions comes from those whose privilege it was to have been your immediate pupils. Of that resolution, as one of the earlier of those pupils, I will say a word. I should be sorry if I thought myself capable of making a formal speech in an hour like this. You are, Mr. President, too largely my creditor for me to judge calmly and wisely. I cannot pay the debt. I do not ask you to forgive it. I can and will confess it. More than twenty years ago it ripened into a judgment, and yet no lapse of time will bar it. Hundreds around you owe the like debt. It grows ever. It is an investment for all time. If you see in it, as I know you do, the true riches, more than the wealth of an Astor is yours. Its bonds are stronger than those of the railroad, its pulse is quicker than that of the telegraph. It is the tribute of loving hearts. It is the debt of filial gratitude.

I came here, to-day, Mr. President, to say now what I have often said at home and to my own pupils, and what this seems to me a fitting occasion to say more publicly.

It has been my privilege for three years to be your pupil. I have seen and have had other eminent masters; Joseph Story, whose name is identified with the jurisprudence of his country; John Hooker Ashmun, who, an invalid for years, and dying at the early age of thirty-three, as a lawyer, left behind him no superior in Massachusetts, whose mind had the point of the diamond and the clearness of its waters; Pliny Merrick, who graces the bench on which I have the honor to sit, but of whom my near relation to him forbids me to speak as I would. A quarter of a century has passed since I left these walls with your blessing. I have seen something of men and of the world since. I esteem it to-day the happiest event of my life that brought me here, the best gift of an ever kind Providence to me, that I was permitted for three years to sit at the feet of your instruction.

Others may speak and think of the writer and scholar, my tribute is to the great teacher; and he is not the great teacher who fills the mind of his pupil from the affluence of his learning or works most for him, but who has the rarer faculty of drawing out and developing the mind of another, and making him work for himself. Rarest of all God's gifts to men. Great statesmen, great orators, great jurists are successful and useful in the degree that they are great teachers. Office of unequalled dignity and worth — even our divine Lord and Master we call the "Great Teacher."

Mr. President, if I have acquired any consideration in my own beloved Commonwealth, if I have worthily won any honor, I can and do with a grateful heart bring them to-day and lay them at your feet; *Teucro duce et auspice Teucro.*

During Dr. Wayland's retirement he pursued his favorite studies, and prepared works for the press, such as "Notes on the Principles and Practices of Baptists," "Sermons to the Churches," "Letters on the Ministry of the Gospel," and "Memoir of the Christian Labors of Chalmers." He revised also his Moral Philosophy, a new edition of which appeared almost simultaneous with his death. He was instrumental in organizing the Brown Street Baptist Church, identifying himself with the movement at great personal sacrifices. . In the early part of 1857, he was invited by the First Baptist Church and Society to supply the pulpit and perform pastoral duties. The conviction had been growing upon him that he had perhaps erred in leaving the pulpit for the Presidency of the College, and he entered upon his new duties with all the ardor and zeal of a young man. He preached with great earnestness and success until June, 1858, when failing health compelled him to retire from active exertions in the cause which he loved so well. He died at his residence in Providence, on Saturday afternoon, September 30, 1865, after a brief illness of a week, having had, like the lamented Manning, an attack of apoplexy or paralysis. His funeral was on the Wednesday following, in the Baptist Church. The spacious house was crowded with mourners, many ministers and alumni of the College coming from Boston and New York, and from more distant points, to pay their last tribute of affection and respect. Thousands, during the hour preceding the services, gazed with sad hearts and tearful eyes upon his majestic form and noble features, now calm in the repose of death. From the eloquent and truthful remarks upon this occasion of the Rev. Dr. Caswell, his life-long associate and most intimate friend, we may be allowed to quote the following:—

His intellect was clear and vigorous, his perceptive powers quick and discriminating, his analysis searching and exhaustive, his generalizations careful, his power of illustration almost unrivalled ; but after all, it was his moral power that left the deepest impression upon those who knew him, or who in any way came within the sphere of his personal influence. In every assembly of citizens, whether for deliberation upon grave public affairs, or for the founding and endowment of hospitals, or providing shelter for orphans, or a home for the aged and infirm. his presence was felt as no other man's was. All waited to hear the utterance of his voice. In every enterprise among us for the moral and religious improvement of the community, in every charity for the relief of the poor, in every effort to succor the fallen and reclaim the wanderer, his counsel was sought almost as an indispensable condition of success. It may justly be said, that he stood among us as the first citizen of Rhode Island.

If we look for the source of this extraordinary power, I think it may be said to spring primarily and mainly from a profound conviction of religious duty. This was the broad basis of his character. This seemed to control all the other elements of his nature, and bring them all into harmonious action. and concentrate them all on a great purpose, that of making men better ; nay, bringing them to the knowledge of the truth as it is in Jesus, and thus making them meet for the Kingdom of Heaven. I need not say in this presence, that Dr. Wayland believed in a Divine revelation. He believed, in his inmost soul, that Jesus Christ spoke as never man spoke, and that he spoke with authority. And hence his profound reverence for the teachings of the New Testament. When he had ascertained the meaning of the sacred text, he held that meaning as a part of God's unalterable truth. He governed himself by it. He pressed it upon the consideration of others. He admitted nothing as a substitute for it. Nothing could supplant it. He held it with the tenacity of a martyr. He believed that there was but one remedy for human wickedness and guilt, and that was, *repentance towards God and faith in our Lord Jesus Christ*. I may say that the cross of Christ stood over before him as the symbol of an undying love and glorious redemption ; and when his great soul, wrapped in devotion, soared highest above the beggarly elements of the world, it approached nearest to the foot of the cross.

The writer of this historical sketch can never forget the joy that beamed in President Wayland's eye and irradiated his countenance, when, as a student, he called at his room and informed him that a class-mate, now a distinguished Professor in a neighboring college, who had been known as a skeptic in his religious views, was deeply anxious about his spiritual welfare ;—and it is pleasant to recall a conversation had with him but a few days previous to his final sickness, on the importance of simple Bible instruction in our Sunday schools, and the need of a suitable question book for this purpose, which, he stated, he had undertaken to prepare.

The following description of Dr. Wayland's personal appearance, character, and habits, we take from a sermon preached by his brother-in-law, the Rev. Dr. C. A. Bartol, of Boston, October 8, 1865: —

His nature was as extraordinary as his character was rare. He was a king by divine anointing — one of the few whose aspect drew attention and fixed every eye. From some persons, we know not how, by a sort of elemental energy, a thrill passes. A slight shudder, half of fear, half of strange attraction, goes through us in their presence. Besides Daniel Webster, I know not who else of our citizens was so charged for this galvanic shock, which his features conducted. His brow, at the orbit of the eye, might have served as an artist's model for Jupiter; and I am not surprised at the story, that, when there was presented to him an exorbitant bill in a foreign land, he looked from the paper to the chafferer, and without speech, the latter fled in terror out of the room. The judgment-seat shone in his eyes for all who ever entered his company.

But the main point is his native energy. What God willed in him, he willed for himself. The first quality I shall specify, had a right to grow in such a soil. It was his justice. He wrote on moral science, and he was the majesty of the moral law in his own person. He walked and spoke and looked and did what he penned. In an acquaintance of nearly thirty years, I have observed in him no deviation from rectitude.

So full of it was he, that he impressed it irresistibly on others. Combined with singular courage and candor, it made him the governor he was. Born to command, of an impassioned soul, with inward fire to drive the bullet and edge the bolt of truth, his conceptions had in them a certain electric swiftness and military force; but righteousness was their range.

Nobody could doubt *he* was President. This gift, thus nursed into a virtue, was the secret of his extraordinary success in administration. I learn, from one of his best students, that, in Brown University, over which he presided for almost a score and a half of years, the new hand at the helm was felt at once. An instantaneous magnetic stroke passed through the buildings. Every inmate was aware of a stringent and wholesome demand of new discipline. Six months had not passed, before the College had risen as by hydrostatic pressure. From no indulgence, but fidelity, ran his scholars' life-long love.

It was this justice which made him such a foe of human slavery. In simple, searching periods, he pointed out its iniquities thirty years ago; though he was, from the same cause, anxious that the evil system should be done away only by means that were lawful and good; and his letters to Dr. Fuller were a valuable contribution to that end. He believed in equity "Corruption wins not more than honesty," was his favorite quotation. But he was no less kind than just. His ethics were set off with such a mien of strictness, that some thought him austere. But that was only the outside. His benevolence was deeper, if possible, than his conscience. He loved to see people about him happy, and to make them so. His glance, that could smite like a cannon-ball, could be gentle too. His voice, which could intone a divine authority, melted with a goodness more divine. I have scarcely listened, in another, to similar accents, which, in private converse, of social and domestic scenes, had a wonderful blending of softness and strength, resembling the mighty and mellow break of the surge on the shore. Mercy was the ground-swell ever heaving up. He was always aiming to bless somebody; and we cannot count the number of those he blessed. If visitors called at his house during his absence, he would, on his return, inquire: "Did you take them into the garden? Did you give them some flowers and some fruit?" Benignity looked out of those keen eyes, and tenderness sat on the lips, which you marvelled could unite such sweetness with their force.

His mood was as perfect as his disposition was fine. I mean he was not, like some kind-hearted men, subject to irritation. Out of temper, he was, I think, never beheld. A hasty word, an uncharitable judgment, I never heard from his mouth. It was not because there was no heat in his soul. A tropical climate prevailed there; but he was a Christian, a great convert of the Pauline stamp. He was so poised he never needed to be on his guard. You would as soon have feared losing the centre of gravity in the globe. He was a man of weight. "When he was in the city," said one, "we always knew it." All the potencies of passion were under his control, as a tame creature keeps not the track like one under the curb. The lion was unmistakable under that tawny skin and shaggy hair; but he had lain down with the lamb; and that lamb was the Lamb of God; and, if the lion's voice was heard, it was no growl, prelude to the devouring leap, but the roar of indignation for a great cause injured or endangered, which made the land resound. He was meek; yet his patience under reproach was not that he lacked a quick sense of what was due to himself, but that he forebore to urge it. Sometimes a bit of friendly irony escaped. When one said to him, "I cannot ask you, with your views, into my pulpit," he simply replied, "Were it not as well to wait till you know I want to enter it?" But he was willing to be chastened, and he told me he was of Dr. Freeman's mind, that a stout mortification occasionally did a man good. Yet no self-denial ever frayed his individuality. As the size of a pyramid or mountain is not incompatible with the definiteness of its lines, so, through all the breadth of his sympathies, stood the independence of his mind. Confessed leader of one of the largest religious denominations in this country, he never lost himself in the million of his followers. No recluse thinker or transcendental essayist was less conventional, or stood stronger on his own feet. He was like an embodied law of nature, a principle of light and life and elevation to his sect, while he was Catholic to all parties * * * * *

Another virtue in him was his *work* In no man's fibre was it ever more stamped. Of what is called terrible toiling, he was a case. If he made any mistake, it was his disallowance of recreation. No theatre, no opera, no concert, no dance for him! His constant look was as one bent to the task, buckling to the oar in a race. I asked him what relaxation was allowed to a minister. He smiled and said, "*A walk.*" When others went a journey, or took a vacation, or staid among the mountains, or by the sea, he remained at home, as in term-time, at his desk. His capacity of persistence I was tempted to envy; but, if I remonstrated with him, he would say, gravely, "It is about as well." He chose a common room, like any under-graduate, within the College precincts, for his study. Hot summer afternoons, I have seen him there, busy in original composition, steadily writing and perspiring, when most men would have considered the stints of the day over. In the morning he would go, for an hour or two, to work in his garden, more vigorously than anybody you employ for such a purpose, and as expertly as if gardening were all his business; for no gardener can show in his grounds a handsomer horticultural monument than still stands of him. He told me he believed in that sort of exercise which was also productive labor; and he alternated this effort of the muscles, with equally severe exertion of the brain. We cannot be saved by our works, say apostle and saint; but if any man could, it was Dr. Wayland. How often I have seen him, spade in hand, advising some caller, who had pursued him from the house! As a specimen of physical, intellectual, and moral ability to achieve, where shall we find his peer?*

A most excellent discourse in commemoration of President Wayland, was delivered before the alumni and friends of the University, Tuesday, September 4, 1866, by Prof. George I. Chace, LL. D.; which discourse has since been published in a pamphlet

---

*The remains of Dr. Wayland lie interred in the North Burial Ground, where also are the remains of Presidents Manning and Maxcy. Over them the family have recently erected to his memory a substantial granite monument or obelisk. During his pastorate in Boston, he married Lucy Lincoln, of that city, sister of the Hon. Heman Lincoln. Two sons, the fruits of this marriage, are living, Judge Francis Wayland, of New Haven, Connecticut, and the Rev. Prof. Heman L. Wayland, of Kalamazoo College, Michigan. His second wife was Mrs. Sage, of Boston, who, with her son, Howard Wayland, survives him.

form. The accompanying likeness was engraved from a photograph, taken in the latter part of the year 1862.

Dr. Wayland was succeeded in the Presidency by the Rev. Barnas Sears, who was elected to this office by a unanimous vote of the Corporation, at the special meeting to which we have already referred, held on the 21st of August, 1855. Mr. Sears was born in Sandisfield, Massachusetts, on the 19th of November, 1802. In 1822, he entered the Sophomore class of Brown University, and graduated in 1825, at the age of twenty-three. His class numbered forty-eight, being the largest class that has ever gone out from the Institution during its entire history. Having finished a course of theological study at Newton, Massachusetts, he, in 1829, became the pastor of the First Baptist Church in Hartford, Connecticut, where he remained two years. At the expiration of this period he accepted an appointment to a professorship in the Hamilton Literary and Theological Institution, now Madison University, New York. In 1833 he embarked for Europe, and spent several years in study at the Universities of Halle, Leipsic and Berlin. While here he laid the foundations for his excellent library, and acquired that taste for the German language and literature, which he has continued to cultivate with such earnestness and enthusiasm. Upon his return to this country he was appointed to a professorship in the Theological Seminary at Newton, where he remained twelve years; during the latter part of this period he was President of the Institution. Upon the resignation of the late Horace Mann, in 1848, he was made Secretary and Executive Agent of the Massachusetts Board of Education. This responsible position he filled with distinguished honor and usefulness for a period of seven years. In these several situations, all of them connected with the interests of learning and religion, Dr. Sears had become widely known to the public, and especially to the religious denomination to which he is attached.

By his professional labors and published writings he had acquired a high reputation for superior talents and varied scholarship; while his persuasive eloquence and genial manners had secured for him in all quarters a host of admiring friends. He was thus preëminently fitted to become the successor of Wayland, Messer, Maxcy, and Manning.

Dr. Sears entered upon his duties at the beginning of the Fall term. The Chancellor of the Institution, Dr. Tobey, attended the services in the Chapel, and in a neat and appropriate speech introduced the new President to the gentlemen of the Faculty, and to the students. In his reply which follows, he gracefully struck the key note of his administration,— popular education, and an earnest devotion to the interests of young men:—

YOUNG GENTLEMEN:—

I am well aware of the grave nature of the duties which I have undertaken to discharge in accepting the office to which I have been called. My humble abilities, too favorably viewed by the Corporation and its official organ who has honored me with this presentation, shall be faithfully devoted to the interests of those committed to my charge. I am greatly encouraged by seeing around me a body of able, and, for the most part, experienced instructors, on whose counsel and coöperation I may safely rely. The general subject to which I am called to direct my attention is, indeed, not new. With education in some form, I have been occupied the greater part of my life. My interest in the subject is second to that of no one. I am deeply interested in young men at that period of life when their characters are formed. In you I see those, who have left their homes and the influence of daily parental example and counsel, perhaps for the first time. Certainly you are now in a situation which requires some independence of character. Your opinions are to be formed anew. Your intellects are to be exercised, and your minds intensely employed in academical study just at the period of their most rapid growth. The intellectual character here formed will probably continue through life. To do what I may to aid you in this important preparatory work will be the object of my highest ambition. I shall rely on the ingenuousness, characteristic of youth, for a reciprocity of feeling and action. While we seek only your good in the highest degree, on broad and generous principles, we may safely trust that you, on your part, will pursue your studies with the same end in view. Yield yourselves, then, confidingly to that honorable career of intellectual and moral improvement in which it will be my delight to aid you, and spend these few golden years, devoted to liberal studies, in such a way that society at large, and yourselves individually, may long enjoy the benefit and rejoice in the fruits of it.

The first decade of President Sears's administration extends through the financial crisis of 1857, and the long and terrible war with the South;—nevertheless, during this period the facilities for instruction have been increased; an elegant and well-appointed Laboratory, for the department of Analytical Chemistry, has been erected at the expense of liberal-minded citizens of Providence; a system of scholarships for meritorious and indigent students has been inaugurated; the Bowen Estate, so called, on the corner of George and Prospect streets, has, through the munificence of a member of the Corporation, been added to the College Green; the Institution has been brought into harmonious relations with the governments of the City and the State, by liberal concessions in the matter of taxation; a debt of twenty-five thousand dollars has been extinguished; and large additions have been made to the College funds. The "New System" introduced by his predecessor has been considerably modified. The increased opportunities for practical education are still offered. But inasmuch as it was found that, while the whole number of students in the partial course increased, those who pursued a full course diminished,—361 students having entered in the years 1850–54, while only 108 were graduated in the full course in the years 1854–58,—it was thought expedient to abandon the three years' course for the degree of Bachelor of Arts, and to diminish the prominence of the partial course. The course of study for academic degrees has therefore returned to its former order and limits. The Bachelor's degree in arts is given at the end of four years of prescribed study; the Master's degree is conferred in course; the Baccalaureate in Philosophy is retained as originally prescribed.

The University has at present, besides a mansion for the President, and a grammar school building erected in 1810, five College buildings or halls, viz.: University Hall, built in 1770, of brick, four stories high, 150 feet long and 46 feet wide, with a projection on the east and west sides of 10 feet by 33, containing 58 rooms for officers and students; Hope College, built in 1822, of brick, four stories high, 120 feet long and 40 wide, containing 48 rooms; Manning Hall, built in 1834, of stone covered with cement, 90 feet in length by 42 in width, two stories high, containing the library room and the chapel; Rhode Island Hall, built in 1840, of stone covered with cement, two stories high, 70 feet long by 42 wide, containing two lecture rooms with apparatus, an ample hall for the cabinet of mineralogy, geology, etc., and a basement fitted up for chemical purposes; and a Chemical Laboratory, built in 1862, of Danvers pressed brick, two stories high, 50 feet long and 40 wide, with a projection on the east side of 35 by 55 feet.

The College library, which from the beginning has been regarded by the friends of the Institution as of the highest importance, and which has always received a large share of their attention and liberality, contains thirty-five thousand carefully selected volumes, including a rich collection of rare and valuable pamphlets. It is open daily for the use of Professors, graduates and undergraduates, between the hours of nine and one. The College grounds comprise about fifteen acres, and are worth, at the present valuation of landed property in their immediate vicinity, upwards of half a million of dollars. These grounds include the University Grammar School lot, about 80 by 138 feet; the President's mansion lot, 80 by 240 feet; the house lots bequeathed to the University by the Hon. Nicholas Brown, 138 feet deep, and extending from a point 119 feet west of Thayer street, eastward to Hope street; the College Green in front of University Hall, the College Campus in the rear, and the College Park, extending from the Campus east to Thayer street. The College enclosure proper comprises the Green and the Campus, and is bounded in general by George, Prospect, Waterman and Thayer streets. The invested funds of the College amount to three hundred and twenty-five thousand dollars; and vigorous efforts are being made to increase them to half a million. In this summary are comprised the original funds, amounting to $21,800; the Nicholas Brown professorship of oratory and belles-lettres, $13,000; the library fund, $25,000; the President's premium fund, $1,000; scholarships, $45,000; aid fund, $5,000; subscription fund for the "New System"; and the one hundred thousand dollars recently given to the College, by Messrs. William Sprague, William H. Reynolds, William S. Slater, Horatio N. Slater, and Earl P. Mason.

From the triennial catalogue published in 1866, it appears that the number of graduates from the beginning is 2,267. In addition to these, many persons have received at the Institution a partial training, remaining within its walls, one, two, or three years, but without receiving any degree;—thus making perhaps three thousand as the quota of educated men which the University has furnished for the country and the world, during the first century of her existence. The academic year is divided into two terms, the first beginning on the first Wednesday in September, and continuing twenty weeks; the second beginning three weeks after the close of the first, (about the middle of February,) and continuing twenty weeks,—to about the second week in July. A recess of one week occurs in the middle of each term. The annual Commencement is on the first Wednesday of September. In the order and the course of study, Brown University does not now differ essentially from her sister colleges of the United States. Her Faculty consists of a President, who is also

Professor of Intellectual and Moral Philosophy, six Professors, three Instructors, and two assistant Instructors. A Librarian and a Register complete her list of officers. Retaining all that the times called for, and all that she found worthy in her "New System," she proceeds, as of old, on the well-tried basis of a sound and thorough Christian, classical and scientific culture; and offers and gives to her pupils an education in keeping with the spirit in which she was founded, and with the intentions of those who have enriched her with ample means, and nurtured her with untiring devotion and zeal.

An extract from President Sears's excellent discourse, delivered at the celebration of the one hundredth anniversary of the founding of the Institution, September 6, 1864, finds here an appropriate place. The author's predictions in regard to an observatory are, we are happy to add, in a fair way of being fulfilled. The Rev. Dr. Caswell, for so many years a Professor in the University, has taken this matter in hand, and has already, it is understood, secured liberal subscriptions for the purchase of a telescope and accompanying instruments, and for the erection of a suitable building. It is earnestly hoped that the picture of the future, so skillfully drawn by the President, will become a reality at some day not far removed from the present:—

New aspects of the place will present themselves to the eye of the spectator who shall stand upon the College campus. As, out of the rough and rocky hill, where Manning took up his abode, with nothing to obstruct his view of the bay, and with only a pathway leading to the neighboring town, an enchanting sight of public buildings, and private residences, and gardens, and broad and beautiful streets, now meets the eye; so, at a future day, not very remote, one will see the vacant plat opposite our beautiful laboratory, occupied by a structure for a kindred purpose, rivalling it in beauty and excellence; and in the rear of both, through a vista formed by them, or elsewhere, a magnificent fire-proof library building, worthy of the precious treasure which it is to protect. On some eminence, not far distant, may, perchance, be seen an observatory pointing its huge telescope to the heavens. Our city itself shall extend eastward, till it reach the river; and, beyond this, shall rise numerous villas, fringing the town.

Let the remaining parts of the picture be filled out by another hand, at some future time; and, before withdrawing from this scene of our fancy, which is sure to be realized in some form similar to what is here sketched, let us leave a cordial welcome to those whom a revolving age shall bring to occupy our places, to the ministers and witnesses of further progress, to be followed, in turn, by others, who, in long succession, shall labor with new devotion and fervor, to perpetuate the blessings and increase the glory of our loved ALMA MATER.

The following presents in a tabular form the number of those who have graduated, from year to year, under the different Presidents:—

MANNING'S ADMINISTRATION.

1769,	- - 7	1773,	- - 5	1777,	- - 7	1787,	- - 10	1791,	- - 16
1770,	- - 4	1774,	- - 6	1782,	- - 7	1788,	- - 20		
1771,	- - 6	1775,	- - 10	1783,	- - 6	1789,	- - 9	Total,	- 165
1772,	- - 6	1776,	- - 9	1786,	- - 15	1790,	- - 22		

MAXCY'S ADMINISTRATION.

1792,	- - 17	1795,	- - 26	1798,	- - 18	1801,	- - 19	Total,	- 227
1793,	- - 12	1796,	- - 17	1799,	- - 24	1802,	- - 28		
1794,	- - 20	1797,	- - 23	1800,	- - 23		—		

MESSER'S ADMINISTRATION.

1803,	- - 23	1808,	- - 33	1813,	- - 35	1818,	- - 18	1823,	- - 27
1804,	- - 22	1809,	- - 60	1814,	- - 47	1819,	- - 20	1824,	- - 41
1805,	- - 28	1810,	- - 20	1815,	- - 22	1820,	- - 29	1825,	- - 48
1806,	- - 19	1811,	- - 24	1816,	- - 33	1821,	- - 40	1826,	- - 28
1807,	- - 28	1812,	- - 23	1817,	- - 25	1822,	- - 30	Total,	- 693

WAYLAND'S ADMINISTRATION.

1827,	- - 30	1833,	- - 20	1839,	- - 35	1845,	- - 28	1851,	- - 32
1828,	- - 25	1834,	- - 23	1840,	- - 36	1846,	- - 32	1852,	- - 38
1829,	- - 19	1835,	- - 15	1841,	- - 31	1847,	- - 33	1853,	- - 24
1830,	- - 20	1836,	- - 24	1842,	- - 35	1848,	- - 30	1854,	- - 40
1831,	- - 13	1837,	- - 38	1843,	- - 29	1849,	- - 27	1855,	- - 35
1832,	- - 23	1838,	- - 30	1844,	- - 26	1850,	- - 22	Total,	- 813

SEARS'S ADMINISTRATION.

1856,	- - 26	1859,	- - 31	1862,	- - 25	1865,	- - 41	Total,	- 369
1857,	- - 30	1860,	- - 29	1863,	- - 28	1866,	- - 42		
1858,	- - 36	1861,	- - 38	1864,	- - 43		—		

We may add, as a sort of appendix to the foregoing, a review of the triennial catalogue, to which reference has already been made. From the summary it appears that the entire number of the sons of Brown University, including not only graduates, but all who have been honored by the Board of Fellows with degrees, or received into her fellowship *ad eundem*, is 2,815; of whom 1,523 are now living. These are scattered over all parts of the globe, and may be supposed to represent fairly the learned professions, and the various callings and pursuits of life.

One of the oldest living graduates, if not the oldest, at the time when the catalogue was passing through the press, was the Hon. Ezekiel Whitman, of the class of 1795, for many years Chief Justice of the Supreme Court of Maine. He has since died, (August 1, 1866,) at his residence in East Bridgwater, Massachusetts, in the ninety-first year of his age. Among other Judges and Chief Justices of the Supreme Court, we notice the names of Samuel Eddy, James Burrill, Tristam Burges, Samuel Randall, Richard Ward Greene, Luke Drury, Job Durfee, Joseph Joslen, William R. Staples, Levi Haile, Samuel Ames, George A. Brayton, Alfred Bosworth, Charles S. Bradley, and Thomas Durfee, of Rhode Island; Marcus Morton, Theron Metcalf, Charles E. Forbes, and Benjamin F. Thomas, of Massachusetts; Asa Aldis, of Vermont; William L. Marcy, of New York; Jabez Bowen, and John G. Polhill, of Georgia. To enumerate judges of the inferior courts, who have received their education at the University, would require more space than can well be spared.

Among those who have filled the office of Governor or Lieutenant-Governor in the several states, we notice in passing, the names of Samuel Coney, of Maine; Jared Warner Williams, of New Hampshire; John H. Clifford, John Reed, and Marcus Morton, of Massachusetts; James Fenner, Philip Allen, John Brown Francis, Jonathan R. Bullock, Nicholas Brown, William Greene,

Elisha Dyer, Henry B. Anthony, and Samuel G. Arnold, of Rhode Island; Ebenezer Stoddard, of Connecticut; James Tallmadge, and William L. Marcy, of New York; Andrew Pickens, of South Carolina; and Pendleton Murrah, the rebel Governor of Texas.

The first President of the College, as has already been stated in the beginning, was a member of Congress in 1786. Of his pupils, and those who have graduated under his successors, thirty-seven appear in the catalogue with the affix "e Cong." to their names. The earliest is James Mitchell Varnum, of the class of 1769, and the latest, Samuel Sullivan Cox, of the class of 1846. Eighteen of the graduates have been honored with a seat in the United States Senate, as follows: Theodore Foster, of the class of 1770; Dwight Foster, class of 1774; James Burrill, class of 1788; James Fenner, class of 1789; James Brown Howell, class of 1789; William Hunter, class of 1791; John Holmes, class of 1796; Nathan Fellows Dixon, class of 1799; Philip Allen, class of 1803; John Brown Francis, class of 1808; William Larned Marcy, class of 1808; John Hopkins Clarke, class of 1809; John Ruggles, class of 1813; Jared Warner Williams, class of 1818; Lafayette Sabine Foster, class of 1828; Henry Bowen Anthony, class of 1833; Samuel Greene Arnold, class of 1841; and John Milton Thayer, class of 1841, recently elected Senator for Nebraska. Of the four delegates to Congress from Rhode Island at the present time, three are graduates of Brown, viz.: Nathan F. Dixon, class of 1833; Thomas A. Jenckes, class of 1838; and Henry B. Anthony.

The entire number of graduates from the beginning, is 2,267. Of this number 583, or more than one-fourth, appear in italics, having been ordained and set apart to the work of the Christian ministry. Ninety-five of this class have been honored at this Institution, and elsewhere, with the degree of Doctor in Divinity. Among the Divines thus honored, we notice the names of Prof.

William Rogers of the first graduating class; Calvin Park, class of 1797, for many years Professor of Moral Philosophy and Metaphysics in the Institution; David Benedict, class of 1806, the venerable Baptist historian; Adoniram Judson, class of 1807, the distinguished missionary to Burmah; Ebenezer Burgess, class of 1809, a tutor of the Institution from 1811 to 1813; Jacob Ide, class of 1809, a son-in-law of the Rev. Dr. Emmons, of Franklin, and the editor of his published works; John L. Blake, class of 1812, author of a General Biographical Dictionary, which has passed through many editions; Romeo Elton, class of 1813, a Professor of Greek and Latin in the Institution from 1825 to 1843; Enoch Pond, class of 1813, Professor in the Theological Seminary, at Bangor; Alvan Bond, class of 1815, formerly a Professor at Bangor; Solomon Peck, class of 1816, for many years Corresponding Secretary of the American Baptist Missionary Union; Benjamin B. Smith, class of 1816, Bishop of the Episcopal church of Kentucky; Swan L. Pomroy, class of 1820, for many years Corresponding Secretary of the American Board of Commissioners for Foreign Missions; Alexis Caswell, also LL. D., class of 1822, Professor of Mathematics and Natural Philosophy in the Institution from 1828 to 1864; George Burgess, class of 1826, late Bishop of the Episcopal church of Maine; Edwards A. Park, class of 1826, the distinguished Professor of Theology at Andover; M. A. DeWolf Howe, class of 1828, recently elected Bishop of Nebraska, but declined; Edward A. Stevens, class of 1833, Missionary at Rangoon; George M. Randall, class of 1835, Bishop of the Episcopal Church of Colorado; Jonah G. Warren, class of 1835, Corresponding Secretary of the American Baptist Missionary Union; Albert N. Arnold, class of 1838, formerly missionary to Greece, and now a Professor in Madison University; Alexander Burgess, class of 1838, recently elected Bishop of Maine as successor to his brother, but declined; Ezekiel G.

Robinson, class of 1838, Professor in the Theological Seminary at Rochester; William T. Brantly, class of 1840, Professor of Metaphysics and Belles-Lettres in Mercer University, Georgia; Kendall Brooks, class of 1841, editor of the National Baptist; Henry Day, class of 1843, for several years a Professor in the Institution; Robinson P. Dunn, class of 1843, Professor of Rhetoric and English Literature since 1851; James P. Boyce, class of 1847, a Professor of Theology in the Furman Institute, Greenville, South Carolina; George P. Fisher, class of 1847, Professor of Ecclesiastical History in Yale College.

Fifty-two of the graduates have received the degree of Doctor of Laws, at this and other institutions of learning. In addition to the names not elsewhere enumerated, we may mention Thomas Park, of the class of 1789; Nathaniel Searle, class of 1794; Abraham Blanding, class of 1796; Benjamin Allen, class of 1797; John Pitman, class of 1799; John M. Williams, class of 1801; John Whipple, class of 1802; William Giles Goddard, class of 1812, for seventeen years a Professor in the University; Zachariah Allen, class of 1813; William Ruggles, class of 1820, Professor of Mathematics and Natural Philosophy in Columbian College; George R. Russell, class of 1821; Isaac Davis, class of 1822; Edward Mellen, class of 1823; George W. Keely, class of 1824, Professor of Mathematics and Natural Philosophy in Waterville College; John Kingsbury, class of 1826, Secretary of the Corporation; Peter C. Bacon, class of 1827; William M. Cornell, class of 1827, Professor of Anatomy and Physiology in Pittsburg, Pennsylvania; John A. Bolles, class of 1829; George Ide Chace, class of 1830, a Professor in the University since 1833; William Gammell, class of 1831, a Professor in the University from 1835 to 1864; John L. Lincoln, class of 1836, a Professor in the University since 1844; David Burbank, class of 1837; Nathan Bishop, class of 1837, for ten years Superintendent of the

Public Schools in Providence, and afterwards Superintendent of the Public Schools in Boston; Samuel P. Bates, class of 1851, Deputy Superintendent of the Public Schools in Pennsylvania.

Among those who have attained to eminence as diplomatists, orators and statesmen, we may mention especially, Gen. James Mitchell Varnum, of the first graduating class, and Col. Samuel Ward, of the class of 1771, both distinguished officers of the revolutionary army; Samuel Eddy, of the class of 1787, for twenty-one successive years Secretary of Rhode Island, and for eight years Chief Justice of the Supreme Court of the State; Jonathan Russell, of the class of 1791, Minister Plenipotentiary to Stockholm, and one of the five commissioners who negotiated the treaty of peace with England, at Ghent, in 1814,—and whose Fourth of July oration, delivered at Providence in the year 1800, has passed through scores of editions, and furnished material for school-boy declamations from that time down to the present day; William Hunter, also of the class of 1791, a distinguished scholar, and for many years *Charge d' Affaires* at the Court of Brazil; the late William Baylies, of the class of 1795, one of the purest-minded and best jurists of the Bay State; Tristam Burges, of the class of 1796, the distinguished orator, whose keen, sarcastic wit proved more than a match for the redoubtable John Randolph, of Virginia; Henry Wheaton, of the class of 1802, Minister Plenipotentiary to Berlin, and author of "Elements of International Law," still the standard book on this subject, and the text-book in the universities and colleges not only of America, but of England; William Larned Marcy, of the class of 1808, Secretary of War under President Polk, and afterwards, under President Pierce, Secretary of State, and author of the famous letter to the Austrian government on the release of Martin Koszta; Lafayette Sabine Foster, whose name we have already mentioned in the list of senators, late President of the United States Senate. To this list we may add George D. Prentice, of the class of 1823, whose witty paragraphs have made the Louisville Journal famous during the last quarter of a century.

Nearly a hundred of the graduates have rendered good service in the cause of learning as tutors and professors in colleges and theological seminaries, while large numbers have distinguished themselves as teachers in the various schools and academies of the land. A score and upwards have served as Presidents of colleges. We may mention the names of Jonathan Maxcy, of the class of 1787, Asa Messer, of the class of 1790, and Barnas Sears, of the class of 1825, in connection with the Presidency of their Alma Mater. Jeremiah Chaplin, of the class of 1799, Rufus Babcock, of the class of 1821, Eliphas Fay, of the class of 1821, and James Tift Champlin, of the class of 1834, in connection with the Presidency of Waterville College; Willard Preston, of the class of 1806, fourth President of the University of Vermont, and James Burrill Angell, of the class of 1849, recently inaugurated President of the same institution; Jonathan Going, of the class of 1809, President of Granville College, Ohio; Jasper Adams, of the class of 1815, President of Geneva College, New York, and afterwards of Charleston College, South Carolina; Wilbur Fisk, of the class of 1815, first President of the Wesleyan University, Middletown, Connecticut; Jesse Hartwell, of the class of 1819, President of Mt. Lebanon University, Louisiana; Horace Mann, of the class of 1819, President of Antioch College; Silas Axtell Crane, of the class of 1823, President of Kemper College, Missouri, and Eleazar Carter Hutchinson, of the class of 1826, President of the same institution; John Pratt, of the class of 1827, President of Granville College; John Brown White, of the class of 1832, President of Wake Forest College; Silas Bailey, of the class of 1834, President of Granville College, now Denison University, and afterwards President of Franklin College, Indiana;

Justin Rolfe Loomis, of the class of 1835, President of the University of Lewisburg, Pennsylvania; and George Whitefield Samson, of the class of 1839, President of Columbian College, Washington.

In looking over the long list of Trustees and Fellows, but few of whom comparatively speaking are among the graduates of the Institution, one can hardly fail to observe how many of the great and good men of the day it comprises. Prominent among the early Fellows are the names of Morgan Edwards, who first proposed to the Philadelphia Association the founding of the College, and who procured in England and Ireland the funds wherewith it was endowed; Doct. Thomas Eyres of Newport, a graduate of Yale, and the first Secretary of the Corporation; Rev. Edward Upham, a Baptist clergyman of Newport, and a graduate of Harvard in the class of 1734; Rev. Dr. Stillman of Boston, the most popular and eloquent preacher of his day; Rev. Dr. Smith of Haverhill, Massachusetts, the brave patriot, and the classmate and intimate friend of President Manning; Jabez Bowen, LL. D., for five years Deputy Governor of Rhode Island; Judge Howell, LL. D., the first Tutor and Professor of the Institution, and for more than half a century a leading man in the affairs of Rhode Island; Doct. Benjamin Waterhouse, the early advocate of vaccination, and the author of the first course of lectures on Botany and Natural History ever delivered in this country; Rev. John Davis, the "pious and learned" defender of civil and religious liberty; Doct. Solomon Drown, a graduate of the College in the class of 1773, and for many years a leading physician of Providence; Rev. Dr. Enos Hitchcock, a graduate of Harvard College, and a leading clergyman of Providence after the Revolutionary war. At the head of the list of Trustees stands the honored name of Stephen Hopkins, LL. D., Governor of the State, and one of the signers of the Declaration of Independence. He was the first Chancellor of the University, and, like the present Chancellor, was an active member of the Society of Friends. Further down the list appears the name of Esek Hopkins, a brother of the Governor, and the first Commodore in the American Navy. We notice also the names of Samuel Ward, Josias Lyndon, Joseph Wanton, Nicholas Cooke, and William Greene, Governors of Rhode Island previous to and during the war, and Daniel Sessions and William Bradford, Deputy Governors; Daniel Jenckes, whose name is so intimately connected with the history of the College charter. He was for forty years a member of the General Assembly, and for nearly thirty years was Chief Justice of the Providence County Court;—his daughter Rhoda was mother of the Hon. Nicholas Brown, from whom the University derives its name, and also of the late Mrs. Hope Ives, after whom Hope College was named. The venerable Isaac Backus, of Middleborough, the Baptist historian of New England, was for thirty-four years an active Trustee of the Institution. But prominent among the early Trustees are the honored names of Nicholas, Joseph and John Brown. To their united efforts and large-hearted benevolence, not only the College, but the City in which it is located, owe much of their present usefulness and prosperity. Of the more recent members of the Corporation, it may be sufficient to say, that they happily represent the piety, the learning and wealth of the four religious denominations recognized in the charter.

The imperfect review which we have thus been enabled to give of the graduates of Brown University, shows that during the first century of her existence she has performed well her part in the great work of diffusing the blessings of learning and religion in the earth, and of "forming," in the language of her charter, "the rising generation to virtue, knowledge and useful literature." Of such a record the friends and patrons of the Institution may well be proud.

58   BROWN UNIVERSITY.

The following ROLL OF HONOR may fitly close this Historical Sketch. It comprises a list of one hundred and thirty-one STUDENTS (including several recent graduates) who left the quiet shades of the Academy to enter upon the field of strife, and aid in putting down the Rebellion. We publish it as it originally appeared in the "Brown Paper"* for 1862, without change or comment. It shows that Brown University, as in the beginning, has been well represented in the struggles of her country for freedom and union. Of this list of students, twenty-one responded at once to the calls of patriotism, and entered the army in the very beginning of the war. How many of her GRADUATES enlisted under the stars and stripes, may never, perhaps, be fully ascertained.

Henry S. Adams, Lieutenant,	45th Massachusetts Volunteers.
Joshua Addeman,	10th Rhode Island "
William Ames, Captain,	2d " " "
William D. Avery, Captain,	United States Navy.
Seth J. Axtell, Corporal,	51st Massachusetts Volunteers.
George H. Babbitt, Sergeant,	39th " "
Charles E. Bailey,	1st Rhode Island "
W. Whitman Bailey,	10th " " "
Daniel C. Ballou,	12th " " "
Orville A. Barker,	39th Massachusetts "
George B. Barrows,	10th Rhode Island "
John T. Blake, Sergeant,	1st Rhode Island Light Artillery.
William W. Bliss, Sergeant,	New York Ironsides Regiment.
James W. Blackwood,	10th Rhode Island Volunteers.
Amos M. Bowen,	1st " " "
Joseph M. Bradley,	1st Rhode Island Light Artillery.
Charles R. Brayton, Captain,	3d Rhode Island Artillery.
Edward P. Brown, Lieutenant,	4th Rhode Island Volunteers.
T. Frederic Brown, Lieutenant,	1st Rhode Island Light Artillery.
William I. Brown, Lieutenant,	9th New Hampshire Volunteers.
Zephaniah Brown,	10th Rhode Island "

* An annual sheet, commenced in November, 1857, and published under the auspices of the students.

HISTORICAL SKETCH.

John K. Bucklyn, Lieutenant,	1st Rhode Island Light Artillery.
Israel M. Bullock,	10th Rhode Island Volunteers.
Henry S. Burrage,	39th Massachusetts "
Christopher C. Burrows, Sergeant,	1st Rhode Island Cavalry.
Charles D. Cady,	1st Rhode Island Volunteers.
Frank H. Carpenter, Steward,	12th " " "
Charles H. Chapman, Adjutant,	5th " " "
Edson C. Chick,	10th " " "
John S. Chick,	" " " "
Charles M Corbin,	" " " "
David P. Corbin, Lieutenant,	22d Connecticut "
Ellmer L. Corthell, Lieutenant,	1st Rhode Island Light Artillery.
Charles C. Cragin,	10th Rhode Island Volunteers.
Harry C. Cushing, Lieutenant,	4th United States Light Artillery.
Augustus N. Cunningham, Major,	78th New York Volunteers.
William P. Davis, Corporal,	9th Rhode Island "
Edward P. Deacon, Captain,	Staff of General Heintzelman.
James A. DeWolf,	1st Rhode Island Volunteers.
Frederic A. Dockray, Lieutenant,	3d Rhode Island Artillery.
Edgar J. Doe,	10th Rhode Island Volunteers.
John K. Dorrance,	" " " "
Samuel R. Dorrance, Sergeant,	" " " "
William W. Douglas, Lieutenant,	5th " " "
Frank W. Draper,	35th Massachusetts "
James G. Dougherty,	10th Rhode Island "
Samuel W. Duncan, Captain,	45th Massachusetts "
G. Lyman Dwight, Lieutenant,	1st Rhode Island Light Artillery.
John D. Edgell, Lieutenant,	53d Massachusetts Volunteers.
Forrest F. Emerson,	10th Rhode Island "
David Fales,	45th Massachusetts "
Hervey A. Foster, Corporal,	10th Rhode Island Volunteers.
Simeon Gallup, Sergeant,	1st Rhode Island Light Artillery.
Clarence T. Gardner, Lieutenant,	3d Rhode Island Artillery.
Henry G. Gay, Sergeant,	26th Connecticut Volunteers.
Edward K. Glezen, Sergeant Major,	10th Rhode Island "
Josiah R. Goddard,	11th " " "
Charles W. Greene,	35th Massachusetts "
James B. M. Grosvenor,	1st Rhode Island Light Artillery.
Albert E. Ham,	10th " " Volunteers.

George B. Hanna, - - - - - "   "   "   "
Charles L. Harrington, - - - - - Illinois Artillery.
Frank T. Hazlewood, - - - - 10th Rhode Island Volunteers.
Charles H. Hidden, - - - - - "   "   "   "
David A. Holmes, - - - - - 3d   "   "   "
John J. Holmes, - - - - - 10th "   "   "
John S. Holmes, - - - - - "   "   "   "
Wendall P. Hood, - - - - - "   "   "   "
William W. Hoppin, - - - - 1st   "   "   "
Charles F. Hosmer, - - - - - 10th "   "   "
William C. Ives, - - - - - "   "   "   "
Hervey F. Jacobs, Lieutenant, - - - 26th Connecticut Volunteers.
Pardon S. Jastram, Lieutenant, - - - 1st Rhode Island Light Artillery.
Leland D. Jencks, - - - - - "   "   "   Volunteers.
Rodolphus H. Johnson, - - - - 9th   "   "   "
Benjamin D. Jones, Corporal, - - - 4th   "   "   "
George H. Kenyon, - - - - 10th "   "   "
Oscar Lapham, Lieutenant, - - - Staff of General Wright.
Frank W. Love, - - - - 10th Rhode Island Volunteers.
Horace W. Love, Lieutenant, - - - 1st   "   " Light Artillery.
Roger W. Love, - - - - - "   "   "   "
Charles F. Mason, Lieutenant, - - - "   "   "   "   "
Matthew M. Meggett, - - - - 10th "   "   Volunteers.
Joshua Mellen, - - - - - "   "   "   "   "
George H. Messer, - - - - - "   "   "   "
Frederic A. Mitchell, Captain, - - - Staff of General Mitchell.
J. Albert Monroe, Major, - - - - 1st Rhode Island Light Artillery.
Elisha C. Mowry, - - - - - 10th "   "   Volunteers.
B. Frank Pabodie, Corporal, - - - "   "   "   "
Robert H. Paine, - - - - - "   "   "   "
Addison Parker, Jr., - - - - - "   "   "   "
Alexander Peckham, - - - - 9th   "   "   "
Stephen F. Peckham, Hospital Steward, - 7th   "   "   "
Duncan A. Pell, Captain, - - - Staff of General Burnside.
S. Hartwell Pratt, - - - - 10th Rhode Island Volunteers.
J. Amon Price, - - - - - "   "   "   "
Hosea M. Quimby, - - - - - Maine Volunteers.
James H. Remington, Captain, - - - 7th Rhode Island Volunteers.
John W. Rogers, Captain, - - - - 40th Massachusetts "

Frederic M. Sackett, Lieutenant,		1st Rhode Island Light Artillery.
Mattson C. Sanborn, Lieutenant,		2d Maine Volunteers.
Nathaniel T. Sanders,		10th Rhode Island Volunteers.
Eugene Sanger,		New Hampshire "
Isaac H. Saunders,		1st Rhode Island "
Livingston Scott,		10th " "
Orville B. Seagraves,		" " " "
Edward H. Sears, Lieutenant.		1st " Light Artillery.
George W. Shaw,		10th " Volunteers.
Sumner U. Shearman, Lieutenant,		4th " " "
A. Judson Shurtleff,		9th " "
T. Delap Smith, Lieutenant,		41st Massachusetts "
Welcome A. Smith,		26th Connecticut
Henry K. Southwick, Lieutenant.		2d Rhode Island
Henry J. Spooner, Lieutenant,		4th " " "
Hebron H. Steere, Sergeant,		1st " " Cavalry.
Orsmus A. Taft, Corporal,		10th " " Volunteers.
John Tetlow, Corporal,		" " " "
Caleb E. Thayer,		" "
Francis M. Tyler,		9th " "
William H. Underhill.		10th " " "
Levi C. Walker,		" " "
Lewis O. Walker,		" " " "
Joseph Ward,		" " " "
Andrew F. Warren,		" " " "
Richard Waterman, Captain,		1st " " Cavalry.
Rufus Waterman, Midshipman,		United States Navy.
John Whipple, Jr., Captain,		1st Rhode Island Cavalry.
Edward N. Whittier, Sergeant,		2d Maine Battery.
James C. Williams, Captain,		Staff of General Mitchell.
William C. Witter,		10th Rhode Island Volunteers.
George T. Woodward,		39th Massachusetts "

The first Seal of the Corporation was procured by the Rev. Dr. Stillman, of Boston, as appears by a vote on record, passed at the second annual meeting, held at Newport on the first Wednesday in September, 1765. At the annual meeting of the Corporation held in 1782, after the war, it is recorded, that

The Chancellor, the President, and Henry Ward, Esq., were appointed a committee to break the old seal of the College, which contains the busts of the present King and Queen of Great Britain; and to agree upon a new seal with suitable devices, to be made of silver, and to report their proceedings therein to this Corporation.

This committee, it appears, failed to do their work, for, at the next annual meeting, it was

Resolved, That the President, Joseph Brown, Esq., Doct. Waterhouse and Doct. Drown, be a committee to devise and get a new seal engraved for the College as soon as may be.

The Seal of the Corporation now in use was devised by a committee consisting of the Rev. Dr. Wayland, President, Rev. Dr. Crocker, Secretary, Moses B. Ives, Esq., Treasurer, and Hon. Judge Pitman. It was adopted September 3, 1834, as appears by the following resolution on record:—

Resolved, That the Seal of the Corporation of this University be a red cross on a white field, between four open books, illuminated by a sun rising amid clouds, bearing the motto, "In Deo Speramus," and surrounded by a band inscribed Sigillum Universitatis Brunensis.

HISTORY

OF THE

COLLEGE LIBRARY.

1770–1866.

LIBRARY.

WITH the exception of a few books procured in England through the agency of the Rev. Morgan Edwards, the College, at the time of its removal from Warren, was destitute of a Library. To supply as far as possible this deficiency, the Providence Library Company, which, according to the late John Howland, was established as early as 1753, tendered to the officers and students the free use of their books — a privilege which they continued to enjoy many years.

The following extract from a letter addressed by the President to Thomas Llewelyn, LL. D., of London, shows the character and the extent of the Library, two years later. The letter is dated at Providence, February 21, 1772: —

> The College edifice is erected on a most beautiful eminence in the neighborhood of Providence, commanding a charming and variegated prospect; — a large, neat, brick building, and so far completed as to receive the students who now reside there, the whole number of whom is twenty-two. To this number we have the prospect of some further additions, although our increase will not probably be large until we are better furnished with a Library and Philosophical Apparatus. At present we have but about two hundred and fifty volumes, and these not well chosen, being such as our friends could best spare.

Dr. Manning, who was distinguished in those early days for his scholarly attainments and liberal views, did not overestimate the value and importance of a Library, in connection with an institution of learning. The following letter, which we find on file, gives the titles of a part of these two hundred and fifty volumes, to which the President, in his correspondence, alludes:—

NEWPORT, May 16, 1771.

REVEREND SIR:—I have received the undermentioned books by the Tristram, which I now send by Mr. Lindsey, as a present to our College; which present, though in itself small, is yet sufficient (perhaps) to testify the great regard and esteem which I have always had, and I hope I always shall have for the Institution. I have examined them, and am very sorry to find several of them soiled by the carelessness of a passenger, which hurts the looks of them somewhat.

LORD KAIMES on Criticism, 2 vols., (4th ed., 8°, Edin., 1769); REID on the Mind, (3d ed., 8°, Lond., 1769); WATTS's Philosophical Essays, (4th ed., 8°, Lond., 1733); GROVE's Moral Philosophy, (2 vols., 8°, Lond., 1749–50); FENNING's Algebra; THOMPSON's Works; WATTS on the Passions, (4th ed., 12°, Lond., 1751); SPECTATOR, (8 vols., 12°, Lond., 1747); ROLLINS's Belles-Lettres, (4 vols., 12°, Lond., 1769–70); PARADISE LOST AND REGAINED; HURRION's Sermons. (2 vols., 8°, Lond., 1727–9); ROBERTSON's History of Scotland, (2 vols., 8°, Lond., 1761); HISTORY OF ICELAND, (By Horrebow, folio, Lond., 1758).

I remain, Reverend Sir, your sincere friend and well wisher,

JOSEPH D. RUSSELL.

Another of the works included in Dr. Manning's enumeration, was LELAND's View of Deistical Writers, third edition, three volumes, 8°, London, 1757, presented to the Library in 1771, by the Rev. John Graves, at that time pastor of the Episcopal church in Providence.

In the latter part of 1772, through the agency, perhaps, of Dr. Llewelyn, the College received from the executors of the Rev. Dr. John Gill, of London, the distinguished commentator, all his published works, together with fifty-two folio volumes of the Fathers, etc. This, in the days of "small things," was a noble gift, and greatly augmented the treasures of the Library.

The following year, the Rev. Benjamin Wallin, of London, presented to the Library his published works in ten volumes, "neatly bound and gilt," together with BUNYAN's Works, in six volumes, BOOTH's Reign of Grace, and WILSON's Sermons. Donations were also received from the Rev. Dr. Stennett, and others.

In 1774, we find on record, a vote of thanks to the Rev. Simon Williams, of Wenham, "for his generous donation to the College Library, of CUDWORTH's Intellectual System, in two volumes, quarto."

On the 6th of December, 1776, immediately after the occupation of Newport by the British troops, the College was disbanded, and the College building, from that time until June, 1782, as stated in our Historical Sketch, was occupied for barracks and afterwards for a hospital. During this confused period, the books were removed to the country for safe keeping, in the care of the Rev. William Williams, of Wrentham, Massachusetts, one of the class of seven that graduated at Warren in 1769, a clergyman of high repute, and for many years a Fellow of the College.

At the reörganization of the College in the Autumn of 1782, the Hon. Asher Robbins, LL. D., late of Newport, was appointed to the office of tutor, and took charge of the Library as librarian. At a meeting of the Corporation held September 5, of this year, it was

Resolved, That the College Library, which, owing to the public confusions, has for several years been in the country, after being compared and examined by the catalogue, be immediately brought with care into town, that the books may be made use of by the students, as formerly. President Manning and John Jenckes, Esq., are requested to see this order forthwith executed.

The Library was then kept in the east chamber, on the second floor of the College building, in what is now known as the Mathematical recitation room. Some idea of its condition at this time may be learned from President Manning's correspondence. "Our Library," he writes to Rev. Dr. Stennett, of London. " consists of about five hundred volumes, most of which are both very ancient and very useless, as well as very ragged and unsightly." At the next annual meeting of the Corporation, held September 3, 1783, it was

Voted, That the Rev. Hezekiah Smith, Doct. Benjamin Waterhouse, Doct. Thomas Eyres, and Doct. Solomon Drown, be a committee to immediately solicit subscriptions for the College, in Providence and Newport.

Voted, That the Chancellor, the President, Joseph Brown, Esq., Mr. Tutor Robbins, Rev. Dr. Stillman, Doct. Waterhouse, and Doct. Drown be a committee to make out a catalogue of philosophical instruments and books, to be purchased by the above subscriptions.

At this meeting, "Mr. John Brown, the Treasurer of the College, offered," says Manning, in a letter to Dr. Stennett, written two months afterward, "to give a sum equal to what all the other members would subscribe, towards procuring an addition to our little Library, and a philosophical apparatus. By this means we obtained subscriptions for near £700 lawful money, six shillings to the dollar, and the catalogues are being made out."

In a letter to the Rev. Dr. Evans, President of the Baptist Academy in Bristol, England, Manning, under date of September 13, 1784, further writes: "We have ordered out from London this Fall about fourteen hundred volumes, * * * a donation from our Treasurer, John Brown, Esq., of Providence. The amount of two hundred pounds sterling was also ordered to be expended in the purchase of a necessary philosophical apparatus, in addition to what we already have, consisting chiefly of a telescope, an air pump and its apparatus, globes, and a thermometer. The money for this order was subscribed by other members of the Corporation last Fall." A list of these fourteen hundred volumes, with the prices, is now, we may add, on file among the College archives. To the bibliographer and the antiquary, it constitutes a document of special interest. The selection was made chiefly by President Manning and the Chancellor, Gov. Hopkins, both of whom were well versed in English literature, and excellent judges of good books.

The following books were imported at this time by Mr. Moses Brown, at a cost of £18 2s 7d sterling, and by him presented to the College Library. Mr. Brown was the younger brother of the Treasurer, and the distinguished patron of the Friends' Boarding School. The books are mostly in illustration of the principles of the religious denomination to which he was attached;—many of them are now rare and of great value. We give the original prices, as we find them in a list on file:—

	£	s.	d.
George Fox's Journal, 3d ed., folio, Lond., 1765,	0	15	0
——— ——— Gospel Truth Demonstrated, folio, Lond., 1706,	0	12	0
Yearly Meeting Epistles, from 1675 to 1759, folio, Lond., 1760,	0	6	0
Robert Barclay's Works, 3 vols., 8°, Lond., 1718–36,	0	13	0
——— ——— Apology, in Latin, 2d ed., 8°, Lond., 1729,	0	4	0
William Penn's Select Works, 5 vols., 8°, Lond., 1782,	1	2	6
Thomas Elwood's Sacred History, 4th ed., 3 vols., 8°, Lond., 1778,	0	15	0
——— ——— Life, 3d ed., 8°, Lond., 1765,	0	3	0
Richard Claridge's Life and Posthumous Works, 8°, Lond., 1726,	0	4	3
——— ——— On the Holy Scriptures, 8°, Lond., 1751,	0	1	6
George Whitehead's Christian Progress, 8°, Lond., 1725,	0	4	6
Alexander Arscott's Considerations, 3d ed., 8°, Lond., 1779,	0	2	6
John Fothergill's Life and Travels, 2d ed., 8°, Lond., 1773,	0	3	3
Dr. John Fothergill's Account of Ackworth School,	0	0	9¼
Hird's Tribute to Memory of Dr. Fothergill,	0	0	9
Sermons of Quakers; taken in Short-Hand, 8°, Lond., 1775,	0	2	6
John Rutty's Materia Medica, 4°, Rotterdam, 1775,	1	0	0
——— ——— Spiritual Diary, 2 vols., 12°, Lond., 1776,	0	6	0
Whiting's Life of John Gratton, 12°, Lond., 1779,	0	1	8
William Crouch on Covetousness, 8°, Lond., 1708,	0	2	3
Sewell's History of the Quakers, 2d ed., folio, Lond., 1725,	1	0	0
Joseph Phipps's Original State of Man, 8°, Lond., 1767,	0	3	0
Samuel Fothergill on Life of Holiness, etc., 2d ed., 8°, Lond., 1761,	0	3	0
John Woolman's Works, 2d ed., 8°, Phila., 1775,	0	6	0
John Churchman's Life,	0	3	6
Piety Promoted, 8th Part,	0	3	0

	£	d.	s.
Bishop's New England judged, (including Whiting's Truth and Innocency defended,) 8°, Lond., 1702-3,	0	6	0
Life of Samuel Bownas, 2d ed., 8°, Lond., 1761,	0	3	0
Life of John Richardson, 3d ed., 8°, Lond., 1774.	0	4	0
John Whiting's Persecution Exposed, 4°, Lond., 1715,	0	6	6
Martin's New Principles of Geography, folio, Lond., 1758,	0	15	0
One old very large map of North America,	0	12	0
Dr. John Fothergill's Works, 3 vols., 8°, Lond., 1783-4,	1	11	6
Two volumes of miscellaneous works by Sophia Hume, Deborah Bell, Mary Brooks, Homes, Claridge, Foster, Wilkinson, Bess, etc.,	1	0	0
	£18	2	7

During this same year, 1784, John Tanner, Esq., of Newport, one of the early members of the Corporation, presented to the Library one hundred and thirty-five volumes of miscellaneous books, most of which, as appears from a list on file, were religious in their character. Many of them are now of special value as illustrating the ecclesiastical history of New England;—among which may be mentioned: Backus's Church History, Sermons by Coleman and Callender, Morton's New England Memorial, Cotton Mather's Remarkables, Morgan Edwards's Materials for Baptist History, Edwards's Narrative, Collection of Sermons by Lathrop, Cooper, Williams, Backus, Mather, etc., etc.

During this same year also, the Hon. Granville Sharp, LL. D., of London, with whom Manning corresponded, presented to the Library his own publications, which were numerous, together with a set of the works of his grandfather, Dr. John Sharp, Archbishop of York. He subsequently sent other valuable presents to the Library. In the correspondence of Manning we also find mention of a set of Saurin's Sermons, presented by Thomas Mullett, Esq., a brother-in-law of Dr. Caleb Evans, of Bristol.

These various donations increased the Library, so that it now contained, says Manning, "upwards of two thousand volumes."

In a letter dated Bristol, September 5, 1785, Dr. Evans thus writes to the President: "At our late annual meeting of the Education Society here, August 24, I obtained a vote in favor of your College, respecting the many valuable books we have to dispose of, and am empowered to send such as I may approve of. I shall take an early opportunity of doing this, and when received shall hope for the favor of a line from you."

This handsome donation—consisting of sixty-one folio volumes, twenty-five quartos, fifty-eight octavos, and five duodecimos, in all one hundred and forty-nine well-bound volumes, including several Fathers of the Church and standard works in science, history, literature and the classics—was received early the following year. Among the folios may be mentioned: WALTON's Biblia Sacra Polyglotta, with CASTELL's Lexicon; BAYLE's Dictionary; CHAMBERS's Cyclopædia; BIOGRAPHIA BRITANNICA; OWEN on the Hebrews, and the Holy Spirit; NESS's History and Mystery of the Bible; POOL's Annotations; CHILLINGWORTH's Works; WHITBY's Commentary; CENTURIATORES MAGDEBURGICI; WYNNE's Life of Jenkins; JOSEPHI Opera; SHAW's and POCOCK's Travels; DIO CASSII Historia Romana; BURNET's Reformation; PLINII Historia Naturalis; WARD's Lives of the Professors of Gresham College; FIDDES's Life of Cardinal Wolsey, etc. SHERIDAN's Lectures, NEAL's History of the Puritans, JORTIN's Life of Erasmus, SALES's Koran, GILL's Body of Divinity, OWEN on Justification, and QUINTILIANI Institutiones, are among the quartos. Such evidences of kind feeling on the part of those with whom this country had so recently been at war, must have been highly gratifying at the time, as they most certainly are even at the present day. This "Education Society" was founded in the year 1780, in aid of the Baptist Academy at Bristol, "to the end that dissenting congregations, especially of the Baptist denomination, in any part of the British dominions, might be more effectually supplied with a succession of able and evangelical ministers." The Society has been eminently useful. It is now in the possession of a very valuable library, containing the collection of books, paintings, etc., of the Rev. Dr. Andrew Gifford, for many years sub-librarian of the British Museum, and also the collection of Dr. Llewelyn.

The following by-laws, adopted by the Corporation at a special meeting held December 23, 1785, may be interesting as a part of our history. They certainly show that the literary treasures of the small and unpretending Library of two thousand volumes, were thoroughly appreciated by its conservators, and guarded with jealous care:—

1. *Voted and resolved*, That in addition to the former regulations for the College Library, the librarian keep the library room neat and clean, and, in delivering out books, he shall suffer none of the students to derange or handle them on the shelves; nor shall the students pass into the library room beyond the table at which the librarian sits, agreeably to a regulation hereafter mentioned; and the students shall be entitled to receive in and deliver out books according to their order of entering the library room.

6. He shall demand and receive a fine of six pence for every time it shall come to his knowledge that any student hath suffered a library book, by him taken out, to be uncovered in his possession, which fine shall be paid under like penalty as money assessed for books damaged.

7. No student or graduate shall presume to lend to any person a book belonging to the Library, on penalty of forfeiting the value thereof, and the privilege of the Library till such forfeiture be paid.

11. He shall deliver the key to none, on any occasion, except to an officer of instruction. And no officer of instruction shall presume to take out a book unless the librarian, or a person deputed by him be present to take the receipt required.

12. He shall open the library room on such day of the week as the President shall from time to time direct, and shall keep it open from one to three o'clock in the afternoon.

16. A standing committee shall be annually appointed to superintend the conduct of the librarian and to audit his accounts, * * * and the President, the Rev. Mr. Hitchcock and the Rev. Mr. Oliver are appointed a committee, etc., till the next annual meeting.

Resolved, That Mr. William Wilkinson be, and he is, hereby elected and appointed librarian.

HISTORY OF THE LIBRARY.

Continuing our extracts from the records of the Corporation, we find, under date of September 6, 1787:—

Voted and resolved, That the thanks of this Corporation be presented to Mr. John Francis, for his valuable donation of books to this College, and that the privilege of the Library be granted to him.

Resolved, That the thanks of this Corporation be presented to Rev. Benjamin Foster, of Newport, for his donation of the Septuagint, and an ancient edition of Horace.

September 4, 1788 : *Voted*, That the graduates of this College write, or procure to be written, fair copies of their Commencement Exercises, and have them bound in a handsome volume, annually, at their expense, to be deposited in the College Library.

Voted, That a particular part of the library room be appropriated for the reception of the works of American authors.

September 2, 1790 : *Voted*, That the thanks of this Corporation be presented by the President to Dr. Hitchcock, for the present of his valuable books entitled, Domestic Memoirs, in 2 vols., 12°, to this College.

September 6, 1792 : *Voted*, That $25 per annum be allowed and paid to each of the former librarians for their attention to and discharge of their duty in that appointment.

April 4, 1793 : *Voted*, That the thanks of this Corporation be presented to the Rev. Dr. Belknap, for the generous and unexpected donation of his History of New Hampshire, and that a copy of this note be delivered Dr. Hitchcock, and he be requested to transmit the same to Dr. Belknap.

Voted, That Mr. Howell, who has now in his possession the valuable donation of law books, presented by Mr. Nicholas Brown to this College, be explicitly informed that the Corporation expect he will take due care of them, by having them covered, that whenever they are deposited in the Library, they may appear in good order, that the donor may not suffer the imputation of presenting books damaged or impaired ; and that Mr. Howell also be informed that the Corporation expect he will attend and read a course of lectures to the students in College, at least once a year, agreeably to his appointment as Professor of Law.

Voted, That the thanks of this Corporation be presented to Mrs. Hope Ives, for her generous and acceptable donation of the American edition of the Encyclopædia Britannica to the College Library, and that the treasurer transmit her a copy of this vote.

Voted, That the librarian be directed to notify by a billet the members of the Corporation, and all others who have had books out of the Library longer than the time allowed by law, that the same must be returned on or before the first day of June next; and that he also inform them that in case of their non compliance with this vote, the money will be demanded of them for said books

Voted, That the thanks of this Corporation be presented to Mr. Nicholas Brown, for his valuable donation of law books to this Institution, and that the secretary deliver Mr. Brown a copy of this vote.

The last-mentioned vote refers to the Hon. Nicholas Brown, from whom, as we have already stated in our Historical Sketch, the University derives its name. He commenced his princely benefactions to the College by the donation of five hundred dollars for the purchase of a law library. In a letter to the Corporation he says: "I make this donation under a deep impression of the generous intentions of my honored father, deceased, towards the College in this town, as well as from my own personal feelings towards the Institution in which I received my education, and from a desire to promote literature in general, and in particular the knowledge of the laws of our country, under the influence whereof not only our property but our lives and dearest privileges are protected."

The books, numbering about three hundred volumes, were purchased of Whieldon & Butterworth, London, at a cost of £112 3s sterling. The selection was made by the Hon. David Howell, to whose care and keeping, it appears, they were for a time consigned. Among the more expensive works, according to the original bill, which is on file, may be mentioned: BACON's Abridgment, 5 vols., folio, £5 15s 6d; COKE upon Littleton, folio, £3 8s; DURNFORD & EAST's Reports, 4 vols., folio, £8 8s; SWINBURNE on Wills, quarto, £3 10s; DOMAT's Civil Law, 2 vols., folio, £2 5s; VINER's Abridgment, 24 volumes, 8", £14 8s; GROTIUS on War and Peace, folio, £2; PUFFENDORF's Law of Nature, folio, £3 3s; BRACTON's De Legibus Angliae, folio, £2 2s, (according to Sir William Jones, "the best of judicial classics"); COKE's Reports, 7 volumes, 8", £4 4s; WESKETT on Insurance, folio, £2 10s; BLACKSTONE's Reports, folio, £2 5s; BROWN's Reports, 2 vols., folio,

£3 10s; CORPUS JURIS CIVILIS, 2 vols., folio, £2 5s; WOODESON'S Lectures, 2 vols., 8°, £1 4s; REEVES'S History of English Law, 4 vols., 8°, £1 10s; ADDINGTON'S Penal Statutes, quarto, £1 9s.

Continuing our extracts from the records, we find, under date of September 4, 1794:—

Voted, That the thanks of this Corporation be presented to Messrs. John Carter and William Wilkinson, for the donation of the following valuable books, to wit: WATSON'S Apology, 1 vol.; PRICE'S Sermons, 1 vol.; MOORE'S Journal, 2 vols.; ORTON'S Letters, 1 vol.; DODDRIDGE'S Sermons, 1 vol.

Voted, That the thanks of this Corporation be presented to Dr. Rippon, of London, for his donation to the College of BICHENO'S Friendly Address to the Jews.

April 26, 1796: *Voted,* That the thanks of this Corporation be presented to Rev. Dr. Prince, for his very valuable donation to the College Library of Lectures on Natural and Experimental Philosophy, by GEORGE ADAMS, comprised in five elegant volumes.

Voted, That the thanks of this Corporation be presented to Mrs. Avis Brown, for her valuable donation to the College Library of DR. CAMPBELL'S Critical Remarks on the New Testament, and his Translation of the Four Evangelists.

September 6, 1796: *Voted,* That the Freshman class be, in future, admitted to the use of the College Library on the same terms as the other students.

It appears by the report of the library committee, that several persons, to whom books have been loaned, neglected to return them, in violation of the laws made to secure a seasonable return of such books; which the Corporation consider as an evil of great magnitude. It is therefore,

Voted, That the librarian be, and he is, hereby directed to apply a speedy and vigorous execution of the enacted laws, and that he fail not to make report of his proceedings at the next meeting of the Corporation.

Voted, That the thanks of this Corporation be presented the Rev. Mr. Backus, for his present to the College Library of the third volume of his Church History of New England.

The following letter from Mr. Benson, who this year resigned his place in the Board of Trustees, is deserving of mention. The author, it may be observed, was formerly a wealthy merchant of Providence; his mansion, on the corner of Prospect and Angell streets, is now occupied by the Watson family:—

SEPTEMBER 3d, 1801.

SIR:— Will you do me the favor to request the Corporation to accept the following trifling donation for the College Library, viz.: Thoughts on Religion, Natural and Revealed, and Reflexions on the Sources of Incredulity, etc , in two volumes, by the Right Honorable DUNCAN FORBES. This is a scarce though celebrated performance. A Vindication of the Divine Inspiration of the Holy Scriptures, in answer to Paine's Age of Reason, by THOMAS SCOTT, chaplain to the Lock Hospital. Discourses on the Genuineness and Authenticity of the New Testament, and on the Nature and Danger of Infidel Philosophy, by the Rev. PRESIDENT DWIGHT. A Summary of the Evidences of Christianity, by JOHN FAWCETT. The Gospel its own Witness, by ANDREW FULLER, D. D., to which is subjoined, a Summary of the Principal Evidences for the Truth and Divine Origin of the Christian Revelation, by the BISHOP OF LONDON.

May the pernicious errors detected and refuted in the preceding productions be forever excluded from the College, and may the important truths they inculcate and enforce, prevail and abound therein.

I am, dear Sir, assuredly your friend,

GEORGE BENSON.

Mr. President Maxcy.

Continuing our extracts, we find as follows:—

September 5, 1805: Mr. Nicholas Brown having offered to this University, in addition to all his other donations, the sum of five hundred dollars, to be vested in books for the Library, it is therefore

Voted, That five hundred dollars be added thereto, payable out of any money in the treasury not otherwise appropriated for the same use. And that Nicholas Brown, Doct. Solomon Drown, Hon. David L. Barnes, and the Secretary be a committee for procuring such books, and causing them to be placed in the Library of the University.

Dr. James Mann, of Wrentham, Massachusetts, having presented to this University GRAVESANDE'S Philosophy, 2 vols., 4°, and SCHLUTTER'S Essay on Mines, (IN FRENCH,) 2 vols., 4°,

Voted, That the President return him the thanks of this Corporation therefor.

September 3, 1807: *Voted*, That the thanks of this Corporation be presented to Doctor Baldwin for the following books presented by him to the University, to wit: BIBLIOTHECA CLASSICA, History of the Reign of Philip III., BALDWIN on Baptism, and the Doctrine of Eternal Misery reconcilable with the Benevolence of God.

The Rev. Isaac Backus, of Middleborough, Massachusetts, author of the Church History of New England, who died in 1806, in the eighty-third year of his age and the sixtieth of his ministry, bequeathed to the College a part of his library. The extent or value of this bequest it is now impossible to determine, as no record was made of it at the time. Among the books thus presented, however, there is one which deserves particular mention. It is a copy of ROGER WILLIAMS's Bloody Tenent yet more Bloody, being the copy originally presented by Williams to his friend and fellow laborer, Dr. John Clarke. On a blank leaf it contains the following words in Roger Williams's hand-writing: " For his honoured and beloved Mr. John Clarke, an eminent Witnes of Christ Jesus, ag'st ye bloodie Doctrine of persecution," etc.

The following appears on record:—

1816, September 5: Dr. Rippon having transmitted to this Corporation, The History of the Human Teeth, by JOSEPH FOX, which book was by Mr. Fox in his life time put into the hands of Dr. Rippon, to be transmitted as a present to this Corporation,

Voted, That the same be received with thankfulness, and placed in the College Library, inscribed with the donor's name, as a donation to this College.

1818, September 3: The Rev. Mr. Bolles having stated that he was authorized by the Rev. Thomas Carlile, of Salem, to say that Mr. Carlile will present to this Institution such theological books as may be desired,

Voted, That the thanks of this Corporation be presented to Mr. Carlile for his generous offer; that a catalogue of the books in the College Library be sent to him, in order that he may furnish the Institution such other books as he may think proper; and that Mr Bolles be requested to present a copy of this vote, and the said catalogue, to the Rev. Mr. Carlile.

Mr. Carlile was a graduate of the College in the class of 1809, and for several years was rector of St. Peter's church in Salem, Massachusetts. Agreeably to his intentions, as expressed in the foregoing vote, he made the following year a splendid donation to the Library, consisting of one hundred and three volumes, mostly in quarto, comprising the best editions of the works of the celebrated French mathematicians, EULER, LACROIX, LAGRANGE, LAPLACE, etc., besides many valuable theological works.

The next, and the most valuable of all the donations to the Library, which we have thus far recorded, is the legacy of the

Rev. William Richards, LL. D., of Lynn, England. Mr. Richards* was a native of South Wales. At the age of twelve he had been at school only one year. From this time till the twenty-fourth year of his age, when he entered the academy at Bristol, he received no instruction. But his application to study was vigorous and persevering. He remained at Bristol two years. After preaching for a short time as an assistant to the Rev. Dr. John Ash, of Pershore, he accepted an invitation from the Baptist church at Lynn, to become their pastor, and entered upon his public ministry in that town, July 7, 1776, where he continued to reside — more than half of the time as pastor of the church — till his death, which occurred in 1818, in the sixty-ninth year of his age.

Mr. Richards seems to have been a man of considerable learning, particularly in English and Welsh history, and in the Welsh language and literature. His writings are historical, political and controversial.† His most important work is the History of Lynn, in two volumes, 8°. Dr. Evans says of it: "It is not only well written, the style perspicuous and manly, but it is replete with information as well as entertainment." His Review of Noble's Memoirs of the Protectoral House of Cromwell, is characterized by Lowndes‡ as "severe, but at the same time just." "His Dictionary of Welsh and English," says Dr. Evans, "a work of minute and wearisome labor, is in high repute." Mr. Richards was of the *General Baptist* denomination, and a strong advocate of religious liberty. It was his love of the liberal character of this Institution, which induced him to bestow upon it his library, as appears from the following passage in his Memoirs: "Mr.

---
* See Memoirs of the Life and Writings of Rev. William Richards, LL. D., by John Evans, LL. D., of Islington. 12mo., Chiswick, 1819.

† For a list of his writings — comprising nearly the whole — see under his name in the Catalogue of the Library.

‡ Bibliographer's Manual.

Richards had corresponded with Dr. James Manning, once President of the Baptist College in Rhode Island. From this gentleman he learned the liberal constitution of that respectable Seminary, and for some years previous to his death meant to bequeath to it his library.* He accordingly made inquiry of Dr. Rogers, (of Philadelphia,) whether it was still conducted on the same liberal footing, in which case he should cherish the same generous intentions towards it." This inquiry was answered by Dr. Messer, then President of the College, in a letter from which we extract the following passage: "Though the charter requires that the President shall forever be a Baptist, it allows neither him, in his official character, nor any other officer of instruction, to inculcate any sectarian doctrine; it forbids all religious tests; and it requires that all denominations of Christians, behaving alike, shall be treated alike. The charter is congenial with the whole of the civil government established here by the venerable Roger Williams, who allowed no religious tests, and no preëminence of one denomination over another; and none has ever been allowed unto this day. This charter is also congenial with the present spirit of this State and of this town."

Gratified with this letter, Mr. Richards bequeathed his library, consisting of about thirteen hundred volumes, to Brown University. The original manuscript catalogue of his library, written in a large round hand, has recently been deposited in the College archives. It is a singular fact that the will of the donor was made on the very day on which the honorary degree of Doctor of Laws was conferred upon him by the College. Mr. Richards had received no intimation that the honor was intended for him, nor did he live to hear that it had been bestowed.

The library which he bequeathed to the College is in many respects valuable. It contains a considerable number of Welsh

* See MANNING AND BROWN UNIVERSITY, pp. 441-47.

books, a large collection of valuable works, illustrating the history and antiquities of England and Wales; besides two or three hundred bound volumes of pamphlets, some of which are very ancient, rare and curious. Not a few of these pamphlets will be prized by the future historian, as illustrations of the progress of civil and religious liberty.

During the year 1824, fifty-four volumes of valuable scientific works, including CLOQUET's Anatomie, LAMARCK's and DECANDOLLE's Flore Française, CUVIER's Règne Animal, and WILKIN's Vitruvius, were presented by Mr. John Carter Brown and Mr. Robert Hale Ives. Often, since that time, the names of these gentlemen appear among the benefactors of the Library.

For the next valuable accession to the Library, designated "the subscription of 1825," the College is indebted to the efforts of Mr. Horatio Gates Bowen, who was librarian of the Institution from 1824 to 1841. At his request several of the friends of the College subscribed eight hundred and forty dollars, which sum was expended in the purchase of books. The following are the names of the subscribers, copied from the original subscription book:—

Edward Carrington, - - - $200	Sullivan Dorr, - - - -	$50
Thomas P. Ives, - - - 200	Thomas L. Halsey, - -	50
Moses B. Ives, - - - - 50	Nathaniel Searle, - - -	10
Robert H. Ives, - - - 50	Tristam Burges, - -	10
James Rhodes, - - - - 50	John D'Wolf, - - - -	10
John Carter Brown, - - 50	Lucius Bolles, - - -	10
Samuel G. Arnold, - - - 50		
Amasa Mason, - - - 50	Total, - - - -	$840

On the return of Professor Elton from Europe, in 1827, donations were received through him, from several distinguished gentlemen in England, in all two hundred and eighty-three volumes; besides eighty-five volumes of classical and miscellaneous works, purchased by him at the order of Messrs. Brown & Ives.

The libraries of the Philophysian and Franklin Societies, composed of undergraduates, when these societies became extinct, were, by a provision in their constitutions, incorporated with the College Library. They together contained three hundred or four hundred volumes.

The government of Great Britain presented during the years 1835-8, one hundred and ten volumes of the publications of the Record Commission.

In 1838, Mrs. Elizabeth H. Bartol, wife of Rev. Cyrus A. Bartol, D. D., of Boston, and Mrs. Hepsy S. Wayland, wife of President Wayland, presented three hundred and fifty-six volumes of standard works in French and Italian literature.

The Rev. Jonathan Homer, D. D., of Newton, Massachusetts, at various times made valuable donations of rare and costly theological books, including some valuable editions of the Bible. Many of these contain copious and useful manuscript annotations by the learned donor.

In January, 1842, the Hon. Theron Metcalf, LL. D., of Boston, a graduate of the College in the class of 1805, presented to the Library a collection of thirty volumes of ORDINATION Sermons. To this he has since added from year to year, until it now numbers sixty-four volumes. These bound volumes contain upwards of fourteen hundred discourses preached in the United States, and mostly in New England, at ordinations, installations and inaugurations, constituting without doubt the largest collection of the kind that has ever been made. He has also presented at various times during the past twenty-five years, one hundred and two volumes of FUNERAL Sermons, arranged in classes as follows, viz.: Ministers, Boston Ministers, Ministers' Wives, Women, Presidents of the United States, Soldiers, College Officers, Miscellaneous, etc. Seven of these volumes, in superior binding, comprise sermons, eulogies, etc., on men who have filled the office of Judge.

The importance of these two thousand pamphlets and upwards, thus arranged and preserved, in connection with the department of special biography, can hardly be over-estimated. In addition to the foregoing, are twenty-two volumes of CENTURY and CENTENNIAL Discourses, abounding in town and local histories, and furnishing rich material for historians and antiquaries; five volumes handsomely bound, containing nearly a hundred HALF-CENTURY Sermons, preached by men who had been settled fifty years over a single parish, and extending over a period of one hundred and fifty years; twenty-four volumes of Discourses delivered at the DEDICATION of Churches, Colleges, School Houses, Hospitals, Cemeteries, Public Halls, Libraries, etc., etc.; ten volumes of ANNIVERSARY Discourses; twelve volumes of MISSIONARY Sermons, including all the printed sermons that have been delivered before the American Board of Commissioners for Foreign Missions, and making, it is believed, the only complete set in existence; twelve volumes of FOURTH OF JULY Orations, including all delivered before the Municipal authorities of Boston (and published) from 1800 to the present time; a complete set, in four volumes, of the annual Sermons and Reports of the MAINE MISSIONARY SOCIETY; five volumes of Discourses on WASHINGTON; five volumes of PHI BETA KAPPA Addresses; besides volumes of MISCELLANEOUS Pamphlets, PLYMOUTH Discourses, Addresses to ALUMNI, FAST and THANKSGIVING Sermons, EDUCATION Sermons, ELECTION Sermons, INTRODUCTORY Sermons, FAREWELL Discourses, THEOLOGICAL Discussions, JUBILEE Discourses, etc., etc. The entire Metcalf Collection now numbers, January 1, 1867, three hundred and fifty-seven bound volumes, comprising nearly ten thousand pamphlets. The labor and patience required in securing these, by diligent inquiry and extensive correspondence, can only be appreciated by those who have been engaged in similar pursuits. In addition to all this, Judge Metcalf has made advantageous purchases of books for the Library Committee from year to year, besides making valuable donations to the Library, including a set of REPORTS of Cases argued and determined in the Supreme Judicial Court of Massachusetts, edited by himself. He has thus shown a spirit of liberal and warm regard for the place of his education, which the lapse of time has not changed, and which is worthy the emulation of all the sons of the College.

A set of the BIOGRAPHIE UNIVERSELLE, fifty-two volumes in twenty-six, in elegant calf binding, was presented to the Library in April, 1843, by Mrs. Hope Ives, Mrs. Charlotte R. Goddard, Mrs. Robert H. Ives, and Mrs. Moses B. Ives.

The donations which have thus far been mentioned were for the most part unsolicited. Some of them at the present day may seem of trifling value. They are not placed on record as possessed of great interest in themselves, but as a just tribute to friends in the mother country, and to men, who, in times of less prosperity than that which the College now enjoys, contributed liberally towards laying the foundations of an honored and useful Institution.

We now come to a new era in our history. Soon after the accession of the Rev. Dr. Wayland to the Presidency of the College, efforts were made to increase the efficiency of the Library, and thus provide enlarged means of liberal and generous intellectual culture, by raising a Fund for the purchase of books. At a meeting of the Standing Committee of the Corporation, held January 10, 1831, it was unanimously resolved:—

1. Tha* immediate measures be taken to raise by subscription, the sum of twenty-five thousand dollars, to be appropriated to the purchase of books for the Library and apparatus for the Philosophical and Chemical departments of Brown University.

2. *Resolved*, That the Chairman and Thomas P. Ives, be a Committee to carry the foregoing resolution into effect.   F. WAYLAND, *Chairman*.

Soon afterwards, a meeting of the friends of the Institution was called, for the purpose of seconding this effort. At this meeting the wants of the Library and the importance of supplying them were presented and urged by President Wayland, Alexis Caswell, D. D., Professor of Mathematics, and John Pitman, LL. D., Judge of the United States District Court, and a member of the Board of Fellows. Previously to this, however, the Hon. Nicholas Brown had, with his wonted munificence, subscribed ten thousand dollars towards the fund. The subscription was opened, with the following conditions:—

1. The whole amount shall be invested in a permanent fund, of which the interest shall be, from time to time, appropriated exclusively to the objects stated in the resolution.

2. The selection of books and apparatus shall be made by a joint committee of the Corporation and Government of the University.

3. One-third of the amount subscribed shall become due on the first day of October, 1832; another third on the first day of October, 1833; and the remainder on the first day of October, 1834.

4. A copy of the subscribers' names, and of the sums subscribed by each, shall be deposited in the Library, and another among the archives of the University.

In stating the object for which the meeting had been called, President Wayland remarked substantially, that all the efforts for the intellectual improvement of mankind were comprehended under two classes. First, effort for the advancement of science, and secondly, for its universal diffusion. In the first instance, he continued, we enter the dominion of knowledge, and discover the laws of the universe, and in the second, we put the knowledge thus attained within the power of every grade of society. It is to the second of these purposes, that the labors of this country have been directed. We have established common schools in every portion of the older states, and by means of them the facilities for acquiring elementary education have become abundant. To the real advancement, however, of science, we have actually done almost nothing. We import our learning scantily, from abroad. Even our universities have employed themselves in the diffusion, rather than in the advancement of science; and even for this comparatively humble effort, they are but ill prepared. Our universities and colleges are at present known principally by the magnitude and the number of their edifices. If the student wishes to push his inquiries into any science beyond the ordinary routine of instruction, where shall he go, in our country, for the means of information? If he enter our college halls and ask for books, he is shown long rows of lodging-rooms. If he inquire for instruments for philosophical research, he is pointed to large piles of brick and mortar. If the teacher desires to investigate truth for himself, and coöperate with the learned of Europe in the advancement of knowledge, where in this country can he go to avail himself of the researches of past ages? The humiliating answer is found in the fact that, in each of the learned professions, the most valuable books with which we enrich our libraries could not have been written in this country, for the knowledge which they embody could not have been found here.

And besides, the speaker added in conclusion, instructors cannot furnish themselves with libraries. Their income does not admit of it, nor can a library, such as the cause of science demands, be collected in a single life time. It must be the accumulated wisdom of past ages, added to the wisdom of our own. Such a library can be procured only by public munificence, and by that munificence so directed as to collect, from time to time, the rich results of the intellectual labor of man.

The following is a list of the subscriptions, most of which were procured by the exertions of Dr. Wayland and Dr. Caswell:—

Nicholas Brown, Providence,	$10,000	Francis Wayland, Providence,	$200
Thomas Poynton Ives, "	1,000	Moses Brown Ives, "	200
John Bowen, New York,	1,000	Robert Hale Ives, "	200
James Arnold, New Bedford,	300	Samuel Ward, New York,	200
Nathaniel R. Cobb, Boston,	250	John B. Jones, Boston,	150

Richard Fletcher, Boston,	$150	Joseph L. Tillinghast, Providence,	$60
Thomas Burgess, Providence,	150	Theron Metcalf, Boston,	51
Amasa Mason, "	150	Zachariah Eddy, Middleborough,	51
William Baylies, Bridgewater,	150	Cyrus Lothrop, Easton,	51
Richard James Arnold, Providence,	150	Samuel Leonard Crocker, Taunton,	50
William Taylor Grinnell, "	150	William Allen Crocker, "	50
William Giles Goddard, "	125	Moses Pond, Boston,	50
Alexis Caswell, "	125	Samuel Hill, "	50
Ebenezer Burgess, Dedham,	100	Peter Pratt, Providence,	50
Sullivan Dorr, Providence,	100	Richard Ward Greene, Providence,	50
Timothy G. Coffin, New Bedford,	100	John Pitman, "	50
John Kelly Simpson, Boston,	100	John Kingsbury, "	50
Heman Lincoln, "	100	Charles Potter, "	50
Lucius Bolles, "	100	Benjamin Hoppin, "	50
Ebenezer Thresher, "	100	Frances R. Arnold, "	50
John Kelly Simpson, Jr., "	100	Timothy R. Greene, New York,	50
Ward Jackson, "	100	James Brown, Providence,	50
Edward Tuckerman, "	100	John W. Francis, New York,	50
William B. Reynolds, "	100	George Colgate, "	50
Levi Farwell, Cambridge,	100	William Colgate, "	50
Ichabod Macomber, Boston,	100	William Larned Marcy, New York,	50
Amos Binney, "	100	Michael Shepard, Salem,	50
Benjamin Shurtleff, "	100	William Leet Stone, New York,	50
Samuel W. Bridgham, Providence,	100	Charles H. Warren, New Bedford,	50
John Brown Francis, Warwick,	100	William Taber Hawes, "	38
George Ide Chace, Providence,	100	John Henry Clifford, "	30
Charles Russell, New York,	100	Harrison Gray Otis Colby, Taunton,	30
John Ward, "	100	John Dix Fisher, Boston,	30
Richard R. Ward, "	100	Elnathan Pierce Hathaway, Assonet,	30
J. & W. Kelly & Co., "	100	John Barstow, Providence,	30
Thomas Purser, "	100	Thomas Francis Carpenter, Providence,	30
William B. Crosby, "	100	Mark A. D'W. Howe, Roxbury,	30
A. M'Intire, "	100	Elisha Dyer, Jr., Providence,	30
Spencer H. Cone, "	100	Horatio Pratt, Taunton,	30
Eliza Ward, Providence,	100	Samuel T. Armstrong, Boston,	27
Solomon Peck, Boston,	75	A. Maclay, New York,	25
John Spence, "	75	Joseph Mauran, Providence,	25
John Sullivan, "	60	Isaac Davis, Worcester,	25
William Tully Dorrance, Providence,	60	Thomas Kinnicutt, Worcester,	25

John Green, Worcester,	$25	Hiram Jacobs, Boston,	$10
Jacob H. Loud, New Bedford,	25	Josiah Robbins, New Bedford,	10
Isaac Davis, Boston,	20	Joseph Sampson, Kingston,	10
John Jeffries, "	20	Joseph Holmes, "	10
William Samuel Patten, Providence,	15	Timothy Gilbert, Boston,	10
William Nichols, Boston,	15		

The sum thus obtained, amounting to nineteen thousand four hundred and thirty-eight dollars, was placed at interest until it had accumulated to twenty-five thousand dollars, and was then invested in a permanent fund, in the stock of the Blackstone Canal Bank, in Providence, according to the provisions of the subscription, as before specified. The first dividend became due in July, 1839. Since that time the proceeds have been regularly appropriated according to the design of the donors.

By a subsequent vote of the Corporation, all the subscribers to the Library Fund, as well as all the subscribers to the fund raised for the erection of Rhode Island Hall, and all donors to the Library to the amount of forty dollars, residing in the city of Providence, were admitted to the free use of the Library.

The room appropriated to the Library, at the time when the Library Fund was raised, " was an apartment in University Hall, crowded to excess, unsightly and wholly unsuited for the purpose to which, from necessity, it was devoted." To remedy this defect, the Hon. Nicholas Brown erected at his own expense a beautiful edifice, for a Library and Chapel; to which, in testimony of veneration for his former instructor, he gave the name of Manning Hall. At the dedication, February 4, 1835, Dr. Wayland delivered a discourse on the " Dependence of Science upon Revealed Religion," which was published in a pamphlet form for circulation.

This hall, the third College building which has been erected, is of the Dorick order, built of rubble stone, and covered with cement. Including the portico, it is about ninety feet in length, by forty-two in width. Its height, from the top of the basement, is forty feet. The Library occupies the whole of the first floor, which is a beautiful room, ornamented in the centre with a double row of fluted columns, from which the shelves extend to the walls, forming twelve alcoves. Its dimensions are sixty-four feet by thirty-eight, and thirteen feet high. Extra shelves for the accommodation of the books have been constructed in every available place throughout, and already they are completely filled. This, together with the fact, that the building is not fire-proof, and, like most library edifices in this country, is constructed with reference to beauty of outward proportion and architectural effect, rather than to convenience of interior arrangements, absolutely essential to the efficient working of a good public library, points to the necessity of a more capacious, convenient, and substantial building.

In 1843, the Library, which, on the 1st of January contained ten thousand two hundred and thirty-five bound volumes, was newly arranged, and a full catalogue of its contents, prepared by Professor C. C. Jewett, now Superintendent of the Free Public Library of Boston, was printed. This Catalogue was favorably noticed in the North American Review, and in other leading periodicals, and drew especial attention to this important department of the Institution. It is alphabetical, according to the names of authors, and has a copious and analytical index of subjects. A supplement, on cards, has been prepared, but it will not probably be printed.

Soon after the publication of the Catalogue, a Chair of Modern Languages was established at the College, and Mr. Jewett was appointed the Professor elect. During his absence in Europe, whither he had gone for the purposes of professional study, and to enable the friends of the Institution to carry out more effectually their wishes for the increase of the Library, a fund of five thousand dollars was raised for the purchase of English books, and the foundations of a French, German and Italian library were laid. The condition and prospects of the Library at this time, may best be learned from the interesting annual report of the Library Committee, presented to the Corporation in September, 1844. We present copious extracts:—

At the regular monthly meeting of the Committee, in November, Mr. Prof. Gammell was requested to prepare a circular, to be addressed to the graduates and friends of the College, and intended to invite their coöperation in the good work of advancing the prosperity of the Library. Mr. Gammell, at a subsequent meeting, reported a draught of the proposed circular, which was adopted by the Committee, and, after being signed by each member, was ordered to be printed. The following extract embraces the substance of this document, and fully explains its design:—

"The Library of Brown University, as is generally known, is dependent for its growth on the proceeds of a fund of twenty-five thousand dollars, which has been raised by subscription, and set apart mainly for this purpose. Some portion of the income of this fund is annually absorbed by appropriations for the increase of the philosophical and chemical apparatus. The remainder is devoted exclusively to the purchase of books for the Library. Under the operation of this new provision for its benefit, the Library, within the last few years, has been considerably enlarged, and its value greatly enhanced. But it will, after all, continue to be lamentably deficient as an aid to public education, and as a depository of learning, unless it obtain from the graduates and friends of the College yet further tokens of their interest in its welfare. From the very excellent catalogue which has just been published, it will be seen what are the actual wants of the Library—how imperfectly supplied are some departments of literature and science, and how entirely destitute are others. The Committee, therefore, while they hope that the permanent character and high usefulness of the Library, and its security as a depository of books for the benefit of other generations, will, at all times, invite frequent and liberal donations from the graduates and friends of the College, venture more particularly, now, to solicit such volumes and pamphlets, as may be willingly spared, of the following or of kindred classes:

"1. Any complete files of American newspapers. 2. Any published discourses, whether sermons, orations or addresses. 3. Any printed pamphlets, not included in the preceding description, which may be illustrative of the character of the times. 4. Any publications relating to the history of collegiate or other education. 5. Ancient pamphlets or other works pertaining to the history of this State, or of any of the United States.

"These several classes of books have been specified by the Committee, but they desire it to be understood that the College will be grateful for any donations which its friends may be pleased to make to its Library.

"The Committee take this occasion to invite the friends and graduates of the College to place in the Library any works which they themselves have published. All such works will be gratefully accepted from their authors as a tribute of respect to the place of their education, and will be faithfully preserved as among the literary fruits which the College has, from time to time, produced."

The Committee have reason to believe, from the number of books and pamphlets which have been presented during the past year, that the foregoing circular has been instrumental, to some extent, in attracting towards the Library the friendly regards of the graduates and friends of the University.

The Committee take great pleasure in inviting the attention of the Honorable Corporation to a very important plan now in progress for the increase of the Library. Deeply sensible of the wants of the Library—wants which the avails of the permanent fund, now much reduced in amount by the low rate of interest, would, under any circumstances, be entirely inadequate to supply—the Committee deemed it to be their imperative duty to appeal to the liberality of friends of the University in behalf of one of its most important interests. More than six months ago, the Committee therefore caused a subscription to be opened for the purpose of raising a sum not less than five thousand dollars, to be expended, as soon as may be, in the purchase of standard works, in the English language. The plan devised by the Committee for supplying the most pressing wants of the Library, met a very cordial and prompt response on the part of those friends of the College who have been solicited to contribute their aid. One gentleman, a citizen of Providence, and a member of the Corporation of this University, imparted to the project a decided impulse, by pledging himself to contribute towards the amount proposed to be raised, the sum of one thousand dollars. A few other gentlemen, some of whom are neither graduates of the University nor members of the Corporation, have likewise pledged themselves in various sums, amounting in all, to two thousand and fifty dollars. The whole amount thus far subscribed towards an object which it is so desirable to accomplish, without delay, is therefore three thousand and fifty dollars. For reasons, which it is unnecessary to state, no progress has for several months been made in the proposed subscription. The graduates and the friends of the University, when they come to learn what has been done in this matter, and what remains to be done, will not, it is confidently believed, suffer a project which promises so much benefit to the Library, to languish for the want of their zealous and efficient coöperation. The Committee cannot dismiss this topic without most earnestly commending to the Honorable Corporation of the University, individually and collectively, the important plan for the increase of the Library which now awaits consummation, and which, with efficient effort, might, ere the lapse of another month, be brought to a successful result. The Librarian, Mr. Jewett, before his return, will visit London. His zeal in behalf of the Library, and his rare skill in the pur-

HISTORY OF THE LIBRARY. 91

chase of books, indicate the wisdom of confiding to him the expenditure of whatever sum may be raised by the subscription now in progress. The Committee have made these suggestions in the belief that the friends of the College will, without delay, make a vigorous effort to place in the hands of Mr. Jewett ample pecuniary means for the purchase of standard works in the mother tongue. Such an opportunity for the judicious and economical expenditure of money, it is not too much to say, has never occurred since the establishment of this University. Such an opportunity may never occur again. Could the sum of ten thousand dollars be raised, the Committee are of the opinion that, in the hands of Mr. Jewett, it might be made adequate to the purchase of not less than ten thousand volumes.

Since the last annual report of the joint Library Committee, 2,201 volumes have been added to the Library—459 by purchase, and 1,742 by donation. The whole number of volumes reported last year as belonging to the Library, was 10,523, exclusive of pamphlets and odd volumes not catalogued. The whole number is now 12,724, exclusive of pamphlets.

The additions which have been made may be classified as follows, viz. : 123 folios; 188 quartos; 1,179 octavos; 690 duodecimos, and smaller; 21 maps, charts, etc.

Among the most valuable works purchased under the direction of the Committee, may be mentioned the GENTLEMAN'S MAGAZINE, in one hundred and twenty-five volumes (well bound) from its commencement in the year 1731, to the year 1820. Regarded simply as an authentic and consecutive record of the great events which signalized the last hundred years, this work may be deemed as essential to every public library. With how much warmer interest do we peruse its various contents, when we recollect that among its early contributors were Johnson and Burke, and others of that constellation of scholars and wits, who illustrated one of the most brilliant epochs in the literary history of England!

The Library has recently undergone an examination, and it speaks well for the care of the Librarian, and for the exact obedience of the under-graduates to the regulations of the Library, that, within the past year, not a book has been lost. The Committee are pleased to add, that to the officers of instruction the Library is becoming, every year, more valuable; and the records of the Library indicate that the under-graduates resort more frequently to its treasures than heretofore, for the purpose of investigating subjects connected with their course of study, and of relaxing their minds, after the fatigues of severe intellectual pursuit.

The scientific and literary departments of the Library have been greatly enriched, during the past year, by the liberal donations of one of the sons of this University. While Mr. Jewett was residing in Paris, a gentleman of Providence, entirely without solicitation from any quarter, placed in his hands ample means for the purchase of such books as he might select to constitute the foundation of a French Library, adequate to the immediate wants of the University. These means were appropriated by Mr. Jewett, under the most favorable circumstances, and with a judgment and taste in the selection of the books which the committee cannot, without the risk of seeming extravagant, sufficiently commend. This most valuable collection embraces eighty-nine folios, eighty-eight quartos, seven hundred and thirty-five octavos, four hundred and eighty smaller sized volumes and twenty maps. Total, one thousand four hundred and twelve, all of approved editions, many of them truly elegant, and all bound in the most neat and thorough style. In this collection are to be found the choicest of the French classics — the best fruits of French genius, in the departments of history, biography, philosophy, eloquence and poetry.

The committee cordially congratulate the Corporation on what must be deemed the *creation* of a most important department in the Library of the University. The French language is hereafter to form a part of the regular academical instructions of the University; and Mr. Jewett, the Professor of Modern Languages, will find, in the Library, ample means not only to facilitate his task as a teacher of the elements of the French language, but to introduce his pupils to an acquaintance with the classical authors of France — to imbue them with a genuine relish for the characteristic beauties of French literature — to render them, in some sort, familiar with the mind of that extraordinary people whose achievements in war, in the fine arts, in the exact and in the physical sciences, and in nearly every department of elegant literature, seem almost to justify their claim to stand at the head of modern civilization.

The scientific collections of the Library have been still farther enriched by the Transactions of the Royal Society, in forty-eight volumes, quarto, likewise presented by a gentleman of Providence, (Mr. Brown.) The remainder of this series, it is understood, has been ordered for the Library.

As Mr. Jewett is now in Germany, where he will continue till he visits Italy, the Committee have authorized the treasurer to remit to him the sum of two hundred pounds sterling, to be invested, at his discretion, in German editions and illustrations of the ancient classics, and likewise in works, which will help to familiarize to the minds of our students the rich and varied literature of that land of authors and scholars. The expediency of this investment requires no vindication. Such is the intrinsic value, and such the wide celebrity of German literature, that a knowledge of the language which embodies it, and to a considerable extent, exclusively embodies it, has come to be considered, in the United States, as an essential part of a liberal education. The Committee rejoice that such is the fact — they welcome it as an indication that our country is beginning to demand of our literary and scientific men a more generous culture, and that a higher standard of scholarship is about to be established in all our institutions of learning. While they would be the last to underrate the wealth of our own language and literature, they believe that the scholar who is familiar with the

German may command access to rich mines of thought and research, in which the English mind has hardly begun to work. They are aware that the German imagination loves to deal sometimes in what is wild and fanciful, and sometimes in what is mysterious and terrific. They are persuaded, however, that its creations, full as they are of beauty and of power, will fail to pervert the sedate and genuine impulses of English thought and fancy and feeling, and that our scholars, and all, indeed, who cultivate the German tongue, will exercise a genuine eclectic spirit — that, fascinated neither by the false philosophy nor by the extravagant fictions of Germany, they will extract from her sterling literature the means for more extended and accurate research in every department of learning; the elements of a truer and less exclusive taste in letters; the materials of a more profound and expansive generalization of the principles which govern human action.

In concluding their report, the Committee commend anew the Library to the favorable regard of the honorable Corporation, as one of the commanding interests of the University. They are solicitous that its importance to the other interests of this Institution — to the cause of sound learning — and to the highest welfare of this community, should not be undervalued. This Institution was founded eighty years ago, for the purpose of promoting, in the language of its charter, "the liberal arts and universal literature." It is mortifying to reflect, how little, till within a few years, has been done to make the Library to correspond, in any sense, to the comprehensive design of the venerable fathers of this University. They were true to the great trust which they undertook to discharge. At an early day, and with limited means, they did what they could to lay broad and deep the foundations of this Institution. Faithful to the high trust committed to our hands, let us, then, in our turn, use the more ample means with which we are endowed, not only in promoting the prosperity of the Library, but in enlarging, in all respects, the capacities of this University to diffuse the blessings of sound learning — to elevate the standard of American scholarship — to invigorate the tone of social morality — and to spread, far and wide, the transforming influences of Christian truth.

The foregoing report, in which the skillful pen of Professor Gammell is readily traced, alludes, it will be seen, to a fund for the purchase of English books. This fund, amounting to five thousand and sixty dollars, was completed early in May, 1845. The following is a list of the contributors, which we gladly place on permanent record, as an act of justice to them, and for the encouragement of future patrons of learning and literature:—

Estate of T. P. Ives, Providence,	$1,200	Abbott Lawrence, Boston,	100
A Friend, (J. C. Brown,) "	1,000	Henry Marchant, Providence,	100
A Friend, "	250	Thomas M. Burgess, "	50
Amory Chapin, "	200	Charles S. Bradley, "	50
Amasa Manton, "	200	Benjamin Cozzens, "	50
Seth Adams, Jr., "	200	William Sprague, "	50
William Appleton, Boston,	200	Owen Mason, "	50
Horatio N. Slater, Providence,	200	Thomas Lloyd Halsey, "	50
Michael Shepard, Salem,	200	William Baylies, Bridgewater,	50
Francis Wayland, Providence,	200	William Foster, Providence,	25
Samuel G. Arnold, "	150	Samuel Hunt, "	25
Isaac Davis, Worcester,	100	Samuel Foster, "	25
Thomas L. Dunnell, Providence,	100	Alvah Woods, "	25
A Friend, "	100	William T. Dorrance, "	10
Mrs. F. Arnold and Mrs. C. E. Green, Providence,	100	Total,	$5,060

The Librarian, Prof. Jewett, having accomplished the object of his visit to Europe, returned in December, 1845, and resumed the duties of his office. The following extracts from his report to the Library Committee, which we find incorporated in the annual report of the joint Library Committee to the Corporation, presented in September, 1846, will furnish a clear and comprehensive account of his purchases while abroad, and be interesting to the bibliographer, and collector of books.

We begin our extracts with a table, showing the number of volumes of the various sizes in each purchase, the whole cost in the currency of the countries where the books were bought, together with the average price per volume of each purchase, and of the whole:—

The whole sum of money is, in Federal currency, say $8,485.41. The whole number of volumes is 7,021. The average price per volume is, therefore, $1.20. It should be observed that this price includes binding, (and the books with few exceptions are substantially and well bound,) and all other expenses of every kind up to the time of shipping.

HISTORY OF THE LIBRARY.

	FOLIO.	QUARTO.	OCTAVO.	DUODECIMO.	Other Articles, MSS, etc.	TOTAL.	Whole cost in money of the country.	Average price per volume in money of the country.	Average price in dollars and cents.
FRENCH BOOKS. Mr. Brown's order,	89	88	735	480	20	1,412	ff 5.459 10	ff 3 64	$ cts. 66
GERMAN BOOKS. Mr. Brown's order,		256	697	218	38	1,209	4,040	3 34	63
ITALIAN BOOKS. Mr. Brown's order,	32	48	295	83	16	474	4,560 89	9 62	1 82
GERMAN BOOKS. College order,	1	10	421	33		465	th. s. gro. 690 15 9	th. 1 12	1 02
FRENCH BOOKS. College order,	8	5	59	5	46	123	ff 1,885 80	ff 15	2 85
ENGLISH BOOKS. College order,	196	235	2,438	444	25	3,338	£ s. d. 1,066 1 7	s. d. q. 6 4 2	1 53
Total,	326	642	4,542	1,263	145	7,021			$1 20

The books lately purchased for our Library, have been selected in view of the previous state of the collection and our own immediate wants, and entirely without reference to the cost. Some books have been purchased which would not have been first chosen; generally because they were bought in lots which contained others more important; but my general rule has been, first to make out with the utmost care a list of the books most needed, and then to purchase those books at the lowest possible prices.

The editions chosen are, for the most part, the very best which have been printed of the respective works. The object was to select editions of standard value for completeness, and elegance, and accuracy of execution; such editions as would always retain their value, even though others, and more costly, and, on the whole, better ones, should be printed. This was in many cases a very difficult part of my duty. This is the part where bibliographical skill and knowledge are most indispensable for a librarian.

I have paid particular attention to the condition of the copies. As far as it was possible, I collated the books myself, page by page, and where it was not possible for me to do it myself, I procured trusty men to collate them, in order to be sure that the copies were perfect and entire.

When I left America, John C. Brown, Esq., requested me to collect all the information which I could in reference to the book trade in France, and communicate with him on the subject; and, at the same time, he intimated his intention to purchase a French Library for the College. I accordingly spent much of my time during the first three months in Paris, in the book shops and libraries, and wrote Mr. Brown the results of my investigations. He immediately forwarded to me a draft for five thousand francs, requesting me to buy with this sum such French books as I might judge most desirable for our Library, directing that such as were purchased should be standard works in good editions and well bound. For about three months I devoted myself almost exclusively to the selection and purchase of the books.

Some of the more important of these works may well be made the subject of special notice.

Among them is a set of the MONITEUR UNIVERSEL, complete from its commencement to 1826, with the introduction, tables, etc., in seventy-seven volumes, folio,—the original edition, a clean copy, well bound, purchased at the sale of the library of an English gentleman who had for several years resided in Paris. This is an invaluable work, of which there are very few copies in the country, and perhaps no copy so perfect as this.

The DESCRIPTION DE L'EGYPTE, one of the most magnificent and costly works ever published, was also purchased at the same sale for about one-quarter of the price at which it is sold at the book auctions in Paris. It is of the second edition, and consists of twenty-six volumes of text and about five hundred folio engravings. Among these books is also a complete set of the new series, of the MEMOIRS, etc., published by four out of five of the Academies of the French Institute, viz.: The ACADEMY OF SCIENCES, the ACADEMY of MORAL AND POLITICAL SCIENCES, the ACADEMY OF THE FINE ARTS, and the FRENCH ACADEMY. This set contains sixty-one handsomely and newly-bound quarto volumes. The ACADEMY OF INSCRIPTIONS AND BELLES-LETTRES can easily be obtained separately.

There is also a collection of Memoirs relative to the history of France, arranged and edited by Messrs. Guizot and Petitot, in one hundred and sixty-two volumes, 8vo, uniformly and elegantly bound. This collection is of the first importance to any one who would acquire a thorough knowledge of French history.

The editions of the French classics are worthy of special attention. They are nearly all of them the best and most costly which have been published. The apparatus for the thorough study of the French language and literature may be regarded as comparatively rich.

After the receipt of the French books, Mr. Brown forwarded me the sum of four thousand francs, to be expended for German books, with instructions similar to those which he had given for the previous purchase. Upon this commission, I bestowed no less time and labor than upon the other. The task of selection was, however, more difficult, owing to the astonishing copiousness of the literature, and the singular destitution of such bibliographical aids as Brunet & Quérard furnished for French literature.

HISTORY OF THE LIBRARY. 97

The German importation contains as large a selection of works from standard German authors as the funds entrusted to me enabled me to purchase. This selection contains a good apparatus for a thorough study of the language. There is a complete set of the ALLGEMEINE DEUTSCHE BIBLIOTHEK, in one hundred and thirty-nine volumes, octavo, and the ALLGEMEINE LITERATUR-ZEITUNG, in one hundred and thirty-four volumes, quarto, the two containing a complete history of German literature for the last hundred years. Also, a set of ERSCH & GRUBER's Encyclopædia, complete, as far as then published, in seventy-two volumes, quarto,—the most extensive and valuable work of the kind ever published, and so far as known, the only copy which has as yet been brought to this country; also, several valuable Maps and Engravings, and a large number of important works in all departments of learning.

I should mention in this connection, that at the suggestion of a friend of mine—an officer in the Royal Guards—I sent a written request to the King of Prussia for a History of the Seven Years' War, published by the Prussian Military Staff;—a work not to be obtained at the shops, but only by application to the King. His Majesty was pleased to present the work, and it has been received through His Excellency Henry Wheaton, late Minister of the United States to Berlin. This is a work indispensable for the thorough study of this important period of history, and is, perhaps, the only copy in the United States.

While in Germany, I also received the sum of one hundred pounds sterling from the Library Committee, with directions to expend the same in the purchase of such books as were immediately needed in the departments of Greek and Latin Classics. Selection here was a most difficult task. A complete apparatus for the study of any one of the more popular authors, would cost more than the whole sum entrusted to me; and it was very difficult to decide what to reject. I have, however, the satisfaction to know that the choice made meets the approbation of the Professors of these departments, and of other eminent linguists who have examined the collection. Indeed, I was very confident it would, as I had made the selection with the assistance of eminent classical scholars. To the Professor of Latin in Brown University, (J. L. Lincoln,) then in Germany, I was particularly indebted for valuable hints, and lists of books. The number of books and the cost per volume, is given in the preceding table. It will be observed that the cost per volume of the books in this department is considerably higher than in any other, excepting that of the fine arts.

Mr. Jewett's account of the Italian purchase is as follows:—

Subsequently to the German purchase, Mr. Brown forwarded to me the sum of six thousand francs, to be expended in Italy for the most valuable Italian books, including some on the fine arts, of which, our Library was lamentably barren. The

Italian Classics purchased are, for the most part, of the choicest library editions, some of them large-paper copies and all well bound. The average price per volume of this importation is very high. This is owing to the large number of elegant illustrated works. Some of these demand particular attention. CANINA's Work on Architecture, Egyptian, Grecian, and Roman, comprising nine volumes, octavo, of text, and three thick volumes folio, of large and handsomely engraved plates, is one of the most magnificent works of the age. This work is not only invaluable to architects; it is of great importance to the classical department, containing, as it does, restorations of all the more important monuments of Greece and Rome, of which, only fragments now remain to us. It also contains plans, on a large scale, of Rome and Athens, and other ancient cities. IL VATICANO, in eight thick volumes, folio, contains a minute description, with beautiful etchings, of St. Peter's church and the Vatican, and all the collections of art which adorn the latter. This superb work was published by order of the Papal Government. The contract for publishing it was given to a bookseller, who agreed to furnish a certain number of sheets if desired, supposing that this number would cover the whole. But the work had advanced only to the middle of the eighth volume, when the number of pages contracted for had been printed. The publisher demanded an additional appropriation for finishing the work. This was refused, and he bound up the number of copies contracted for by the government and delivered them in their unfinished state. He subsequently completed the work at his own expense. It is important, therefore, in purchasing the work, to shun the government copies. Our copy is complete. IL CAMPIDOGLIO, in two large volumes, folio, is a work upon the Capitol, similar to that upon the Vatican, which has just been described.

The MUSEO BORBONICO contains an account of all the collections of the Naples Museum; and it should be remembered that all the movable articles which have been recovered from Herculaneum and Pompeii are deposited there. Of this work, there are several editions more or less complete. The most perfect in all respects, is that published by the Neapolitan Government, of which ours is a copy. This edition is very rare and costly everywhere out of Italy. I do not know of any other copy than ours in this country, though it is possible there are others. It is in thirteen volumes, quarto. The work is not yet completed.

The works of THORWALDSEN, in two volumes, folio, and those of CANOVA, in four volumes, octavo, are also in the collection, besides a large number of views in Italy, and engravings. There is also a large map, more than eight feet square, of ancient Rome, by CANINA, a panoramic map of modern Rome eight and one-half feet long and four wide, and a large collection of works illustrating the typography and history of the eternal city. I also obtained from the collection of the Prince of Canino a few small Etruscan vases, genuine antiques.

On my return to Paris, continues Prof. Jewett, in the summer of 1845, I received a draft from the Committee for three thousand francs, with instructions to purchase with the same, a telescope for twelve hundred francs, and a list of scientific books, and to expend the balance on the purchase of such works, particularly such relating to the fine arts, as I might judge most needed. With the balance of the funds I purchased, among other works, the Musée Français and Musée Royal, in six volumes, folio, of beautiful engravings with letter press. This splendid work printed by order of the French government, contains engravings of all the best paintings and statues in the vast museum collected in Paris by Napoleon, and now distributed to its original owners, in all parts of Europe. The work may be considered as quite indispensable in every public library. To us who cannot see the originals, such a collection of engravings of all the choicest monuments of ancient and modern art is of the greatest interest. It cannot fail to have a strong influence in forming and cultivating a taste for art among our students.

The following English books are mentioned by Prof. Jewett, as worthy of special notice:—

A complete set of Hansard's Parliamentary History and Debates, from 1066 to the close of the last session, in one hundred and seventy-eight large octavo volumes, uniformly bound in half Russia; a complete set of the Monthly Review and the Gentleman's Magazine, (in continuation of the parts already in the Library); the complete works of the most prominent English authors (not before had) in every department of literature, in the best editions; a complete set of the Encyclopædia Metropolitana, substantially bound in half Russia, besides many valuable maps and engravings. There are also many costly scientific works, some elegant works on the fine arts, as the National Gallery, Hogarth's works, valuable architectural works, Lodge's Portraits, Sir William Gell's Pompeiana, etc. There is also a very valuable selection from the Reports of the British Parliament, in upwards of one hundred folio volumes, well bound, purchased at the sale of the library of William Seymour Blackstone, M. P., grandson of the illustrious Sir William Blackstone. It may not be amiss to mention, that several of the books purchased derive additional interest from their containing autographs of distinguished individuals to whom they belonged.

While in London, I received from Moses B. Ives, Esq., the sum of one hundred pounds sterling, with the request that I would expend the same in the purchase of books for the Library. At this time I had the rare good fortune to find a collection containing nearly all that has ever been published in the form of a separate essay or treatise relating to Shakspeare and his works. This collection was commenced more than twenty years ago, by Mr. Thomas Rodd, one of the most intelligent booksellers, and probably the best bibliographer in London. It is almost perfect. Mr. Rodd possessed facilities for making such a collection which no other man enjoyed. It lacks but few, and those unimportant publications, known to exist in this department. The collection is, without doubt, by far the richest in this country, and perhaps the richest in the world. It does not contain all the editions of the works of the immortal bard. A collection of *them* would be quite beyond our present means. A good copy of the first edition has been sold for about a thousand dollars. Copies of the first edition of the separate plays are worth from ten to twenty or thirty guineas each. We have a fac simile of the first edition, which, for critical purposes, is very valuable. We have also the edition called "Stevens Own," Boswell's, Malone's and Knight's. These, with Collier's, are the most valuable that have been published

This collection of Shakspeariana contains one hundred and ninety-six volumes, bound in full calf. One of them is IRELAND's original copy of his CONFESSIONS, inlaid, as the book-binders term it, with marginal notes in his own hand-writing. An addition has recently been made to the collection, of one hundred and fifty volumes, purchased at the sale of Burton's Shakspeariana, in New York; and also of BOYDELL's Illustration of Shakspeare, in two immense folio volumes, presented by Mr. Ives. In 1852, Mr. Ives presented to the Library twenty-five bound volumes of the PROVIDENCE JOURNAL, from 1838 to 1850, and seven volumes of the PROVIDENCE MORNING COURIER, from 1836 to 1840. These volumes of which, he continued the Journal from year to year, are of obvious importance, as a continuous record of events pertaining to the annals of the city and the State, and especially of all the public occasions of the University, and of all facts and incidents belonging to its current history. Mr. Ives was a graduate of the College in the class of 1812, and for nearly thirty-two years was the efficient Treasurer of the Corporation. He died in 1857.* He was an

* Mr. Ives died on the 7th of August, at the age of sixty-three. A discourse, in commemoration of his life and character, was delivered by the Rev. Dr. Wayland, from which we cannot forbear making the following extract: "As Treasurer of the University, he was brought into more intimate relations with the officers of instruction. No one of them will, I am sure, forget the fraternal care with which he watched over their interests. Was any of them sick,— he was the first person to visit him, with offers of assistance. Was any one borne

upright man, a model merchant, and, a warm, steadfast friend of the Institution.

In March, 1844, Mr. Brown presented to the Library a set of the YEAR BOOKS, from Edward I. to Henry VIII., in ten volumes, small folio, London, 1596–1640. In Wallace's Reporters chronologically arranged, (third edition, page sixty-seven,) we find respecting them the following note: "In 1689 the thirteen Judges of England had occasion to lament how scarce the older editions of the Year Books had become in the country where they were printed; to an extent, say they, which had proved, 'of no small detriment' to the study of the law itself. It was a somewhat striking incident of a summer ramble in the North, that, in 1847, far along the track of two hundred years afterwards, and when nearly twice as long a term as had intervened between the date when the Year Books were printed and that in which the Judges complained of their scarceness—I should note a copy of them in a college library of the United States, the gift to it of an American merchant. In the Library of Brown University, Providence, Rhode Island, bound in as fragrant Russia as ever shed its odors through the palace workshop of Hayday, M'Kenzie or Riviere, may be seen an edition of the Year Books, the gift of Mr. John Carter Brown," etc.

Mr. Brown has continued to present, from year to year, valuable donations to the Library, chiefly of rare and costly books.

down with labor, and in need of relaxation,— he was the first to suggest the remedy, and the most active in providing the means for its accomplishment. In all the efforts made, for the last thirty years, to increase the Library, and improve the facilities for education, he ever bore a prominent part. His interest never flagged, when anything could be suggested to improve the condition of the Institution which he loved so well. If, in any respect, Brown University has gained in favor with the public; if it has taken a more honorable rank among the Colleges of New England; if its means of education have been rendered, in any respect, ample, and its Board of Instruction such as would adorn any similar Institution in our country; to no one are we more indebted for all this, than to the late Treasurer of the University."

Among them may be mentioned, in illustration, the following, viz.: JUSTINIANI INSTITUTIONES, large folio, Venetiis, N. Jenson, 1477,—a splendid copy of one of the old illuminated books, bound in full Russia; BABYLONIAN TALMUD, twelve volumes, folio, bound in full goat gilt,—a sumptuous copy; BARNARD'S Catalogus Bibliothecæ Regiæ, large paper, six volumes, folio; MURATORI'S Rerum Italicarum Scriptores, with TARTINI's Continuation, thirty volumes, folio; JOURNAL DES DEBATS, Paris, 1800–36, seventy-four volumes, folio; PANZER'S Annales Typographici, eleven volumes, quarto; LIVY'S Decades a Lucca Porro Recognitæ, folio, Tarvisi, J. Vercellius, 1482,—an uncommonly fine specimen of ancient typography; the LONDON CHRONICLE, 1757–98, eighty-three volumes, quarto,—a fine clean copy, edges untrimmed; ARINGHI'S Roma Subterranea post Bossium, etc., two volumes, folio, 1659; COLLECTION DE DOCUMENTS Inédits sur l'Histoire de France, ninety-two volumes, quarto; Continuations down to the present time of TRANSACTIONS OF THE ROYAL SOCIETY, MÉMOIRES de l'Institut National de France, LE MONITEUR UNIVERSEL, and REAL MUSEO BORBONICO; NICHOL'S Virgilii Maronis Hexaglotta, edited by Sotheby, folio, large paper, London, 1827; additions to the SHAKSPEARIAN Collection, etc., etc.

During the year 1844, Mr. Philip Allen, Jr., presented to the Library, VIE DE NAPOLÉON, recontée par lui-même, four volumes; JOMINI'S Précis de l'Art de la Guerre, two volumes; TRAITÉ DES GRANDES OPERATIONS MILITAIRES, four volumes; HISTOIRE DES GUERRES DE LA RÉVOLUTION, fifteen volumes; KAUSLER'S Great Military Atlas, with two hundred colored plates; and a fine copy of the GENERAL ATLAS of the Society for the Diffusion of Useful Knowledge.

The Class which graduated in 1821, held a meeting in Providence, a quarter of a century from the time of their graduation, at which a considerable sum of money was subscribed for the benefit of the Library, in token of their grateful interest in the

HISTORY OF THE LIBRARY. 103

Institution at which they were educated. The money thus obtained was placed in the hands of Dr. Thomas H. Webb, of Boston, who purchased, with excellent judgment, about five hundred volumes, mostly from the library of the Hon. John Pickering. They comprise a variety of works in history, literature and science, of standard character and of permanent value. Among them are fifty volumes of the HISTOIRE DE L'ACADÉMIE Royal des Inscriptions et Belles-Lettres, FABRICII Bibliotheca Græca, fourteen volumes, quarto, and a large thick volume of PLUTARCH's Lives, in Latin, published at Rome, in 1471. This last volume is one of the oldest books in the Library. Such rare instances of liberality on the part of a class is deserving of special commendation. We hope to chronicle many similar instances in the future. In arranging the alcoves of a college library it would be wise to reserve shelves to be filled by the contributions of graduates.

The next year, 1847, a valuable addition of patristic works was made to the Library, through the agency of several of the leading clergymen of the city. The history of this movement may be found in the annual report of the joint Library Committee to the Corporation, an extract from which may be interesting to the general reader:—

> The deficiency of American libraries in the best editions of the early Christian Fathers, has often been made a subject of public regret and complaint. The deficiency of our own Library in this respect, though probably not greater than that of most others, yet had often been remarked by those whose studies had led them to investigate the antiquities of the Christian church. The means of pursuing such inquiries here, in the original editions of authors, were exceedingly limited and unsatisfactory. The attention of the friends of theological learning in this city was first publicly called to this fact by the Rev. Mr. Osgood, minister of the second Unitarian Church, (now Rev. Dr. Osgood, pastor of the Church of the Messiah, in New York,) and the proposition was made that a sum of money be raised in the several parishes of the city for the supply of this deficiency, and for furnishing the means of prosecuting ecclesiastical studies to the clergy of the several Christian denominations here. An opportunity of purchasing the works of the leading Christian Fathers, was soon afterwards

presented in the sale of the valuable library of the Rev. Matthias Bruen, in the city of New York. A subscription was immediately set on foot by several clergymen of this city, in their respective parishes, and the sum of twelve hundred and fifty dollars was soon raised for the purpose above mentioned, and placed at the disposal of the Committee. Of this sum, one thousand dollars was collected by Rev. Mr. Granger, one hundred and fifty dollars by Rev. Mr. Osgood, and one hundred dollars by Rev. Mr. Hall. Subscriptions are also understood to have been commenced in other parishes, which, it has been intimated, may be filled up at a future day. In the disposition of the funds furnished by this subscription, the Committee expended about nine hundred dollars at the sale of the Bruen library; the remaining three hundred and fifty dollars is in the hands of the Treasurer, to be appropriated to the purchase of similar works, whenever a favorable opportunity shall be presented. The collection of patristic literature which has thus been added to the Library, comprises in all, one hundred and eighty-four volumes, viz.: Folios, one hundred and thirty; quartos, twenty-nine; octavos, twenty-three; duodecimos, two. Among them are the BIBLIOTHECA MAXIMA VETERUM PATRUM, in twenty-seven volumes, folio; the works of AUGUSTINE, of AMBROSE, of BERNARD, of CHRYSOSTOM, of ALCUIN, of the GREGORIES, of EUSEBIUS, of PHILO, of JEROME, and of many others of the early Fathers of the Christian church. These works are all of the Paris Benedictine editions, and are in excellent condition. They have greatly enhanced the value of the Library to all students of ecclesiastical and patristic literature, and have placed it among the very best libraries in the country, so far as this department of learning is concerned. It is hoped by the Committee, that the volumes which have thus been added may accomplish the benevolent design of the contributors, and for a long succession of generations, furnish incitement and aid to the clergy of this city and its vicinity, in studying the writings which relate to the origin and early history of Christianity.

To this collection of the Fathers, we may remark, important additions were afterwards made. The sum of money eventually collected by the clergymen of the city for the encouragement of patristic learning, amounted to about two thousand dollars.

The purchases made for the Library during the year 1851 now claim our attention. And here we may be allowed to quote at length from the annual report of the joint Library Committee presented to the Corporation in September, 1852:—

The Committee call attention, in the first place, to a collection bought at the sale in New York, of the library of the late Rev. Dr. Jarvis. Aware of the great value of this library, probably the most valuable private collection ever offered at auction in this country, the Committee made out from the catalogue a list of works which they wished to secure, and authorized the Librarian to attend the sales, and make the purchases under the advice of the sub-committee on books. The Librarian executed his commission with fidelity and good judgment, and was successful in procuring most of the works which had been selected. There were purchased three hundred and eighty-six volumes, which cost altogether nine hundred and eight dollars. They are mostly rare works, difficult to be obtained even in Europe; they are almost exclusively folios and quartos, in the best editions, with the binding and all outward appointments, for the most part, of the first quality and in excellent condition. Among them are about thirty volumes of the Greek and Latin Fathers, which go far towards completing the patristic collection in the Library, especially of the writers of the first six centuries. There are also among them extensive historical collections, of which we select for mention the following, viz. : —

DUCHESNE's Ancient Norman Historians, from 888 to 1220, folio; DUCHESNE's French Historians, down to the time of Philip IV., five volumes, folio; SCHOTT's Spanish Historians, four volumes, folio; PISTORIUS's Body of Polish History, three volumes in one, folio; PISTORIUS's German Historians, four volumes, folio; PANTANUS's Danish History, folio; also a THESAURUS of Swiss History, in one volume, folio; and the great Historical Dictionary of MORERI, in ten volumes, folio. Belonging to the department of ecclesiastical history, may be mentioned the thirteen folio volumes of the MAGDEBURGH CENTURIATORS,—the foundation work of protestant church history; also ARNOLD's Impartial History of Church and Heretics, four volumes, folio; NATALIS ALEXANDER's Ecclesiastical History, nine volumes, folio; and SUICER's Thesaurus Ecclesiasticus, two volumes in one, folio. Still other works worthy of mention, are a fine copy of FOLARD's Polybius, seven volumes, quarto; BROTIER's Tacitus, four volumes, quarto; CALVIN's works, nine volumes, folio,—a fine copy of the now scarce Amsterdam edition of 1671; MARVILIUS's Leipsic edition of the Theodosian Code, six volumes in seven, folio; and SPANHEIM's Dissertation on Ancient Coins, two volumes, folio,—a copy which belonged to Gibbon's private library.

These books have cost the Library a large outlay of money, and it may be justly said that they will be rarely used; but these facts are not the criterion of their value to our Library. Belonging as they do, to the class of books which are indispensable instruments of extensive research, and which, by furnishing the requisite materials and authorities, are essential means for the production of original and elaborate works on the various subjects of which they treat, they mark, by their introduction to our alcoves, an auspicious event in the history of the Library; they indicate a great step of progress, in the right direction, of the Library of a learned Institution. It has often been mentioned as a reproach, or at least as an evil attaching to our public libraries, that they are quite deficient in the needful materials for extensive scientific and literary investigations. Many years ago, it was said by Fisher Ames, that "all our universities would not suffice to supply the authorities for such a work as Gibbon's"; and a remark of the same import was made in a literary address delivered a few years since by the late Mr. Justice Story. Prof. Jewett, of the Smithsonian Institution, asserts in one of his annual reports, after a careful examination, that "Mr. WHEATON's History of International Law could not have been written in this country from the materials contained in our public libraries." Similar assertions have been made respecting Mr. TICKNOR's History of Spanish Literature, and the historical works of PRESCOTT, and of BANCROFT; and it is well known that these eminent authors were obliged to import from abroad expensive books, and to go to Europe themselves to collect materials for the composition of these works, which do so much honor to the literature of the country. And it is certainly incumbent upon the managers of public libraries to aim to remove, by pursuing a systematic plan from year to year, the great evil which is illustrated by all these facts. It is with such a view as this, that the works above described have been purchased for our Library, as well as others of similar character, mentioned in former reports of the Library Committee. While we would not neglect other acknowledged objects of the Library, we would aim to make it as rapidly as possible a great repository of learning; into whose inclosures shall gradually be gathered from the wide domains of literature all works which are of ultimate authority in every department of knowledge; all works, whatever they may be, whether the minutest tract or the amplest folio, which can facilitate the progress of the future historian, and cast a sure and faithful light on his pathway. We may mention, in fortunate coincidence with these remarks, that some of the books purchased at the Jarvis sale formerly belonged to Gibbon's own collection; indeed we may say, that by means of the additions made during the past year, and of other recent years, the significant remark above quoted from Fisher Ames and Judge Story, has already lost well nigh all its force in its bearings upon our Library; and we need only follow out on a systematic plan the course we have already commenced, and the period is not far distant, when the writers of our own land and of other lands, who may aspire to rival in industry and in fame the Gibbons of former times, may find in the treasures here accumulated the amplest views for the attainment of their noble ends.

The report from which the foregoing extract has been taken, was prepared by Professor Lincoln. It embodies sound wisdom, and presents views worthy the consideration of the managers of our public libraries. It is in accordance with these views that the Librarian was authorized to expend the Tallmadge bequest, in the purchase of duplicates from the Astor Library. The Hon. James Tallmadge, LL. D., to whom we have referred in our Historical Sketch, was a graduate under President Maxcy. Upon his death, in September, 1853, he bequeathed to the University one thousand dollars, for the improvement of the Library. At the annual meeting of the Corporation held in September, 1854, it was—

Resolved, That this Corporation would express their deep gratitude for this token of remembrance from one of their most distinguished graduates and firmest friends.

Resolved, That the Library Committee be requested to appropriate the amount of this bequest to the purchase of books, and to take such measures as shall indicate the source from whence they have been derived.

This bequest, as we have already stated, was expended in the purchase of choice duplicates. For this valuable purchase the Library is greatly indebted to the courtesy and professional skill of Dr. Coggeshall, the late efficient Superintendent of the Astor Library.

We may be pardoned for adding another extract from Professor Lincoln's admirable report, referring as it does to the need of a new Library building, constructed in accordance with the most approved principles of library architecture; a need which the lapse of fifteen years has only increased. Such a building, well filled with useful books, would become a centre of influence, and the home and resort of students and literary men. It would be instrumental of the highest good to the community, and reflect lasting credit upon the liberality of the friends of the Institution, through whom we trust it may ere long be built:—

The Committee cannot close this report without adverting to a subject of great and growing importance to the Library and to the University, and one that has forced itself anew upon their attention in preparing these returns, namely, the desirableness of taking early measures for either enlarging the present Library hall, or what is far better, if practicable, of erecting a new Library building. The considerations which prompt such a suggestion lie very near at hand, and seem to the Committee to be of the most pressing character. The first and most obvious is the absolute incapacity of the present hall to meet even the existing wants of the Library. The space for folios and quartos is already entirely occupied. * * * Again, the present building is very insecure. As is well known, it is not fire-proof. It is obviously very unsafe for a valuable Library to be deposited in a building furnished with no provisions against the casualities of fire, especially when it is used, as is ours, for various other College purposes. The recent case of fire in the Congress Library teaches an impressive lesson on this point. It is also insecure against other dangers; it might be entered at ease from nearly any point, and robbed of its most valuable treasures. To these considerations it may be added that the present hall is, on many accounts, inconvenient for a large and growing Library. The shelves are quite too high, and they ought to be so arranged as to obviate the necessity of the ladders* now in use. There are also no suitable accommodations for pictures, maps, plates, etc., of which we have now a very numerous and costly collection. All these facts clearly indicate the great desirableness of endeavoring to take early measures for a new and lasting improvement in this most important department of the University. It is believed that, in the present state of the University, no more signal service could be conferred upon it by its patrons and friends, than the erection, on some suitable part of the College grounds, of a new edifice, skillfully planned and constructed, and furnished with all the requisite appointments for the exclusive uses of the Library; one that shall be capacious enough to accommodate a hundred thousand volumes, and so built as to be capable of indefinite enlargement. The consummation of a great enterprise like this would be a most propitious event in the history of the College. It would place the fortunes of the Library upon a firm and permanent basis; and the most sober-minded of its friends might indulge in brilliant visions of its future prosperity and usefulness.

In looking over the records of the Corporation, we find under date of September 5, 1856, the following preamble and resolution, offered by Samuel G. Arnold:—

Whereas, Don Geronimo Urmeneta, an alumnus of this University, and late Minister of Finance of the Republic of Chili, has sent through Samuel W. Greene, Esq., the elegant works of Claudio Gay, entitled, Historia fisica y politica de Chile, in twenty-three octavo volumes of text, and two quarto volumes of plates, Paris. 1845–54, as a present to the Library of Brown University,

Resolved, That the President be requested to acknowledge the receipt of the same, and convey the thanks of this Corporation to Señor Urmeneta, for his munificent gift.

*The present Librarian, in 1858, sprained his ankle badly by falling from one of these high ladders, from the effects of which fall he has not yet entirely recovered. Dr. Ebert, the distinguished German Bibliographer and Librarian, is said to have lost his life in this way.

Señor Urmeneta is a native of Santiago, Chili, and one of the most distinguished men of that country. He entered the Sophomore class at Brown in 1832, but did not graduate. In 1851 he received the honorary degree of A. M., and in 1859 the degree of LL. D. He has continued to manifest a warm regard for the place of his education, by sending to the Library repeated donations of valuable books. Some of these are worthy of special notice, being elegantly printed, on large paper, of superior quality. Among them are GALERIA NACIONAL o Coleccion de Biografias i Retratos de Hombres Celebres de Chile, edited by Hermojenes de Irisarri and Miguel Luis Amunátegui, two volumes, folio, Santiago, 1854, large type and thick heavy paper, with forty-eight portraits; COLECCION DE TRATADOS celebrados por la República de Chile, quarto, Santiago, 1857; OBSERVACIONES ASTRONÓMICAS, por el Dr. Cárlos Guill? Mœsta, quarto, Santiago, 1859.

In 1863, the late venerable Dr. Crocker presented to the Library a noble folio, bound in full Turkey morocco and richly gilt, entitled BIBLIA SACRA POLYGLOTTA BAGSTERIANA, London, 1831. This work presents eight languages at each opening of the volume. It comprises the Samaritan Pentateuch, the Septuagint Greek version of the Old Testament, the Vulgate Latin, Diodati's Italian, Scio's Spanish, Ostervald's French, Luther's German, the authorized version of the English Bible, the original Greek text of the New Testament, and the venerable Peshito, or old Syriac version. Mr. Crocker was a graduate of Harvard University in the class of 1802. In 1808 he was elected to a Fellowship in Brown University, which position he held until his death in 1866, a period of fifty-eight years. He was one of the original members of the joint Library Committee, which was organized in 1840, and for nearly a quarter of a century he devoted himself to the interests of the Library with earnestness and zeal. His portrait graces the Collection in Rhode Island Hall.

Among the recent purchases for the Library are a special selection of about five hundred volumes of works on Chemistry, and a costly collection of Architectural books, including DALY's Revue Générale de l'Architecture et des Travaux Publics, in twenty-two quarto volumes; CANINA's Edifizi di Roma Antica, six volumes, folio; the Architecture of LEON BAPTISTA ALBERTI, in three volumes, folio; BOWMAN & CROWTHER's churches of the Middle Ages, two volumes, folio; BRUYÈRE's Études relatives a l'Art des Constructions, two volumes, folio; CALLIAT's Parallèle des Maisons de Paris, folio; CARTER's Ancient Architecture of England, folio; CASTERMAN's Parallèle des Maisons de Bruxelles, folio; CONEY's Ecclesiastical Edifices of the Olden Time, two volumes, folio; D'AGINCOURT's Storia dell' Arte, six volumes, royal octavo of text, and one volume, folio, of plates; DAHLBERG's Suecia Antiqua et Hodierna, three volumes, folio; DELAMOTTE's Original Views of Oxford, folio; DUGDALE's Monasticon Anglicanum, eight volumes, folio; DURAND's Recueil et Parallèle Édifices en tout Genre, folio; FRANCHETTI's Storia e Descrizione del Duomo di Milano, quarto; GAILHABAUD's Architecture du Vme au XVIIme Siècle et les Arts qui en dépendent, four volumes, quarto, and one volume, folio; GAUCHEREL's Examples de Décoration, folio; GAUTHIER's Plus beaux Édifices de la Ville de Gênes, two volumes, folio; GOURLIER's BIET's, etc., Choix d' Édifices Publics, three volumes, folio; GRAFFENRIED & STURLER's Architecture Suisse, folio; GWILT's Encyclopædia of Architecture, thick octavo; GYFFORD's Designs for small picturesque Cottages, quarto; HIRT's Geschichte der Baukunst bei den Alten, three volumes, quarto, and one volume, folio; HOPE's Historical Essay on Architecture, two volumes octavo; ISABELLE's Édifices Circulaires et les Domes, folio; KRAFFT's Recueil d' Architecture, folio; LETAROUILLY's Édifices de Rome Moderne, three volumes, quarto, of text, and three volumes, folio, of plates; LOUDON's Encyclopædia of Cottage, Farm and Villa

Architecture, thick octavo; NASH's Architecture of the Middle Ages, folio; NICHOLSON's Encyclopædia of Architecture, two volumes, quarto; PAPWORTH's Rural Residences, (twenty-seven colored plates,) quarto; PENROSE's Investigation of the principles of Athenian Architecture, folio; PLAW's Ferme Ornée, or Rural Improvements, quarto; PLAW's Rural Architecture, quarto; POCOCK's Architectural Designs, quarto; PUGIN's True Principles of Pointed or Christian Architecture, quarto; RAWLINSON's Designs for tall Chimney Shafts, folio; REYNAUD's Traité d' Architecture, two volumes, quarto, of text, and one volume, folio, of plates; RICHARDSON's Studies from old English Mansions, four volumes, folio; RONDELET's Art de Batir, five volumes, quarto, of text, and one volume, folio, of plates; RUSCA's Raccolta dei Disegni di diverse Fabbriche in Pietroburgo, folio; SHAW's Encyclopædia of Ornament, quarto; SHAW's Civil Architecture, quarto; SIMMS's Public Works of Great Britain, folio; SMILLIE & WALTER's Mount Auburn Illustrated, quarto; SOANE's Sketches in Architecture, folio; TURNER's Domestic Architecture, two volumes, octavo; The Civil Architecture of VITRUVIUS, by Wilkins, quarto; WEALE's Theory, Practice and Architecture of Bridges, three volumes, octavo; WEALE's Examples in Architectural, Engineering and Mechanical Drawing, folio; WEALE's Public Works of the United States, folio; WICKES's Spires and Towers of the Mediæval Churches of England, two volumes, folio; WORNUM's Analysis of Ornament, octavo; WYATT's Metalwork and its Artistic Design, (printed in colors,) folio.

But our limits will not admit of further details. From this imperfect sketch it will be seen, that the Library of Brown University, although not large, numbering but about thirty-five thousand volumes, is unusually choice and valuable. A large proportion of the books have been selected with special reference to the wants of students, and gentlemen engaged in literary and scientific research. The departments of bibliography, the classics,

English history and literature, ecclesiastical history, patristics, mathematics, the modern languages, and the fine arts, are quite full, and comparatively complete. The Library has a good collection of books pertaining to the history and literature of the English Dissenters. In modern law books, in works on anatomy and medicine, botany, natural history, and the mechanical arts, there are lamentable deficiencies. The Library has comparatively but few duplicates. In addition to the Metcalf collection already described, it has a large number of bound and unbound pamphlets, " those leaves of an hour, and volumes of a season, and even of a week," which, says D'Israeli, "slight and evanescent things as they appear, and scorned at by opposite parties, while each cherishes its own, are in truth the records of the public mind, the secret history of a people, which does not always appear in the more open narrative."

Several of the College Professors have good libraries in the specialities to which they are devoted. That of President Sears is deserving of notice. It contains upwards of seven thousand volumes, the greater part of which are in the German and Latin languages. The most valuable part of it consists of SPECIAL HISTORIES and BIOGRAPHIES, particularly those relating to the period of the Reformation, and what preceded and followed it. The Rev. Dr. Dunn, Professor of Rhetoric and English Literature, has an excellent Belles-Lettres library of about three thousand volumes, including a choice collection of German Exegetical works, and books adapted to the critical study of the Scriptures. The Rev. Mr. Diman, Professor of History and Political Economy, has a fine collection of books in his department, and especially rich in Metaphysics and German Philosophies. Professors Lincoln and Harkness have also, each of them, a good working apparatus for the study of the Greek and Latin classics.

In this connection it may not be improper to refer to the private collection of Mr. Brown, to whose liberality, as we have already seen, the College Library is so greatly indebted. It contains upwards of ten thousand volumes, mostly rare works pertaining to early American history. As an illustration of its character and value, we may be allowed to quote from our Librarian's Manual,* a work recently published: "These two Catalogues, (Rich's Bibliotheca and Supplement,) although they contain two thousand five hundred and twenty-three articles, are far from being complete. A merchant of Providence, well known to the amateurs of this class of books, has in his own private collection three thousand two hundred and thirty-one early works upon America, published between the years 1700 and 1800, of which one thousand five hundred and twelve are not mentioned by Rich. He has also one thousand one hundred and seventy-four works published *previous* to the year 1700, of which five hundred and nine are not mentioned by Ternaux; thus making four thousand four hundred and five separate works relating to America and published previous to the year 1800, of which two thousand and twenty-one were unknown to the eminent American bibliographers, whose catalogues are described in this list." The most costly of all collections of books is the one of which Hariot's Virginia forms a part, and which is known as DE BRY'S VOYAGES. This is a collection of voyages and travels in Asia, Africa, and America. Its publication was commenced in the year 1590, by De Bry, an eminent engraver and bookseller at Frankfort-on-the-Main, and continued by himself and his successors for forty-four years. It is copiously illustrated with maps and the finest engravings executed at that period. The series make twenty-five folio

---

*THE LIBRARIAN'S MANUAL; a Treatise on bibliography, comprising a select and descriptive list of bibliographical works; to which are added, sketches of Public Libraries. Illustrated with Engravings. 4to., New York, C. B. Norton, 1858, pp. 314.

volumes, thirteen of which relate to America. It was published in Latin and in German, and in French and English in part. It also underwent many changes and variations. A complete set of this exceedingly rare work, including every edition and variation known, making nearly a hundred volumes, forms a part of Mr. Brown's library.

Previous to the year 1824, the duties of the Librarian were performed by one of the College tutors. The following are the names of those who have filled this office, viz.: Hon. Asher Robbins, William Wilkinson, President Maxcy, President Messer, Rev. Otis Thompson, Prof. Calvin Park, William Emmons, Hon. John Bailey, Doct. Caleb H. Snow, Peter Pratt, Aaron Brooks, Hon. Horace Mann, and C. Sumner Smith. From 1824 till 1840, the office was filled by Prof. Horatio G. Bowen. He was succeeded by Prof. C. C. Jewett, who held the office seven years. The present incumbent entered upon his duties in March, 1848. Prof. William Gammell, was Librarian *pro tem*, from September 14, 1840, to June 3, 1841, and the Rev. Dr. Caswell, from June 3, 1841, to October 11, 1841, when Prof. Jewett commenced his services. The Rev. Dr. Dunn, was chosen Assistant Librarian, September 26, 1843, and took charge of the Library during Mr. Jewett's absence in Europe. The following graduates have also acted as Assistant Librarians, viz.: Asa H. Gould, Charles J. Muenscher, Judson Benjamin, Franklin J. Dickman, Reuben A. Guild, James B. Angell, Heman L. Wayland, William H. Mills, Samuel Brooks, Edward T. Caswell, Samuel C. Eastman, and Edward H. Cutler.

The Library is open during term-time, daily, from nine till one; during vacations, weekly, on Saturdays, from ten till one. The members of the Corporation and Faculty; all resident graduates; all donors to the Library fund; all donors to the fund for building Rhode Island Hall; and all donors to the Library to the amount of forty dollars, residing in Providence, are entitled to the use of the Library without expense. Undergraduates are entitled to the use of the Library, and are charged therefor the sum of three dollars per annum.

The privilege of consulting the Library is extended, under ordinary restrictions, to all graduates of the University; to all settled clergymen, of every denomination, residing in the city of Providence and the vicinity; and to all other persons on whom, for the purpose of advancing the arts, science or literature, the Corporation or Library Committee may, from time to time, confer it. Books are occasionally loaned to persons at a distance, by special permission.

The following are some of the general regulations of the Library, established by a vote of the Corporation of Brown University, at their annual meeting, September 2, 1841:—

No book shall be borrowed from the Library or returned to it without the knowledge and presence of the Librarian or his assistant, who shall take particular notice of the state of each book, when delivered out, and when returned. And every book, when lent, shall, if the Librarian so direct, have a proper cover on it, which shall be returned undefaced, with the book. And the Librarian shall require of the borrower a receipt for every book, if he be present; otherwise the book may be delivered on his written application. In no case, however, shall books be lent to undergraduates, unless they are present to sign a receipt for the same.

No person except officers of instruction shall borrow from the Library more than one folio, which he may keep four weeks; or one quarto, which he may keep three weeks; or two octavos or two duodecimos, which he may keep two weeks.

For every book not returned at the time specified, the person borrowing it shall pay for each folio or quarto, three cents; and for each octavo or duodecimo, two cents, for every day, until it shall be returned.

All the books, whether in possession of undergraduates, resident graduates, officers of instruction, members of the Corporation, or others, shall be returned to the Library, on or before the Friday preceding the close of each Collegiate term. Any person who may fail to comply with this requirement, shall pay twenty-five cents for each volume of which he retains possession.

If any book borrowed from the Library be injured or defaced by writing in it or otherwise, or be lost, the Librarian shall make immediate report of it to the Library

Committee. And if the borrower be a graduate or undergraduate, the Library Committee shall oblige him to replace it as soon as possible, with one of equal value; or they may punish him by fine or otherwise; and if such volume be part of a set, the borrower shall be obliged to replace the whole set, or be punished, as above; and until this be done, he shall not be allowed to borrow any other book.

No book can be renewed to any undergraduate or resident graduate, unless it be brought to the Library.

No undergraduate, while receiving books, shall take down any book from the shelves without special permission from the Librarian.

No person shall lend to any other a book which he has borrowed from the Library, nor let it go from under his personal custody. And no book shall, by any person, be carried out of the city of Providence, without the special permission of the Corporation or of the Library Committee.

Inasmuch as the Librarian is held specially responsible for the safe keeping of the books, etc., belonging to the Library, no person shall be allowed to enter the Library, unaccompanied by him or by his authorized agent.

If any undergraduate desires to borrow a book, which is lent out of the Library, he may leave his name and the title of the book with the Librarian, and when the book shall be returned, the Librarian shall reserve it for the person so applying; provided he call for it at his next time of receiving books from the Library.

Such books, maps, charts, etc., as have been, or which may be presented, with the intention or request that they shall not be lent from the Library, shall in no case be lent therefrom. Books which are valuable for their plates, or for their rarity or antiquity, and all others which the Library Committee may designate as works of reference, shall not be lent; but may be freely consulted in the Library.

The privileges of the Library shall be withdrawn from all such persons as may incur fines under the preceding regulations, until such fines shall have been paid. And the Librarian is authorized to suspend or withdraw the privilege of borrowing books from the Library, or of reading books therein, from any person who may wilfully violate any of its regulations.

The joint Library Committee are authorized to establish, from time to time, such additional regulations, not incompatible with the laws of the University, as shall be found proper and necessary, for the safety of the Library and the due administration of its concerns. All such additional regulations shall, however, be reported to the Corporation.

HISTORY

OF THE

COLLEGE CHARTER.

1763–1863.

CHARTER.

THE history of the Charter of Brown University is one of struggle against opposing influences, arising in part from the sectarian feeling so prevalent throughout New England a century ago, and which appears to have been particularly bitter towards the denomination under whose auspices the College in Rhode Island was founded. The LIFE AND CORRESPONDENCE OF MANNING abounds in illustrations of this feeling towards the Institution over which he presided, and also of ecclesiastical oppression, to resist which was one of the main causes that led to the formation of the Warren Association. In the light of an advancing civilization all this has now passed away;—if occasionally recalled to remembrance, it is only in the spirit of kindness, as an impressive admonition to the fuller exercise of that charity which "beareth all things." A faithful account of the College Charter, must of necessity reflect somewhat upon the character of great and good men, whose names have passed into history, and whose memories are precious. On this point we may be allowed to quote the remarks of Professor Knowles, in his preface to the Memoir of Roger Williams. "We must not," he says, "in order to promote or defend religion, attempt to conceal events which history has already recorded, and much less to palliate conduct which we cannot justify. Let us rather confess, with frankness and humility, our own faults, and those of our fathers; learn wisdom from past errors; and bring ourselves and others, as speedily as possibly, to the adoption of those pure principles by which alone Christianity can be sustained and diffused. The book of God records, among its salutary lessons, the mistakes and sins of good men."

In the cabinet of the Rhode Island Historical Society is a manuscript volume by the Rev. Morgan Edwards, entitled, MATERIALS TOWARDS A HISTORY OF THE BAPTISTS IN RHODE ISLAND, in which the author gives a sketch of the early history of the College. This sketch, which is published in Staples's Annals of Providence, contains a narrative by President Manning, written a few years after the occurrence of the events described. This narrative is incorporated in our former work, and reproduced here in order to give completeness to this chapter of our College History:—

In the month of July, 1763, we arrived at Newport, and made a motion to several gentlemen of the Baptist denomination — whereof Col. Gardner, the Deputy Governor, was one — relative to a seminary of polite literature, subject to the government of the Baptists. The motion was properly attended to, which brought together about fifteen gentlemen of the same denomination at the Deputy's house, who requested that I would draw a sketch of the design, against the day following. That day came; and the said gentlemen, with other Baptists, met in the same place, when a rough draught was produced and read.— the tenor of which was, that the Institution was to be a Baptist one, but that as many of other denominations should be taken in as was consistent with the said design. Accordingly, the Hon. Josias Lyndon and Colonel Job Bennet, were appointed to draw a Charter to be laid before the next General Assembly, with a petition that they would pass it into a law. But the said gentlemen pleading unskillfulness touching an affair of the kind, requested that their trusty friend, the Rev. Ezra, now Dr. Stiles, might be solicited to assist them. This was opposed by me, as unwilling to give the Doctor trouble about an affair of other people; but they urged that his love of learning and catholicism would induce him readily to give his assistance. Accordingly their proposition was consented to, and his assistance obtained; or, rather, the draughting of the Charter was left entirely to him, after being told that the Baptists were to have the lead in the Institution, and the government thereof,

HISTORY OF THE CHARTER. 121

forever; and that no more of other denominations were to be admitted than would be consistent with that. The Charter was drawn, and a time and place were appointed for the parties concerned to meet and hear it read. But the vessel in which I was to sail for Halifax going off that day, prevented my being present with them long enough to see whether the original design was secured; and as the Corporation was made to consist of two branches, Trustees and Fellows, and these branches to sit and act by distinct and separate powers, it was not easy to determine, by a transient hearing, what those powers might be. The Trustees were presumed to be the principal branch of authority; and as nineteen out of thirty-five were to be Baptists, the Baptists were satisfied, without sufficient examination into the authority vested in the Fellowship, which afterwards appeared to be the soul of the Institution, while the Trusteeship was only the body. Placing, therefore, an entire confidence in Dr. Stiles, they agreed to join in a petition to the Assembly to have the Charter confirmed by authority.*

* Prof. Kingsley, in his life of Dr. Stiles, states that "a committee of Baptists and Congregationalists was appointed to draft a Charter of a College; and of this body, Mr. Stiles and Mr. William Ellery were designated to prepare such an instrument for their consideration." "It is highly probable," he further adds, "from internal evidence, that the Charter was drawn principally by Mr. Stiles; Mr. Ellery having little concern in preparing it, except to see to the correctness of the legal language. Whoever drew it, he had obviously before him the charters of Yale College, and was familiar with the questions which had arisen with respect to them. The privileges secured to the University by this Charter are very ample; and the language of the several provisions is remarkably full, precise, and explicit. It is, undoubtedly, in many respects, one of the best college charters in New England."

From Prof. Kingsley's statements, it would appear that Baptists and Congregationalists were alike interested in the movement, and that a joint committee representing the two denominations was appointed to draft the Charter. From the statements, however, of Backus, Edwards, Manning, and Jenckes, it is evident that Baptists alone were the originators of the undertaking; that Baptists alone met at the Deputy Governor's house, in Newport, in July, 1763; that, of their number, Lyndon and Bennet were appointed to draft a Charter in accordance with a plan sketched by Manning; that these gentlemen, "pleading unskillfulness," requested that Dr. Stiles "might be solicited to assist them"; and that this was at first opposed by Manning, who was "unwilling to give the Doctor trouble about an affair of other people." The following memorandum, found among the papers of Dr. Stiles, furnishes the key to Professor Kingsley's narrative, and leaves, says President Sears, no room to suspect any want of candor on the part of the latter: "A Charter draughted by a committee of Baptists and Presbyterians, for a College in Rhode Island, was preferred to the Assembly, August, 1763, read and continued. After this, the Baptists deserted the Presbyterians, and prepared the same Charter, with the alteration of the proportions of the denominations in the Corporation. This passed the Assembly at their session at Greenwich, by adjournment last Tuesday, February, 1764." See appendix to President Sears's Centennial Discourse, page 65. The original Charter is published in the appendix to MANNING AND BROWN UNIVERSITY, (pages 465-82,) together with the alterations to which Dr. Stiles refers. These alterations were many and important, as the reader may see at a glance.

16

The following is the petition to which Manning in his narrative refers, copied from the original document. The signatures to the document, it may be remarked, are genuine:—

To the Honorable, the General Assembly of His Majesty's Colony of Rhode Island, to be held at Newport on the first Monday of August, A D. 1763, by adjournment.

THE PETITION OF DIVERS OF THE INHABITANTS OF SAID COLONY.

Whereas, Institutions for liberal education are highly beneficial to society by forming the rising generation to virtue, knowledge, and useful literature, and thus preserving in a community a succession of men qualified for discharging the offices of life with usefulness and reputation, and have always merited and received the public attention and encouragement of every wise, polite and well regulated State : And whereas a public school or seminary erected for this purpose within this Colony, to which the youth may freely resort for education in the vernacular and learned languages, and instruction in the liberal arts and sciences, would be for the general advantage and honor of this government : And whereas there is a confessed absence of polite and useful learning in this Colony, your petitioners, affected with a deep sense thereof, and prompted alone by motives drawn from the public good, and desirous, as far as in them lies, to subserve the political interests of this His Majesty's Colony, and solicitous for cultivating the morals and informing the knowledge of the rising generation, upon which foundation the harmony, good order, and reputation of society depend,— HUMBLY show, that for the good intents and purposes above mentioned they have concerted and planned the Charter herewith presented, and the same, having carefully considered and revised, do propose and submit it to the consideration of this honorable Assembly, requesting your Honors that, out of your great regard for useful literature, and the good morals of the youth of this Colony, and others that may resort to this same for the advantages of education, you would give your assent to and grant and confirm the aforesaid Charter, with all its powers, privileges and immunities, as amply and fully as in said Charter is specified and expressed : And your petitioners as in duty bound will ever pray.

Nicholas Tillinghast, Charles Wickham, Silas Cooke, Peter Mumford, Samuel Fowler, Joseph Clarke, Thomas Rodman, Thomas Wickham, Jr., Benjamin Mason, Thomas Rodman, Jr., Henry Ward, John Bowers, Oliver Arnold, William Burroughs, Standford Wyatt, William Taggart, Jonathan Easton, Jonathan Otis, Nicholas Ward, Jr., Jonathan Rogers, Robert Potter, Samuel Ward, Job Bennet, Joshua Clarke, Gardner Thurston, Josias Lyndon, John Wheaton, William Ellery, Jr., Jonathan Willson, Gideon Cornell, Martin Howard, Israel Brayton, Paul Coffin, Charles Bardin, John Freby, Benjamin Sherburne, Sylvester Child, Caleb Gardner, Jonathan

Nichols, Shubael Barr, Cromel Child, William Vernon, J. Gardner, Joseph Sanford, John Tillinghast, Nicholas Easton, Joshua Saunders, James Tanner, John Tanner, Robert Stevens, Samuel Greene, Joseph G. Wanton, David Moore, Samuel Lyndon, Elnathan Hammond, Nathan Rice, James Gardner, Clarke Brown, Benjamin Hall, Esek Burroughs, Joseph Rodman, William Rogers.

The petition, continues Manning, in his narrative, was preferred, and cheerfully received, and the Charter read; after which a vote was called for, and urged by some to pass into a law. But this was opposed by others, particularly by Daniel Jenckes, Esq., member for Providence, who contended that the Assembly required more time to examine whether it was agreeable to the design of the first movers for it, and therefore prayed the house to have the perusal of it while they adjourned for dinner. This was granted, with some opposition. Then he asked the Governor, who was a Baptist, whom they intended to invest with the governing power in said Institution? The Governor answered, "The Baptists, by all means." Then Mr. Jenckes showed him that the Charter was so artfully constructed as to throw the power into the Fellows' hands, whereof eight out of twelve were Presbyterians, usually called Congregationalists, and that the other four might be of the same denomination, for aught that appeared in the Charter to the contrary. Convinced of this, Governor Lyndon immediately had an interview with Dr. Stiles, the Presbyterian minister of Newport, and demanded why he had perverted the design of the Charter. The answer was, "I gave you timely warning to take care of yourselves, for that we had done so with regard to our society";* and finally observed, "that he was not the rogue." When

---

* In Prof. Kingsley's Life of Dr. Stiles, to which reference has already been made, we find it stated that the project of a College in Rhode Island had been the subject of serious deliberation a considerable time before the Charter was actually granted by the legislature, and that in this matter Dr. Stiles had taken a prominent part, collecting statistics, etc. His plan, as stated by Kingsley, was, to unite several denominations of Christians in the enterprise, both in America and in Great Britain, and thus, by proper care, to make the dissenting interest eventually exceed the Episcopal establishment. The whole number of churches of the Congregational, Presbyterian, and Baptist denominations, not only in the colonies, but in great Britain and Ireland, he ascertained to be three thousand six hundred and thirty-eight. "He supposed that all these churches might be induced to contribute to the establishment and support of an institution which would so greatly subserve their interests." The arrival at Newport of Mr. Manning, and the proposition made by him for the establishment of a Baptist College, interferred, of course, with his cherished views and plans. It is therefore not surprising that he should have been unwilling to see them defeated, without a struggle on his part to carry them into effect. We can understand how an attempt should have been made, either by Dr. Stiles or his associates, in drafting an act of incorporation for a College in Rhode Island, to pay special "regard" to the interests of their own "society." That there was disappointment on both sides, and at the time mutual recrimi-

the Assembly was convened again, the said Jenckes moved that the affair might be put off to the next session; adding, that the motion for a College originated with the Baptists, and was intended for their use, but that the Charter in question was not at all calculated to answer their purpose; and since the committee intrusted with this matter by the Baptists professed they had been misled, not to say imposed upon, it was necessary that the Baptists in other parts of the Colony should be consulted previous to its passing into a law, especially as few, if any of them except himself, had seen it; and he prayed that he might have a copy for the said purpose, which he promised to return. All which was granted. When the Charter came to be narrowly inspected, it was found to be by no means answerable to the design of the agitators, and the instructions given the committee. Consequently, application was made to the Philadelphia Association, where the thing took its rise, to have their mind on the subject, who immediately sent two gentlemen* hither to join with the Baptists of this

nations, is evident from the narrative. Under similar circumstances there doubtless would be again, human nature being very much the same now as in the days of our ancestors. It is due to Dr. Stiles, to state that he afterwards appeared to cherish friendly feelings towards the Institution. Having been elected to a Fellowship in the College, and solicited by repeated deputations from the Corporation to accept the trust, he thus writes to the Chancellor and Trustees: "I was too firm a friend to literature not to have taken part in the Institution at first upon my nomination in the Charter, had I not been prevented by reasons which a subsequent immediate election could not remove. * * * * With the greatest pleasure and alacrity I could have joined with you in so noble a work, but that I am obstructed by reasons which, however they may justly influence *Congregationalists* in general, ought not *now* to have any weight with you *as a body*." Whatever were the "reasons" which "obstructed" Dr. Stiles, one of which, it is stated, was "the offence he should give his brethren should he accept it," (MANNING AND BROWN UNIVERSITY, page 215,) they still influenced him to decline the office to which he was invited, with suitable acknowledgments of the politeness and respect with which he was treated on this occasion. His letter concludes with the catholic and pious wish, that "the Father of lights, from whom comes down every good and perfect gift, may excite the public munificence, and raise up benefactors, through whose liberalities this Institution shall be completed with an ample endowment."

* On the margin of the Morgan Edwards MS., in the hand-writing of the Rev. Dr. Jones, who was Edwards's intimate friend, is the following, namely: "Why their names are not mentioned, I cannot say. However, there was no one sent but myself, although Mr. Robert Strettle Jones was so kind as to bear me company to Rhode Island on the occasion.— SAMUEL JONES." Mr. Jones, it will be remembered, in connection with Mr. Edwards, had been intrusted by the Association with the business in general of founding a Baptist college or university. He had, at this date, but recently been ordained in Philadelphia. He was a young man of liberal education, and a ready and skillful writer; hence his special fitness for the duty assigned him in this emergency. The following extract from notes to a century sermon delivered by him before the Philadelphia Baptist Association, October 6, 1807, nearly fifty years afterwards, shows the manner in which he performed his

Colony in making such alterations and amendments as were to them specified before their departure. When they arrived, Dr. Eyres,* of Newport, was added to the committee, and they happily draughted the present Charter, and lodged it, with a new petition, in proper hands. The most material alterations were, appointing the same number of Baptists in the Fellowship that had been appointed of the Presbyterians, by Dr. Stiles; settling the Presidency in the Baptist society; adding five Baptists to the Trustees and putting more Episcopalians than Presbyterians in the Corporation.

Among the alterations not here enumerated by Manning, were, electing the President by the Corporation instead of exclusively by the Trustees; providing for convoking an assembly of the Corporation on twenty days notice instead of six; making five a quorum of the Board of Fellows instead of eight; and striking out the clause making the places of Trustees or Fellows who should remove out of the State, vacant. By confining membership in the Corporation to persons residing within the limits of the Colony, the original Charter excluded the originators and founders of the College. Hence, in the list of names proposed by Dr. Stiles to be incorporated, the following, which we find in the printed Charter, as suggested by the committee, are omitted; namely, Rev. Morgan Edwards, Rev. Samuel Jones, Rev. James Manning, Rev. Isaac Eaton, Rev. John Gano, Rev. Samuel Stillman, Rev. Jeremiah Condy, and Robert Strettle Jones, Esq. The names of Hezekiah Smith, Isaac Backus, William Williams, and others from out of the State, who rendered such signal service in the early history of the College, would also have been excluded from membership in the Corporation, by the Charter as originally drafted.

mission: "In the Fall of 1763, the writer of these sheets, on request, repaired to Newport, in Rhode Island, and new-modelled a rough draught they had of a Charter of incorporation for a College, which soon after obtained legislative sanction."

* Thomas Eyres, a physician, the first Secretary of the Corporation, and a Fellow of the College from 1764 until his death in 1788. He was graduated at Yale College, in the class of 1754. His father, Elder Nicholas Eyres, was pastor of the Second Baptist Church, in Newport, from 1731 until his death, February 13, 1759.

The Hon. Daniel Jenckes, Esq., to whom Manning refers in his narrative, was a wealthy merchant of Providence, and a man of undoubted integrity. He died July 7, 1774, in the seventy-third year of his age, having continued, says the record,—a member of the Baptist church forty-eight years "without censure." He was for forty years a member of the General Assembly, and for nearly thirty years Chief Justice of the Providence County Court. His daughter, Rhoda, was the wife of Nicholas Brown, the eldest of the "Four Brothers," to whom the College is so much indebted for its early prosperity and success. Among the manuscript writings of Morgan Edwards, we also find, in the same volume from which Manning's narrative is taken, a history of the College Charter, by Judge Jenckes, which reads as follows:—

While I attended the business of the Assembly, held August, 1763, Capt. William Rogers came to the Council Chamber and presented me with a paper, with a design I should sign it; adding, that, as it was a petition for a Baptist college, he knew I would not refuse. Business not permitting me to attend to it immediately, I requested he would leave with me the petition and Charter. Meanwhile, the sergeant made proclamation requiring the members to take their seats. In my seat I began to read the papers, but had not done before the petition and Charter were called for, which I gave to the sergeant, and he to the speaker at the board. The petition being read, a motion was made to receive it, and grant the Charter. After some time I stood up to oppose, proceeding immediately on the petition, giving my reason in words to this effect: "I understood that the College in question was sought for by the Baptists; and that it was to be under their government and direction, with the admission only of a few of other religious denominations to share with them therein, that they might appear as catholic as could be, consistent with their main design; but, on the contrary, I perceived by glancing over the Charter, while I sat in my place just now, that the main power and direction is vested in twelve Fellows, and that eight out of the twelve are to be Presbyterians; and that the others may or may not be of the same denomination; but of necessity, none of them are to be Baptists. If so, there is treachery somewhere, and a design of grossly imposing on the honest people who first moved for the Institution. I desire, therefore, that the matter may lie by till the afternoon." This was granted. In the afternoon the matter was resumed, with a seeming resolution in some to push it through at all events; but I had influence enough to stop proceedings then also. That evening and the next morning, I made it my business to see Governor

Lyndon and Col. Bennet, and to inform them of the construction of the Charter. They could not believe me, for the confidence they had in Dr. Stiles's honor and integrity, until seeing convinced them ; what reflections followed may be better concealed than published. However, we all agreed to postpone passing the Charter into a law, and did effect our purpose for that session, notwithstanding the attempts of Mr. Ellery and others of the Presbyterians to the contrary. Before the breaking up of the Assembly, the house, at my request, directed the speaker to deliver the Charter to me, after I had made a promise that it should be forthcoming at the next meeting of the Assembly.

I took the Charter to Providence, and showed it to many who came to my house ; others borrowed it to peruse at home. Meanwhile, the messengers from the Philadelphia Association arrived in Newport, which occasioned the committee of Newport to send to me for the Charter. I asked for it of Dr. Ephraim Bowen, who had borrowed it last. The doctor said he lent it to Samuel Nightingale, Esq. Search was made for it there, but it could not be found ; neither do I know to this day what became of it. When the next General Assembly met, (last Wednesday in October, 1763,) the second Charter was presented ; which was much faulted, and opposed by the gentry who concerned themselves so warmly about the other. And one in particular demanded that the first Charter, which had been entrusted to me, might be produced. Then I related, as above, that it was lost, and the manner how it was lost ; but the party, instead of believing this, very rudely suggested that I had secreted the Charter, and in the face of the court charged me with a breach of trust ; which brought on very disagreeable altercations and bickerings, until, at last, I was necessitated to say, that "if there had been any foul doings, it was amongst them of their own denomination at Providence." Their clamors continued ; and we gave way to them that session for peace sake. Meanwhile, Dr. Bowen, who is a man of strict honor and integrity, used all means to recover the former Charter, posting an advertisement in the most public places in town, and making diligent inquiry ; but to no purpose. At the next Assembly, which met in February, 1764, the new Charter was again brought on the carpet ; and the same clamor against it, and unjust reproaches against me, were repeated. It was said that the new Charter was not like the old, and was constructed to deprive the Presbyterians of the benefit of the institution. To which it was replied, "that it was agreeable to the designs of the first undertakers, and if calculated to deprive the Presbyterians of the power they wanted, it was no more than what they themselves had attempted to do to the Baptists." After much and warm debate, the question was put and carried in favor of the new Charter, by a great majority.

It is not a little remarkable that this important document, after having been lost for a century, should have come to light in the year of the celebration of the one hundredth anniversary of the College. It is now handsomely bound and lodged among the library archives. For generations it slept among the old papers of the church over which Dr. Stiles was pastor; then it found its way into the hands of the Rev. Dr. William B. Sprague, the great collector of autographs, at Albany, who generously presented it to the University, upon being made acquainted with its historical value. The place of its deposit clears Mr. Jenckes of the charge brought against him by one of the "gentry." Into whose hands it fell after it was lent to Mr. Jabez Bowen, and by him to a third person, must now of course be a matter of conjecture. It is certain that it in some way came into the possession of Dr. Stiles, for upon the back of it, in his own clear and distinct hand-writing, are the following remarks:—

For the Rev. Dr. Charles Chauncy, Boston:—This Charter was presented to the Assembly August, 1763; recopied, with some alterations by the Baptists, in October; and passed the Assembly February, 1764. Principal alterations were:—

1. By omitting "To all people, etc., Greeting," in the initiatory address, the subsequent insertion in the body of the Charter, "Now, therefore, know ye," is an impropriety in clerkship.

2. The Baptists have shown a greater affection for all other denominations than for the Congregationalists.

3. Instead of eight or a majority of Congregationalists in the branch of the Fellowship, according to the original agreement, they have inserted eight Baptists; thus assuming a majority of about two-thirds in both branches, hereby absorbing the whole power and government of the College, and thus, by the immutability of the numbers, establishing it a party College more explicitly and effectually than any college upon the continent. This is the most material alteration.

4. Most of what is contained between the marginal crotchets in page six is omitted; and the whole paragraph for securing the freedom of education with respect to religion, so mutilated as effectually to enable and empower the Baptists to practise the arts of insinuation, and proselyting upon the youth by private instruction, without the request of the parents.

What "original agreement" was violated by the adoption of the present Charter; in what respects Rhode Island College was established "a party college more explicitly and effectually than any college upon the continent," referring, of course, to the six colleges in existence in the year 1764; and how the paragraph pertaining to religious freedom and sectarian differences of opinion "enables and empowers the Baptists to practice the arts of insinuation and proselyting," we leave to the judgment and candor of our readers to decide. Either Dr. Stiles was in an irritable mood, when he appended these notes, or he was more unfriendly to the Institution than has been generally believed. His manuscript papers, it may not be improper to mention, abound in expressions of ill feeling towards both the College and its President. (See appendix to President Sears's Centennial Discourse, pp. 65–70.) The original Charter drafted by Dr. Stiles, is published entire, as has already been stated, in the appendix to MANNING AND BROWN UNIVERSITY. The corrections and alterations made by the committee from Philadelphia, and which are now incorporated in the present Charter, are also published in a column by the side of the original paragraphs.

From the foregoing accounts, or narratives, it appears, (1) That President Manning drew up a plan of the College, and presented it to a company of Baptist gentlemen, at Newport, in the month of July, 1763. (2) That the Hon. Josias Lyndon and Col. Job Bennet were appointed to draw a Charter, in accordance with said plan, to be laid before the next General Assembly, with a petition that it might be made a law. (3) That the assistance of the Rev. Dr. Stiles, afterwards President of Yale College, was solicited and obtained. (4) That the drafting of the Charter was left entirely to Dr. Stiles; and that he, in turn, was assisted by the Hon. William Ellery. (5) That the Charter was accordingly drawn, and a time and place were appointed for the parties concerned to meet and hear it read. (6) That Manning, being obliged to leave on that day for Halifax, was unable to be with the committee long enough to see whether the original design was secured, and that the Baptists, being satisfied, without sufficient examination into the authority vested in the Fellowship, and reposing entire confidence in Dr. Stiles, agreed to join in a petition to the General Assembly to have the Charter confirmed by authority. (7) That the petition and Charter were accordingly presented to the General Assembly in August, 1763, but that action thereon was postponed until the next session, through the influence of the Hon. Daniel Jenckes, the attempts of Mr. Ellery and others of the Presbyterians to the contrary notwithstanding. (8) That the Charter was found on inspection to be so drawn as to vest the main power and direction of the Institution in a board of twelve Fellows, eight of whom were to be Congregationalists or Presbyterians, and the other four of the same denomination for aught that appeared to the contrary; and that in general it did not answer to the original design. (9) That in this emergency application was made to the Philadelphia Association, "where the thing took its rise," to have their mind on the subject. (10) That they immediately sent to Newport the Rev. Samuel Jones, who was accompanied by Robert Strettle Jones, and that when they arrived, Dr. Eyres, of Newport, was added to the committee. (11) That, meanwhile, the original copy of the Charter, presented to the General Assembly in August, and intrusted by that body to Mr. Jenckes, had been lost. (12) That the committee found at Newport a rough draft of this Charter, which they happily remodelled, and that the most material alterations were, appointing the same number of Baptists in the Fellowship that had been appointed of the Presbyterians by Dr. Stiles; settling the Presidency in the Baptist society; adding five Baptists to the Trustees; putting more Episcopalians than Presbyterians in the Corporation; and extending the membership of the Corporation to persons residing out of the Colony or State.

The foregoing statements of Edwards, Manning and Jenckes respecting the origin of the College and the history of the Charter, are fully established and confirmed by the historian Backus, whose accuracy, we believe, has never been called in question. Being in the prime and vigor of life when the College was founded, and one of its first Trustees, he was, of course, familiar with all the facts pertaining to its early history.

The following letter, which forms a part of the Manuscript to which we have referred, and which appears to have been addressed to President Manning by Morgan Edwards, may with propriety be introduced here, although portions of it belong to a later period. The author was accustomed to express his opinions without reserve, and sometimes, perhaps, with a little too much pungency:—

I should not have ventured to oppose my opinions to yours, had not facts, recent facts, decided the matter in my favor; and shown that the goodness and candor of the President have imposed on his judgment. Remember you not the first Charter? While the Baptist College was yet in embryo they very disingenuously opposed it, as such, and contrived to make it their own, since which disappointment, Dr. Stiles would have nothing to do with it, though courted again and again to accept even a Fellowship therein. And when the present Charter was presented to the Assembly at South Kingstown, remember you not what clamor they raised against it there? And what stout opposition they made to the passage of it, insomuch that its friends thought it best to desist? And how they triumphed afterwards? And when the affair was brought on again at East Greenwich, the next session, you can never forget with what heat and coarse expression the same oppositions were renewed, nor the mortification and murmurings which the passing of it occasioned. It is true, while the Charter lay dormant they remained easy; and, as you say, appeared well pleased when you had set it on foot at Warren. But the reason of that is obvious. They knew that while the College stood friendless and moneyless, as it then did, they should have the pleasure to see it fall, and to mock those who began to build a tower and were not able to finish it. But seemed they good humored when money came thither from Europe? or did they look as the man of Bristol did, at your first Commencement, and put the same invidious construction upon everything, that he did on the complacence you showed him that day? Their good affection toward the College edifice was but varnish; for while with specious arguments they would have it here, and anon there, and then, in another place, they were only working to prevent it being anywhere; and soon as it had a locality and the beginning of its existence at Providence, did they not, with some misled Baptists, attempt to get another college, to destroy yours, and actually carried their design through the lower house? This also failing, what remains but to prevent youth from resorting to it. Their slandering the officers of instruction, as insufficient; the town where it is in, as a lawless place; the College, as wanting government; their representing it as a nest of Anabaptists, calculated to make proselytes; their visiting grammar schools and tampering with masters and parents; their scolding Presbyterian youth, when they enter with you, as your neighbor Rowley did, who is capable of nothing but what is gross and indelicate; their refusing to pay their subscriptions, etc.,—are all intended to hurt what they could neither prevent nor destroy. Think you that their present opposition to the College is the effect of those newspaper complaints and threatenings of Presbyterian oppression in New England? Why, then, did they oppose it before those complaints and threatenings had existence? Think you they will be friends should we desist from these complaints and court their favor? It cannot be, except God should once teach them to love their neighbors as themselves, and do as they would be done by. Destroying the Baptist College will pacify them, and nothing else. The existence of that on the hill of Providence is a Mordecai in the gate. I told you, long ago, that if you could not do without the Presbyterians, you could not do at all. I need not inform you that I deal in generals. I except the honest, the trusty, and the good, and some such Presbyterians I have met with, in their connections with this College. God send us more, and mend the rest.

The following is the Charter of Brown University, which was presented to the General Assembly in October, 1763, and adopted at an adjourned session, held in East Greenwich, in February, 1764:—

At the General Assembly of the Governor and Company of the English Colony of Rhode Island and Providence Plantations, in New England, in America, begun and holden by adjournment, at East Greenwich, within and for the Colony aforesaid, on the last Monday in February, in the year of our Lord one thousand seven hundred and sixty-four, and fourth of the reign of his most sacred Majesty George the Third, by the grace of God, King of Great Britain, and so forth.

AN ACT FOR THE ESTABLISHMENT OF A COLLEGE OR UNIVERSITY, WITHIN THIS COLONY.

WHEREAS institutions for liberal education are highly beneficial to society, by forming the rising generation to virtue, knowledge, and useful literature; and thus preserving in the community a succession of men duly qualified for discharging the offices of life with usefulness and reputation, they have therefore justly merited and received the attention and encouragement of every wise and well-regulated State: And

HISTORY OF THE CHARTER. 133

whereas a public school or seminary, erected for that purpose within this Colony, to which the youth may freely resort for education in the vernacular and learned languages, and in the liberal arts and sciences, would be for the general advantage and honor of the government : And whereas Daniel Jenckes, Esq., Nicholas Tillinghast, Esq., Nicholas Gardner, Esq., Col. Josias Lyndon, Col. Elisha Reynolds, Peleg Thurston, Esq., Simon Pease, Esq., John Tillinghast, Esq., George Hazard, Esq., Col. Job Bennet, Nicholas Easton, Esq., Arthur Fenner, Esq., Mr. Ezekiel Gardner, Mr. John Waterman, Mr. James Barker, Jr., Mr. John Holmes, Solomon Drown, Esq., Mr. Samuel Winsor, Mr. Joseph Sheldon, Charles Rhodes, Esq., Mr. Nicholas Brown, Col. Barzillai Richmond, Mr. John Brown, Mr. Gideon Hoxsey, Mr. Thomas Eyres, Mr. Thomas Potter, Jr., Mr. Peleg Barker, Mr. Edward Thurston, Mr. William Redwood, Joseph Clarke, Esq., Mr. John G. Wanton, and Mr. Thomas Robinson, with many other persons, appear as undertakers in the valuable design : And thereupon a petition hath been preferred to this Assembly, praying that full liberty and power may be granted unto such of them, with others, as are hereafter mentioned, to found, endow, order and govern a college or university within this Colony ; and that, for the more effectual execution of this design, they may be incorporated into one body politic, to be known in the law, with the powers, privileges and franchises, necessary for the purposes aforesaid.

Now, THEREFORE, KNOW YE, That being willing to encourage and patronize such an honorable and useful institution, we, the said Governor and Company, in General Assembly convened, do, for ourselves and our successors, in and by virtue of the power and authority within the jurisdiction of this Colony, to us by the Royal Charter granted and committed, enact, grant, constitute, ordain and declare, and it is hereby enacted, granted, constituted, ordained and declared, that the Hon. Stephen Hopkins, Esq., the Hon. Joseph Wanton, Jr., Esq., the Hon. Samuel Ward, Esq., the Hon. William Ellery, Esq., John Tillinghast, Esq., Simon Pease, Esq., James Honyman, Esq., Nicholas Easton, Esq., Nicholas Tillinghast, Esq., Darius Sessions, Esq., Joseph Harris, Esq., Francis Willett, Esq., William Logan, Esq., Daniel Jenckes, Esq., George Hazard, Esq., Nicholas Brown, Esq., Jeremiah Niles, Esq., Joshua Babcock, Esq., Mr. John G. Wanton, the Rev. Edward Upham, the Rev. Jeremiah Condy, the Rev. Marmaduke Brown, the Rev. Gardner Thurston, the Rev. Ezra Stiles, the Rev. John Graves, the Rev. John Maxson, the Rev. Samuel Winsor, the Rev. John Gano, the Rev. Morgan Edwards, the Rev. Isaac Eaton, the Rev. Samuel Stillman, the Rev. Samuel Jones, the Rev. James Manning, the Rev. Russel Mason, Col. Elisha Reynolds, Col. Josias Lyndon, Col. Job Bennet, Mr. Ephraim Bowen, Joshua Clarke, Esq., Capt. Jonathan Slade, John Taylor, Esq., Mr. Robert Strettell Jones, Azariah Dunham, Esq., Mr. Edward Thurston, Jr., Mr. Thomas Eyres, Mr. Thomas Hazard, and Mr. Peleg Barker, or such or so many of them as shall, within twelve months from the date hereof, accept of this trust, and qualify themselves

134 BROWN UNIVERSITY.

as hereinafter directed, and their successors, shall be forever hereafter one body corporate and politic, in fact and name, to be known in law by the name of TRUSTEES AND FELLOWS OF THE COLLEGE OR UNIVERSITY IN THE ENGLISH COLONY OF RHODE ISLAND AND PROVIDENCE PLANTATIONS, IN NEW ENGLAND, IN AMERICA; the Trustees and Fellows, at any time hereafter, giving such more particular name to the College, in honor of the greatest and most distinguished benefactor, or otherwise, as they shall think proper; which name, so given, shall, in all acts, instruments and doings of the said body politic, be superadded to their corporate name aforesaid, and become a part of their legal appellation, by which it shall be forever known and distinguished: And that, by the same name, they and their successors, chosen by themselves, as hereafter prescribed, shall and may have perpetual succession; and shall and may be persons able and capable, in the law, to sue and to be sued, to plead and to be impleaded, to answer and to be answered unto, to defend and to be defended against, in all and singular suits, causes, matters, actions and doings, of what kind soever: And also to have, take, possess, purchase, acquire, or otherwise receive and hold lands, tenements, hereditaments, goods, chattels, or other estates; of all which they may, and shall, stand and be seized, notwithstanding any misnomer of the College, or Corporation thereof; and by whatever name, or however imperfectly the same shall be described in gift, bequest, and assignment, provided the true intent of the assigner or benefactor be evident: Also the same to grant, demise, aliene, lease, use, manage and improve, according to the tenor of the donations, and to the purposes, trusts and uses, to which they shall be seized thereof. And full liberty, power and authority, are hereby granted unto the said Trustees and Fellows, and their successors, to found a College or University within this Colony, for promoting the liberal arts, and universal literature: And with the moneys, estates and revenues, of which they shall from time to time become legally seized as aforesaid, to endow the same: And erect the necessary buildings and edifices thereof on such place within this Colony as they shall think convenient: And generally to regulate, order and govern the same, appoint officers, and make laws, as hereinafter prescribed; and hold, use and enjoy all the liberties, privileges, exemptions, dignities and immunities enjoyed by any college or university whatever.

And furthermore, That the said Trustees and Fellows, and their successors, shall, and may, forever hereafter have a public seal, to use for all causes, matters and affairs whatever, of them and their successors, and the same to alter, break and make anew, from time to time, at their will and pleasure; which seal shall always be deposited with the President, or senior Fellow

And furthermore, by the authority aforesaid, it is hereby enacted, ordained and declared, That it is now, and at all times hereafter shall continue to be, the unalterable constitution of this College or University, that the Corporation thereof shall consist of two branches, to wit: That of the Trustees, and that of the Fellowship, with distinct, separate and respective powers: And that the number of the Trustees shall and may be thirty-six; of which twenty-two shall forever be elected of the denomination called Baptists, or Antipædobaptists; five shall forever be elected of the denomination called Friends or Quakers; four shall forever be elected of the denomination called Congregationalists, and five shall forever be elected of the denomination called Episcopalians: And that the succession in this branch shall be forever chosen and filled up from the respective denominations in this proportion, and according to these numbers; which are hereby fixed, and shall remain to perpetuity immutably the same. And that the said Stephen Hopkins, Joseph Wanton, Samuel Ward, William Ellery, John Tillinghast, Simon Pease, James Honyman, Nicholas Easton, Nicholas Tillinghast, Darius Sessions, Joseph Harris, Francis Willet, Daniel Jenckes, George Hazard, Nicholas Brown, Jeremiah Niles, John G. Wanton, Joshua Clarke, Gardner Thurston, John Graves, John Maxson, John Gano, Samuel Winsor, Isaac Eaton, Samuel Stillman, Russel Mason, Elisha Reynolds, Josias Lyndon, Job Bennet, Ephraim Bowen, John Taylor, Jonathan Slade, Robert Strettell Jones, Azariah Dunham, Edward Thurston, Jr. and Peleg Barker, or such or so many of them as shall qualify themselves as aforesaid, shall be and they are hereby declared and established the first and present Trustees. And that the number of the Fellows, inclusive of the President (who shall always be a Fellow) shall and may be twelve; of which, eight shall be forever elected of the denomination called Baptists, or Antipædobaptists; and the rest indifferently of any or all denominations. And that the Rev. Edward Upham, the Rev. Jeremiah Condy, the Rev. Marmaduke Brown, the Rev. Morgan Edwards, the Rev. Ezra Stiles, the Rev. Samuel Jones, the Rev. James Manning, William Logan, Esq., Joshua Babcock, Esq., Mr. Thomas Eyres, and Mr. Thomas Hazard, or such or so many of them as shall qualify themselves as aforesaid, shall be, and they are hereby declared the first and present Fellows and Fellowship, to whom the President, when hereafter elected, (who shall forever be of the denomination called Baptists, or Antipædobaptists) shall be joined to complete the number.

And furthermore, it is declared and ordained, That the succession in both branches shall at all times hereafter be filled up and supplied according to these numbers, and this established and invariable proportion, from the respective denominations, by the separate election of both branches of this Corporation, which shall at all times sit and act by separate and distinct powers: And in general, in order to the validity and consummation of all acts, there shall be in the exercise of their respective, separate and distinct powers, the joint concurrence of the Trustees and Fellows, by their respective majorities, except in adjudging and conferring the academical degrees, which shall forever belong, exclusively, to the Fellowship, as a learned Faculty.

And furthermore, it is constituted, That the instruction and immediate government of the College shall forever be and rest in the President and Fellows or Fellowship.

And furthermore, it is ordained, That there shall be a general meeting of the Corporation on the first Wednesday in September, annually, within the College edifice, and until the same be built, at such place as they shall appoint, to consult, advise, and transact the affairs of the College or University: At which, or at any other time, the public Commencement may be held and celebrated. And that, on any special emergencies, the President, with any two of the Fellows, or any three of the Fellows, exclusive of the President, may convoke, and they are hereby empowered to convoke, an assembly of the Corporation on twenty days notice: And that, in all meetings, the major vote of those present of the two branches respectively, shall be deemed their respective majorities aforesaid: Provided, That not less than twelve of the Trustees, and five of the Fellows, be a quorum of their respective branches: That the President, or, in his absence, the Senior Fellow present, shall always be Moderator of the Fellows: That the Corporation, at their annual meetings, once in three years, or oftener in case of death or removal, shall and may choose a Chancellor of the University, and Treasurer, from among the Trustees, and a Secretary from among the Fellows: That the nomination of the Chancellor shall be in the Trustees, whose office shall be only to preside as Moderator of the Trustees; and that, in his absence, the Trustees shall choose a Moderator for the time being, by the name of Vice-Chancellor: And at any of their meetings, duly formed as aforesaid, shall and may be elected a Trustee or Fellow, or Trustees or Fellows, in the room of those nominated in this Charter, who may refuse to accept, or in the room of those who may die, resign or be removed.

And furthermore, it is enacted, ordained and declared, That this Corporation, at any of their meetings, regularly convened aforesaid, shall and may elect and appoint the President and Professors of languages, and the several parts of literature: And upon the demise of him or them, or either of them, their resignation or removal from his or their office, for misdemeanor, incapacity or unfaithfulness (for which he or they are hereby declared removable by this Corporation) others to elect and appoint in their room and stead: And at such meeting, upon the nomination of the Fellows, to elect and appoint tutors, stewards, butlers, and all such other officers usually appointed in colleges or universities, as they shall find necessary, and think fit to appoint for promoting liberal education, and the well ordering the affairs of this College; and them, or any of them, at their discretion, to remove, and substitute others in their places. And, in case any President, Trustee or Fellow, shall see cause to change his religious denomination, the Corporation is hereby empowered to declare his or their place or places vacant, and may proceed to fill up it or them accordingly, as before directed, otherwise each Trustee and Fellow, not an officer of instruction, shall continue in his office during life, or until resignation. And further, in case either of the religious denominations should decline taking a part in this catholic, comprehensive and liberal

HISTORY OF THE CHARTER.

institution, the Trustees and Fellows shall and may complete their number, by electing from their respective denominations, always preserving their respective proportions herein before prescribed and determined: And all elections shall be by ballot, or written suffrage: And that a quorum of four Trustees and three Fellows may transact any business, excepting placing the College edifice, election of Trustees, President, Fellows and Professors, that is to say, so that their act shall be of force and validity, until the next annual meeting, and no longer.

And it is further enacted and ordained by the authority aforesaid, That each Trustee and Fellow, as well those nominated in this Charter, as all that shall hereafter be duly elected, shall, previous to their acting in a corporate capacity, take the engagement of allegiance* prescribed by the law of this Colony to his Majesty King George the Third, his heirs and rightful successors to the crown of Great Britain, which engagement shall be administered to the present Trustees and Fellows, by the Governor or Deputy-Governor of this Colony, and to those from time to time hereafter elected by their respective Moderators, who are hereby empowered to administer the same

And still more clearly to define and ascertain the respective powers of the two branches, on making and enacting laws, it is further ordained and declared, That the Fellowship shall have power, and are hereby empowered from time to time, and at all times hereafter, to make, enact, and publish, all such laws, statutes, regulations, and ordinances, with penalties, as to them shall seem meet, for the successful instruction and government of said College or University, not contrary to the spirit, extent, true meaning and intention, of the acts of the British Parliament, or the laws of this Colony; and the same laws, statutes and ordinances, to repeal: Which laws, and the repeals thereof, shall be laid before the Trustees, and with their approbation shall be of force and validity, but not otherwise. And further, the Trustees and Fellows, at their meetings aforesaid, shall ascertain the salaries of the respective officers, and order the moneys assessed on the students for tuition, fines and incidental expenses, to be collected by the Steward, or such other officer as they shall appoint to collect the same; and the same, with their revenues, and other College estates in the hands of the Treasurer, to appropriate in discharging salaries and other College debts: And the College accounts shall be annually audited and adjusted in the meeting of the Corporation.

And furthermore, it is hereby enacted and declared, That into this liberal and catholic institution shall never be admitted any religious tests: But, on the contrary, all the members hereof shall forever enjoy full, free, absolute and uninterrupted liberty of conscience: And that the places of Professors, Tutors, and all other officers, the

---

* A substitute for this engagement of allegiance to the King of Great Britain was adopted soon after the Declaration of American Independence.

President alone excepted, shall be free and open for all denominations of Protestants: And that youth of all religious denominations shall and may be freely admitted to the equal advantages, emoluments and honors of the College or University; and shall receive a like fair, generous and equal treatment, during their residence therein, they conducting themselves peaceably, and conforming to the laws and statutes thereof. And that the public teaching shall, in general, respect the sciences; and that the sectarian differences of opinions, shall not make any part of the public and classical instruction; although all religious controversies may be studied freely, examined and explained, by the President, Professors and Tutors, in a personal, separate and distinct manner, to the youth of any or each denomination: And above all, a constant regard be paid to, and effectual care taken of, the morals of the College.

And furthermore, for the honor and encouragement of literature, we constitute and declare the Fellowship aforesaid a learned faculty; and do hereby give, grant unto, and invest them and their successors with full power and authority, and they are hereby authorized and empowered by their President, and in his absence by the senior Fellow, or one of the Fellows appointed by themselves, at the anniversary Commencement, or at any other times, and at all times hereafter, to admit to and confer any and all the learned degrees, which can or ought to be given and conferred in any of the colleges or universities in America; or any such other degrees of literary honor as they shall devise, upon any and all such candidates and persons as the President and Fellows, or Fellowship, shall judge worthy of the academical honors: Which power of conferring degrees is hereby restricted to the learned Faculty, who shall or may issue diplomas or certificates of such degrees, or confer degrees by diplomas, and authenticate them with the public seal of the Corporation, and the hands of the President and Secretary, and of all the Professors, as witnesses, and deliver them to the graduates as honorable and perpetual testimonies.

And furthermore, for the greater encouragement of this seminary of learning, and that the same may be amply endowed and enfranchised with the same privileges, dignities and immunities, enjoyed by the American colleges, and European universities, we do grant, enact, ordain and declare, and it is hereby granted, enacted, ordained and declared, That the College estate, the estates, persons and families of the President and Professors, for the time being, lying and being within the Colony, with the persons of the tutors and students, during their residence at the College, shall be freed and exempted from all taxes, serving on juries, and menial services: And that the persons aforesaid shall be exempted from bearing arms, impresses and military services, except in case of an invasion.

And furthermore, For establishing the perpetuity of this Corporation, and in case that at any time hereafter, through oversight, or otherwise through misapprehensions and mistaken constructions of the powers, liberties and franchises, herein contained,

HISTORY OF THE CHARTER.

any laws should be enacted, or any matters done and transacted by this Corporation contrary to the tenor of this Charter, it is hereby enacted, ordained and declared, That all such laws, acts and doings, shall be in themselves null and void: Yet, nevertheless, the same shall not, in any courts of law, or by the General Assembly, be deemed, taken, interpreted or adjudged, into any avoidance, defeasance or forfeiture of this Charter; but that the same shall be and remain unhurt, inviolate and entire, unto the said Corporation, in perpetual succession; which Corporation may, at all times, and forever hereafter, proceed and continue to act: And all their acts, conformable to the powers, tenor, true intent and meaning of the Charter, shall be and remain in full force and validity; the nullity and avoidance of any such illegal acts to the contrary in any wise notwithstanding.

And lastly, we the Governor and Company aforesaid, do, for ourselves and our successors, forever hereby enact, grant and confirm, unto the said Trustees and Fellows, and to their successors, That this Charter of incorporation, and every part thereof, shall be good and available in all things in the law, according to our true intent and meaning: And shall be construed, reputed and adjudged, in all cases, most favorably on the behalf and for the best benefit and behoof of the said Trustees and Fellows, and their successors, so as most effectually to answer the valuable ends of this useful Institution.

In full testimony of which grant, and of all the articles and matters therein contained, the said Governor and Company do hereby order, That this act shall be signed by the Governor and Secretary, and sealed with the public seal of this Colony, and registered in the Colony's records: And that the same, or an exemplification thereof, shall be a sufficient warrant to the said Corporation to hold, use and exercise, all the powers, franchises and immunities, herein contained.

Signed and sealed at Newport, the twenty-fourth day of October, in the year of our Lord one thousand seven hundred and sixty-five, and in the fifth year of [L. S.] His Majesty's reign, George the Third, by the grace of God, of Great Britain, etc., King.

EDWARD THURSTON, JR., Deputy Secretary.   SAMUEL WARD, Governor.

The provision in the foregoing Charter, exempting from taxation the estates, persons and families of the President and Professors, has given rise to unhappy discussions throughout the State, and alienated, doubtless, the sympathies of many from the University. It was so in the beginning. As early as June, 1772, in regular town meeting, the words "all taxes," in the College Charter, were considered as implying nothing more than "all taxes due to the Colony," and the annual town tax was ordered to be assessed and levied on the estates of the President and Professor. The same thing was done in the two following years. In 1774, the assessors (Messrs. Joseph Brown, Christopher Sheldon and Nathaniel Wheaton) omitted to assess President Manning and Professor Howell, on the ground that they were legally and properly exempted by Charter. Thereupon ensued a long and protracted discussion, which was carried on in the columns of the PROVIDENCE GAZETTE, to which the reader is referred. (See numbers for February 5, February 12, April 16, April 30, and May 28, 1774.) Much bitterness and not a little personal feeling were developed. It was proposed at one time to call a special town meeting on the subject, but wiser counsels prevailed, and the action of the assessors was sustained, and followed in succeeding years. The war which soon broke out with the mother country, and the great personal influence which Manning exerted over all classes of men, contributed not a little, perhaps, to this result.

Among the archives of the University we find the following document, which may properly appear in connection with this subject:—

> In order to give satisfaction to the town of Providence, we whose names are under written, do declare and make known, that it is our real sentiment that the College estate within this town, (the edifice itself, the President's house and garden, and the land appropriated to the use of a yard to the College excepted,) together with the persons and estates of the President and Professors, are in law and justice bound to pay their equal proportion of the town rates. Therefore we do publicly and solemnly promise unto the freemen of the town now in town meeting assembled, that we will both in our public and private capacities exert ourselves to the utmost of our abilities to cause for the future all taxes that shall be levied on the persons and estates aforesaid by this town, to be punctually paid. In witness whereof, we have hereunto set our hands in Providence, this 10th day of April, A. D. 1774.

The original document, of which the foregoing is a copy, is signed by Thomas Green, who, at the time of writing, was a member of the Corporation.

HISTORY OF THE CHARTER.   141

Of late years this controversy in regard to the taxation of the President and Professors has been revived. Finally, during the progress of the recent civil war, a bill was introduced into the General Assembly to repeal the obnoxious provision of the Charter. The President of the University, it was well known, favored some movement of this kind, having a regard for the future good of the Institution over which he presided rather than his own immediate advantage. He argued, and with reason, that wealthy Professors, who were able to pay their taxes, were mainly benefited by the exemption, and not those who had but little if any property to be taxed. A public institution, he moreover contended, under a republican form of government like our own, could not really thrive without the good will of the public upon whose benefactions and sympathies it was dependent. On the other hand, it was contended that the General Assembly had never made any appropriation for the College, which had conferred lasting benefits upon both city and State, and that any movement on the part of the assembled legislators, to interfere with the chartered rights and privileges which the Professors had enjoyed for a century, would be ungrateful and unjust. By wise concessions and judicious action on the part of the Corporation, the excitement and ill feeling incident to the discussion of this question were allayed, and the most friendly relations between the College and the public at large were established. The President and Professors generously waived their rights under the Charter, and empowered the Trustees and Fellows to adopt any measures that might forward the interests of the University. A committee of the Corporation, in conference with a committee of the Legislature, secured the passage of an act, by which exemption from taxation was not to cover over ten thousand dollars. The validity of this act was made to depend on the assent of the Corporation, so that the inviolability of the Charter was thus recognized and preserved. In this form it secured a unanimous vote in the General Assembly, and also in a very large meeting of the Corporation convened expressly for this purpose. It is now, therefore, a law. So important a movement is worthy of special mention, and we therefore proceed to give at length the details.

By a resolution of the City Council of Newport, passed on the 4th of March, 1862, their State Senator was instructed to endeavor to procure the alteration or repeal of so much of the Charter of Brown University, as exempts the property of the President and Professors from taxation;—the Council stating that in their opinion, there was no justifiable reason for such an exemption, especially at a time when all kinds of property were necessarily and heavily taxed for the support of government and the preservation of the Union. This resolution was presented to the Senate on the day following, and referred to the Committee on the Judiciary for consideration. This Committee, at a special session of the General Assembly, submitted to the Senate, on the 26th of August, 1862, a lengthy report, drawn up by the Hon. Elisha R. Potter, of South Kingstown, together with an act or bill for repealing the obnoxious clause in the Charter, which reads as follows:—

An Act to amend the Charter of Brown University by repealing so much thereof as exempts the estates, persons and families of the President and Professors from taxation.

WHEREAS, in times of public danger all persons ought to bear their share of the public burdens in proportion to their ability, and this General Assembly have full confidence in the patriotism of the said President and Professors, and in their willingness to bear their proper share of the taxation necessary for the preservation of our Union and Constitution, therefore

IT IS ENACTED BY THE GENERAL ASSEMBLY AS FOLLOWS:

So much of the act entitled "An act for the establishment of a College or University within this Colony," passed at the February session, A. D. 1764, as exempts the estates, persons and families of the President and Professors of said Institution, now known as Brown University, from taxation, is hereby repealed.

The act was passed, and the report, entitled, "Right of a Legislature to grant a Perpetual Exemption from Taxation," was ordered to be printed.

In the House, however, after a spirited debate, the matter was finally referred to the Committee on the Judiciary, with instructions for the Chairman, Hon. Richard W. Greene, LL. D., of Warwick, to present the whole subject to the Corporation of the University, of which he was himself a member, at their approaching annual meeting. This he accordingly did, and on the 4th of September, the Corporation referred the subject to a Select Committee of five, with instructions to report at a special meeting of the Corporation to be held on the 21st of January, 1863. This Committee consisted of Dr. Samuel Boyd Tobey, Chancellor; Hon. John Kingsbury, LL. D., Secretary; Hon. William S. Patten; Hon. Isaac Davis, LL. D.; and Hon. Benjamin F. Thurston. They prepared an elaborate and comprehensive report, which was duly presented at the special meeting of the Corporation. This Body, however, after a lengthy session, adjourned without action, leaving the matter still in the hands of the Committee. Meanwhile the House of Representatives, on the 9th of February, 1863, passed the following act, emanating, it is understood, from the Select Committee of the Corporation, the Senate, ten days afterwards, unanimously concurring in the same:—

An Act to limit the exemption from taxation of the estates, persons and families of the President and Professors of Brown University.

IT IS ENACTED BY THE GENERAL ASSEMBLY AS FOLLOWS:—

SECTION 1. The Corporation of Brown University in Providence consenting hereto, That the estates, persons and families of the President and Professors for the time being of said University, and of their successors in office, shall not hereafter be freed or exempted from taxes for more than the amount of ten thousand dollars for each of such officers, his estate, person and family included.

SECTION 2. The vote of said Corporation, under the seal and certified by the Secretary thereof, declaring that the Corporation being authorized by the President and Professors of said University, does in behalf of the President and Professors and in behalf of said Corporation consent to this Act, shall be deemed and taken to be proof of their consent thereunto, when said vote shall have been filed in the office of the Secretary of State.

The Corporation of the University, at a second special meeting, held Wednesday, February 11, which was largely attended, adopted the following by a unanimous vote:—

WHEREAS, The General Assembly of the State of Rhode Island, at its present session on the 11th day of February, 1863, has passed an Act, the principal section of which is in the following words, viz. :—

"SECTION 1. The Corporation of Brown University in Providence, consenting hereto, That the estates, persons, and families of the President and Professors for the time being, and of their successors in office, shall not hereafter be freed and exempted from taxes, for more than the amount of ten thousand dollars for each of such officers, his estate, person and family included,"

AND WHEREAS, The Institution of Brown University was established by its founders, was incorporated with liberal franchises by the State, has been maintained solely by private benefactions; all uniting for the same noble object, that is, to create and promote a Seminary of religion and learning within this State, whose beneficent influences should be diffused, at home and abroad, through all time,

AND WHEREAS, Those influences can and will be most happily diffused and continued by a cordial good will and a harmonious coöperation between the General Assembly and citizens of this State and the University,

AND WHEREAS, The General Assembly by its Act aforesaid, has expressed the opinion that the President and Professors should bear a portion of the burdens of taxation from which they are exempted by our Charter, and has made the validity of its said Act to depend upon the consent of this Corporation thereto, thereby affirming and maintaining the inviolability of said Charter,

Therefore, in order to manifest our cordial compliance with a reasonable wish of the General Assembly, as expressed in said Act,

It is hereby voted and declared by the Corporation of Brown University, that being authorized by the President and Professors of said University, this Corporation does, in behalf of the President and Professors, and in behalf of said Corporation, consent to the said Act, passed by the General Assembly of the State of Rhode Island at its present session, as aforesaid ; and the Secretary of this Corporation is hereby instructed to file a copy of this vote, under the seal of the Corporation, and certified by himself, in the office of the Secretary of State, as proof of the consent of this Corporation thereto.

HISTORY OF THE CHARTER. 145

Thus a vexed and difficult question was happily settled, and the Charter itself preserved intact. The removal, in consequence, of long-existing prejudices in the minds of the people towards the College, and the restoration of mutually cordial and friendly relations, are auspicious omens for the future. That the University may keep on the even tenor of her way, diffusing throughout the State and the land sound learning and religion, and that the citizens, without distinction of sect or party, may hereafter honor and cherish her as "their own," is a consummation most earnestly to be desired by all her graduates, benefactors and friends.

The following names of members of the Corporation at the time of the removal of the College to Providence, classified according to the religious denominations which they represented, as specified in the Charter, may be useful for reference, as also the names and residences of the present members:—

BOARD OF FELLOWS.—1770.

BAPTISTS.
Rev. James Manning, *President*.
Rev. Morgan Edwards, Philadelphia.
Rev. Edward Upham, Newport.
Rev. Samuel Stillman, Boston.
Rev. Hezekiah Smith, Haverhill.
Rev. John Davis, Boston.
Doct. Joshua Babcock, Westerly, (Seventh Day Baptist.)
Doct. Thomas Eyres, Newport.

EPISCOPALIANS.
Rev. Marmaduke Browne, Newport.
Henry Ward,* Esq., Newport.

FRIEND.
Doct. Jonathan Easton, Newport.

CONGREGATIONALIST.
Doct. Jabez Bowen, Providence.

BOARD OF FELLOWS.—1867.

BAPTISTS.
Rev. Barnas Sears, D. D., LL. D., *President*.
Hon. James H. Duncan, LL. D., Haverhill.
John Carter Brown, A. M., Providence.
Hon. Isaac Davis, LL. D., Worcester.
Rev. Baron Stow, D. D., Boston.
Rev. Alvah Woods, D. D., Providence.
Rev. Samuel L. Caldwell, D. D , Providence.
S. S. Bradford, A. M., Providence.

CONGREGATIONALISTS.
Rev. Edwards A. Park, D D., Andover.
Hon. John Kingsbury, LL. D., Providence.

EPISCOPALIANS.
Alexander Duncan, A. M., Providence.
Hon. Charles S. Bradley, A. M., Providence.

* Mr. Ward resigned his Fellowship in 1771, and was elected a Trustee in place of Robert Strettle Jones, of Philadelphia, a Baptist. Mr. Ward's place in the Fellowship was filled by the election of the Rev. George Bisset, of Newport.

BOARD OF TRUSTEES.—1770.

BAPTISTS.
Hon. Samuel Ward, Newport, (Seventh Day
Daniel Jenckes, Esq., Providence. Baptist.)
Nicholas Brown, Esq., Providence.
Rev. Gardner Thurston, Newport.
Rev. John Maxson, Newport, (Seventh Day
Rev. John Gano, New York. Baptist.)
Rev. Samuel Winsor, Johnston.
Hon. Josias Lyndon, Newport.
Simon Pease, Esq., Newport.
Rev. Joshua Clarke, Hopkinton, (Seventh
Col. Job Bennet, Newport. Day Baptist.)
Peleg Barker, Esq., Newport.
Rev. Russell Mason, Swansea.
Rev. Isaac Backus, Middleborough.
Sylvester Child, Esq., Warren.
John Tanner, Esq., Newport.
Joseph Brown, Esq., Providence.
Nathan Spear, Esq., Boston.
Capt. John Warren, Newport.
William Brown, Esq., Swansea.
John Tillinghast, Esq., Newport.
———— ———— (One vacancy.)

FRIENDS.
Hon. Stephen Hopkins, Providence.
John G. Wanton, Esq., Newport.
Nicholas Easton, Esq., Middletown.
Edward Thurston, Jr., Newport.
Thomas Greene, Esq., Providence.

EPISCOPALIANS.
Gov. Joseph Wanton, Newport.
Hon. James Honyman, Newport.
George Hazard, Esq., Newport.
Joseph Russell, Esq., Providence.
———— ———— (One vacancy.)

CONGREGATIONALISTS.
Doct. Ephraim Bowen, Providence.
Hon. Nicholas Cooke, Providence.
Hon. Darius Sessions, Providence.
James Helme, Esq., South Kingstown.

Hon. Stephen Hopkins, *Chancellor.*
Hon. Samuel Ward, *Vice-Chancellor.*
Doct. Thomas Eyres, *Secretary.*
Col. Job Bennet, *Treasurer.*

BOARD OF TRUSTEES.—1867.

BAPTISTS.
Rev. David Benedict, D. D., Pawtucket.
Richard J. Arnold, A. M., Newport.
Rev. Rufus Babcock, D. D., New York.
Rev. William Phillips, A. M., Providence.
Rev. William Hague, D. D., Boston.
Rev. Arthur S. Train, D. D., Framingham.
Horatio N. Slater, Esq., Webster.
Hon. Samuel G. Arnold, A. M., Providence.
Hon. Charles Thurber, A. M., Brooklyn.
Hon. Albert Day, Hartford.
Rev. C. W. Flanders, D.D., Kennebunk Port.
Gardner Colby, Esq., Newton Centre.
Rev. John C. Stockbridge, D. D., Portland.
Marshall Woods, A. M., Providence.
Rev. Jonah G. Warren, D.D., Newton Centre.
Rev. Heman Lincoln, D. D., Providence.
Hon. Thomas G. Turner, Warren.
Rev. A. H. Granger, D. D., Providence.
Jefferson Borden, Esq., Fall River.
Hon. J. Warren Merrill, Cambridge.
John B. Hartwell, Esq., Providence.
Hon. William Sprague, A. M., Providence.

FRIENDS.
Samuel Boyd Tobey, M. D., Providence.
Hon. Richard W. Greene, LL. D., Warwick.
Hon. Geo. Howland, A. M., New Bedford.
Stephen A. Chase, Esq., Salem.
George L. Collins, M. D., Providence.

EPISCOPALIANS.
Zachariah Allen, LL. D., Providence.
Robert H. Ives, A. M., Providence.
William A. Crocker, A. M., New York.
Hon. Thomas P. Shepard, A. M., Providence.
William Goddard, A. M., Providence.

CONGREGATIONALISTS.
Hon. Edward Mellen, LL. D., Worcester.
Hon. William S. Patten, A. M., Providence.
Rev. Thatcher Thayer, D. D., Newport.
Earl P. Mason, Esq., Providence.

Samuel Boyd Tobey, M. D., *Chancellor.*
Hon. John Kingsbury, LL. D., *Secretary.*
Marshall Woods, A. M., *Treasurer.*

SUBSCRIPTIONS

OBTAINED IN

ENGLAND AND IRELAND.

BY

Rev. MORGAN EDWARDS.

1767-1769.

EARLY SUBSCRIPTIONS.

AT the first meeting of the Corporation, held in Newport on the first Wednesday in September, 1764, measures were taken to obtain funds for the endowment of the infant College. Committees to receive subscriptions, including in all the names of sixty-nine gentlemen, were appointed for Rhode Island, the states of Massachusetts and Connecticut, and the southern and western parts of the Continent. In the Philadelphia, Charleston, and Warren Associations, and throughout the Baptist churches of America, the Institution was warmly commended, and every individual member thereof was recommended to contribute annually a small sum for its support, and the encouragement of learning.

Among the gentlemen with whom the Corporation corresponded on the subject of obtaining subscriptions for the College, was the Rev. Morgan Edwards, who had first proposed the founding of the Institution to the Philadelphia Association. He at once resolved to go on a mission to Great Britain and Ireland, where he had received his birth and education. The following "authorization" we copy from the records:—

By the Honorable Samuel Ward, Esquire, Vice-Chancellor, and the Reverend James Manning, President of the College or University in the English Colony of Rhode Island and Providence Plantations, in New England, in America. To the Reverend Morgan Edwards, A. M., of the City of Philadelphia, in the Province of Pennsylvania, GREETING:—

WHEREAS, The General Assembly of the Colony aforesaid, did, by an act passed at their session held on the last Monday in February, 1764, incorporate certain persons therein named into one body corporate and politic; and granted them a Charter, authorizing and empowering them and their successors to found, endow, order and govern a College or University within said Colony, as in and by the said Charter, reference thereto being made will fully and clearly at large appear: And whereas, the Corporation of the said College or University, reposing special trust and confidence in your abilities and integrity, and convinced of your disinterested zeal and ardor for promoting and completing the design of the General Assembly, did, at their meeting held by authority of, and agreeable to their Charter, at Newport, in the said Colony, on the day of the date hereof,* unanimously resolve, that you, the aforesaid Morgan Edwards, should be requested and empowered to proceed to Europe to solicit and receive donations for the aforesaid purpose: These are therefore to authorize and empower you, the said Morgan Edwards, to proceed with all convenient speed to Europe, and in any part of his Majesty's dominions, or elsewhere, to urge, solicit, and receive from the friends of useful literature, and other well disposed persons, donations and benefactions for the founding and endowing the College or University aforesaid: For all which donations and benefactions you are to be accountable to the Treasurer of said Corporation for the time being; your reasonable charges and expenses in soliciting the same being first deducted.

In testimony whereof, the said Vice Chancellor and President have hereunto set their hands, and caused the seal of the Corporation to be affixed, in Newport aforesaid, this twentieth day of November, 1766, and in the seventh year of
[L. S.] the reign of our Sovereign Lord George the Third, by the grace of GOD, King of Great Britain, etc.

JAMES MANNING, President.
SAMUEL WARD, Vice-Chancellor.

The following letter to the General Assembly of the Church of Scotland, commending to their regards Mr. Edwards and his mission, we copy from an original document on file. Mr. Edwards, it appears, confined his solicitations to England and Ireland. The

---

*The date of the document, it will be observed, is November 20, 1766;—but the annual meeting of the Corporation was held on the first Wednesday in September, 1766.

letter is remarkably well expressed, and deserves a place in this documentary history of the College:—

To the very Reverend, the Moderator, and the other members of the General Assembly of the Church of Scotland. The Memorial of the Honorable Stephen Hopkins, Esq., Governor of the Colony of Rhode Island and Providence Plantations, in New England, and Chancellor of the College in the said Colony, and of the Reverend James Manning, President of the same, in behalf of the Corporation of the said College, sheweth:

That the General Assembly of the said Colony, taking into consideration the disadvantages the inhabitants thereof lie under from the want of a College for the education of youth, and the great benefits that arise to society from a well ordered and liberal education, granted a charter incorporating the persons therein mentioned, and empowering them to erect, found and endow a College in the said Colony, for the promotion of learning upon a plan so extensive and charitable that protestants of all denominations may there freely be initiated in the useful arts and sciences, as by the charter will fully appear.

The persons so appointed have accepted the trust reposed in them; but being sensible that in this small Colony alone, it would be impossible to raise a sufficient fund for the purposes aforesaid, found themselves under a necessity to make application to the friends of literature in other parts of His Majesty's dominions, for their charitable assistance.

Accordingly they have appointed and empowered the Reverend Mr. Morgan Edwards to solicit and receive donations for this Institution in Great Britain and Ireland; whom we have desired to make application to you; and take the liberty to recommend him as a gentleman of great merit, and a faithful minister of Jesus Christ. It will be in his power to give you every necessary information for forming a true judgment of this affair.

To gentlemen of your piety and learning it is needless to attempt to point out the great utility of a good education, and we have only to request that you will take this matter into consideration, and give Mr. Edwards such assistance and encouragement in the prosecution of this business as you shall think it deserves

We are, with great respect, Reverend Gentlemen, your most humble servants,

JAMES MANNING, President.
STEPHEN HOPKINS, Chancellor.

Mr. Edwards set out for Europe in the month of February, 1767. He appears to have been well received by his brethren in England, as is manifest from the following printed document:—

The credentials of the Rev. Morgan Edwards, of Philadelphia, being satisfactory to this assembly of General Baptists, (met at Horsly-down, May 25, 1768,) and he having laid before us a printed state of the Baptist College, in Rhode Island, and the design being approved by us, we do recommend the same to the serious consideration of the several congregations belonging to this assembly, to make collections and promote private contributions for the same, (the immediate expense of which is supposed to require about £2,000,) and that the money so collected be remitted to the Rev. Dr. Jeffries or the Rev. Daniel Noble, in London. Signed by order and in behalf of the whole,

GRANTHAM KILLINGWORTH.

LONDON, May 27, 1768: We whose names are underwritten having perused the charter of the Baptist College in Rhode Island government, and the Rev. Morgan Edwards's authority (under the seal of said College) to solicit donations towards endowing it, and having (some of us) been personally acquainted with Mr. Edwards, as well before his going to America, as since, do earnestly recommend his useful undertaking to the friends of religion and learning.

John Gill, D. D., Samuel Stennett, D. D., Rev. Benjamin Wallin, Joseph Jeffries, D. D., Rev. C. Bulkley, Rev. Thomas Towle, William Langford, D. D., Thomas Gibbons, D. D., John Conder, D. D , Andrew Kippis, D. D., Rev. H. Evans, of Bristol.

Mr. Edwards thus writes from London, to his friend, President Manning, at Warren, respecting the progress of the subscriptions:—

LONDON, April 26, 1768.

MY DEAR FRIEND:—I long to hear from you. Your last was of October 12, 1767. Why are you so slack? I informed you by post, January 7, of my compliance with your request touching Mr. Keith's demand; and of a draught on you, value £66 14s 2d sterling. The duplicate of same draught I sent by a Boston vessel which sailed about the latter end of the same month. I hope one or the other is come safe to Mr. Tillinghast's hands. Since that I have sent to Philadelphia, £219 10s 4d. I might have sent more were I not suspicious that the exchange is low by reason of the number of vessels that sailed for that port for flour. Mr. Miles informed me that he had sold one of my Irish bills, value £83 10s 1d, for £138 12s 4d currency, which gained for the College upwards of £13. I have not had any account of the sale of the other bill from the same country. I want much to hear how you intend to put the money out.

Last week a banker gave me twenty guineas, with a promise of much more, on condition that the College, from time to time, will correspond with him, and show fairness and fidelity in the management of what money he and others intrust us with.

EARLY SUBSCRIPTIONS.

I must desire, therefore, that the College will embrace the first opportunity to begin that correspondence, and acknowledge his kindness. You may direct to Mr. Samuel Roffey, banker in Lombard street, London. You must observe, also, that in England, as in Ireland, I solicit for money towards endowing the College, and therefore take care that you all attend to the design of the donors.

Inclosed you have a list of all the sums I received in Ireland, which list was distributed in the several places where I have been. The design was to let every one of them see that I gave true credit for what I have received. Had Tenn–nt, D–vis, and Be–ty, and Whit–r* done so they would have prevented suspicions very injurious to themselves and to those that come after them on the like errand. Mr. Raffey told me that he has been called a rogue for aiding the said persons to raise money in London.

If I were to stay in London ever so long I believe I should get money, but it comes so slowly and by such small sums that I cannot spare the time. However, I may depend on the friendship of two or three when I leave the kingdom, who have promised to solicit for us, and do not doubt but they will do more than I shall be able to accomplish, as they may watch convenient seasons. There have been no less than six cases of charity pushed about town this winter, viz.: two from Germany, two from the country of England, and two from America. The unwearied beneficence of the city of London is amazing!

Your newspapers, and letters from your government, published in other papers, have hurt me much. You boast of the many yards of cloth you manufacture, etc. This raises the indignation of the merchants and manufacturers. I have been not only denied by hundreds, but also abused on that score. My patience, my feet, and my assurance are much impaired. I took a cold in November, which stuck to me all winter, owing to my trampoosing the streets in all weathers. Pray let me hear from you by every opportunity. My love to Mrs. Manning, and believe me to be, with affection and esteem, your brother and humble servant, MORGAN EDWARDS.

P. S. I see in the York paper, an advertisement signifying that infant baptism is from heaven, proved at Newburyport. But the people of Haverhill do not seem to believe

---

* In 1753, by request of the Trustees of the College of New Jersey, the Presbyterian Synod of New York appointed the Rev. Gilbert Tennent, in conjunction with the Rev. (afterwards President) Samuel Davies, to cross the Atlantic and solicit funds for that Institution. The mission was eminently successful; but the only account of it that remains is found in the diary of Mr. Davis. About the same time, or a little later, the Rev. Nathaniel Whitaker, accompanied by Samson Occum, an Indian preacher, solicited funds for Moor's Indian Charity School, afterwards Dartmouth College. Who the other person was to whom Edwards refers, we are not informed.

that this image came down from Jupiter; for the brave Hezekiah Smith, I hear, frequently uses the baptism of John.

The following is the list to which Mr. Edwards refers in the foregoing letter:—

A list of persons in Ireland, who have contributed towards endowing the College in Rhode Island government. Published, according to promise, partly for the honor of the benefactors, and partly to satisfy them and the College of the fidelity of their humble servant, by whom the money hath been collected. The sums are put down in English currency, because better known in America:—

CORK.

	£	s	d
Joseph Fowke,	2	2	0
Stephen Mills,	8	8	0
John Osburn,	1	1	0
William Harrington,	1	1	0
Mary Murphy,	1	1	0
Thomas Bible,	0	10	6
Susanna Pilson,	1	1	0
Rev. Walter Richards,	1	1	0
Riggs Falkiner,	3	3	0
William Dixon,	1	1	0
James Rains,	1	1	0
Thomas Strettell,	2	2	0
Henry Wannell,	0	2	6
Thomas Rogers Trayer,	0	5	0
John Elliott,	0	10	6
Abraham Lane,	0	10	6
Robert Stevelly,	0	10	6
Francis Carleton,	1	1	0
Joshua Harmon,	0	10	6
Richard Pope,	1	1	0
James Aickin,	0	5	0
James Emerson	0	10	6
Mathew O. Dwyer,	0	10	6
Mary Newth,	0	2	6
John Rolt,	0	5	0
William Dobbin,	1	1	0
Gerard Fehrman,	0	10	6
Abraham Fuller,	0	5	0
Samuel Beale,	0	2	6
Francis Allin,	1	1	0
Francis McCarthy,	0	6	9
George Eveleigh,	1	1	0
William Lawton,	0	10	6

	£	s	d
Ebenezer Pike,	1	1	0
Caleb Beale,	0	10	6
Humphry Crowly,	1	1	0
Benjamin Pike,	0	10	6
Daniel Jones,	0	6	0
Nathaniel Lavit,	2	2	0
William Parks,	1	1	0
Peter Cambridge,	1	1	0
James Ellis,	0	10	6
George Randall,	1	1	0
Joseph Abell,	0	5	0
John Devroux,	1	1	0
Luke Grant,	1	1	0
Nicholas Howell,	0	5	0
Thomas Price,	0	5	0
Thomas Jones,	1	1	0
Samuel Neale,	0	10	6
John Dennis,	1	1	0
George Newenham,	1	1	0
	50	10	9

WATERFORD.

	£	s	d
William Emerson,	1	1	0
Elizabeth Brown,	1	1	0
Josiah Porter,	1	1	0
Rev. James Edwards,	1	1	0
Hans Wallace,	0	10	6
E. Edwards, M. D.,	0	10	6
Hugh Ramsey,	0	10	6
John Lyon,	0	10	6
Thomas Jones,	0	10	6
William Hammond,	0	10	6
Rev. John Brown,	1	1	0
	8	8	0

EARLY SUBSCRIPTIONS.

DUBLIN.

Name	£	s.	d.
Joseph Agitt,	1	1	0
Mary Wilkinson,	1	1	0
Mrs. Luke Kelly,	0	5	6
Richard White,	0	10	6
Samuel Powell,	0	8	3
Robert Moore,	2	2	0
Abraham Wilkinson,	2	2	0
Mary Thomas,	1	1	0
John Atkinson,	1	1	0
John Fawcett,	1	1	0
William Coates,	1	1	0
Robert Montgomery,	0	10	6
George Wilson,	0	10	6
John Allen,	1	1	0
William Hunt,	1	1	0
Peter Wilkinson,	1	1	0
George Gibson,	1	1	0
Rachel Connor,	1	1	0
Samuel Tyndall,	1	1	0
Richard Maxwell,	1	1	0
B—— G——on,	1	1	0
William McGowan,	0	10	6
Benjamin Nun,	1	1	0
Nathaniel Stakes,	0	10	6
James Booth,	0	10	6
Samuel Gough,	0	10	6
Thomas Hatfield,	0	10	6
Beau Champe,	0	1	0
Elizabeth Benn,	0	10	0
Thomas Booth,	0	10	6
Rev. John Haughton,	1	1	0
Thomas Bible,	0	5	0
Thomas Bond,	0	10	6
Rebecka Gibbon,	2	2	0
William Gibson,	0	5	0
Elizabeth Brabing,	1	1	0
James Manypeny,	0	10	6
Rev. Thomas Vance,	1	1	0
Rev. William Boulton,	1	1	0
Robert McGregor,	0	10	6
James Goodman,	0	10	6
John Reilly,	1	1	0
Robert Riky,	1	1	0
Thomas Vickers,	0	5	0
Edward Hincks,	0	10	6
Isaac Simon,	1	1	0
William Jackson,	0	10	6
George Maquay,	1	1	0
Joseph Nun,	1	1	0
Col. James Dunn,	1	1	0
John Walker,	0	5	0
John Fury,	0	1	0
Nathaniel Mackay,	0	5	0
Anthony Grayson,	1	1	0
Nathaniel Garner,	0	10	6
Benjamin Page,	0	10	6
John Barrow,	0	5	0
Mary McMaster,	2	2	0
John Armstong,	1	1	0
James Lang,	1	1	0
James Young,	0	1	0
James Martin,	0	5	0
S. Bushell,	0	10	6
Hester Hewetson,	0	10	6
Robert Jaffray,	1	1	0
David Aigoin,	0	10	6
Jeremiah Vickers,	0	10	6
Thomas Read,	1	1	0
Thomas Garner,	0	2	6
Miss Aigoin,	0	10	6
William Grubb,	0	10	6
Thomas King,	1	1	0
John Stewart,	1	1	0
Samuel Edwards,	0	10	0
	57	16	3

BELFAST.

Name	£	s.	d.
Greggs and Cunningham,	2	2	0
Rev. Thomas Drennan,	1	1	0
Gilbert Orr,	1	1	0
Robert Armstrong,	0	10	6
Rev. James Saurin,	1	1	0
The first and second Presbyterian Churches,	13	9	0
Third Presbyterian Church,	14	15	4
	33	19	10

LISBURN.

Name	£	s.	d.
William Nevill,	1	1	0
Rev. James Bryson,	0	10	6
James Down and Connor,	3	3	0

BROWN UNIVERSITY.

	£	s.	d.		£	s.	d.
John Hill,	1	1	0	Rev. Robert Higinbothom,	0	10	6
Jacob Hancock,	0	10	6	Rev. Arthur Kyle,	0	10	6
Francis Burden,	1	1	0	James Thomson,	0	10	6
David Wilson,	1	1	0	William Mitchell,	0	2	6
Henry Bell,	0	16	3	Shuma White,	0	5	0
William Macten,	0	10	6	Alexander Patrick,	1	1	0
Alexander Legg,	1	1	0	William Galt,	0	10	6
				Henry Newton,	0	1	0
	10	15	9	John Hunter,	0	2	6
ANTRIM.				James Hamill,	0	2	7
Thomas Thompson,	1	1	0				
John Gilmore,	0	5	0		8	0	1
John Thompson,	1	1	0	LONDONDERRY.			
Thomas Hoope,	0	10	6	Rev. John Torrens,	1	1	0
Charles Bell,	0	10	6	William Hogg,	0	10	6
Rev. William Williamson,	0	5	0	William Caldwell,	1	1	0
Samuel McCormick, M. D.,	1	1	0	John Fairly,	1	1	0
Thomas Bell,	0	10	6	Samuel Hadfield,	1	1	0
Thomas Shaw,	0	10	6	William Scott,	1	1	0
George Young,	0	10	6	Robert Fairly,	0	10	6
John Meek,	0	2	6	Rev. John Hood,	0	10	6
William Meek,	0	5	0	Rev. David Harvey,	1	1	0
Alexander McBurney,	0	5	0	John Atchison,	0	10	9
James Duncan,	0	5	0	John Knox,	1	1	0
John Blackley,	0	5	0	Robert Alexander,	0	10	6
James Watt,	0	2	6	James Thompson,	0	10	6
				William McKean,	1	1	0
	10	6	7				
BALLYMONY.					11	11	0
Thomas Leiky,	0	2	6				
Rev. Laurence Grace,	1	1	0	NEWRY.			
Gift of the Presbyterian Church,	4	6	3	Richard ap Richard,	1	1	0
				George Glenny,	0	5	0
	5	9	9	James Pollock,	1	1	0
COLERAINE.				Thomas Stewart,	0	5	0
				Samuel McDowell,	0	5	0
Hugh Lyle,	1	1	0	William Beath,	0	10	6
Alexander Lawrence,	0	10	6	George Scott,	0	2	6
William Smith,	0	5	0	Rev. James Moody,	0	10	6
John Galt,	1	1	0	John Pollock,	1	1	0
Charles Haslett,	0	10	6				
Robert Rice,	0	2	6		5	1	6
Susanna Ferguson,	0	2	6	WESTMEATH.			
Fred. Ferguson,	0	2	6	Timothy Bagnal,	1	1	0
John Clarke Lewis,	0	3	0	Timothy Bagnal, Jr.,	0	10	6
John Bell,	0	2	6	Joseph Lemmon,	1	1	0
Alexander McKachan,	0	2	6	Mrs. Knowland,	1	1	0

EARLY SUBSCRIPTIONS. 157

	£	s.	d.		£	s.	d.
Thomas Booth,	0	10	6	John Cornwall,	0	5	0
James Brennon,	0	5	0	Alexander Cornwall,	0	5	0
John Codd,	0	5	0	Thomas Ashton,	0	10	6
By sundry,	0	13	0	John Lemmon,	0	10	6
	5	7	0	Joseph Smith,	0	10	6
ORMOND.				Nicholas Middleton,	1	1	0
Rev. James North,	1	1	0	James Shortt,	1	1	0
Daniel Rogers,	1	1	0		9	12	0
Mich. Lewis,	1	1	0	Rev. Phil. Dixon of Tullemore,	1	1	0
William Shortt,	1	1	0	Rev. Jas. Deaves of Garryard,	0	10	6
Anna Wilkinson,	0	5	0	Thomas Foucee of Tyrrels-pass,	0	10	6
Thurgood North,	0	10	6		2	2	0
William Rhodes,	0	2	6				
Grace Otway,	0	6	6	Sum total collected in Ireland,	116	4	5

Remitted to the College by Mr. Thompson of Derry, June 26, 1767,	26	5	0
By Greggs and Cunningham of Belfast, July 13, 1767,	44	4	3
By Falkiner and Mills from Cork, September 16,	84	0	0
By ditto, October 5, 1767,	21	0	0
By Captain Seymore Hood, from Newry,	8	8	0
By Richard Lemmon, from Cork,	2	2	0
Sum total remitted,	185	19	3
Not yet received of the above subscriptions,	2	7	0
Necessary expenses,	27	18	2
	216	4	5

P. S. Mr. Edwards begs the excuse of those gentlemen on whom he has not been able to wait a second time to receive their subscriptions; and desires they will be pleased to pay the same to Mr. Abraham Wilkinson of Park Street, or Mr. John Pym Joshua, of Ushers Quay, Dublin, who will soon be authorized by the College to solicit, receive, and remit money for its use. Mr. Edwards has also heard, since he left Ireland, of several who expressed a willingness to become benefactors to said College. He thanks them for their good will; and entreats them to deposit their gifts, whether money or books, with the above mentioned merchants in Dublin. This list may be had of the Rev. W. Boulton, in Golden Lane, Dublin.

Mr. Edwards also published and circulated a second list, as follows:—

A list of the gentlemen and ladies in England who have contributed towards endowing the College in Rhode Island government. In this list the publisher hath endeavored to give honor to whom honor is due, but if he hath failed in any instances, he hopes the party concerned will excuse it:—

BROWN UNIVERSITY.

LONDON.

Name	£	s.	d.	Name	£	s.	d.
Rev. Dr. John Gill,	5	5	0	Messrs. Lane, Son, and Fraser,	5	5	0
Rev. Dr. Samuel Stennet,	10	10	0	Mr. Isaac Wane,	5	5	0
Rev. Dr. Andrew Gifford,	10	10	0	Messrs. Champion and Dickason,	5	5	0
Rev. Dr. Joseph Jeffries,	5	5	0	Mr. Edward Jeffries,	5	5	0
Rev. Daniel Noble,	5	5	0	Mr. Bartholomew Pomeroy,	5	5	0
Rev. Charles Bulkley,	5	5	0	Mr. Granger,	4	10	0
Rev. John Stevens,	3	3	0	J. Shearwood, Esq.,	3	3	0
Rev. Dr. John Conder,	1	1	0	Mr. Joseph Flight,	3	3	0
Rev. Dr. Thomas Gibbons,	1	1	0	Mr. Thomas Weston,	3	3	0
Rev. Thomas Towle,	1	1	0	Mr. Thomas Flight,	3	3	2
Rev. William Clarke,	1	1	0	Mr. Robert Keen,	3	3	0
Rev. John Potts.	1	1	0	Mr. Vaughan,	2	2	0
Rev. Joseph Jenkins,	1	1	0	Mr. John Hamman,	2	2	0
Ditto in Books,	2	10	0	Thomas Nash, Esq.,	2	2	0
The Hon. Thomas Penn,	20	0	0	Mr. John Gill,	2	2	0
Thomas Llewelyn, Esq.,	21	0	0	Mr. J. Mabbs,	2	2	0
Ditto in Books,	10	10	0	Miss Flights,	2	2	0
Samuel Roffey, Esq.,	21	0	0	Mr John Flight,	2	2	0
Benjamin Franklin, Esq.,	10	10	0	Mrs. Prudence Davis,	2	2	0
Frederick Bull, Esq.,	10	10	0	Mrs. Elizabeth Wilkinson,	2	2	0
Robert Barlow, Esq., of Boston,	10	10	0	Mr. Joseph Robarts,	2	2	0
Thomas Hollis, Esq.,	10	10	0	Mr Thomas Pewtress,	2	2	0
Stephen Williams, Esq.,	10	10	0	Mr. George Keith,	2	2	0
Thomas Watson, Esq.,	10	10	0	Mr. Joseph Burch,	2	2	0
Messrs. D. and J. Barclay,	10	10	0	Mr. Alexander Scott,	2	2	0
Mr. Benjamin West,	10	10	0	Mr. Nicholas Beekman,	2	2	0
William Stead, Esq.,	10	10	0	Mr. Thomas Bell,	2	2	0
Mr. Stephen Lowdell,	10	10	0	Mr. Stephen Dendy,	2	2	0
Jenkin Jones, Esq.,	10	10	0	Mr. John Bowles,	1	1	0
James Vere, Esq.,	10	10	0	Mr. Samuel Williams,	1	1	0
Grantham Killingworth, Esq.,	10	10	0	Mr. Clement Bellamy,	1	1	0
Messrs. Harford and Powell,	10	10	0	Mr. Joseph Perry,	1	1	0
Messrs. Mildred and Roberts,	10	10	0	Mrs. Ann Perry,	1	1	0
John Mills, Esq.,	10	10	0	Mr. Joseph Perry, Jr.,	1	1	0
John Thornton, Esq.,	10	10	0	Mr. James Pearson,	1	1	0
Timothy Hollis, Esq.,	5	5	0	Mrs. Flight,	1	1	0
Dr. John Fothergill,	5	5	0	Mr. Flight,	1	1	0
George Baskerville, Esq.,	5	5	0	Mrs. Mackmerds,	1	1	0
Mr. William Weare,	5	5	0	Mr. James Smith,	1	1	0
Samuel Stinton, Esq.,	5	5	0	Miss Elizabeth Butler,	1	1	0
Mr. David Langton,	5	5	0	Mr. William Mace,	1	1	0
Mrs. Elizabeth Halsey,	5	5	0	Mr. George Darby,	1	1	0
Mrs. Martha Adams,	5	5	0	Mr. Ra. Jackson,	1	1	0
Rev. John Potts,	1	1	0	Mr. Edward Robarts,	1	1	0
Mr. George Wilkinson,	5	5	0	Mr. John Wollaston,	1	1	0
				Mr. William Taylor,	1	1	0

EARLY SUBSCRIPTIONS. 159

	£	s.	d.		£	s.	d.
Mr. James Cahuel,	1	1	0	Miss Guertz, -	0	10	6
Mr. William Brittain,	1	1	0	Mr. John Young,	0	5	3
Mr. Charles Barton,	1	1	0	Mr. Evan Davis, -	0	5	3
Mr. Eldridge. -	0	10	6	Mr. Thomas Holford, -	0	5	3
Mr. Thomas Nichols,	1	1	0	Mr John Shenston,	0	5	3
Mr. John Hattersley, -	1	1	0	Mr. John Williams, -	0	5	0
Mr John Cooper, -	1	1	0	Mr. Robert Sargeant,	0	5	3
Mr. Benjamin Forsitt,	1	1	0	Mr. T. Treadway,	0	5	3
Mr. T. Crawley, -	1	1	0	Mr. James Murrey,	0	5	3
Mr William Straphan,	1	1	0	Mrs. Mayor, -	0	5	3
Mr. Henry Rutt, -	1	1	0	Mr. John Burnside,	0	5	3
Mr. Alexander Clunie,	1	1	0	Mr. John Edwards, -	0	5	3
Mr. John Wells, -	1	1	0	Mrs. Huslet,	0	2	6
Mr. Hugh Humston, -	1	1	0	Mr. Joseph Sargeant, -	0	2	6
Mr. Carrington Bowles, -	1	1	0	Mr. Richard Rust,	0	2	0
Mr. Isaac Jemmett, -	1	1	0	Mr. Abraham King, -	0	1	0
Mr. Robert Plimpton,	1	1	0	Mr. John Letham,	0	2	6
Mr. Jeremiah Ridout,	1	1	0				
Isaac Hollis. Esq.,	1	1	0		492	9	0
Miss Sarah Wiggins, -	1	1	0	BRISTOL.			
Mr. Thomas Cox, -	1	1	0	Rev. William Foot, -	2	2	0
Mr. T Scofield, -	1	1	0	Rev. John Needham, -	0	10	6
Mr. Henry Keene,	1	1	0	Rev. Hugh Evans,	1	1	0
Mrs. Jane Knightly, -	1	1	0	Rev. Caleb Evans,	2	2	0
Mr. William Grace,	1	1	0	Rev. James Newton,	1	1	0
Mr. Guy Bryan,	1	1	0	Rev. Dr. Stonehouse, -	1	1	0
Leader Cox, Esq.. -	1	1	0	Rev. John Thomas,	0	10	6
Mr. Henry Williams, -	0	10	6	Rev. Jonathan Watts,	0	5	0
Mr. Thomas Kitchen,	0	10	6	Messrs. John and Fred. Bull, -	5	5	0
Mr. Robert Hill,	0	10	6	Miss Sarah Brown,	0	3	0
Mr. Job Heath,	0	10	6	Mr. John Harris, -	2	2	0
Mr. S. Williams,	0	10	6	Mr. Thomas Ludlow, -	2	2	0
Mr. John Davis, -	0	10	6	Dr. Joseph Mason, -	2	2	0
Mr. Per. Mann,	0	10	6	William Lunell, Esq.,	1	1	0
Mrs. Elizabeth Fawconer,	0	10	6	Mr. Abr. Rich. Hawksworth, -	1	1	0
Mr. Combes,	0	10	6	Mr. J. Champion,	1	1	0
Mrs. Stiles, -	0	10	6	Mr. J. Banister, -	1	1	0
Mrs. Mary Brine,	0	10	6	Mrs. Ann Noble,	1	1	0
Mr. John Williams,	0	10	6	Mr. Abr. Ludlow, -	1	1	0
Mr. John Everard,	0	10	6	Mr. William Ludlow, -	1	11	6
Mr. Thomas Yeoman, -	0	10	6	Mr. John Page, -	1	1	0
Mr. John Banett,	0	10	6	Mr. John Stock, -	1	1	0
Mr. Carlton,	0	10	6	Mrs. Mary Stokes, -	1	1	0
Mr. John Allen,	0	10	6	Mr. William Reeve, -	1	1	0
Mr. George Warren,	0	10	6	Mr. John Moore, -	0	10	6
Mr. John Muggeridge,	0	10	6	Miss Pages, -	0	10	6

160 BROWN UNIVERSITY.

	£	s.	d.		£	s.	d.
Mr. John Edye,	0	10	6	Mr. John Parslow,	0	2	6
Mr. Robert Cottle,	0	10	6	Mr. John Brimble,	0	2	6
Miss Sarah Farley,	0	10	6	Mrs. Sarah Burdock,	0	1	0
Mr. William Hazle,	0	10	6				
Mr. Joseph Grimes,	0	10	6		55	1	0
Mr. Anthony Henderson,	0	10	6	EXETER.			
Mr. John Page,	0	10	6	Rev. Thomas Lewis,	1	7	0
Mr. Robert Coleman,	0	10	6	By his Deacon,	3	6	3
Miss Eliz. and Rebecca Brown,	0	10	6	Rev. Thomas Twining,	1	1	0
Mrs. Dorcas Jolleff,	0	10	6	By his Deacon,	1	10	2
Mr. Joseph Green,	0	10	6	Mr. John Holmes, Jr.,	2	12	6
Mr. Francis Collins,	0	10	6	Master and Miss Weymouth,	1	11	6
Mr. Joseph Sevier,	0	10	6	Mr. Samuel Weymouth,	1	1	0
Mr. Samuel Waterford,	0	10	6	Mrs. Mary Buckland,	0	10	6
Mr. William Frampton,	0	10	6	Mrs. Mary Maunder,	0	10	6
Mr. John Brown,	0	10	6	Mr. Joshua Williams,	0	10	6
Mrs. Mary Poole,	0	10	6	Mr. A. H. Groth,	0	10	6
Mr. B. Chandle,	0	10	6	Mrs. Ann Jones,	0	10	6
Mr. William Cowles,	0	10	6	Mr. Samuel Dunsford,	0	5	3
Mrs. Susanna Rogers,	0	10	6	Mr. Joseph Pope,	0	5	3
Mr. Nath. Wraxall,	0	10	6	Mr. John Carely,	0	5	3
Mr. Edward Daniel,	0	10	6	Mr. Robert Manning,	0	5	0
Mr. Nath. Watkins,	0	10	6	Mr. Caleb Blight,	0	5	0
Mr. Philip Rose,	0	10	6	Mr. Richard Strong,	0	2	6
Mr. Joseph Whittuck,	0	9	0	Mr. James Newman,	0	2	6
Mr. Samuel Welton,	0	5	3				
Mr. Samuel Allen,	0	5	3		16	12	8
Mr. Benj. King,	0	5	3	TAUNTON.			
Mr. John Winwood,	0	5	3	Rev. Joshua Toulmin,	1	1	0
Mr. Benj. Brock,	0	5	3	Rev. Richard Harrison,	0	10	6
Mr. John Morgan,	0	5	3	Rev. William Johnson,	0	10	6
Mrs. Ele. Howldy,	0	5	3	Rev. John Ward,	0	10	6
Mr. Edward Ransford,	0	5	3	Rev. Mal. Blake,	1	1	0
Mr. David Cherry,	0	5	3	Ebenezer Jeffries, Esq.,	2	2	0
Mr. Joseph Shapland,	0	5	3	Mr. Joseph Jeffries,	2	2	0
Mr. Lewis Watkins,	0	5	6	James Kirkpatrick, Esq.,	1	1	0
Mr. George Harris,	0	5	3	Mr. Thomas Newcomen,	1	1	0
Mr. Thomas Allard,	0	5	3	Col. John Roberts,	1	1	0
Mr. William Edwards,	0	5	3	Mrs. Noble,	1	1	0
Mr. William Garnsey,	0	5	3	Mr. John Westcott,	1	1	0
Mr. Thomas Evans,	0	5	3	Mr. Benjamin Jeffries,	0	10	6
Mr. John Stych,	0	5	3	Mrs. Totterdale,	0	10	6
Mr. David Jones,	0	5	0	Mr. Caleb Bryant,	0	10	6
Mr. Thomas Adlam,	0	5	0	Mr. Thomas Pope,	0	10	6
Mr. James Norton,	0	2	6	Mr. John Cole,	0	10	0
Mr. Ch. Whittuck,	0	2	6	Mr. Abraham Sheppard,	0	10	6

EARLY SUBSCRIPTIONS.

	£	s.	d.
Mr. Nehemiah Bewfey,	0	5	3
Mrs. Ann Smith,	0	5	0
Mr. Caleb Stower,	0	3	0
Mr. Edward Cornish,	0	2	6
Mrs. Ann Cross,	0	2	6
Mr. William Stone,	0	3	0
Mr. Samuel Smith,	0	5	0
Mr. Benjamin Boon,	0	1	0
	17	12	9

ABINGDON.

	£	s.	d.
Rev. David Turner,	1	1	0
Joseph Butler, Esq.,	10	10	0
Jos. Tompkins, Esq.,	10	10	0
William Tompkins, Esq.,	10	10	0
Benjamin Tompkins, Esq.,	5	5	0
Mr. Nat. Roberts,	5	5	0
Mr. Joseph Fuller,	0	10	6
	43	11	6

RYE.

	£	s.	d.
Mr. David Guy,	1	1	1
Mr. Peter Jerman, of Breed,	1	1	0
Dr. Thos. Frewen, of Northiam,	0	10	6
Mr. Richard Batchellor, of ditto,	0	5	6
Mr. George Quested,	0	5	0
By Rev. Mr. Purdey's Deacon,	2	5	6
	5	8	6

HYTHE.

	£	s.	d.
Rev. Thomas Piety,	5	5	0
Gift of the Church,	4	4	0
	9	9	0

FOLKSTONE.

	£	s.	d.
Rev. Thomas Whitehead,	0	10	6
By his Deacon, (gift of Church,)	11	11	0
Mr. Robert Howard,	0	5	3
	12	6	9

SMARDIN.

	£	s.	d.
Jenkin Hague, Esq.,	2	2	0
Mr. Russel,	1	1	0
Gift of the Church,	2	5	4
	5	8	4

OXFORD.

	£	s.	d.
Mr. William Plater,	1	1	0
Mr. Samuel Fox,	1	1	0
Archdale Rooke, Esq.,	0	10	6
Mr. Thomas Plater,	0	10	6
Mrs. John Clarke,	0	10	6
Mr. Richard Williams,	0	10	6
Miss Mary Fox,	0	5	3
Mr. John Voysey,	0	4	0
	4	13	3

CIRENCESTER.

	£	s.	d.
Mr. Joseph Freeman,	1	1	0
Mr. William Wilkins,	0	10	6
Mr. Thomas Dawson,	0	10	6
Mrs. Jane Overbury,	0	10	6
Mr. Henry Wavel,	0	10	6
	3	3	0

TEDBURY.

	£	s.	d.
Mr. Nath. Overbury,	1	1	0
Mr. John Overbury,	1	1	0
Mr. William Overbury,	0	10	6
	2	12	6
Gift of the Church of Ashford,	3	17	6
Mr. John Brown of Canterbury,	1	1	0
By the Rev. Mr. Benge's Deacon,	1	6	6
	6	5	0

	£	s.	d.
Sum total collected in England,	675	14	3
Remitted to the College by Mr. John Strettell, January 26, 1768,	40	0	0
By ditto, Feb. 15,	22	0	4
By Mr. George Keith, January 1,	66	14	2
By Messrs. Pewtress and Robarts, March 25,	52	10	0
By Mr. George Wilkinson, April 1,	52	10	0
By ditto, April 26,	52	10	0
By ditto, May 26,	100	0	0
By ditto, August 12,	52	10	0

	£	s.	d.
By Rev. Caleb Evans, of Bristol, June 27,	52	10	0
By the Rev. Thomas Piety, of Hythe, May 12,	5	5	0
By Mr George Wilkinson, August 12,	14	8	0
In Books, some not yet sent,	14	5	0
Sum total remitted,	525	2	6
Necessary expenses hitherto,	89	16	9
Cash in hand,	60	15	0
	675	14	3

P. S. Mr. Edwards did intend to give receipts for all the sums he should receive, but finding that would be too tedious, he thought it best to print and publish the above list, which will answer the same end, as therein every benefactor will find that just credit is given him. It is possible that Mr. Edwards may be detained in England by contrary winds some time after the printing of this list, and in that time receive more donations; if so, he will take care to give the public an account thereof, along with what money his friends may raise after his departure. Circular letters are sent to most parts of England and Wales, in hope that deficiencies may be made up, and Dr. Gill, Dr. Stennett, Dr. Jeffries, and Rev. Daniel Noble are appointed to receive and remit what may be gathered, whether money or books. Finally, Mr. Edwards takes this opportunity, in the name of the College to thank the benefactors to our infant Seminary, and most earnestly to entreat his reverend brethren, who shall receive his letters, to exert themselves in favor of a most liberal and catholic Institution.

N. B. This list may be had of Mr. George Keith, Grace-church street.

LONDON, August 22, 1768.

Mr. Edwards returned to America during the latter part of 1768, and at the annual meeting of the Corporation in 1769, presented his account with the vouchers; an abstract of which account we copy from the records:—

RHODE ISLAND COLLEGE TO MORGAN EDWARDS,   DR.
To sundries and accounts rendered,   £896 16s. 6d.

RHODE ISLAND COLLEGE,   CR.
By amount of donations in Ireland,   £213 17s. 5d.
"   "   "   England,   665 4 3
By sundry smaller donations, as per accounts exhibited, inclusive of his own subscription,   9 8 6
    888 10 2

Balance due to Morgan Edwards,   £8 6s. 4d.

Which being referred to the committee appointed to examine the College accounts, they made the following report, viz. :—

WARREN, September 6, 1769.

The subscribers being a committee to examine the above accounts, have compared it with the vouchers, and find the above sum of eight pounds six shillings and four pence sterling due to Mr. Edwards.

      Edward Upham,   Nicholas Brown,
      Joseph Russell,   Jabez Bowen Jr.,
             Archibald Campbell.

Which report was unanimously accepted by the Corporation.

From the foregoing it appears that Mr. Edwards obtained for the College the sum of £888 10s. 2d. sterling, which, he remarks in his narrative, was succeeding "pretty well, considering how angry the mother country then was with the colonies for opposing the stamp act."

In order that this sum might constitute a permanent fund for the support of the President, it was

Voted, That the certificate presented to this Corporation by the Rev. Morgan Edwards, be recorded, which is as follows, viz. :—

Whereas, a law of the College, (made at Newport, September, 1, 1768,) secures the money raised in Europe for the purpose for which it was intended by the donors, this certifies that their design was, That the interest thereof should forever go to pay the salary of the President.

WARREN, September 7, 1769.   MORGAN EDWARDS.

The original subscription book of Morgan Edwards, somewhat the worse for wear, is now among the College archives. This important document, we may add, was presented to the Library in the year 1849, by Mr. Joshua Edwards, through the Rev. Richard Webster, pastor of a Presbyterian church in Mauch Chunk, Pennsylvania. This Mr. Edwards was the son of Rev. Morgan Edwards. He was then living, although upwards of eighty years of age. The certificate, form of a receipt, and introduction are printed;—the rest is in manuscript. The subscriptions are mostly in the hand-writing of the subscribers, and the document is therefore one of exceeding great value as a collection of autographs.

The reader will not fail to observe how prominent the name of Morgan Edwards appears in the early history of the College. He first proposed the founding of it to the Philadelphia Association; he was particularly active in obtaining a charter from the General Assembly, and in procuring the first funds for the endowment of the Institution, deeming this, to use his own language, "the greatest service he has done or hopes to do for the Baptist interest;"* he attended the early meetings of the Corporation, and was in communication with the Browns in regard to the matter of location; he preached the first "Commencement Sermon," and when the President seemed in doubt whether to go with the College to Providence, or retain his pastoral relations with the church at Warren, he wrote him from Philadelphia a vigorous letter of remonstrance, to which we have referred in our history of the Charter:—

> I cannot help being angry with you when you talk of another President. Have you endured so much hardship in vain? We have no man that will do as well as you. Talk no more, think no more of quitting the Presidency, unless you have a mind to join issue with those projectors and talkers who mean no more than to hinder anything from being done. If you go to Providence, the Warren people may have a supply; if they were willing to part with you, it is likely the College would have no reason to covet you.

Before taking our leave of Mr. Edwards, we may add a few particulars respecting his early life and professional career. He retained his connection with the church in Philadelphia ten years, during the latter part of which time his relations, it is understood, were not entirely harmonious. In the year 1770, he preached a new years sermon from the text, "This year thou shalt die." He

* "Materials towards a History of the Baptists in Pennsylvania," page 48.

had, from some unaccountable impulse, been led to believe that he should die on a particular day, and this sermon was supposed by some to have been intended as his own funeral sermon. This circumstance could not but affect his reputation injuriously. In addition to this, he is said to have indulged, occasionally, in the excessive use of intoxicating drinks. Under these circumstances, he voluntarily resigned his charge, preaching occasionally until the settlement of his successor, Dr. Rogers, in 1772. The following extracts from letters in our possession addressed to the Rev. Hezekiah Smith, by the Rev. Messrs. Francis Pelot and Oliver Hart, of South Carolina, show Mr. Edwards's position at this time in a friendly light. The first is dated October 28, 1771. "I then wish" (referring to the Philadelphia church) "they would agree with their Mr. Edwards again. Thus I argue to myself: 'If he may preach occasionally, why not steadily?' 'Oh! but he has not behaved as well as he should.' I reply, 'There cannot be anything immoral, or he would not be allowed to preach occasionally, and the mantle CHARITY would easily cover small imperfections. Besides, the present dissatisfaction, no doubt, would make him more cautious for the future, and might be a means of preserving the usefulness of a talented man—a man who has scarce his fellow in a warm attachment to the Baptist interest." In a letter dated April 8, 1772, Mr. Pelot adds: "We were favored with the company of Rev. Morgan Edwards at my house for about a week in last January. We also had his company at our Association. We all esteem him as a sensible, good man, and he left us all full of love to him." Rev. Oliver Hart, of Charleston, in a letter dated February 27, 1772, thus writes: "Rev. Mr. Edwards, from Philadelphia, has been here, and tarried with us about three weeks. He is a great good man, but some say he preaches too slow." And in a second letter, written the next month, he further adds: "In my last I informed you that we had the pleasure of Mr. Edwards's company at our Association. He is a great good man; firmly attached to the Baptist interest, to promote which he cheerfully encounters all difficulties." These testimonials, coming voluntarily from two of the most prominent Baptist ministers of the South, show that Mr. Edwards, even at a time when his sun appeared to be obscured, was a man highly esteemed, and that he was worthy of the honor, which is accorded to him, of having been the prime mover in originating and founding Brown University.

In the year 1772, he removed with his family to Newark, Delaware, and was occupied in preaching in a number of vacant churches till the commencement of the Revolutionary war. He then remained silent until the war was over, owing, doubtless, to the fact that he adhered to the cause of Great Britain, and was justly ranked with the Tories; although it is understood that his Toryism was rather a matter of principle than of action. President Manning, in his diary,* speaks of visiting Col. Miles, in the year 1779, at his "elegant seat," thirteen miles from Philadelphia, in company with Edwards and Dr. Jones, thus showing that political differences did not interrupt their friendship. After the Revolution, Mr. Edwards occasionally read lectures on Divinity in Philadelphia, and other parts of Pennsylvania; also in New Jersey, Delaware and New England; but, owing to the unhappy fall already alluded to, as well as to his political sentiments, he declined ever after to resume the active duties of the ministry. From passages in the correspondence of Manning, it appears, furthermore, that he sympathized with Elhanan Winchester, whose "apostasy," as it was termed, and his conduct in relation to the church at Philadelphia, caused him to be excluded from fellowship with the Baptist associations. In a letter to the Rev.

* MANNING AND BROWN UNIVERSITY, pp. 279–80.

John Rippon, of London, dated August 3, 1784, Manning thus writes:—

Mr. Morgan Edwards has not printed in vindication of his (Winchester's) principles, but he read me a manuscript more than a year since on that subject, which he did not own, though charged then with being the author. He did not deny it; whereby he was entreated not to add the printing of this to the long list of imprudent things which had already so greatly grieved his friends and so injured his reputation. This plainness did not please him, but I thought the use of it was duty.

Mr. Edwards died at a place then called Pencader, Delaware, January 28, 1795, in the seventy-third year of his age. His funeral sermon was preached by the Rev. Dr. William Rogers, of Philadelphia, on II. Cor. vi. 8:—"By honor and dishonor; by evil report and good report; as deceivers and yet true." The text was selected by himself, and designed, as some suppose, to have a bearing upon his own peculiar history. A portion of this discourse, which was published in Dr. Rippon's Annual Register, a work printed in London, may fitly close this chapter:—

Honor, Mr. Edwards certainly had, both in Europe and America. The college and academy of Philadelphia. at a very early period, honored him as a man of learning and a popular preacher, with a diploma, constituting him Master of Arts: this was followed by a degree ad eundem, in the year 1769, from the College of Rhode Island, being the first commencement in that Institution. In this Seminary he held a Fellowship, and filled it with reputation, till he voluntarily resigned it in 1789; age and distance having rendered him incapable of attending the meetings of the Corporation any longer.

He also met with dishonor; but he complained not much of this, as it was occasioned by his strong attachment to the Royal Family of Great Britain, in the beginning of the American war, which fixed on him the name of a Tory: this I should have omitted mentioning, had not the deceased expressly enjoined it upon me. For any person to have been so marked out in those days was enough to bring on political opposition and destruction of property: all of which took place with respect to Mr. Edwards, though he never harbored the thought of doing the least injury to the United States by abetting the cause of our enemies.

A good report our departed brother also had: the numerous letters brought with him across the Atlantic from the Rev. Dr. John Gill, and others, reported handsome things of him; and so did, in return, the letters that went from America to the then parent country. Evil reports also fell to his share; but most of these were false reports, and therefore he gave credit for them as a species of persecution; and even the title of a deceiver did not escape him. Often has he been told that he was an Arminian, though he professed to be a Calvinist; that he was an Universalist in disguise, etc., yet he was true to his principles. These may be seen in our confession of faith, agreeing with that republished by the Baptist churches assembled at London in the year 1689. He seldom meddled with the five polemical points; but when he did, he always avoided abusive language. The charge of Universalism brought against him was not altogether groundless; for though he was not an Universalist himself, he professed a great regard for many who were, and he would sometimes take their part against violent opposers, in order to inculcate moderation.

Mr. Edwards was born in Trevethin parish, Monmouthshire, in the Principality of Wales, on May 9, 1722, old style; and had his grammar learning in the same parish, at a village called Trosnant: afterwards he was placed in the Baptist seminary at Bristol, in Old England, at the time the President's chair was filled by the Rev. Mr. Foskett. He entered on the ministry in the sixteenth year of his age. After he had finished his academical studies, he went to Boston, in Lincolnshire, where he continued seven years, preaching the gospel to a small congregation in that town. From Boston he removed to Cork, in Ireland, where he was ordained June 1, 1750, and resided nine years. From Cork he returned to Great Britain, and preached about twelve months at Rye, in Sussex. While at Rye, the Rev. Dr. Gill, and other London ministers, in pursuance of letters which they received from this church, (Philadelphia,) urged him to pay you a visit. He complied, took his passage for America, arrived here May 23, 1761, and shortly afterwards became your pastor. He had the oversight of this church for many years; voluntarily resigned his office when he found the cause, which was so near and dear to his heart, sinking under his hands; but continued preaching to the people till they obtained another minister, the person who now addresses you, in the procuring of whom he was not inactive.

After this, Mr Edwards purchased a plantation in Newark, Newcastle county, state of Delaware, and moved thither with his family in the year 1772; he continued preaching the word of life and salvation in a number of vacant churches till the commencement of the American war. He then desisted and remained silent till after the termination of our revolutionary troubles, and a consequent reconciliation with this church: he then occasionally read lectures in Divinity in this city, and other parts of Pennsylvania; also in New Jersey, Delaware, and in New England; but for very particular and affecting reasons, could never be prevailed upon to resume the sacred character of a minister.

EARLY SUBSCRIPTIONS. 169

Our worthy friend departed this life, at Pencader, Newcastle county, Delaware state, on Wednesday the 28th of January last, in the seventy-third year of his age, and was buried, agreeably to his own desire, in the aisle of this meeting-house, with his first wife and their children; her maiden name was Mary Nun, originally of Cork, in Ireland, by whom he had several children, all of whom are dead, excepting two sons, William* and Joshua: the first, if alive, is a military officer in the British service; the other is now present with us, paying this last public tribute of filial affection to the memory of a fond and pious parent! Mr. Edwards's second wife was a Mrs. Singleton, of the state of Delaware, who is also dead, by whom he had no issue.

Several of Mr. Edwards's pieces have appeared in print; namely: (1.) A farewell discourse delivered at the Baptist meeting in Rye, on February 8, 1761, on Acts xx. 25, 26. This passed through two editions, 8vo. (2.) A sermon preached in the college of Philadelphia, at the ordination of the Rev. Samuel Jones, A. B., (now D. D.,) with a narrative of the manner in which the ordination was conducted, 8vo. (3.) The Customs of Primitive Churches, or a set of Propositions relative to the Name, Materials, Constitution, Power, Officers, Ordinances, etc., of a Church, to which are added, their Proofs from Scripture, and historical narratives of the manner in which most of them have been reduced to practice, 4to. This book was intended for the ministers of the Philadelphia Association, in hopes they would have improved on the plan, so that their joint productions might have introduced a full and unexceptionable treatise of church discipline. (4.) A New Year's Gift; a sermon preached in this house, January 1, 1770, from these words: This year thou shalt die; which passed through four editions. What gave rise to this discourse will probably be recollected for many years to come. (5.) Materials towards a History of the Baptists in Pennsylvania, both British and German, distinguished into First day—Keithian— Seventh day—Tuncker and Mennonist Baptists, 12mo. 1770. (6.) Materials towards a history of the Baptists in New Jersey, distinguished into First day—Seventh day— Tuncker and Rogerene Baptists, 12mo. 1792. The motto of both volumes is, Lo! a people that dwell alone, and shall not be reckoned among the nations. (7.) A Treatise on the Millennium. (8.) A Treatise on the New Heaven and New Earth: this was reprinted in London. (9.) Res Sacra, a translation from the Latin: the subject of this piece is an enumeration of all the acts of public worship which the New Testament styles offerings and sacrifices; among which, giving money for religious

---

* William graduated in the class of 1776, under President Manning, at the very early age of fourteen. An account of the Commencement for 1770, published in the PROVIDENCE GAZETTE, says: "The business of the day being concluded, and before the assembly broke up, a piece from Homer was pronounced by Master Billy Edwards, one of the Grammar School boys, not nine years old."

uses is one; and therefore, according to Mr. Edwards's opinion, is to be done in the places of public worship, and with equal devotion.

Besides what he gave to his intimate friends as tokens of personal regard, he has left behind him forty-two volumes of sermons, twelve sermons to a volume, all written in a large print hand: also about a dozen volumes in quarto, on special subjects; in some of which he was respondent; and therefore they may not contain his own real sentiments: these, with many other things, unite to show that he was no idler.

He used to recommend it to ministers to write their sermons at large, but not to read them in the pulpit; if they did, he advised the preacher to write a large, fair hand, and make himself so much master of his subject, that a glance might take in a whole page. Being a good classic, and a man of refinement, he was vexed with such discourses from the pulpit as deserved no attention, and much more to hear barbarisms; because, (as he used to say,) "They were arguments either of vanity or indolence, or both; for an American, with an English grammar in his hand, a learned friend at his elbow, and close application for six months, might make himself master of his mother tongue."

The Baptist churches are much indebted to Mr. Edwards. They will long remember the time and talents he devoted to their best interests both in Europe and America. Very far was he from being a selfish person; when the arrears of his salary, as pastor of this church, amounted to upwards of £372, and he was put in possession of a house by the church till the principal and interest should be paid, he resigned the house, and relinquished a great part of the debt, lest the church should be distressed.

The College of Rhode Island is also greatly beholden to him for his vigorous exertions at home and abroad, in raising money for that Institution, and for his particular activity in procuring its Charter; this he deemed the greatest service he ever did for the honor of the Baptist name. As one of its first sons, I cheerfully make this public testimony of his laudable and well-timed zeal.

In the first volume of his Materials, he proposed a plan for uniting all the Baptists on the continent in one body politic, by having the Association of Philadelphia (the centre) incorporated by charter, and by taking one delegate out of each Association into the corporation; but finding this impracticable at that time, he visited the churches, from New Hampshire to Georgia, gathering materials towards the history of the whole. Permit me to add, that this plan of union, as yet, has not succeeded.

Mr. Edwards was the moving cause of having the minutes of the Philadelphia Association printed, which he could not bring to bear for some years; and therefore, at his own expense, he printed tables, exhibiting the original and annual state of the associating churches

There was nothing uncommon in Mr. Edwards's person; but he possessed an original genius. By his travels in England, Ireland, and America, commixing with all sorts of people, and by close application to reading, he had attained a remarkable ease of behavior in company, and was furnished with something pleasant or informing to say on all occasions. His Greek Testament was his favorite companion, of which he was a complete master : his Hebrew Bible next ; but he was not so well versed in the Hebrew as in the Greek language ; however, he knew so much of both as authorized him to say, (as he often did,) that the Greek and Hebrew are the two eyes of a minister ; and that translations are but commentaries, because they vary in sense as commentators do. He preferred the ancient British version above any other version that he had read ; observing, that the idioms of the Welsh fitted those of the Hebrew and Greek like hand and glove. Perhaps, no other language corresponds so well with them, except the Arminian ; of which L'Enfant and Beausobre, in the preface to their new French translation, say " that the Arminian Testament is a literal version, without the alteration of phrases, or supplements to help out the sense."

Our aged and respectable friend is gone the way of all the earth ; but he lived to a good old age, and with the utmost composure closed his eyes on all the things of time. Though he is gone, this is not gone with him ; it remains with us, that the Baptist interest was ever uppermost with him, and that he labored more to promote it than to promote his own ; and this he did, because he believed it to be the interest of Christ above any in Christendom. His becoming a Baptist was the effect of previous examination and conviction, having been brought up in the Episcopal Church, for which church he retained a particular regard during his whole life.

ACCOUNT

OF THE

FINAL LOCATION.

1768–1770.

LOCATION.

SOON after the founding of the College, an important question arose in regard to the most eligible and desirable place for its permanent Location. This question divided for awhile the exertions of its friends, and created enemies, who, defeated in their plans, sought to establish a rival seminary of learning. The Rev. Morgan Edwards, in his brief historical sketch, written, probably, in the year 1771, thus narrates the progress of events:—

To the year 1769, this Seminary was for the most part friendless and moneyless, and therefore forlorn, in so much that a College edifice was hardly thought of. But Mr. Edwards making frequent remittances from England, some began to hope, and many to fear, that the Institution would come to something and stand. Then a building and the place of it were talked of; which opened a new scene of troubles and contentions that had well nigh ruined all. Warren was at first agreed upon as a proper situation, where a small wing was to be erected in the spring of 1770, and about £800 raised toward effecting it. But soon afterwards some who were unwilling it should be there, and some who were unwilling it should be anywhere, did so far agree as to lay aside the said Location, and propose that the county which should raise most money should have the College. Then the four counties went to work with subscriptions. That of Providence bid high for it; which made the county of Newport, which is jealous of Providence on account of trade, exert itself to the utmost. However, Providence obtained it; which so touched the jealousy and piqued the pride of the Islanders, as to make many of them enemies to the Institution itself. The same is too much the case with the other disappointed counties. Nevertheless, by the adventurous and resolute spirit of the Browns, and some other men of Providence, the edifice was begun in May, 1770, and roofed by the fall of the year. The next summer the inside was so far finished as to be fit for the reception of scholars.

The first mention of the Location of the College, to be found in the records of the Corporation, is as follows:—

The Hon. Josias Lyndon, Esq., the Hon. Stephen Hopkins, Esq., the Hon. Samuel Ward, Esq., the President, Nicholas Easton, Esq., Nicholas Brown, Esq., and the Rev. Russell Mason, were appointed a Committee to examine what place is most suitable to fix the College edifice upon, and to make report to the next annual meeting.

This was on the first Wednesday in September, 1768. At the next meeting of the Corporation, which was held in Newport, it was ordered:—

That the Secretary notify the members of the Corporation of their next annual meeting at Warren, six weeks successively previous to their meeting, by an advertisement in the Newport and Providence newspapers, and at which time it is proposed to take into consideration a proper place for the erecting a College edifice upon.

At the annual meeting, which was, for the first time, held in Warren, on the 6th of September, 1769, the Committee on Location thus report:—

We, the subscribers, being appointed to consider the most suitable place to erect the College edifice on, are of opinion that said edifice be placed in some part of the County of Bristol, and that a committee be appointed to point out such a place as shall be most convenient, and that may be had on the best terms.

James Manning,   Russell Mason,
Stephen Hopkins, Nicholas Brown.
Josias Lyndon.

Whereupon it was voted:—

That the foregoing report be accepted. Resolved, That Sylvester Childs, Esq., Mr. John Brown, Capt. John Warren, and Mr. Nathan Miller, be a committee to purchase materials, agree for a suitable place to erect the edifice on, to take a deed of the same in behalf of the Corporation, and to carry said building into execution as soon as they can, and that any three of them be a quorum; and that they be empowered to solicit and receive subscriptions. Resolved, That Archibald Campbell, Esq., be added to the committee for placing the College edifice.

FINAL LOCATION.

The church in Warren, anticipating, perhaps, the action of the Corporation, had already voted:—

That the meeting house in this town be, and is for the use of the Corporation and President at Commencement times, and oftener, if wanted by either, only so as not to interfere with Divine worship, provided, that the College edifice be founded and built in the county of Bristol; and that the parsonage house in said Warren be for the use of the President, so long as the President be our minister.

Soon after this meeting, the following citation appeared in the Providence and Newport papers:—

This is to notify the members of the Corporation of the College within this Colony, that application has been made, by the gentlemen of the county of Kent, setting forth, that they have opened a subscription for founding and endowing said College, on condition that the edifice be erected in the county of Kent; and desiring an opportunity of assigning their reasons to the Corporation, for a reconsideration of the vote at their last meeting, for erecting the edifice in the County of Bristol. This is therefore to desire all the members of the said Corporation, to meet at the Court House, in Newport, on Tuesday, the 14th of November next, at 10 o'clock, A M., to hear such propositions as shall be laid before them, relative to placing said edifice, and transacting any other necessary business: At which time and place, the gentlemen concerned in procuring subscriptions for the different places, are desired, by themselves, or their committees, to appear, present their several subscriptions, and offer their reasons in favor of the respective places. By order, THOMAS EYRES, *Secretary*.
October 18, 1769.

The dispute about the final Location of the College appears to have been confined thus far to the towns of Warren and East Greenwich. The first motion to have the College in Providence, came, so far as we can learn, from Mr. Moses Brown. In a letter to his brothers, dated Newport, October 23, 1769, he writes:—

I had, yesterday, on the road, a full conversation with Mr. Sessions on affairs of the College. His objections are such to Warren, that he says he cannot encourage it if set there, but if it could be erected at Providence, he would give one hundred dollars, and engage to procure one or two scholars from the country; and should there be a vacancy in the Corporation, he would, if desired again, accept a place therein, and, as a member, do all he could for the College. And when we consider the number of advantages which Providence has over Warren, I am much inclined to think that it is yet within our reach.

Governor Sessions, agreeably to Mr. Brown's suggestion, was made a Trustee of the College, in 1770. His views in general in regard to a suitable place for the location of a seminary of learning, which we find preserved on file, are original, to say the least, as well as entertaining and instructive. They were prepared, it appears, with a view to the special meeting of the Corporation about to be held in Newport:—

Since the late dispute with respect to the situation of a college, between the towns of Warren and Greenwich, people have naturally been engaged to take under consideration the several arguments that have been advanced; that is to say, the advantages and disadvantages that may necessarily attend the institution in each of those places, or any other place within this Colony:—and I believe the more this matter is debated and considered, the more every unprejudiced person will be convinced that it ought not to be erected in either of those towns. In the erecting of a college the natural as well as artificial advantages of its situation should be the primary object, and by all means ought to determine the limits of its establishment. Now, if it can be made to appear that any town in the Colony is happily so situated by nature and improved by art, as to render a seminary for learning and the instruction of youth, of greater public benefit than any other town, then I believe it must be granted by every candid person, that in that same spot it ought to be erected. Most people are tinctured with a bias in favor of the towns where they live, but the impartial will make up judgments from matters of fact, which ought in every controversy to be of the greatest weight. At present I shall waive nominating any town calculated for the aforesaid use, but shall content myself by observing what accommodations may be necessary for the increase of a useful and learned seminary.

In the first place it should be founded in a clear and wholesome air, not subject to epidemical disorders. 2d. It should be in a town where the principles of Christianity are openly professed and constantly practiced; where good orders are kept; where the morals of the inhabitants are not corrupted; where virtue of every kind is encouraged, and vice in every shape discountenanced; where civil and religious liberty is encouraged and defended; where the first day of the week is duly observed; where there are assemblies of the different denominations of Christians, who regularly meet on that day, among whom the doctrines of Christianity and morality are intelligibly and faithfully taught, so that the young collegians may join with them in the several modes of worship in which they have been educated, and which may be consonant with their dictates of conscience.

3d. It should be built in a town where the materials for building are good and cheap; where the workmen are skillful and experienced, and their demands moderate; where the necessaries of life, such as diet, fuel and clothing are good in kind, plentiful, and the price reasonable; where the trade of the town is so extensive and the consumption so considerable, that almost any American or country produce imported by land or water may find a good market, so that the parents or friends of the students may support them at college in the least burthensome manner. The town should be large and populous, so that upon commencements, or other public occasions, the large number of people that usually attend may be agreeably entertained and provided for. The conversation of the inhabitants should be civil, polite and courteous, so as to induce gentlemen from all the American colonies at times to take up their residence in the town, where they might be entertained, and gain an acquaintance with the seat of the muses, which would have a great tendency to promote its prosperity. The interior business of the town should consist of the various branches of trade and commerce, carried on by persons of every legal employment and character, so that the students may become thoroughly acquainted with men as well as books, that when their academical studies are finished, they may not be finished blockheads.

4th. In the infant state of a college, where there is but a small library, and probably no mathematical or philosophical apparatus, and no Professors in the learned sciences, it would certainly be the most desirable to have it fixed in a town where these disadvantages might in some measure be remedied. But can they be at Warren or Greenwich? Have they a town library as some other towns have? Are there a number of gentlemen there who have large private libraries of the best authors, and who would readily lend them for the public good, as there are in some of our towns? Is there any philosophical or mathematical apparatus, or are there any persons to show youth the use of the same, or to teach in any of the branches of these useful sciences? Are any of the youth disposed to apply to the study of physic;—where are they likely to make the greatest proficiency—in a town where there is scarce a regular physician, and probably no anatomical or physical authors, or where they abound with all of them? Are any of the students prosecuting the study of the law;—where can it be effected with advantage, but in some towns where there are eminent lawyers, good libraries of lawbooks, and where the practice is constantly kept up in the various courts that are held in the shire town of a large county?

5th. Another necessary accommodation for a college is its being seated in a town where there is an open, convenient and extensive communication both by land and water. Most people would choose to put children to college where they could send to them, visit them, hear from them, and have them brought home with the most ease and the least expense. A college should not be erected where the communication is liable to be interrupted by a hard frost, or high and contrary winds, for that would not only prevent the mutual intercourse which ought to be kept up, but might greatly affect the institution, by cutting off all supplies of fuel, provisions and other necessaries.

We of the present day can hardly realize the force of Gov. Sessions's last argument against Warren, or East Greenwich. How a "hard frost," or "high and contrary winds," could interrupt communication with the Institution, and thus cut off "all supplies of fuel, provisions and other necessaries," can be seen only by the aid of an uncommonly vivid imagination.

At the meeting of the Corporation held in Newport, November 14, 1769, agreeably to the citation, the following members were present, viz.: —

TRUSTEES: — The Chancellor, (Stephen Hopkins,) Hon. Samuel Ward, Esq., Hon. Josias Lyndon, Esq., Ephraim Bowen, Esq., Rev. Gardner Thurston, Rev. Samuel Winsor, Job Bennet, Esq., Nicholas Brown, Esq., Nicholas Easton, Esq., Mr. Joseph Brown, Mr. Edward Thurston, Jr., Mr. Peleg Barker, Rev. Joshua Clarke, Rev. John Maxson, Hon. Joseph Wanton, Jr., Esq., Thomas Green, Esq., Joseph Russell, Esq., Sylvester Child, Esq., John Tillinghast, Esq., James Honeyman, Esq., Mr. John Warren, Mr. John Tanner, Mr. John G. Wanton.—23. FELLOWS: — President Manning, Rev. Edward Upham, Mr. Jabez Bowen, Jr., Henry Ward, Esq., Dr. Thomas Eyres.—5.

The meeting was continued three days. Wednesday morning it was resolved: —

> To recede from the vote of the last meeting, to erect the College edifice in the County of Bristol.

In the afternoon it was voted: —

> That the business of the Corporation be *not* postponed to a distant adjournment.

FINAL LOCATION.

Thursday morning it was resolved:—

That the place for erecting the College edifice be now fixed. But that nevertheless the committee who shall be appointed to carry on the building do not proceed to procure any other materials for the same, excepting such as may be easily transported to any other place, should another hereafter be thought better, until further orders from this Corporation; if such orders be given before the first day of January next. And that in case any subscription be raised in the County of Newport, or any other county, equal or superior to any now offered, or that shall then be offered, and the Corporation be called in consequence thereof, that then the vote for fixing the edifice shall not be esteemed binding; but so that the Corporation may fix the edifice in another place in case they shall think proper. Voted, That the College edifice be at Providence. Voted, That the President, Job Bennet, Esq., Mr. John Brown, Mr. John Warren, and Mr. John Jenckes be a Committee to fix a suitable place for building the edifice.

The following is the memorial from Providence, which was presented to the Corporation on the second day of the meeting:—

To the Chancellor, President, and the other gentlemen of the Corporation for founding and endowing a College within the Colony of Rhode Island and Providence Plantations, convened at Newport, the 14th of November, 1769.

The Memorial of John Cole, Moses Brown and Howard Smith, in behalf of the principal inhabitants of the town of Providence, represents, That it will be most for the advantage of the College of which you have the government, that it be erected in the town of Providence, for the reasons we shall now offer:—

First, that it is absolutely necessary that there be money enough collected for erecting the College edifice and other buildings. Sensible of this, the inhabitants we represent generously subscribed eight hundred pounds, lawful money, upon principles of regard and esteem for so useful and necessary an Institution; but finding this sum, with the other subscriptions of the different towns in the Colony upon like disinterested principles, insufficient for the purpose, anxious that the Institution should be carried fully into execution, and finding the conditional subscription in other parts still insufficient, they were induced to begin one among themselves, which is so far completed as to amount to six thousand two hundred and sixty dollars, which, with the former unconditional subscription, is, as we apprehend, fully adequate for the purpose, with this single provision, that the College edifice be erected in the town of Providence, which will be a still further advantage to the Institution, as you must be sensible, from the following considerations:—

The principal benefit to a College is the number of its students, which may rationally be supposed to be greater at Providence than at either of the other places proposed. To show this, we beg leave to observe, that the intention of the Charter was to found a College or University upon the most catholic and free principles, agreeable to that invaluable principle upon which this Colony was founded, and yet it was necessary to put the government principally into the hands of one society, at whose expense it would be chiefly supported. This being the case, makes it a matter of the greatest necessity that the edifice be erected where youth of all denominations of Christians may resort and attend the public worship of the Supreme Being in the way their parents or their own consciences may direct, and thereby free, catholic and open principles be carried into practice in this noble Institution to the latest posterity; which, we apprehend, cannot be if the edifice be erected where there are only one or two societies. Providence has this advantage so essentially necessary to the freedom of the Institution, there being places of public worship of all the various denominations of Christians in America. Hence people differing in persuasion from the President and principal part of the governors, will be induced greatly to prefer Providence to either of the other places proposed. Instances of this have already happened, as has been verbally communicated.

The central situation of Providence, the free, cheap and easy communication between the northern colonies and the several towns in this and the neighboring governments, must be allowed to exceed either of the places proposed. To this may be added the greater plenty and cheapness of all kinds of provisions, fuel, clothing and cheapness of board.

The ease and convenience with which parents may visit their children to see their proficiency, as well as in case of sickness or accidents, where the best physicians and remedies are at hand, must afford a peculiar satisfaction to all tender parents who regard the comfort and health of their children as well as their education.

We have four public school houses, one of which* is calculated to contain four masters, including one for the languages, and one for the mathematics and other branches of learning preparatory to a liberal education;—as also a public library,† which, in the

* Commonly called the "Brick School House." It was erected in the year 1768, on Meeting street, where it now stands. At present it is occupied as a free school for colored children. In 1770, the upper part of it, which was owned by individuals, (the lower part only belonging to the town,) was occupied by the College, upon its removal to Providence. Where the other three houses were, to which the memorialists refer, we are unable to determine. They were, without doubt, small buildings, and occupied, if at all, by private scholars, as public schools were not introduced in Providence until nearly half a century later.

† "The Providence Library," says the late venerable John Howland, was first established in the year 1753, and placed in the Town House. On the night of December 24, 1758, the House, together with the greater portion of the Library, was destroyed by fire. In 1762, by great exertions on the part of several of the proprietors, it was reestablished, and books

infant state of the Seminary, must be very useful to all the scholars;—and particularly for those who may incline to the study of the law or physic, (either before the first or between that and their second degree,) we have not only large and useful libraries in both these faculties, but gentlemen of eminence who would be very useful in the prosecution of such studies.

The further usefulness and prosperity of the College depending upon the preservation of the freedom of the Institution, we are constrained from our respect to this distinguishing advantage over other institutions of like purpose, to mention this for their consideration, that the Charter leaves the tutors, Professors, and all other officers, (the President excepted,) at large to be of any denomination of Christians, no doubt with this good intent, that they should be of the various persuasions;—but can it be expected that gentlemen confirmed in their religious sentiments, and who value the attendance upon public worship in their own way, as their greatest privilege and blessing, will reside at the College where they cannot have this privilege, or that they will attend upon this duty under these circumstances on the same terms as they would if the College was placed where they might attend upon Divine worship agreeably to their own minds? We have two printing offices, which will much contribute to the emolument of the College, there being thus published a weekly collection of interesting intelligence, which not only tends to the enlargement of the minds of the youth, but which will give them early opportunities of displaying their genius upon any useful and speculative subjects, and which must excite in them an emulation to excel in their studies.

All the materials necessary to erect the buildings we have as plenty and as cheap, at least, as any of the other places; and we think we may claim more, better and cheaper workmen, and can, therefore, erect the edifice sooner, and with more convenience than it can be done in either of the other places proposed.

We conclude by observing, that it is necessary in the execution of all matters of a public nature, that the undertakers have a zeal for promoting it. This qualification, so requisite for the perfecting of the College institution, we are conscious we have, as has been made manifest by the people of Providence from the very beginning to this time, not only by their liberal subscriptions, amounting to more than all the money that has been subscribed within the Colony, but, every other mark of respect for the Institution and the favorers of it.

for it were imported from London. These, in 1764, were placed in the east end of the New Court House. In 1770, the Library Company offered the use of the books to the officers and students of the College, "until a Library could be procured for that respectable establishment."

From all which we are confident it must be the opinion of the Corporation, that it will be most for the benefit of the College to be placed in the town of Providence, and have, therefore, full assurance that you will order it to be erected there accordingly.

We are, Gentlemen, your most obedient servants,

JOHN COLE,
MOSES BROWN,
HAYWARD SMITH.

Newport, November 15th, 1769.

The argument of the memorialists based upon the "two printing offices," has at least the merit of novelty. Whether the "early opportunities of displaying their genius" thus afforded the students, would be recommended by the modern Professor of Rhetoric, or satisfactory to the learned readers of the Providence Journal, we will not attempt to say. John Milton's "Speech for the Liberty of Unlicensed Printing" may possibly have had something to do with the suggestion of this argument.

From the foregoing it appears that the inhabitants of Providence had subscribed for the College eight hundred pounds, lawful money, equal to two thousand six hundred and sixty-six dollars and sixty-seven cents; and in addition, six thousand two hundred and sixty dollars, on condition that the Institution should be located in their town. Their main reliance, however, it is evident was not their subscriptions, but their disinterested zeal, and the entire religious freedom which prevailed among them, so entirely in harmony with the spirit of the College Charter, and in accordance with the principles upon which the Colony had been founded. Providence contained at this time about four thousand inhabitants, and five hundred families. The religious complexion of these families, Dr. Stiles estimated to be as follows: "One hundred families real Baptists; one hundred and forty political Bapists and Nothingarians; one hundred and forty of Mr. Snow's congregation, two-thirds Baptists, one-third Presbyterians; sixty Pedobaptist Congregationalists; forty Episcopalians; twenty families Quakers, a few Sandemanians, and about twenty or forty

FINAL LOCATION. 185

persons Deists." Mr. Cole, it may be added, whose name appears at the head of the committee from Providence, was at this time Postmaster of the town, and a member of the General Assembly.

The following memorial from East Greenwich, appears to have been presented to the Corporation on the last day of the meeting:—

To the Honorable Members of the Corporation of the College, convened at Newport ye 16th day of November, 1769.

Your memorialists beg leave to represent that they conceive that the County of Kent is the most proper place for erecting said College edifice, for the following reasons:—

First: It is situated nearly in the centre of the Colony. This will more effectually accommodate each respective County than any other place that can be fixed upon, and therefore if the Corporation should ever petition for the aid and assistance of government, it is more probable they will unite in forwarding and promoting such grants.

Secondly: The local subscriptions of Kent united with the several general subscriptions, are sufficient to build and complete said College, and those temporary subscriptions will be found altogether insufficient for keeping up and perpetuating the Institutional expenses. It is therefore necessary to place it where the government will be most likely to take it under their consideration and immediate protection, that being, as we think, very justly urged by certain gentlemen before the General Assembly to be the most probable means of enlarging the donations from abroad. These advantages considered together, which will result to the Institution by its being fixed at Kent, we trust will be thought by the Corporation a matter of more consequence than large sums raised by local subscriptions.

Thirdly: As Institutions of this kind have been found by experience not to prosper in popular towns, we think the town of Providence too large now in its present condition; as it is a place well calculated for trade, it is altogether reasonable from thence to conclude that the growth and enlargement of it in a very few years will render it quite unsuitable for seminaries of learning to be placed in. The town of East Greenwich, on the contrary, is well situated as to pleasantness, surrounded with a large country abounding with every necessary supply to render the scholars comfortable, the town being large enough to accommodate the students effectually, and situated upon the post road, so that an easy correspondence might be had with any part of the continent,—there being likewise a post office in the town, and every other advantage as to communication with other governments that Providence can urge.

Furthermore, as it hath been strongly argued, this Institution is founded upon the most catholic plan, therefore they say they have singular advantages over Kent as to the accommodations of the different religious denominations. In answer to this we can say, in behalf of Kent, we have a Friends and a Baptist meeting house nearly situated to the place where the College is proposed to be set; also a meeting house of the Separates within three miles of East Greenwich, upon a good road, free from ferries; and it is highly probable, if the College is fixed at Kent, there will be a Church and Presbyterian meeting house built soon.

WILLIAM GREENE,
NATHANAEL GREENE, JR.,
PRESERVED PEARCE,
CHARLES HOLDEN, JR.,

Committee.

It will be observed that while Gov. Sessions urged that the Institution should be located in a large town, where the necessaries of life could be readily obtained, where trade was extensive, and where the students could have facilities for studying medicine and law, which reasons were further urged by the memorialists from Providence, who claimed all these advantages for the College, and, in addition, four school houses, a public library, and the two printing offices to which we have already referred, the memorialists from East Greenwich contended that Providence was too large a town for an institution of learning. Chief Justice Greene, whose name appears at the head of the committee, was, in 1778, elected Governor of Rhode Island, which office he held eight years. He was elected a Trustee of the College in 1785, as the successor of Gov. Hopkins, deceased. It seems hardly necessary to add that the second name upon the list is that of one who afterwards became the distinguished Major-General in the army of the Revolution, and who was now about to take his first lessons in public life as a member of the General Assembly from Coventry. Mr. Pierce, or Major Pierce, as he was called, was at this time a member of the Assembly from East Greenwich, while Mr. Holden, a few years later, represented the town of Warwick.

The increasing interest taken in the Location of the College by the various contending parties, and the general views and considerations which influenced their actions, may be readily inferred from a communication which appeared in the Newport Mercury of November 20, 1769. The writer presents his arguments with great force and clearness:—

I am informed, that the Corporation of the College, at their meeting here this week, came to a resolution, that six weeks should be allowed the inhabitants of the County of Newport to raise a subscription, and put in their claim for building it in this County.

The great benefits of a liberal education are so well known and allowed, that it is not necessary to enlarge upon this head; and I shall only mention, very briefly, some of the advantages which will accrue to this Institution, and to this town, from fixing the College here.

From the smallness of the College funds, it is certain that its principal and surest support must arise from the number of students; and whoever considers the number of inhabitants in Newport, the reputation of the island for health and pleasantness, the easy communication we have with all parts of this government, and with the western and southern colonies, and the cheapness with which pupils may be boarded, must confess that no place in this Colony is so proper to fix the College in, nor so likely to afford a sufficient number of students, as this town of Newport.

Besides, a considerable advantage may be derived to the Professors and students from the library* in this town. A library calculated for men of learning, consisting of a great number of well chosen books, upon all arts and sciences, as well as a very great number in the learned languages; the use of which may be allowed the pupils, under the discreet care of the President and tutors. This, in the infant state of the College, must be allowed to have great weight.

The advantages to this town and county from fixing the College here would be many. I have only time and room to mention two.

*The Redwood Library at this time was considered one of the largest and best of the public libraries in America, containing about fifteen hundred volumes of standard books. Of these the classical and theological books were the most valuable. The Rev. Dr. Stiles, who officiated as Librarian during the greater portion of his twenty years residence in Newport, is said to have derived largely from this collection his great and varied stores of learning. The Library owes its origin to a literary and philosophical society established in 1730, of which Bishop Berkeley was a prominent and active member. It was incorporated in 1747. receiving its name from Abraham Redwood, Esq., its most liberal benefactor. The building, a beautiful specimen of the Doric order, was completed in 1750. It has recently been greatly enlarged and improved. The Library now contains upwards of twelve thousand volumes, besides many choice pictures and works of art.

Supposing this College to flourish equally with those in Cambridge and New Haven, (which is highly probable,) it is evident, that the interest of the town and county would be greatly promoted by boarding and supplying so many persons coming from abroad, and spending their money among us; and by the employment they would necessarily give to the tradesmen and artificers.

But this, though very great, is by no means equal to the advantage the inhabitants of this town would receive from the opportunity of bringing up their children in the useful arts, with very little expense. For instance, the people in this town might board their sons at home, and bring them up at College, with the small additional expense of twelve dollars a year, and less than half so much for books and necessary instruments. And after they had finished their education, which might be at sixteen, seventeen, or eighteen years of age, according to their forwardness, they would then not only be qualified for any of the learned professions, but if the inclination of their parents or their own genius should lead them, they would be much better qualified for the compting-house, the shop, the sea, or for any trade; and in case of misfortunes, which might render them incapable of bodily labor, they would find, in their learning, resources to support themselves reputably.

Every thinking man will readily suggest to himself other advantages, which cannot be added here. And, as a friend to learning, to the Institution, and to this town, I earnestly recommend the consideration of this matter to the inhabitants; and doubt not but a regard to their own interest, and the interest of their posterity, will induce them to exert their ancient spirit, and raise such a subscription as will be sufficient to establish the College here.

I am, Sir, your constant reader and humble servant,   A. B.

In the Diary of Dr. Stiles, under the date of January 3, 1770, about six weeks after the publication of the foregoing communication, is an important entry pertaining to this subject:—

Dr. Eyres visited me this morning to discourse about the place of the Baptist College. He tells me that Providence has subscribed £3,090, lawful money; of which about £2,200 is truly conditioned that the College edifice be erected there; but, of the £800 they had before subscribed unconditionally, they had the subscription papers for £300 in their own hands, and refused to deliver them,—holding in this manner about £500 conditioned. Dr. Eyres said that the Newport subscription was about $9000, (£2700,) but said they did not choose to mention the amount exactly, nor how much conditionally. The case is this: Mr. Redwood and some others have said they would give largely, in case it was here; but that Providence, by artifice and stratagem, would eventually get it there; and yet, would not subscribe, but will undoubtedly give liberally. So there is a real uncertainty. They are endeavoring to get a meeting of the Corporation, but Providence opposes it. Mr. Manning, the President, is for Providence.

The main contest from this time onward, appears to have been between Providence and Newport. The following is the preamble to the subscription book in the latter place, which we copy from an original paper. Among the largest subscribers was Abraham Redwood, Esq., founder of the "Redwood Library." He afterwards subscribed, says the Providence GAZETTE, five hundred pounds sterling towards a second college or university, which it was proposed to erect in Newport:—

Whereas the Governor of the English Colony of Rhode Island and Providence Plantations, in New England in America, by an act passed at their session in February, 1764, incorporated certain persons, therein mentioned, into a body politic, and granted them full power, and ample authority, to found and endow a College or University in said Colony: And whereas a sufficient number of the persons so appointed have qualified themselves agreeable to said act; and are taking the most probable measures for forming so useful and honorable an Institution, which will necessarily be attended with considerable expense: We, therefore, the subscribers, sensible that nothing hath a greater tendency to adorn human nature, and to promote the true interest and happiness of mankind, than useful literature, and that the fixing the College in the town of Newport will be attended with the greatest advantages to the said Institution, do, in consideration thereof, each one for himself, promise and engage to give, and accordingly to pay unto Job Bennet, Esq., treasurer of the said Corporation, or his successor in said office, or order, the several sums affixed to our names, respectively, to be applied primarily to the building a suitable College edifice, and the surplus in such a manner as the said Corporation shall think most conducive to answer the ends of their Institution.

Provided, nevertheless, and this subscription is made upon express condition, that the College edifice be erected in the said town of Newport; otherwise the same shall be void.

The preamble to the Providence subscription book, was the same, except the paragraph at the close, which reads thus:—

Part of the following subscriptions to the amount of eight hundred pounds lawful money, is absolute let the College be built anywhere in the Colony; the remaining sum is on condition that the College edifice be erected in the town of Providence.

The progress of this important contest, which waxed warmer and warmer till its close, may best be learned from some documents on file, and which we present in the order of date. The first is a letter to Mr. Moses Brown, from one of the Judges in the County of Kent, declaring his preference for Providence over Newport. The writer signs himself, "A man who raised just 2604 pounds of tobacco." We thus learn that the staple product of Virginia was cultivated quite extensively in Rhode Island at this period: —

WARWICK, December 1st, 1769.

SIR: — We are informed that the County of Newport are raising money by subscription, in order to over-bid you and place the College at Newport. If that should be really the case, I believe there may be one thousand dollars raised in the town of Warwick, if the old town at the east end can be properly animated, which I think is not hard for Providence to do. The reasons that are given at the west part of the town are too many to enumerate. But this is one that governs me: — Newport and Kings Counties admit the necessity of a college, and appear almost agreed that our County is the most suitable place in the Colony, (at least the major part by far say it is their opinion); — Now, if it is necessary to build a college, and our County is the most proper place, if the County of Newport and Kings County would subscribe no more than their real proportion would be to build such an edifice in the Colony, upon condition it was placed in the County of Kent, the spot where they say it ought to be built; — if they would do that, it is in their power to give it to us. But if they refuse to do that, they say themselves it is right and put us out of the question. I am sure Warwick in general will do their endeavors to promote Providence before Newport, and so will East Greenwich, save them that always were bitter against you.

Your humble servant, etc.

A communication, signed by Gov. Hopkins and the Browns, is addressed to the Town Councils of Glocester and Scituate, urging their coöperation in securing for Providence the Location of the College, on the ground that it would be the means of bringing "great quantities of money into the place," and thus of increasing the value of all estates in the country for which the town was a market. How much the vast increase of wealth and influence in Providence and the towns adjoining, during the century past, may be owing to the College, we leave for our readers to decide:—

PROVIDENCE, December 8th, 1769.

GENTLEMEN :—We make no doubt but you must have heard before now that a college is about to be built somewhere in this Colony, and that a vote hath been obtained that it shall be erected in the town of Providence, on condition that there be more money subscribed toward building it in this County than in the County of Newport, on the first day of January next; but if that County's subscription be then highest, the matter is to be reconsidered, and the College will without any question be removed thither. When we consider that the building the College here will be a means of bringing great quantities of money into the place, and thereby of greatly increasing the markets for all kinds of the country's produce; and, consequently, of increasing the value of all estates to which this town is a market; and also that it will much promote the weight and influence of this northern part of the Colony in the scale of government in all times to come, we think every man that hath an estate in this County who duly weighs these advantages, with many others that will naturally occur to his mind, must, for the bettering of his own private interest, as well as for the public good, become a contributor to the College here, rather than it should be removed from hence.

The inhabitants of this town, fully sensible of these advantages, have subscribed very freely, and indeed very largely on condition the College be erected here, as you will see by the enclosed lists; and we have taken the freedom to address ourselves to you, hoping you will exert yourselves in this interesting affair as well by your own benefactions as by procuring subscriptions among your neighbors, and be good enough to let some one of us know before the first of January what is done.

We are the more zealous in this matter as we have certain intelligence that the people in Newport, who are become sensible of the importance of this matter, are very diligently using every method in their power to carry the prize from us, and as the few remaining days of this month is the whole time in which we can work to any purpose, we hope none will slumber or sleep. We think ourselves in this matter wholly engaged for the public good; and therefore hope to be borne with when we beg of you and all our neighbors, to seriously consult their own interest and pursue it with unremitted zeal.

We are, very respectfully, your assured friends,
STEPHEN HOPKINS,
NICHOLAS BROWN & Co.

N. B. Any materials useful about the building will be received on account of the subscription.

From a letter addressed by Messrs. Nicholas, John and Moses Brown, to their brother Joseph, then in Newport, it appears that the Providence subscriptions at the close of the year 1769, had reached the sum of £3,424, or $11,413.33. At the last meeting of the Corporation, they had voted, with a proviso, to fix the College at Providence; and a part of the manœuvering on the part of the worthy President and his zealous coadjutors, the Browns, Hopkins, Jenckes, etc., seems to have been to prevent another meeting. An allusion in the letter to Morgan Edwards, shows that he was kept duly informed of the progress of events:—

PROVIDENCE, December 30th, 1769.

BROTHER JOSEPH:—This evening we compared our subscriptions, and found the whole, including unconditional subscriptions and Whipple's land, three thousand four hundred and twenty-four pounds lawful money, reckoning the land as we wrote, viz., four dollars; but Mr. Jenckes, upon recollection of the goodness of the land, says it could not be bought for that, it being a very good tract; from what we otherwise hear, it may be worth six dollars, but five at least, which will make forty-three dollars and fourteen cents more. This sum of three thousand four hundred and twenty-four pounds, is one-hundred and sixty more than when you went away. We hope you will be able to stop the meeting being called, as it will put us to much trouble in getting further subscriptions, which to raise very considerable will be difficult. However, you may, if you can stop the meeting there, add fifty pounds lawful money, which our M. B. will see paid, but make no use of this unless you find it absolutely necessary, as he proposes to make use of it on the spot where to set the edifice, if it comes here, as it certainly will be necessary then. If the calling of the meeting, etc., be given up, perhaps it may not be best for the committee to come up till the beginning of next week, or until we get the plan secured, but this is a matter submitted to you. Please inquire whether there is any vessel in from Philadelphia, to know about the cedar, and whether a vessel be going to York through which I may convey my packet to Mr. Edwards, with the intelligence about the College. If you have any time, inquire how the H matter stands, etc., etc. Yours,

NICHOLAS BROWN & Co.

Our compliments, etc., to Col. Wanton.

As an illustration of the zeal and energy of the Providence people, we copy from the GAZETTE:—

FINAL LOCATION.

WHEREAS, it is now determined that the College about to be built in this Colony shall be erected in the town of Providence;—and as many gentlemen have been so generous to this very useful Institution as to become benefactors to it, and have subscribed considerable sums for carrying it on;—therefore we, in behalf of the Committee for providing materials and overseeing the work, hereby give public notice to all who are already subscribers, and to those whose beneficent minds may incline them to become such, to give us, as soon as they possibly can, as the season is far advanced, an account of such materials fit for the building as they would choose to furnish in lieu of their subscriptions; all which will be very gratefully received by their very humble servants,

STEPHEN HOPKINS,
JOHN BROWN.

Providence, January 12, 1770.

The friends of the College, in Newport, now redoubled their exertions, and soon raised by subscription a sum larger than had been raised in Providence. Notwithstanding the exertions of the Browns to "stop the meeting," a citation for the Corporation to assemble at Warren, was published in the papers of the day:—

WHEREAS, the County of Newport hath raised a larger sum than any that hath yet been offered to the Corporation of the College in this Colony, to be paid to the Treasurer upon condition that the College edifice be erected in the town of Newport: This is therefore to notify members of the said Corporation to meet together at Warren, on Wednesday, the 7th day of February next, at ten o'clock in the forenoon, to take into consideration any proposals that may be made for placing the College edifice, and to transact any other necessary business. At which time and place, the persons concerned in procuring subscriptions are desired to attend, by themselves or their committees.

JOSHUA BABCOCK,
THOMAS EYRES,   } *Fellows.*
HENRY WARD,

On the Monday previous to the final meeting of the Corporation, on this exciting question of Location, the following printed handbill was circulated all over the town:—

PROVIDENCE, Monday, February 5, 1770.

The inhabitants of this town and County are desired to meet at the Court House, this afternoon, at two o'clock, to hear and consider of some effectual plan for establishing the College here.

As this is a matter of the greatest consequence, and the Corporation is to meet on Wednesday next, a general attendance is earnestly requested.

In accordance with this call, a large number of the inhabitants assembled at the place designated, and the Hon. Stephen Hopkins, Esq., was chosen Moderator. John Cole and Moses Brown were continued a committee to lay the subscriptions before the Corporation, and the following gentlemen were added thereto, viz.: Hon. Darius Sessions, John Andrews, Joseph Nash, David Harris, Daniel Tillinghast, John Jenckes, Amos Atwell, Joseph Bucklin, Jeremiah Whipple, Esq., and Knight Dexter.

The following spirited letter from President Manning, addressed to "Mr. Nicholas Brown, in Providence," shows that he was a skillful tactician, and that he used his great influence in favor of Providence. It gives an animated view of the nature of the contest, and of the earnest determination of the parties at issue:—

SIR:—The time is now at the doors when it will be determined whether Providence or Newport shall have the College; and as I think that the former is the fittest place for it, I would give you a gentle hint, that you may be prepared in the best manner to stand your ground I expect Newport will exceed you in the largeness of their subscriptions, for they gave bonds last week for three thousand two hundred pounds, and had not rendered the subscriptions from Block Island, South County, nor from the eastern shore, in all which places there was money subscribed for Newport. Neither can I tell whether the Warren subscriptions were contained in that bond. Besides, they were still subscribing in Newport. Redwood has at last subscribed his five hundred pounds sterling, etc. Now, as I am a friend to the College, and think your place the best for its settlement, I would advise you to get every farthing you can subscribed. But if, when you come to compare notes, you should fall behind them, they will make a great noise if you take in your unconditional subscriptions and plead your agreements for materials, etc., etc.

Now, as I think you have the good of the College at heart more than they, it will stand you in hand to demonstrate this in the clearest light; and this you can do by proffering to build the College yourselves, without even taking their unconditional subscriptions in Newport. Say nothing about the President's house; but consult how large a house you can build, and finish two stories with your own money, in as short a time as you possibly can accomplish it, and engage to finish the rest as fast as wanted; for here you know you may have your own time, since boarding can always be had in town, and many will always choose to board there. So that the President can help you here to sufficient time to pick up money from other parts, or even enable you to finish the other rooms with the rent of those that are finished. Two advantages will result from such a proposal. First, you will throw your unconditional subscription out of their light, and give it its full weight in favor of Providence. Secondly, you can here make all the advantage to yourselves, from lying handy to the materials; the whole weight of this will be thrown directly into your scale, and you can promise just as much more than they can, as the edifice can be erected cheaper with you than them, and as you will prosecute it with more spirit and do the bargaining and work with less expense. Here, too, you will have the advantage of them, as you have made out bills of everything, and bespoke the materials and workmen, and can push it immediately into execution. You might reason a month on these advantages and not make some dull souls see the force of it, so well as you can demonstrate it in this way in ten minutes. And I think you will be equally as safe in this way as in giving bonds, and it must weigh much with the gentlemen who have the welfare of the College at heart. Besides, you will take them here at unawares. Give up the other subscriptions in the Colony to the Corporation, and let them dispose of them as they think best, and it will be a wonder if they don't find out by next May session, that there will be necessity of a house for the President, and very probably will lay it out that way. If you fall in with this proposal, it will be proper for four, five or six of you to oblige yourselves to the performance under a proper penalty. What I have heretofore said is to secure you against the first onset; but if you should be driven from your post, the next thing is to secure your retreat. If, therefore, your vote should be receded from, your hopes must lie in dividing the members between the four places; for it would be imprudent to fight Newport singly. It is possible you may have address enough to get Providence and Greenwich highest here, for the Newport members who favor you at heart, may vote for Warren and Kent without having their hopes torn down; and if the contest should finally fall between you and Kent, you may guess how it would terminate by the last meeting; and in this way I think all your members in Newport who favor Providence, may vote for it without incurring any damage;—I mean at your final issue. I think you could beat Kent with greater ease than Warren or Newport; but of this you are the best judge, being an experienced soldier.

There will many attend the meeting from Newport, for their spirits are very high in the cause. Proposals, too, will doubtless be made for an accommodation half way. But how great a sum will be offered for this is uncertain as yet. But should I persist in spilling ink and spoiling paper longer you may be weary of reading my jargon, and be solicitous to know my name, which at present I choose not to reveal. But am, to all intents,

      Your Friend, if not Humble Servant.

N. B. You will excuse the omission of date, as it is quite unnecessary.

The great and final meeting of the Corporation on the question of Location, was held in the Baptist Meeting House, in Warren, on the 7th of February, 1770. Thirty-five members were present, as follows:—

FELLOWS:—The President, Rev. Edward Upham, Rev. Samuel Stillman, Thomas Eyres, Joshua Babcock, Henry Ward, and Jabez Bowen, Jr.—7. TRUSTEES:—The Chancellor, (Hon. Stephen Hopkins,) Hon. Samuel Ward, Hon. Josias Lyndon, Hon. Joseph Wanton, Jr., Rev. Russell Mason, Rev. Gardner Thurston, Rev. Samuel Winsor, Rev. Isaac Backus, Rev. John Maxson, Nicholas Brown, Joseph Brown, William Brown, Joseph Russell, George Hazard, Peleg Barker, John Warren, Nathan Spear, Nicholas Cooke, Sylvester Child, John Tanner, Thomas Greene, Ephraim Bowen, Edward Thurston, Jr., John G. Wanton, Daniel Jenckes, Job Bennet, James Helme, and Darius Sessions.—28.

Says Manning, in a letter to his friend, Hezekiah Smith:—

The dispute lasted from Wednesday last, ten o'clock A. M., until the same hour on Thursday, P. M. The matter was debated with great spirit, and before a crowded audience. The vote was put, Recede or Not. It went Not, by twenty-one against fourteen. You asked me in your last whether it had not raised a party in the government. I answer, no; but it has warmed up the old one something considerable. I was greatly censured by people in Newport, for not joining to call a meeting about the 1st of January, and a great noise was made because I would not act contrary to an express vote of the Corporation, at the meeting on the 10th of November. But at our last meeting, the house gave me liberty to attempt a vindication of my conduct, and after hearing me through the matter, they came to a vote, *nemine contradicente*, that they saw no reason why I should be blamed in this matter, and that they approved of my conduct. In the course of the debates there was sometimes undue warmth, but, upon the whole, it subsided, and all parties seemed much more unanimous than I expected, in after business. Many of the gentlemen of Newport said they had had a fair hearing, and had lost it; but their friendship to the College remained, and they would keep their places, pay their money, and forward to their utmost the design. * * * * * * Messrs. Stillman and Spear were up from Boston, and Backus from Middleborough. It is said that the eight ministers at the Corporation meeting, were all for Providence. This I shall not assert, however. But I believe the Baptist Society in general, are not dissatisfied at the determination.

Returning now to the meeting—The following is the Memorial presented from East Greenwich:—

To the Honorable, the Board of Trustees and Fellows of Rhode Island College, present at Warren, this 7th day of February, A. D., 1770:—

We, the subscribers, being appointed a committee, by a large number of the inhabitants of the County of Kent, who were latterly concerned in a local subscription relative to erecting the College edifice, to wait upon this Honorable Board, and make such representations as comport with the real sentiments of our said constituents, do beg liberty humbly to revive our claim to the College, by continuing said subscription. For that, whereas, it yet remaineth a matter of uncertainty in what County the College edifice will be erected, and as the present contest subsisteth between the respectable Counties of Newport and Providence, and each of those Counties being actuated by a laudable design of promoting the future interest and prosperity of the Institution, we humbly conceive they will both, upon mature deliberation, resign their claims, and concede that it shall be placed in some other part of the Colony. The reasons which induced us to form this conclusion are many, some of which, with the greatest deference, we shall take the freedom to offer. We are fully convinced that no seat of literature in America, has ever arrived to any considerable degree of eminence and utility, but what hath received large donations from Great Britain. The institution of science, therefore, which fails of that source, must remain in infancy and obscurity. But, if the very creators of such an Institution, cease to patronize and protect it, surely strangers will have no powerful motive left to encourage or assist it; consequently it must be placed in such a part of that Colony which gave it being, as best to commode the whole; otherwise, the greater part being disappointed, will abandon it to its own impotence. But, were a College to be erected in Newport or Providence, it must fail of countenance from the Colony, both being situated so far from its centre.

It is likewise well known that Newport and Providence have ever been the capital sources of party in this Colony; and consequently the Institution must annually be subject to the attacks of one party or the other if placed in either, and so, liable to continual vicissitude, if not demolition itself; to avoid which, the wisdom and prudence of Newport and Providence will both be exerted. Should these contending parties mutually resign it to another place, it will be sufficiently removed from any domestic obstructions of this sort; and both being sincere friends to the Institution, they have it in their power, as both would be happily agreed in the same thing, by their concurrent influence to cause it to enjoy the favorable smiles of this Colony, and therefore of Great Britain, if by any means Great Britain would be excited to shelter and defend it. By this method, it will undoubtedly arrive to such a degree of superior grandeur as to command veneration and esteem from all its neighbors;—a consideration of the last importance. It is also a general maxim and a very true one, that such is the fluctuating disposition of youth, that a considerable degree of retirement is very requisite in order to acquire any great proficiency in literary pursuits. The subjects of science are so numerous, the prospects so extensive and the researches so deep, that a young mind entangled by the more captivating allurements of life, will never soar to those sublime heights, as to answer the noble ends of a college education. But is there sufficient retirement in Newport or Providence? With the greatest modesty it may be asserted, that every populous town affords all those opportunities for avocation and amusement, that a luxuriant imagination can aspire after. Moreover, as the enlargement of useful knowledge and promotion of religion are the principal ends for which all seats of learning ought to be established; so that place in a Colony which is best situated for these purposes, is most eligible to be fixed upon; but that convenient place which is nearest the centre of the Colony is best adapted therefor, from whence its salutary influences may equally be extended to every part.

Money, after all, must be had, and we doubt not (should we be indulged with an opportunity of dispersing our subscriptions through the whole Colony) but we could procure a sum almost equal (if not superior) to any that has been already presented; for the encouragements we have received from every County in this Colony, (Bristol only excepted,) are very promising. Our own subscribers are reänimated with a desire to promote the good of the Institution, even to such a degree that many of them would largely add to their subscriptions. Many there are likewise in the same County that have not yet subscribed, who express their warmest desires to become subscribers, should Kent ever have another opportunity to exert its generosity.

Upon the whole, Sirs, the encouragement and assurance we had afforded us by some of the principal gentlemen in Providence, joined by many in Newport, were originally the moving cause that excited us to propagate a local subscription. Had we been in the least apprised that either Newport or Providence would ever lay a claim, we should have immediately desisted from such an undertaking. And for the same reason we make not the least pretension, while the contest remains between them; but should they now relinquish their claims, we cordially hope and fully expect that the same benevolence that first befriended us will again be exerted, and by that means that you, gentlemen, will grant us indulgence; in the mean time, reserving to ourselves the advantage of all further necessary suggestions.

JAMES M. VARNUM,
NATHANAEL GREENE, JR.,
CHARLES HOLDEN, JR.,
ADAM MAXWELL

In the specious reasoning and well expressed language of the foregoing memorial, we recognize the skillful pen of him whose name appears at the head of the signatures, and who had but recently graduated at the Institution. He afterwards established himself in East Greenwich, as a lawyer, where he rapidly rose to distinction in his profession, his extraordinary talents procuring for him an extensive practice.

The Providence memorial is without signatures. It appears to be mainly a complaint against Newport:—

To the Chancellor, President, and other gentlemen of the Corporation, for founding and endowing a College within the Colony of Rhode Island and Providence Plantations, convened at Warren, the 7th of February, 1770.

The Memorial of the subscribers in behalf of the inhabitants of the town of Providence, etc., represent:—

That, notwithstanding the great majority of voices at the last meeting for erecting the College edifice in Providence, we were unexpectedly surprised with an advertisement in the Newport Mercury of the 15th ult., which came to hand not till the 23d, for calling your present; and particularly at the assertion therein that the County of Newport hath raised a larger sum than any that hath yet been offered to the Corporation of the College. The facts, (though certified by three of the respectable branch of the Fellows,) we apprehend, and think we can clearly show, were not at that time so,—as before that date, the subscription for Providence amounted to three thousand and ninety pounds, for which a bond was duly sealed and executed, payable to the Corporation upon express condition that the edifice be erected in the town of Providence. Besides, there was a deed of land amounting to one hundred and seventy-one pounds more, made to the Corporation on the like conditions, and delivered into the Treasurer's hands Whereas, the subscription for Newport at that time was not even pretended to contain a sum exceeding two thousand six hundred pounds, including Mr. Redwood's generous donation of five hundred pounds sterling, and Mr. Easton's of the —— acres of land, valued at —— pounds, both which, as we are well advised, were not executed until long since.

We consider this pretence of having a greater sum, not only as doing injustice to us, but really injuring the valuable Institution itself; and whether it be not imposing on this respectable Corporation to call them together at this difficult season, and upon so slight a pretence, we leave to your determination. We apprehend had Doct. Babcock known every circumstance attending the matter, he would have refused signing an advertisement, as some others of the Fellows did; and more especially as a major part of the members of both branches have actually been consulted upon the same matter. Upon this, you are now met and advised that it was not necessary, or that there was not that especial emergency required by the charter to induce the calling of a meeting;—and this must evidently appear upon reflection on the vote previous, in regard to placing the College at Providence—wherein the 1st of January last was the longest time allowed for the Corporation to counter order the vote for placing and carrying on the building of the edifice. In consequence, thereof, it became necessary, before the Corporation could legally be by charter convened at the said 1st of January, that the notification be given twenty days before.

This, every member present must be sensible, could be the only true construction of the vote;—but compliance with this request could not be, as there was a still further reasonable injunction laid on those who should require a meeting, viz.:—That they should first raise a subscription equal or superior to any before, or that should then be offered to the Corporation; which was so far from being the case, that, at that junction, there was scarcely any sum subscribed, as we have been well informed: or, at least, not a sufficiency to make even a pretence for application.

This being the case, it appears evident that some gentlemen of Newport, even from their first perceiving the College was like to be erected at Providence, were induced by their unreasonable aversion to every emolument of Providence, to do that which the good of the Institution itself could not have induced them to do.

The Chancellor, Gov. Hopkins, thus states the case of the two rival claimants, presenting in a clear and concise manner the controversy from the beginning:—

The zeal and spirit of the people here, more than at Newport, for promoting the College is certainly most evident:—First, by the unconditional subscription, which, in Providence, was nearly double to that in Newport; whereas, if their zeal for the Institution had been equal to ours, the number of the people and their abilities compared, their subscriptions ought to have been much more than double to ours. And, as this was coolly transacted in both towns, before any kind of strife was begun or emulation was raised about the place where the College should be erected, it is the strongest proof imaginable that the ardor of the Providence people, while no by-ends biased, was infinitely greater than that of the gentlemen of Newport.

Again, if we consider the conditional subscriptions of both towns, we shall evidently find the same superiority in the Providence people's zeal for the College, for this subscription was set on foot and principally filled in Providence, from the very laudable motive of promoting the Institution and putting it in a condition that the

College edifice might be erected somewhere, and not with the least view of circumventing any other place, as some have too uncharitably represented.

We first with grief observed the very little progress of the unconditional subscriptions, after the Commencement, and that there was very little hope, within any reasonable time, that a sum in any degree equal to erect a building, which might be tolerably decent and useful, would be obtained. This being also observed by the late ingenious Mr. Campbell, induced him to promote a conditional subscription in King's County and Kent, which, as soon as we had knowledge of, we also encouraged, in hopes that it might have answered the purpose arrived at. But when that had been fully tried, we found that the sum likely to be raised by it would be altogether inadequate to the design in hand.

Things being in this situation, and after divers consultations had about it, we at length determined to open a conditional subscription in Providence, which filled beyond our warmest expectations, and seemed to promise that a College edifice might be soon erected. This subscription we offered to the Corporation at their meeting in November last, and they then approved of it.

But some gentlemen of Newport perceiving a probability that the College might be erected at Providence, were moved by their unreasonable enmity to that town, to do that which the good of the Institution itself could never have induced them to do. They accordingly desired that time might be allowed to the people of the town and county of Newport, to see if they could not raise a larger sum for the College than any that was then offered; and accordingly the time they asked was allowed, so long as not to delay carrying on the building longer than the 1st of January past. Yet, although they have taken near double the time allowed them, and the generous and public-spirited Mr. Abraham Redwood hath given more than a fifth part of the whole sum, yet their whole subscription doth not exceed ours, from which it is quite plain that their zeal for the College, even when whetted by their aversion to Providence, has fallen greatly short of ours in the conditional subscriptions also.

From all which reasons, with some others too invidious to mention, but which will naturally occur to all who are acquainted with the proceedings in this matter, it must be very evident the College edifice will be much sooner built and the Institution much more encouraged and supported, if it be left in the care of the people at Providence, who have from the beginning shown so much zeal and attention to it, than if it should be removed and put under the care of those people of Newport, who have shown so little regard for it in any other light than in making a matter of contention about it.

Gov. Hopkins alludes to the "unreasonable enmity" of the people of Newport to Providence. It is evident, from the early history of the College, that there had long existed an unpleasant state of feeling between the two towns, and that this feeling entered into the contest respecting the final Location. The famous Ward and Hopkins controversy, commenced in 1755, and continued for thirteen years, with all the bitterness of the most partizan strife, served, doubtless, to stimulate the zeal and passions of the parties now contending for the College. Gov. Ward, who was an active member of the Corporation, represented the people in the southern counties of the State, while the voters in the northern counties supported his more successful rival. The reasons "too invidious to mention," which determined the Corporation to locate the College in Providence, cannot now, perhaps, be definitely known. The decided preference of the President, as indicated in his letter to Nicholas Brown, doubtless had great influence with his friends, and especially with those of his own religious denomination. "The eight Baptist ministers" who were present at the final meeting, viz., Russell Mason, of Swansea, Gardner Thurston, of Newport, Samuel Winsor, of Providence, Isaac Backus, of Middleborough, John Maxson, of Newport, Edward Upham, of Newport, Samuel Stillman, of Boston, and the President, "were all for Providence," as appears from Manning's letter to Smith, to which we have already referred. This is worthy of special notice, because three of these ministers belonged in Newport. It is a matter of regret that, among the documents on file, there should be no memorial or paper giving more particularly the views of the Newport people in regard to this vexed question of Location.

The following account of the final meeting of the Corporation, was written by Mr. Moses Brown, on Thursday, February 9th, being the next day after the adjournment:—

WARREN, February 7th, 1770.

The Corporation met, swore in George Hazard, and chose Darius Sessions as one of the Trustees. The gentlemen from Newport kept off from laying before the Corporation their reasons for asking a remove until after "candle light," and after we insisted that they should lay these subscriptions on the table. They handed a bond from sundry persons for £3,100, lawful money, being £10 more than our former bond. We insisted then that as that did not amount to so much as ours, with the land, that they should give up their claim, agreeable to promise, but after some debate adjourned at about ten o'clock in the evening, to nine in the morning. When met, they presented two papers, but insisted on knowing the amount of our subscription; which we had before told them was to the amount of the bond, and the unconditional subscription of £800 besides. At length Henry Ward took me out towards the door, and declared there was all they had, and that they had no orders to go any higher, and proposed if we would not lodge any further subscriptions, they would lay down their papers, and proceed to trial accordingly. We agreed. William Ellery then lodged the papers before held, and would not deliver to anybody, being one bond for £150, lawful money, and one other for £300. When we came to foot our sums we had about £226 more than they, ours being £4,175. Hereupon they delayed by many evasions proceeding to business, and insisted for adjournment to dinner; after which the meeting met, and after waiting three-quarters of an hour, Samuel Ward, Doct. Babcock, Henry Ward, etc., came in and presented a security for their unconditional subscription, which they said was £508 14s., and a bond for £500 more. All this time no subscriptions were produced, they alleging they had left them at home, and none were finally produced. By this last bond they exceeded our subscriptions, land and all, about £385. Whereupon, it was thought advisable to lodge the last subscription we had to be made use of upon this occasion, amounting to £226, with the Treasurer, not caring to trust the vote, they being so much ahead, especially as they insisted that our unconditional subscriptions ought not to tell anything; whereby they would be about £1,235 over us. This reduced it, so that reckoning the whole of their sum and the whole of ours, they were £158 more than we. We presented a calculation in the arguments, of the amount of the building if at Newport more than if at Providence, amounting to £574 lawful money, which we insisted should be added to ours, leaving a balance in our favor of £415. The vote came on after long litigation and argument, both Kent and Warren putting in their claims. The vote was, "Repeal, or Not;" it passed in the negative by twenty-one to fourteen votes. So the merits of the Newport arguments made by Henry Ward, etc., replied to by self, Gov. Hopkins, etc.

February 9th, 1770.
MOSES BROWN.

The reader will not fail to observe how active and zealous was the author of the foregoing account, in securing for Providence the final Location of the College. He was never a member of the Corporation, although elected a Trustee, and repeatedly urged by his associates to accept the position. In 1773, at the age of thirty-five, he became a member of the Society of Friends. Withdrawing, at this time, from the bustle of commerce and trade, he sought that retirement to which his feeble health invited, and which was more congenial to his early-formed taste for intellectual pursuits. Here on his beautiful estate in the environs of Providence, in rural quiet and simplicity, he spent a long and useful life, aiding by his judicious counsels and abundant wealth in the promotion of intelligence, piety, and freedom among men. One of his latest acts was to collect and arrange a file of papers relating to the early history of the College, for which the Corporation passed a vote of thanks at their annual meeting in 1833. To these papers we have been specially indebted for this documentary chapter of our work.

One of the results of the Location of the College at Providence, was a movement on the part of the defeated contestants to establish a college in Newport. Dr. Stiles states in his Diary, February 23, 1770: "Mr. Ellery came to discourse about the charter of another college, on the plan of equal liberty to Congregationalists, Baptists, Episcopalians and Quakers." And, April 1, 1770, he adds: "There is now pending before the General Assembly of Rhode Island, a petition for a charter for a college here in Newport, since the first Rhode Island College is fixed at Providence. College enthusiasm!" The application was favorably received in the House, and a charter was granted by a vote of twenty majority. In the Senate, however, it was either rejected or indefinitely postponed. The following action of the Corporation, at a special meeting held in Warren, on the 2d of April, is the probable explanation of the defeat of this project:—

RESOLVED, That this Corporation make application to the General Assembly, and pray that a petition now before the Assembly for granting a charter to another college, be rejected.

VOTED, That Chancellor Hopkins, President Manning, Hon. Darius Sessions, Rev. Samuel Stillman, Col. Job Bennet, and Secretary Eyres, be a Committee to draw up a memorial to the General Assembly, pursuant to the preceding vote."

The said memorial, or remonstrance, having been prepared and approved, it was—

VOTED, That the Hon. Stephen Hopkins, Hon. Samuel Ward, Hon. Darius Sessions, Job Bennet, Moses Brown, Daniel Jenckes, John Tillinghast, Oliver Arnold, and James Mitchell Varnum, be, and they or the major part of them are, appointed a Committee to be present at the General Assembly, and enforce the said remonstrance.

This remonstrance we are happy to be able to present to our readers. It is an exceedingly valuable document, inasmuch as it settles points in regard to the origin of the College, which have sometimes been disputed, giving the reasons why it was founded, stating clearly, in connection with previous narratives or accounts, by whom it was founded, when it was founded, and where the plan originated:—

To the Honorable the General Assembly of the Colony of Rhode Island, to sit at Newport, on the first Wednesday in May, 1770.

The Remonstrance of the Trustees and Fellows of the Corporation of the College in said Colony humbly sheweth:—

That the several denominations of Baptists residing in most of the British Northern Colonies, are, taken collectively, a considerable body of Christians; and these people having of late years taken into consideration that there are no public seminaries for the education of youth, where those of that persuasion can enjoy equal freedom and advantages with others, were thereby induced to form a resolution to erect a college, and institute a seminary for the education of youth somewhere in North America, to be effected chiefly, if not altogether, by the application, and at the cost and expense of the Baptist churches.

That having proceeded thus far, they began to inquire after the most convenient place for executing their design; and on deliberation, finding that the Colony of Rhode Island was first settled chiefly by Baptists, that a very considerable part of its inhabitants are still of that persuasion, and that a universal toleration of liberty of conscience hath from the beginning taken place in it, they had great hope it would prove a proper place for founding a College, and in which the infant Institution might be most encouraged; and accordingly they applied to the General Assembly of said Colony for a charter of incorporation, which they thankfully acknowledge was freely granted them.

That in forming this charter care was taken, that, notwithstanding the burden of expense was to fall chiefly on the Baptists, yet, no other Christian society should be excluded from the benefits of it; and accordingly, a sufficient number from each of the principal of them were taken in to be Trustees and Fellows in the Corporation, as might be able to take care of, and guard their interest in it, in all time to come. And the youth of every denomination of Christians are fully entitled to, and actually enjoy equal advantages in every respect, as the Baptists themselves, without being burdened with any religious test or complaint whatsoever.

That, since granting the charter aforesaid, several considerable men among the Baptists have taken great pains, as well in Europe as in America, to solicit benefactions for endowing said College, and have collected considerable sums for that purpose; and many others of the same Society, have become very large contributors towards the expense of erecting the College edifice.

All this being known and understood, we confess our surprise at the thoughts of those, who are pleased to look upon this as a very contracted plan; and this surprise becomes a real concern on being informed that a petition hath been set on foot, and subscribed by a great number of persons, praying the General Assembly to grant another charter for instituting a college within the said Colony, different and separate from that already granted and established, and pretended to be on a more liberal and catholic plan; and our concern is increased to a real anxiety, on perceiving the General Assembly entertained the said petition with some kind of approbation.

Permit us, therefore, to remonstrate, that, as we had firm reliance on the lasting faith and credit of the Legislative Body of the Colony of Rhode Island, that faith and credit hath by us as a Corporation, been asserted, and pledged, in most parts of England, and Ireland, and in many parts of America; and, on that foundation large sums of money have been given, and more subscribed towards this Institution. That, should a charter be granted for erecting another corporation of the same kind in this Colony, all those who have been benefactors to this will think themselves deluded, and deceived; notwithstanding, we have acted under the faith of the government; and all those that hereafter might become benefactors, will be discouraged, and hindered. That the granting of our Charter, being for erecting and endowing a College in the Colony Rhode Island, must, rationally, and justly, be considered as exclusive of any other college being erected within it.

Therefore, your Remonstrants humbly pray, that you would be pleased to countenance and encourage the present Institution and College in this Colony; and not permit, or suffer, any other to be set up and established to rival and ruin it.

And your Remonstrants will ever pray.

A manuscript in the hand-writing of the Rev. Dr. Stiles, purporting to be the charter for another college which the petitioners failed to secure from the General Assembly, is, we understand, in the possession of Dr. David King, of Newport.

Allusion has been made to the file of papers relating to the Location of the College, preserved by Mr. Brown. Our readers will peruse with pleasure the following interesting letter respecting them from the venerable philanthropist, written, it may be added, when in his ninety-fifth year. We publish it entire, although the latter part belongs rather to the history of Roger Williams and the First Baptist Church:—

PROVIDENCE, 25th of 5th month, 1833.

ESTEEMED FRIEND, FRANCIS WAYLAND:—

Agreeable to encouragement given thee when at my house, I herewith send thee a file of papers containing copies of originals, which I preserved at the time of their transactions, respecting the removal of the College from Warren, after the Corporation had set the Location of it at liberty from Warren, where it had been concluded to place it, and where the first Commencement was held. I had them copied soon after we conversed about them, when thou seemed, as I thought, to have a choice for them. I wish they were better done, but such as they are, after comparing, I leave them at thy disposal. I presume there are no other writings or copies that contain the same, or so full accounts of the progress, labor, and I may say, anxiety which occured on the subject at and about that business. When the fixing of the College edifice here was firmly settled, rather than at Warren, Newport, or East Greenwich, which all claimed the preference, our house, then composed of four brothers, viz., Nicholas, Joseph, John and Moses Brown, concluded to take charge of building the necessary buildings, purchasing land for the same, etc. At that time, gardens and buildings were to be purchased and removed, besides the site for the College; for we then knew the lot from Main street to the neck road on the east was the original home lot of our ancestor, Chad Brown, of whom we had the tradition that he was the first Baptist ELDER in Providence. Doct. Edwards when collecting materials for the history of the Baptists here, and examining all the elderly people he could find here, on which business I accompanied him, was informed that Chad Brown was the first ELDER, although Roger Williams being a preacher before he came here, was a preacher and continued it here for some time. Richard Scott says he was with him in the Baptist way three or four months, when Roger left them, and went in a way of seeking. Roger's testimony respecting Chad Brown, I have under his own hand, in a plea of his before the Court of the four New England Colonies, saying, " Chad Brown a wise and godly soul, (now with God,) with myself brought the first twelve and the after comers to a oneness by arbitration." Chad and his wife were buried in their own lot near the northwest corner of the now town house, and had a large square monument of granite over them, till by the request of the town to widen that street, their bones were taken up and interred in the North Burying Ground, and head and foot stones were erected over them by the town. I saw their remains when taken up. His son John Brown (his eldest) was also a preacher, but not an elder, and was the father of James Brown, long a Baptist elder until his death. Thou may see by all this our family had an interest in promoting the Institution now called Brown University, besides the purchase of the name by my worthy nephew Nicholas; and I hope it may continue useful to posterity and retain the liberal principles of the founders of the State and Institution. Here I may mention that Chad Brown was one, who, in 1640, as a committee-man of the town, reported a plan for the peace of the then town and the establishment of liberty of conscience, and who, in 1643, was appointed to mediate between the Governor of Massachusetts and the settlers in Warwick. These, however, are matters of history, the first in "Simplicity's Defence," the other in "Hazard's State Papers." Possibly thou may not have known he also appears on our town records to have been a surveyor of land in early times.

When I began this letter, I had nothing more in view than a few lines to introduce the copies of the minutes, letters, etc., respecting the removal of the College here, but as I have gone further, I conclude to give thee my own knowledge respecting the changes and alterations in the Baptist church in this town, which was in very early time known by the name of Six Principle Baptist. In proof of this, I have an original letter of Elder Pardon Tillinghast, signed by himself, Gregory Dexter and Aaron Davis, in behalf of the brethren of the church in this town, dated in the 5th month, then July, 1681; and this is confirmed by Elder Tillinghast's deed of the Baptist meeting house and lot to the church. Their views are explained by the passage in Hebrews. 6: 2. "laying on of hands." This was the agreed practice in 1732. at a special meeting of the ministers and elders at Elder Brown's, signed by ten ministers and fourteen other members on this subject.* Also I have a pamphlet written by James Manning, to a minister desiring his views on the subject, as appears by comparing the manuscript with other writings of his. I mention these facts, not that I consider them otherwise than historical facts, which in the modern history of the society are contrarily represented to support the present ruling writers. Indeed, the difference is marked between the old church of the Baptists in this town and after Elder Manning, a worthy godly

---

*This letter is published in MANNING AND BROWN UNIVERSITY, page 154.

man and an excellent preacher, whom I attended in his last moments, and whom we all loved. In divers respects, however, his practice was different from the church here, and much difficulty was in the meeting upon the subject of singing and the contribution box, these being never before known. To give a vote of the church in favor of the first more particularly, the female members were called upon to vote, though not usual, and my mother and sister attended accordingly. This occasioned a serious division with the old deacons and members. Elder Manning having powerful aid from some of the old members, and being prudent enough to keep himself out of the strife, preserved the affection most generally of the church. At length a separation was concluded on, the meeting house and lot were sold, the money was divided, the meeting house in Johnston on the plain was built, and also the house now called the First Baptist. My brother Joseph was a member of the church, and when he brought his contribution box to my mother's pew, I now remember my reluctant feelings for him, our family and the church never having seen the like in our meeting, though often in the Congregational and other churches. And though much has been said of Roger Williams as being a Baptist,* yet in his book of "Hireling Ministry none of Christs," printed in 1652, on page 8, he says, "Jesus Christ never made bargains with his messengers or pastors;" and on page 14, he says, "Universities as to the ministry of Jesus Christ are none of his institutions; the title scholar appointed to the ministry is a sacrilegious and thievish title, robbing all believers and saints." These views of Roger I believe are little known by Baptists, as the book is out of print. Were these and

---

* Mr. Williams, according to Winthrop, was baptized, with eleven others, on or previous to March 16, 1639, thus constituting the First Baptist Church of Providence. He may, therefore, with propriety be regarded as the founder of the Baptist denomination in America. It is not, however, contended that he thereby assumed the pastoral relation, as he did not long retain his connection with the church. He had doubts, it appears, in regard to the validity of his baptism, in consequence of the absence of "a visible succession" of authorized administrators of the rite. His views too in regard to the Christian ministry underwent a change, as is indicated in "The Hireling Ministry," to which Mr. Brown refers. His mission was to establish in the New World a government on the principles of entire civil and religious freedom. He was, however, a man of genuine piety, and he adhered through life, so far as we may judge from his published writings, to the sentiments which he advocated in his earlier years. He believed in CONVERSION AS A CONDITION OF CHURCH MEMBERSHIP; this is evident from all his controversial works. In regard to what is known as the distinguishing sentiment or doctrine of Baptists at the present day, viz., BAPTISM BY IMMERSION, he thus writes, more than ten years after the founding of the Providence church: "I BELIEVE THEIR PRACTICE" (referring to the Baptists at Seekonk) "COMES NEARER THE FIRST PRACTICE OF OUR GREAT FOUNDER, CHRIST JESUS, THAN OTHER PRACTICES OF RELIGION DO." See Biographical Introduction to the Writings of Roger Williams, in the Publications of the Narragansett Club, pp. 35-8.

27

other things more fully known, I presume he would not stand in the Society as an example. His early and latter writings are very different, showing his instability as to his claims of religion. If any information to thee should be derived, my object in relating them with Christian freedom will be answered.

I conclude and remain thy friend,
MOSES BROWN.

SUBSCRIPTIONS

OBTAINED IN

SOUTH CAROLINA AND GEORGIA,

BY

REV. HEZEKIAH SMITH.

———

1769–1770.

EARLY SUBSCRIPTIONS.

WHEN the Corporation met at Warren, in 1769, to decide upon the Location of the College, they voted :—

That the Rev. Hezekiah Smith be desired by this Corporation to solicit benefactions for their use, in the southern and western provinces on this continent, or elsewhere, and that suitable credentials be given him for that purpose, by the Chancellor and President, with the seal of the Corporation annexed.

The following is a copy of the "credentials," from a rough draft on file :—

By the Honorable Stephen Hopkins, Esquire, Chancellor, and the Reverend James Manning, President of the College or University in the English Colony of Rhode Island and Providence Plantations in New England in America. To the Rev. Hezekiah Smith, of Haverhill, in America, GREETING:

WHEREAS, the General Assembly of the Colony aforesaid, taking into consideration the many advantages derived to society from educating youth in useful literature, did grant a charter incorporating the persons therein named into a body politic, and empowering them to erect, found and endow a College or University in said Colony: And whereas, the said Corporation from the smallness of their funds, have found themselves under a necessity of requesting the generous assistance of the friends of religion and learning without the said Colony: And whereas, the said Corporation at their annual meeting at Warren, on the first Wednesday in September, instant, being well convinced of your affection and regard to the said College or University, and of your integrity and ability, did unanimously appoint and request you to solicit and receive benefactions in any part of America for the benefit of the said Institution. These are, therefore, to empower and authorize you, the said Hezekiah Smith, to receive all such charitable donations as shall be made in America, for the erecting, founding or endowing the said College or University; assuring the donors that their benefactions shall be religiously applied by the said Corporation to the purposes they shall direct.

In testimony whereof, we, the said Chancellor and President, have hereunto set our hands and caused the seal of the said College or University, to be affixed [L. s] this —— day of September, in the ninth year of the reign of His Most Sacred Majesty George the Third, by the Grace of God, King of Great Britain, etc., Anno Domini, 1769.

By order, STEPHEN HOPKINS, *Chancellor*,
JAMES MANNING, *President.*

Mr. Smith, whose relations with President Manning from early manhood down to the close of life, were those of the greatest intimacy, was born on Long Island, New York, on the 21st of April, 1738. In his youth he became pious, and at the age of nineteen he joined the Baptist church in New York city, then under the pastoral care of the Rev. John Gano. He commenced his classical education at Hopewell, entered the College of New Jersey at Princeton, and graduated in the year 1762, in the same class with Manning. After leaving college, he travelled through the southern provinces, in order to recover his health, which had become somewhat impaired by a too close confinement to his studies. In a single year he made a tour of four thousand miles, and laid the foundations of lasting friendship with the Rev. Messrs. Hart, Pelot, and others of a kindred spirit, whose intercourse and correspondence proved a delight to him in his riper years. At Charleston, South Carolina, he was ordained by several ministers of the Charleston Association. The Baptist church in Haverhill, Massachusetts, gathered through Mr. Smith's instrumentality, was organized on the 9th of May, 1765, and he was chosen the pastor. Here he labored as an earnest and effective preacher of the Gospel, during a period of forty years, or until his death, which occurred January 22, 1805. For a fuller account of him, together with extracts from his correspondence while serving as a chaplain in the American army, see MANNING AND BROWN UNIVERSITY, pages 135–142.

Mr. Smith left home on his important mission for the College, October 2, 1769, and returned June 8, 1770, having been absent from the people of his charge a little over eight months. He travelled extensively through South Carolina, and Georgia, preaching as he had opportunity, and prosecuting with energy and zeal the work to which he had been appointed. His fervid piety, his eloquence, his commanding presence and genial manners, gained him hearers, and rendered him everywhere a welcome guest. He succeeded in obtaining subscriptions to the amount of £3,710 17s 6d, South Carolina currency, of which he collected £2,523 8s 6d, as appears from his final accounts, which were submitted to the Corporation at their annual meeting in 1770. In a letter to Dr. Stennet, dated June 7, 1770, President Manning writes:—" Our brother, Hezekiah Smith, of Haverhill, has collected and obtained subscriptions in South Carolina and Georgia, from whence he has just returned, to the amount of about £500 sterling." From Mr. Smith's diary we select for publication that portion relating to this journey:—

OCTOBER 1, in the evening preached at Mr. Thomas Osgood's, from Psalms, 45:13. Monday, 2, went to Medfield and lodged for the night at Nathan Plimpton's. Tuesday, 3, went to the Rev. Mr. Manning's, in Warren. Wednesday, 4, went to Col. Bennet's, in Newport. Thursday, 5, in the evening preached in Mr, Thurston's pulpit, from Genesis, 45 : 4. Friday, 6, went to Jonas Belton's, in Groton. Saturday, 7, went to Rev. Jonathan Todd's, in East Gilford ; tarried there till Monday. Sunday, 8, preached two sermons in Mr. Todd's pulpit ; in the forenoon from Genesis, 45 : 4, and in the afternoon from Titus, 3 : 7. The assembly were much affected, and I can but think and hope that God blessed these discourses to some souls. Monday, 9, went to Mr. Nichols's, in Stratford. Tuesday, 10, went to East Chester, to Mr. Butler's. Wednesday, 11, went to New York. Thursday, 12, embarked for Charleston, on board the sloop Sally, Capt. Peter Schermerhorn. Arrived at Charleston, South Carolina, on the 20th ; went to Rev. Oliver Hart's, and there tarried. Sunday, 22, preached two sermons from Genesis, 45 : 4, and Romans, 5 : 1. Monday, 23, Tuesday, 24, Wednesday, 25, and Thursday, 26, solicited donations for Rhode Island

College. Thursday evening, preached a sermon in Rev. Oliver Hart's pulpit, from Zechariah, 3 : 9. Friday, 27, and Saturday, 28, solicited donations for the College. Sunday, 29, preached two sermons, from Mark, 8 : 38, and Habakkuk, 11 : 16. Monday, 30, and so through the whole week solicited donations. Tuesday and Wednesday evenings, preached from 1st Corinthians, 9 : 24, and Genesis, 24 : 49. Sunday, NOVEMBER 5, in the evening preached in the Rev. Mr. Hart's pulpit, from Solomon's Song, 5 : 2. Monday, 6, to Saturday, 11, solicited benefactions for Rhode Island College, though Thursday evening preached from Isaiah, 23 : 1. Sunday, 12, preached three sermons in Rev. Mr. Hart's pulpit, from Romans, 12 : 2, John, 18 : 4, and Revelations, 14 : 15. Monday, 13, and all the week, solicited benefactions for the College. Thursday evening preached a sermon from John, 3 : 14. Saturday, 18, married Nathan Ellis and Mary Drysdel, both of Charleston. Sunday, 19, preached two sermons in Rev. Mr. Hart's pulpit, from Deuteronomy, 32 : 2, and Acts, 13 : 41, and heard Mr. Done preach one. Monday, 20, collected money for the College. Tuesday, 21, went to Mr. Bee's, at Pon Pon. Wednesday, 22, went to Mr. Jordon's, at the Saltcatchers. Thursday, 23, went to Rev. Francis Pelot's, in Eutaw. Friday, 24, went to Mr. Screven's in Georgia, and tarried there till Monday, when I went to Mr. Stirk's. Tuesday, 28, went to Savannah, to Mr. Bolton's. Wednesday, 29, went to Rev. Mr. Osgood's, at Midway. Tarried there two days. Friday, DECEMBER 1, went to Sunsbury to Rev. Mr. Edmund's, and preached in the evening from "So run that ye may obtain." Saturday, 2, went to Rev. Mr. Osgood's. Sunday, 3, preached two sermons in Rev. Mr. Osgood's pulpit, from Deuteronomy, 32 : 2, and Romans, 5 : 1. Monday, 4, detained at Mr. Osgood's on account of rain. Tuesday, 5, went to Savannah and lodged at Rev. Mr. Zubly's. Wednesday, 6, solicited benefactions for the College. Thursday, 7, went to Benjamin Stirk's, at Leeds, in St. Matthews, and preached from John, 5 : 10. After sermon, baptized Elizabeth Williams, of Gosham, in St. Matthews Parish. Friday, 8, and Saturday, 9, solicited benefactions for the College. Met with good success. Sunday 10, preached one sermon in Rev. Mr. Zubly's pulpit, from Song of Solomon, 5 : 16. He preached in the afternoon. Monday, Tuesday and Wednesday, solicited benefactions for the College, though on Tuesday afternoon went to Rev. Mr. Whitefield's Orphan House, where I delivered two discourses,—one the same evening I got there, from Romans 5 : 1, and the other the next morning, from Deuteronomy 32 : 2. After the morning service, breakfasted and took a view of the buildings and the wings which were then building, and then returned to Savannah. Wednesday, 13, had the pleasure to sup with Mr. Whitefield, and also to breakfast with him the next morning, at James Habersham's. Thursday, 14, went on boat to go to Hilton Head, and lodged the night on Bloody Point. Friday, 15, got to the island Hilton Head and went to Capt. Samuel Green's. Lodged there till morning. Saturday, preached on the muster field to the company assembled for exercise, from Ephesians 6 : 11. Then the Captain exercised his company, after which I got £100, Southern currency, subscribed for the Rhode Island College. Sabbath, 17, preached from Luke 14 : 18. Monday, December 18, went to Rev. Mr. Pelot's, at Eutaw. Tuesday, 19, collected for the College. Wednesday, 20, set out to Charleston; the first night lodged at Mr. Main's, in Indian Land, the second night at Mr. Branford's, at Pon Pon; Friday evening, reached Charleston. Saturday, September 23, among my friends and in my study. Sunday, 24, preached three times; first from Isaiah 40 : 1, then from Zechariah 9 : 12, and in the evening from Luke 13 : 25. Monday, 25, in the forenoon, heard Mr. Caldwell preach, and in the evening married John Gowrlay and Elizabeth River. Tuesday, 26, to Saturday, 30, collecting for the College, visiting and studying, though Thursday evening I preached from Hebrews 12 : 25. Sabbath, 31, preached three sermons, from Revelation 5 : 12, and John 6 : 37.

Monday, JANUARY 1, preached from Hebrews 13 : 5. Tuesday, January 2, collecting for the College. Wednesday, January 3, visiting and getting bills of exchange. Thursday, 4, and Friday, 5, engaged in collecting for our College. Saturday, 6, in Mr. Hart's study. Sunday, January 7, preached three sermons in Mr. Hart's pulpit; two from 2d Peter 1 : 10; and one from Revelation 12 : 11. Monday, 8, and through the week, endeavoring to collect. Sunday, 14, preached two sermons; one in the forenoon, from Leviticus 25 : 9, and in the evening from Matthew 5 : 20. Mr. Done preached in the afternoon. Monday, 15, endeavoring to collect for the College as opportunity served, though Friday evening preached in Mr. Hart's meeting house, from Isaiah 30 : 10. Saturday, 20, in Mr. Hart's study. Sunday, 21, preached in the forenoon from Jeremiah 31 : 20. Mr. Done preached in the afternoon, and I in the evening from Jeremiah 3 : 22. Monday, 22, to Wednesday, 24, waiting a passage to St. Helena. Thursday, 25 to Saturday, 27, among my friends and in my study. Sabbath, 28, preached in the forenoon from Job 23 : 3. Heard Mr. Matthews preach in the afternoon, and I preached in the evening from Proverbs 3 : 17. Monday, 29, went to Pon Pon, to Mr. Ezekiel Brandford's. Tuesday, 30, to the Horse Shoe, to Mr. Josiah Pendervise's; lodged there two nights. Thursday, FEBRUARY 1. went to Mr. Bulline's, in Stono. Friday, February 2, went to Charleston. Succeeded very well in collecting for the College this week. Saturday, February 3, at Mr. Hart's. Sunday, 4, heard Mr. Matthews and Mr. Hart preach during the day, and I preached in the evening from John 7 : 37. Monday, February 5, met in Association with the churches of South Carolina, in Charleston, and in the evening preached from Job 23 : 4. Tuesday, February 6, met in Association. Wednesday, 7, collecting for the College. Thursday, 8, preached Mr. Edmund Matthew's ordination sermon, from 2d Timothy 2 : 24,—" Apt to teach." Friday and Saturday, detained in town by bad weather. Sunday, February 11, in the evening preached from 1st Corinthians 2 : 14. Monday, 12, in Charleston. Tuesday, 13, left Charleston and got to Georgetown on Thursday. Friday, February 16, preached at Mr. Flin's, the tavern, from Isaiah 28 : 16. Saturday, 17, left Georgetown and went in the evening to Mr. Wetherspoon's, on Lynch Creek. Sunday, 18th, went to Tilman Cobb's, on Pedee. Monday, 19, went to Peter Cobb's Tuesday, 20, went to Capt. George Hick's. Wednesday, 21, to Mr. Pegue's. Thursday, 22, collecting. Friday, 23, preached at Mr. Bedingfield's, from "So run that ye may obtain." Saturday, 24, went to Rev. Mr. Bedgegood's; preached for him on Lord's day, from Romans 5 : 1. Monday and Tuesday at Mr. Bedgegood's. Wednesday, 28, went to Arthur Hart's, and preached from Hebrews 12 : 1.

Thursday, MARCH 1, went to Malachi Murfee's. Friday, 2, went to Benjamin James's, in Cashway. Saturday, 3, Preached in Cashway meeting house from "Is all well." Sabbath, 4, preached in Casway from 2d Corinthians, 13 : 11. Monday, 5, went to Capt. Thompson's, at Swift Creek; to get to his house from Peter Cobb's, I went by the Devil's Wood Yard and over Belly Ache Run. Tuesday, March 6, I went to John Perkins, after crossing Lynch's Creek. Wednesday, 7, went to Capt. Cartee's, in Camden, or at the Pine Tree. Thursday, March 8, went to Capt. Howard's at the High Hills of Santee. The Santee is formed by the Wateree and the Congree. The Congree is formed by Saluda and Broad rivers The Catawba river runs into the Wateree. Friday, 9, I preached at Dr Howard's, from "What think ye of Christ?" A blessed appearance of religion was among the people. I trust God is about to gather in some of his elect in this place. Saturday, 10, preached from Acts 16 : 30. Sabbath, 11, preached two sermons, one from 1st Corinthians 9 : 24, and another from Romans 6 : 23. Monday, March 12, went to Mr. Sumpter's, on the Santee, and preached the same evening from John 3 : 7 Tuesday, 13, went to Monk's Corner. Wednesday, 14, went to Charleston. Thursday, 15, to Saturday, 17, in town among my friends, and settling my business for my departure. Sabbath, 18, preached from Malachi 4 : 2. Monday, Tuesday and Wednesday, collecting for the College. Thursday evening, preached from Hosea 10 : 12. Friday and Saturday, in town and in my study. Sunday 25, preached three sermons from 1st Timothy 1 : 8, Ezekiel 17 : 23, and Revelation 20 : 12. Monday and Tuesday, in the country collecting Wednesday and Thursday, in town and on James Island. Thursday evening I preached in Mr. Hart's pulpit from Luke 5 : 31. Friday and Saturday, collecting. Sunday, APRIL 1, preached three sermons, from Luke 10 : 30–36, Hebrews 2 : 3, and Revelation 1 : 7. Monday and Tuesday, collecting. Wednesday, preached in the Baptist meeting house on James Island, from Titus 3 : 7. Thursday, collecting, and in the evening preached from Solomon's Song 1 : 5. Friday and Saturday, collecting, visiting and in my study. Sunday, 8, heard Mr. Stirk and Mr. Hart preach during the day, and I preached in the evening from Proverbs 28 : 26.

EARLY SUBSCRIPTIONS.

Monday and Tuesday, collecting and visiting. Wednesday, visiting and in my study. Thursday, 12, in the evening preached from Ezekiel 36 : 26. Friday and Saturday, getting ready for my departure, and in the study preparing for the Lord's day. Sunday, 15, preached in the forenoon in Mr. Hart's pulpit from Ecclesiastes 11 : 1, and in the evening from Revelation 2 : 17. Monday, 16, preparing to embark for New York. Tuesday, 17, in the evening preached my farewell sermon from 2d Corinthians 13 : 11. Wednesday, Thursday and Friday, in town waiting a passage. Saturday, 21, left Charleston, and lay in the Rebellion Road until Sunday, 22 ; went over the Bar and arrived at New York the last day of April. Found my friends well. Tuesday, May 1 preached in the evening in Mr. Gano's pulpit from Ezekiel 36 : 26. Wednesday, in New York. Thursday, went to New Jersey. Friday, visited my parents. Saturday, back to New York. Sunday, 6, preached three times in Mr. Gano's pulpit, from Jeremiah 31 : 20, Jeremiah 3 : 22, and Revelation 1 : 7. Monday, Tuesday and Wednesday, among my friends. Thursday evening, preached in Mr. Gano's pulpit from Ezekiel 47 : 8. Friday, went to New Jersey. Saturday, at my brothers. Sunday, 13, preached three times at Lion's Farms, from Jeremiah 3 : 22, Jeremiah 31 : 20, and Revelation 1 : 7. Monday, at Connecticut Farms. Tuesday, preached at Short Hill, from John 15 : 10. After service went to my father's, where I preached Thursday evening from John 7 : 37. Friday, at my father's. Saturday, 19, went to Newark. Sunday, 20, preached three sermons in the Lion's Farms Baptist meeting house, from Malachi 4 : 2, and Philemon 1 : 21. Monday, 21, preached at the Scotch Plains Baptist meeting house, from 1st Corinthians 9 : 24. Tuesday, 22, went to New York. Wednesday, 23, preached in Mr. Gano's church in the evening, from Revelation 2 : 17. Thursday, went to my brother Jeremiah's, Connecticut Farms, and there tarried until Saturday, when I went to New York. Sunday, 27, preached three times in Mr. Gano's pulpit, from Job 23 : 3–4, and Romans 9 : 33. Monday, set out for Haverhill. Lodged the night at Mr. Dehart's, on Long Island. Tuesday night, lodged at Mr. Smith's. Wednesday, 30, went to Southhold, and preached a sermon at John Simm's, from Matthew 22 : 42. Thursday, went to Sterling, and there tarried the night. Friday, June 1, went to the Rev. Mr. Lee's, at Oyster Pond. Preached in the evening at his house from 1st Corinthians 9 : 24. Saturday, crossed the Ferry to New London. Sunday, 3, preached in Mr. Woodbridge's meeting house from Romans 5 : 1 ; in the Poor House from Luke 5 : 31 ; and in the Court House from 1st Corinthians 9 : 24. Monday, 4, went to Providence ; lodged two nights at Mr. Nicholas Brown's. Tuesday, 5, in the evening preached in Mr. Winsor's meeting house from Revelation 1 : 7. Wednesday, went to Charlestown, and lodged at Mr. Brown's. Thursday, went to Capt. White's, in Methaven. Friday, 8, went home to Haverhill, and found things in quietness. Rejoiced to see my good friends, to whose souls I long to be of service.

From the foregoing diary, it appears that Mr. Smith was absent from his home two hundred and fifty days, and that during this period he preached just one hundred times. The following letter from the Rev. Oliver Hart, shows how he was received, and the manner in which he performed the duties of his mission:—

CHARLESTON, April 17, 1770.

DEAR MR. MANNING:— As our good friend, Mr. Smith, is now almost ready to embark for your northern clime, I embrace the opportunity of sending you a few lines, which I hope you will accept as a superadded token of my unfeigned regard. I am sorry Mr. Smith is obliged to leave us so soon. His labors have been acceptable to my people universally, and many others have constantly crowded to hear him. Some, I trust, have received advantage by his faithful preaching. Two young men were to see him last night under soul concern. May the good work be carried on in their hearts, and may we yet hear of many more being awakened to a sense of their lost state by nature. As to his endeavors to serve the College, they have been indefatigable, and his success has been more than equal to what could have been expected, all things considered. I am sure he has merited the grateful acknowledgments of the Corporation. No man could have done more, and few would have done so much as he has, to serve the Institution. He has met with much opposition, and borne many reflections, but none of these things have discouraged him. I heartily wish the benefactions of this province may greatly promote the welfare of the College. Great grace be with you.

I am yours, etc., OLIVER HART.

The document, of which the following is an exact title, is among the archives of the University. It gives not only the names of benefactors, with the several amounts subscribed, but also the names of others upon whom Mr. Smith called, with remarks added, such as, "No money," "Doubtful," "Probable," "Call again," "Out of town," "Go thy way for this time," etc., etc. These latter names, which constitute the bulk of the document, are here omitted for want of room. The original paper from which the document in question was carefully copied, in the hand-writing of Mr. Smith, has recently been presented to the University, by the Rev. Ebenezer Thresher, of Dayton, Ohio, a graduate in the class of 1827. It is a small duodecimo manuscript of twenty-six pages, and bears the marks of age and use:—

AN EXACT LIST OF BENEFACTIONS, ETC., TO THE RHODE ISLAND COLLEGE, COLLECTED AND GOT SUBSCRIBED IN SOUTH CAROLINA AND GEORGIA, BY HEZEKIAH SMITH.

SOUTH CAROLINA.—CHARLESTON.

[South Carolina Currency], £ s. d.

	£	s.	d.
Hon. Wm. Bull, Lieut-Gov.,	50	0	0
Hon. Othniel Beal, Member of the Council,	25	4	0
Hon. Peter Manigault, Speaker,	50	8	0
Gabriel Manigault, Esq.,	100	16	0
David Graeme, Esq.,	50	0	0
Barnard Elliott, Esq.,	100	0	0
Christopher Gadsden, Esq.,	20	0	0
Col. Henry Laurens,	50	8	0
Hopkin Price,	25	4	0
John Hodsden,	50	0	0
Thomas Lamboll, Esq.,	17	0	0
Col. Probet Howarth,	12	12	0
Thomas Farr,	7	7	0
Rebekah Holmes,	10	0	0
William Burrows, Esq., Master in Chancery,	12	12	0
Rev. Mr. Emly,	11	10	0
Alexander Perronneau,	5	15	0
Capt. Thomas Tucker,	10	0	0
Thomas Young,	25	0	0
Stephen Townsend,	7	7	0
Justinus Stoll,	50	0	0
Thomas Sereven,	50	0	0
Ichabod Atwell,	10	0	0
Oliver Cromwell,	5	0	0
James Johnson,	5	0	0
Charles Crouch,	5	0	0
David Williams,	126	0	0
Judith Ball,	8	5	0
James Phillips,	30	0	0
Wm. Edwards, one Bridle,	5	0	0
James Richards,	5	0	0
Samuel Cords,	5	0	0
Doct. John De Lahoe,	10	0	1
Susanna Walker,	1	10	0
Sarah Lessene,	1	0	0
George Cooke,	5	0	0

[South Carolina currency], £ s. d.

	£	s.	d.
Elisha Poinsett,	5	0	0
Brailsford & Munereeff,	10	0	0
Simmons & Co.,	3	2	0
Leger & Co.,	5	15	0
Francis Gutter,	5	0	0
Major Fuller,	12	12	0
Matthias Hutchinson,	4	13	0
Solomon Legare,	8	5	0
Francis Nicholson,	1	0	0
Benjamin Wish,	7	7	0
Israel Joseph,	3	0	0
Michael Lazarus,	1	10	0
Barnard Young,	1	0	0
Thomas Eustace,	1	0	0
Milchar Warley,	5	15	0
Bulliott,	10	0	
John Laughton,	5	0	0
Stephen Devall,	7	7	0
William Clarkson,	1	12	0
Edward Dempsey,	12	12	0
Mrs. Kinlock,	4	2	6
Benjamin Warring,	25	0	0
Jeremiah Theus,	5	0	0
Elizabeth Coon,	12	12	0
Robert Sherman,	10	0	0
John Boyd,	10	2	0
Charles S. Stocker,	7	7	0
Charles Reily,	12	12	0
Charles Grimball,	50	0	0
Patrick Hinds,	50	0	0
William Millar,	12	12	0
Robert Clarke,	5	0	0
William Creighton,	2	17	6
John Fullarton,	8	17	0

GEORGIA.

[Sterling], £ s. d.

	£	s.	d.
Doct. Stout, of Sunbury,	10	0	0
His Excellency James Wright,	5	0	0
Hon. James Habersham,	2	0	0
Rev. John Joachim Zubly,	10	0	0

	[Sterling,] £	s.	d.
Capt. James Habersham, paid,	1	0	0
" " " subscribed,	5	0	0
John Stirk,	10	0	0
Benjamin Stirk,	20	0	0
Doct. James Cuthbert,	5	5	0
Hon. Jona. Bryan, Esq.,	10	0	0
James Devereaux, Ass't Judge,	15	0	0
Lachlum McGilvery,	5	0	0
Hon. Noble Wimberly Jones, Tr.,	5	0	0
Rev. Samuel Frink,	5	0	0
Philip Box, Esq.,	5	0	0
Matthew Roach, Esq.,	5	0	0
James Mossman,	5	0	0
John Rae, Esq.,	5	0	0
John Smith, Esq.,	2	0	0
William Spencer,	2	10	0
William Gibbons,	5	0	0
Benjamin Andrews.	5	0	0
John Stophius,	5	0	0

SOUTH CAROLINA.—HILTON HEAD.

	[South Carolina currency,] £	s.	d.
Capt. Samuel Green,	33	0	0
Lieut. Thomas Bull,	7	9	0
Ensign Daniel Savage,	5	0	0
Sergeant Philimon Parmenter,	5	0	0
Isaac Parmenter,	10	0	0
Benjamin Parmenter,	2	0	0
John Parmenter, Sen.,	5	0	0
Jacob Neal,	3	2	0
Francis Martin Angelo,	3	0	0
Richard Bland,	5	0	0
Thomas Scott,	5	0	0
Henry Toomer,	2	0	0
Lancelot Bland,	3	0	0
John Gregory,	3	0	0
James Welsh,	1	11	0
Philip Martin Angelo,	1	0	0
Merideth Rich,	3	0	0
Dominick Johnson,	3	0	0

EUTAW.

Col. Daniel Heyward,	20	0	0
Capt. William Hazzard,	20	0	0
John Grimball,	5	15	0

CHARLESTON.

William Cuttins,	5	0	0
James Brisbane,	20	0	0

	[South Carolina currency,] £	s.	d.
Charles Atkins,	10	0	0
Plowden Weston,	10	0	0
John Beal,	3	13	6
Richard Burhloe,	3	0	0
John Gowrlay	5	0	0
James Hinds,	5	0	0
Rebeckah Tubbs,	2	0	0
Doct. Isaac Chandler,	3	13	6
Abraham Walcutt, Hilton Head,	5	0	0
Matthew Witter, of James Island,	5	0	0
John Rivers, " "	10	0	0
Isaac Rivers, " "	15	0	0
Henry Smith, Esq., Goose Creek,	20	0	0
Thomas Rivers, Jr.,	50	0	0
William Bee, Pon Pon,	10	0	0
Thomas Jones, Horse Shoe,	7	7	0
Josiah Pendarvis, " "	25	0	0
Samuel Boswood, Pon Pon,	10	0	0
Ezekiel Branford, " "	10	0	0
John Bulline, Stono,	15	0	0
William Bulline, "	7	7	0
Robert and Sarah Cattle,	20	13	0
Capt. I. Ladson, Ashley River,	20	0	0
Susanna Ballantine, Stono,	2	0	0
John Morris,	12	12	0
Doct. John Harrison,	50	0	0

GEORGETOWN.

Joseph Brown,	3	2	0
Samuel Wragg,	12	12	0
John Dickey,	3	2	0
William Dewett,	5	0	0

PEDEE.

John Williams,	100	0	0
Alexander Mackintosh, Esq.,	25	0	0
John Chisolme,	3	2	0
Richard Raines, Black Swamp,	6	4	0
Claudius Pegues, Esq.,	25	0	0
Thomas Williams,	10	0	0
William Pegues,	20	0	0
Thomas Wade, Esq.,	8	2	0
John Jenkins,	1	7	0
Ely Kershaw,	25	4	0
Thomas Lide,	5	15	0
Benjamin Rogers,	20	0	0
Philip Pledger, Esq.,	5	15	0
George Hicks,	20	0	0
Sarah James,	12	12	0

EARLY SUBSCRIPTIONS.

[South Carolina currency, £ s. d.

Name	£	s.	d.
Hugh Dillon,	5	0	0
Magnus Cargill,	1	11	0
Rev. Nicholas Bedgegood,	22	1	0
William Dewitt,	20	0	0
John Mackintosh,	7	7	0
Howell James,	10	0	0
William Tarral,	5	0	0
Abel Edwards,	5	0	0
William James,	5	0	0
Thomas Evans,	25	0	0
Thomas James,	12	12	0
Arthur Hart,	20	0	0
John Davies,	1	10	0
Thomas Edwards.	15	0	0
Charles McCall,	10	0	0
John Kimborough,	25	4	0
James Dozer,	5	0	0
Rev. Evan Pugh,	5	0	0
Manuel Cox,	1	0	0
Samuel Russel,		11	0
Robert Lide,	1	11	0
Martin Cobb,	5	0	0
Benjamin James,	1	11	0
Thomas Wiggins,	1	11	0
James Thomson, Swift Creek.	25	0	0
Charles Dewett,	10	0	0
Lewis Perkin, Swift Creek,	5	0	0
Robert Thomson, "	5	0	0
John Chisnut, Camden,	12	12	0
Capt. Isaac Ross, "	5	15	0
Capt. John Canty, "	5	15	0
Benjamin Hart, Wateree,	16	9	4
Capt. Henry Hunter, "	7	0	0
Joseph Kirkland, "	5	15	0
Thomas Sumter, Santee,	10	0	0
Doct. Joseph Howard, "	7	7	0
Anthony Pouncy,	20	0	0

CHARLESTON.

[South Carolina currency, £ d. s.

Name	£	s.	d.
Hon. Joseph Kershaw, Camden,	3	10	8
Moses Lindo,	20	0	0
John Savage, Esq.,	20	0	0
Doct. John Swint,	10	0	0
Nathaniel Fuller, Ashley River,	20	0	0
John Screven, James Island,	10	0	0
William Axson, Jr.,	5	0	0
William Morgan,	14	14	0
Josiah Smith, Jr.,	25	0	0
Susanna Baddeley,	3	2	0
Daniel Stephens,	5	0	0
Joseph Marrion,	5	0	0
William Fitch, Sen.,	20	0	0
William Fitch, Jr.,	10	0	0
Augustine Stillman,	10	0	0
Capt. James Matthews, of Boig Sally,	3	13	6
Torrans, Poaug & Co.,	10	0	0
Joseph Creighton,	3	10	0

SUMMARY.

	£	s.	d.
Charleston,	1,841	16	2
Hilton Head,	100	2	0
Eutaw,	45	15	0
Georgetown,	18	16	0
Pedee,	640	3	4
Georgia £147 15s. sterling, equal in S. C. currency to	1,034	5	0
Total,	3,680	17	6
Received in South Carolina,	2,136	10	6
" Georgia,	227	10	0
Total,	2,364	0	6
Balance due in S. Carolina,	510	2	0
" " Georgia,	806	15	0
Total,	1,316	17	0

1769. November 20, remitted to Rev. John Gano, bill of exchange on Lawrence Kortright, merchant in New York, drawn by Savage & Legare, £200 New York money, which is - - - - £800 0 0

1770. January 4, remitted to Rev. Samuel Stillman, bill of exchange on Thomas Russell, merchant in Boston, drawn by Torrans, Poaug & Co., £40 sterling, which is - - - - - - 280 0 0

1770. February 8, ditto, bill of exchange on Nathaniel Coffin, Esq., in Boston, drawn by John Morris, Esq., £50 sterling, which is 350 0 0

1770. March 30, remitted to Rev. John Gano, bill of exchange on Lawrence Kortright, merchant in New York, drawn by Savage & Legare, 214⅜ dollars, which is - - - - - - £332 5 7½
1770. April 2, ditto, bill of exchange on Messrs. Greg, Cunningham & Co., merchants in New York, drawn by Torrans, Poaug & Co., 675 sterling, which is - - - - - - - - 525 0 0
Total amount remitted, - - - - - - 2,287 5 7½
Hezekiah Smith to account for - - - - - - - 76 14 10½

Total received, - - - - - - - - 2,364 0 6
Total amount subscribed, - - - - - - - - 3,680 17 6
John Alran, Pedee, - - - - - - - - 5 0 0
Gid. Gibson, " - - - - - - - - 20 0 0
John Hitchcock," - - - - - - - - 5 0 0

Total, South Carolina currency, - - - - - £3,710 17 6

The following is a true copy of what was inserted in the South Carolina newspapers:—

The subscriber begs leave, in this public manner, gratefully to return his humble and hearty thanks to the benefactors of Rhode Island College, whom he has met with since his first arrival in this Province. And as he expects to leave the Province soon, those gentlemen who were so kind as to promise to send their benefactions for the College to him, at Rev. Oliver Hart's, may now have an opportunity before his departure.

HEZEKIAH SMITH.

N. B. I shall leave a list of the subscribers names, together with their benefactions, in the hands of Mr. David Williams. So that each benefactor may hereafter see that his donation goes towards making up the sum I have collected since my arrival here.

Here follows a copy of what was inserted in the Georgia GAZETTE:—

Hezekiah Smith, sensible of the kindness he met with when in Georgia, begs leave to present his sincere thanks to the benefactors of Rhode Island College in that place; any of whom, by applying to Benjamin Stirk, Esq, (in whose hands is lodged the subscription paper,) may see that his donation goes towards making up the sum he collected and got subscribed there.

The following, which we take from a Charleston paper, dated October 26, 1769, does not appear to be mentioned in this interesting document of Mr. Smith's:—

EARLY SUBSCRIPTIONS.

In the sloop Sally, Capt. Peter Schermerhorn, from New York, who arrived here last Friday, came no less than forty-five passengers; amongst them, John Smith, Esq., and Mrs. Smith, of New York; Capt. Elijah Steel, Mr. Thomas Ivers, of this place; and the Rev. Hezekiah Smith, who, we hear, is commissioned to solicit benefactions towards establishing a College at Warren, in Rhode Island Government, while such a necessary institution is entirely neglected here. Surely, charity should begin at home.

The account submitted by Mr. Smith to the Corporation, at a meeting held in Providence, Thursday, September 6, 1770, is as follows:—

Dr.	Rhode Island College in account with Hezekiah Smith.			Cr.		
	£	s.	d.	£	s.	d.
1770. April 17. To five bills of exchange remitted at sundry times, - - - -	2,287	5	7½	1770. April 17. By cash received of sundry benefactors in South Carolina, as per account rendered, - -	2,136	10	6
To £8 per cent. given for bill of exchange of £30 sterling, purchased of Ambrose Wright, in Georgia, £48 sterling,	16	16	0	By ditto, received in Georgia,	227	10	0
To my necessary expenses, as per account, added, - -	208	12	6	By cash gained upon a bill drawn upon Lawrence Kortright, in New York, of 214½ dollars, - - - -	10	14	4½
To cash gained upon a bill drawn upon Lawrence Kortright, in New York, of 214½ dollars, - - - -	10	14	4½	By cash received upon the bills drawn upon Lawrence Kortright, and Messrs. Greg, Cunningham & Co., in N. York, to help bear my expenses,	119	0	0
	2,523	8	6		2,493	14	10½
To balance due H. Smith, as per contra, - - -	£29	13	7½	By balance due H. Smith,	29	13	7½
					£2,523	8	6

Whereupon it was voted:—

That the accounts presented by the Rev. Hezekiah Smith, of the donations and subscriptions by him received in the provinces of South Carolina and Georgia, be accepted, and that the Corporation highly approve of his conduct, and return him their hearty thanks for his great and generous services.

Voted, also, that as Mr. Smith was long absent from his people, in the service of the Corporation, and his salary during that time would have amounted to sixty-six pounds thirteen shillings and four pence, that the Corporation would willingly make up the sum to him, but as he generously refuses to receive anything on that account more than a remission of his subscription of forty dollars to the College, the said subscription is accordingly remitted, and the Corporation gratefully consider the remainder of said sum which he would have received for his salary, as a donation to the Institution.

Voted, that the sum of twenty-nine pounds thirteen shillings and seven and one-half pence, South Carolina currency, due the Rev. Hezekiah Smith on settlement of his account, be paid him out of the Corporation treasury.

It would thus appear that Mr. Smith succeeded in obtaining benefactions for the College to the amount of about twenty-five hundred dollars, a large sum of money at that early period. While the forty-five hundred dollars obtained by Mr. Edwards was constituted a permanent fund for the support of the President, the money obtained by Mr. Smith was mostly expended upon the College buildings, agreeably to a suggestion made by Manning in his letter to Nicholas Brown, published in the preceding chapter. See pages 194–5. This we infer from the fact that in 1775, when Col. Bennet resigned his office as Treasurer, the permanent funds of the College amounted to but £1,349 14s 8d, lawful money, or about forty-five hundred dollars. Only a small part of the balance of subscriptions due, amounting, according to Mr. Smith's report, to £1,316 17s, South Carolina currency, was probably ever collected.

ACCOUNT

OF THE

COLLEGE BUILDINGS.

1770–1862.

UNIVERSITY HALL.

ERECTED IN 1770.

IN the journal, or dairy of the Rev. Hezekiah Smith, occurs the first mention that we find of a College building. Under date of September 5, 1765, he thus writes:—

> I was with the Corporation at Newport which sat upon the College business, and was elected one of the Fellows of the College. Although but part of the Corporation, we subscribed nineteen hundred and ninety-two dollars for the BUILDING, and for endowing the College.

This, it will be observed, was at the second annual meeting of the Corporation. The following extracts from the records, relate to the subject before us:—

September 5, 1768. The Hon. Josias Lyndon, Esq., the Hon. Stephen Hopkins, Esq., the Hon. Samuel Ward, Esq., the President, Nicholas Easton, Esq., Nicholas Brown, Esq., and the Rev. Russell Mason, were appointed a committee to examine what place is most suitable to fix the College edifice upon, and to make report to the next annual meeting.

This Committee reported Thursday, September 7, 1769, whereupon it was

Voted, That the foregoing report be accepted. Resolved, That Sylvester Childs, Esq., Mr. John Brown, Capt. John Warren, and Mr. Nathan Miller, be a committee to purchase materials, agree for a suitable place to erect the edifice on, to take a deed for the same in behalf of the Corporation, and to carry said building into execution as soon as they can; and that any three of them be a quorum; and that they be empowered to solicit and receive subscriptions.

September 8, 1769: Resolved, That the Hon. Stephen Hopkins, Esq., Mr. Joseph Brown, and the Rev. John Davis, be a committee to draught instructions and prepare a model of the house proposed to be erected, which, if approved by the Corporation, is to serve as directions to the committee appointed to carry the same into execution.

Resolved, That Archibald Campbell, Esq., be added to the committee for placing the College edifice.

The Committee appointed to draft instructions and prepare a model, etc., made the following report:—

1st. That a suitable place be procured for erecting the College edifice on the easiest terms; and that the title be indisputable; and that proper and sufficient deeds of conveyance of said land be taken for the Corporation.

2d. That the building do not exceed sixty-six feet long, and thirty-six feet wide, and three stories high;—that it be a plain building, the walls of best bricks and lime, the doors and window frames of red cedar;—that there be a cupola for a bell;—that the first building be so situated as to be one wing of the whole College edifice, when completed.

3d. As there is a want of time at present, that a committee be appointed to furnish the committee for building with a complete draught of the whole building.

4th. That the committee for building procure the best materials, on the best and easiest terms.

5th. That the committee for building make provision this year, that the workmen may begin earlier in next.

STEPHEN HOPKINS, JOSEPH BROWN,
JOHN DAVIS.

September 8, 1769.

The foregoing report having been "read, considered, accepted and agreed to," it was

Voted, That the Chancellor, the President, and Mr. Joseph Brown be a committee to prepare a complete model of the building, according to the report of the aforesaid committee, and deliver the same to the Committee for Building.

Voted, That the Committee for Building be empowered to draw upon the Treasurer for money from time to time to carry on said building, and that they render accounts to the Corporation at each of their meetings, which the Secretary is hereby ordered to notify successively in the public papers for three weeks before their meetings.

Thursday, November 16, 1769 : Voted, That the President, Job Bennet, Esq., Mr. John Brown, Mr. John Warren, and Mr. John Jenckes, be a committee to fix a suitable place for building the edifice.

Voted, That the Chancellor, Mr. John Brown, Mr. John Warren, and Sylvester Child, Esq., be a committee to carry on the building of the College edifice; and that the Treasurer empower the said committee to collect all such sums of money as have been or shall be subscribed towards carrying on said building; and that these two committees ascertain the model and bigness of the College edifice, and also the house for the President, and make report of their doings to the next meeting of the Corporation.

This, it will be observed, was before the final decision to locate the College at Providence. On Friday, February 9, 1770, the day after the question of location had been settled, it was

Voted, That the College edifice be built according to the following plan, viz.: That the house be one hundred and fifty feet long and forty-six feet wide, with a projection of ten feet on each side, (ten by thirty,) and that it be four stories high.

Resolved, That Mr. John Jenckes be added to the Committee for building the College edifice; and that any three of them be a quorum, with power to act.

The gentlemen appointed for carrying on the building, or in other words the Building Committee, consisting of Stephen Hopkins, John Brown, John Warren, Sylvester Child, and John Jenckes, "appeared," says the record, "before the Corporation, and generously offered to do the same without charging any commissions therefor."

The President declined to be chairman of the committee on locating the building, and Mr. Joseph Russell was appointed in his stead. This committee, therefore, consisted of Joseph Russell, Job Bennet, John Brown, John Warren and John Jenckes. The lot selected for the building comprised originally about eight acres, and included a portion of the "home-lot" of Chad Brown, whom the late Moses Brown designates as "the first Baptist Elder in Rhode Island." It was for this reason purchased through the agency of the Brown family, in order that the College might stand on the "original house-lot or home-share, so called," of their pious ancestor.* The following extract from the Record of Deeds, Book 19, page 108, will be found interesting. It presents a clear and accurate account of the southern half of the original College lands:—

TO ALL PEOPLE TO WHOM THESE PRESENTS SHALL COME: We, John Brown and Moses Brown, both of Providence, in the County of Providence and Colony of Rhode Island and Providence Plantations, merchants, send greeting:—Know ye, that we, the said John and Moses Brown, for and in consideration of the sum of three hundred and thirty dollars, to us in hand already paid by the Trustees and Fellows of the College or University in the English Colony of Rhode Island and Providence Plantations in New England in America, the receipt whereof, by a discount out of the sums we have severally subscribed to the College, we do hereby acknowledge, have given, granted, bargained, sold, aliened, enfeoffed, conveyed, and confirmed, and by these presents do give, grant, sell, alien, convey, and confirm unto said Trustees and Fellows, and to their successors and assigns forever, one certain piece or parcel of land lying in the town of Providence, bounded * * * * * which said piece of land contains about four acres, and became the property of us, said Moses and John Brown, by a deed of bargain and sale from Samuel Fenner, of Cranston, who received it as one of the legatees of Daniel Abbott, Esq., late of said Providence, deceased, who received the northerly third part thereof from his father, Daniel Abbott, by descent, who purchased the same of James Brown, who received it of his brother John Brown, the present grantor's great-grandfather, who received it by descent from his father Chad Brown, who was one of the original proprietors after the native Indians of whom it was purchased, and is the middle part of that which was his house-lot or home-share of land so called; the other two-thirds being the middle part of the original house-lot or home-share of George Rickard, since called John Warner's, which part was con-

---

* See Mr. Brown's letter to President Wayland, page 207.

COLLEGE BUILDINGS. 233

veyed by the said Rickard to the said Chad Brown, from whom it descended to his aforesaid son John, who conveyed it to his brother Jeremiah Brown, who conveyed the same to the aforesaid Daniel Abbott, the elder, from whom it descended to Daniel Abbott, the younger, and became Samuel Fenner's as aforesaid: the whole of this piece of land making the southern half of the lot and highway leading to it whereon the College edifice is now erecting.

The foregoing deed was signed August 1, 1770, by John Brown and his wife Sarah, Moses Brown and his wife Anna, and Stephen Hopkins, Chief Justice. It was recorded January 7, 1771. The northern half of the lot, consisting of about four acres, was purchased by the Corporation, as per deed recorded in Book 19, page 106, of Oliver Bowen, of Providence, one of the legatees of Daniel Abbott, for the sum of four hundred dollars. Mr. Abbott, says the record,

Took it by descent from his father Daniel Abbott, who received two-thirds part of it, being on the north side, from Robert Williams, by deed of gift, who purchased it by deed of bargain and sale of Robert Morrice, who purchased it of Daniel Abbott the first, who was an original proprietor after the native Indians. The other third part the second named Daniel Abbott purchased, by deed of bargain and sale, from his brother John Brown, who took it by descent from his father Chad Brown, who was the first proprietor after the Indians, the whole of this parcel of land making the northern half of the lot and highway leading to it, which hath been purchased to erect the College edifice upon.

It will thus appear that Chad Brown owned two-thirds of the original College grounds. The "highway" leading from Benefit street to the lot, is now College street. Mr. Edwards describes the location as "remarkably airy, healthful, and pleasant; being the summit of a hill pretty easy of ascent, and commanding a prospect of the town of Providence below, of the Narragansett Bay and the islands, and of an extensive country, variegated with hills and dales, woods and plains," etc. Surely, he adds, "this spot was made for a seat of the Muses."

The plan or "model" adopted by the Building Committee and approved by the Corporation, was that of NASSAU HALL, Princeton, which was then regarded as one of the finest structures in the country. They broke ground on Tuesday, March 27, 1770, and on the 14th of May following, the corner stone of the new edifice was laid by John Brown. This, Mr. Howland states, was the first one laid in the foundation, at the bottom of the cellar wall, in the southwest corner of the building. Tradition adds that Mr. Brown, in accordance with the customs of the times, generously treated the crowd with punch, in honor of the joyful occasion. The progress of the building was greatly accelerated by the disturbances in Boston and the consequent interruptions of business, enabling the Committee to secure from that place an ample supply of skillful workmen.

President Manning, in writing to his friend the Rev. Dr. Stennett, of London, under date of June 7, 1770, thus describes the edifice: "The foundation of the College is now laid, and the building proceeds faster than could have been expected, its magnitude considered, which is one hundred and fifty by forty-six feet, with a projection in the middle of ten feet on each side (east and west sides, ten by thirty-three feet) for the public rooms. It is to be four stories high, with an entry of twelve feet through the middle of each, and is to be built of brick. It will contain fifty-six rooms in all. The town of Providence itself has nearly provided for the building, as they have raised by subscription near four thousand pounds, lawful money, at six shillings per dollar. The beneficence of a few Baptists in this place, their fortunes considered, is almost unparalleled."

Continuing our extracts from the records we find:—

Thursday, April 26, 1770: Voted, That Joseph Russell, David Harris, Esq., and Mr. Daniel Tillinghast, or the major part of them, be a committee to hire a suitable habitation for the President in Providence, until one can be built for him, and that it be at the charge of the Corporation.

Thursday, September 6, 1770: Voted, That the Corporation do approve of what the Committee for building the College and the President's House have done in that business:—That they be empowered to continue to carry on said buildings in the best manner they can:—That they be empowered to cause the stones on the College lands to be made into wall, to fill up the holes from whence said stones were dug, and to move and repair the barn on said land, and to make such other improvements thereon as to them may appear to be necessary.

Thursday, September 5, 1771: The following report, with the annexed state of accounts, was presented to the Corporation:—

Dr.	THE COLLEGE IN ACCOUNT WITH NICHOLAS BROWN & Co.		Cr.
1771. March 11. To sundry supplies, as per annexed account, £2,844 5 3¼		1771. March 11. By sundry subscriptions received as per account rendered, - - £2,121 4 10	
		By balance due to N. B. & Co. 623 0 5¼	
£2,844 5 3¼		£2,844 5 3¼	

We, the subscribers, being appointed by the Corporation of the College, at their meeting in April last, to audit the accounts of the Committee for building said College—

Have, in obedience to said order, carefully examined their respective accounts, with the several vouchers thereto annexed; and we find a balance from the subscribers for building said College due to Nicholas Brown & Co., of six hundred and twenty-three pounds five pence and one farthing, lawful money, agreeably to the above account current.

And here upon this occasion, we think it our duty to inform all the benefactors to this Institution, that the materials for said College, appear to us to have been purchased, collected, and put together with good judgment, prudence and economy; and that this Committee, for their great application, disinterestedness and activity, are justly entitled to the thanks of every one who wishes well to so arduous and important an undertaking.

Providence, March 11, 1771.
NICHOLAS COOKE, DARIUS SESSIONS, JOSEPH RUSSELL.

Which report, being read, was universally accepted and ordered to be recorded.

Ordered, That the Secretary give a fair copy of the above report to each of the Committee for purchasing materials and building said College, as a testimony of their entire approbation of their conduct.

The Hon. Nicholas Cooke, Hon. Darius Sessions and Mr. Joseph Russell are continued a committee to audit the accounts of the Building Committee from time to time as shall be thought necessary, with the understanding that they report to the next meeting of the Corporation.

Up to March 11, 1771, the amount expended on the College edifice and the President's house, for the two buildings were carried on together, and included in the subscriptions, was, as has already been stated, two thousand eight hundred and forty-four pounds, five shillings three and one-quarter pence, lawful money, equal to about nine thousand four hundred and eighty dollars. The original account of "sundry supplies" furnished by Nicholas Brown & Co., including all moneys expended by the Building Committee, is exceedingly full and minute, filling sixteen pages of folio ledger paper. Some of the items may interest the general reader as well as the antiquarian. They illustrate the progress of the buildings, and throw light on the habits and customs of our fathers:—

1770. Jan. 1.	To cash paid Robert Currie, for passage of Joseph Brown, Jonathan Hamman, and Zeph. Andrews to Cambridge, to view the colleges, 12 dollars,	- - - -	£3	12	0
"	" To cash, Joseph Brown paid the expenses in said journey,		2	16	0
"	" To John and Moses Brown's horses to Samuel Fenner's to purchase the lot for the College, and from thence to Jonathan Randall, Esq., and then to Fenner's again, in all seven miles, - - - - -			5	3
"	" To John Brown's horse and ferriage to Elisha Burr's, in Rehoboth, to contract for brick, nine miles, - -			3	7
"	" To Nicholas Brown's horse to Jeremiah Williams, -			1	6
"	" To cash paid for the postage of a letter to the Corporation,			1	6
1770. April 2.	To cash, Zeph. Andrews paid for expenses in Boston, besides what Joseph Brown paid, - - - -			15	6½
"	7. To postage of a letter from the Architect of Philadelphia,			1	4
"	17. To paid Wm. Compton for calling a meeting of the subscribers, - - - - - - - - -			2	6
"	" To paid ditto for his attendance at a meeting at the Court House, and bill, - - - - - - -			3	0
"	" To refuge boards judged by Hamman to be worth, to stick boards on, etc., - - - - - - -			4	0
"	" To one-quarter load of wood of N. B. to lay boards on,			1	6
" May 17.	To 3 qts. rum allowed Cole & John Jenckes, - -			1	8
"	24. To 3 pts. rum allowed John Jenckes for the scow men,			0	10
"	25. To Town scow two days fetching stones, - - -			6	0

COLLEGE BUILDINGS.

1770. May 25. To one-half day's work of Earle's negro,		1 6
" " To cash paid Comstock for one-half day's carting with three creatures,		3 0
" June 1. To paid Henry Paget, Esq., for twelve and one-half day's work of his negro Pero, and bill at 3s,		1 17 6
" 9. To one wheelbarrow, new, but broke to pieces in the service,		10 6
" 19. To paid James and Abraham Littlehale for one month's work of each at 30s, at the foundation,		3 0 0
" " To one pail allowed A. Cole for the people to carry water to drink in,		1 6
" " To ½ gall. West India rum for the digging of the well,		1 9
" " To 1 qt. ditto allowed by John Jenckes,		1 0
" 21. To ½ gall. ditto at twice for the well,		2 0
" 28. To ½ gall. rum for the well diggers,		1 1
" " To 1 gall. West India rum when laying the first floor,		3 6
" Aug. 2. To 2 galls. ditto and 2 lbs. sugar, second floor,		8 0
" 6. To 3 pints ditto allowed Simmons for "extraordinary services,"		1 6
" 21. To 2 galls. good rum and 2 lbs. sugar when raising the President's house,		9 8½
" 25. To 4 galls. West India rum, very good and old, and 1 lb. sugar, third floor,		15 7½
" Sept. 14. To 4 galls. ditto and 1 lb. sugar, fourth floor,		14 7
" " To 1 pt. ditto allowed the carpenters gratis,		0 7
" Oct. 9. To 7¾ galls. old West India rum and 2 lbs. sugar when raising the fifth floor,		1 8 4
" 13. To 3 galls. West India rum when raising roof,		10 6
1771. Jan. 7. To cash paid Oliver Bowen for the College land, the remainder, £30 15s 7d, paid by John Jenckes, the whole £84,		53 4 5
" " To 5 acres land bought of Samuel Fenner, at 90 dollars per acre, is £135; to one year's interest, 8s 2d,		143 2 0
" Feb. 7. To 1 box glass for President's house,		3 3 0
" " To paid Benjamin Mann, for setting seven squares glass in Mr. Snow's meeting house, broke at Commencement,		4 8
" March 8. To paid Ebenezer Leland, for painting the College and President's house,		9 0 0

From the foregoing account, it will appear, that the amount paid for the original College lands was four thousand three hundred and eighty pounds, or seven hundred and thirty dollars; being about ninety dollars per acre, for what is now valued at one dollar, and upwards, per square foot.

The last item of expenditure which we have copied from the original account, is for painting, March 8, 1771. The buildings had, therefore, at this date, approached completion. Dr. Stiles, in his diary, November, 1771, thus writes:—

> On Monday I went to visit the College, where five or six lower rooms are finished off. They have about twenty students, though none yet living in the College edifice.

The amount of subscriptions paid, it appears, up to March 11, 1771, was £2,221 4s 10d, or about $7,404, leaving a balance due Nicholas Brown & Co., of $2,076. The following is the "College Credit," as exhibited by them in their account. We present it entire, as it includes the only list known to exist of the original subscribers for building the College edifice and the President's house. It will be observed that the names of all the subscribers are not included, but only of those who had paid, up to date:—

1770.	£	s.	d.	1770.	£	s.	d.
Richard Knight's subscription,	2	8	0	Seven squares glass, 8 by 10,			
Cash received of W. Wheaton,				for John Brown,		4	2½
for lime			4?	One gallon W. I. rum returned,		3	6
William Wheaton for lime.		9	0	Thirty-six feet 3 by 7 inch joist			
William Logan,	2	8	0	and do. 13 feet, charged to			
Two hhds. lime of J. Jenckes,	1	10	0	Jos. and Wm. Russell,		3	7½
Two hhds lime of Doct. Jno.				One house plank, charged to			
Jenckes,	1	10	0	Insig Elizabeth,		1	3
Jona. Jenckes, Jr.,	3	0	0	Elisha Mowry's subscription,	4	1	3
Cash received of Job Bennet,	16	4	0	Nich's Power, 220 ft. timber,		8	3
" " Robert Stery,	3	12	0	Andrew Cole, for 24 feet refuge			
Ten squares glass, 8 by 10,				boards,			6
sold Col. Wanton,		6	0	Robert Carver's subscription,	6	0	0
Benoni Pearce,	3	0	0	John Field's "	6	9	0
200 bricks, John Jenckes had,		4	6	Oliver Whipple's "	4	8	0
Warner & Tillinghast,	4	16	0	Ezek Eddy's "	3	0	0
Mary Brown, wid. of Obadiah,	12	0	0	2500 shingles charged to John			
Wilson Jacobs,	2	10	0	Smith and Bacon, at 15d,	1	17	6
Gov. Wanton's subscription,				Joshua Spooner's subscription,	3	15	0
paid in a Treasury note,	30	0	0	Cash received of Job Bennet,	48	0	0

COLLEGE BUILDINGS. 239

1770.	£	s.	d.	1771.	£	s.	d.
John Fenner,	3	0	0	Lime and sand to mend mother's			
Oliver Fuller,	1	10	0	oven,	1	0	
124 feet timber to David Harris,	4	8		Col. John Waterman,	3	15	0
200 feet house plank to N. Brown,	9	0		Abraham Belknap,	5	0	0
60 feet timber to Henry Bacon,				Jacob Belknap,	2	0	0
at 3s 6d per foot,	2	2	0	Job Randall,	3	0	0
Eph. Wheaton's subscription,	4	0	0	Abel Perry,	2	8	0
Messrs. Stewart & Taylor's do.,	4	16	0	William Wheaton,	51	0	0
Isaac Brayton,	2	10	0	Nathan Angell,	15	0	0
Samuel Thurber,	6	8	0	Molly Brown, for daughters of			
Samuel Thurber, Sen'r,	3	0	0	Obadiah,	15	0	0
James Olney,	3	0	0	Jno. Waterman, paper mill,	6	0	0
Clarke & Nightingale,	4	16	0	Timothy Gladding's subscription,	2	8	0
Andrew Waterman,	8	0	0	Caleb Greene,	9	0	0
John Peck,	3	0	0	John Hoppin,	3	18	0
John Smith, Jr.,	2	10	0	White & Waterman,	4	16	0
1771.				Thomas Sabin,	6	10	0
Samuel Nightingale, Jr.,	12	0	0	2,086 bricks, charged to Jno.			
John Batty,	3	0	0	Smith, at 18d,	1	17	5
Nicholas Clarke,	4	10	0	Daniel Larned,	2	8	0
Nathanael Greene,	5	0	0	Jabez Bowen, Jr.,	60	0	0
William Earle,	12	0	0	30 feet timber for sloop Caty,			
Jno. B. Hopkins,	9	0	0	at 3s 6d per ——	1	0¼	
James Field,	2	10	0	Mary Young,	6	0	0
John Petty,	3	16	0	Daniel Thornton,	1	4	0
George Brown,	4	4	0	Joseph Arnold,	3	0	0
Nathan Arnold,	2	8	0	Edward Spaulding,	6	0	0
Thomas and Benjamin Lindsey,	10	0	0	Samuel Young,	4	16	0
Jas. Hoyle paid Wm. Wheaton,	3	0	0	Nicholas Cooke, Esq..	45	0	0
Paul Allen,	2	16	0	Benjamin Mann,	15	0	0
Martin Simmons,	3	0	0	Edward Hawkins,	3	15	0
James Andrews,	1	4	0	Ephraim Walker,	4	0	0
Eleazer Hardin & Son,	7	8	0	Ephraim Peabody,	2	15	0
John Pitcher,	3	15	0	Joshua Hacker,	3	10	0
Christopher Arnold,	3	0	0	Knight Dexter,	18	0	0
George Makepace,	6	0	0	Jona. Arnold,	14	0	0
Simon Smith,	6	0	0	Welcome Arnold,	3	16	0
8 lb. lead to make a hand-lead,	2	0		Daniel Jackson,	3	0	0
Thurber & Cahoon,	46	0	0	Elijah Bacon,	6	6	0
2500 shingles to Edward Hawkins, at 15s.	1	17	6	Benjamin Waterman, Jr.,	2	8	0
				Job Smith,	21	0	0
William Chickley,	3	0	0	Abner Thayer, paid J. Smith,	2	8	0
Samuel Ingraham,	3	0	0	David Harris,	30	0	0
Christopher Williams,	3	0	0	Thomas Greene,	15	0	0
Benjamin Whipple,	1	4	0	Jona. and Christ'r Olney,	8	0	0
Phineas Brown,	5	0	0	Stephen Whipple,	13	12	0

1771.	£	s.	d.
Dexter Brown,	7	10	0
William Brown,	2	8	0
William Morris,	2	8	0
Jona. Hamman,	6	0	0
James Sabin,	12	8	0
Benjamin Stelle,	7	10	0
What Jno. Jenckes paid William Wheaton,	16	16	11½
Nicholas Power,	10	8	0
Lewis Bosworth,	2	10	0
Benjamin Whipple,	2	10	0
Daniel Whipple,	1	0	0
Josiah King's subscription,	3	0	0
Sylvanus Sayles,	7	16	0
Thomas Bennet,	4	10	0
Jeremiah Brown,	6	0	0
Henry Sterling,	7	16	0
Benjamin Coate's note,	4	0	0
Jacob Whitman,	13	0	0
William Spencer,	1	10	0
Abraham Winsor,	7	0	0
Gideon Brown,	3	0	0
What John Jenckes paid Jno. Smith towards brick,	11	16	6
Christopher Lippitt,	5	0	0
Rufus Hopkins,	5	0	0
Stephen Colvin,	2	8	0
Joseph Remington,	2	8	0
Thomas Harris,	3	0	0
James Arnold,	11	8	0
Ebenezer Thompson,	8	8	0
James Burrill,	2	8	0
Jona. Holden,	1	10	0
James Lovett,	33	15	0
Abraham Angell,		12	0
Peter Randall,	3	10	0
44 lbs. strips of lead cut by the carpenters, at 3d,		11	0
Chad Brown,	3	0	0
William Gully,	3	0	0
Mortar, charged Wm. Wheaton,		18	7
James Barry,	2	8	0
Amos Kimball,	2	8	0
Nicholas Brown's subscription,	200	0	0
Charged Eleazer Harding for 136 squares sash contained			

1771.	£	s.	d.
in his bill vs. President's house, more than delivered, at 4s 4d,	2	8	2
Moses Brown's subscription,	200	0	0
John Brown's "	200	0	0
Joseph Brown, £100; the other £100 to be paid in philosophical apparatus according as subscribed for, at the first cost, as soon as a proper place is provided to put them in,	100	0	0
The carting of the 26 boxes of glass as is contained in Dexter Brown's account,	2	12	0
Zephaniah Andrews,	10	0	0
Charles Angell,	1	0	0
Benjamin Allen,	4	0	0
James Arnold, Jr.,	4	0	0
John Aplin,	2	8	0
Richard Brown,	2	10	0
Samuel Butler,	30	0	0
James Burrough,	3	0	0
Solomon Bradford,		12	0
Samuel Coy,	2	8	0
Benjamin Cushing,	30	0	0
Andrew Cole,	3	0	0
Richard Collier,		12	0
John Fritton,	3	0	0
Richard Godfrey,	2	8	0
Richard Eddy,	3	0	0
John Gibbs,	2	8	0
James Greene,	1	10	0
Levi Hall,	3	0	0
Amos Horton,	5	0	0
Henry Jenckes,	1	16	0
Christopher Jenckes,	1	16	0
Seth Knap,	2	8	0
Ebenezer Leland,	2	8	0
Nathaniel Metcalf,	3	0	0
Daniel Manton,	6	0	0
Allen Peck,	4	10	0
Nathaniel Packard,	2	8	0
William Pearce,	2	8	0
Peter Ritto,	1	4	0
Jehu Smith,	2	15	0
Jno. Jenkins,	3	0	0

COLLEGE BUILDINGS.

1771.	£	s.	d.	1771.	£	s.	d.
Jno. Smith, Cranston,	2	8	0	5833 shingles, charged of Robert Carver the 11th of Sept., and afterwards charged in his whole bill, amounting to £64 5d,	5	5	0
Christopher Sheldon,	9	0	0				
Jeremiah Scott,		12	0				
Paul Tew,	7	10	0				
Benjamin Tallman,	2	8	0				
Comfort Wheaton,	6	0	0				
Nathan Waterman,	2	8	0	Total, £1,958 2 8¾			
Jeremiah Whipple,	9	0	0	Deduct out of the foregoing subscriptions, the whole being not yet paid,	148	11	4¾
Otis Whipple,	4	10	0				
Nahum Wilder,	1	4	0				
David Whipple, charged Jere.,	2	8	0				
Isaac Woodroof,	2	8	0	Total, £1,809 11 4			
Oliver Bowen's subscription,	9	0	0	Parts of sundry subscriptions received but not credited in this amount,	411	13	6
John Smith the 3d do.,	2	8	0				
Paid John Smith, towards brick by Jenckes, besides what is credited,	2	13	0	Total, £2,221 4 10			

Continuing our search among the records, we find:—

Thursday, September 3, 1772. Voted, That the tiles for covering the College edifice shall be retained for that use.

Whereas a sum of money is immediately wanted to defray the expense of slating the College edifice, it is resolved, That the Rev. John Gano be appointed to solicit donations for that purpose in this or the other colonies; and that he be requested to proceed upon that business as soon as may be.

Voted, That the sum of five dollars be taken for the use of each room in the College edifice annually, from those who live in them.

Thursday, September 2, 1773: Voted and resolved, That the offer of the Secretary (Doct. Thomas Eyres) be accepted, that he would pay the interest of one hundred dollars for three years to any gentleman who will advance said sum towards finishing the rooms in the College edifice, after the balance in Mr. Howell's hands was expended, the Corporation being security for the original sum.

Thursday, September 8, 1774: Voted, That the thanks of this Corporation be presented to the Rev. John Gano, for his having used his best endeavors to promote a subscription for this College in the southern colonies;—that the manner in which he has proceeded is approved by the Corporation; and he is hereby requested to proceed upon the same business in any other places and methods which he shall judge most beneficial towards the advancement of the College; and the Secretary is ordered to give him a copy of this vote.

On Saturday, December 7, 1776, Sir Peter Parker, the British commander, with seventy sail of men-of-war, anchored in Newport harbor, landed a body of troops and took possession of the place. "The country," says President Manning, "immediately flew to arms and marched to Providence. There, unprovided with barracks, they marched into the College, and dispersed the students, about forty in number." From this time the College continued to be occupied for barracks, and afterwards for a hospital, by the American and French forces, until May 27, 1782, when the edifice was left in a most ruinous condition. "The Corporation," Manning continues, advanced out of their own pockets near one thousand dollars for the most necessary repairs, and ordered the course of education to recommence." March 4, 1785, he writes, "Mr. John Brown is about finishing the third story, which we expect to want in the course of the year." From this it would seem that only two stories were finished at first. The fourth story was finished in 1788, as appears from the following records:—

September 4, 1788: Voted, That the Treasurer of this Corporation be authorized to contract with such persons as may offer to furnish the fourth story of the College edifice, or any part of it, on such terms as he shall judge proper.

The following petition to the General Assembly, copied from a rough draft on file in the hand-writing of President Manning, will repay perusal. The friends of the College might well object to the building being put to such uses as are here set forth in detail. No date is found on the document, but the petition was probably presented in the year 1780. "President Manning," says Backus, referring to this period, "now engaged again in the work of education. But further interruptions were in store for him. On the 25th of June, 1780, while he was preaching at the church, it being Sunday, the College edifice was a second time seized, by the order of the council of war, for a hospital for the French troops, who held it until May 27, 1782":—

The Petition of the members of the Corporation of Rhode Island College, whose names are hereunto annexed, humbly showeth : —

That the College edifice was first taken in December, 1776, for the use of barracks and an hospital for the American troops, and retained for that use until the Fall before the arrival of his most Christian Majesty's fleets and armies in this State ;—that, by our direction, the President resumed the course of education in said College, and took possession of the edifice on the 10th of May, 1780; and continued so to occupy it until the authority of this State, in a short time after, granted it to the French army as an hospital, who continued to hold and use it for said purpose until the last week, when the Commissary of War of the French army delivered it up, with the keys, to his Honor the Deputy Governor; they having previously permitted the officers of the French ships in this State to place their sick in it, who still continue there ;—that the building was in good repair, and occupied by upwards of thirty students when first taken for the public service;—that great injury hath been done to every part of it since taken out of the hands of the Corporation ; especially by two buildings adjoining it, one an house of offal at the north end, with a vault fifteen feet deep under it, having broken down the wall of the College to facilitate the passage of the invalids from the edifice into it ; from which addition the intolerable stench renders all the northern part uninhabitable ; and the other an horse stable, built from the east projection to the north end, by which the house is greatly weakened ; many of the windows are also taken entirely out of the house, and others so broken, as well as the slate on the roof, that the storms naturally beat into it. As your Honors must be sensible that the interests of literature in this State must generally suffer, as well as the building erected for its promotion; and the Corporation conceiving that there cannot be the shadow of a reason for detaining any longer the College edifice from them, who now want to apply it immediately to the uses for which it was erected, do request the Legislature to deliver them the house, and order all their buildings taken down and removed from the College lots, such repairs as are absolutely necessary to be made at the public expense ; and to pass an order that it shall not again be appropriated as an hospital or barracks. And your petitioners, as in duty bound, will ever pray.

At the annual meeting of the Corporation in 1783, it was

Resolved, That an application be made to his most Christian Majesty to patronize this College ; and that the President, Rev. Mr. Stillman and Doct. Waterhouse be a committee to draught a petition to him for this purpose.

At a special meeting held January 7, 1784, quoting from the records,

The address to his most Christian Majesty, drawn up by the Rev. Samuel Stillman and Doct. Benjamin Waterhouse, was read and approved.

Voted, That the Chancellor, the President, Hon. Jabez Bowen and Doct. Solomon Drown, be a committee to draught a letter to Doct. Benjamin Franklin, to accompany the address to his most Christian Majesty.

The address to which reference is here made, is given entire in MANNING AND BROWN UNIVERSITY, pp. 401-3. The following, copied from a rough draft of the letter to accompany the address, deserves a place here, not only from its connection with the history of University Hall, but also from its statements respecting the history and condition of the College:—

SIR:—In compliance with the request of the Honorable the Corporation of the College at Providence in the State of Rhode Island, transmitted in their vote of the 7th of September last, we take the liberty to inform your Excellency that the College under their direction was founded in 1764, and received the small endowment of which it is now possessed solely from the beneficence and contributions of individuals, the government not being sufficiently impressed with an idea of the importance of literature to afford its patronage or lend it any further assistance than that of granting it a charter. With these small beginnings, however, at the commencement of the late war the Corporation had the pleasure to see that beautiful edifice erected on the hill at Providence, and upwards of forty students matriculated, together with a large Latin school as a nursery to supply it with scholars. The whole endowment consisted of one thousand pounds, lawful money, as a fund, besides the lot of six acres of land.* At that period the young Institution was speedily growing in reputation as well as in number of scholars. But on the arrival of the enemy in that State, in the year 1776, it was seized by the public for barracks and an hospital for the American army, and continued to be so occupied until a little before the arrival of the armaments of his most Christian Majesty, upon which it was again taken out of the hands of the Corporation by an order of government, and delivered up to our allies for the same uses to which it had been applied by the American army. They held it till their army marched for the Chesapeake. To accommodate it to their wishes they made great alterations in the building, highly injurious to the designs of its founders. This, with the damages done to it by the armies of both nations while so occupied, subjected the Corporation

---

* The College lands originally comprised eight acres, according to the recorded deeds and the "College Credit" submitted by Nicholas Brown & Co. to the Corporation in 1771. See pages 232-3 and 237-8. The highway thereto, which is now a part of College street, was of course included in these eight acres. The writer speaks of the "lot" without probably taking into account the "highway." The funds, it may be added, amounted at this time to more than one thousand pounds, as will appear in a succeeding chapter.

to a heavy expense to repair it; and that when the deranged state of our finances prevented us from making scarcely any advantage of the interest of our little fund in the State treasury. Having at their own expense made the repairs, they applied first to the Legislature of the State, and repeatedly to Congress for some compensation; but have not been able to obtain the least assistance. Thus circumstanced they think it their duty to solicit the patronage of his most Christian Majesty in the manner they have done in the memorial which accompanies this letter.

We have the pleasure to inform your Excellency that there are upwards of fifty students now belonging to the College, with flattering prospects of an increase.

The above is a brief account of the origin and present state of the College at Providence. We only add, that this Institution embraces in its bosom and holds out equal privileges to all denominations of protestants; and its Corporation, agreeably to charter, is, and must forever be composed of some of all denominations of Christians.

We have the honor to be, Sir, your very humble servants.

After many and fruitless applications to Congress by the President and Corporation, for remuneration on account of damages and loss of rent, all of which we have detailed in our former work, an act was passed by the United States government, April 16, 1800, entitled,

AN ACT FOR THE RELIEF OF THE CORPORATION OF RHODE ISLAND COLLEGE.

BE IT ENACTED, etc., That the accounting officers of the Treasury be, and they are, hereby authorized and directed to liquidate and settle the claims of the Corporation of Rhode Island College, for compensation for the use and occupation of the edifice of said College, and for injuries done to the same, from the tenth day of December, one thousand seven hundred and seventy-six, to the twentieth day of April, one thousand seven hundred and eighty, by the troops of the United States; and that the sum which may be found due to the said Corporation for damages done to and occupation of the said edifice, as aforesaid, be paid them out of any moneys in the Treasury not otherwise appropriated.

How much compensation the College finally received, we are unable at present to determine. Dr. Benedict, in his History, states it to have been two thousand dollars.

In January, 1823, this venerable edifice received the name of UNIVERSITY HALL, by a special vote of the Corporation. In 1850, important changes were made in the interior of the building.

The old chapel, the walls of which had so long resounded with the voices of eloquence and the utterances of prayer and praise, was converted into recitation-rooms. The dining hall too, where the stewards of a former day were accustomed to preside during the hours for meals, with all the dignity of their position, was remodelled, while "commons," in accordance with the progressive spirit of the age, were abolished. And recently the long and spacious entry halls, where mischievous students too often delighted in midnight revels, have been disfigured by the introduction of suitable partitions. In this instance utility and expedience have been consulted rather than beauty, and a regard for time-honored associations.

The President's house, we may add in conclusion, which formerly stood on the College Green directly in front of Manning Hall, was removed in 1839, and the new and elegant mansion on the corner of Prospect and College streets was erected in its place.

BAPTIST MEETING-HOUSE.

ERECTED IN 1775.

GOVERNOR WINTHROP, under date of March 16, 1639, states that Roger Williams "was rebaptized by one Holliman, a poor man, late of Salem. Then Mr. Williams rebaptized him and some ten more." For more than sixty years the church thus founded held meetings in the open air, or worshipped beneath the friendly shelter of groves and trees. There was no public building at this time in the town even for civil purposes. After Philip's war, in June, 1676, the annual town-meeting was held, says Staples, "before Thomas Field's house, under a tree, by the water-side."

In the year 1700, the Rev. Pardon Tillinghast, the minister of the church, built at his own expense a meeting-house, on a lot near the corner of North Main and Smith streets. This house and lot he afterwards generously deeded to the church. The building, according to tradition, was small and rude, "in the shape of a hay-cap, with a fire-place in the middle, the smoke escaping from a hole in the roof."

At the time of President Manning's removal to Providence the church, which consisted of but one hundred and eighteen members living widely apart, were worshipping in a small house thirty-five by forty-one feet in dimensions, erected in the year 1726. A brief description of the building and of the mode of worship, which we find in Stone's "Life and Recollections of John Howland," may be appropriately introduced in this connection:—

At high water the tide flowed nearly up to the west end of the building. * * * From the front door, opening on Main street, an aisle extended to the pulpit, which was raised three or four steps from the floor. On each side of the aisle benches extended north and south to the walls of the house, and there were benches in the gallery, which was entered by narrow stairs from a door on the south side of the house. * * * They did not approve of singing, and never practiced it in public worship. When more than one elder was present, and the first had exhausted himself, he would say: "There is time and space left if any one has further to offer." In that case, another and another would offer what he had to say; so there was no set time for closing the meeting. * * * The house could not contain a large congregation, nor did the number present seem to require a larger house, as they were not crowded, though many of them came in from the neighboring towns on horseback, with women behind them on pillions.

Under the pastoral care of Manning the church and society greatly increased in numbers and efficiency, so that ere long it became necessary to erect a new house of worship. With a view to the accommodation of the College, it was determined to build it in such a style of elegance, and of such dimensions, that it should surpass any edifice of the kind connected with the Baptist denomination in the colonies.

In looking over the records of the society, we find that, at a meeting held at the house of Mr. Daniel Cahoon, on Friday evening, February 11, 1774, it was

RESOLVED, That we will all heartily unite as one man, in all lawful ways and means, to promote the good of this society; and particularly attend to and revive the affair of building a meeting-house for the public worship of Almighty God, and also for holding Commencements in.

In accordance with this resolve, the society, with unanimity and promptness, entered upon the prosecution of their labors. A committee of two persons, Messrs. Joseph Brown and Jonathan Hammond, were immediately appointed to proceed to Boston, "in order to view the different churches there, and to make a memorandum of their several dimensions and forms of architecture." The old house and lot were sold at public auction, and the present spacious lot, bounded by Thomas, Benefit, President and North Main streets, was purchased of Mr. John Angell. In this latter transaction very important service appears to have been rendered by Mr. William Russell.*

According to a letter from Mr. Moses Brown, published in a previous chapter, (pages 207-10,) it appears that the church in its earlier periods was of the "Six Principle" order, so called, and that at this time a separation took place, a part of the members, under the guidance of Elder Winsor, contending for the practices and usages of their fathers, and the remainder adhering to Manning, and the views more generally entertained by the Baptist denomination at the present day. The money obtained from the sale of the old house and lot being divided between the two parties, the former built a house in Johnston upon the plain, and established a "Six Principle" church.

On the 25th of April, 1774, at a meeting of the Society, of which Dr. Manning was Moderator, and Benjamin Stelle, Clerk, it was resolved:—

1. That a petition be presented to the honorable General Assembly, praying that a charter, containing certain privileges and immunities, may be granted to the Baptist society in Providence.

2. That the Rev. James Manning, Ephraim Wheaton, Nicholas Brown, David Howell, and Benjamin Thurber be a committee to draft a plan of a charter, and present the same to the society for approbation as soon as may be.

3. That Mr. John Brown be the committee man for carrying on the building of the new meeting-house for said society.

4. That Messrs. John Jenckes, Daniel Cahoon, Ephraim Wheaton, Nathaniel Wheaton, Daniel Tillinghast, Joseph Brown, William Russell, Edward Thurber, Nicholas Brown, Christopher Sheldon, and Benjamin Thurber, they or the major part

---

* Judge Staples in his "Annals," gives the tradition that Mr. Angell, who was a "Gortonian and the last of the sect," would not sell his orchard for a Baptist meeting-house for any consideration. It is certain, from the records, that Mr. Russell first bought the land by request, and then conveyed it to the Society. Being an Episcopalian in his religious views, and a wealthy merchant, the owner of the land would naturally suppose that it was wanted for a private residence, rather than for the use to which it was put.

of them, be a standing committee to assist and advise with Mr. John Brown, in locating and carrying into execution the building of the new meeting-house.

Thus, while a large committee of eleven was chosen for assistance and advice, the carrying on of the building, and the execution of the plan was wisely left to a committee of one. There was hence a unity of purpose, and a success in the final results, which a large and divided committee could never have attained. In this matter our fathers have left on record an example which societies of the present day may do well to imitate. It is pleasing to notice in this record, the unlimited confidence reposed in the abilities and discretion of Mr. Brown. Had there been informers in those days of trial and peril, the large reward offered by the British government for the apprehension of the leader in the destruction of the Gaspee, might have seriously interferred with the plans of the society.

In order to defray the additional expense of purchasing a lot, and of building a house sufficiently large to accommodate the College, recourse was had to a lottery. This was in accordance with the universal practice in Rhode Island and throughout the colonies, at this period. The lottery was divided into six classes, the time and place of drawing which were notified from time to time in the PROVIDENCE GAZETTE. Eleven thousand nine hundred and seventy tickets were sold, at prices ranging from two and one-half to five dollars each. The sum proposed to be raised by this scheme was two thousand pounds, lawful money, or about seven thousand dollars. The managers appointed by the General Assembly, were Nicholas Brown, John Jenckes, William Russell, Benjamin Thurber, Edward Thurber, Nathaniel Wheaton, Daniel Tillinghast, William Holroyd, James Arnold, and Nicholas Power. In their announcement of June 25, 1774, they ask for the

Cheerful assistance and encouragement of the public, especially when it is considered that this is the first time the Baptist society have solicited their assistance in this way, which they can assure them would not now have been the case had they not purchased as much more land, and designed a house as much larger than the society required for their own use (purposely to accommodate public Commencements), as will amount to the full sum proposed to be raised by this lottery.

On Monday, August 29, was the "raising" of the new meeting-house, due notice of which had been given in the papers. A large crowd assembled, and the occasion seems to have been made a general holiday throughout the town.

During the following year the house was so far completed that it was occupied by the society. It was opened for public worship on Sunday, May 28, 1775, when Dr. Manning preached the dedication discourse, from Genesis xxviii, 17:—"And he was afraid, and said, How dreadful is this place! this is none other but the house of God, and this is the gate of heaven." On Tuesday, June 6, the raising of the steeple, which occupied nearly four days, was finished. The plan of this most elegant piece of architecture was taken from the middle figure in the thirtieth plate of Gibbs's " Designs of buildings and ornaments," representing the steeple of St. Martin's in the Fields, one of the finest churches in London.* It measures one hundred and eight feet from the top of the tower, and one hundred and eighty-five feet from the ground to the top of the vane. The total height of the steeple is one hundred and ninety-six feet. The house itself is eighty feet square. The roof and galleries are supported by twelve fluted pillars, of the Doric order. The weight of the original bell was two thousand five hundred and fifteen pounds, and upon it was the following motto:—

> For freedom of conscience the town was first planted;
> Persuasion, not force, was used by the people;
> This church was the eldest, and has not recanted,
> Enjoying, and granting, bell, temple, and steeple.†

* See Knight's " London Illustrated," volume V., page 195.
† Dissenters in Great Britain were not allowed to have steeples or bells to their churches. To this prohibition reference is undoubtedly had in this inscription.

Fronting each of the four streets that surround the house is a door, and fronting Benefit street are two doors. Thus on Commencement days, and on other public occasions, it can be readily vacated. Mr. Joseph Brown, a member of the church, was the principal architect, and Mr. James Sumner* superintended the building. The entire expense of the edifice and lot was upwards of twenty-five thousand dollars. When we consider the value and scarcity of money in those days, the perils and dangers of an impending war with the mother country, and also the fact that Providence was then a small town, containing, when the building was commenced, a population of only four thousand three hundred and twenty-one, according to the official numeration of the inhabitants, we are amazed at the genius which could conceive, and the energy, enterprise, and skill which could successfully complete so great an undertaking. Even at the present day, the venerable structure, with its tall, graceful spire, and its spacious enclosure, shaded by stately elms, constitutes one of the chief attractions of the city. In the beginning and progress of this enterprise, we have an illustration of the remarkable influence which Manning must have exerted over the people of his care.

Sunday morning, May 28, 1865, just ninety years after the first dedication of the house, the Rev. Dr. Caldwell, pastor of the church, preached an historical discourse which was afterwards published. An extract from this discourse may fitly close the present account:—

You can follow the eighty-two commencements with which this house is associated in the memory of so many children of the College; you would like to review the great public events which have been here commemorated,—the treaty of peace in 1783, the adoption of the constitution in 1789, the death of Washington in 1800; the civic and

* Mr. Howland states, (Stone's Life, etc., page 37,) that the Boston Port Bill drove many carpenters and masons away from that town, who came to Providence and were employed upon the meeting-house; and that Mr. Sumner, who superintended the erection of the steeple, was one of them.

religious occasions, when, in praise and prayer, when, in jubilee or humiliation, the people have here, as in some common temple, acknowledged the God of power and of mercy.

There are the common as well as uncommon days and Sabbaths; the words of how many lips, once eloquent with authority or persuasion, now hushed in death. What a history is enclosed within these walls! What a shadowy procession of persons and events going in and out here,—funerals and weddings and baptisms; sermons whose memory lingers yet, whose influences will never die; and then the more spiritual and interior events and experiences which have passed through the souls of these three generations; the souls which have here bowed to the authority of God, and melted into love before the Saviour's cross here lifted up to faith; the vows, uttered and unuttered, in which they have given themselves to God and to duty; the viewless winds of the Spirit breathing here, and leaving blessed fruits which ripen glorious and abundant in the house not made with hands!

The fine steel engraving accompanying the present sketch was designed, it may be added, by James S. Lincoln, an artist of Providence, and engraved by Messrs. G. G. Smith and J. W. Watts, of Boston.

UNIVERSITY GRAMMAR SCHOOL.

ERECTED IN 1810.

IN the month of April, 1764, the Rev. James Manning, as we have already stated in our Historical Sketch, opened a Latin School in the town of Warren, Rhode Island, with a view to the beginning of college instruction. This School, therefore, was the germ of the future College. In 1770, it was removed to Providence, and for two years was carried on in one of the chambers of the Brick School House, so called, now the Meeting Street Grammar School. The first allusion that we find concerning it, after its removal, appears in the GAZETTE, in an account of the first Commencement held in Providence:—" The business of the day being concluded, and before the assembly broke up, a piece from Homer was pronounced by Master Billy Edwards, one of the Grammar School boys, not nine years old." This Edwards was a son of the Rev. Morgan Edwards, one of the founders of the College. He graduated in 1776, at the early age, it appears, of fourteen. In 1772, the School was removed to a room on the lower floor of the new College edifice, as we learn from the following notice, which was also published in the GAZETTE:—

Whereas several gentlemen have requested me to take and educate their sons, this may inform them, and others disposed to put their children under my care, that the Latin School is now removed, and set up in the College edifice; where proper attention shall be given, by a master duly qualified, and those found to be the most effectual methods to obtain a competent knowledge of grammar steadily pursued. At the same time, spelling, reading, and speaking English with propriety, will be particularly attended to. Any who choose their sons should board in commons, may be accommodated at the same rate with the students,—six shillings per week being the price. And I flatter myself that such attention will be paid to their learning and morals as will entirely satisfy all who may send their children. All books for the School, as well as the classical authors read in College, may be had, at the lowest rate, of the subscriber,

Providence, July 10, 1772.
JAMES MANNING.

The following year, May 20, 1773, President Manning thus writes to his friend the Rev. John Ryland: "I have a Latin School under my care, taught by one of our graduates, of about twenty boys." This graduate was the Rev. Ebenezer David, of the class of 1772. How long he continued in charge of the School we are not informed. The next mention of it appears in the following advertisement, which we also copy from the Providence GAZETTE:—

A Grammar School was opened in the school room within the College edifice on Monday the 11th instant, in which the same mode of teaching the learned languages is pursued, which has given such great satisfaction to the inhabitants of this town.

The scholars are also instructed in spelling, reading, and speaking the English language with propriety, as well as in writing and arithmetic, such part of their time as their parents or guardians direct.

College Library, March 22, 1776.

Under date of November 8, 1783, President Manning writes to his friend Dr. Stennett, "I have the assistance of a Tutor, and a Grammar Master keeps School in the College edifice." This was William Wilkinson, who had just graduated at the Commencement in September. In 1784, Manning writes, "He is a good Master. The School is nearly up to twenty." Mr. Wilkinson retained the charge of the School until 1792. He was eminently successful as a teacher, and fitted for College many of its distinguished alumni. In 1786, the School was removed from the College edifice, back to the Brick School House, on Meeting street, as appears from the following advertisement published in the GAZETTE:—

William Wilkinson informs the public, that, by the advice of the School Committee, he proposes removing his School from the College edifice, on Monday next, to the Brick School House; and sensible of the many advantages resulting from a proper method of instruction in the English language, he has, by the Committee's approbation, associated with him Mr. Asa Learned, as an English instructor. Those gentlemen and ladies who may wish to employ them in the several branches of the Greek, Latin, and English languages taught grammatically, arithmetic, and writing, may depend on the utmost attention being paid to their children. Greek and Latin at twenty-four shillings per quarter; English at sixteen shillings.

Providence, October 20, 1786. WILKINSON AND LEARNED.

From this it appears that the immediate connection of the School with the College was for a time dissolved. The first mention that we find of the School in the records of the Corporation, appears under date of September 4, 1794:—

Voted, That the President use his influence and endeavor to establish a Grammar School in this town, as an appendage to this College, to be under the immediate visitation of the President and the general inspection of the town's School Committee, and that the President also procure a suitable master for such School.

In accordance with this vote the School was again established in the College. In a recent notice of the late Philip Allen, a graduate in the class of 1803, it is stated that "he was prepared for College in the Latin School, then kept in the north-west corner-room of the lower story of the old College building, by Jeremiah Chaplin, afterwards President of Waterville College."

Under the date of September 7, 1809, we find upon the records the following:—

Voted, That a suitable building, in which to keep a Grammar School, be erected on the College lands, provided a sum sufficient to defray the expense of erecting said building can be raised by subscription, that said School be under the management and control of the President of the College, and that Thomas P. Ives, Moses Lippitt, and Thomas Lloyd Halsey, Esqrs., be a committee to raise said sum, and cause said building to be erected, and that they erect the same on the west line of the Steward's garden.

COLLEGE BUILDINGS.   257

Voted, That the President be authorized to procure a master to teach the Grammar School ordered at this meeting, and that if a sufficient sum be not raised from the scholars to pay the salary of the master, the deficiency be paid out of the funds of this University.

In accordance with the foregoing instructions the committee, consisting of Messrs. Ives, Lippitt and Halsey, proceeded at once to procure subscriptions, and to erect a house suitable for the purpose in view, on a part of the College grounds directly opposite the present mansion-house of the President. It was built of brick, twenty-four and one-half by thirty-three feet, and two stories in height. The whole expense was $1,452,86, which amount was obtained from one hundred and eighteen subscribers, mostly citizens of the town, in sums ranging from one hundred dollars down to five, three and two. The following are their names, which we copy from an original document on file:—

Nicholas Brown,	$100 00	Williams Thayer,		$15 00
Thomas P. Ives,	100 00	Moses Eddy,		10 00
Thomas L. Halsey,	50 00	George A. Hallowell,		8 00
Moses Lippitt,	50 00	William Church,		10 00
Richard Jackson, Jr.,	20 00	James B. Mason,		20 00
Samuel G. Arnold,	30 00	Adams & Lothrop,		10 00
John Rogers,	30 00	Jonathan Russell,		20 00
John Corliss,	20 00	Benjamin Hoppin,		10 00
John S. Carlile,	20 00	Benjamin Clifford,		10 00
Sullivan Dorr,	30 00	Caleb Earl,		5 00
Thomas Arnold,	10 00	Isaac Boorom,		10 00
James Brown,	20 00	William Taylor,		5 00
William Holroyd,	10 00	Sanford Branch,		5 00
Ephraim Bowen,	20 00	Salmon Arnold,		10 00
Alexander Jones,	10 00	Stephen Tillinghast,		10 00
George Jackson,	10 00	Richmond Bullock,		10 00
William Wilkinson,	10 00	Ephraim Talbot,		10 00
Nehemiah Dodge,	10 00	G. W. Page,		5 00
Samuel Ames,	10 00	Burrows Aborn,		5 00
Asa Ames,	10 00	John Bowers,		5 00
William Blodget,	10 00	Jacob Scesman,		12 50
Samuel Eddy,	10 00	Thomas Thomson,		10 00
James Rhodes,	20 00	Gustavus Taylor,		10 00
William Jones,	10 00	Benjamin & Charles Dyer,		10 00
Peter Grinnell,	10 00	Olney Winsor,		5 00

BROWN UNIVERSITY.

Christopher Rhodes,	$5 00	Samuel Wheaton,	$5 00
Thomas Sessions,	10 00	Samuel N. Richmond,	5 00
Benjamin T. Chandler,	10 00	Joseph S. Martin,	10 00
Nathaniel Searle, Jr.,	10 00	Cash.	3 00
Obadiah M. Brown,	15 00	George Earle,	5 00
William H. Mason,	10 00	Israel Bullock,	5 00
James Burrill, Jr.,	10 00	George W. Hoppin,	3 00
H. P. Franklin,	5 00	Charles Low,	7 50
Young Seamans,	10 00	Cash.	2 00
Moses M. Atwell,	10 00	Jesse Comstock,	5 00
Tristam Burges,	10 00	Earle & Branch,	7 13
Samuel Bridgham,	5 00	William Snow,	5 53
Wheeler Martin,	5 00	Seth Adams,	2 00
Cash,	3 00	Joseph Martin,	3 33
Ebenezer Thomson,	5 00	John Carlile,	5 00
William Bowen,	10 00	Asa & Smith Bosworth,	20 00
Thomas S. Webb,	10 00	Asa Ames,	10 00
Taft & Waterman,	5 00	T. P. Clarke,	3 00
Oliver Earle,	5 00	William Almy,	5 00
Thomas Coles,	10 00	Stephen Dexter,	10 00
Philip Allen,	10 00	Edward Dexter,	8 00
Samuel Dexter,	5 00	David L. Barnes,	10 00
William Valentine,	15 00	Robert Rogers,	5 00
Nathaniel G. Olney,	10 00	Thomas Tillinghast,	5 00
Nicholas Power,	10 00	John T. Child,	5 00
Greene & Carter,	5 00	William Patten,	5 00
John Dorrance,	10 00	Lucius Bolles,	10 00
Thomas C. Hoppin,	5 00	Asa Messer,	10 00
Nathaniel Searle,	10 00	Simeon Martin,	10 00
D. C. Cushing,	5 00	Nathan B. Crocker,	10 00
Samuel P. Allen,	5 00	Henry Edes,	5 00
Samuel Aborn,	10 00	Moses Lippitt, additional.	1 57
Joshua B. Wood,	5 00	Brown & Ives, additional, (they	
Walter Paine,	5 00	having in vain attempted to	
Cash,	3 00	get part of the same sub-	
Alexander Adie,	5 00	scribed by others,)	90 30
Isaac Pitman,	10 00		
Nathaniel Pearce,	5 00	Total.	1,452 86

We should be glad in this connection to present a complete list of all the Masters of the Latin or Grammar School from the beginning; the means for this, however, are not at hand, no mention whatever being made of them in the records and files of the Corporation. The following names have already been alluded to, viz.: Rev. James Manning, D. D., 1764-70; Rev.

Ebenezer David, 1772—; William Wilkinson, A. M., 1783-92; Rev. Jeremiah Chaplin, D. D. Mr. Chaplin graduated in 1799, and as he instructed Mr. Allen, who was admitted to the College in September of this year, he must have devoted a portion of his time to the Grammar School while an undergraduate. The President of the College, it will be observed, had the general care and oversight of the School, employing such Masters as he pleased. In the early catalogues of the College we find the following names of "Preceptors of the Grammar School," appended to the list of College officers, viz.: Wood Furman, A. M., 1808; Rev. Ebenezer Burgess, D. D., 1809; Rev. Harvey Jenks, 1810; David Avery, 1811–12; George Fisher, 1813; Rev. Solomon Peck, D. D., 1816; Rev. Willard Pierce, 1818; Rev. Jesse Hartwell. D. D., 1819–21; Hon. Isaac Davis, LL. D., 1822; Rev. Silas A. Crane, D.D., 1823; Prof. George W. Keely, LL. D., 1824.

Whether the School was continued regularly from this date, we have not the means of determining. It is probable, however, that there were interruptions. For many years after the completion of the building, the upper part was used for the Medical Lectures that were formerly given in connection with the College. In 1837, Mr. Benjamin H. Rhodes, of the class of 1833, took charge of the School and continued it two years. In 1839, he was succeeded by Mr. Joseph S. Pitman, who taught it for a short time. In 1843, Mr. Elbridge Smith, who had been a Tutor in College during the two preceding years, assumed the charge, and the following year Mr. Henry S. Frieze, a graduate in the class of 1841, was associated with him. In 1845, Mr. Smith left the School, and his place was supplied by Mr. Merrick Lyon, also a graduate in the class of 1841. Under their joint management the UNIVERSITY GRAMMAR SCHOOL had a brilliant and successful career. The number of pupils greatly increased, so that in the year 1852 they were encouraged to make, at their own expense, an addition to the building of thirty-five feet, and to supply the commodious halls and rooms thus obtained, with all the modern conveniences and appointments of a first class school. The present dimensions of the building, therefore, are twenty-four and one-half feet by sixty-eight. In 1854, Mr. Frieze accepted a Latin Professorship in the University of Michigan, at Ann Arbor, and his place was supplied by Dr. Emory Lyon, who, from that time onward, has had charge of the English and mathematical departments, while his brother has had charge of the classical department. Under their skillful management the School has increased in usefulness and reputation. As it was in the beginning, so is it now, a most important help to the College, training for admittance thereto large numbers of scholars, who take high rank in their respective classes, and thus do honor to their early instructors. As an illustration, we may mention that during the past twenty years two hundred and twelve young men have entered the University, who were prepared for College at the University Grammar School.

HOPE COLLEGE.

ERECTED IN 1822.

THE first mention made of this building, appears on the records under date of September 6, 1821:—

Voted, That the President, and Messrs. Brown, Ives, Halsey, Rhodes, Jackson and Dorr, be a Committee to consider on the propriety of erecting another College edifice, or other building or buildings, a suitable place on which to erect the same, with a plan of the building or buildings, and generally such information on the subject as they may think proper; and that said Committee report at the adjourned meeting of this Corporation.

At the adjourned meeting aforesaid, held on the 10th of October following, it was

Voted, That the President and Messrs. Brown, Ives, Halsey, Rhodes, Jackson and Dorr, be a Committee to select and if necessary to purchase a suitable site for another College edifice, and that they be authorized to erect the edifice on such plan and of such dimensions as they may think proper.

Voted, further, That said Committee be authorized to solicit donations and draw on the treasury for the above purpose.

At an adjourned meeting of the Corporation held on the 13th of January, 1823, the Committee made the following report, viz.:—

The Committee appointed in September, 1821, to procure a suitable piece of land and erect thereon a College edifice, beg leave to refer to the treasurer's report for the 3d of September, 1822, for particulars concerning the lot purchased of Mr. Nathan Waterman. On this lot an elegant brick building of the following dimensions, has been erected by Nicholas Brown, Esq., the distinguished patron of the University, in length one hundred and twenty feet, width forty feet, four stories high, and containing forty-eight rooms; the object therefore is accomplished, and no part of the funds placed at the disposal of the Committee by the Corporation, has been used towards said building. Mr. Brown, it is understood, will make a communication on the subject of the new College edifice, at the meeting to be holden by adjournment in the University Chapel, on Monday, the 13th of January instant, to which communication the Committee invite the attention of the Corporation.

Respectfully submitted by

THOMAS LLOYD HALSEY,
RICHARD JACKSON,
SULLIVAN DORR,
THOMAS P. IVES,
ASA MESSER,
JAMES RHODES,
} Committee.

Brown University, January 11, 1822.

Mr. Daniel Hale, it may be added, was the master mason, and Mr. Samuel Staples, the master builder.

The following is Mr. Brown's communication to which the Committee refer in the foregoing report:—

TO THE CORPORATION OF BROWN UNIVERSITY:—

It affords me great pleasure, at this adjourned meeting of the Corporation to state, that the College edifice, erected last season, and located on the land purchased by the Corporation of Mr. Nathan Waterman, is completed.

Being warmly attached to the Institution where I received my education, among whose founders and benefactors was my honored father, deceased, and believing that the dissemination of letters and knowledge is the great means of social happiness, I have caused this edifice to be erected wholly at my expense, and now present it to the Corporation of Brown University, to be held with the other corporate property, according to their charter.

As it may be proper to give a name to this new edifice, I take leave to suggest to the Corporation that of "Hope College."

I avail myself of this occasion to express a hope that Heaven will bless and make it useful in the promotion of virtue, science and literature, to those of the present and of future generations who may resort to this University for education. With respectful and affectionate regards to the individual members of the Corporation,

I am their friend,

NICHOLAS BROWN.

The above communication having been read by the Chancellor pro tem, Hon. Richard Jackson, it was thereupon,

Resolved, That the members of this Corporation entertain a very high sense of the liberality of this patron of science, in the gift of this new building, in addition to his former large donations to this University.

Resolved, That in compliance with the suggestion of the donor, the new edifice be denominated HOPE COLLEGE.

It is further Resolved, That, the Honorable David Howell, Rev. Henry Edes, and Stephen H. Smith, Esq., be a Committee to devise and report at our next annual meeting the most eligible means to manifest our gratitude for this illustrious instance of public munificence.

At this meeting it was also

Voted, That the old College edifice be named UNIVERSITY HALL.

Mrs. Hope Ives, for whom the new edifice was named, was the only surviving sister of Mr. Brown. Their grandparents were Judge Daniel Jenckes, whose name appears conspicuous in connection with the history of the College charter, and Joanna Scott, a descendant of Richard Scott, who was one of the original founders of the Colony and a contemporary of Roger Williams. Mrs. Ives was born on the 22d of February, 1773. In the year

1792, March 6, she was married to Thomas Poynton Ives, Esq., by the Rev. President Maxcy. Of their six children, the first born was Mrs. Charlotte R. Goddard, and the fourth, Mr. Robert H. Ives, both still living. The second child, the late Moses B. Ives, died August 7, 1857, as has already been stated in our History of the College Library. Their mother died August 21st, 1855, at the age of eighty-two, "venerated," says the late Dr. Wayland, "by the public, beloved by the good, and mourned by the widow and orphan."

No sum is anywhere named in the records as the cost of Hope College. From other sources, however, it is ascertained that the bills for its erection amounted to about twenty thousand dollars. For many years the upper rooms of the north division of the building, have been occupied by the Philermenian and United Brothers Societies.

This building, the fourth that has been erected exclusively for the College, came very near being destroyed by the devouring element a few months ago. On Wednesday, December 5, 1866, at a quarter to twelve, while the students were engaged in recitation, a fire broke out in room number fifteen, south division. The alarm was given, and through the vigorous exertions of the students it was speedily subdued, without the aid of the fire department, which was promptly on the ground. Had it been discovered half an hour later, or had there been a high wind at the time, Hope College, and perhaps Manning Hall adjoining, must have been destroyed. As it was, considerable damage was done in the room where the fire originated.

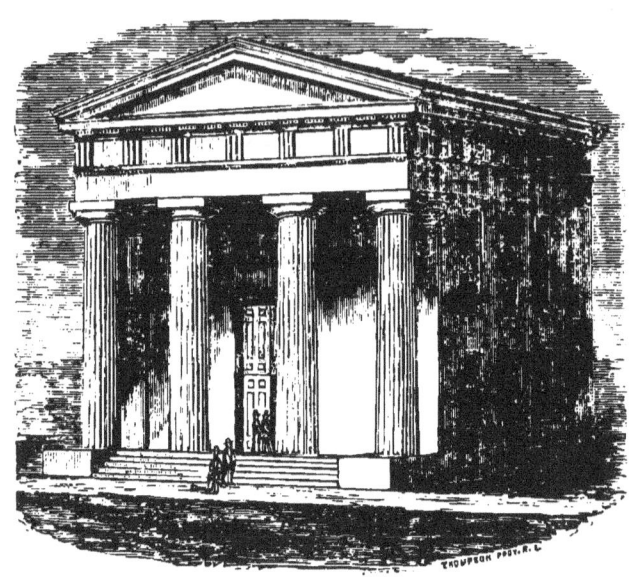

MANNING HALL.

ERECTED IN 1834.

THIS building, as has already been stated in our History of the College Library, was erected solely at the expense of the Hon. Nicholas Brown, and by him presented to the Corporation, with a request that it might be called MANNING HALL, in honor of his distinguished instructor and revered friend, President Manning. By a singular oversight, no mention is made of this munificent gift in the records. The only allusion which we find to the building, is under date September 4, 1834: "Voted, That the Librarian, after the books shall have been removed to the new building, be required to attend in the Library room from ten to twelve o'clock, A. M., during the ordinary College terms." At the next annual meeting it was "Resolved, That the Hon. Nicholas Brown be requested by this Corporation to sit for his portrait." This is the portrait that now graces the collection in Rhode Island Hall.

Manning Hall is composed of two spacious apartments, one of which was designed for the Library, and the other for the purposes of a College chapel. To these uses it was dedicated by appropriate literary and religious exercises, on the 4th of February, 1835, at which time a discourse was delivered by President Wayland, on the "Dependence of Science upon Revealed Religion." This discourse was afterwards published. The following original ode, by Albert G. Greene, Esq., of the class of 1820, was sung on the occasion:—

> To thee, fair Science, to thee,
> In thy courts we with joy and with gratitude come;
> To thee, fair Science, to thee,
> With song and with music to offer the dome,
> A temple for thee, for thy children a home:
> For this, to its portals we gladly repair,
> And make vocal its walls with thanksgiving and prayer.
>
> To thee, loved Freedom, to thee,
> We offer the tribute and hallow the fane:
> And hence may the sons of the free
> Go forth, thy great cause o'er the earth to maintain:
> Oh! ne'er be their hopes nor their labors in vain—
> Nor this roof ever echo the tread of the slave,
> Which is reared for the home of the free and the brave.
>
> To thee, pure Religion, to thee,
> We have built the fair temple, made sacred the shrine:
> And ever, blest faith, may it be
> Kept holy to thee and thy service divine;
> It is Learning's—'tis Freedom's—'tis Thine.
> Through ages unborn, let its altar still be,
> Thou God of our fathers, kept holy to thee.

The following original ode, by another Alumnus of the College, (the late Bishop Burgess, of Maine,) was sung at the close of the exercises:—

  Ages after ages urge
   On and on, like ocean waves;
  Soon shall break the future surge
   O'er our long-forgotten graves:
  Yon bright bay as bright shall gleam,
   Yon fair city rise as fair,
  Yon rich meads as richly teem;—
   Other eyes shall see them there.

  Yet shall Learning's hoary halls
   Win the vot'ry step of youth;
  Yet shall speak these echoing walls,
   Sacred still to sacred truth:
  And must ours be voiceless sleep,
   Ours an image left on nought,
  Lost beneath the whelming deep
   All we were and all we wrought?

  No! through many a distant age,
   Each and all unchang'd may live;
  No! to form the future's page
   Each and all have much to give:
  Patient toils and worthy aims,
   Guarded trusts and cherish'd powers,
  Blameless lives and stainless names,
   These we give, if these be ours.

  Clasp we then the brother hand,
   Seal the compact, fair and fast;
  Long as these lov'd walls shall stand,
   That unsullied gift shall last!
  Thou, whose truth is saving might,
   Thou, whose love is strong defence,
  Lift the Cross of life and light,
   Lift it here, and send it hence!

The cost of Manning Hall is stated by Professor Gammell, in his "Sketch of the educational and other Benefactions of the late Hon. Nicholas Brown," to have been eighteen thousand five hundred dollars. It is an exact model of the temple of DIANA-PROPYLEA, in Eleusis, being just twice the size of the original. The plan and details were obtained from a work entitled, "The Unedited Antiquities of Attica, comprising the Architectural Remains of Eleusis, Rhamnus, and Thericus. By the Dilettanti Society." Folio, London, 1817. The following description of the building is taken from one of the notes in President Wayland's published discourse:—

This College edifice, the third which has been erected, is built of stone. Including the portico, it is about ninety feet in length, by forty-two in width. Its height, from the top of the basement, is forty feet. The Library occupies the whole of the first floor, and is a beautiful room. In the centre, it is ornamented with a double row of fluted columns. The Library is sixty-four feet by thirty-eight, and is thirteen feet high. The Chapel is on the second floor It exhibits the most graceful proportions. Its length and breadth are the same as those of the Library. Its height, however, is not less than twenty-five feet. The front of the edifice is ornamented with four fluted columns, resting on a platform projecting thirteen feet from the walls. Manning Hall is situated between University Hall and Hope College, equidistant from each. It is of the Doric order, and is said to be one of the finest specimens to be found in the country. Mr. Russell Warren was the architect; Mr. Daniel Hale, the master mason; and Messrs. Tallman & Bucklin, the master builders.

In 1857, the Chapel was embellished and greatly improved at the expense, it is understood, of Messrs. Brown and Ives. The walls were painted, the ceiling was frescoed, and the windows were removed to give place to new ones, with ornamental sashes, and flock and stained glass. On the east wall, directly over the pulpit, an elegant and costly mural tablet was erected in honor of Nicholas Brown, by his nephews, Moses B. and Robert H. Ives. The tablet was made at the marble works of Tingley Brothers, who furnished for it the design. Upon it is the following inscription:—

COLLEGE BUILDINGS.   269

NICOLAUS. BROWN. A. M.
VIR. INTEGRITATE. INCORRUPTA
SUMMA. IN. HOMINES. BENEVOLENTIA
PIETATE. ERGA. DEUM. EXIMIA
PRÆDITUS
VERE. BEATUS. NON. QUOD. MULTA. POSSEDERIT
SED. QUIA. DEI. MUNERIBUS. UTI
SCIVIT. CALLUITQUE
UT. NON. SIBI. VIVERET. SED. ALIOS. BEATOS. REDDERET
PLENA. MANU. ANIMOQUE. LIBENTE. INOPES. ADJUVABAT
ET. OMNIA. CONSILIA. ATQUE. OPERA
RELIGIONI. MORIBUSQUE. PUBLICIS. SECUNDA
PROMOVERE. SEMPER. LABORABAT
DOCTRINAE. AE. LITERARUM
OMNIUMQUE. VERAE. HUMANITATIS. STUDIORUM
FAUTOR. ERAT. MUNIFICUS
ATQUE. HUIC. UNIVERSITATI. QUAE. EJUS. NOMINE. GAUDET
PATRONUS. ET. INSIGNE. PRAESIDIUM
NATUS. IV. APRILIS. M. DCC. LXIX
OBIIT. XXVII. SEPTEMBRIS. M. DCCC. XLI

And on the lower part of the Tablet:—

MOSES. BROWN. IVES. ET. ROBERTUS. HALE. IVES
AVUNCULI. SUI. IN. PIAM. MEMORIAM
HANC. TABULAM
PONENDAM. CURAVERUNT
M. DCCC. LVII

In 1866, a handsome tablet of white marble was placed on the north side of the Chapel, in memory of the students and graduates of the University, who have fallen in the recent civil war. It was dedicated with appropriate services, on Tuesday afternoon, September 4. Prayer was offered by Rev. Prof. Dunn, and remarks were offered by Mr. J. B. Mustin, chairman of the committee of undergraduates, by whom, and at whose expense mainly, the enterprise had been carried forward. Remarks were also made by Rev. Prof. Diman, Gen. A. B. Underwood, of Newton Centre, Massachusetts, Bishop B. B. Smith, of Kentucky, Abraham Payne, Esq., of Providence, and Rev. J. B. Simmons, of Philadelphia, all graduates of the University.

The inscription reads thus:—

IN MEMORIAM FRATRUM SUORUM
QUI PRO LIBERTATE
ET PRO REIPUBLICAE INTEGRITATE
IN BELLO CIVILI CECIDERUNT
LITERARUM STUDIOSI
IN HAC UNIVERSITATE COMMORANTES
HANC TABULAM POSUERUNT
MDCCCLXVI.

No names have yet been inscribed upon the tablet, in consequence of the difficulty of procuring a complete list of the graduates who have fallen in battle. The following are the names reported by the committee at the dedication, viz.: Sullivan Ballou, of Pawtucket, a member of the Sophomore class in 1849; Charles Bertrand Randall, of Somerset, Massachusetts, class of 1852; Robert Hale Ives, of Providence, class of 1857; William H. Kneass, of Philadelphia, who left College in 1858, while a member of the Junior class; James Clark Williams, of New York city, class of 1861; William Ide Brown, of Fisherville, New Hampshire, class of 1862; and James Peck Brown, of Rehoboth, Massachusetts, class of 1863. To this list should be added the name of Thomas Poynton Ives, of the class of 1854. He did not, it is true, fall in battle, but his recent untimely death was undoubtedly occasioned by exposure and fatigue during the war. Additional names will be found when the roll of honor for Brown University, now in course of preparation by Major Henry S. Burrage, shall be fully made up.

Within a few years the exterior of Manning Hall has been thoroughly repaired and painted, at an expense of thirty-five hundred dollars, the amount having been generously subscribed for this purpose by Mr. John Carter Brown.

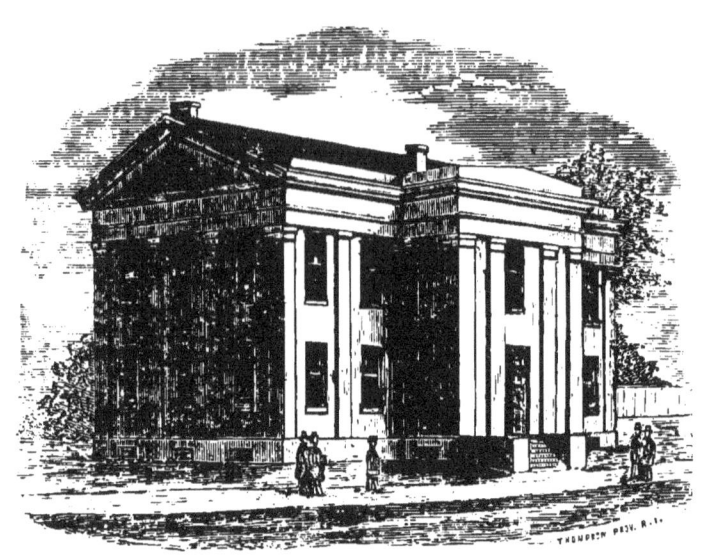

RHODE ISLAND HALL.

ERECTED IN 1840.

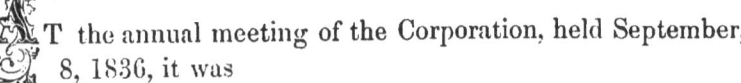T the annual meeting of the Corporation, held September, 8, 1836, it was

Voted, That a Committee be appointed to devise means for erecting a building for lecture rooms, and rooms for the reception of geological and physiological specimens; and that Messrs. Richard J Arnold, Timothy R. Greene, and James H. Duncan, be that Committee.

The following year it was

Voted, That the Committee, appointed last year, to devise means for erecting a building for lecture rooms, etc., be continued; and that John C. Brown be added to that Committee.

Voted, That the treasurer (Moses B. Ives, Esq.) be requested to consider and report on the expediency of improving the College grounds.

September 6, 1838, it was

Voted, That the existing Committee on the subject of devising means for erecting lecture rooms, etc., be requested to proceed; and that the Rev. Dr. Wayland be added to that Committee; and that they have authority to erect a building, as soon as means may be obtained.

The Committee now consisted of Messrs. Arnold, Greene, Duncan, Brown, and Wayland. The history of the new enterprise from this point, may best be given in an extract from the President's annual report of the Faculty for 1839:—

Nearly two years since, the President of the University received a letter from a lady interested in the prosperity of the Institution, generously offering the sum of five hundred dollars, to be appropriated to the increase of the means of instruction in physical science, provided the additional sum of fifteen hundred dollars, should, within a specified time, be subscribed towards the same object. An effort was made to raise the requisite sum, but it unfortunately failed. The lady then expressed her willingness to contribute the same amount, in aid of any other effort which might be made, to promote the interests of learning in the University.

At the very time when this subject was in agitation, several benevolent gentlemen in Providence privately expressed to some members of the Corporation, a willingness to unite in any attempt that might be thought important to promote the prosperity of the Institution. Soon after the last Commencement, (1838,) these gentlemen met at the house of the President, and the sum of twenty-five hundred dollars (including the offer before mentioned) was subscribed towards the erection of an additional building to be devoted to the purposes of physical science. After considerable effort had been made, and it seemed impossible to raise the subscription to the required amount, the treasurer of the University received from the munificent benefactor of this Institution, the Hon. Nicholas Brown, a letter, of which the following is a copy:—

"PROVIDENCE, March 18, 1839.

"MOSES BROWN IVES, ESQ., TREASURER OF BROWN UNIVERSITY—

"DEAR SIR:— In common with a number of the friends of Brown University, I desire the erection of a suitable mansion-house for the President, and likewise of another College edifice for the accommodation of the departments of Natural Philosophy, Chemistry, Mineralogy, Geology, and Natural History. As it is highly important that these buildings, so necessary to the welfare of the Institution, should be erected without delay, I hereby tender to the acceptance of the Corporation, two lots of land on Waterman street, as a site for the President's house, and the lot of land called the Hopkins estate, on George street, as a site for the College edifice; and I hereby pledge myself for the sum of ten thousand dollars, viz.: seven thousand dollars for the President's house, and three thousand dollars towards the erection of the College edifice, the suitable improvement of the adjacent grounds, and the increase of the permanent means of instruction in the departments of Chemistry, Mineralogy, etc., provided an equal amount be subscribed by the friends of the University before the first of May, next.

"I am, with affectionate regards, and great personal respect for all the friends and patrons of the University,

Respectfully,   NICHOLAS BROWN."

Encouraged by this munificent offer, a vigorous effort was at once made to secure Mr. Brown's donation. Within the time specified the requisite sum was subscribed, the friends of the University cordially coöperating in a movement so auspicious to the cause of good learning. The following are the subscribers' names:—

Nicholas Brown,	- - - $10,000	Zachariah Allen, - - - $100
Amasa Manton,	- - - 1,000	James Rhodes, - - - 100
Hope Ives,	- - - 1,000	Horatio N. Slater, - - - 100
Thomas J. Stead,	- - 500	Samuel W. Bridgham, - 100
Amory Chapin,	- - 500	John Barstow, - - - 100
Richard J. Arnold,	- - 500	Peter Pratt, - - - 100
Francis Wayland,	- - 500	Josiah Chapin, - - - 100
Moses B. Ives,	- - 500	Benjamin Aborn, - - - 100
Robert H. Ives,	- - 500	Matthew Watson, - - - 100
William G. Goddard,	- - 500	Benjamin Hoppin, - - - 100
Philip Allen & Son,	- - 500	Richard W. Greene, - - 100
William Sprague,	- - 500	Richard Waterman, - - 100
Samuel Ward & Brother,	- 500	James H. Duncan, - - 100
John Whipple,	- - - 300	Lyman Tiffany, - - - 100
Seth Adams, Jr.,	- - 200	Samuel F. Man, - - - 100
Thomas Burgess,	- - 200	Alexis Caswell, - - - 100
Peter Grinnell & Sons,	- - 200	George I. Chace, - - - 60
Truman Beckwith,	- - 100	Sarah J. Slater, - - - 50
Thomas L. Halsey,	- - 100	Samuel B. Tobey, - - - 50
Samuel Larned,	- - 100	Thomas M. Burgess, - - 50

Henry A. Rogers,	$50	William Gammell,	$40
Henry P. Franklin,	50	Joseph Balch, Jr.,	20
Elisha Dyer, Jr.,	50	Walter S. Burges,	20
John L. Hughes,	50	Ezra W. Howard,	20
Thomas C. Hoppin,	50	William P. Bullock,	20
John Kingsbury,	50	Henry B. Anthony,	10
Thomas F. Carpenter,	50	Allen O. Peck,	10
William T. Dorrance,	50	Samuel W. Peckham,	10
Samuel N. Richmond,	50	C. A. Ballou,	10
Isaac Brown,	50	Henry Earle,	10
Lemuel H. Elliot,	50	Gamaliel L. Dwight,	10
Joseph Mauran,	50		
James F. Simmons,	50	Total,	$20,890
Elizabeth Waterman,	50		

With the exception of about six hundred dollars, the whole of the foregoing sum was subscribed by citizens of Providence and vicinity. Rhode Island Hall was opened for public inspection on Commencement day, September 3, 1840; and, on the day following, it was dedicated to the uses for which it was built, by an appropriate address from the late Professor William G. Goddard. Owing to the sudden illness of the author, the difficult task of reading the manuscript was kindly undertaken by the Rev. Dr. Crocker. The subject of the address was, THE SOCIAL INFLUENCE OF THE HIGHER INSTITUTIONS OF LEARNING. It was discussed in a most skillful and thorough manner, and the thoughts were expressed in the peculiarly classical and elegant language for which the writer was distinguished. We sincerely regret that the address has never been published, in accordance with the unanimously expressed wishes of the Corporation. The building is of stone covered with cement, seventy feet long by forty-two feet wide, with a projection in front of twelve feet by twenty-six. The first floor is divided into two lecture rooms, one for the Professor of Chemistry, the other for the Professor of Natural Philosophy. The second story is thrown into an ample and beautiful hall, of chaste proportions, for the cabinet of Mineralogy, Geology, and other similar collections of the University.

Its walls at present are adorned with the portraits of distinguished graduates and friends of the College, and those who have acquired a name in the history of the State. This hall is open to the public on Saturdays in the afternoon, and is often visited by citizens and strangers. There is also a commodious basement, with an entrance on George street, containing a chemical laboratory, and other apartments suitable for conducting chemical analysis, and the various processes of Chemistry applied to the arts. Messrs. Tallman & Bucklin were the builders.

We may add, in this connection, a brief account of the apparatus for the two lecture rooms in Rhode Island Hall. The Rev. Dr. Benedict, in his account of Brown University, in 1813, published in his "General History of the Baptist Denomination," says:—

> The philosophical apparatus, though not so large as those of older universities, is yet respectable for its extent It consists of an orrery, a theodolite, a reflecting telescope, solar and double microscopes, convex and concave mirrors, lenses, globes, an air pump, the gift of the late Nicholas Brown, Esq., machinery for Hydrostatics, Electricity and Mechanics, together with such other articles as are necessary to a respectable course of experiments in Natural Philosophy. A number of these articles were purchased with a donation of five hundred dollars from the late Samuel Elam, Esq.

Mr. Elam was a resident of Newport. He made the donation to which Benedict refers, in 1799, "for the purpose of purchasing a philosophical apparatus for the use of Rhode Island College." Whereupon, the Corporation, at a special meeting held October 14,

> RESOLVED, That the thanks of this Corporation be returned to Mr. Elam, for his generous and very acceptable donation; and also that the Hon. Jabez Bowen, Esq., Chancellor of the College, be authorized to accept of Mr. Elam the above mentioned donation in behalf of the Corporation.

President Wayland, in his Discourse on the Life and Character of the Hon. Nicholas Brown, published in 1841, further remarks:—

The philosophical apparatus, which had been purchased at different times, and most of it at a remote period, had become, from ordinary wear and accident, almost unfit for use. With the exception of a valuable astronomical clock, and an excellent transit instrument, by Troughton, the gift of Mr. J. C. Brown and Mr. R. H Ives, the whole of it was, I think, inferior to that which at present we frequently see in the possession of many of our high schools and academies By the liberality of Mr. Brown and his brother-in-law, Mr. Thomas P. Ives, this department was at once placed in its present advantageous position. These gentlemen directed the Faculty to order, at their expense, such a set of apparatus, in all the departments of experimental science, as the wants of the University seemed to require. These instruments were received in the year 1829. The University was thus furnished at once with as ample means for philosophical illustration as almost any in our country, and superior, in fact, to those possessed by many similar institutions in Europe.

To the apparatus thus furnished, large additions have been made from year to year, from the income of the Library fund, which income, according to the original conditions of subscription. is "to be appropriated to the purchase of books for the Library, and apparatus for the philsosophical and chemical departments of Brown University."

Within the past year an important addition has been made to this department through the liberality of Messrs. J. C. Brown and R. H. Ives. It consists of Melloni's heat apparatus, Ruhmkorff's induction coil for Electricity, Duboscq's lantern, Bunsen's battery, fifty cups, and a nine prism spectroscope. The expense of this addition, it is understood, was about two thousand dollars. The University, therefore, has now excellent facilities for illustrating the latest discoveries in light and heat, and in general for the study of the natural and physical sciences.

PRESIDENT'S HOUSE.

ERECTED IN 1840.

THIS is a commodious house of graceful proportions, built of wood, as the engraving represents. Its dimensions are forty-six by thirty-seven feet, with an octagonal projection in front, forming a vestibule. The lower story is twelve feet high, and the chambers are ten feet. Over the front door is an Ionic portico, eight by seven feet. The addition is twenty-one by eighteen feet, the lower story being eight feet high, and the chambers seven feet. Attached to this is a wood-house, eighteen by seventeen feet. The builders were Messrs. Tallman & Bucklin.

The house fronts on George street, the lot being bounded on the north, east and south by Waterman, Prospect and George streets. It was occupied by President Wayland upon its completion; and here he held his customary reception or levee on Commencement evening, September 3, 1840. Immediately afterwards the old house, which stood directly opposite, was removed to College street, a little below Benefit, where it now forms a part of the wooden block of buildings in that vicinity.* A solitary pump without a handle still indicates the former site.

Agreeably to the original design, as has already been stated, the grounds in front of the University buildings were at this time graded and adorned with gravelled walks; the Lombardy poplars, planted in 1803, by Ezekiel Robins, according to the records, were removed, and their places supplied by the hardy and graceful elms; and the whole College enclosure was surrounded by a new and handsome paling, making it, in the language of President Wayland, "an ornament to the city of Providence, and one of the loveliest spots in New England."

In the year 1854, the Corporation erected a substantial brick barn for the accommodation of the President, on Prospect street, at the rear end of the Grammar School lot. The cost of this improvement, as appears from the Treasurer's report for September, 1855, was a little less than twenty-five hundred dollars.

* On page 246, it is stated inadvertently that the old house was removed in 1839. President Wayland occupied the old house until the new one was completed.

CHEMICAL LABORATORY.

ERECTED IN 1862.

GREAT advances have been made in the science of Chemistry within the past few years, creating a demand for improved facilities for instruction in this department of learning, intimately connected as it is with manufacturing interests and industrial pursuits. To this demand the Corporation of Brown University have promptly responded. A neat and substantial Laboratory, combining utility, economy and beauty, in harmonious proportions, has been erected on the east side of the College campus, at an expense, including the cost of apparatus and fittings, of about fifteen thousand dollars. Subscriptions for this object, to the amount of fourteen thousand two hundred and fifty dollars, were obtained mostly through the exertions of Nathaniel P. Hill, formerly the Professor of Chemistry applied to the arts. The additional expense of about one thousand dollars, was provided for from the general funds of the University. The following are the names of the subscribers:—

Seth Padelford,	$5,000	Julia Bullock,	$500
John Carter Brown,	2,000	Royal C. Taft,	300
Thomas P. Shepard,	1,000	Cyrus Taft,	100
Horatio N. Slater,	1,000	John F. Chapin,	100
Amos D. & James Y. Smith,	1,000	J. P. Balch & Son,	100
Cash, (to be expended by Prof. Hill,)	1,000	Cash,	100
Robert H. & T. P. Ives,	1.000	"	50
Earl P. Mason,	500		
Nathaniel P. Hill,	500	Total,	$14,250

The building was completed and occupied in the early part of 1863. It is of the mediaeval Italian style, or more strictly speaking, the Italian Gothic. Its dimensions are, two stories in height, fifty by forty feet, with a projection on the east side thirty-five by fifty-five feet. The walls are of brick, built hollow, faced on the outside with Danvers pressed bricks, and "rendered" on the inside with plaster. The roofs are covered with Vermont slates, laid in alternate bands of purple and green. The underpinning of the entire structure consists of red granite from the Westerly quarries, capped with olive-colored freestone. The window openings have segment or semi-circular heads, with olive and brown freestone voussoirs, the extrados of which are cut to form a pointed arch. The principal entrance doorway is decorated with olive-colored freestone. The band course beneath the main cornice and window sills, are of the same material, from the Albert Quarry, so called, in Nova Scotia. The chairman of the building committee, Thomas P. Shepard, Esq., superintended the work, to whose unwearied pains, and especially to the professional labors of the architect, Mr. Alpheus C. Morse, the friends of the University are largely indebted, for the substantial character of the building, the thoroughness of its workmanship in its several parts, and the economy and skill shown in all its financial details and results.

For all the interior arrangements, as well as the general plans of the building, credit is justly due to Professor Hill, and to his associate, Prof. John Peirce. These gentlemen had for several years given great attention to this department of science, the former having visited the best laboratories in the country, with a view to the ultimate erection of a suitable laboratory at Brown University, while the latter had spent some time in Europe. They were therefore enabled to introduce into it the best features of those which they had examined, together with important improvements.

The appointments of the Laboratory are:—

1. An analytical laboratory, capable of accommodating thirty-four students.
2. A technical laboratory, for special investigations.
3. A library room. Here are already upwards of five hundred volumes of choice works on Chemistry, together with delicate balances, and other costly instruments.
4. An apparatus room.
5. The private laboratories of the professors.
6. A lecture room, with which are connected two preparatory rooms.
7. A photograph room.
8. A dark room for photometric experiments.
9. Five large basement rooms for storage.

The apparatus and fittings for these rooms were made by Thomas Phillips & Co., of Providence, from plans furnished by Prof. Hill. From these same plans, it may be added, these gentlemen have recently furnished the laboratories of Columbia, Yale, and Amherst Colleges, and the Rensselaer Polytechnic Institute, of Troy.

We close this account of the Laboratory, with the following extract from the annual catalogue:—

CHEMISTRY APPLIED TO THE ARTS.

The Chemical Laboratory is open to students (except on Saturdays) from 9 to 12 A. M., and from 3 to 6 P. M.

It is the design of this department to teach students, first, Analytical Chemistry, and then to direct their studies to the practical applications of Chemistry. Particular attention is given to Metallurgy, Pharmacy, Medical Chemistry, and to the applications of Chemistry to manufacturing processes.

The course is not confined to undergraduates; other persons, if prepared to pursue the study to advantage, are admitted to the Laboratory. A knowledge of General Chemistry, however, is necessary to profitable study in this department.

The expenses for students who take a course of two hours daily, are (for a term of twenty weeks) as follows:—

Tuition,	$15.00
Charge for Gas, Chemicals, etc ,	18 33
To this must be added, the charges for breakage, (varying with the student's care,) about	3.00
Total,	$36.33

Students who take courses of four hours or of six hours daily, pay respectively double or treble the above amounts.

JOHN H. APPLETON, Instructor in Analytical Chemistry.
CHARLES M. STILLWELL, Assistant Instructor.

COLLECTION OF PORTRAITS

IN

RHODE ISLAND HALL.

COLLECTION OF PORTRAITS.

THE Collection of Portraits in Rhode Island Hall now comprises thirty-one, many of them painted from life. They represent men of all ranks and professions, and include not only benefactors, officers and graduates of the College, but also soldiers, statesmen and divines, who have distinguished themselves in the annals of Rhode Island. Most of them have been obtained, it will be observed, through the active exertions of the Hon. John R. Bartlett, to whom the thanks of a grateful public are justly due. An enterprise so auspiciously begun, should be continued from year to year, until the Collection shall at least approach more nearly to completion. The following brief historical account will, it is hoped, be useful for reference, and help to awaken new interest in this department of the College :—

1. REV. JAMES MANNING, D. D., first President of the College. Born, 1738; graduated at College of New Jersey, 1762; died, 1791.

An uncommonly fine portrait of the distinguished scholar and divine, to whose untiring and philanthropic exertions the College may be said to owe, if not its origin, at least its continued existence and prosperity for more than a quarter of a century. It was painted from life in the year 1770, by Cosmo Alexander, a Scotch artist, who came from Edinburgh to Newport about this time, and who is said to have been the patron of Gilbert Stuart, giving him his first lesson in drawing. An account of Alexander may be found in "Dunlap's History of the Arts of Design in the United States." From this portrait was engraved the excellent likeness accompanying MANNING AND BROWN UNIVERSITY, and also the present work. In the summer of 1864 it was restored to its original freshness and beauty, by George Howorth & Son, of Boston, and encased in an elegant modern frame, at the expense of Mr. John Carter Brown. A portrait of the wife of President Manning, also painted by Alexander, is in the possession of Mrs. Eliza B. Rogers.

2. REV. DR. MANNING. A second portrait.

This was painted from the original by Mr. James S. Lincoln, of Providence, at the expense of Messrs. Brown & Ives, and by them presented to the Corporation about the year 1840.

3. HON. NICHOLAS BROWN, the distinguished benefactor of the University, and from whom it derives its name. Born, 1769; graduated, 1786; died, 1841.

At the annual meeting of the Corporation, held September 3, 1835, it was resolved, "That the Hon Nicholas Brown be requested by this Corporation to sit for his portrait," and "That Messrs. Robert E. Pattison and Moses B. Ives be a committee to present this request and to carry the resolution into effect." In accordance with this resolve a full length portrait of Mr. Brown was painted during the following year, by Chester Harding, of Boston, the distinguished American portrait painter.

4. REV. FRANCIS WAYLAND, D. D., LL. D., fourth President of the College or University. Born, 1796; graduated at Union College, 1813; died, 1865.

This is a full length portrait, by George P. A. Healy, of Boston. The subject is represented as standing on the platform in front of the pulpit of the First Baptist Church, with his Commencement robe and cap, in the act of giving to the graduating class the customary rolls of parchment. It was painted at the expense of Mr. John Carter Brown, and by him presented to the Corporation about the year 1846.

5. REV. ADONIRAM JUDSON, D. D., the distinguished missionary to Burmah. Born, 1788; graduated, 1807; died, 1850.

This is a half length portrait also by Healy. It was presented to the Corporation in September, 1846, as appears by the following extract from the records: "The

President read a letter from Rev. Dr. Caswell, Rev. Dr. Granger, and Deacon James H. Read, committee of the First Baptist Church, presenting to the Corporation a splendid portrait of the Rev. Adoniram Judson, D. D., and requesting, that, if accepted, it may be placed in a conspicuous place in some of the halls of the College.''

6. WILLIAM CODDINGTON, the first Governor of Rhode Island. Born, 1601; died, 1678.

This was copied from an original portrait in the Council Chamber in Newport, by Thomas Mathewson, Esquire.

7. ESEK HOPKINS, the first Commodore in the American Navy. Born, 1718; died, 1802.

Painted by Mr. M. J. Heade, of Providence, from a mezzotint engraving executed in London, and now in the possession of Mr. John Carter Brown. Commodore Hopkins was a brother of Governor Stephen Hopkins, the signer of the Declaration of Independence. His daughter Susan was married to the Rev. Dr. Maxcy, the second President of the College.

8. ABRAHAM WHIPPLE, the daring Commodore in the American War. Born, 1733; died, 1819.

This is a full length portrait, copied by Mr. Heade from an original in the possession of his grandson, Dr. William Comstock, of Middletown, Massachusetts.

9. MOSES BROWN, the youngest of the "Four Brothers," and a munificent patron of the Friends' Yearly Meeting Boarding School. Born, 1738; died, 1836.

Painted by Mr. Heade, from an original sketch by W. J. Harris.

10. COLONEL WILLIAM BARTON, the daring captor of Major-General Prescott. Born, 1747; died, 1831.

Copied by Mr. Lincoln, from an original portrait in the possession of his daughter, Mrs. Cushman.

11. GILBERT STUART, the celebrated American portrait painter. Born, 1756; died, 1828.

Painted by his daughter, Miss Jane Stuart, from an original miniature in her possession.

12. SAMUEL SLATER, the father of American manufactures. Born, 1768; died, 1835.
   Painted by Mr. Lincoln, from an original portrait also by him.

13. THOMAS POYNTON IVES, a distinguished Providence merchant, and a benefactor of the College. Born, 1769; died, 1835.
   Copied by Mr. Lincoln, from an original picture by Harding.

14. HON. TRISTAM BURGES, LL. D., the distinguished orator and statesman. Born, 1770; graduated, 1796; died, 1853.
   An original portrait painted by C. B. King, Esq., of Washington, and presented by him to the Corporation.

15. HON. HENRY WHEATON, LL. D., the distinguished author of "Elements of International Law." Born, 1785; graduated, 1802; died, 1848.
   Copied by Mr. Heade, from an original portrait by Healy, in the Council Chamber, of Providence.

16. COMMODORE OLIVER HAZARD PERRY, the hero of the naval engagement on Lake Erie. Born, 1785; died, 1820.
   Painted by Miss Jane Stuart, from an original portrait by her father, Gilbert Stuart.

The following letter addressed to the Secretary of the Corporation, gives the history of the portraits numbered 6 to 16:—

PROVIDENCE, August 21, 1857.

SIR:—I am directed by the gentlemen at whose expense the portraits of the distinguished men of Rhode Island have been presented, to place them at the disposal of the Corporation of the University, with the desire that they may be arranged in some suitable hall where they may at all times be accessible. The Collection includes the portraits of Gov. Coddington, Com. Hopkins, Com. Whipple, Com. Perry, Col. Barton, Moses Brown, Henry Wheaton, Gilbert Stuart, Samuel Slater, Thomas P. Ives, and Tristam Burges.

The following are the names of those at whose expense the Collection has been made, viz.: John Carter Brown, Moses B. Ives, Robert H. Ives, Amos D. Smith,

James Y. Smith, Philip Allen & Son, Elisha Dyer, Benjamin Hoppin, Horatio N. Slater, Charles B. King, Mrs. Charlotte R. Goddard.

I am, respectfully, your obedient servant,
JOHN R. BARTLETT.

The three following portraits, and those numbered 21-26, were also obtained through the exertions of Mr. Bartlett:—

17. HON. ASHER ROBBINS, LL. D., a distinguished scholar and statesman, and the first Librarian of the College. Born, 1757; graduated at Yale College, 1782; died, 1845.

Painted from life by the late Charles King, of Newport, and by him presented to the University.

18. REV. GEORGE BERKELY, D. D., the celebrated Irish prelate and philosopher. Resided at Newport in the years 1729-31.

Painted by Henry C. Pratt, of Boston, from an original by Smibert, a Scotch artist, who died in Boston, in 1751. Mr. Smibert came to this country with Berkely, and for a time resided with him as a member of his family.

19. REV. WILLIAM ELLERY CHANNING, D. D., the distinguished Unitarian divine. Born, 1780; graduated at Harvard College, 1798; died, 1842.

This is a fine painting, copied from an original, by Henry C. Pratt.

20. REV. NATHAN B. CROCKER, D. D., the venerable Rector of St. John's Church. Born, 1781; graduated at Harvard College, 1802; died, 1865.

A full length portrait, painted from life by Mr. D. Huntington, of New York.

The following communication respecting it deserves a place in a documentary history of the College. We give it to our readers in full:—

TO THE CORPORATION OF BROWN UNIVERSITY:—

In the month of May last a few gentlemen of this city met by common agreement for the purpose of considering in what manner there might be appropriately expressed to Rev. Nathan B. Crocker, D. D., the venerable Rector of St. John's Church, the high respect and esteem in which his character and services have long been held by his fellow-citizens of Providence. The gentlemen thus meeting were not connected with Dr. Crocker by ecclesiastical associations, and their only object was to devise a suitable mode of giving expression to what they well knew to be the common sentiment among all classes of the community. At this meeting it was determined to request Dr. Crocker to sit for his portrait, to be executed by some artist of distinction, and to be placed, when finished, with the consent of the Corporation, in Rhode Island Hall, with the other portraits belonging to the University. At the same time the undersigned were appointed a committee to carry this determination into immediate execution. In order to give as general a character as practicable to the proceeding, it was also decided to fix the subscriptions for accomplishing the purpose at the uniform rate of one dollar for each person.

In accordance with the general idea thus indicated, the undersigned have performed the grateful duty which was assigned to them. Immediately on obtaining the consent of Dr. Crocker, they engaged the services of Mr. D. Huntington, of New York, an artist of high reputation in this department of his art. They also set on foot, in different portions of the community, the subscriptions which were required for defraying the expense. The portrait has now been executed by Mr. Huntington with eminent success. It possesses not only great fidelity to the form and features it was designed to portray, but also superior excellence as a work of art, and it will not fail to commend itself to those who may look upon it, as a beautiful specimen of artistic execution.

The entire professional life of Dr. Crocker has been spent among the people of Providence. In an age that has been filled with changes, it has been distinguished for its uniform and unambitious fidelity, and it strikingly illustrates the happy results of permanence and stability in the relations of a Christian minister to the community in which his lot is cast. He was born in Barnstable, Massachusetts, July 4, 1781. He graduated at Harvard College in 1802, and in October of the same year he came to Providence, and conducted public worship in St. John's Church as Lay Reader until the following May, when he was ordained a Deacon in the Episcopal Church. In June, 1804, he was ordained a Presbyter, and soon afterwards was established as Rector of the parish of St. John's — the office in which he has continued to the present time. He is now the oldest clergyman of the Protestant Episcopal Church of the United States, and for more than fifty years he has been a member of each of its triennial conventions, excepting only the last. At Commencement, in 1808, he was elected a member of the Board of Fellows of Brown University — a post which he still continues to fill, and which has connected him with the government and care of the University for a longer period than any other person, whether living or dead, whose name is recorded in its annals. Within this period he has also been Secretary of the Corporation fifteen years, and a member of the library committee more than sixteen years. This briefest outline of his long career, extending through nearly two generations, will suggest to every mind the services which constitute his preëminent title to the gratitude and honor both of this city and the University.

Having now fulfilled the purpose for which we were appointed, it only remains that we present the work, with whose execution we have been intrusted, to the body for whose custody it was originally designed. We, therefore, respectfully request the Corporation to accept this portrait for the University, in behalf of the numerous subscribers whose names are herewith communicated, as a token of the respect and esteem which are cherished for this venerable gentleman by his fellow-citizens in Providence and its vicinity. It is designed to be a testimonial to his pure life and worthy example; to the fidelity and usefulness of his life-long services among us, as a minister of the gospel, and to the sympathy which he has always manifested with the well being, both moral and social, of this community. We ask that this portrait may be suspended with those already collected in Rhode Island Hall, and we earnestly hope that it may remind the scholars of the University and all who in the present or future time shall gaze upon it, how beautiful and venerable is a serene and unostentatious life spent in the performance of elevated duties, and in labors for others' good.

In behalf of those for whom we have acted, we have the honor to remain, very respectfully,

JOHN KINGSBURY, WILLIAM S. PATTEN,
JOHN R. BARTLETT, WILLIAM GAMMELL,
SAMUEL G. ARNOLD.

Providence, September 4, 1860.

The foregoing communication having been read and accepted, the following preamble and resolutions were adopted:—

Whereas, as appears by the foregoing communication, there has been presented to this University, in the name and behalf of a large number of the people of Providence and vicinity, a well executed portrait of Rev. Nathan Bourne Crocker, D. D., as a tribute of the respect and esteem which are cherished for his character and services as a Christian minister and as a man, during his long residence in this city; it is therefore

RESOLVED, That we, the members of the Corporation, gratefully accept this valuable work of art, and that we delight to recognize it as a tribute of respect, for one, who, during a period of fifty-two years, has been intimately connected with us and our predecessors in the councils of the University.

RESOLVED, That we honor the sentiments which have prompted the people of Providence and its vicinity thus to express their grateful appreciation of the character and life of this venerable minister of the gospel, and that in placing his portrait in Rhode Island Hall, they have most fittingly indicated the relations which he has so long sustained, alike to the city and the University.

21. MAJOR-GENERAL AMBROSE E. BURNSIDE, Governor of Rhode Island. Born, 1824; graduated at West Point, 1847.

A full length portrait, by Emanuel Leutze, of New York. The subject is represented in military costume, in the act of carrying the Stone Bridge at the battle of Antietam. The painting was presented to the Corporation by the persons whose names are here given, with the amount of their subscriptions:—

John Carter Brown, - - - $100	Seth Padelford, - - -	$50
Henry Butler, - - - 100	Thomas P. Shepard & Co., -	50
James Y. Smith, - - - 100	Moses B. Jenkins, - - -	50
Earl P. Mason, - - - 100	William Grosvenor, - - -	50
A. & W. Sprague, - - - 100	William Goddard, - - -	50
William H. Reynolds, - - 100	James T. Rhodes, - - -	50
Jabez C. Knight, - - - 100	T. P I. Goddard, - - -	50
Amos D. Smith, - - - 100	Elisha Dyer, - - - -	50
Robert H. Ives, - - - 100	Henry Lippitt, - - -	25
Thomas P Ives, - - - 100	Thomas F. Hoppin, - - -	25
Burnside Rifle Co., - - - 100	Julia Bullock, - - -	25
Charlotte R. Goddard, - - 50		
Thomas A. Jenckes, - - - 50	Total, - - - -	$1,675

22. BRIGADIER-GENERAL ISAAC P. RODMAN, who fell at the battle of Antietam. Born at South Kingstown, 1822; died September 30, 1862.

Painted by Mr. J. S. Lincoln, from a photograph   Presented to the Corporation of the University by the following subscribers:—

William Sprague, - - - $20	Jabez C. Knight, - - -	$20
William H. Reynolds, - - 20	Ambrose E. Burnside, - - -	20
James Y. Smith, - - - 20	Robert H. Ives, - - -	20
Seth Padelford, - - - 20		
C. F. Harris, - - - - 20		$160

23. LIEUT.-COL. CHRISTOPHER GREENE, a distinguished Rhode Island officer of the Revolutionary war. Born, 1737; died, 1781.

Painted by Mr. Lincoln from an original in the possession of Simon Henry Greene, Esq., a grandson of Col. Greene, by whom it was presented to the University.

24. DR. SOLOMON DROWNE, a Surgeon in the American army, and an early Professor in the College. Born, 1753; graduated, 1773; died, 1834.

Painted by C. C. Ingham, of New York, from an original in the possession of Dr. Drowne's family. It was presented to the University by Dr. Drowne's son, Henry B. Drowne, and by his grandsons, Henry T., Thomas S., Christopher R, and George R. Drowne.

25. CHARLES II., KING OF ENGLAND.
26. CATHERINE OF BRAGANZA, HIS QUEEN.

It was from Charles II. it will be remembered that Rhode Island received her glorious Charter, dated July 8, 1663, a charter which has been the fruitful theme of praise from historians and statesmen for more than two centuries. These valuable portraits are originals, painted it is supposed by John B. Gaspars, an artist of Belgium, who visited England during the Civil War, and who, after the Restoration, became an assistant to Sir Peter Lely and afterwards to Sir Godfrey Kneller. They are of the ordinary size, being rather more than half length, Charles being painted with the robes and insignia of the Garter. They were obtained in England by Ethelbert R. Billings, Esq., of Providence, through the influence of the Secretary of the National Picture Gallery. Mr. Billings had them restored to their original freshness and beauty, and presented them to the Corporation of the University.

27. REV. WILLIAM ROGERS, D. D., the first student of Brown University. Born, 1751; graduated, 1769; died, 1824.

The Rev. Dr. Rogers was matriculated by President Manning September 3, 1765, and from that time until June 20, 1766, a period of nine months and seventeen days, he was the first and only student of "Rhode Island College." For many years he was Professor of Oratory and Belles-Lettres in the University of Pennsylvania. This picture was painted by his only surviving daughter, Miss Eliza J. Rogers, and was by her presented to the University in the summer of 1864. It was copied from an original portrait by Remembrandt Peale, taken in the year 1795, when the subject was in the prime and vigor of life.

28. DR. LEVI WHEATON, an early graduate of the College. Received the degree of A. B. in 1782; died, 1851.

Painted by Healy in 1846, and presented to the Corporation in the summer of 1865, by his two granddaughters, Mrs. Charles C. Little, of Boston, and Miss Martha B. Wheaton, of Cambridge. Dr. Wheaton was a Professor in Brown University from 1815 to 1828.

29. GEN. JAMES TALLMADGE, LL. D., Lieut.-Governor of New York. Born, 1778; graduated, 1798; died, 1853.

A small steel engraving, presented to the University by Mrs. James Ludlow, of Newport, in November, 1865. Gen. Tallmadge bequeathed to the Library of the University one thousand dollars.

30. OLIVER CROMWELL, Lord Protector of the English Commonwealth. Born, 1599; died, 1658.

A faithful and life-like portrait, painted by Mr. Heade. The following letter from the artist will be interesting to our readers:—

PROVIDENCE, R. I., April 28, 1866.

MR. GUILD—

DEAR SIR:—My picture of Cromwell was painted from two miniatures by Samuel Cooper; the one belonging to Earl De Grey, and the other to the Duke of Buccleuch. I was assisted also by a cast taken from Cromwell's face after his death, which Bell, the sculptor, kindly loaned me for the purpose. From this cast I copied the following evidences of its authenticity:—

"This mask is from the original one in possession of Mrs. Russell, Chest. Park; traced authentically from Richard, Protector. Richard left them to his dear Elizabeth. She left the mask to her cousins, Richard and Thomas. The first left the mask, with other things to Annie Elizabeth and Letita, (his daughters.) They left them to their cousin, Oliver Cromwell, Chest. Park; he to his daughter, Mrs. Russell."

Very truly yours,

M. J. HEADE.

The picture, it may be added, was painted by Mr. Heade at the request of Mr. Bartlett, who wrote him while in London on behalf of the University. By accident Mr. Heade learned that an original portrait by Cooper, was in the possession of the Duke of Buccleuch. Mr. Cooper, who, it appears, was one of the most eminent artists of his day, had been employed to paint a full length portrait of the Great Protector; and while engaged in his work, he privately painted a miniature picture for himself, in which all natural blemishes and defects were faithfully delineated. A knowledge of this fact coming to Cromwell, the artist was summoned into his presence, and required to give up the too truthful portrait before it was half finished. This is the original, now in the possession of the Duke of Buccleuch, who kindly allowed it, for the first time, to be copied, on learning the destination of the picture. The painting was purchased of Mr. Heade for three hundred and fifty dollars, and placed in Rhode Island Hall in April, 1866. The funds used for this purpose, by permission of the donors, were a part of a subscription for a military school, which it was proposed to establish in connection with the University. An account of this subscription may be found in another chapter.

31. GENERAL ANDREW JACKSON, seventh President of the United States. Born, 1767; died, 1845.

COLLECTION OF PORTRAITS. 295

A full length portrait of this distinguished statesman, painted from life by Amans, January 8, 1840, and presented to the Corporation by Col. William H. Reynolds, of Providence. In a letter to President Sears, accompanying the gift, dated June 14, 1866, the donor says:— "This picture was presented to one of the ex-Mayors of New Orleans, and purchased of his family by myself some three years since. At the time of its purchase the owner was confined in Fort Jackson for disloyalty to the government."

A prominent object of interest in Rhode Island Hall is a fine marble bust of the late DR. WAYLAND, executed by Thomas Ball, of Boston, in the year 1861. This bust is pronounced by all who have seen it to be, both as a likeness and a specimen of the sculptor's art, a work of rare and extraordinary merit. The expense, including pedestal, was six hundred and fifty-five dollars, to defray which five dollar subscriptions were obtained among the widely-scattered sons of the University who had been the pupils of the lamented President.

The following communication respecting the bust was presented to the Corporation by the Hon. Samuel G. Arnold, at the annual meeting held September 5, 1861:—

TO THE PRESIDENT AND CORPORATION OF BROWN UNIVERSITY:—

The undersigned, acting in behalf of a large number of the graduates of Brown University who were pupils of President Wayland, have procured a marble bust of our venerated and distinguished Instructor, which we now have the pleasure of presenting for the acceptance of the Corporation, with the request that it may be carefully preserved in one of the halls of the University. Twenty-nine classes of graduates received their degrees from the hands of President Wayland, and since his retirement from office a desire has been very widely felt among them that there might be placed at this scene of his long and illustrious services some memorial of the estimation in which those services are held, and of the respect which is entertained for his personal character among the widely-scattered men who were once his pupils.

It is in accordance with this pervading sentiment, that those whom we represent have caused this bust to be procured. It has been executed by Mr. Thomas Ball, of Boston, an artist of well known reputation, and by the common voice of all who have seen it, it has been pronounced, both as a likeness and a specimen of the sculptor's art, to be a work of rare and extraordinary merit. It has been procured by the ready coöperation of gentlemen representing nearly every class of President Wayland's pupils from the class of 1827 to the class of 1855, and residing in every geographical division of the country. It may, therefore, well be regarded as an expression of the filial respect and reverent honor with which his pupils in every part of the land cherish the name and character of their early "Guide, Philosopher and Friend."

In now presenting it to the Corporation, we desire, in behalf of our brethren, that it may be accepted and preserved to future times as an humble tribute of the affectionate respect which is felt for Dr. Wayland among those over whose education he so faithfully presided; and also, as an expression of their grateful appreciation of the distinguished services he has nobly and heroically performed, not for themselves alone, for the University, for our country, and for the age in which he has lived.

With our warmest wishes for the continued and ever increasing prosperity of the University, we have the honor to be, Gentlemen, with great respect, your obedient servants,

ELISHA DYER,	MARSHALL WOODS,
GEORGE I. CHACE,	REUBEN A. GUILD,
WILLIAM GAMMELL,	JAMES TILLINGHAST,
THOMAS P. SHEPARD,	CHARLES H. PARKHURST,
ABRAHAM PAYNE,	JOHN W. VERNON,
SAMUEL G. ARNOLD,	*Committee.*

Providence, Wednesday, September 4, 1861.

The Hall during the greater part of the year is open to the public on Saturday afternoons, and also every day during Commencement week. The Librarian of the University has charge of the Collection of Portraits as Keeper of the Cabinet, and reports upon the same to the Corporation, at their annual meetings.

FINANCIAL HISTORY

OF THE

COLLEGE.

1764—1867.

COLLEGE LANDS.

HE first purchase of land for the College comprised, as has already been stated in connection with our account of University Hall, about eight acres, being the middle portion of the home-lots of Chad Brown, Daniel Abbott, George Rickard and John Warner. The price paid, as appears from the Record of Deeds, and also from the accounts of Nicholas Brown & Co., was two hundred and nineteen pounds, or seven hundred and thirty dollars, being a little more than ninety dollars per acre. These home-lots, as they were called, extended from the Main street, now North and South Main streets, eastward to Hope street. The original College estate included the Grammar School lot, and that portion of College street extending from the College to Benefit street.

It appears from the records that the College in the beginning owned lands in some of the towns adjoining Providence, which lands were finally sold, and the proceeds applied to increase the resources of the Institution.

The first addition to the College estate was made in the year 1815. From a deed dated August 9, it appears that the Corporation bought of Sylvanus G. Martin, for six hundred dollars, a lot on George street, fifty feet on said street, and extending north to the College lands one hundred and thirty feet.

In 1822, April 15, the Corporation purchased of Nathan Waterman, for the sum of five thousand one hundred and eighty-nine dollars and sixty-six cents, a piece of land on which to erect Hope College, extending one hundred and twenty-three feet north and south, and four hundred feet east and west; bounded by Prospect, Waterman and Brown streets, and the original College estate.

In 1826, May 31, the Hon. Nicholas Brown deeded to the Corporation of the University, the estate known as the Hopkins estate, on George street, lying between the Cady and Bowen estates, and extending north to the College premises one hundred and thirty feet. This deed was not recorded until the 14th of July, 1840. Rhode Island Hall was erected upon this lot, in accordance with the wishes of the benevolent donor.

In 1839, June 12, Mr. Brown deeded to the Corporation two lots of land lying between Waterman, Prospect and College streets, as an eligible site for the President's house. The estimated value of these lots, at the time when they were presented to the Institution, was seven thousand dollars.

In 1840, July 29, Mr. Brown purchased of Caleb Earle the Bussey lot, so called, on George street, fifty feet by one hundred and thirty, for the sum of seventeen hundred dollars, and presented the same to the University. He also presented one other lot on the same street. The estimated value of these two lots, together with the Hopkins estate which we have already described, was twenty-five thousand five hundred dollars.

In 1843, Mr. John Carter Brown deeded to the Corporation a lot of land fifty by one hundred and thirty feet, bequeathed to him in trust by his father, the Hon. Nicholas Brown, for the "improvement of the College estate." This lot is now included in the extension of Prospect street from College street to George.

In 1851, the University came into possession of one-half of the Corliss lots, so called, lying between the College premises and Hope street, bequeathed to the Corporation by the Hon. Nicholas

Brown. These lots, by an amicable division of land made in 1854, between the University and the heirs of Thomas P. Ives, and recorded in Record of Deeds, Book 142, page 25, are located on the north side of Manning street, between Thayer and Hope streets. The area, including Thayer, Brook, and one-half of Manning streets, is one hundred and sixty-one thousand five hundred and ninety-seven square feet, or nearly four acres. The estimated valuation of these lots at the time when they were bequeathed to the University, as stated by Prof. Gammell in his sketch of Mr. Brown, was forty-two thousand five hundred dollars.

The latest addition to the College estate was in 1860. On the 8th of March, as appears from the records, Mr. Seth Adams deeded to the Corporation of the University, in consideration of the sum of ten thousand dollars paid him by Mr. John Carter Brown, the lot on the corner of George and Prospect streets, seventy by one hundred and thirty feet, formerly known as the Bowen estate. This act of munificence on the part of Mr. Brown, makes an open enclosure of the "College Green," and provides that it always be kept open and free from all encumbrances and buildings.

The present College enclosure, comprising about ten acres, is bounded in general by George, Prospect, Waterman and Thayer streets. Beginning at the Pearce estate opposite Brown street, it extends west on George street four hundred and eleven feet; thence north on Prospect street five hundred and sixty feet; thence east on Waterman street four hundred and twelve feet; thence south on Brown street one hundred and twenty-seven feet; thence east five hundred and sixty-eight feet, to within one hundred and nineteen feet of Thayer street; thence south three hundred and thirty-two feet; thence west five hundred and forty-two feet; thence south to the starting point on George street, one hundred and thirty-two feet. In addition to this is the

Grammar School lot, about eighty by one hundred and thirty-eight feet, the mansion house lot, eighty by two hundred and forty feet, and the house lots bequeathed to the University by the Hon. Nicholas Brown, lying on the north side of Manning street, one hundred and thirty-eight feet deep, and extending from the College enclosure, one hundred and nineteen feet west of Thayer street, east to Hope street. The entire College lands comprise about fifteen acres, and are worth at the present valuation of landed property in their immediate vicinity, not far from three-quarters of a million of dollars.

We may add here, that within the past three years, nearly five hundred trees of various kinds, have been planted by a skillful gardener, in that part of the College enclosure which lies east of the new chemical laboratory. The funds for this purpose were furnished through the liberality of Mr. John Carter Brown. The students of a future generation, as they walk through the "College Park," or recline with their books in hand beneath the cooling shade of the graceful firs and elms, will bless the far-sighted wisdom of this benefactor. The "College Green" was graded and adorned with elms, and also the "College Campus," as we have already stated, at the time when Rhode Island Hall and the President's house were erected.

AGRICULTURAL LANDS.

IN the year 1862, Congress passed an act, which was approved on the 2d of July, donating public lands to the several states and territories, which should provide colleges for the benefit of Agricultural and the Mechanic Arts. The provisions of this act are fully stated in Chapter CXXX., of the Statutes of the United States. One of them is as follows:—

SECTION 4. AND BE IT FURTHER ENACTED, That all moneys derived from the sale of the lands aforesaid, by the states to which the lands are apportioned, and from the sales of land scrip hereinbefore provided for, shall be invested in stocks of the United States, or of the states, or some safe stocks, yielding not less than five per centum upon the par value of said stocks; and that the moneys so invested shall constitute a perpetual fund, the capital of which shall remain forever undiminished, (except so far as may be provided in section fifth, of this act,) and the interest of which shall be inviolably appropriated, by each state which may take and claim the benefit of this act, to the endowment, support, and maintenance of at least one college where the leading object shall be, without excluding other scientific and classical studies, and including military tactics, to teach such branches of learning as are related to Agriculture and the Mechanic Arts, in such manner as the legislatures of the states may respectively prescribe, in order to promote the liberal and practical education of the industrial classes in the several pursuits and professions in life.

The following resolutions, accepting the grant of land made by the United States for an Agricultural College, were adopted by the General Assembly of Rhode Island, at its January session, in 1863:—

RESOLVED, The Senate concurring with the House, in the passage hereof, that the General Assembly of the State of Rhode Island, does hereby express its acceptance in behalf of the State, of the benefit of the provisions of Chapter CXXX., of the Statutes of the United States, passed at the second session of the thirty-seventh Congress, and approved July 2d, A. D. 1862, donating public lands to the several states and territories, which may provide colleges for the benefit of Agriculture and the Mechanic Arts, upon the terms and conditions in the said act, contained and set forth ; and that the faith of the State be, and is hereby pledged to the United States that, upon the receipt of the scrip provided to be issued under the said act of Congress, it will faithfully apply the proceeds thereof to the objects, and in the manner prescribed by the said act.

RESOLVED, That His Excellency the Governor be, and that he hereby is, requested to notify the President of the United States, without delay, of the accepting by the Legislature of this State of the donation of scrip for one hundred and twenty thousand acres of the public lands of the United States, (that quantity being thirty thousand acres for each senator and representative in Congress from this State,) made by the provisions of Chapter CXXX., of the Statutes of the United States, approved July 2d, 1862, donating public lands to the several states and territories, which may provide colleges for the benefit of Agriculture and the Mechanic Arts, upon the terms and conditions in the said act, contained and set forth, and to furnish at the same time a copy of said notification for the Secretary of the Interior.

RESOLVED, That His Excellency the Governor be, and he hereby is, fully authorized and empowered by himself or his order, to receive from the Secretary of the Interior, or any other person authorized to issue the same, the land scrip to which this State is entitled, under the provisions of Chapter CXXX., of the Statutes of the United States, passed at the second session of the thirty-seventh Congress, and approved July 2d, A. D. 1862, donating public lands to the several states and territories, which may provide colleges for the benefit of Agricultural and the Mechanic Arts, and to hold the said scrip subject to the future order of this General Assembly.

These one hundred and twenty thousand acres of the public lands, the Legislature proposed to transfer to Brown University. At a special meeting of the Corporation held on the 21st of January, 1863, the subject was presented and discussed. The action relating thereto, we copy from the records:—

WHEREAS, The House of Representatives of the State of Rhode Island, on the fourteenth of January instant, passed an act to transfer and assign to Brown University the Land Scrip, together with the benefits and responsibilities of the provisions of Chapter CXXX., of the Statutes of the United States, passed at the second session of the thirty-seventh Congress, and approved July 2, 1862, donating public lands to provide colleges for the benefit of Agriculture and the Mechanic Arts, upon the terms and conditions of said act; and,

WHEREAS, Should such act be perfected by the concurrence of the Senate, it will be necessary for the same to be accepted or declined before the next meeting of the Corporation; and,

WHEREAS, The accepting or declining the same involves questions of great importance, both to the State and to the University, and requires more knowledge of facts, and more deliberate consideration of consequences than this Corporation now have, or can give, therefore it is

VOTED, That the whole subject be referred to the Executive Board, and that the full power and authority of this Corporation be, and is, hereby given to said Executive Board, to accept or decline the transfer of said grant by the General Assembly to this Corporation; this Corporation hereby ratifying and confirming the action of said Executive Board by virtue of this vote.

The Executive Board accepted of the transfer of Land Scrip upon the following conditions, as set forth in the resolution finally passed by the General Assembly:—

RESOLVED, That His Excellency the Governor be, and he hereby is, authorized and appointed on the part of the State, to transfer, assign, and set over to the Corporation of Brown University, in the city of Providence, the scrip now in the possession of the Governor, or which may hereafter come into his possession from the government of the United States, under and by virtue of a resolution passed by this General Assembly, at its present session, upon receiving from the said Corporation, or its duly authorized agent, the following stipulations; which stipulations shall be as and for a perpetual agreement, by and between said Corporation and State as aforesaid, and shall be in form substantially as follows, that is to say:—

SAID CORPORATION DOES HEREBY AGREE—

1. To provide a college or department in said University, the leading object whereof shall be, without excluding other scientific and classic studies, and including military tactics, to teach such branches of learning as are related to Agriculture and the Mechanic Arts, in such manner as hereinafter stated, in order to promote the liberal and practical education of the industrial classes in the several pursuits and professions of life.

2. To locate without unnecessary delay, and at their best discretion, the said scrip upon some of the public lands of the United States, properly open to be located upon, and from time to time to sell and dispose of the lands so to be located upon, so that the largest price can be obtained for the same.

3. To invest and to keep invested the proceeds of the said sales in stocks or securities of the United States or of this State, but if this should be impracticable, so that an income therefrom of at least five per centum per annum upon their par value could not be realized, then to invest such proceeds in some other safe stocks, (the safety of which other stocks the University shall guarantee,) upon which an income of at least five per centum, as aforesaid, can be realized.

4. To pay all expenses of locating and selling said lands, and all taxes which may be assessed thereon or upon the proceeds thereof.

5. To apply faithfully the income arising from the avails of the sales of said lands in endowing, maintaining and supporting a college in said Univerisity as aforesaid, for the objects as aforesaid, so that no portion of said proceeds or income therefrom shall be used in the erection, preservation, purchase or repairing of any building or buildings, for College or other purposes; PROVIDED, however, that a portion of said proceeds of said sales, not exceeding one-tenth part thereof, may, at the discretion of said Corporation be expended according to said act of Congress, in the purchase of lands for sites, or an experimental farm, whenever said Corporation shall so determine.

6. To educate scholars, each at the rate of one hundred dollars per annum, to the extent of the entire annual income from said proceeds, subject to the proviso as aforesaid; the Governor and Secretary of State, to have the right on or before Commencement day of each year, and in conjunction with the President of the University, to nominate candidates for vacancies occurring in said college or department as aforesaid, at the beginning of each collegiate year, and students admitted to said college, and pursuing studies therein by virtue of said fund, are not to be excluded from the regular scientific and classic studies of said University, and are to be subject to the laws and regulations of the University in entering and remaining thereat, and are to be graduated with the degree of Bachelor of Philosophy or Bachelor of Arts, or are to receive a certificate for a partial course, according as the case may be.

7. To assume upon itself all the responsibilities and duties which are imposed upon the State by the said act of Congress, and also all the duties imposed upon colleges endowed under the provisions of the said act, and to be entitled to all the privileges and immunities conferred thereby upon the State, and upon institutions endowed thereunder.

8. To make to the Governor of the State an annual report, a copy of which shall be communicated to the General Assembly, of all lands located and sold, until the whole is disposed of, the amount received for the same and how invested, and of the appropriations made of the proceeds therefrom, and stating the number of the students to whom the same have been applied, and of all other matters prescribed by said act of Congress as aforesaid.

Another resolution was adopted by the General Assembly, providing for the nomination of State scholarships at Brown University:—

RESOLVED BY THE GENERAL ASSEMBLY AS FOLLOWS:—

That the Senators and Representatives from the several towns in the the General Assembly, for the time being, are constituted a Board of Commissioners, whose duty it shall be during the January session in each year, to present to the Governor and Secretary of State the names of worthy young men from the several towns, to be educated as State beneficiaries in Brown University, according to the act of Congress donating land to the several states and territories which may provide colleges for the benefit of Agriculture and the Mechanic Arts. And the said Commisssioners are hereby instructed, after one candidate has been presented from each town in the State, (the order of the towns to be determined by lot,) to select the candidates as far as may be from the several towns in the ratio of their representation in the House of Representatives, and from that class of persons who otherwise would not have the means of providing themselves with the like benefits; and that the Governor and Secretary of State be, and they are hereby, instructed to select candidates from the names presented, in such manner as that whenever for any reason any town shall not have received its just quota of those admitted to said University, such town shall, in the nomination of subsequent candidates, have priority over those towns which have received their full quota.

Thus the University came into possession of Land Scrip for one hundred and twenty thousand acres of public lands, which lands were eventually located in Kansas. By a written contract made on the 31st of January, 1865, these lands were sold to Horace T. Love for the sum of fifty thousand dollars, payable, without interest, as follows:—

One thousand dollars on the 20th of August, - - - 1866.
Four " " " - - - 1867.
Five " " " - - - 1868.
Ten " " " - - - 1869.
Thirty " " " - - - 1870.

United States seven-thirty bonds of an equal value with the above, were deposited with the Treasurer of the University, as security for the payment of Mr. Love's notes.

SCHOLARSHIPS.

MR. NICHOLAS BROWN, at his death in 1841, bequeathed one-half the net income of the rents and profits of certain estates, to the Corporation of Brown University, directing that the same should be paid by his executors, as the rents should be collected from year to year, until his grandson, Nicholas, should attain to the age of twenty-one years, which he did on the 16th of September, 1853. This net income, during the twelve years as specified, was to be appropriated by the Corporation, in the language of the Will, "to the charitable purpose of aiding deserving young men in obtaining their education while members of said University." In a codicil to his Will, Mr. Brown adds:—

> And I do hereby recommend to said Corporation, and to the Faculty thereof, to accept of the advice and recommendation of the Warren Education Society, (now called the Rhode Island Baptist Education Society,) as to the persons who shall receive the benefit of such aid and assistance, when said Society shall offer their advice and recommendation in relation thereto.

A portion of the income thus bequeathed to the University was appropriated, in accordance with the advice and suggestions of President Wayland, to be awarded in premiums, as we learn from the following announcement in the annual catalogue published in 1842:—

> The Corporation of Brown University, desirous of cultivating a generous love of science, and of rewarding with marks of distinction those students who have attained to distinguished excellence in scholarship, and who have, also, sustained an unblem-

ished moral character,—have appropriated two hundred dollars, to be awarded in premiums, either in money or books, to such competitors as may by examination prove themselves most meritorious.

This sum thus appropriated was afterwards increased to four hundred and twenty dollars. In 1850, the "New System" went into operation, the standard of scholarship was changed, and the following statutes regulating the award of the "University Premiums," were adopted:—

1. The competition for the University Premiums is open only to those students who are candidates for some one of the degrees conferred by the University.

2. No student shall be admitted as a candidate for a premium, who does not sustain an irreproachable moral character, and who is not punctual in his attendance upon all Collegiate exercises.

3. No student shall be a competitor for a premium whose average standing for the year is below fifteen, the maximum of standing being twenty.

4. No student shall be a competitor for more than one premium, whose average standing for the year is below eighteen.

In 1858, the Corporation voted to apply the fund derived from the bequest of Nicholas Brown, and now amounting to upwards of eleven thousand dollars, to scholarships of one thousand dollars each, the income thereof to be appropriated "to the charitable purpose of aiding deserving young men in obtaining their education while members of the University." It was also voted, on motion of the Rev. Dr. Babcock—

That the Corporation and Faculty be recommended to accept the advice and recommendation of the Rhode Island Baptist Education Society, (which now holds the place of the late Warren Education Society) as to persons who shall receive such aid and assistance, when said Society shall offer their advice and recommendation relative thereto.

The establishing of a system of Scholarships to aid deserving young men in obtaining an education, is justly regarded by President Sears as perhaps the most important act of his administration. His large experience as an educator had long since convinced him, that distinction in the various walks of literary and professional life attends, most frequently, those whose early years are full of struggle against the difficulties of pecuniary embarrassment. Without the timely aid of a charitable endowment, such men as Sir Isaac Newton, the "judicious" Hooker and Jeremy Taylor, might never have graduated from the Universities of Oxford and Cambridge. The Hon. Isaac Davis, when in England, remarked to one, who for thirty years had been entrusted with the care of the Register of Cambridge University: "I suppose you have many sons of Dukes, Earls and Lords among the graduates who have distinguished themselves." "No, sir," says the Registrar, "if you want to consult the record of our distinguished scholars and great men, look to the SCHOLARSHIPS, Sir, look to the SCHOLARSHIPS."

In addition to these general considerations, the system of Scholarships inaugurated by President Sears aids especially pious students who have the ministry in view, and thus secures the main object which the Philadelphia Association had in founding the College. That this was the original design of the Institution, the LIFE, TIMES AND CORRESPONDENCE OF JAMES MANNING affords ample proof. In a letter to the Rev. Dr. Stennett, of London, dated November 8, 1783, Manning develops a plan for the assistance of young men preparing for the ministry, very similar to the views which President Sears has embodied in his system.

The following are the Scholarships of Brown University at the present time:—

1. THE NICHOLAS BROWN SCHOLARSHIPS, (eleven,) - - $11,000
    Founded by the Corporation in 1858, from funds derived from a bequest of the late Hon. Nicholas Brown.

2. THE PRESIDENT'S SCHOLARSHIP, - - - - - - - - 1,000
    Founded by Barnas Sears, September 1, 1859.

3. THE ALVA WOODS SCHOLARSHIPS, (three,) - - - - $3,000
Founded by Alva Woods, September 22, 1859, and June 13, 1865.

4. THE SLATER SCHOLARSHIP, - - - - - - - - - 1,000
Founded by Horatio N. Slater, May 9, 1860.

5. THE EARL P. MASON SCHOLARSHIP, - - - - - - 1,000
Founded by Earl P. Mason, May 10, 1860.

6. THE DUNCAN SCHOLARSHIP, - - - - - - - - 1,000
Founded by James H. Duncan, of Haverhill, Mass., Sept. 5, 1860.

7. THE HEZEKIAH S. CHACE SCHOLARSHIP, - - - - - 1,000
Founded by Hezekiah S. Chace, of Boston, November 16, 1860.

8. THE ARNOLD WHIPPLE SCHOLARSHIP, - - - - - 1,000
Founded by Mrs. Phebe Whipple, January 28, 1861.

9. THE JOSEPH BROWN SCHOLARSHIP, - - - - - - 1,000
Founded by Mrs. Eliza Brown Rogers, January 28, 1861.

10. THE PARDON MILLER SCHOLARSHIP, - - - - - 1,000
Founded by Mrs. Ann Eliza Miller, January 30, 1861.

11. THE ISAAC DAVIS SCHOLARSHIP, - - - - - - - 1,000
Founded by Isaac Davis, of Worcester, Massachusetts, May 21, 1861.

12. THE GARDNER COLBY SCHOLARSHIP, - - - - - 1,000
Founded by Gardner Colby, of Boston, May 3, 1862.

13. THE EPHRAIM WHEATON SCHOLARSHIP, - - - - 1,000
Founded by James Wheaton, September 29, 1862.

14. THE JAMES Y. SMITH SCHOLARSHIP, - - - - - - 1,000
Founded by James Y. Smith, September 15, 1863.

15. THE S. S. BRADFORD SCHOLARSHIPS, (two,) - - - 2,000
Founded by S. S. Bradford, September 18, 1863, and June 23, 1865.

16. THE FRANCES R. ARNOLD SCHOLARSHIP, - - - - 1,000
Founded by Mrs. Frances R. Arnold, September 18, 1863.

17. THE CORNELIA E. GREEN SCHOLARSHIP, - - - - - $1,000
    Founded by Mrs. Cornelia E. Green, September 18, 1863.
18. THE CHARLES THURBER SCHOLARSHIP, - - - - -   1,000
    Founded by Charles Thurber, of Brooklyn, N. Y., Oct 15, 1863.
19. THE CROCKER SCHOLARSHIP, - - - - - - - -   1,000
    Founded by Robert H. and Thomas P. Ives, October 20, 1863.
20. THE CLARK SCHOLARSHIP, - - - - - - - - -   1,000
    Founded by Robert H. and Thomas P. Ives, October 20, 1863.
21. THE ALBERT DAY SCHOLARSHIP, - - - - - - -   1,000
    Founded by Albert Day, of Hartford, Connecticut, March 28, 1864.
22. THE HENRY P. KENT SCHOLARSHIP, - - - - - -   1,000
    Founded by Henry P. Kent, of Suffield, Connecticut, July 25, 1864.
23. THE ROMEO ELTON SCHOLARSHIP, - - - - - - -   1,000
    Founded by Romeo Elton, of Exeter, England, August 13, 1864.
24. THE ANN E. WATERS SCHOLARSHIPS, (five,) - - -   5,000
    Founded by Mrs. Ann E. Waters, of Brooklyn, New York, January 6, and May 1, 1865.
25. THE L. FAIRBROTHER SCHOLARSHIP, - - - - - -   1,000
    Founded by Mrs. L. Fairbrother, of Pawtucket, April 3, 1865.
26. THE GEORGE LAWTON SCHOLARSHIP, - - - - - -   1,000
    Founded by George Lawton, of Waltham, Mass., April 10, 1865.
27. THE JOHN P. CROZER SCHOLARSHIP, - - - - -   1,000
    Founded by his daughter, Mrs. Margaret C. Bucknell, of Philadelphia, October 10, 1866.
28. THE DAVID HOWELL SCHOLARSHIP, - - - - - -   1,000
    Founded by his great-grandson, Gamaliel Lyman Dwight, April 1, 1867.
29. UNIVERSITY SCHOLARSHIPS, (two,) - - - - - -   2,000
    Founded by the Treasurer April 1, 1867, from uninvested scholarship funds, and also from the unexpended income of Scholarships.

Total, forty-seven Scholarships, - - - - - - - - $47,000

In addition to the foregoing are the following Scholarships not yet available, and from which no income has thus far been received:—

1. THE GEORGE L. SHERMAN SCHOLARSHIPS, (two,) - - $2,000
   Founded by George L. Sherman, April 19, 1860, and payable within six months after the decease of himself and wife.

2. THE JAMES N. GRANGER SCHOLARSHIP, - - - - - 1,000
   Founded by Mrs. Ann B. Granger, January 12, 1861, and payable on or before September 1, 1870.

3. THE HAZLETINE SCHOLARSHIP, - - - - - - - - 1,000
   Founded by S. E. Brooks, of Cambridge, Massachusetts, September 24, 1862, and payable within one year after his decease.

4. THE WILLIAM COOLIDGE RICHARDS SCHOLARSHIP, - - 1,000
   Founded by William C. Richards, of Lynn, Mass., May, 4, 1863, and payable within one year after the decease of himself and wife.

Total, five Scholarships, - - - - - - - - - - $5,000

The income of a Scholarship, it may be stated in closing, is sixty dollars.

AID FUND.

SOME account of the AID FUND established by Miss Lydia Carpenter, of Pawtucket, may naturally be expected in connection with the Scholarships. The following letter, which was read to the Corporation at its annual meeting held in September, 1860, presents in brief the facts pertaining to the history of this Fund:—

REV. BARNAS SEARS, PRESIDENT OF BROWN UNIVERSITY—

RESPECTED SIR:—Miss Lydia Carpenter, of Pawtucket, Rhode Island, requests me to place in your possession the inclosed note of the Corliss Steam Engine Co., for $4,000, dated December 3, 1859, payable in four months from date, (3–6 of April next.) She also incloses $83.10, the four months interest thereof.

This note, with the $1,000 heretofore (in March, 1858) placed by her at your disposal, making the principal sum of $5,000, is a donation from her to the University, under the following arrangements and conditions:—

To establish a fund to be called the AID FUND, which is to be applied to help deserving students, who may need aid after their admission into Brown University, to obtain a Collegiate education therein, by loans or gifts from the Fund, or from its income.

The principal sum of Fund never to be reduced by its use below four thousand dollars.

The Fund to be invested and kept by the Treasurer separate from other funds of the University, and payments on account thereof to be made only on the written order of the President of the University, actual or acting as such; and no payments to be made which shall reduce the Fund below, or when it is below, $4,000.

All appropriations out of the Fund shall hereafter be made according to the direction of a standing committee of three persons, of which the President of the University, acting or officiating as such, shall be chairman, and Thomas Carpenter, of Pawtucket, Rhode Island, shall be one, and William S. Patten, of Providence, shall be one.

When a vacancy occurs in the committee by the death, resignation, or disability of either or both of the last named members, the Chancellor of the University shall fill the first vacancy, and the Secretary of the Corporation the second; and thereafter the committee shall be the President, and the Chancellor and the Secretary of the Corporation "ex officiis."

The committee shall keep minutes of their doings, without giving unnecessary publicity thereof. Their high official stations will insure impartiality in the administration of the Fund.

By not calling the Fund by the name of any person, it is left an open fund, inviting increase by contributions from others, who will be at liberty to identify their donation to the AID FUND by such name and subject to such mode of application, not inconsistent with the general object, as they shall appoint.

The appropriations already made by the President out of the $1,000 heretofore given, are approved and adopted by the donor, and are made in conformity with this donation and her intentions.

I am requested to ask that no needless notoriety be given to the name of the person who has employed my agency in this communication.

       Respectfully yours,
                 WILLIAM S. PATTEN.
Providence, March 9, 1860.

Upon the receipt of the foregoing communication by the Executive Board, the following votes were passed:—

VOTED, That the Executive Board of Brown University accept the gift from Miss Lydia Carpenter, of Pawucket, Rhode Island, of $5,000 to the University for an AID FUND, and on the terms thereon.

VOTED, That this University hereby express with gratitude the obligations of the University to her for her unexpected and munificent gift; aware that words of praise can add but little to the conscious enjoyment of one who conceives and performs so noble a benefaction, the influence of which will not cease to cheer the depressed spirits and smooth the toilsome way of the indigent student, as he labors to obtain knowledge and virtue, so long as they are dispensed by this University.

VOTED, That a copy of these votes be sent to Miss Carpenter, signed by the President and Secretary of this Board, and that the letter with the action of this Board thereupon, be communicated by the President to the Corporation at their next meeting.

The Corporation fully approved of the action of the Executive Board, accepting the donation of five thousand dollars from Miss Carpenter, with all its conditions and restrictions. Miss Carpenter afterwards presented to the Treasurer of the University the sum of three hundred and fifty-eight dollars to make up the cost of a certificate of United States six per cent. stock, for the sum of five thousand dollars, which sum now constitutes the AID FUND.

The founder of the AID FUND, it may be added, is a maiden lady upwards of seventy years of age, and a worthy member of the First Baptist Church in Pawtucket. She was baptized by the Rev. Dr. Benedict, during the early part of his ministry in that town.

It may be proper to state here, that previous to the establishment of the AID FUND, Mr. Seth Padelford paid into the Treasury the sum of three hundred dollars, to be expended under the direction of President Sears and Professor Hill, in settling the College bills of meritorious students.

FUNDS AND TREASURERS.

SUBSCRIPTIONS for the endowment of the College in the beginning were obtained, as we have already seen, by the Rev. Messrs. Edwards and Smith. The amount of benefactions thus secured, a part of which constituted the first permanent funds of the College, was about seven thousand dollars. To increase these funds, and also to aid in defraying the current expenses of the Institution, subscriptions were solicited throughout the State and colonies, especially among the Baptists. The records of the Philadelphia, Charleston, and Warren Associations have frequent mention of the College, and of efforts on its behalf. In 1774, these Associations recommended "every member to pay SIXPENCE STERLING annually, for three years successively, to their Elder, or some suitable person; this money to be paid to the Treasurer of the College." At the same time, says Benedict in his history, the Rev. Messrs. John Gano, Oliver Hart and Francis Pelot were appointed to address the various Baptist associations throughout America, and urge their coöperation in procuring funds for Rhode Island College. To what extent these efforts were successful, we have no means at hand for ascertaining. The disturbances of this early period, the breaking out of the American war, and the consequent interruption of Collegiate exercises, turned the thoughts of the people into other channels, and institutions of learning were for a time forgotten.

The first Treasurer of the College was John Tillinghast, Esq., of Newport, who was elected to this office at the annual meeting of the Corporation held in 1764. His duties it is to be presumed were not especially arduous, as College instruction did not begin until the following year, when Mr. Manning was formally appointed President. No annual reports of his appear on file, and no further mention is made of the Treasurer until 1767, when, his term of service having expired, Col. Job Bennet, also of Newport, was appointed his successor. According to the record —

The Rev. Edward Upham and Mr. Edward Thurston, Jr., were appointed a committee to receive of John Tillinghast, Esq., late Treasurer of this College, his accounts and papers, and deliver them to Job Bennet, Esq., the present Treasurer.

Mr. Tillinghast attended the meeting at Warren which determined the location of the College, after which his name does not appear in the records of the Corporation until 1776, when having deceased, Mr. Cahoon was appointed a Trustee in his place. From the reports of his successor in office, it appears that he subscribed and paid towards founding and endowing the Institution one hundred pounds.

We present a few extracts from Col. Bennet's reports, in order to place on permanent record the names of some of the early benefactors of the College. The amounts, it will be observed, are in New England currency, six shillings to the dollar : —

			£	s.	d.
1766.	Sept. 4.	Rev. Samuel Stillman,	12	0	0
1767.	" 4.	Rev. Hezekiah Smith,	0	15	0
"	" 14.	Rev. Gardner Thurston,	1	11	0
"	Oct. 5.	Joshua Babcock, Esq.,	1	10	0
"	" 5.	Rev. John Maxson,	0	6	0
"	Nov. 6.	Joseph Wanton, Esq.,	1	10	0
"	Dec. 25.	John Tillinghast, Esq.,	5	0	0
1768.	Jan. 9.	Josias Lyndon, Esq.,	1	10	0
"	" 9.	Job Bennet,	0	18	0
"	Aug. 9.	Nicholas Brown, Esq.	2	10	0

FINANCIAL HISTORY. 319

				£	s.	d
1768.	Sept. 8.	Samuel Ward, Esq.,		1	4	0
"	" 9.	Rev. John Maxson,		6	12	0
"	" "	Rev. Isaac Backus,		6	6	0
"	" "	Rev. Hezekiah Smith,		0	16	0
"	" "	Job Bennet,		3	10	3
"	" "	Rev. James Manning,		3	12	0
"	" "	Rev. Gardner Thurston,		6	0	0
"	" "	John Tillinghast, Esq.,		5	0	0
"	" "	Josias Lyndon, Esq ,		3	0	0
"	" "	Mr. Peleg Barker,		3	7	6
"	" 12.	Nicholas Easton. Esq.,		2	2	0
"	Oct. 27.	Samuel Brocks, of Elizabethtown,		3	12	0
1769.	Sept. 8.	Rev. John Gano,		4	10	0
1770.	April 2.	Job Bennet,		12	14	7
"	Aug. 2.	Josias Lyndon,		12	0	0
"	" 10.	Peleg Barker,		4	2	6
"	Sept. 20.	John Tillinghast, Esq.,		14	8	0
"	" 20.	Governor Wanton,		30	0	0
"	Oct. 18.	Rev. John Ryland, of England, (his annual subscription of five guineas for President Manning,)		6	10	0
"	Dec. 4.	John Tillinghast, Esq.,		30	0	0
"	" "	Simon Pease, (in part of his father's donation,)		18	0	0
"	" "	Col. Josias Lyndon,		13	10	0
"	" 19.	John Tanner,		18	15	0
1771.	Feb. 19.	Rev. John Maxson,		0	18	0
"	April 16.	John Tillinghast, Esq.,		45	10	0
"	May 13.	Nicholas Easton, Esq.,		12	18	0
"	June 24.	Joseph Wanton, Jr.,		28	10	0
	Total,			£312	17	10

Mr. Bennet resigned his office as Treasurer in 1775. He died in 1784, and at the annual meeting of the Corporation for that year, Col. Daniel Tillinghast, of Providence, was appointed a Trustee in his place. His last annual report represents the permanent funds of the College as amounting to £1,349 14s 8d, or about forty-five hundred dollars, which was the sum obtained in

England and Ireland by Morgan Edwards. It would thus appear that the money obtained by Hezekiah Smith in South Carolina and Georgia, had been expended in defraying current expenses, and in erecting the College buildings.

Col. Bennet was succeeded as Treasurer by John Brown, one of the "Four Brothers" whose names appear so conspicuous in the early history of the College, as well as of the town in which the College is located. A full account of these brothers and of their ancestors, may be found in our former work, pp. 143–176. For twenty-one years, during the most trying periods of the country's history, Mr. Brown conducted the financial affairs of the College, displaying a skill in their management and a fertility in resources, for which he was distinguished in the management of his own affairs, and contributing freely to the funds of the Institution from his ample fortune. He resigned the Treasurership September 8th, 1796, whereupon the Corporation passed a vote of thanks "for his long and faithful services." He retained his place in the Corporation a few years longer, but the infirmities of age pressing heavily upon him he at length resigned, in the following interesting letter, which well deserves a place in a documentary history of the College. The reader will not fail to notice the allusion to oratory, or "handsome speaking," for which Presidents Manning and Maxcy were especially distinguished, and which doubtless prepared the way for the NICHOLAS BROWN PROFESSORSHIP:—

PROVIDENCE, September 6, 1803. }
TUESDAY MORNING. }

GENTLEMEN:— Finding the state of my health fast declining, which, together with my inactivity of body and long-continued lameness, has rendered and will continue to render me a useless member of the Corporation, and wishing, as I do, that some one who may have it in his power as well as inclination to promote the welfare of the Institution should be elected in my place, I now take this early opportunity to resign my seat in the Corporation, desiring that it may be filled as your wisdom shall direct, during the present annual Commencement.

In small states like ours, where the legislature gives but little pecuniary aid to found literary institutions or endow them, there remain, of course, greater exertions for well-disposed individuals to bring to maturity such seats of learning as we wish our College to become. But when we consider that thirty-three years only have passed since the foundations of our College edifice were laid, the progress of the Institution has not been very inconsiderable, though many impediments during that time have much retarded the wished for increase of students. The great Revolutionary war, in which we obtained our independence, was a great stagnation to our Institution, the College edifice having been taken and applied to the use of a hospital and for barracking the troops nearly one-sixth part of the whole time from its foundation to this day. This circumstance, with others, furnishes certainly sufficient motives to induce us to hope for, and expect, many more patrons and promoters of literature to step forward and advance the College, under your directions. Being located in the centre of New England, and with one of the most liberal charters that has ever been granted, to warrant and secure a fair and generous equality to be extended to every religious sect, I do most sincerely recommend the promotion of its highest interests to every branch in the government of the College. And as the most beautiful and handsome mode of speaking was a principal object, to my certain knowledge, of the first friends of this College, I do wish that the honorable the Corporation may find means during their deliberations of this week, to establish a Professorship of English Oratory, and that suitable funds for the purpose may be so placed, that the annual income only can be touched for the salary pertaining to such a Professorship.

I am, Gentlemen, with great regard, your obedient servant,

JOHN BROWN.

The letter having been read, it was

VOTED, That the President, Dr. Stillman and Dr. Benjamin Bourne be a committee to wait on Mr. Brown, to communicate to him the high sense this Corporation entertains of his very important services rendered to the public in the establishment and very liberal patronage of this College; and that they deeply regret his absence from this annual meeting, and much more so the cause of it; and to assure him that they hope and trust that his health may be restored, and his life and usefulness long protracted; and to request of him liberty to continue his name as a Trustee of the College.

Mr. Brown died a few days afterwards, and the following year his son-in-law, Mr. James Brown Mason, a graduate of the College in the class of 1791, was appointed a Trustee in his place.

From the annual reports of Mr. Brown on file, and also from his accounts, we gather a few names to record among the benefactors of the Institution:—

			£	s.	d.
1775.	Sept. 14.	Hezekiah Smith,	1	4	0
"	" "	John Stites, of Elizabethtown,	1	2	11
1783.	" 2.	Thomas Gair, (collections,)	13	7	4
"	" 6.	"Worthy Mr. Longfray's donation,"	12	0	0
"	Oct. 2.	Caleb Blood, of Newton, (collections,)	8	15	9
"	Dec. 30.	Rev. Benjamin Wallin's legacy,	33	6	8
1788.	Sept. 9.	Rev. William Vanhorn, (collections in Pennsylvania and New Jersey,)	21	12	0
1791.	May 3.	Miss Hannah Ward, legacy,	12	0	0
"	Sept. 8.	Rev. William Vanhorn, (collections,)	21	10	8
"	" "	William Holroyd, (collections,)	34	4	0
	Total,		£159	3	4

Mr. Wallin, whose name is included in the foregoing list, was a clergyman of London, and a correspondent of Dr. Manning. He died near the close of the Revolutionary war, bequeathing to the College the sum of twenty-five pounds, sterling. Some of his letters are published in MANNING AND BROWN UNIVERSITY. Miss Ward, who left a small legacy to the College, was probably a relative of Governor Ward, and a resident of Newport. It is to be regretted that such instances of remembrance among the early friends of the Institution are not more frequent in these later times.

Mr. Brown was succeeded in the Treasurership by his nephew, the Hon. Nicholas Brown. His accession to office marks an era in the history of the University. For twenty-nine years he conducted its financial affairs with unsurpassed zeal and efficiency, contributing to its funds and resources during this period, and until his death, in money, lands and buildings, upwards of one hundred and sixty thousand dollars. He began his benefactions in February, 1792, by presenting to the Corporation, as has already been stated in a previous chapter, the sum of five hundred dollars, for the purchase of law books for the Library. In 1803, the Corporation

VOTED, That the donation of five thousand dollars, if made to this College within one year from the late Commencement, shall entitle the donor to name the College.

This was in accordance with a provision of the charter, authorizing the Trustees and Fellows to name the Institution in honor of its most distinguished benefactor. Several previous votes of this kind appear on record. To the wishes of his friends, as implied in the foregoing vote, Mr. Brown gracefully responded, by making to the College a donation of five thousand dollars, to remain in perpetuity, as a fund for the establishment of a Professorship of Oratory and Belles Lettres. The letter accompanying this donation has already been given in our "Historical Sketch." The fund thus established, was allowed to accumulate from year to year, until it had more than doubled. In 1826, one hundred shares in the stock of the Bank of North America, amounting to ten thousand dollars, were purchased by the Treasurer, which shares constituted for many years the SPECIAL FUND for the said Professorship.

In 1825, Mr. Brown was elected a Fellow of the University, and the office of Treasurer being thus made vacant, his place was filled by the election of his nephew, the late Mr. Moses Brown Ives. The first annual report made by Mr. Ives, was in September, 1826. From it we learn that the permanent funds of the University, at that time, were as follows:—

100 shares in Bank of North America, (Special Fund,)	$10,000
3 shares in Providence Bank,	1,200
21 shares in Rhode Island Union Bank,	2,100
150 shares in Union Bank,	7,500
25 shares in Manufacturers Bank,	2,500
James Rhodes's note on demand,	8,000
Total,	$31,300

The Special Fund of ten thousand dollars has already been accounted for. Of the twenty-one thousand three hundred dollars, four thousand five hundred dollars were obtained in the beginning by the Rev. Morgan Edwards, two thousand dollars were obtained from Congress in 1800, for damages done to the College edifice during the war, and the balance of fourteen thousand eight hundred dollars was obtained from small donations and legacies, and the accumulations of interest, but mainly through lotteries. Lotteries, it will be remembered, were formerly a very common method of obtaining funds for charitable and religious purposes, not only in Rhode Island but throughout the country. At a special meeting of the Corporation held December 23, 1795, it was

VOTED, That the Chancellor, together with the Rev. Dr. Hitchcock, Messrs. John Brown, Joseph Nightingale, John Smith, Welcome Arnold, David Howell and Nicholas Brown, be a committee to apply to the General Assembly of this State at their ensuing session, praying, in behalf of the Corporation, for the grant of a lottery to raise a sum not exceeding twenty-five thousand dollars, to be applied to the use of this Institution.

The application, it appears, was successful, for at the annual meeting of the Corporation in 1798, it was

VOTED, That the College lottery shall commence drawing the second Wednesday in October next.

In 1811, it was

VOTED, That Nicholas Brown, James B. Mason, James Rhodes, John T. Child, and Moses Lippitt, Esquires, be appointed a committee to apply to the General Assembly of this State at the next session, for liberty to raise by lottery twenty thousand dollars, for the advancement of the interests of this Institution. That said committee be also requested to apply to the legislatures of Massachusetts, New York and Connecticut, for permission to sell tickets in those states.

Whether this last lottery scheme was ever carried out, we have no means at hand for determining.

In 1850, important changes were made in the system of instruction, and large additions were made to its permanent funds. As this constitutes an important part of the financial history of the University, we incorporate into our present work most of the printed report of the committee appointed to raise a fund of one hundred and twenty-five thousand dollars, the statement of facts therein contained being taken chiefly from the report of President Wayland, made to the Corporation at a special meeting held March 28, 1850:—

In the year 1827, the property of the University consisted of the College premises; two buildings, used as lecture rooms and dormitories for students; and funds to the amount of $34,500.

Since that time, two edifices, one for the Library and Chapel, the other for lecture rooms and cabinet, and a house for the President, have been erected by the liberality of the late Hon. Nicholas Brown, and other friends of the Institution. Also a fund of twenty-five thousand dollars has been raised by private munificence for the improvement of the Library, and for procuring suitable apparatus for Chemistry and Natural Philosophy.

These contributions, though indispensable to the well-being of the University, have added nothing to the income by which the cost of tuition could be reduced, or the salaries of the officers of instruction increased.

A considerable portion of the income of the fund has, by necessity, been consumed in repairs and other incidental expenses. The residue, and the receipts for tuition, have constituted all the means in the hands of the Corporation for the support of the President and other officers of instruction. The salaries which were paid twenty years ago, are now rendered wholly inadequate, by the increased expensiveness of living; and for a considerable period the officers have been obliged to support themselves, in part, from their own funds.

Such being the circumstances, the Professors presented, in the year 1848, a memorial to the Corporation, asking for an increase of their salaries. The case was so urgent, that the committee of advice was directed to comply with their request. The salaries were therefore raised two hundred dollars each. It was, however, found that this increased compensation would exhaust the existing fund, and soon render the College bankrupt.

To prevent a result so disastrous, and at the same time to afford the Professors a reasonable compensation, the Corporation resolved to raise, by subscription, the sum of

FIFTY THOUSAND DOLLARS to meet the pressing wants of the University. This effort proposed no material change in the system of instruction, nor any increase in the number of officers; and, as is well known, it resulted in failure.

At the annual meeting of the Corporation in 1849, President Wayland tendered his resignation. He was urged to reconsider the subject; a committee of conference was appointed, and the Corporation adjourned to meet in December of the same year. At this adjourned meeting the President made a verbal statement of his views in reference to some changes in the system of instruction, and a committee, of which he was chairman, was appointed to report more fully at an adjourned meeting to be held in March, 1850.

This report, drawn up by Dr. Wayland, was printed, and has been widely circulated. It proposed material changes in the system of instruction; that the range of studies be greatly extended; and as a basis for carrying the plan into effect, that the sum of one hundred and twenty-five thousand dollars be raised by subscription. The report was unanimously adopted, and a committee of solicitation appointed, who entered immediately upon the discharge of their duties. The success of the subscription was, at the outset, rendered almost certain by the munificence of a few individuals, who came forward, without solicitation, and nobly pledged sums to the amount of sixty-five thousand dollars, on condition that the remainder should be subscribed by responsible persons on or before the 5th day of September, 1850. The committee were met both in this city and in other places by a cheerful liberality, which made the work of solicitation a pleasure; and at a meeting of the Corporation held on the stipulated day, the committee had the satisfaction to announce that the entire sum had been subscribed.

The subscriptions are as follows:—

John Carter Brown, Providence,	$20,000	Zachariah Allen, Providence,	$1,000
Alexander Duncan, "	20,000	James Arnold, New Bedford,	1,000
Estate of Thos. P. Ives, (Mrs. Hope Ives, $6,000; Mrs. C. R. Goddard, $1,000; M. B. Ives, $9,000; R. H. Ives, $4,000,) Providence,	20,000	Isaac M. Bull, New York.	1,000
		William P. Bullock and Julia Bullock, Providence,	1,000
		Crocker & Brothers, Taunton,	1,000
		George Cummings, Cambridge,	1,000
H. N. Slater, Providence,	5,000	Jacob Dunnell & Co., Providence,	1,000
Estate of Samuel G. Arnold, do.	2,000	George W. Hallett, "	1,000
Isaac Davis, Worcester,	2,000	George Howland, New Bedford,	1,000
Amasa Manton, Providence,	2,000	Earl P. Mason, Providence,	1,000
A. & W. Sprague, Warwick,	2,000	John A. Parker, New Bedford,	1,000
Marshall Woods, Providence,	2,000	Thomas Richardson, Boston,	1,000
Edward Carrington, "	1,500	George R. Russell, West Roxbury,	1,000
Seth Adams, Jr., "	1,000	A Friend, by George R. Russell.	1,000
Philip Allen, "	1,000	Robert G. Shaw, Boston,	1,000
Philip Allen, Jr., "	1,000	Michael Shepard, Salem,	1,000

FINANCIAL HISTORY. 327

Name	Amount	Name	Amount
Esther Slater, North Providence,	$1,000	Joseph W. Fearing, Providence,	$225
A. D. & J. Y. Smith, Providence,	1,000	John Barstow, "	200
Francis Wayland, "	1,000	Nathan Bishop, Boston,	200
William Baylies, West Bridgwater,	700	William J. Cross, Providence,	200
Nathan Appleton, Boston,	500	John Farnum, Philadelphia,	200
Samuel Appleton, "	500	William Gammell, Providence,	200
William Appleton, "	500	Thomas L. Halsey, "	200
William Blake, "	500	Edward Harris, Woonsocket,	200
Isaac Brown, Providence,	500	Edwin Hoyt, New York,	200
Thomas Burgess, "	500	Shubael Hutchins, Providence,	200
Josiah Chapin, "	500	John Kingsbury, "	200
James W. Converse, W. Roxbury,	500	Amos Lawrence, Boston,	200
Richard Fletcher, Boston,	500	Samuel Lawrence, "	200
John B. Francis, Warwick,	500	Moses B. Lockwood, Providence,	200
I. P. & R. G. and Rowland Hazard,		George C. Nightingale, "	200
South Kingstown,	500	John Oldfield, "	200
Benjamin Hoppin, Providence,	500	William H. Potter, "	200
Charles T. James, "	500	Providence Journal, "	200
Moses B. Jenkins, "	500	David Sears, Boston, "	200
Edward King, Newport,	500	Charles N. Talbot. New York,	200
Daniel Paine, Providence,	500	John E. Thayer, Boston,	200
E. R. & J. B. M. Potter, S Kingstown,	500	Amos C. Barstow, Providence,	150
James T. Rhodes, Providence,	500	James P. Boyce, Charleston, S. C.	150
Eliza B. Rogers, "	500	Walter S. Burges, Providence,	150
Robert Rogers, Bristol,	500	Fales, Lothrop & Co., Philadelphia,	150
Orray Taft, Providence,	500	Seth Padelford, Providence,	150
Samuel Boyd Tobey, Providence,	500	Jonathan Pike, "	150
Richard Waterman, "	500	Henry Anthony, "	100
Matthew Watson, "	500	Hezekiah Anthony, "	100
Benjamin R. Almy, "	300	Tully D. Bowen, "	100
Richard J. Arnold, "	300	Joseph Carpenter, "	100
Babcock & Moss, Westerly,	300	Royal Chapin, "	100
Charles S. Bradley, North Providence,	300	W. & G. Chapin, "	100
Alexis Caswell, Providence,	300	George Carlton, Boston,	100
George I. Chace, "	300	H. S. Chase, "	100
Fearing & Hall, New York,	300	T. P. Cushing, "	100
P. Grinnell & Sons, Providence,	300	A. B. Dike, Providence,	100
Thomas J Hill, "	300	Byron Diman, Bristol,	100
George G. King, Newport,	800	Alexander DeWitt, Worcester,	100
Henry A. Rogers, Providence,	300	Benjamin Finch, Newport,	100
Charles Potter, "	300	E. W. Fletcher, Providence,	100
Alvah Woods, "	300	James N. Granger, "	100
William T. Dorrance, "	250	John Green, Worcester,	100
Thomas R. Hazard, Portsmouth,	250	George B. Holmes, Providence,	100
Lawrence, Trimble & Co., New York,	250	Ezra W. Howard, "	100
Edward Pearce, Providence,	250	Henry L. Kendall, "	100
Thomas P. Shepard, "	250	H. R. Kendall, Brookline,	100

Jacob H. Loud, Plymouth,	$100	Prudence C. Loring, Boston,	$50
Marsh, Booth & Co., New York,	100	H. & R. Lippitt, Providence,	50
John H. Mason, Providence,	100	Merrick Lyon, "	50
Owen Mason, "	100	Silvanus G. Martin, "	50
Joseph Mauran, "	100	Pardon Miller, "	50
John Norris, Bristol,	100	George Owen, "	50
Samuel M. Noyes, Matanzas, Cuba,	100	Smith Owen, "	50
U. & C. W. Parsons, Providence,	100	Samuel W. Peckham, "	50
Sackett, Davis & Potter, "	100	Isaac Ray, "	50
Francis G. Shaw, Boston,	100	Henry Simon, "	50
Quincy A. Shaw, "	100	P. Tillinghast, New York,	50
S. G Shipley, "	100	Isaac Thurber, Providence,	50
J. Smith, Barre,	100	Elisha Watson, South Kingstown,	50
Otis Tufts, Boston,	100	Benjamin F. Thomas, Worcester,	30
Thomas & Martin, Philadelphia,	100	Charles Washburn, "	30
Sally Thompson, Providence,	100	Ellis Ames. Canton,	25
Elizabeth Waterman, Providence,	100	Francis W. Bird, Walpole,	25
Resolved Waterman, "	100	Alfred Bosworth, Warren.	25
Stephen Waterman, "	100	J. D. Burgess, Providence,	25
Charles H. Welling, Philadelphia,	100	Henry Chapin, Worcester,	25
Samuel K Williams, Boston,	100	Ira Cleaveland, Dedham,	25
John Winthrop, New Orleans,	100	Robert B. Cranston, Newport,	25
Charles Thurber, Worcester,	65	William Douglass, Providence,	25
A. F. Adie, Providence,	50	William F. Dow, New Bedford,	25
Bradford Allen, "	50	Barnum Field, Boston,	25
James B. Ames, Mobile,	50	Johnson Gardner, Seekonk,	25
Jacob Babbitt, Bristol,	50	George Hunt, Providence.	25
George M. Bartol, Lancaster,	50	W. W. Keach, "	25
Thomas Brown, Providence,	50	Nehemiah Knight, New York,	25
James W. Cooke, New York	50	Whiting Metcalf, Providence,	25
Gilbert Congdon, Providence,	50	Hugh Montgomery. Boston,	25
Charles H. Childs, "	50	Ezekiel Owen, Providence,	25
James F. DeWolf, Bristol,	50	Payton & Hawkins, "	25
William B. DeWolf. "	50	L. R., Boston,	25
William Fales, "	50	Luther Robinson, Boston,	25
Thomas Fletcher, Providence,	50	Henry S. Washburn, Worcester,	25
Henry S. Frieze, "	50	Lucy Snow, Boston,	20
William S. French, "	50	Crawford Allen, ($1,000, to be paid	
A. M. Gammell, Warren,	50	in yearly installments of $50,)	
M. A. D'W. Howe, Philadelphia,	50	paid in	50
Thomas A. Jenckes, Providence,	50		
Thomas Kinnicutt, Worcester,	50	Total,	$127,995

It was during this year, 1851, that the University came into possession of ten thousand dollars, bequeathed to the Corporation by the Hon. Nicholas Brown. In 1843, President Wayland presented to the University forty shares in the Blackstone Canal Bank, amounting to one thousand dollars, the income thereof to be annually appropriated in premiums, to be called the "President's Premiums." This class of premiums, we may add, is awarded to those members of the Freshmen class who attain to the highest excellence in the studies preparatory to admission.

A portion of the subscription fund of 1850 was expended in improvements and necessary repairs, as was contemplated upon the adoption of the "New System." The following abstract from the Treasurer's report for September, 1854, will show the condition of the finances of the University at that time, and also where the funds were invested : —

1. COMMON FUND.
    3 shares Providence Bank, par value, - - - - - $1,200
    21 shares Rhode Island Union Bank, par value, - - - 2,100
    150 shares Union Bank, par value, - - - - - 7,500
    25 shares Manufacturers Bank, par value, - - - - 2,500
    9 bonds New York Central Railroad Co., - - - - 8,500

    Total, - - - - - - - - $21,800

2. NICHOLAS BROWN PROFESSORSHIP.
    13 bonds Providence & Worcester Railroad Co., payable in 1860, 13,000

3. NICHOLAS BROWN BEQUEST.
    6 bonds Second Mortgage New York & Erie Railroad Co., - - 6,000
    4 bonds First Mortgage Hudson River Railroad Co., payable in 1860, 4,000

    Total, - - - - - - - - $10,000

4. LIBRARY FUND.
    1,000 shares Blackstone Canal Bank, - - - - - 25,000

5. UNIVERSITY PRIZE FUND.
    4 bonds Second Mortgage Hudson River Railroad Co., payable in 1860, 4,000
    4 Convertible Bonds New York & Erie Railroad Co., payable in 1871, 4,000
    1 Booth Mills Note, J. Pickering Putnam, Treasurer, dated July 1,
        1853, two years, - - - - - - - 4,000

    Total, - - - - - - - - - $12,000

6. PRESIDENT'S PREMIUM FUND.
   40 shares Blackstone Canal Bank, - - - - - - $1,000 00
7. SUBSCRIPTION FUND OF 1850.
   1 note Amoskeag Manufacturing Co., dated November 22, 1852,
      five years, William Amory, Treasurer, - - - 13,000 00
   1 note Stark Mills, dated November 22, 1853, five years, William Amory, Treasurer, - - - - - - 13,000 00
   3 notes, $5,000 each, Amoskeag Manufacturing Co., dated January 11, 1851, five years, - - - - - 15,000 00
   1 note Bay State Mills, dated December 1, 1852, five years, Samuel Lawrence, Treasurer, - - - - - 6,500 00
   80 shares Bank of Commerce, Boston, - - - - 8,000 00
   300 shares Bank of Commerce, Providence, - - - - 15,000 00
   1 note Booth Mills, J. Pickering Putnam, Treasurer, dated July 1, 1853, - - - - - - - - 7,500 00
   1 note Blackstone Manufacturing Co., C. H. Dabney, Treasurer, on demand, - - - - - - - - 1,759 25
   35 bonds Providence & Worcester Railroad Company, due in 1860, 35,000 00
   1 bond Worcester & Nashua Railroad Co., payable May 1, 1855, 1,000 00
   3 notes belonging to Subscription Fund, due September, 1854, December, 1854, and June, 1855. - - - - 800 00

   Total, - - - - - - - - - - $116,565 25

SUMMARY.

Common Fund, - - - - - - - - - - $21,800 00
Nicholas Brown's donation, (for Professorship,) - - - - 13,000 00
Nicholas Brown's bequest, - - - - - - - - 10,000 00
Library Fund, - - - - - - - - - - 25,000 00
University Prize Fund, arising from the Hon. Nicholas Brown's bequest, saved from collections of one-half the rents of the Blackstone Canal Bank estate, from September, 1841, to September, 1853, (now constituting the Nicholas Brown Scholarships,)* - - 12,000 00
President's Premium Fund, - - - - - - - 1,000 00
Subscription Fund of 1850, - - - - - - - 115,759 25
Notes due in 1854 and 1855, - - - - - - - 800 00

   Total, - - - - - - - - - - $199,465 25

*$323.93 was due to the Providence Bank from this Fund, August 31, 1854.

Mr. Ives died on the 7th of August, 1857, having managed the finances of the University during a period of thirty-two years, with rare devotion and skill. Not only in the discharge of the onerous duties of the Treasurership, for which he received no pecuniary compensation, but on all occasions, during the whole period of his life, he showed himself a firm and steadfast friend of the Institution where he received his education.

He was succeeded by his brother, Mr. Robert Hale Ives, who was elected Treasurer at the annual meeting of the Corporation held the following month. He graduated at the University in the class of 1816. His large experience in financial affairs, and the warm regard which he, in common with his family and ancestors, had ever shown for the Institution, preëminently fitted him for the Treasurership, a position which he held nearly ten years, or until the close of 1866.

At the time when he entered upon his duties as Treasurer, the income of the College was not sufficient to meet its current expenses, and a debt in consequence accumulated, which threatened, in a few years, to impair seriously its resources and usefulness. In this emergency it was determined to endeavor to raise by subscription the sum of one hundred and fifty thousand dollars, for the payment of the debt, and for the general purposes of instruction. A part of the plan was to secure Scholarships of one thousand dollars each, the income of which, sixty dollars, should be appropriated to aid indigent and meritorious students in obtaining an education. On the 19th of August, 1859, an arrangement was made with the Rev. Horace T. Love, a graduate in the class of 1836, and formerly a Baptist missionary to Greece, to act as soliciting agent for both Brown University and Waterville College, now Colby University. He immediately entered upon his work, in the prosecution of which he was aided by President Sears, who labored with untiring energy and zeal to place the Institution over which he presided, upon a good financial basis. Through their united efforts subscriptions amounting to upwards of ninety thousand dollars were secured, a part of which were applied to the extinguishment of the debt, a part to the building of the new Chemical Laboratory, and the remainder, with the exception of several conditional subscriptions not yet paid, were applied to Scholarships, an account of which, and of the Laboratory, we have already given. See pages 279 and 308.

The following is a list of the subscriptions, in addition to subscriptions for Scholarships and the Laboratory, obtained by Messrs. Love and Sears, (mostly by President Sears,) between the years 1859 and 1865:—

John Carter Brown,		$30,000
($15,000 for the erection of a new Library Building. 10,000 for purchase of the Bowen lot. 3,500 for repairs on Manning Hall. 1,000 for New Chemical Laboratory. 500 for planting trees in College Park. $30,000)		
Robert H. & Thomas P. Ives,		16,000
($5,000 for extinguishing the debt. 2,000 for Scholarships. 1,000 for New Chemical Laboratory. 10,000 not specified. $16,000)		
Samuel G. Arnold,		1,000
Jefferson Borden, Fall River,		1,000
James G. Bolles, Hartford,		1,000
Gardner Colby, Boston,		1,000
Isaac Davis, Worcester,		1,000
Jacob Dunnell, Pawtucket,		$1,000
Edward Harris, Woonsocket,		1,000
John B. Hartwell,		1,000
Jabez C. Knight,		1,000
Horatio N. Slater		1,000
A. & W. Sprague,		1,000
Samuel Boyd Tobey,		1,000
Marshall Woods,		1,000
Matthew Howland, New Bedford,		500
George Howland, " "		500
Samuel M. Noyes,		500
James T. Rhodes,		500
Total,		$61,000

In October, 1865, the Treasurer received from the executor of the late Hon. William Baylies, of Bridgewater, Massachusetts, the sum of two thousand dollars, the same having been bequeathed by him to the University. Mr. Baylies, to whom we have already alluded in our review of the triennial catalogue, graduated under President Maxcy, in the class of 1795. He died in Taunton, Massachusetts, September 27, 1865, aged eighty-nine years and twelve days. Such instances of remembrance on the part of the alumni of the University are pleasant to record.

Notwithstanding the improved condition of the University, the increasing number of students, and the additions made to the funds, the Professors were ill paid for their services, and the progress of the Institution was greatly retarded for want of a more complete endowment. It was determined, therefore, to make another vigorous effort on its behalf, and raise by subscription the sum of two hundred and fifty thousand dollars. The wise and patriotic course of President Sears during the late war, his rare attainments as a scholar, and his distinguished services in the cause of popular education, had gained him warm friends on every hand, and favorably disposed the minds of the public, to whom he now appealed, towards the Institution over which he presided. His appeal met with a ready and generous response. Five gentlemen of Providence cheerfully subscribed twenty thousand dollars each, on condition that the required sum should be secured. This condition they afterwards relinquished on learning the urgent needs of the University, paying to the Treasurer the amount of their subscriptions, or giving security therefor, and paying interest from September 1, 1866. The President, assisted by Professor S. S. Greene, has also obtained liberal subscriptions in Massachusetts, mostly on condition that the required sum of two hundred and fifty thousand dollars be secured in full. We give the names of the subscribers thus far, remarking that the undertaking is still in progress, and that encouragement has been received of subscriptions from parties who are not yet prepared to put their names upon the President's book :—

Horatio N. Slater, paid,	$20,000	J. Warren Merrill, Cambridge,	$5,000
William Sprague, "	20,000	Samuel Davis, Boston,	2,000
William S. Slater, "	20,000	Charles S Kendall, "	1,000
Earl P. Mason, "	20,000	James Upton, Salem,	1,000
Wm. H. Reynolds. (interest paid,)	20,000	Joseph Sawyer, Boston,	1,000
Gardner Colby, Newton Centre,	10,000	Lyman Tiffany, Cambridge,	1,000
Jefferson Borden, Fall River,	9,000	Stephen G. Allen, Boston,	1,000
Isaac Davis, Worcester,	*5,000	Mrs. Margaret Wood, "	1,000

334 BROWN UNIVERSITY.

J. W. Converse,	"	$1,000	John Holman, Boston, $250
Matthew Bolles,	"	1,000	Jonah G. Warren, Newton Centre, 250
George K. & H. A. Pervear, Lynn,		1,000	B. F. Brooks, Boston, 250
Hezekiah S. Chase, Boston,		1,000	J. E. Taylor, Springfield, 250
Joseph H. Converse, Cambridge,		1,000	N. P. Mann & Co., Boston, 200
John R. Deane, Boston,		500	Geo. C. Goodwin and Geo. D. Edmunds, Charlestown, 200
E. C. Fitz, in behalf of the Carey Avenue Baptist Church, Chelsea,		500	John C. Pratt, Boston, 200
D. S. Ford & J. W. Olmstead, for Watchman & Reflector, Boston,		500	Edwin Hall, Philadelphia, 200
			Joseph A. Pond, Brighton, 100
Henry R. Glover, Cambridge,		500	John Hanna, Philadelphia, 100
Gardner Chilson, Mansfield,		500	John C. Davis, " 100
Benjamin F. Brown, Boston,		500	J. G Chase, Springfield, 100
Thomas Griggs, Brookline,		500	Thomas E Evans, Boston, 100
Cash, paid September 24, 1866,		500	S. G. Bowdlear, " 100
Benjamin F. Thomas, Boston,		500	Benjamin B. Converse, Roxbury, 50
H. N. Tinkham, Springfield,		500	
S. A. Caldwell, Philadelphia,		300	Total, - - - - $150,050
Ezekiel Blake, Springfield,		300	

In the summer of 1865, a subscription was started by President Sears to obtain funds " to pay the expense of providing for instruction in military tactics by Col. F. Lippitt, for one year." The plan of thus establishing a military school in connection with the University, was for a time, however, abandoned. There is now, we are informed, an encouraging prospect of accomplishing in the most effective manner the object of such a school, under the auspices and general direction of the United States government. The names of the subscribers for this military fund are hereby given, in accordance with the general plan of our work. Several of the persons named, it will be observed, have paid their subscriptions, the amount, three hundred and fifty dollars, having been expended by consent of the parties, in the purchase of the Cromwell portrait for Rhode Island Hall. The balance of the subscriptions will doubtless be cheerfully paid, whenever funds shall be needed for the purposes above specified:—

Ambrose E. Burnside,	- - - $50	E. P. Taft,	- - - -	$50
Tully D. Bowen,	- - - 50	John F. Chapin,	- - -	50
Earl P. Mason,	- - - 50	Henry B. Anthony,	- -	50

A. S. Gallup,	- $50	Truman Beckwith,	- $50
Rufus Waterman,	50	Samuel Foster,	50
Royal C. Taft, paid,	50	Robert H. Ives,	- 50
Jacob T. Seagrave,	50	William Goddard,	50
William M. Bailey,	50	J. P. Balch & Son,	- 50
H. A. Hidden,	50	Amos D. Smith & Co., paid,	50
Cyrus Taft,	50	Thomas A. Jenckes,	- 50
Henry Anthony, paid,	50	Usher Parsons,	50
Seth Adams, Jr.,	50	Amos C. Barstow,	- 50
John M. Mason,	50	E. K. Glezen,	50
J. Dunnell,	50	Seth Padelford, paid,	- 50
W. T. Dorrance, paid,	50	Elisha Dyer,	25
William Sprague, "	50		
William B. Weeden, paid,	50	Total,	$1,575

At the annual meeting of the Corporation held in September, 1866, Mr. Ives resigned the Treasurership. For nearly a century the financial affairs of the College had been managed, as we have seen, with uncommon wisdom and skill, by the representatives of a single family. It is doubtful if a similar instance can be found in the history of any other College;—and it is certain that four successive treasurers thus related cannot be found, who have displayed such remarkable munificence, ability, and zeal in promoting the welfare of an institution of learning. For this the names of John Brown, Nicholas Brown, Moses Brown Ives, and Robert Hale Ives will be held in everlasting remembrance, by the graduates and friends of Brown University.

An abstract from Mr. Ives's last annual report to the Corporation, presents a brief statement of the invested funds of the University, and also of the receipts and expenditures for the year ending August 31, 1866:—

INVESTED FUNDS.

1. Common Fund,	- $173,800	6. Scholarships Fund,	- $38,000
2. Library Fund,	25,000	7. Agricultural Fund,	1,000
3. President's Premium Fund,	1,000	8. New Subscription,	- 20,000
4. Aid Fund,	5,000		
5. Jackson Prize Fund,	1,250	Total,	- $265,050

BROWN UNIVERSITY.

RECEIPTS FOR THE CURRENT YEAR.

Collected from students through the Register,	$14,408 14	Bequest of William Baylies,	$2,000 00
Income of invested Funds,	14,340 43	Old debit to Scholarships transferred,	2,841 55
Orders on Scholarships,	3,040 00		
Orders on Aid Fund,	485 00	Total,	$37,115 12

DISBURSEMENTS.

Repairs,	$3,041 92	Interest on Draft,	29 03
Expenses,	5,938 91	Loan from Library Fund repaid, with interest,	1,456 41
Salaries,	18,127 50		
Balance of Laboratory account transferred,	8,467 55	Total,	$37,061 41

Mr. Ives was succeeded in the Treasurership by Marshall Woods, M. D., a graduate of the University in the class of 1845. He entered upon his duties soon after his return from Europe, or about the 1st of January, 1867. Mr. Woods, it may be remarked, is allied to the Brown family, having married Anne Brown Francis, a descendant, on her father's side, of John Brown, the third Treasurer of the College, and on her mother's side, of the Hon. Nicholas Brown.

The following is the Treasurer's statement of the invested funds of the University April 12, 1867, the time when these sheets are passing through the press:—

Common Fund, including the amount of new subscription paid in,	$213,853 75	Jackson Prize Fund,	$1,250 00
		President's Premium Fund,	1,000 00
		Agricultural Fund,	1,000 00
Scholarships Fund,	40,797 50		
Library Fund,	25,000 00	Total,	$288,901 25
Aid Fund,	6,000 00		

The following is a brief summary of all the legacies and bequests that have been made to the College during the first century of its existence, or at least all of which we have any knowledge:—

1772. Rev. Dr. John Gill, of London, books.
1783. Rev. Benjamin Wallin, of London, - - - - - $125
1791. Miss Hannah Ward, - - - - - - - 40

FINANCIAL HISTORY. 337

1806. Rev. Isaac Backus, of Middleborough, books.
1818. Rev. William Richards, LL. D., of Lynn, England, books.
1841. Hon. Nicholas Brown, - - - - - - - $22,000
  "   "   " lands, estimated present value, -   -   150,000
1853. Hon. James Tallmadge, LL. D., of New York, - - - - 1,000
1865. Hon. William Baylies, LL. D., - - - - - - 2,000

Total, 1400 volumes, and lands and money to the amount of - - $175,165

The following is a summary of the various subscriptions for the College, or University, of which an account is given in the present work:—

1766–71.	Miscellaneous subscriptions, (pages 318–19,) - - -	$1,043
1767–68.	Subscriptions obtained in England and Ireland by Morgan Edwards, (pages 149–63,) - - - - -	4,500
1769–70.	Subscriptions obtained in South Carolina and Georgia by Hezekiah Smith, (pages 113–226,) - - - -	2,500
1770–71.	For the erection of the College buildings, (pages 235–41,)	9,480
1775–91.	Miscellaneous subscriptions, (page 332,) - - -	530
1783.	For the purchase of Philosophical Apparatus, (page 68,)	1,000
1784.	To purchase books for the Library, (page 68,) - -	2,300
1809–10.	For the University Grammar School, (pages 257–8,) -	1,452
1825.	For the Library, (page 80,) - - - - - -	840
1831–2.	For the Library Fund, (pages 83–7,) - - - -	19,438
1838–9.	For Rhode Island Hall and the President's House, (pp. 272–4,)	20,890
1854–5.	For the purchase of English books, (pages 90–4,) - -	5,060
1847–8.	Subscriptions of Providence churches for the encouragement of patristic learning, (pages 103–4,) - -	2,000
1850–1.	To raise a fund of one hundred and twenty-five thousand dollars, (pages 325–8,) - - - - -	127,995
1857–66.	For portraits and bust in Rhode Island Hall, (pages 285–97,)	6,400
1859–62.	For the Chemical Laboratory, (pages 279–80,) - -	14,250
1859–65.	Subscriptions obtained by President Sears and Mr. Love, to extinguish debt, etc., and not included in other subscriptions here enumerated, (pages 321–2,) - -	57,000
1859–67.	Subscriptions for Scholarships, (pages 308–13,) - -	41,000
1865.	For military instruction, (pages 334–5,) - - - -	1,575
1866–7.	New Subscriptions, (pages 333–4,) - - - -	150,050
	Total, - - - - - - - - - -	$469,303

43

We close this chapter with such extracts from the last will and testament of the Hon. Nicholas Brown as pertain to the history of the University:—

To my grandson Nicholas Brown, son of my oldest son Nicholas Brown, now living near the city of New York, I give, devise and bequeath my Brick House estate, situated in said Providence, and extending from South Main street to the river, the said house being now occupied by the Blackstone Canal Bank; he my said grandson to come into the possession and enjoyment thereof, when he shall arrive to the age of twenty-one years; and that the said estate shall not, for any cause or under any pretence, be sold before my said grandson shall arrive at the age of twenty-one years, should he so long live; and that until that period, the one-half of the rents and income of said estate, after deducting the repairs, taxes and insurance, be by my said executors kept separate and apart, as a fund to accumulate, and on his arrival at that age, the same be paid over to him my said grandson, for his own use and benefit; and the other half of the said rents and income on said estate, after deducting as aforesaid, to be paid, as the same shall be collected, to the Corporation of Brown University, to be by them appropriated to the charitable purpose of aiding deserving young men in obtaining their education while members of said University.

To the Corporation of Rhode Island College or Brown University, established at Providence, I give, devise and bequeath my undivided half part of the Corliss lots, so called, situated in Providence, and adjoining to their other College lots, and extending easterly therefrom to Hope street, to be and remain to them, their successors and assigns forever, they to come into possession and enjoyment of the same, in ten years after my decease. Also I give, devise and bequeath to the Corporation of Rhode Island College or Brown University, the further sum of five thousand dollars, to be applied to building a house for the President of the Institution, on the Waterman lot, on Waterman and Prospect streets, unless I shall have erected such house in my lifetime. Also the additional sum of five thousand dollars, to be appropriated in the erection of an edifice for minerals; these two last sums to be paid in one year after my decease. Also the sum of one thousand dollars towards making up the library fund, payable in eighteen months after my decease. Also the sum of twenty thousand dollars in cash, payable by my executors in ten years from my decease. Also I give, devise and bequeath to the Corporation of Rhode Island College or Brown University, the Hopkins estate and wall lots, situated south of the Colleges and on the northerly side of George street, in said Providence.

CODICIL.

I have also in my said Will, and on the fourth page thereof, devised and bequeathed to the Corporation of Rhode Island College or Brown University, among other things,

the sum of five thousand dollars to be applied to building a house for the President of
the Institution, on the Waterman Lot; also the sum of five thousand dollars to be
appropriated to the erection of an edifice for minerals; also the sum of one thousand
dollars towards making up the Library fund; all which things have been done, and to
which I have contributed; and the said bequests are therefore hereby revoked. And
I have given to said Corporation of Brown University, by my said Will, and on the
third page thereof, one-half of the net income of the rents and profits of my Brick
House estate with the buildings thereon, extending from South Main street to the
water, for and during the minority of my grandson Nicholas Brown, to whom the
estate is devised in fee; the half of said net income to be by said Corporation appropriated to the charitable purpose of aiding deserving young men in obtaining their
education while members of said University. And I do hereby recommend to said
Corporation, and to the Faculty thereof, to accept of the advice and recommendation
of the Warren Education Society, as to the persons who shall receive the benefit of
such aid and assistance, when said Society shall offer their advice and recommendation
in relation thereto.

I have also by my said Will, on the fourth page thereof, given and bequeathed to
said Corporation of Brown University, the sum of twenty thousand dollars in cash,
payable in ten years after my decease, by my Executors. Now therefore, as a
substitute and lieu of the said sum of twenty thousand dollars, I do hereby give and
bequeath unto said Corporation of Brown University the sum of ten thousand dollars,
to be paid by my Executors, within the time mentioned in said Will.

To the Northern Baptist Education Society, in Massachusetts, I give and bequeath
in addition to what I have before given to that Society, the sum of one thousand
dollars, to be paid in ten annual payments of one hundred dollars each; under the
hope and expectation that said Society will assist such charity scholars as contemplate
finishing their education at Brown University.

COMMENCEMENT EXERCISES.

1769—1866.

COMMENCEMENT EXERCISES.

WARREN, as we have already stated, was the cradle of the infant College, and here the first Commencement was held, in the Baptist meeting-house, Wednesday, September 7. 1769. The occasion drew together a crowd of people from all parts of the Colony, inaugurating, says the historian Arnold, the earliest State holiday in the history of Rhode Island. Seven young men, having completed the required course of study, took their "Bachelor's degree in the arts." Their names are thus entered by President Manning on his "Matriculation Roll":—

WILLIAM ROGERS, - - entered September 3, 1765, Newport, Rhode Island.
RICHARD STITES, - - -   " June 20, 1766, Elizabethtown, New Jersey.
JOSEPH BELTON, - - -   " November 4, 1766, Groton, Connecticut.
JOSEPH EATON, - - -   " November 10, 1766, Hopewell, New Jersey.
WILLIAM WILLIAMS, - -   " November 10, 1766, Hilltown, Pennsylvania.
CHARLES THOMPSON, - -   " November 10, 1766, Amwell, New Jersey.
JAMES MITCHELL VARNUM,   " May 23, 1768, Dracut, Massachusetts.

Four out of these seven students came, it will be observed, from New Jersey and Pennsylvania, where the College had its origin. Rogers, the FIRST STUDENT, and the only one from Rhode Island, became distinguished as a man of letters and as a preacher. He was chaplain of a brigade in the Continental army, and for many years was Professor of Oratory and Belles Lettres in the University of Pennsylvania. He was also for some time previous to the war, pastor of the First Baptist Church in Philadelphia. Stites was a brother-in-law of President Manning. He studied medicine and became a practising physician in the State of his birth. Dr. Stephen Gano, so long the pastor of the Baptist Church in Providence, studied medicine under him two years. Of Belton's personal history we have been unable to learn any particulars. Eaton was a son of the Rev. Isaac Eaton, to whom belongs the distinguished honor of founding Hopewell Academy. Williams settled in Wrentham, Massachusetts, as pastor of a Baptist church, and the principal of an academy, which, in his day, attained to high distinction as a literary institution. Of the many youth under his care upwards of eighty were fitted for his alma mater, among whom may be mentioned the Rev. Dr. Maxcy, successor to Manning, the Hon. David R. Williams, Governor of South Carolina, and the Hon. Tristam Burges. Thompson, the valedictorian of the class, was a successful pastor of the Baptist Church in Warren, and afterwards for many years, of the church in Swansea. He was also a chaplain in the American army. Varnum became a successful lawyer and one of the most celebrated orators in the Colony of Rhode Island. He was also noted as a military man, and in 1777 was promoted by Congress to the rank of Brigadier-General. His biography, together with that of Rogers, Thompson, and Williams, may be found in our LIFE OF DR. MANNING.

The following is the order of exercises for this Commencement, taken from the PROVIDENCE GAZETTE AND COUNTRY JOURNAL. The valedictory oration in the hand-writing of the author, is among the documents preserved in the Library of the University. The publication of this oration, together with the Latin Salutatory, and the addresses of Williams, Varnum, and Rogers, we are reluctantly compelled to omit for the present:—

1769.

1. The Salutatory Oration in Latin. - - - - - Richard Stites.
2. The Americans, in their present Circumstances, cannot, consistent with good Policy, affect to become an Independent State; a Forensic Dispute.
James M. Varnum, William Williams.
3. An Oration on Benevolence. - - - - - - William Rogers.
4. Materia cogitare non potest; a Syllogistic Disputation in Latin.
William Williams, Joseph Belton, Joseph Eaton, William Rogers, James M. Varnum.
5. The Oratorial Art; an Oration, with the Valedictory Addresses.
Charles Thompson.

Before proceeding to give in their order the exercises of the various Commencements that have been held since the memorable "First Commencement," we may allude to some of the "acts and resolves" pertaining thereto. In looking over the records of the Corporation, we find under date of March 13, 1786, the following:—

RESOLVED, That in future, the candidates for Bachelor Degrees, being alumni of the College, shall be clad at Commencement in black flowing robes and caps, similar to those used at other universities.

RESOLVED, That an exclusive right of furnishing such robes and caps, for the use of the candidates, be granted and confirmed to an undertaker for the space of fifteen years; and that Mr. Asher Robbins be authorized to inquire for an undertaker, and find out the lowest terms on which such robes and caps may be obtained, and to report the same to the Faculty of the College for the time being, who are hereby authorized to complete the contract.

The President now wears the classic "gown and cap," while half a dozen robes, worn in turn by successive speakers of the graduating class, serve to perpetuate the customs and usages of the past. In accordance with the so called progressive spirit of the age, we may expect ere long to see these badges and symbols of scholastic life in the older universities of Europe, abolished in this democratic country of ours, which requires its representatives abroad to dispense with ceremonial court dresses, and such like insignia of office and rank.

Under date of September 6, 1787, we find it

RESOLVED, That in future the Salutatory Oration at public Commencements, be assigned by the President; that the Valedictory and Intermediate Orations be assigned by the classes; and that the Syllogistic and Forensic Disputes, and such other exercises as they may judge necessary, be assigned by the President and Tutors; and that in case any student shall refuse, or neglect to exhibit his part, or any of said exercises, in writing, at or before the time of the examination of his class for the honors of the College, the President and Tutors shall assign the part or parts of such delinquent or delinquents, to such others of the same class as they may think proper.

It would thus appear that the Valedictorian was formerly appointed by his classmates, not so much perhaps on account of superior scholarship, as the possession of popular gifts and the graces of oratory. In this connection we may add, that the expenses of Commencement were, in the early history of the College, defrayed by the graduating class, those having the highest parts paying the largest sums. Thus we find it stated in Bowen's Memoir of Tristam Burges, that this distinguished orator paid one hundred dollars, or nearly one-half the expenses of Commencement, in 1796, for the valedictory honors to which he had been assigned, while the Salutatorian paid eighty dollars.

The following resolution, passed by the Corporation, September 2, 1790, reads strangely to those who are accustomed to the quiet Commencements of the present day :—

RESOLVED, That it be recommended to the Baptist Society, in future, to take effectual measures to prevent the erection of booths, or receptacles for liquors, or other things for sale, and all disorderly practices on the Baptist Meeting House lot, on Commencement days.

Until within a comparatively recent period Commencement has been a general holiday, manufacturing establishments in the city and vicinity being closed, and the people crowding the streets to witness the PROCESSION escorted by Col. Tillinghast's "Company of Cadets," or the "United Company of the Train of Artillery." Tents and booths were everywhere erected, and the day was given to mirth and enjoyment. Tuesday the undergraduate societies had their celebrations, and in the evening, from the beginning of Maxcy's administration down to the accession of Dr. Wayland to the Presidency, there were transparencies and an illumination of the College buildings, by the students. The change of time made in 1851, from September to July, tended to destroy much of the popular element of this Collegiate anniversary. After a short experience of two years the Corporation wisely returned to the time honored "first Wednesday in September," but in the estimation of the masses of the people, the glory of "Rhode Island Commencement" has departed.

For more than half a century the exercises of Commencement were continued during both forenoon and afternoon, with an interval between. The present mode of conducting them was adopted in September, 1829. Since that time, and especially since about the year 1840, the "Commencement Dinner," at the CLOSE of the literary exercises in the church, has been a prominent feature of the day.

The earliest printed "Order of Exercises" of which we have any knowledge, is dated 1795. The account of Commencements previous to that year has been obtained with great difficulty, mainly from files of the PROVIDENCE GAZETTE, and from Rippon's BAPTIST ANNUAL REGISTER, published in London. A complete set of the printed Exercises from the year 1800, bound in a handsome quarto volume, is among the documents that are carefully preserved in the archives of the University.

The second Commencement of the College, and the first in Providence, was held in Mr. Snow's meeting-house, on the west side of the river, this being, at the time, the largest house in town. Here subsequent Commencements were held until 1776, when the new Baptist meeting-house was ready for use. The following are the anniversary exercises of the College for nearly a century, arranged in the order of their successive years:—

1770.

1. The Salutatory Oration in Latin. - - - - - John Dennis.
2. A Forensic Dispute. - - - - John Dennis, Theodore Foster, Samuel Nash, Seth Read.
3. An Intermediate Oration on Catholicism. - - - Theodore Foster.
4. A Syllogistic Disputation in Latin. - - Theodore Foster, Respondent; Samuel Nash, Seth Read, John Dennis, Opponents.
5. The Valedictory Oration. - - - - - - Seth Read.

"The business of the day being concluded," says the GAZETTE, "and before the Assembly broke up, a piece from Homer was pronounced by Master Billy Edwards, one of the Grammar School boys, not nine years old." This Edwards was a son of the Rev. Morgan Edwards. He graduated, it will be observed, in the class of 1776.

1771.

1. The Salutatory Oration in Latin. - - - - - Samuel Ward.
2. A Dialogue, on the necessity of perpetuating the Union between Great Britain and her Colonies. - - - - Thomas Arnold, Micah Brown.
3. An Intermediate Oration on the Advantages of Peace. - Thomas Ustick.
4. Justitia punitiva Dei est attributum; a Syllogistic Disputation.
    Thomas Arnold, Respondent;
    Micah Brown, Ranna Cossit, Benjamin Farnham, Opponents.
5. A Forensic Dispute on Literature. - - Samuel Ward, Ranna Cossit, Benjamin Farnham.
6. The Antiquity and Usefulness of Civil Law; an Oration with the Valedictory Addresses. - - - - - - - Thomas Arnold.

1772.

1. The Salutatory Oration in Latin. - - - - Joseph D. Russell.
2. An Intermediate Oration on History. - - - - Elias Howell.

COMMENCEMENT EXERCISES.   349

3. Soliloquy on Solitude. - - - - - Joseph Appleton.
4. An Oration on Agriculture, and the Pleasures of a Country Life. Joseph Harris.
5. The Origin, Nature and Design of Civil Government; an Oration for the Master's Degree. - - - - - James M. Varnum, (class of 1769.)
6. Miracula extitisse humano Testimonio probari potest; a Syllogistic Disputation
    Elias Howell, Respondent;
    Joseph Appleton, Benjamin Greene, Ebenezer David, Opponents.
7. Female Education; an Oration for the Master's Degree.
    Richard Stites, (class of 1769.)
8. The Incomparable Advantages of Religion; an Oration with the Valedictory Addresses. - - - - - - - - Ebenezer David.

1773.

From a "Remonstrance of the Senior Class of Rhode Island College to the respectable the President and Professor of the same," bearing date February 19, 1773, it appears that serious objections had been made to a Commencement for this year, on the ground mainly that the graduating class were not "orators." These objections were finally overruled, and Commencement was held as usual. The following account from the Diary of the Valedictorian, Doct. Solomon Drowne, is kindly furnished us by his grandson, Rev. Thomas S. Drowne, of Brooklyn. We publish it, instead of the regular Order of Exercises. The author, it may be observed, was an intimate friend of President Manning, and for many years was a Professor in the College. His portrait is in the Collection in Rhode Island Hall:—

WEDNESDAY, SEPTEMBER 1. At length the day, the great, the important day, is come. O may it prove propitious. Now we must pass from easy college duties into the busy, bustling scenes of life. At about ten o'clock, the Corporation being assembled, we walk in procession from the College Hall to the Rev. Mr. Snow's meeting-house, where the President introduces the business of the day by Prayer; after which Nash addresses the assembly in a Latin Salutatory Oration; then follows an English Oration, pronounced by Mr. Foster, upon the Discovery, progressive Settlement, present State and future Greatness of the American Colonies; which is succeeded by a Syllogistic Disputation in Latin, (the Theses being previously distributed,) "An Voluntati competit Libertas?" wherein Litchfield is the Respondent, and myself, Padelford and Tillinghast, the Opponents. After this, Tillinghast delivers an Oration on Politeness, which finishes the exercises of the forenoon.

The afternoon exercises begin with an English Oration for the Master's degree, upon Civil Liberty, by Mr. Dennis. The degree of A. B. is then conferred on myself, Joseph Litchfield, Jacob Nash, Philip Padelford and Henry H. Tillinghast; and the degree of A. M. on Messrs. John Dennis, Theodore Foster, Samuel Nash and Seth Read; also on Doct. Thomas Eyre, Secretary of the College, and late of Yale College; to which succeeded my Valedictory Oration; and then a most solemn and pathetic charge by the President to our class. The whole is concluded by Prayer.

Now our palpitation and anxiety are over. * * Thus ends a day which has been long expected, but has passed forever.

The following is President Manning's charge, to which allusion is made in the foregoing account, and for which we are indebted to Henry T. Drowne, Esq., of New York, also a grandson of Doct. Drowne.

The practice of delivering a BACCALAUREATE ADDRESS, inaugurated by Manning, and followed by his successor, Maxcy, and for a time by President Messer, was afterwards discontinued.

PRESIDENT MANNING'S ADDRESS.

You will naturally expect that I should express the same affectionate regard for your welfare, as for that of those who have before shared the honors of this College, by giving you a parting charge. But if I thought you would expect and imagine I would give it as a mere thing of course, and with unfeeling formality, I should either entirely omit it, or endeavor to conceive it in such terms and utter it with such tones as would convince you of my earnestness. But even to suggest that you were all capable of such unaccountable insensibility, would be highly injurious to your character, for which I publicly profess the most tender concern.

With you I consider the scene now shifted, and you to have exchanged the retirement of a college for the clamorous, or at least busy, scenes of life;—that agitated ocean on which, unless Providence is distinguishingly propitious, you may expect to find full exercise for all your abilities, and at last perhaps scarce weather out the storms, with honor and advantage, which will gather and thwart even a virtuous course.

To lay down general rules and useful maxims for your future conduct, is a matter extremely easy; for you to adopt and apply them, untutored by experience, is not so easy.

Experience is a kind of knowledge that is purely personal, and hence arise the numberless mistakes of inadvertent youth; yet, from an attentive view of life, much may be learned from others, for causes similar will be productive of similar effects. The same course of action which has brought infamy on others, will involve you also; and the virtuous, useful life of others points you directly to that reputation which they have acquired. So far, then, success may be hoped for from wholesome lectures read to docile minds, and a suitable charge given to those who aim to tread the path of virtue and climb to solid reputation.

The sagacious public will not only discern your quantity of capacity, but decide who of you have most exerted yourselves to improve in knowledge; and, small as this class is, and numerous as the disadvantages under which it has labored are, I am not without hopes of seeing at least some of its members distinguish themselves amongst the sons of science.

If a proper foundation has not been laid in your first studies to initiate you into the knowledge of letters, I believe you will do your Instructors the justice to impute it to something else as the cause, rather than to their inattention to your interest or their duty

And though a course of four years in college without forfeiting a standing by vicious conduct is generally thought sufficient to entitle to a degree, yet something more than possessing a diploma must prove that you merit it. I therefore charge you to press forward with hasty steps in the road to knowledge, and if an immature age, a fickle and indolent temper, or but a moderate capacity has distanced you in the race, let more confirmed age, future activity and redoubled diligence urge you on with a noble ambition at once to even outdo yourselves, and agreeably disappoint the expectations of your friends.

In forming your connections, as well as in all your undertakings, proceed with the utmost caution. The neglect of this has proved the ruin of thousands.

Be slow to speak, but swift to hear; be angry only when absolutely necessary, and then you will not be likely to exceed due bounds. Despise the narrow, contracted principle which actuates the selfish, and only think you deserve the character of men when you affectionately love and glow with ardor to promote the happiness of all mankind. Your personal wants are few, unless unnecessarily multiplied by yourselves, and consequently you may expend much on the public.

Remember that the lowest calling in life may be honored by a proper attention paid to the duties of it, and that the highest may be degraded by the neglect of them. Aspire not, therefore, to an exalted station without conscious worth to entitle you to it, and an unshaken resolution to support it.

Despise as well those fetters of the mind forged by devoted bigots to opinion, as those for the body by tyrannic princes and legislatures.

Challenge the glorious prerogative of thinking for yourselves in religious matters, and generously grant to others without a grudge what you yourselves deem the dearest of all blessings.

I have a right to expect your friendship for this College, and your strenuous exertions in its just vindication, while I interdict an ungenerous partiality.

Make religion your first, your great, your only concern. Converse intimately with death by devout meditation. Read with the closest attention the Scriptures of God, and by their aid realize the awful, glorious realities of eternity. Make them alone the standard of both your faith and your practice. Refute the daring, licentious infidel with a holy life, without which the most holy profession is both utterly incredible and unavailing.

And should any of you assume the character of a Christian preacher, I warn you to beware of touching this sacred Ark with unhallowed hands. Remember the awful, ever memorable fate of those who offered strange fire; such will yours be, except your hearts are purified with the faith of the Gospel.

Finally, we must all meet at the august tribunal of the Supreme Judge, to hear the decisive sentence according to our characters. May this, my dear pupils, be to you an introduction into everlasting joy.

1774.

1. The Salutatory Oration in Latin. - - - - - Timothy Jones.
2. Theatrical Exhibitions corrupt the Morals of Mankind, and are prejudicial to the State; a Disputation. - - - - Dwight Foster, Respondent.
Elias Penniman, Opponent.
3. An Oration on the Necessity and Advantages of Cultivating our own Language.
John Dorrance.
4. An Dictamina Conscientiae sunt semper obtemperanda? a Syllogistic Dispute.
John Dorrance, Respondent.
Barnabas Binney, Dwight Foster, Timothy Jones, Elias Penniman, Opponents.
5. Patriotism; an Oration for the Master's Degree. Samuel Ward, (class of 1771.)
6. Plea for Religious Liberty; an Oration with the Valedictory Addresses.
Barnabas Binney.

1775.

There was no Commencement this year, although the graduating class consisted of ten, being the largest class that had thus far been connected with the Institution. The recent battles of Lexington and of Bunker Hill had electrified the public, and turned their attention from literary performances to the stern realities of civil war. For an interesting correspondence between the Senior Class and the President, in reference to Commencement, and the great and perilous issues of the day, see MANNING AND BROWN UNIVERSITY, pp. 24–41.

1776.

1. The Salutatory Oration in Latin. - - - - - John P. Mann.
2. An Oration on the Advantages of Literature. - - - Jabez Thayer.
3. An Oration on Toryism and Negro Slavery. - - Abraham Cummings.
4. An Leges Divinae aliquid ultra Vires humanas ab Hominibus exigunt; a Syllogistic Dispute. - - - - Jabez Thayer, Abraham Cummings.
5. An Oration on the Education of Youth of both Sexes. - - - Curtis Coe.
6. An Oration in Hebrew. - - - - - - Abraham Cummings.
7. An Oration on Liberty; with the Valedictory Addresses. Ebenezer Dutch.

1777—1782.

During these years there was no Commencement. From December 7, 1776, until May 27, 1782, the course of studies was suspended, and the College edifice was occupied for barracks, and afterwards for a hospital, by the American and French forces.

1783.

No record has been preserved of the order of exercises of this Commencement. The PROVIDENCE GAZETTE says: "As soon as the Corporation had taken their seats, the audience were entertained with an anthem; after which, the President made a prayer well adapted to the occasion. The candidates then proceeded to perform their respective parts, which consisted of several orations on different subjects, and a forensic disputation. An oration was likewise delivered by Dr. James Mann, of Harvard College."

The degree of Bachelor of Arts was conferred on Jacob Campbell, George Tillinghast, John Tillinghast, Othniel Tyler, and William Wilkinson.

In the evening, the Rev. Dr. Stillman preached an animating sermon from Luke 15 : 32 :—" It was meet that we should make merry and be glad; for this thy brother was dead and is alive again, and was lost and is found."

1784—1785.

The old stock of undergraduates, so to speak, having become exhausted, there was no further Commencement until the Freshmen Class that entered in 1782, were prepared to take their Bachelor's degree.

1786.

1. The Salutatory Oration in Latin. - - - - - James Manning.
2. An Oration on the Study of History. - - - - - Oliver Bowen.
3. A Dialogue upon the Four Elements.   Benjamin B. Carter, Joseph Mason, Jairus Hall, Robert L. Annan.
4. An Oration on the Advantages of Commerce. - - Nicholas Brown, Jr.
5. The Rise and Progress of Science ; an Oration for the Master's Degree.
   Othniel Tyler, (class of 1783)
6. A Forensic Dispute on the Question :—Whether it would not have been better for America to have remained dependent on Great Britain ?
   Benjamin Woods, Edmund Freeman, Jonathan Gould, Timothy Greene.
7. Reflections upon Governments, and a Tribute to the Memory of our late departed friend, General Greene; an Oration for the Master's Degree.
   George Tillinghast, (class of 1783.)
8. The Valedictory Oration. - - - - - - Lemuel Kollock.

N. B. A Syllogistic Dispute between Messrs. Amos Wood, Preserved Smith and William Annan, was omitted for want of time.

1787.

1. An Oration in Greek on Rhetoric. - - - - Abraham Crouch.
2. An Oration on the present Appearance of public Affairs in the United States of America ;—portraying the superior advantages to be enjoyed by this country, and the public happiness rationally to be expected, in case the States shall harmoniously agree on the great Federal measures necessary for the good of the whole, whereon the Convention have been some time deliberating at Philadelphia, and recommending industry, the manufactures of our country and

the disuse of foreign goods; and soliciting the fair daughters of America to set the patriotic example by banishing from their dress the costly gewgaws and articles of foreign production. - - - - Nathaniel Lambert.
3. An Oration on Agriculture; its Antiquity, Importance, Advantages, and modes of Culture. - - - - - - - Oliver Leonard.
4. A Forensic Dispute on the Question: Whether it be good Policy in the States on the Atlantic Shore, to promote an immediate Settlement on the Western Territory? - Eli King, Negative, Jonathan Maxcy, Affirmative, Abraham Crouch, Negative, Oliver Leonard, Affirmative.
5. An Oration on the Equality of Mankind as to Natural Talents, considered without Reference to Education. - - - - - - Oliver Hawes.
6. An Oration on the Necessity in Republics of diffusing knowledge among the People. - - - - - - - - Abner Alden.
7. A Panegyric on the Policy and Conduct of the Athenians in encouraging Literature and the useful Arts. - - - - - - - Eli King.
8. The Prospects of America, a Poem; with the Valedictory Addresses.
Jonathan Maxcy.

Among the College documents, are "Proposals for printing by subscription" President Maxcy's Poem, which "gained," the paper states, "the universal applause of a large, crowded and polite assembly." It was published in a duodecimo form, with an appendix containing an historical account of the College and the State of Rhode Island. Signatures C and E of the work are on file in the Library of the University.

1788.

1. The Salutatory Oration in Latin; a Retrospect on the Ages of Learning.
Simeon Doggett.
2. An Oration in Hebrew, on the Eloquence of the Scriptures. Samuel Mead.
3. A Forensic Dispute on the Question:— Whether those Nations which have been most eminent for Knowledge, have also been most eminent for Virtue?
Joshua Leonard, James Burrill.
4. An Oration in Greek, on the Importance of Encouraging Genius.
Josias Holbrook.
5. A Dialogue in Blank Verse, on the Situation and Prospects of America. (Written by John Turner.) - - - Benjamin Adams, Jesse Blackinton, Jabez P. Fisher, John Turner.

6. A Sketch on Creation. - - - - - - - Jabez Bowen.
7. An Oration in French, on Letters in General. - - - George Jackson.
8. A Burlesque Poem on Political Projectors. - - - Stephen Tillinghast.
9. An Essay on Original Genius. - - - - - Hermann Daggett.
10. A Comic Dialogue to ridicule False Learning. (Written by Harding Harris.)
John Briggs, Harding Harris, George Jackson, Ebenezer Lazell, Benjamin Whitman.
11. A Tribute to the Memory of our Departed Heroes. - - William Barton.
12. A Poem on Liberty; with the Valedictory Addresses. Amos Maine Atwell.

1789.

1. The Salutatory Address in Latin, with an English Oration on the Progress and Improvement of the Arts and Sciences in America. John C. Nightingale.
2. A Forensic Dispute on this Question:— Whether Columbus by discovering America benefited mankind? - - Edward Richmond, Paul Draper.
3. An Oration on Patriotism. - - - - - Jeremiah B. Howell.
4. A Funeral Oration on the Death of Levi Hayes, once a member of the graduating class. - - - - - - - - - Nicholas Power.
5 An Oration on Liberty. - - - - - - - Thomas Park.
6. An Oration on the Pleasures of the Imagination. - - Edward Richmond.
7. The Propriety and Importance of the Establishment of a Gymnasium for the Education of American Youth; an Oration for the Master's Degree.
Lemuel Kollock, (class of 1786.)
8. A Poem; with the Valedictory Addresses. - - - James Fenner.

President Manning's BACCALAUREATE ADDRESS for this year is published in our former work, pp. 425–7.

1790.

1. The Salutatory Address in Latin, with an English Oration, congratulating the State of Rhode Island upon her Accession to the Federal Government, and the Completion of the Union of the States. - - - - Peter Hawes.
2. An Oration on the bad Effects of Party in a State. - - William Allen.
3. An Oration in Greek, on the Slave Trade. - - - - Jacob Convers.
4. A Forensic Dispute on the Question:— Would Mankind have been more happy than they now are, had the Earth spontaneously yielded her Fruits necessary for the Support of Man? - - - - Job Nelson, Asa Messer.
5. An Oration in French, in Praise of Eloquence. - - Benjamin H. Hall.
6. The Second Intermediate Oration— Reflections on Happiness. - John Fitch.

COMMENCEMENT EXERCISES. 357

7. The First Intermediate Oration — On the History of Commerce and Navigation.
Moses Brown.
8. An Oration on the Progress of Man from an uncivilized to a civilized State, comparing his Happiness in those different States. - Nathaniel Drinkwater.
9. A Forensic Dispute on the Question :—Is that generally received Maxim, "Honesty is the best Policy," founded in Truth? - - Nehemiah Shumway,
Thomas Cobb.
10. An Oration on the Benefit of Men of Genius to the World, exemplified particularly in the Life of Dr. Franklin, with a Panegyric upon that truly great man.
John Waldo.
11. The Expediency of establishing a Federal University in America; an Oration for the Master's Degree. - - - Oliver Leonard, (class of 1787.)
12. The Importance of subjecting the Passions to the Control of Reason, with the Influence of Education in producing this effect; an Oration for the Master's Degree. - - - - - Abraham Crouch, (class of 1787.)
13. An Oration on the Pleasures of the Fine Arts, and the Importance of making them a Branch of Study; with the Valedictory Addresses. Abijah Whiting.

President Messer, it will be observed, graduated with this class.

1791.

1. The Salutatory Oration in Latin, on the History of Eloquence. William Hunter.
2. A Dissertation :— Comparison of Ancient and Modern Literature.
Samuel W. Baylies.
3. An Oration on the Causes of the Difference of the Moral Faculty.
George R. Burrill.
4. A Dissertation on Civil Liberty. - - - - - - James Ellis
5. A Dissertation on the following Question :— Is Fashion, everything considered, Beneficial to Mankind? - - - - Elisha Fairbanks, John Morse.
6. An Oration on Villainy considered as the Source of Empire. James B. Mason.
7. An Oration in Greek :— Comparison of Demosthenes and Cicero.
Chiron Penniman.
8. An Oration on the Influence of the Fine Arts on Society. Samuel King.
9. The Difference between Law and Constitution ;— an Oration for the Master's Degree. - - - - - James Burrill, (class of 1788.)
10. An Oration on the Death of the Rev. President Manning.
Simeon Doggett, (class of 1788.)
11. The Past, Present and Future Prospects of America ;— an Oration for the Master's Degree. - - - - - Jabez Bowen, (class of 1788.)

12. The Rights of Brutes;—an Oration for the Master's Degree.
          Hermann Daggett, (class of 1788.)
13. The Difference in the Spirit of Heroism in the Different Periods of Society;— an Oration for the Master's Degree.
        Josias L. Arnold, (a graduate of Dartmouth.)
14. The Valedictory Oration. - - - - - Jonathan Russell.

At this Commencement the Hon. Judge Howell, who had long been connected with the College as Tutor and Professor, and afterwards as a Fellow of the Corporation, presided. His ADDRESS to the graduates, which we copy from Rippon's BAPTIST ANNUAL REGISTER, has been deservedly admired for its excellent counsel, and as a specimen of English undefiled. The Oration by Simeon Doggett, on the death of President Manning, is among the documents on file in the Library of the University. Extracts from this Oration, it may be added, are published in our former work, pp. 455-7.

JUDGE HOWELL'S ADDRESS.

YOUNG GENTLEMEN:—The occasion which has devolved on me the duty of addressing you, cannot fail to impress your minds with an uncommon degree of seriousness.

Your beloved President, from whose lips you have been accustomed to receive lessons of wisdom, is not here to give you his last benediction; he is gone to the world of spirits; and, as we hope and trust, to receive the rewards of his labors of love and of virtue.

The patrons of the College could not, however, permit you to bid adieu to this Institution without authorizing one of their number to address you.

Although I have not a personal acquaintance with all of you, and cannot, therefore, be supposed to entertain such an affectionate solicitude for your welfare as your immediate Instructors; yet the part I have taken, as an overseer of your progress in learning, and the former relation I sustained to this College for many years, as a teacher, awaken in me, on this solemn occasion, the most tender and sincere concern for your future welfare in life.

The pittance of time alloted to a collegiate education, can suffice only to lay the foundation of learning: the superstructure must be reared by the assiduous attention of after years.

This day enlarges you into the world. Extensive fields open to your view. You have to explore the scenes, and to make an election of the character that best pleases you on the great theatre of life.

"Seekest thou great things for thyself? Seek them not," said the ancient prophet to Baruch, his scholar and scribe. An overweening fondness for our own abilities, leads us, in the ardor of youth, to portray in our imagination future greatness. Time and experience only can correct the error, and reduce us to think of ourselves soberly, and as we ought. Human life is full of disappointments.

A readiness to listen to counsel is the surest mark of wisdom in youth. "In the multitude of counsellors there is safety." When, therefore, you are about to take any important step in life, omit not to consult your friends; and let your decision be the result of deep reflection, and the most careful circumspection.

If you wish for prosperity in your worldly affairs, rise early in the morning, and attend to your own business with diligence, punctuality, and order; pay a sacred regard to truth and justice; live temperately, and moderate your passions by listening to the voice of reason. Take not the lead in fashions, nor suffer yourselves to be noted for singularity. Discover your knowledge on proper occasions, but avoid an affected and pedantic display of it.

Let the rights of man ever be held sacred. A moment's reflection will convince you, that others' rights are as inviolable as your own; and a small degree of virtue will lead you to respect them. He that serves mankind most successfully, and with the best principles, serves his Creator most acceptably. Be cautious of bandying into parties; they regard neither the abilities nor virtues of men, but only their subserviency to present purposes; they are a snare to virtue and a mischief to society. With this caution on your mind, you will never revile or speak evil of whole sects, classes, or societies of men.

In the choice of friends and companions, rather aspire to those above you in life, than sink to those below; the former line of conduct will mark a generous ambition, the latter indicates baseness and exility of thought: from the former you are to expect advantages, and from the latter an incumbrance. To obtain this object, will require the extension of your abilities and the growth of your virtues.

Never aim to rise in life by depressing others; it is more manly to rely on the strength of one's own abilities and merit. Avoid publishing, or even listening to scandal. To mention, with pleasure, the virtues even of a rival, denotes a great mind.

Trifle not with yourselves, nor suffer yourselves to be trifled with by others. If you rightly estimate your own merit, the world will not long differ from you. Avoid contradictions, or soften them. Aim to instruct and entertain your company, rather than to divert them with the affectation of wit, and scurrility of a droll.

Render to your superiors due respect. Order is Heaven's first law. Nature teaches subordination; society demands it. The best soldiers make the best officers; and the best citizens the best rulers. Yet carefully distinguish the honors paid to rank and office, from those paid to personal merit; and let the latter be the principal object of your ambition.

Forget not this precious motto: "Nihil humanum a me puto alienum." Consider every one in human shape as your brother; and "let charity in golden links of love connect you with the brotherhood of man." Let your benevolence be broad as the ocean; your candor brilliant as the sun, and your compassion and humanity extensive as the human race.

The brevity and uncertainty of life, should admonish us never to procrastinate the duties of the present time. Of all things, our salvation is of the greatest moment. Man is fallen into a wretched state of sin and depravity, and needs a renovation of nature—the implantation and cultivation of the sublime virtues of Christianity to restore him to his true dignity—to qualify him for happiness. The very natures of God and his creatures give birth to fixed and immutable relations between them. These are the foundations of virtue, and as solid as those of the everlasting mountains. It is not possible for man to become happy otherwise than by conforming to the laws of his nature; by becoming really and truly such as man ought to be, in thought, word, and deed.

The sacred Scriptures are to be the study of your lives; nor let it be thought an employment beneath a gentleman; Newton, Locke, and the most eminent philosophers studied and wrote commentaries on them. It is a mark of vanity to speak lightly of revelation. Not to admire those ancient and sublime books shows a want of taste in fine writing, as well of real judgment in discerning the truth. And here let me caution you never to ridicule whatever may be held sacred by any devout and judicious man. If you cannot join with him, at least do not disturb him by your irreverence.

Young gentlemen, it is your good fortune to enter on life in a country peculiarly favored by the bounteous hand of Nature, and blessed with the best government in the world. Your education distinguishes you among your fellows; the eyes of many are fixed on you. Your parents and friends have, no doubt, the most flattering hopes of your future eminence: Do not disappoint them. The patrons of this College also feel a peculiar interest in your prosperity; let me entreat you, therefore, as you esteem your friends, as you respect the place of your education, resolve to act your parts in life well, and may Heaven strengthen you with grace so to do.

The day is at hand when all of us, whether young or old now, must appear, and give an account of our conduct, before the Creator and Governor of the World. "That is the day of days; the important day," as the Poet says, "for which all other days were made." Time, with all its concerns and enjoyments, will then vanish from our eager grasp—Eternity will then commence, and a solemn COMMENCEMENT will THAT be. Your worthy President has gone before you. If you loved him, or if you even love yourselves, let me, in the most earnest and solemn manner, call on you to recollect, and imprint on your memory, his pious care over you, his faithful admonitions, and his amiable example; and to prepare to follow him.

In behalf the Corporation, Young Gentlemen, I bid you FAREWELL.

COMMENCEMENT EXERCISES. 361

1792.

1. The Salutatory Address in Latin, and an English Oration on the French Revolution. - - - - - - - - - - Bildad Barney.
2. An Oration on the Advantages of Good Government. - - Paraclete Tew.
3. A Dissertation in Greek on the Effects of Luxury. - - Richard M. Stites.
4. An Oration on the Rise and Progress of Astronomy. - William W. Folwell.
5. A Dispute on the Justice and Policy of emancipating the Slaves in America.
   William V. King, Eli Smith, Peter O. Alden.
6. An Oration on the Improvement of the Mind. - - Ebenezer Withington.
7. An Oration on French Air Balloons. - - - - - David Leonard.
8. A Dissertation on prosecuting the War with the Indians. - Elijah D. Green.
9. An Oration on the Theatre. - - - - - Thomas C. Hazard.
10. An Oration recommending Rhode Island College to the Patronage of the State.
    Jahaziah Shaw.
11. An Oration on the Wealth of Nations. - - - Nathanael Hazard.
12. An Oration on the Establishment of Societies in America. George Larned.
13. An Oration on the Pleasures of the Imagination; with the Valedictory Addresses.
    Thomas M. Clark.

At this Commencement Judge Howell also presided, by special request of the Corporation.

1793.

1. The Salutatory Oration in Latin on the Importance of Education to a Republican Government. - - - - - - - Wilkes Wood.
2. First Intermediate Oration, on the French Revolution. - Gilbert Dench.
3. A Forensic Dispute on the Question: — Is it for the Interest of the United States to assist the French Revolution against its Enemies in the present War?
   William A. Leonard, Paul Allen, Jr.
4. A Dissertation on the Importance of uniting Political Virtue with Political Power. - - - - - - - Zephaniah Leonard.
5. An Oration in Latin, showing that Anticipation is preferable to Enjoyment.
   George C. Bowen.
6. A Dissertation on Moral Agency. - - - - Lemuel Wadsworth.
7. Fourth Intermediate Oration on the present State and Prospects of America.
   Isaiah Weston.
8. An Oration on the comparative Advantages of Savage and Civilized Life.
   Thomas L. Halsey, Jr.

46

9. Third Intermediate Oration on the Superiority of Agriculture to other Arts.
John Hathaway.
10. Second Intermediate Oration on Ecclesiastical Tyranny. William A. Leonard.
11. A Dispute on the Question : — Ought the Ministers of the Gospel to be supported by Civil Government? - - - Isaiah Weston, George C. Bowen.
12. An Humorous Dialogue. - - Zephaniah Leonard, John Hathaway, Lemuel Wadsworth, John Merrill.
13. A Poem on the Happiness of America. - - - - Paul Allen, Jr.
14. An Oration on the Philosophy of the Mind; with the Valedictory Addresses.
John Merrill.

1794.

1. The Salutatory Address in Latin, with an English Oration on the Progress of Reason. - - - - - - - - Jeremiah Bailey.
2. The Fifth Intermediate Oration on the Pleasures of Philosophy, with its Advantages to Government. - - - - - - - Enoch Hazard.
3. An Oration in Greek, on the Wealth of Nations. - - William Briggs.
4. The Fourth Intermediate Oration, on the Effects of Luxury in Empires.
Daniel Warren.
5. A Dispute on this Question : — Whether the Use of Spirituous Liquors is advantageous to Mankind? - - John Miles, John P. Little, Mason Shaw.
6. The Second Intermediate Oration, on Science as the Source of Empire.
Nathanael Searle.
7. The Eleventh Intermediate Oration, on Simplicity. - - William Grant.
8. The Seventh Intermediate Oration, on Education. - Stephen S. Nelson.
9. The Tenth Intermediate Oration, on the Progress of Revolutions in Nations.
Samuel Watson.
10. The Sixth Intermediate Oration, on the Absurdity of paying Deference to Custom and Precedent. - - - - - - - Zenas L. Leonard.
11. The First Intermediate Oration, on the Political Influence of the Clergy.
Timothy Briggs.
12. An Oration in Latin, on Superstition. - - - William T. Hazard.
13. The Ninth Intermediate Oration, on the Pleasures and Advantages of History.
John W. Richmond.
14. A Dialogue designed to ridicule Quackery in Professions.
Samuel W. Brigham, Jeremiah Bailey, Mason Shaw, Enoch Hazard.
15. The Eighth Intermediate Oration, on the Difficulty of obtaining and the Necessity of maintaining our Liberty. - - - - - Joseph Rawson.
16. The Third Intermediate Oration, on the Theatre. - - Solomon Sibley.

17. The Inexpediency of the Americans engaging in the European War; an Oration for the Master's Degree.   -   -   -   James Ellis, (class of 1791.)
18. An Oration on the Power and Improvement of Reason; with the Valedictory Addresses.   -   -   -   -   -   -   -   Samuel W. Brigham.

1795.

1. The Salutatory Address in Latin, with an English Oration on the Impolicy of opposing Opinion by Force.   -   -   -   -   -   -   John Smith.
2. An Intermediate Oration, on National Greatness.   -   -   Joseph Eaton.
3. An Intermediate Oration, showing that Literature is the most permanent Basis of Felicity.   -   -   -   -   -   -   -   Charles O. Screven.
4. An Oration on the general effects of Luxury on Science.   -   Isaac Averell.
5. A Dispute on this Question:—Whether the Love of Fame is advantageous to Mankind?   -   -   John Luscomb, Peleg Chandler, John A. Hazard.
6. An Oration on Deism, considered as a Prelude to the Universal Establishment of Christianity.   -   -   -   -   -   -   -   Amos Hopkins.
7. An Intermediate Oration, on Commerce.   -   -   -   Thomas Screven.
8. An Oration, on the Death of Stephen Torrey.   -   -   Stephen Cutler.
9. An Oration, on the State of Literature in the United States. -   Gaius Deane.
10. An Oration, on the Immortality of Brutes.   -   -   -   Simeon Marcy.
11. An Oration, on the Progress of Science.   -   -   -   James Gurney.
12. An Intermediate Oration, on the Origin and Evils of Political Oppression.
Joseph W. Crossman.
13. An Intermediate Oration, on Faction.   -   -   -   -   James Gordon.
14. A Dissertation, on the Theatre.   -   -   -   -   Abiel Williams.
15. A Dissertation in Latin, on War.   -   -   -   -   -   Isaac Briggs.
16. An Oration on the Advantages resulting from the Art of Printing.
Oliver Wiswell.
17. An Intermediate Oration, on the Necessity of submitting the Passions to Reason.
Erastus Larned.
18. An Intermediate Oration, on the Advantages of Commerce. Samuel G. Arnold.
19. An Intermediate Oration, on the Advantages of Men of Genius to Mankind.
Elisha Fisk.
20. An Oration, on the Influence of Government on the Spirit of Nations.
Andrew Morton.
21. An Oration, on Mental Improvement; with the Valedictory Addresses.
William Baylies.

1796.

1. The Salutatory Address in Latin, with an English Oration on the Drama.
   Benjamin B. Simmons.
2. An Intermediate Oration, on the Importation of Foreign Luxuries.
   Abraham Blanding.
3. An Intermediate Oration, on the Importance of the Knowledge of Civil Rights.
   Nathan Whiting.
4. The Second Dispute, on the Policy of establishing a uniform System of Education throughout the United States.   -   Horace Senter, Joseph Holmes, Asa Kimball.
5. An Oration against Religious Establishments.   -   -   -   John Holmes.
6. An Oration on the Manifestation of Deity in his Works.   John M. Roberts.
7. Astronomy burlesqued; a Conference.   Abraham Blanding, Nathan Whiting.
8. An Oration on the Necessity of subjecting the Passions to Reason.   Daniel Crane.
9. An Intermediate Oration, on Attachment to particular Systems of Religious Opinions.   -   -   -   -   -   -   -   -   Asa Aldis.
10. An Intermediate Oration, on Individual and National Greatness.
    Philip Hayward.
11. The First Dispute, on this Question:—Whether Christianity has augmented the temporal Happiness of Man?   Benjamin Shurtleff, Oliver Cobb, Bezer Bryant.
12. A Dialogue.   -   -   -   David King, John M. Roberts, John Holmes.
13. A Dissertation in Favor of Female Education.   -   -   -   David King.
14. An Oration, pleading the Cause of Man, together with the Valedictory Addresses.
    Tristam Burges.

Mr. Burges's Valedictory Oration was justly regarded, at the time of its delivery, as a remarkable production. The paragraph beginning, "Guided by reason, man has travelled through the abstruse regions of the philosophic world"; and that succeeding it, "By imagination, man seems to verge towards creative power," have been selected as exercises for declamation, in various schools and colleges throughout the land. The greater part of the Oration is published in Bowen's "Memoir of Tristam Burges."

1797.

1. The Salutatory Address in Latin, and an English Oration on Independence.
   James Ervin.
2. An Intermediate Oration, on the Liberty of the Press.   -   - John Simmons.

COMMENCEMENT EXERCISES. 365

3. An Intermediate Oration, on the Advantages resulting from the Study of History.
Nathan Holman.
4. An Oration on the Importance of Education to the Union of Republican Governments. - - - - - - - Richard George.
5. An Intermediate Oration, on the present prosperity of the United States.
John Baldwin.
6. A Dissertation on War. - - - - - - Horatio G. Bowen.
7. A Forensic Dispute on the Question :— Whether it would be more advantageous for Mankind if the Earth should produce her Fruits spontaneously?
Liberty Bates, Nathan Carey.
8. An Oration on the Love of Glory. - - - - Abijah Draper.
9. A Poem. - - - - - - - - - Paul Dodge.
10. A Dissertation on the Prospects of America. - - - Horace Everett.
11. An Oration on the Infallibility of the Understanding. - - John Sabin.
12. A Dissertation on the Pleasures of the Imagination. - Francis Howard.
13. A Dialogue; "The World's infectious." - - Liberty Bates, Paul Dodge, Francis Howard, Samuel Ervin, John D. Witherspoon.
14. An Intermediate Oration, on the Love of Power, considered as a Principle of Action. - - - - - - - - Calvin Park.
15. An Oration on the Necessity of maintaining the Dignity of the United States.
Jairus Ware.
16. An Oration on the Advantages of Mental Improvement. Drury Fairbanks.
17. An Oration on the Indignities offered America by France. Samuel Ervin.
18. A Forensic Dispute on the Question :— Does the Light of Nature afford Evidence that God will pardon Sin ? Abel Richmond, William Collier, Joseph B. Cook.
19. An Oration on Oratory. - - - - - John D. Witherspoon.
20. A Conference on Education. - - Horatio G. Bowen, Horace Everett, Drury Fairbanks, Jairus Ware.
21. The Necessity of Political Union at the Present day; an Oration for the Master's Degree. - - - - - Paul Allen, Jr., (class of 1793.)
22. The Propriety of introducing the Science of Jurisprudence into a Course of Classical Education; an Oration for the Master's Degree.
Samuel W. Bridgham, (class of 1794.)
23. An Oration in Defence of Revelation; with the Valedictory Addresses.
Benjamin Allen.

1798.

1. The Salutatory Address in Latin, with an English Oration, on the Importance of Science and Religion, particularly to the Youth of America.
Andrew Dexter, Jr.

2. An Intermediate;—a Poem on Faction. - - - - Lucius Cary.
3. First Dispute on this Question:—Are Capital Punishments justifiable?
William H. Sabin, Rodolphus H. Williams, William P. Maxwell.
4. A Dissertation in Latin, on the Conduct of France since the Commencement of the Revolution. - - - - - - - Theodore D. Foster.
5. A Dissertation, on Attachment to particular Systems of Religion.
Sylvanus Waterman.
6. A Dialogue:—The Bachelors. - - - Morrill Allen, Nathaniel Bullock, James Tallmadge, Lucius Cary.
7. A Dissertation on the Evils of Luxury. - - - Alvan Underwood.
8. A Dispute on this Question:—Which is the most conducive to Virtue, Adversity or Prosperity? - - - - Nathanael G. Olney, Abraham Gushe, William E. Green, John Fessenden.
9. An Intermediate Oration, on the Immortality of Brutes. Nathaniel Bullock.
10. A Dissertation on the Diversity of Religious Opinions. - - Morrill Allen.
11. An Intermediate Oration, on the Infringement of the Rights of Men.
James Tallmadge.
12. A Dialogue:—The Jacobin Reformed. John Fessenden, William E. Green, Otis Thompson.
13. An Intermediate Oration, urging the Necessity of Religion as the only permanent Basis of Civil Government. - - - - - Otis Thompson.
14. An Oration on Union considered as the only Safety of the United States; together with the Valedictory Addresses. - - - - Conrade Webb.

1799.

1. The Salutatory Address in Latin, with an English Oration on the dangerous Consequences of Foreign Influence. - - - - Zechariah Eddy.
2. An Intermediate Oration, on Superstition. - - - Lemuel LeBaron.
3. An Oration in Greek, on the Necessity of Virtue. - - Alvan Tobey.
4. An Oration on the Manners and Principles of the Times.
Paul L. A. Auboyneau.
5. An Intermediate Oration, on the Necessity of uniting Habits of Industry with Religion. - - - - - - - Judah A. McClellan.
6. A Dissertation, showing that Man is actuated more by Passion than by Reason.
John Pitman.
7. An Oration on Enthusiasm of Opinion. - - - - Daniel Turner.
8. An Oration on the Advantages of a Navy to the United States. Allen Bourne.
9. A Dissertation on the Utility of a general Diffusion of Political Knowledge.
Nathan F. Dixon.

10. An Intermediate Oration, on the Necessity of Science to Support the Government of the United States. - - - - - James Thompson.
11. A Political Dissertation. - - - - - Whipple Aldrich.
12. A Dissertation in Latin, on the Necessity of Virtue to the Support of Civil Government. - - - - - - - - Franklin Greene.
13. An Intermediate Oration, on the Establishment of a National University.
Wood Furman.
14. An Intermediate Oration, on the Importance of Philosophical Improvement.
Abraham B. Story.
15. A Dissertation on the Impossibility of Exterminating Christianity.
Joshua Bradley.
16. War; an Oration for the Master's Degree. Tristam Burges, (class of 1796.)
17. An Oration on the Proneness of Men to fall into Extremes; with the Valedictory Addresses. - - - - - - Jeremiah Chaplin.

1800.

1. Salutatory Oration, on Slavery of Opinion, comprehending the usual Addresses.
Paris J. Tillinghast.
2. An Intermediate Oration, on the Importance of Historical Information.
Gaius Conant.
3. A Dissertation in Latin, on the Rise and Fall of Empires. - Daniel Loring.
4. Dispute on this Question: — Would passive Commerce be more advantageous to the United States than their present active Commerce? Theodore A. Foster, Thomas Burgess, Abiel Russell.
5. An Intermediate Oration, on the Influence of the Passions. John M. Bradford.
6. An Oration on the Pleasures of Sensibility. - - - - Levi Tower.
7. A Dissertation in Greek; — Union necessary to the Support of Republican Government. - - - - - - - Andrew Rawson.
8. A Dissertation on the Utility of Science in a Republican Government.
Daniel Young.
9. An Intermediate Oration, on Female Education. - - - Calvin Tilden.
10. An Oration on Party Spirit. - - - - - - Nathaniel Todd.
11. An Intermediate Oration on the Advantages of Prejudice. Moses Miller.
12. A Dissertation on the Necessity of Religion to the Support of Government.
Gravenner Taft.
13. An Oration on Civil Dissensions, considered as a Prelude to a Change in Government. - - - - - - - - Thomas Burgess.
14. A Dissertation on Atheism. - - - - - - Enos Cutler.

15. A Dispute on this Question:—Is Marriage conducive to Happiness?
Royal Farnum, John M. Bradford, Calvin Tilden.
16. An Intermediate Oration, on the Influence of Improved Taste on Society.
Abiel Russell.
17. An Intermediate Oration, on the Constitution of the United States, and the Influence it has on the Spirit of the People. - - Theodore A. Foster.
18. An Intermediate Oration, on Literature as the Basis of Happiness.
Royal Farnum.
19. Dialogue;—The Fall of Fashion. - - Benjamin F. Bourne, Moses Miller, Gravenner Taft, William R. Theus, Nathaniel Todd.
20. A Dissertation on Instrumental Music, showing its Effects on the Passions.
Liberty Rawson.
21. An Oration, on Literature as necessary to the Support of Independence.
Benjamin F. Bourne.
22. An Intermediate Oration, on Mental Improvement. - - William R. Theus.
23. Valedictory Oration, on Political Economy, comprehending the usual Addresses.
John Mackie.

1801.

1. The Salutatory Address in Latin, and an English Oration on Noble Blood.
Andrew Pickens.
2. An Oration on Religious Establishments. - - - Lucius Bolles.
3. An Intermediate Oration, on the Influence of Superstition on the Human Mind.
Enoch Brown.
4. An Oration in Latin, on the Propensity of Mankind to Society. Ezra Leonard.
5. An Oration on the Impartial Administration of Justice. - Lemuel Bishop.
6. An Oration on the Necessity of Union to support the Peace and Happiness of Society. - - - - - - - Jonathan Nye.
7. A Poem. - - - - - - - Philo H. Washburn.
8. A Discussion of the comparative Advantages of Theology, Natural Philosophy, Moral Philosophy, and History. - - George Barstow, Enoch Brown, James Lesley, Robert Sterry.
9. An Oration on Democracy. - - - - - - Gad Tower.
10. A Dialogue on Profession. - - Andrew Pickens, George W. Perkins, Samuel Dexter, Lemuel Bishop.
11. An Intermediate Oration, on Religion considered as the Basis of Civil Government. - - - - - - - - - George Barstow.
12. A Intermediate Oration:—The Equality of Rights consistent with the good Order of Society. - - - - - - James Lesley.

COMMENCEMENT EXERCISES.   369

13. A Dispute on the Question:—Is it reasonable to sacrifice Convenience to Fashion?   William Blanding, Joseph Cheney. Samuel Dexter, Samuel V. Medbery.
14. An Intermediate Oration on Slander.   -   -   -   -   Robert Sterry.
15. The Influence of the Female Character on Society; an Oration for the Master's Degree.   -   -   -   -   -   Lucius Cary, (class of 1798.)
16. A Poem; with the Valedictory Addresses.   -   -   John M. Williams.

1802.

1. Salutatory Addresses, and an Oration on the Spirit of Enquiry.   Alfred Metcalf.
2. An Intermediate Oration, on Patriotism.   -   -   -   Samuel M. Pond.
3. A Dissertation.   -   -   -   -   -   -   Samuel Perry, Jr.
4. A Dissertation.   -   -   -   -   -   -   -   Levi Hart.
5. An Oration on the Abuse of Power.   -   -   -   Gardner Daggett.
6. An Oration on the Necessity of Science and Virtue to the Support of good Government.   -   -   -   -   -   -   Melatiah Everett.
7. A Conference on the comparative Advantages of the Invention of Printing, the Discovery and Use of the Compass, the Discovery and Use of Metals, and of Architecture.   -   -   -   Paul Jewett, Sumner Bastow, Warren Rawson, Benjamin Gleason.
8. A Poem.   -   -   -   -   -   -   -   Richard Waterman.
9. An Intermediate Oration:—Progress of the Mathematical and Physical Sciences during the Eighteenth Century.   -   -   -   -   Henry Wheaton.
10. An Oration on the Amelioration of Man.   -   -   -   Samuel Bugbee.
11. A Dissertation on the Decline of Slavery.   -   -   -   Frederick W. Bottom.
12. An Oration on National Virtue.   -   -   -   -   -   John Godfrey.
13. An Intermediate Oration, on War.   -   -   -   -   Henry Bowen.
14. A Poem on the Times.   -   -   -   -   -   Benjamin Gleason.
15. An Intermediate Oration, on Republican Policy.   -   -   Sumner Bastow.
16. An Oration.   -   -   -   -   -   -   -   John Whipple.
17. A Poem:—The Rewards of Ambition.   -   -   -   Milton Maxcy.
18. An Intermediate Oration, on the Patronage of Literature.   John Holroyd.
19. An Intermediate Oration, on the Productions of Genius and Taste united. Warren Rawson.
20. An Intermediate Oration, on the Evils of Democracy.   William W. Bowen.
21. An Oration on Politics. John Pitman, candidate for the Degree of Master of Arts.
22. An Oration:—Happiness attendant on Virtue; and the Valedictory Addresses. Ferdinand Ellis.

This is the last Commencement at which Dr. Maxcy presided, having been elected to the Presidency of Union College, Schenectady, New York. His BACCALAUREATE ADDRESS for this year, and also for the years 1794, 1798, and 1801, may be found in an octavo volume of four hundred and fifty-two pages, published in New York, in 1844, entitled, "The Literary Remains of the Rev. Jonathan Maxcy, D. D., with a Memoir of his Life, by Romeo Elton, D. D."

1803.

1. Salutatory Addresses in Latin, and an Oration in English, on Self-Abuse.
Lemuel Paine.
2. An Intermediate Oration: — The Intelligence of Deity evident from the Origin of Motion. - - - - - - - Zabdiel Sampson.
3. An Intermediate Oration, on Prejudice. - - - Thompson Miller.
4. An Intermediate Oration, on Ambition. - - - David Holman, Jr.
5. An Oration on Man. - - - - - - - Philip Allen.
6. An Oration on the Ruling Passion. - - - Benjamin Cowell.
7. An Oration on Dissimulation. - - - - Samuel H. Lothrop.
8. A Theological Essay. - - - - - - Jason Sprague.
9. A Forensic Dispute: — Is a Public preferable to a Private Life.
Aaron Blake, Levi H. Perkins.
10. An Oration on Fashion. - - - - - - Philip M. Fiske.
11. An Intermediate Oration, on Sensuality. - - - Elnathan Walker.
12. An Intermediate: — A Poem on Art. - - - - Daniel Thomas.
13. A Syllogistic Dispute: — Is the Newtonian Astronomy true?
Thompson Miller, Chandler Flagg, Aaron Blake, Christopher Webb.
14. An Intermediate Oration: — Equanimity the source of Happiness.
Christopher Webb.
15. An Intermediate Oration, on National Depravity. - - Chandler Flagg.
16. An Intermediate Oration, on the Abuse of Religion. Jonathan Thayer.
17. An Oration on Civil War. - - - - - George T. Olney.
18. A Dialogue: —The Pedant. - - Daniel Thomas, Zabdiel Sampson, Samuel H. Lothrop, Benjamin Cowell.
19. An Oration on National Prosperity. - Theodore A. Foster, candidate for the Degree of Master of Arts.

20. An Oration on Taxation. - - Benjamin Bourne, Jr., candidate for the
Degree of Master of Arts.
21. An Oration on Candor, and the Valedictory Addresses. John Reed, Jr.

Dr. Maxcy, as we have stated in our "Historical Sketch," was succeeded by the Rev. Dr. Messer, who presided over the Institution from 1802 until 1826, or nearly a quarter of a century. His first BACCALAUREATE ADDRESS, delivered at this Commencement, and which was published at the time by request, will be read with interest by his pupils, especially as very few of his productions have found their way to the public.

PRESIDENT MESSER'S ADDRESS.

At this time, young Gentlemen, your situation is peculiarly critical. Having just finished your collegiate studies, you are now ready to enlarge on the world, and to become personal actors in those important scenes, where thousands, for lack of skill, have been ruined. In discharging this last official duty, I feel solicitous to guard you against similar disasters, and to point you to a course which shall be safe and happy. You must all be sensible that in this favored land the field of honor and promotion is open only to personal acquisition. Unless a man inherits the virtues, he inherits not the immunities of his parents. You must, therefore, stand on your own feet. Hence it is especially important that you secure the approbation of the wise and worthy; and this you can secure only by adorning your characters with a virtuous, persevering industry. A life of indolence was never designed for man. His external situation and internal constitution both require that he should be active. Let the circle in which he moves be high or low, he must, if devoid of industrious habits, be devoid of substantial enjoyment. You must not think, therefore, that because you have devoted yourselves to literature, you are free from the necessity of labor. No man feels that necessity more than the scholar. Whether you enter on public or private life, therefore, let me advise you never to imagine that you have any time to spare for useless indulgencies; but bear it ever in mind that the most industrious man is, other things being equal, the most happy in himself, and the most respected by others.

Like all other habits, however, a habit of industry can be produced only by a regular, persevering attention. Let this be remitted but for a short period, and a habit of opposite tendency will unavoidably begin to grow. Hence in the very outset you should be careful to place yourselves in the view of such objects as are fitted to excite constant exertion. On this account it is highly important that you delay not to draw the plan of your pursuit for life. Until you do this, you will be living without an object; and, your minds being in constant vibration, you will scarcely know what to do with yourselves. You will be more likely to envy the condition of others, than to better your own; and more to subvert, than to promote the end of your existence. Though, therefore, you may find it difficult to draw this plan, let me advise you to draw it soon. Indeed, you will not gain so much by procrastination as you imagine. Perhaps you may not, after ten years consideration, be more prepared than you now are, to bring your minds to the proper point. At the same time let me advise you in this case to guard yourselves against rash precipitation. A wrong step taken here may seriously affect you during life. That profession which is the best for others, may not be the best for you. Nature has formed different men for different stations; and no man will appear well in a station differing from the intentions of nature. As it is of the greatest importance that you should ascertain what these intentions are in this particular, you will be careful to examine, not the honor and emolument attached to any station, but the nature and extent of its duties; and to compare them with the tendencies of your own minds. You may be certain that nature never intended you for a station which you are not qualified to fill; and you may be certain also, that you are not qualified to fill a station which involves duties at invincible variance with your own minds. In this case, let the success of others be ever so great, you must expect none for yourselves; for no man, unless he loves his duty, will discharge it with advantage. Hence, if you should think of entering on the profession of law, you should examine, not what others have done or gained in that profession, but what you yourselves can do or gain; not what a highway it has opened for the promotion of others, but whether you yourselves are pleased with the study and practice of law; and whether you can qualify yourselves to discharge with honor the arduous duties of the profession.

To those who think of entering on the profession of theology, an examination of this kind becomes very solemnly proper and important. No arrogance can be more censurable or wicked than that, which will allow men, for the sake of lucre, to thrust themselves into the ministry. A law of nature in man renders it impossible that he should be indifferent to theological truth. In his view that truth must ever be attractive, or repulsive. No prospect of honor, or emolument can alter this law. Hence, while a man's heart is not attracted by the solemn truths of theology, must he not, by attempting to explain or enforce them, exhibit himself in a very awkward and melancholy posture? Can an office for propagating humility be gratifying to a man of pride? Or will he discharge its duties with faithfulness and success? As the doctrines of theology are fitted to exalt the character of God, and to abase the character of man, it seems impossible that any man should inculcate those doctrines with satisfaction to himself, or edification to others, until he imbibes the spirit of them, and loves them. Notwithstanding my warm attachment, therefore, to a theological profession, and my earnest wishes to see it filled with respectable characters, I must still entreat you, both on account of your own personal felicity, and on account of the prosperity of true religion, never to step your feet on the sacred threshold of that profession, until you are fully satisfied that the solemn duties of it will themselves delight your hearts, and that you are prepared to discharge them with advantage to your fellow-men.

The imperfections of human nature are such that but few men can render themselves eminent in many things. They who grasp at a knowledge of everything, may generally expect to be skillful in nothing. You will find ample room for the exertion of your talents in a single profession. Whatever that may be, you will be careful to give it your principal attention. Yet, as there is a strong connection between all the branches of knowledge, you cannot render yourselves skillful in any one of them, while wholly ignorant of the rest. No man, indeed, can acquit himself respectably in any literary performance, until his mind is enlarged with a stock of general truths. Be guarded, then, against these two extremes; against distracting your minds by roaming at random among all subjects indifferently; and against contracting them by attending only to a few subjects exclusively.

It is the general expectation that men will acquit themselves according to the advantages they have had. Hence but few apologies are made for the ignorance of those who have had the opportunity of acquiring knowledge. It is, therefore, important that you, who have had this opportunity, should give full proof that you have improved it well; and hence that you should still persevere in the pursuit of knowledge. For if, calculating on your present acquisitions, you remit your attention to study, you must soon forget what you have already learned, and revert back to the point from which you started, when you first began your literary course.

In your intercourse with men, you have need of great circumspection and sagacity. You will find them perhaps different from what you now expect; and, unless you are especially guarded, you may find yourselves obliged to purchase a knowledge of them at a dear rate. Notwithstanding the maxim which is good in law, that "a man is innocent until he is proved guilty," you will find it dangerous to confide in any, until you have proof that they are worthy. Fatal experience has convinced many that selfish principles have an extensive influence on human actions. You will find most men alive to their own interest; and in general it will be the most safe to commit yourselves to them only so far as that interest may induce them to befriend you. Yet you will find some in whom you may ever confide; men who would not injure you sooner than they would themselves; and who in adversity as well as prosperity, will ever exhibit themselves the patrons of truth, integrity and benevolence. Whenever you find such men, give them your warmest friendship. Value them more than the wealth of India; and let their virtues be the patterns of your own. Think not, however, that men of this character dwell only in a certain place, or bear only a certain name. Names differ greatly from things; though prejudice would often confound them together. As you are privileged with a liberal education, you will banish prejudice from your breasts. It is fit only for the ignorant. You will think on a liberal scale. You will view men and things through the medium of candor. According to the advice which the excellent Dr Watts has given you in his chapter on prejudice, which I beg you never to forget, you will divest yourselves of those youthful prepossessions, and local attachments, which becloud the mind, and render it unfit for the perception of truth; and you will ever rejoice when the truth is discovered, even though it should condemn yourselves. You will then be able to guard yourselves against deception, and to confide only in the worthy. You will also discover that these must be ascertained, not by invidious distinctions, but by personal character; and that true worth often dwells with him whom prejudice has marked with infamy.

Your own personal characters should be a prime object of your attention. No splendor of talents, nor advances in knowledge can compensate for the want of moral principles. Even vicious men, if they would tell the truth, would tell you that they cannot give their confidence to the vicious. The immutable distinction between right and wrong is so forcibly impressed on the minds of men, that, however wrong themselves, they require what is right in others. Be careful then to cultivate a fair, moral character. Let no temptations seduce you from the path of rectitude. Hold the rights of others as sacred as you hold your own; and remember that you have no more right to injure them than they have to injure you. As you abhor those who injure you, you must expect the abhorrence of those whom you may injure. Ever place before yourselves the golden maxim of doing to others as you wish they should do to you; and never forget that the way of the transgressor of this maxim is ever hard.

In this connection it is important to be remembered that there is a strong intimacy between moral character and the belief of truth. That must be a singular infatuation, indeed, which can induce any to expunge the doctrine of belief from their system of morals. Let it only be granted that it is no matter what a man believes, and it must be granted also that, in a moral view, it is no matter what he does. If a man's belief has no influence on his practice, that practice will be as destitute of moral quality, as is the running of a horse, or the flouncing of a whale. If you wish, therefore, to consider yourselves as rational moral beings, you will give no countenance to that most gross, barbarous absurdity. Indeed, there appears to be the same connection between the belief and practice of a rational being as there is between a cause and an effect; and therefore, while I exhort you to give diligent attention to the things which you practice, let me exhort you to give the same attention to the things which you believe.

Hence, I must commend to your belief the important principles of our holy religion; entreating you to receive them into your hearts and to follow them in your lives. These principles received in this way, will give you a high elevation on the scale of moral excellence. They will incite you ever to act in character; and they will ensure you the good will of all the amiable beings in existence. They will support you in the hour of adversity; and, when your part on earth is acted, they will unfold to you a more exalted and happy scene, where there will be no tears, nor sorrow, nor sickness, nor death; where friends will never separate, but where an uninterrupted blaze of glory will forever irradiate and enrapture their souls.

For these precious principles, my respected young friends. I must persuade myself you will cultivate a constant veneration. Into this persuasion I am unavoidably led by a reflection on the very laudable manner in which you, as a body, have acquitted yourselves, while members of this Institution. While I keep in mind your regular, studious and friendly deportment, and your zealous attachment to law, order and morals, I will not, I cannot allow the fear that you will ever disgrace yourselves by adopting infidel principles, or licentious practices. May the rich benedictions of heaven attend you, while passing through life; and may the precious promises of the gospel support you in the hour of death. With these reflections, and hoping that you will receive them as coming from a friend, I must now bid you an AFFECTIONATE FAREWELL.

1804.

1. Salutatory Addresses in Latin, and an Oration in English, on National Economy.
    Marcus Morton.
2. An Oration on the Science of Medicine. - - - - Elias Frost.
3. An Oration on Hypocrisy. - - - - - Silas Tobey.
4. An Oration on the Importance of a General Diffusion of Knowledge through the United States - - - - - Lemuel W. Briggs.
5. A Forensic Dispute: — Which is the most injurious, Hypocrisy or Pride?
    Richard Briggs, Samuel Randall.
6. An Oration: — The Wisdom and Goodness of God, manifested in his Works.
    Warren Preston.
7. An Oration on the Evils of Persecution. - - - Tisdale Hodges.
8. An Intermediate Oration on the Abuse of Merit. Jason Chamberlain, Jr.
9. An Oration on the Sugar Cane. - - - - - Thomas H. Sill.
10. A Dispute: — Would not Married People be as happy, if their Partners, instead of being chosen by themselves, were appointed by Civil Authority?
    William D. Williamson, Oliver Hayward,
    Lemuel Williams, Jr., Samuel K. Williams.
11. An Intermediate Oration: — Reflections on History. Samuel K. Williams.
12. An Oration on the Soul. - - - - William D. Williamson.
13. An Intermediate Oration, on Misanthropy. - - - Oliver Hayward.

14. An Intermediate Oration, on Partiality. - - Lemuel Williams, Jr.
15. A Dialogue. - - - Richard Briggs, Elias Frost, George Norton, Samuel Randall, Thomas H. Sill.
16. An Oration on the Abuse of Civil Privileges, with the Valedictory Addresses.
Benjamin Hobart.

1805.

1. Salutatory Addresses in Latin, and an Oration in English:—Disputes on the Principles of Government dangerous. - - - - Williams Emmons.
2. An Intermediate Oration:—Selfishness the Source of political Contentions.
Samuel P. Loud.
3. An Oration on Diversity of Opinions. - - - Sylvester F. Bucklin.
4. An Intermediate Oration, on the Tendency of false Opinions. - John Shaw.
5. An Intermediate Oration, on the Spirit of Innovation. - - John B. Snow.
6. An Oration on the Character of Roger Williams. - - Thomas D. Webb.
7. A Poem on the Inexpediency of Capital Punishments. - Benjamin James.
8. An Oration on Female Excellency. - - - Walter R. Danforth.
9. An Oration on modern Patriotism. - - - - - Joseph F. Lippitt.
10. An Oration encouraging Attempts at Excellence in Oratory. - Amasa Fisk.
12. An Oration on the Abuse of Genius. - - - - Stephen W. Eddy.
12. A Poem, Intermediate, on Gratitude. - - - - - Samuel Deane.
13. A Syllogistic Dispute:—Is Sincerity always the best Policy?
Jared Whitman, Aaron Hobart, John Howe, Samuel P. Loud.
14. An Intermediate Oration, on the Love of Fame. - - - John Howe.
15. An Intermediate Oration, on the Abuse of Liberty. - - Aaron Hobart.
16. An Intermediate Oration, on the Bias of Passion. - - Jared Whitman.
17. Dialogue. - - Sylvester F. Bucklin, Walter R. Danforth, Samuel Deane, Stephen W. Eddy, Benjamin James, Joseph F. Lippitt.
18. An Oration showing the Superiority of Biography to History.
John Holroyd, Esq., candidate for the Degree of Master of Arts.
19. An Oration on Energy of Character, with the Valedictory Addresses.
Theron Metcalf.

1806.

1. The Salutatory Address in Latin, with an English Oration, on the Influence of Courage on Society. - - - - - - Daniel March.
2. An Intermediate Oration, on the Pleasures and Pains of Memory.
Richard B. Bedon.
3. An Oration on Dissimulation. - - - - - Daniel Johnson.
4. An Oration on the Influence of Religion in Society. - - Noah Whitman.

COMMENCEMENT EXERCISES. 377

5. An Intermediate Oration, on Mental Improvement. - Louis R. Sams.
6. An Oration on Natural History. - - - - - John G. Dean.
7. An Oration on Ecclesiastical History. - - - - David Benedict.
8. A Forensic Dispute on the Question : — Is the Imprisonment of Bankrupts expedient? - - - - - Palmer Cleveland. Henry D'Wolf.
9. An Intermediate Oration, on the Impropriety of Public Punishments.
Willard Preston.
10. A Poem.   Daniel Thomas, candidate for the Master's Degree, (class of 1803.)
11. Reason ; — An Oration for the Master's Degree.
John Reed, Jr., (class of 1803.)
12. An Oration on Defamation ; with the Valedictory Addresses.   Jacob Eames.

1807.

1. Salutatory Addresses in Latin, and an Oration in English, on Mental Preparation.
John Bailey.
2. An Oration on Literary Excellence. - - - - Bailey Loring.
3. An Oration on the Dignity of Man. - - - - - Eliab Whitman.
4. An Intermediate Oration, on Political Virtue. - - - Jacob Hill.
5. An Oration on the Cultivation of the Mind. - - - Oliver Angell.
6. An Oration on the Influence of Novelty. - - - Elisha P. Fearing.
7. Oratio Latina de Mentis Industria. - - - - Ezekiel R. Wilson.
8. An Oration on the Durability of the Christian Religion.   Charles Wheeler.
9. An Intermediate Oration : — National Honor dependent on Energy of Government. - - - - - - - - - - Cyrus Alden.
10. A Poem on Science. - - - - - - - Samuel Bloss.
11. An Oration : — Effects of Infidelity on Society and Government.
Ebenezer Stoddard.
12. An Oration on Diversity of Opinion. - - - - Zedekiah Sanger.
13. A Dispute : — Which is the most desirable, Confidence or Diffidence?
Charles Manton, Samuel I. Thurston.
14. An Oration on the Influence of Adversity on the Character of Man.
Luther Barstow.
15. An Intermediate Oration, on the Rising Glory of America. Nahum Harrington
16. An Essay on Jurisprudence. - - - - - - Cyrus Alden.
17. An Oration on the Fine Arts. - Henry Wheaton, Esq., (class of 1802,) candidate for the Degree of Master of Arts.
18. An Oration on Free Inquiry ; with the Valedictory Addresses.
Adoniram Judson.

1808.

1. Salutatory Addresses in Latin, and an Oration in English :— Industry essential to Mental Greatness. - - - - - Bradford Sumner.
2. An Oration on the Patronage of American Literature. Jeremiah Mayhew.
3. An Oration on Self-Approbation. - - - - - Luther Bailey.
4. An Essay on Mathematics. - - - - - - Abiel Bolles.
5. An Oration on Self-Knowledge. - - - - Seth Chapin.
6. An Oration on the Pleasures of Literature. - - - John Rogers, Jr.
7. A Poem on Music. - - - - - - - Thomas Power.
8. A Syllogistic Dispute :— Is the Philosophy of Mind preferable to the Philosophy of Matter ? - - - - - Benjamin Rice, Josiah J. Fiske.
9. A Oration :— Bigoted Credulity the product of Monkish Ignorance.
  Henry T. Cooke.
10. An Oration :— Knowledge essential to Liberty. George W. R. Corlis.
11. An Essay on History. - - - - - Dutee J. Pearce.
12. Oratio Latina de Modo Mercaturam defendendi. - Nathaniel S. Spooner.
13. An Essay on Ethics. - - - - - - - Ezekiel Rich.
14. An Oration on the Love of Power. - - - - George Willard.
15. An Oration on Religious Freedom. - - - - - William Barker.
16. An Oration on Modern Philosophy. - - - - Jeremiah Lippitt.
17. A Forensic Dispute :— Is the Slanderer as criminal as the Assassin ?
  Isaac Porter, William G. Field, Otis Briggs.
18. An Oration on Mental Energy. - - - - Josias H. Coggeshall.
19. A Dispute :— Is a Delicate Sensibility desirable ?
  Jacob Corey, William L. Marcy.
20. An Oration :— The Deception of Ambitious Characters. John B. Francis.
21. An Oration on Science ; with the Valedictory Addresses. John B. Wight.

1809.

1. Salutatory Addresses in Latin, and an Oration in English, on the Patronage of Science. - - - - - - - - - Elijah Morse.
2. An Oration on National Energy. - - - - - David Delano.
3. An Oration on Thinking. - - - - - Thomas Williams.
4. An Oration on Martial Spirit. - - - - Henry F. Clark.
5. An Essay on Natural Theology. - - - - Ebenezer Burgess.
6. An Oration on Force of Character. - - - - Daniel F. Harding.
7. An Oration on Political Union. - - - - - Thomas Pope.
8. A Poem on the Progress of Refinement. - - - - Joshua Dean.

9. An Oration :— The Influence of Governments on Society.   William Haven.
10. An Oration :— Civil Society essential to the Happiness of Man.
　　　　　　　　　　　　　　　　　　　　　　　　Samuel S. Wilkinson.
11. Oratio Latina :— Luxuria privatæ tam quam publicæ Felicitati perniciosa.
　　　　　　　　　　　　　　　　　　　　　　　　Joseph Randall.
12. A Poem on Resignation. - - - - - - Henry Goodwin.
13. An Oration on Bar Eloquence. - - - - William Tyler.
14. An Oration on Wine - - - - - Robert Hume.
15. An Oration on the Mental Cultivation of Brutes. - - Silas Hall.
16. A Syllogistic Dispute :— Ought Application to be more respectable than Talents ?
　　　　　　　　　　　Jonathan Going, Jabez Fox, Gardner Burbank.
17. An Oration on Foreign Influence. - - - - James B. Dorrance.
18. An Oration on the Vicissitudes of Life. - - - John H. Clarke.
19. An Oration on Civil Government. - - - - Thomas Carlile.
20. An Oration :— The Union of Talents and Virtue ; with the Valedictory
　　Addresses. - - - - - - - - Jacob Ide.

1810.

1. Salutatory Addresses in Latin, and an Oration in English, on Sophistry.
　　　　　　　　　　　　　　　　　　　　　　　　Hervey Jenks.
2. An Oration on National Honor. - - - - Collins Darling.
3. Oratio Latina de Rationis Abusu. - - - - David Reed.
4. An Oration on the Abuse of Liberty. - - - Francis D. Wait.
5. An Oration on Commerce. - - - - - Martin Moore.
6. An Essay on the Being of God. - - - - Daniel Kendrick.
7. An Essay on the Utility of Natural Philosophy. - - Philip R. Hopkins.
8. An Oration on the Advantages of Literature. - - Charles Roby.
9. An Oration on Biography. - - - - - George W. Spencer.
10. An Essay on the Philosophy of Mind. - - - David Avery.
11. An Oration on the Rights of injured Africans. - - Cyrus Lothrop.
12. An Oration on National Growth and Decay. - - Abel Cushing.
13. Oratio Græca de Hominis Dignitate. - - - - William Reed.
14. An Oration on Events in Europe. - - - Henry K. McClintock.
15. An Eulogy on the Character of Cicero. - - - Simon R. Greene.
16. An Essay on Rhetoric. - - - - - - William Bates.
17. An Oration on the Permanency of the Present Form of Government in the
　　United States. - - - - - - - Isaac Bailey.
18. An Oration on the Attainment of Excellence ; with the Valedictory Addresses.
　　　　　　　　　　　　　　　　　　　　　　　　Appleton Downer.

1811.

1. The Salutatory Addresses in Latin, and an Oration in English, on the Utility of Scientific and Literary Knowledge. - - - - - Arnold Gray.
2. An Oration :—The Union of the United States essential to the Preservation of their Liberty. - - - - - - - Nicholas Brown.
3. An Oration in Latin, on the Importance of the Execution of Laws. Joshua P. Dickinson.
4. An Oration :— Curiosity, guided by Reason and Common Sense, the Source of Mental Improvement. - - - - - - Israel Alger.
5. An Oration on American Literature. - - - Oliver H. Kollock.
6. An Oration on the Evidence in Support of Divine Revelation. George Phippen.
7. A Dissertation on the Immortal Nature of Man. - - - Hartford Sweet.
8. An Oration on the Corruption of American Principles and Manners. Charles N. Tibbitts.
9. An Eulogy on the Character of Fisher Ames. - - William H. Allen.
10. An Essay on the Study of Belles Lettres. - - - Thomas Russell.
11. An Oration on Superstition. - - - - Latham A. Burrows.
12. An Oration on an Athenæum. - - - - - Thomas Rivers.
13. An Oration on the Veracity of the Sacred Scriptures. - - David March.
14. An Oration on Free Thinking. - - - - Aaron Putnam.
15. An Oration in Greek, on the Utility of Civil Law. - - Ezra Hutchins.
16. A Dispute :— Which form of Government is preferable, a Republican or a Monarchical? - - - - Peter Wheelock, Daniel Wardwell.
17. A Poem on Fashionable Manners. - - - - Luther M. Harris.
18. An Oration on the Permanency of the American Republic. Benjamin W. Cozzens.
19. A Poem on Social Intercourse. - - - - - Thomas Tolman.
20. An Oration on Liberty. - - - - - Dexter Randall.
21. An Oration on the Means of Establishing the Literary Character of America; with the Valedictory Addresses. - - - - William Winsor.

1812.

1. Salutatory Addresses in Latin, and an Oration in English, on the Obstacles to American Literature. - - - - - - - Isaac Fiske.
2. An Oration :— Man by Nature formed to be Virtuous. Ephraim Randall.
3. The Progress of Modern Infidelity, an Oration. - - John L. Blake.
4. An Oration on Chivalry. - - - - - - Moses B. Ives.
5. An Essay on the American Constitution. - - Richard W. Greene.

6. A Latin Oration on the Character of Man. - - - Samuel Phinney.
7. Advantages arising from the study of Geography :—An Oration. James Sanford.
8. An Oration :—The Influence of Religious Opinions on Society.
    James M. Winchell.
9. An Essay on the Influence of a cultivated Imagination. William G. Goddard.
10. A Greek Oration, on the Love of Glory. - - - Preserved Smith.
11. An Oration on Reason and Fancy. - - - - - Ralph Gilbert.
12. A Dissertation on the Rank of the Fair Sex in the Scale of Being.
    John L. Parkhurst.
13. A Poem. - - - - - - - - Henry C. Knight.
14. An Oration on Religious Freedom. - - - - Daniel Hewett.
15. An Oration on Enthusiasm of Character. - - Christopher C. Dexter.
16. An Oration on the Influence of erroneous Opinions imbibed in early Life.
    Josephus Wheaton.
17. An Oration :—National Virtue essential to National Prosperity.
    Bradford Sumner, Esq., candidate for the Degree of Master of Arts.
18. An Oration on the Cultivation of a Genius for Discovery and Invention; with the Valedictory Addresses. - - - - - Cyrus Kingsbury.

1813.

1. Salutatory Addresses in Latin, and an Oration in English, on the Progressive Improvement in the Condition of the Human Species. - - Joel Hawes.
2. Decision of Character :—An Essay. - - - - Timothy G. Coffin.
3. An Essay on the Importance of Evangelizing our Frontier Natives.
    Thomas Shepard.
4. A Dispute :—Has Civil Government any Right to interfere in matters of Religion ? - - - - - Amherst Wight, Ebenezer Force.
5. An Essay on the Ingratitude of Republics. - - Benjamin I. Gilman.
6. An Oration on the Influence of the Reformation in the Revival of Learning.
    Caleb H. Snow.
7. Anticipation contrasted with Reflection :—An Essay. - Joseph K. Angell.
8. A Greek Essay on the Love of Novelty. - - Benjamin D. Weeden.
9. An Essay on the Patronage of Literature. - - - Zachariah Allen.
10. Female Genius :—A Poem. - - - - - - Daniel Knight.
11. An Essay on Jurisprudence. - - - - - - Earle P. White.
12. An Essay on the Political and Religious State of the World. Romeo Elton.
13. An Essay on Manufactories. - - - - - - Jerome Loring.
14. An Essay on the Progress of Liberty in South America. Jonas L. Sibley.
15. A Dispute :—Which were the more Justifiable in commencing the First Punic War, the Romans or Carthagenians? Samuel Atkinson, Joshua Morton.

16. A Poem :— The Powers of Fancy. - - - - Job Durfee.
17. An Oration :— The Reward of Merit. - - - - Emerson Paine.
18. An Oration :— Disinterested Benevolence essential to Perfect Society.
Jonas Perkins.
19. A Dispute :— Which is the most Prolific of Enjoyment, the Life of the Scholar or of the Statesman? - - - - George Fisher, Morgan Nelson.
20. Great Occasions productive of eminent Characters :— An Oration ; with the Valedictory Addresses. - - - - - - Enoch Pond.

1814.

1. An Oration, on the Rise and Decline of Reason. - - - James Ford.
2. An Oration on the Perversion of Power. - - - - James Barker.
3. An Oration on Antiquity. - - - - - Anson G. Chandler.
4. An Oration on the Government of the Passions. - - Seth Alden.
5. A Dispute :— Are Factories beneficial to the United States?
John F. Williams, Samuel Y. Atwell.
6. An Essay on Refinement of Taste. - - - - William Richmond.
7. An Oration on Political Science. - - - - - Andrew Mackie.
8. A Greek Dissertation on Theological Wars. - - Samuel Angell.
9. An Oration on Selecting an Object of Pursuit. - Manning Belcher.
10. " Know Thyself " :— An Essay. - - - George H. Tillinghast.
11. An Essay on Anticipation. - - - - - Richard J. Arnold.
12. An Essay on Sociability. - - - - - Alexander Jones.
13. Thoughts on the Dignity of Christianity. - - - Thomas B Ripley.
14. A Dispute :— Which Profession requires the most extensive Information, that of the Physician, the Divine, or the Lawyer? - - - George O. Strong, Willard Holbrook, Reuel Washburn.
15. An Essay on the Disgrace attending unsuccessful Merit. Charles F. Tillinghast.
16. An Oration :— The Practical Atheist. - - - - Elijah F. Willey.
17. War considered in its Effects on Literature. - - - Lemuel Parkhurst.
18. An Oration :— The future Character of America. - Goodwin Allenton.
19. An Oration on the Ardor of Youth. - - - - Joseph Joslen.
20. An Oration on the Literature of Ancient Greece. - - James Thayer.
21. An Oration on the Abuse of Reason ; with the Valedictory Addresses.
Ansel French.

1815.

1. The Salutatory Addresses in Latin, and an Oration in English :— Preëminence of Modern Genius. - - - - - - Jasper Adams.

2. An Oration : — Man Formed for Happiness. - - - John E. Howard.
3. An Oration on Elective Governments. - - - - Crawford Allen.
4. An Oration : — Influence of Science on Liberty. - - Dana A. Braman.
5. A Greek Oration : — Battle of Bridgewater. - - William A. Shepard.
6. An Oration : — Oriental Idolatry. - - - - John B. Warren.
7. Hero of the South : — A Poem. - - - - - Alvan Bond.
8. An Essay on Party Spirit. - - - - - - John Seamans.
9. An Essay : — Uniformity of Conduct. - - - George Copeland.
10. A Latin Oration. - - - - - - Silas P. Holbrook.
11. War considered in its Relation to Natural and Revealed Religion : — An Essay.
    Ebenezer Coleman.
12. Means of Preserving Peace : — An Oration. - - - Abijah Pond.
13. "The Star in the East : " — An Oration. - - - George Taft.
14. An Oration : — The Fine Arts, - - - - - John E. Holbrook.
15. The Pursuit of Fame : — An Oration. - - - - Joseph Thayer.
16. Hero of the North : — A Poem. - - - - Benjamin Whitman.
17. The Ravages of Time : — An Oration - - - - Wilbur Fisk.
18. National Importance of the Fine Arts : — An Oration. - Joseph Clark.
19. Remarks on the Federal Constitution, as connected with the American Union.
    Charles Fobes.
20. Patriot's Vision : — A Poem. - - - - - John G. Polhill.
21. An Oration on Mental Improvement.
    Benjamin W. Cozzens, Esq., candidate for the Degree of Master of Arts.
22. Influence of the Study of Philosophy : — An Oration ; with the Valedictory
    Addresses, - - - - - - - Charles Turner.

1816.

1. Salutatory Addresses in Latin, and an Oration in English : — Defence of Criticism.
   Thomas Vernon.
2. Reality and Imagination contrasted. - - - - Lewis W. Fisher.
3. An Essay on the Influence of Social Affections. - - George L. Barnes.
4. An Essay on Creation. - - - - - - Thomas P. Bancroft.
5. An Oration on Talent. - - - - - - Nathaniel Searle.
6. An Oration on the reciprocal Obligations of Learning and Religion.
   Abner Morse.
7. Constituent Principles of Government - - - Joseph W. Torrey.
8. Latin Oration on Eloquence. - - - - - Frederick Crafts.
9. Education essential to Political Union. - - - Joseph Mauran.
10. Sketch of the Progress of Society in New England. - Eliab Kingman.

11. Virtue and Science :— An Oration. - - - - - Peter B. Hunt.
12. Science and Religion :— An Oration. - - - - James Hubbard.
13. An Oration on War. - - - - - - Elisha Atkins.
14. Ravages of Despotism. - - - - - S. Augustus Arnold.
15. The Effects of Perseverance. - - - - - Jason H. Archer.
16. Union of Philosophy and Virtue. - - - - - Reuben Torrey.
17. Reflections on the Powers of the Mind. - - - John M. Chisolm.
18. Greek Oration on Intemperance. - - - - John Cooke Brown.
19. The Influence of Prejudice on American Literature :— An Oration.
Hezekiah Battelle.
20. Acquirement of Preëminence. - - - - - - Isaac Bowen.
21. Hero of the Mediterranean :— A Poem. - - - - Avery Briggs.
22. Cultivation of Taste :— An Oration. - - - - - Peter Pratt.
23. Revolution of Empires :— An Oration. - - - John Carter Brown.
24. South American Revolution :— An Oration. - - - Solomon Peck.
25. The Effects of early Habits on the Imagination :— An Essay.
Benjamin B. Smith.
26. Hints on restricting the Imagination. - - - - Benjamin F. Hallett.
27. The American Dead :— A Poem. - - - - Alexander Wood.
28. An Oration on the Eccentricity of Genius. - - - - Robert H. Ives.

1817.

1. The Salutatory Addresses in Latin, and an Oration in English, on Genius.
Aaron Brooks.
2. Origin and Influence of Error :— An Oration. - - Charles Jackson.
3. Eulogy on Fulton. - - - - - - - Everett Balcom.
4. Science of Geology :— An Oration. - - - Jonathan Bigelow.
5. Latin Oration, on the Dark Ages. - - - - Lewis L. Miller.
6. Struggle for Freedom :— A Poem. . - - Jonathan P. Crafts.
7. Influence of Learning on Society :— An Oration. - Henry Jackson.
8. Obstacles to the Progress of American Literature :— An Oration.
Joseph F. Martin.
9. Greek Oration. on the Powers of the Mind - - Pardon B. Farrington.
10. Divine Immutability deduced from the Order of the Celestial Bodies.
Abel Manning.
11. National Honor :— An Oration. - - - - - Elisha Hayward.
12. Dispute :— Which is the more Useful Member of Society, the Poet or the Orator ? - - - - - Samuel Ashley, Stephen Rawson.
13. Spirit of Patriotism. - - - - - - - Joseph Patrick.

COMMENCEMENT EXERCISES.   385

14. Victories of the Redeemer : — A Poem.   - - -   Isaac Kimball.
15. Dispute : — Has the French Revolution been beneficial to Mankind ?
Edward R. Lippitt, Warren Lovering.
16. Danger of American Liberty : — An Oration. - -   William R. Staples.
17. American Star : — An Oration.   - - - - -   Elipha White.
18. Fate of Genius : — An Oration.   - - - -   Benjamin F. Allen.
19. An Oration on the Abuse of Intellectual Powers ; with the Valedictory Addresses.
William Greene.

1818.

1. Salutatory Addresses in Latin, and an Essay in English, on Early Prejudice.
Thomas F. Carpenter.
2. The Influence of Moral Obligation on Society : — An Oration.
Jared W. Williams.
3. An Oration on the Nature and Importance of Truth and Goodness. Elias Fiske.
4. Independence of Character.   - - - -   Walter P. B. Judson.
5. An Oration on the Study of Metaphysics.   - - -   Jabez Porter.
6. The Moral Influence of Memory : — An Oration.   - -   Martin Snell.
7. A Latin Oration, on Greek and Roman Eloquence.   - .   Stephen M. Rogers.
8. Utility of Monuments : — An Oration.   - - -   William Watson.
9. Study of Natural History.   - - - - -   Alva Carpenter.
10. Reason and Fancy : — An Oration.   - - -   William S. Patten.
11. The Atheist : — An Oration.   - - - -   John W. Whitman.
12. An Oration on the Causes of the Decay of Genius   - -   Azel Utley.
13. The Present Situation of America.   - - - - -   Esek Aldrich.
14. Love of Truth the Philosopher's Guide : — An Oration.   Willard Pierce.
15. The Mutual Influence of Literature and Civil Government. Solomon L. Wildes.
16. An Oration on the Policy of Acknowledging the Independence of South
America.   - - - - - -   Elnathan P. Hathaway.
17. The Influence of Individual Character on National Prosperity.
Dutee J. Pearce, Esq., candidate for the Degree of Master of Arts.
18. Natural Dignity of Man : — An Oration ; with the Valedictory Addresses.
Jedediah L. Stark.

1819.

1. Salutatory Addresses in Latin, and an Oration in English, on the Origin and
Effects of Modern Scepticism.   - - -   - George Fisher.
2. An Oration on the Decline of Infidelity.   - - - -   Francis Wood.
3. An Oration on the Influence of Toleration on Individual and National Character.
James S. Holmes.

4. A Latin Oration, on the Value and Immutability of Truth.   Jesse Hartwell.
5. An Oration on the Moral Influence of Pagan Philosophy.   Joseph Merriam.
6. A Dispute : — Are the Inducements for cultivating Science in the United States, equal to those of Great Britain?   -   Thomas Backus, Samuel B. Shaw.
7. An Oration on the Influence of Curiosity.   -   -   -   Nathaniel Helme.
8. A Greek Oration : — Freedom essential to Eloquence.   Daniel G. Sprague.
9. An Oration : — Diversity of Opinion favorable to the Interests of Society.
   David Torrey.
10. An Oration on the Advantages of War.   -   -   -   Elijah L. Hamlin.
11. A Poem : — The Phenix from her Ashes.   -   -   -   Jairus S. Keith.
12. An Oration on the Utility of Mathematical Studies.   -   Steuben Taylor.
13. An Oration : — Philosophy, the only Permanent Basis of Political Institutions.
   Ira M. Barton.
14. An Oration on the Fine Arts.   -   -   -   -   -   William Ennis
15. An Oration : — The gradual Advancement of the Human Species in Dignity and Happiness; with the Valedictory Addresses.   -   Horace Mann.

1820.

1. Salutatory Addresses in Latin, and an Oration in English, on the Science of Human Nature.   -   -   -   -   -   -   -   William Ruggles.
2. Cultivation of the Imagination.   -   -   -   -   -   Henry A. Rogers.
3. The principal Causes of Human Instability.   -   -   Charles B. Halsey.
4. Freedom of Inquiry.   -   -   -   -   -   -   John Goldsbury.
5. Characteristics of the Philosopher.   -   -   -   -   Ebenezer Stone.
6. A Greek Oration on Ancient Authors.   -   -   -   -   Lemuel Hall.
7. The Character of Mahomet.   -   -   -   -   Benjamin G. Church.
8. Which has a just Claim to Superiority in Literature and Science, Greece or Rome? A Dispute.   -   -   -   Swan L. Pomroy, Joseph M'Clintock.
9. Attention to particular rather than to general Literature, essential to extensive Usefulness.   -   -   -   -   -   -   -   Horatio G. Wheaton.
10. Impediments to the Progress of Literature.   -   -   -   Henry Hersy.
11. Triumph of Reason   -   -   -   -   -   -   -   Abiel Childs.
12. Prospects of African Aggrandizement.   -   -   -   Joseph J. Fales.
13. The Analytic Science.   -   -   -   -   -   -   George Gary.
14. Defence of the American Character.   -   -   -   Joseph Hathaway.
15. The Dignity and Importance of Astronomy.   -   -   -   Enoch Sanford.
16. Patronage of Genius.   -   -   -   -   -   Augustus W. Roberts.
17. The Resurrection and Judgment : — A Poem.   -   -   Albert G. Greene.
18. An Oration on National Permanency; with the Valedictory Addresses.
   Welcome A. Burges.

COMMENCEMENT EXERCISES. 387

1821.

1. The Salutatory Oration in Latin. - - - - - - Levi Haile.
2. An Oration on Political Constitutions. - - - John L. Doggett.
3. A Greek Oration on Ancient Poetry. - - - Samuel B. Parris.
4. An Oration on the Political State of France. - - Simeon Tucker.
5. A Conference on the Moral Law and the Gospel. - Nathaniel Cobb, Augustus B. Reed, Moses Thatcher.
6. An Oration : — Reflections on Italy. - - - - - Oliver Everett.
7. A Latin Oration on the Progress of Christianity. - - Thomas H. Webb.
8. An Oration on the Spirit of Despotism. - - Thomas J. Humphrey.
9. An Oration on the Connection between Learning and Fame. Eliab Williams.
10. A Philosophical Dispute : — Do Meteorites originate from Sources connected with the Earth? Eliphas Fay, Joseph Muenscher, William G. Hammond.
11. An Oration on the Influence of early Impressions. - - Eliphalet P. Crafts.
12. An Oration on the relative Importance of Natural and Intellectual Philosophy. Increase S. Smith.
13. An Oration on the Progressive Improvement of Man. - - Lucius Alden.
14. A Conference on Architecture, Sculpture, Painting and Poetry. George Griswold, Rufus Babcock, George R Russell.
15. An Oration on Religious Philosophy; with the Valedictory Addresses. Levi Packard.

1822.

1. Salutatory Addresses in Latin, and an English Oration, on the Influence of Learning in the Development of National Resources. Samuel Starkweather
2. A Forensic Dispute : — Would a general Diffusion of Knowledge contribute to the Permanency of the Monarchies of Europe? - - William Barry, Joseph W. Farnum, Samuel Presbury, Richard E Eddy.
3. Poetic Excitement. - - - - - - Daniel L. Goodwin.
4. An Oration in Latin : — The Elegant Arts of Ancient Rome. William A. Crocker.
5. The Family of the Medici. - - - - - Solomon Lincoln.
6. Recollections of Athens : — An Oration in Greek. - - Jacob H. Loud.
7. Intellectual Philosophy. - - - - - - John Pierce.
8. The Philosopher, a correct Theorist and a skillful Practitioner. John Wilder.
9. Theological Conference : — The Excellence, History and Prospects of Christianity. George W. Hathaway, Samuel Kingsbury, Preston Cummings.
10. Comparative Advantages of Europe and America for Poetical Description. Thomas Kinnicutt.

11. Philosophical Forensic : — Which Country has contributed most to the Promotion of Physical Science, France or Great Britain ? - Thomas M Burgess, Isaac Davis, Henry H. F. Sweet.
12. The Old Age of the Scholar. - - - - Benjamin C. Cutler.
13. An Oration on the Influence of American Literature on the Permanency of the American Union; with the Valedictory Addresses. - Alexis Caswell.

1823.

1. Salutatory Addresses in Latin, and an English Oration, on Political Science.
Silas A. Crane.
2. An Oration : — Scottish Literature. - - - - John W. Tenney.
3. A Dispute : — Has the reign of Napoleon been advantageous to Europe ?
William Badger, Joseph W. Fearing, James Plaisted.
4. An Oration : — Influence of Education on National Happiness. Elias Bullard.
5. A Latin Oration : — The Augustan Age. - - - William Magoun.
6. An Oration : — Literature indebted to Religion. - Charles Dresser.
7. A Dispute : — Are Capital Punishments useful ? - - Caleb Belcher, Aholiab Johnson.
8. A Dissertation on the Science of Mind - - - Joseph P. Tyler.
9. An Oration : — Pleasures of Hope. - - - George D. Prentice.
10. A Greek Oration : — Spartan Institutions. - - - Benjamin Norris.
11. Conference : — On Chemical, Mechanical, and Intellectual Philosophy.
Seth Miller, Edward Mellen, Rufus Hodges.
12. An Oration : — Influence of Curiosity in the Acquisition of Knowledge.
Baalis Sanford.
13. Conference on Fiction, Poetry, and Eloquence. Samuel Ames, Asa M. Bolles, William R. Watson.
14. An Oration : — Influence of Situation on the Character of Nations ; with the Valedictory Addresses. - - - - - - Henry S. Fearing.

1824.

1. Salutatory Addresses in Latin, and an English Oration, on the Effects of the Crusades on the Refinement of Europe. - - - Joseph S. Jenckes.
2. An Oration : — The Influence of Luxury on National Prosperity.
George A. Brayton.
3. A Dispute : — Is the Present Condition of America favorable to the Advancement of Literature and Science ? - - Luther Smith, Shubael Peck.
4. An Oration : — Wonders of the Age. - - - William P. Bullock.
5. A Latin Oration, on the former and present Condition of Italy. Allen O. Peck.

COMMENCEMENT EXERCISES. 389

6. An Oration: — Defence of the Irish Character. - - Ezra Wilkinson.
7. A Dissertation on the Advantages of Biography. - John P. Turney.
8. A Dispute: — The comparative Advantages of Peace and War.
    William H. Judd, Henry C. Jewett, George Mann.
9. An Oration: — Literary Eminence dependent on Persevering Industry.
    Tyler Thatcher.
10. A Greek Oration: — Ancient and Modern Greece contrasted.
    Richard F. Sweet.
11. An Oration: — The Precariousness of Intellectual Sovereignty.
    Aruna C. H. Smith.
12. An Oration: — The final Causes of the Diversity of Talent. David Daniels.
13. A Conference on Navigation, Agriculture and Mechanics.
    Phineas Savory, George Dyer, Charles R. Fisk.
14. An Oration: — Christianity favorable to the Advancement of Literature.
    William Leverett.
15. A Conference on Fiction, Poetry and Eloquence.
    William H. Waterman, George A. Bucklin, Eliphalet W. Hervey.
16. An Oration: — The Spirit of the Times. - - - - Asa Potter.
17. An Oration: — Union of Intellectual and Moral Excellence George Leonard.
18. An Oration on the Present Disinclination for Scientific Research; with the Valedictory Addresses. - - - - - George W. Keely.

1825.

1. The Salutatory Addresses in Latin, and an Oration in English: — The Influence of Circumstances on Character. - - - - George G. King.
2. An Oration, on some of the Prominent Events of the Age. Samuel T. Wilder.
3. A Latin Oration, on the Study of the Latin and Greek. - George Fiske.
4. A Conference: — Sketches of France, England, Scotland, and America.
    Sidney Williams, Benjamin Willis, John B. Herreshoff, Jared D. Richmond.
5. An Oration: — Preëminence of Modern Times. - William T. Hawes.
6. An Oration: — Unlimited Improvement the Prerogative of Man.
    Moses G. Thomas.
7. A Greek Oration, on Grecian Literature. - - - George W. Briggs.
8. A Dispute: — Is Sensibility the Source of Excellence? - John Burrage,
    Henry B. Goodwin, William W. Hall, Nathaniel E. Johnson.
9. An Oration: — Literature of the Fifteenth Century. Christopher Robinson.
10. A Conference: — The Anxieties of Youth, Manhood and Old Age, with a view of Futurity. - - - Lewis W. Clifford, Jerathmel B. Jenckes,
    William Pratt, George W. Patten.

11. A Dispute on the Comparative Beauties of Nature and Art. Hermon Bourne, Thomas J. Forbes, Thomas Snow, William S. Stanley.
12. A Dispute: — Does Despotism or Licentiousness present the greater Obstacle to the Establishment of Free Government? - - - Lucius W. Clark, Theodore L. Lincoln, Samuel Plaisted.
13. A Conference on Civil and Religious Freedom. - - Joseph Green, Hugh Montgomery, Benjamin C. Wade.
14. An Oration: — The Troubadours. - - - - Sands G. Cole.
15. An Oration: — The Triumphs of the Scholar. - - - Horatio Pratt.
16. A Conference on Painting, Sculpture, Poetry, and Architecture. Charles C. P. Hastings, Solon Hill, Onslow Peters, Samuel Watson.
17. An Oration: — The Influence of Association upon the Intellectual Character. Barnas Sears.
18. An Oration: — The Difficulty and Glory of subduing the Passions. David Sanford.
19. An Oration: — American Feeling. - - - - Joseph H. Price.
20. An Oration: — The Ravages of War. - - - - James B. Prince.
21. An Oration: — National Enthusiasm the source of National Greatness; with the Valedictory Addresses. - - - - - Ira Cleaveland.

President Sears, it will be observed, was a member of this class, being the largest class, without exception, that has ever graduated from the Institution.

1826.

1. An Oration on the Importance of Correct Principles of Philosophizing. Henry Williams.
2. A Dissertation on the Utility of Ancient Classics. - - George B. Peck.
3. A Dissertation on Early Recollections. - - - Jason B. Blackington.
4. A Dissertation: — Enthusiasm, Complex and Diversified in its Operation. Thomas Wilson.
5. A Dissertation: — The Beneficial Effects of the Fine Arts on Society. Gilbert Fay.
6. A Dispute: — Has the Reign of Napoleon been Advantageous to Europe? Walter W. Dalton, Benjamin R. Dean.
7. Oratio Græca de Rebus Græcorum. - - - Henry W. Thayer.
8. A Dissertation on the Progress of Literature. - George W. Messenger.
9. A Dissertation: — The Influence of Theatrical Exhibitions on a Nation. Zenas Bliss.

COMMENCEMENT EXERCISES.   391

10. An Oration on the Diversities of National Character. - - John Daggett.
11. A Conference on Mental Discipline, and the Progress of American Improvement. - - - - - - William Phillips, Francis Deane.
12. An Oration on the Influence of Early Associations in the Formation of Character.
    Charles J. Warren.
13. Oratio Latina de Præstantia Antiquorum. - - - Calvin P. Fiske.
14. A Dissertation : — A Knowledge of Human Nature the Glory of the Scholar.
    Eleazar C. Hutchinson.
15. A Poem : — Last of the Carribbes. - - - - - Nathan Willis.
16. An Oration on the Benefit of Men of Genius to the World. Jonathan Aldrich.
17. A Conference on the Value of Philosophy and Classic Literature.
    Nathan Ball, Lewis Washburn.
18 An Oration on Hypothetical Philosophy. - - - Cyrus W. Allen.
19. An Oration : — Distinction often the Result of Accident.   Isaiah L. Green.
20. An Oration on the Natural Right of Man in relation to Political Reformation.
    Samuel Ames, (class of 1823,) candidate for the Degree of Master of Arts.
21. An Oration on the Institution of Free Schools. - - William R. Watson,
    (class of 1823,) candidate for the Degree of Master of Arts.
22. An Oration : — The Life of the Man of Letters. - - George Burgess.

This is the last Commencement at which Dr. Messer presided. He resigned the Presidency of the University in a letter dated September 23, 1826, which letter is published in our "Historical Sketch." (Page 28.) A prominent member of the class of 1826, was the Rev. Dr. Edwards A. Park, of Andover. He declined speaking at Commencement, and the valedictory honors were assigned to the late Bishop Burgess. John Kingsbury, LL. D., the present efficient Secretary of the Corporation, was also a member of this class.

1827.

1. Salutatory Addresses in Latin, and an Oration in English, on American History.
    Joseph F. Phillips.
2. Medical Science : — An Oration. - - - - - Noah Warner.
3. A Dissertation. (Excused.) - - - - - Peter C. Bacon.
4. A Dissertation. (Excused.) - - - - - Simeon B. Carpenter.
5. Philanthropy Interwoven with the Destiny of Man : — An Oration.
    Peter R. Minard.

6. Natural Science : — An Oration. - - - - Williams Latham.
7. A Dissertation. (Excused.) - - - - - Justin Hammond.
8. The Attainment of Excellence : — An Essay. - Thomas J. Coggeshall.
9. An Essay. (Excused.) - - - - - - Israel Putnam.
10. The Foundation of True Greatness : — A Dissertation. James W. Thompson.
11. An Essay. (Excused.) - - - - - - Charles Wadsworth.
12. An Essay. (Excused.) - - - - - - Charles Gilman.
13. Domestic Manufactures : — An Essay. - - - Thomas R. Hunter.
14 A Dissertation. (Excused.) - - - - - Zaccheus Colburn.
15. A Dissertation. (Excused.) - - - - - Sylvanus Morse.
16. The Fall of Mexico : — A Poem. - - - - Charles Thurber.
17. A Dissertation. (Excused.) - - - - - William M. Cornell.
18. The Future Drama of our Country : — A Dissertation - John H. Clifford.
19. The Mathematical Oration. - - - - - William H. Spear.
20. The Oration on Classical Literature. - - - - Elam Smalley.
21. The Spirit of the Crusaders : — An Oration. - - - Isaiah Moody.
22. An Oration. (Excused.) - - - - - - James Bishop.
23. An Oration. (Excused.) - - - - - Mellen Chamberlain.
24. Advantages of America for awakening Poetic Genius : — An Oration.
H G. Otis Colby.
25. The Oration on Moral Science. - - - - Ebenezer Thresher.
26. The Memory of Roger Williams ; with the Valedictory Addresses.
John H. Weeden.

The Rev. Dr. Wayland, who succeeded President Messer, presided for the first time at this Commencement.

1828.

1. The Nature and Benefits of Revolutions ; with Salutatory Addresses.
Samuel West, Jr.
2. The Freedom of the Press : — A Dissertation. - - Lucius S Bolles.
3. The Oration on the Character of Columbus. - - - Daniel C. Burt.
4. The Oration on Popular Education. (Excused.) - - Maturin L. Fisher.
5. Influence of Love of Country on National Character : — An Essay.
Gamaliel L. Dwight.
6. Simple Classification of the Powers and Operations of the Human Mind : — A
Dissertation. - - - - - - - Francis W. Emmons.
7. Causes for the Progress of Infidelity : — A Dissertation. Albert C. Ainsworth.
8. Pulpit Eloquence : — An Oration. - - - - Francis Horton.

COMMENCEMENT EXERCISES.   393

9. American Literature : — An Oration. (Excused.) - - James C. Roy.
10. The Influence of Climate on Intellectual Character :—An Oration. (Excused.)
    Milton Bradford.
11. Influence of Moral Cultivation upon the Prosperity and Perpetuity of Governments : — An Essay. (Excused.) - - - - Samuel Lamson.
12. Internal Navigation : — An Essay. (Excused.) - - Daniel M. Hale.
13. American Manufactures : — An Essay. (Excused.) - George A. Rhodes.
14. Defence of the Revolutionary Tories : — A Dissertation. Ephraim Munroe.
15. The Effects of Music on the Passions : — An Oration. John Winthrop.
16. The Word "Farewell" : — A Poem. - - - Mark A. D. Howe.
17. Oration : — Influence of Natural Scenery on Character. Henry F. Edes.
18. Oration : — Utility of Intellectual Philosophy. - - Joseph T. Robert.
19. Oration : — Force of Character. - - - - - Archer B. Smith.
20. Oration : — The Education of Nature contrasted with the Education of Art.
    Amos Lovering.
21. Eulogy on DeWitt Clinton. - - - - - - Joseph Roby.
22. The New England Character; with the Valedictory Addresses.
    Lafayette S. Foster.

1829.

1. Oration on the Extent of Individual Influence; with the Salutatory Addresses.
   William B. Carpenter.
2. The Pleasures of a Literary Life : — A Dissertation. - - John H. Bird.
3. Oration on the Economical Effects of Intellectual Culture. Benoni Carpenter.
4. Causes of Commercial Depression :—A Dissertation. (Excused.) Elisha Dyer, Jr.
5. What would be the most suitable Form of Government for Independent Greece ?—
   A Dissertation. - - - - - - Charles H. Holmes.
6. Oration on the Dignity of the Medical Profession. - - Charles Gordon.
7. Oration on the Permanency of the Union. (Excused.) Samuel Coney, Jr.
8. Religious Principle, the last Hope of Empire : — An Oration. Stephen P. Hill.
9. Oration on the Means of Perpetuating our Civil Institutions. James W. Cooke.
10. The Old Age of the Scholar : — An Intermediate Oration. (Excused.)
    Nathan Dresser, Jr.
11. Moral Effects of the Catholic Emancipation : — An Oration. Isaac D. Wilson.
12. Progress and Effects of Free Inquiry : — An Oration. - Henry A. Miles.
13. The Atheist : — An Intermediate Oration. - - William T. Dorrance.
14. The Modern Literature of Germany : — An Oration. - John E. Sweet.
15. Oration : — The Memory of the Dead. - - - John A. Bolles.

16. Oration on the comparative Effects of Poetry and Painting. (Excused.)
Theophilus P. Doggett.
18. Oration on the Causes permanently influencing American Literature; with the Valedictory Addresses. - - - - - Charles W. Crouch.

Up to this time it had been the invariable practice to have Commencement exercises during both forenoon and afternoon, with an interval between. This year the exercises were continued, as they have been since, without interruption until the close.

1830.

1. Salutatory Addresses. - - - - - Christopher M. Nickels.
2. Social Provisions of Christianity :— An Oration. - Samuel B. Swaim.
3. Criminal Jurisprudence :— An Oration. - - Benjamin F. Thomas.
4. The Study of the Mathematics :— An Oration. (Excused.) Elisha Stevens.
5. Moral Courage of Legislators essential to National Greatness :— A Dissertation.
Benjamin H. Hathorne.
6. Improvement of Taste :— A Dissertation. (Excused.) Lucius Kingman.
7. Character of Roger Williams :— An Essay. - - Joseph Moriarty.
8. Influence of the Love of Fame on the Development of Genius :— An Oration.
Ebenezer Smith, Jr.
9. Christian Patriotism :— An Oration. (Excused.) - - Gideon Dana.
10. Southern Slavery :— An Intermediate Oration. - Hazell W. Crouch.
11. Ancient and Modern Eloquence compared :— A Dissertation. Ellis Ames.
12. Excellence Attainable by All :— An Essay. - - Francis J. Lippitt.
13. Festivals, Patriotic and Literary :— An Oration. - - Richard S. Edes.
14. Sectional Prejudice :— An Intermediate Oration. - Albert G. Wakefield.
15. Superiority of Moral Power :— An Oration. - - - Spencer A. Pratt.
16. The Eras of Poetry :— An Oration. - - - - Christopher G. Perry.
17. An Oration on National Attachments. Harrison G. O. Colby, (class of 1827,)
candidate for the Degree of Master of Arts.
18. An Oration on the Perils of Professional Life. - - John H. Clifford,
(class of 1827,) candidate for the Degree of Master of Arts.
19. Oration :— The Results of Improvements in the Science of Education; with the Valedictory Addresses. - - - - - - George I Chace.

1831.

1. Study essential to Poetical Excellence :— An Oration; with the Salutatory Addresses. - - - - - - - David King, Jr.

COMMENCEMENT EXERCISES. 395

2. Consecrated Talent : — An Intermediate Oration. - Edward Otheman.
3. Literary History : — An Oration. - - - - William H. Eddy.
4. The Bible a Classic : — An Intermediate Oration. - Francis W. Bird.
5. Causes of the Superiority of Modern Society :—An Essay. Joseph M. Church.
6. The Christian Statesman : — An Oration. - - - Henry Waterman.
7. The Spirit of Chivalry : — An Essay. - - - William F. DeWolf.
8. An Oration on the Political Character of Milton. - - Nicholas Hoppin.
9. Character of Bishop Heber : — An Oration. - - - Francis Peck.
10. Natural Science : — An Intermediate Oration. - - Walter S. Burges.
11. Oration : — The Influence of the Scholar on the Advancement of Political Freedom. - - - - - - Joseph L. Jernegan.
12. The Power of Conscience : — A Poem. Mark A. D. Howe, (class of 1828,) candidate for the Degree of Master of Arts.
13. Oration : — The Causes of a Diseased Imagination ; with the Valedictory Addresses. - - - - - - - William Gammell.

1832.

1. Salutatory Addresses. - - - - - - Oren A. Ballou.
2. Poetry of Religion : — The Salutatory Oration. - - Jonathan E. Arnold.
3. The Importance of our Political Union : — An Oration. Erasmus D. Miller.
4. Influence of Periodical Reviews : — A Dissertation. - - Henry Earle.
5. Christianity favorable to Political Economy : — An Oration. Warren Leverett.
6. Effects of Polemical Theology : — An Oration. (Excused.) Thomas B. Newhall.
7. Moral Influence of Fiction : — An Oration. - - Oren A. Ballou.
8. Modern Education : — An Oration. - - - - Isaac E. Heaton.
9. Moral Prospects of our Country : — An Oration. (Excused.) James Huckins.
10. Autobiography of Men of Science : — An Oration. (Excused.) Samuel W. Peckham.
11. Prospects of Europe. Affirmative : — An Intermediate Oration. Obadiah W. Albee.
12. Prospects of Europe. Negative : — An Oration. - Charles N. Fearing.
13. Moral Excellence necessary to true Greatness : — A Dissertation. Samuel W. Bridgham, Jr.
14. Incentives to Benevolent Enterprise : — A Dissertation. - Jacob White.
15. Mental Improvement the Safeguard of our Country : — An Oration. (Excused.) Jonathan R. Harding.
16. Spirit of Enterprise necessary to a flourishing Community : — A Dissertation. John K. Simpson, Jr.
17. Pleasures of a Cultivated Taste : — A Poem. - - Charles Holden, Jr.

18. Love of Truth :— An Intermediate Oration. - - - Salmon C. Perry.
19. Sanguinary Punishments :— An Intermediate Oration. (Excused.)
    Joseph Farnum, Jr.
20. Uses of History :— An Oration. (Excused.) - - John B. White.
21. Character of Lord Brougham :— An Oration. - - Samuel Randall, Jr.
22. Waste of Mind :— An Oration. - - - Washington Leverett.
23. The Humility of True Science :— An Oration. (Excused.) John M. Mackie.
24. Voluntary Associations :— An Oration. John A. Bolles, (class of 1829,) candidate for the Degree of Master of Arts.
25. Valedictory Addresses to the Corporation. (Excused.) Washington Leverett.
25. Valedictory Addresses to the Class. (Excused.) - - John M. Mackie.

1833.

1. Salutatory Addresses. - - - - - - Arthur S. Train.
2. Influence of Moral upon Intellectual Cultivation :— An Intermediate Oration.
    William B. Jacobs.
3. History the Grand Inquest of Character :— A Dissertation.
    Nathan F. Dixon, Jr.
4. Influence of Religious Belief upon the Emotions of Taste :— A Dissertation.
    Ebenezer P. Dyer.
5. Object of a Liberal Education :— An Intermediate Oration. (Excused.)
    Nehemiah G. Lovell.
6. Materials for American Literature :— An Intermediate Oration. George F. Pool.
7. An Active Profession the best Discipline for Intellectual Character :— An Oration.
    Benjamin H. Rhoades.
8. Pulpit Eloquence :— An Oration. - - - - Edward A. Stevens.
9. The Study of History :— An Oration. (Excused.) - Horatio A. Wilcox.
10. Consecrated Genius :— A Poem. (Excused.) - Lorenzo O. Lovell.
11. Decline of American Patriotism :— An Oration. - Lemuel W. Washburn.
12. Popular Superstitions :— An Intermediate Oration. - Nehemiah Knight.
13. Poetical Character of Scott and Byron :— A Dissertation. Peres Simmons.
14. Consistency of Character :— An Essay. (Excused.) Edward Freeman.
15. Scottish Covenanters. (Excused.) - - - - Henry G. Wiley.
16. Labor the only True Genius. - - - - - George T. Metcalf.
17. Egyptian History :— An Oration. - - - - Henry B. Anthony.
18. The Power of Humility :— An Oration. - - - - Arthur S. Train.
19. Character of Robert Hall; with the Valedictory Addresses. (Excused.)
    Jabez Taber.

1834.

1. Salutatory Addresses. - - - - - Pardon D. Tiffany.
2. Martial Spirit unfavorable to the Permanence of Free Institutions: — An Oration. Jonathan R. Bullock.
3. The Study of Natural Science: — A Dissertation. - Crawford Nightingale.
4. Love of Power: — An Oration. - - - - - Hervey S. Dale.
5. Influence of National Intercourse on the Progress of Society: — An Intermediate Oration. - - - - - - - - Charles W. Wood.
6. Patient Thought: — An Oration. - - - - Joseph Bridgham.
7. The Education of Mercantile Men: — A Dissertation. Daniel P. Simpson.
8. Early Character of Rhode Island: — A Dissertation. - Edward H. Hazard.
9. Causes of the Decline of Nations: — A Dissertation. (Excused.) Carrington Hoppin.
10. The Choice of a Profession: — A Dissertation. (Excused.) Augustus Leland.
11. Moral Reasoning superior to Demonstration: — An Oration. (Excused.) Oliver Ayer.
12. Value of the Ancient Classics to the American Student: — An Oration. Ephraim Ward.
13. Advantages of the Study of Phrenology: — A Dissertation. David Perkins.
14. Obstacles to the Progress of American Literature: — An Oration. Pardon D. Tiffany.
15. Progress of Science: — An Oration. (Excused.) - - George Cole.
16. System in Intellectual Labor essential to Success: — An Oration. (Excused.) Silas Bailey.
17. Hostility to Truth: — An Oration. • • • Joshua W. Downing.
18. Tendency of Revolutions: — An Oration. - - Charles K. Johnson.
19. Responsibilities of American Young Men: — An Oration. William H. Wood.
20. Study of Political Economy: — An Oration. (Excused.) Edward A. Lotbrop.
21. Study of Physical Science: — An Oration. (Excused.) Luther Robinson.
22. The Philosopher and the Philanthropist Compared; with the Valedictory Addresses. - - - - - - James T. Champlin.

1835.

1. The Condition and Prospects of Africa: — An Oration. - Jonah G. Warren.
2. Causes of the Superiority of Ancient Eloquence: — An Oration. Edward Stone.
3. Characteristics of True Patriotism: — An Oration. - Samuel S. Sumner.
4. The Influence of Progressive Civilization on Poetry: — An Oration. John M. Mackie, (class of 1832,) candidate for the Degree of Master of Arts.

5. The Political Principles of Chief Justice Marshall: — An Oration.
    William F. DeWolf, A. M., (class of 1831,)
    candidate for the Degree of Bachelor of Laws.

This has sometimes been called the CONSCIENTIOUS CLASS. It appears from the record, that they were unwilling to accept of parts at Commencement, unless the distribution of them on the principle of scholarship were relinquished. This could not be done consistently with President Wayland's views of the matter, and consequently all but three of the class declined being candidates for degrees.

The following are the names of the members of the class, as they are given in the annual catalogue. Fifteen of them appear in the triennial catalogue recently published, with the years when they took their degrees:—

Leonard Bliss,	Otis Fisher,	Joshua M. Macomber,	Edward Stone,
Alfred Bosworth,	Josiah Goddard,	Reuben Morey,	Samuel S. Sumner,
Nathan Brittan,	Samuel L. Gould,	Elias Nason,	William D. Upham,
Henry Chapin,	Levi H. Holden,	Zenas B. Newman,	Geronimo Urmeneta,
Joshua B. Chapin,	Dwight Ives,	George M. Randall,	George G. Warren,
George W. Cross,	Charles C. Jewett,	Edward T. Richardson,	Jonah G. Warren,
Samuel Curry,	Justin R. Loomis,	William R. Saxton,	John Waterman.
Giles M. Eaton,			

1836.

1. Salutatory Addresses. - - - - - - Charles Chamberlain.
2. Oration : — The Source of Fanaticism. - - - William L. Brown.
3. The Periodical Literature of the Present Day : — An Oration.
    Thomas L. Dunnell.
4. Paul in Athens : — A Poem. - - - - - Jacob R. Scott.
5. Eulogy on William Wirt (Excused.) - - - John G. Jones.
6. The Moral Uses of Emulation : — An Oration. (Excused.) Henry Smith.
7. Political Patronage : — An Oration. (Excused.) - William C. Mellen.
8. Oration : — The Qualifications for a Modern Reformer. Stephen O. Shepard.
9. Oration : — The Influence of Men of Genius on their Age. (Excused.)
    William H. Potter.

10. The Effects of Natural Agents upon the Progress of Society : — An Oration.
Samuel Clarke.
11. The Importance of Cultivating Social Feeling : — An Intermediate Oration.
Thomas L. Randolph.
12. The Dignity of the Medical Profession : — An Oration. (Excused.)
Jotham Lincoln.
13. Oration : — The Progress of Physical Science. (Excused.) Caleb Farnum.
14. The Ultimate Success of great Minds : — An Intermediate Oration.
John L. Lincoln.
15. Oration : — Enthusiasm of Genius. - - - - Silas B. Randall.
16. Oration : — The Social Influence of an Aristocracy. (Excused.)
Thomas P. Shepard.
17. Oration : — Benevolence and Justice, the true Principles of National Policy.
Wilbur Tillinghast.
18. Mental Refinement : — An Oration. (Excused.) - Charles H. Waterbury.
19. Reverence for Antiquity : — An Intermediate Oration. (Excused.)
John G. Douglass.
20. The Connection between Science and Christianity : — An Intermediate Oration. (Excused.) - - - - - - Edward A. Bennett.
21. The Influence of the Fine Arts : — An Intermediate Oration. (Excused.)
Charles J. Everett.
22. The Progress of British Reform : — An Intermediate Oration. (Excused.)
George Jacques.
23. Oration : — Causes of the Decline of Poetry. Charles Chamberlain.
24. The March of Mind. - - - - - - John P. Knowles.
25. Causes of the Decline of Pulpit Eloquence : — An Oration. Arthur S. Train, (class of 1833,) candidate for the Degree of Master of Arts.
26. Oration : — The Field of Philosophical Research not explored ; with the Valedictory Addresses. - - - - - - - Horace T. Love.

1837.

1. Salutatory Addresses. - - - - - - - Edwin Noyes.
2. The Importance of an Enlightened Literary Criticism : — A Dissertation.
Charles W. Reding.
3. The Eloquence of the Revolution : — An Essay. Alexander G. Henshaw.
4. The Spirit of Party : — A Dissertation. - - - George Griggs.
5. Rome : — An Essay. - - - - - - - George W. Peck.
6. The Orator : — An Essay. - - - - - - Erasmus D. Fish.

7. The Influence of the Imagination on the Spirit of Enterprise : — An Oration.
Francis Smith.
8. The Character of Mirabeau : — A Dissertation. - - Charles R. Train.
9. Money : — A Poem. - - - - - - David A. Putnam.
10. The Importance of the Union : — An Oration. - - James W. Dallam.
11. The Power of the Past : — A Dissertation. - - William S. Child.
12. Consistency of Poetry with Philosophy and Religion : —An Oration.
Joseph Smith.
13. The Crusades : — An Oration. - - - - Thomas S. Sommers.
14. The Profession of Law : — An Intermediate Oration. Lambert J. Jones.
15. Vindication of Poetry : — An Intermediate Oration. Nicholas P. Tillinghast.
16. Oration : Moral Courage in the Character of the American Citizen demanded by the Circumstances of the Country. - - - William R. Babcock.
17. Oration : — Transcendental Philosophy. - - - James T. Champlin,
(class of 1834,) candidate for the Degree of Master of Arts.
18. Oration : — Caution requisite in the Character of the Philosopher ; with the Valedictory Addresses. - - - - Samuel S. Greene.

1838.

1. Salutatory Oration in Latin. - - - - - William S. Ames.
2. Florence and its Associations : — A Dissertation. John C. Stockbridge.
3. Influence of the Classic Mythology upon the Character of the People : — An Essay. - - - - - - - - Samuel F. Dike.
4. The Principles of Modern Patriotism : — A Dissertation. Charles M. Bowers.
5. The value of Metaphysical Speculations : — A Philosophical Dissertation.
George Young, (excused,) Ezekiel G. Robinson.
6. Early Memoirs : — A Poem. - - - - Henry C. Whitaker.
7. Importance of carrying into Manhood the Feelings of early Youth : — An English Oration. - - - - - - - Alfred Colburn.
8. The Career of the English People : — A Dissertation. James M. Clarke.
9. The Power of the Old and the New : — A Conference.
John W. P. Jenks, (excused,) Edward D. Pearce, Alexander Burgess.
10. Character of Nathaniel Bowditch : — An English Oration. Azel D. Cole.
11. Moral Progress : — An English Oration. - - George V. N. Lothrop.
12. Limitations of Scientific Enquiry : — An English Oration. Albert N. Arnold.
13. Moral Uses of the Fine Arts : — An Essay. (Excused.) Ezra W. Howard.
14. Characteristics : — A Poem. - - - - Thomas A. Jenckes.
15. Classical Oration : — The Mingling of Literary with Professional Studies.
Marcus Morton.

16. Features in the present Stage of Social Progress: — An English Oration; with the Valedictory Addresses. - - - - - Charles S. Bradley.

1839.

1. Salutatory Oration in Latin. - - - - - William T. Wilson.
2. The slow Development and Prevalence of Correct Principles: — An English Oration. - - - - - - - Charles C. Burnett.
3. Political Degeneracy: — A Dissertation. (Excused.) Ebenezer L. Shepard.
4. Physical Science, the Useful Arts, and the Fine Arts, considered as Subjects of Popular Education: — A Conference. - - - Henry G. Steward, Joseph S. Pitman, John W. Dodge.
5. The Age of Charles I: — An Essay. (Excused.) - - - Seth Mann.
6. The Political Character of Milton: — An Essay. - - Henry C. Dorr.
7. The Moral Spirit required in the Investigation of Truth: — A Dissertation. William Douglas.
8. The Value of Antiquarian Labors: — A Dissertation. (Excused.) Frederic L. Batchelder.
9. Can the Fine Arts be usefully employed as Aids in Devotion? — A Forensic Discussion. - - - - George W..Patch, Thomas S. Malcom.
10. The Religious Influence of Modern Philosophy: — A Dissertation. George W. Packard.
11. Moral Courage essential to the Character of the Statesman: — An English Oration. - - - - - - - James B. M. Potter.
12. Value of Literary Education to Men of Business: — A Dissertation. (Excused.) Albert T, Elliott.
13. The Waste of Intellect: — An English Oration. (Honorary.) Ezra W. Fletcher.
14. The Philosophical Oration:—The Spirit of the Philosopher. George W. Samson.
15. The Classical Oration:—The Moral Lessons to be derived from the Ancient Classics. - - - - - - - - Samuel Glover.
16. Self-Reliance: — An English Oration; with the Valedictory Addresses. Francis E. Hoppin.

1840.

1. Salutatory Oration in Latin. - - - - - James R. Boise.
2. Parallel between the United States and the Empire of Russia: — A Dissertation. Frank Griffin
3. Sympathy with Men of Genius: — An Essay. - - Henry G. Weston.
4. Political Integrity: — An Intermediate Oration. - - Jonas D. Sleeper.

5. A Discussion. (Excused.) - - - Oliver Fisk, Thomas W. Wood.
6. The Re-Interment of Napoleon in Paris: — An Essay. James H. Coggeshall.
7. Enthusiasm : — An English Oration. - - - Benjamin Franklin.
8. Popular Delusions : — A Dissertation. - - - William N. Sage.
9. An Intermediate Oration. (Honorary.) - - - - Nathan H. Dow.
10. The Power of Personal Character : — A Dissertation. - Ebenezer Dodge.
11. The Historian : — An Intermediate Oration. - - Obiel W. Briggs.
12. The Influence of a Skeptical Spirit on the Progress of Truth : — A Dissertation. George H. Browne.
13. The Influence of Intellectual Culture on the Moral Character : — An English Oration. - - - - - - - William T. Brantly.
14. The Value of Private Life : — An English Oration. - Edward C. Larned.
15. An English Oration. (Excused.) - - - - - William Dutton.
16. An English Oration. (Honorary.) - - - - Edward W. West.
17. Character of the English Puritans : — An English Oration. Heman Lincoln.
18. The Social Theorists of the Age : — An English Oration. - William Gaston.
19. The Philosophical Oration : — The Elements of Intellectual Success. Abraham Payne.
20. The Classical Oration : — The Influence of Ancient Mythology upon Literature, compared with that of Christianity. - - - James R. Kendrick.
21. The Study of the Past: — An English Oration; with the Valedictory Addresses. Nathaniel Morton.

1841.

1. Salutatory Oration in Latin. - - - - - Kendall Brooks.
2. The Idea of Fate in the Grecian Drama : — The Classical Oration. Franklin Wilson.
3. The Fall of Italian Freedom : — An Intermediate Oration. James B. R. Walker.
4. The Reign of Charles I : — An English Oration. - - Augustus Mason.
5. Writers of the Reign of Queen Anne : — An Intermediate Oration. Charles Hart.
6. An English Oration. (Excused.) - - - - James N. Sikes.
7. A Discussion. (Excused.) - - Asa M. Gammell, George W. Brown.
8. The Harmony of Religion and Philosophy : — An English Oration. Merrick Lyon.
9. The Martyr Spirit : — An Intermediate Oration. - - Jonas R. Perkins.
10. Social Change : — An English Oration. - - - Samuel S. Mann.

11. Orators of the American Revolution : — An English Oration.
   Thomas C. Campbell.
12. Professional and Political Eminence : — An English Oration.
   Benjamin A. Edwards.
13. An Essay. (Excused.) - - - - - - Asa P. Taylor.
14. An Essay. (Excused.) - - - - - - William M. Hale.
15. An Essay. (Excused.) - - - - - - David Haynes.
16. An Essay. (Excused.) - - - - - - Henry S. Wheaton.
17. An Essay. (Excused.) - - - - - Alanson H. Tinkham.
18. The Age and Poetry of Dante : — An Intermediate Oration.
   Samuel G. Arnold.
19. The Sources of the Poet's Power : — An English Oration.   Richard C. Hall.
20. The Importance of Liberal Studies to the Statesman : — An English Oration.
   Frederic W. Coffin.
21. The Spirit of Philosophical Inquiry : — The Philosophical Oration.
   Elbridge Smith.
22. Characteristics of the Present Age : — An English Oration ; with the Valedictory Addresses. - - - - - - Henry S. Frieze.

1842.

1. Salutatory Oration in Latin. - - - - - Joseph R. Manton.
2. The Conflicts of Truth : — An Oration of the Second Class. Zuinglius Grover.
3. The Spirit of the Man of Letters : — An Intermediate Oration.
   Stephen E. Brownell.
4. Military Power in Free States : — A Dissertation   -   Amasa S. Westcott.
5. The Pursuits of the Naturalist : — A Dissertation   -   Peter F. Mackie.
6. The Decline of the Tragic Drama : — An Intermediate Oration.
   George M. Bartol.
7. The Intellectual and Social Influence of the Pulpit : — An Intermediate Oration.
   Asa H. Gould.
8. The Benefits and Evils of Political Associations : — A Dissertation.
   Christopher S. Tillinghast.
9. The Economy of Christian Missions : — An Oration of the Second Class.
   John S. James.
10. The Eloquence of Thought : — An Oration of the First Class.   Henry H. Button.
11. The Introversive Habits of the Age : — An Oration of the First Class.
   Cornelius G. Fenner.
12. The Moral Dignity of the Federal Judiciary : — An Oration of the Second Class.
   George S. Stevenson.

13. The Egotism of Scholars: — An Oration of the First Class. Edwin Metcalf.
14. The Philosophical Oration: — The Uses of the Imagination in Philosophical Inquiry. - - - - - - - - Charles K. Colver.
15. The Classical Oration: — Vindication of Classical Studies Noah F. Packard.
16. Life a Season of Education: — An English Oration; with the Valedictory Addresses. - - - - - - - - Albert Harkness.

Parts for Commencement were also assigned to the following members of the Class, who were excused from speaking, viz.: —

1. A Dissertation. - - - - - - - Isaac J. Burgess.
2. A Dissertation. - - - - - - - Albert E. Dennison.
3. An Oration of the Second Class. - - - - - James W. C. Ely.
4. An Intermediate Oration. - - - - Charles G. W. French.
5. An Oration of the First Class. - - - - - - John Parsons.
6. An Oration of the First Class. - - - - - James M. Phipps.

1843.

1. Salutatory Oration in Latin. - - - - - - Henry Day.
2. The American Navy: — An Oration of the First Class. - George D. Miles.
3. The Judicial Character: — An Intermediate Oration. - Charles W. Hewes.
4. The Cultivation of Pulpit Oratory: — An Essay. - - Isaac F. Jones.
5. Causes of the Permanence of the Roman Catholic Church. Edwin T. Winkler.
6. The Career of the Duke of Wellington: — A Dissertation. Daniel F. Morrill.
7. Intellectual and Social Benefits of Commerce: — A Dissertation.
   Benjamin N. Lapham.
8. Genius a Creative Power: — An Essay. - - - William Knowles.
9. College Memories: — A Poem. - - - - Tracy P. Cheever.
10. The Power of Ceremonial Forms: — An Oration of the First Class.
    Harrison V. R. Lord.
11. The Sway of Original Thought: — An Oration of the First Class.
    Harrison C. Page.
12. The last Days of Lord Byron: — An Oration of the First Class.
    William W. Whitman.
13. The Philosophical Oration: — The Prophetic Power of Philosophy.
    Percival W. Bartlett.
14. The Classical Oration: — The Claims of Liberal Studies upon Professional Men.
    Andrew Croswell.
15. The Education of the Sentiments: — An English Oration; with the Valedictory Addresses. - - - - - - - Robinson P. Dunn.

Parts for Commencement were also assigned to the following members of the Class, who were excused from speaking, viz.:—

1. An Intermediate Oration. - - - - Benjamin Gardner.
2. An Oration of the Second Class. - - - - Lyman Jewett.
3. An Intermediate Oration. - - - - Austin Norcross
4. An Essay. - - - - - - - William R. Pierce.
5. An Oration of the First Class. - - - - Robert B. Smith.
6. An Intermediate Oration. - - - - - Harvey D. Walker.
7. An Oration of the Second Class. - - - - William Walker.

1844.

1. Salutatory Oration in Latin. - - - - Alfred E. Giles.
2. The Trusts committed to the Scholar : — A Disquisition. - Cyrus Bentley.
3. The Poems ascribed to Ossian : — A Dissertation. - Jonathan E. Whitaker.
4. Florence and its Associations : — An Essay. - Elisha D. Vinton.
5. Appeals to Popular Passions : — A Dissertation. - - Cyrus Bean.
6. The Prospects of American Sculpture : — A Disquisition. William S. Barton.
7. The Value of Liberal Education to Mercantile Men : — An Essay.
William G. Pierce.
8. The Courage which arises from fixed Principles : — An Essay. Richard Lentell.
9. The Christian Gladiator : — A Poem. - - - Sylvanus D. Phelps.
10. The Influence of the Imagination upon Moral and Social Character : — An English Oration. - - - - - - Lewis H. Boutell.
11. The Sympathy between Literature and Art : — An English Oration.
William H. Davol.
12. The Principle of Association, and its Influence upon Intellectual Character : — An English Oration. - - - - - Willard Sayles.
13. The Philosophical Oration : — The Metaphysician - Richard Cushman.
14. The Classical Oration : — The Perpetuity of the Ancient Classics.
Joshua P. Converse.
15. The Characteristics and Destiny of American Civilization : — An English Oration ; with the Valedictory Addresses. - - - - James H. Morton.

Parts for Commencement were also assigned to the following members of the Class, who were excused from speaking, viz.:—

1. A Dissertation. - - - - - - - Lucius Lyon.
2. A Dissertation. - - - - - - - William J. Gatling.

1845.

1. Salutatory Oration in Latin. - - - - - - Eli Thayer.
2. The true Culture of the Moral Sentiments: — An Oration of the First Class.
   Samuel Haskell.
3. The Basis of true Soul-Liberty: — A Dissertation. William H. Eaton.
4. Unity of Opinion, not Attainable and not Desirable: — An Oration of the Second Class. - - - - - - - - David B. Ford.
5. The Influence of National Song: — A Dissertation. Thomas S. Drowne.
6. The Progress of American Art: — An Oration of the First Class.
   William H. Fuller.
7. The Influence of a Belief in Man's Immortality, upon Literature: — A Dissertation. - - - - - - - - Solon W. Bush.
8. The Importance of a Right Direction in Social and Philanthropic Efforts: — A Dissertation. - - - - - - - James Andem.
9. Loyalty in a Republic: — An Oration of the Second Class. James M. Keith.
10. The Effects of widely extended Territory upon National Character: — An Oration of the First Class - - - - - George Parks.
11. The First Age of English Literature: — An Oration of the First Class.
    William F. Hansell.
12. The Leading Theories in Geology: — An Oration of the First Class. Isaac F. Cady.
13. The Rise of British Commerce: — An Oration of the Second Class.
    Marshall Woods.
14. The Classical Oration: — The Age of Longinus. James M. Symonds.
15. The Philosophical Oration: — The Results of the Baconian Philosophy.
    John D. E. Jones.
16. The Life of the Man of Genius: — An Oration; with the Valedictory Addresses.
    Charles J. Muenscher.

Parts for Commencement were also assigned to the following members of the Class, who were excused from speaking, viz.:—

1. An Oration of the Second Class - - - - Levi W. Meech.
2. An Oration of the Second Class. - - - - - Cyrus Knowlton.
3. A Dissertation. - - - - - - - Edwin M. Snow.
4. A Dissertation. - - - - - - - Joseph E. Putnam.

1846.

1. The Salutatory Oration in Latin. - - - Franklin J. Dickman.
2. The Influence of Public Libraries: — An Oration of the First Class.
   Elisha C. Mowry.

3. The Spirit of Chivalry in our own Age: — An Essay.   -   James C. Fletcher.
4. The Existing School of English Humorists: — An Oration of the Second Class.
   William W. Pearce.
5. "Non omnis moriar": — An Oration of the Second Class.   Francis Wayland.
6. Hero Worship: — An Intermediate Oration.   -   -   -   Samuel S. Cox.
7. The Manufactures of New England: — A Dissertation.   Thomas C. Greene.
8. The Doom of the Jewish Race: — An Oration of the Second Class.
   Benjamin B. Babbitt.
9. The Political Destinies of Italy: — An Essay.   -   -   William Goddard.
10. The Equality of Human Destiny: — An Oration of the First Class.
    Raymond Lopez.
11. The Restoration to Italy of her Works of Art: — An Oration of the First Class.
    John F. Chapin.
12. Prospective Results of Pacific Relations between England and America: — An Intermediate Oration.   -   -   -   -   -   Aaron W. Chaffin.
13. Faith, the Basis of great Actions: — An Oration of the First Class.   Thomas Durfee.
14. The Classical Oration: — The Power of the Ancient Classics, as tested at the Revival of Learning.   -   -   -   -   -   Stephen Waterman.
15. The Philosophical Oration: — The Philosophy of the Schoolmen.
    Frank W. Anthony.
16. The Friendships of Men of Letters: — An Oration; with the Valedictory Addresses.   -   -   -   -   -   -   Henry I. Coe.

Parts for Commencement were also assigned to the following members of the Class, who were excused from speaking, viz.: —

1. An Intermediate Oration.   -   -   -   -   -   Judson Benjamin.
2. An Intermediate Oration.   -   -   -   -   -   Ebenezer Dawes.
3. A Dissertation.   -   -   -   -   -   -   Francis E. Prevaux.
4. A Dissertation.   -   -   -   -   -   -   Calvin H. Topliff.
5. A Dissertation.   -   -   -   -   -   -   James S. Rogers.
6. An Essay.   -   -   -   -   -   -   Thomas P. I. Goddard.
7. An Essay.   -   -   -   -   -   -   Nathaniel W. Metcalf.
8. An Essay.   -   -   -   -   -   -   Henry L. Rider.

1847.

1. The Salutatory Oration in Latin.   -   -   -   -   Phineas Howe.
2. The Learning of the Arabians: — An Intermediate Oration.   George Capron.
3. Want of National Spirit in American Literature: — A Dissertation.
   Nicholas Hathaway.

4. The Sources of the Scholar's Power: — An Essay. - Charles J. Bowen.
5. International Charity: — An Oration of the First Class. - James P. Boyce.
6. Romance of Uncivilized Life: — An Essay. - - Charles M. Allin.
7. The Permanence of English Civilization: — An Oration of the Second Class.
Edwin Dibell.
8. The Victories of War and the Victories of Peace: — A Poem.
Samuel H. Judson.
9. The Judiciary, as affected by National Character: — An Oration of the First Class, - - - - - - - Thomas H. Ripley.
10. Spanish Colonization in America: — An Oration of the Second Class.
Thomas S. Anthony.
11. The Eloquence of Silence: — An Intermediate Oration. - Joshua J. Ellis.
12. The Scientific Artizan: — An Intermediate Oration. - Elijah B. Stoddard.
13. The Emigrations of our own and of earlier Ages: — An Oration of the First Class. - - - - - - - - Cyrus Garnsey.
14. Utilitarian Education: — An Oration of the First Class. Reuben A. Guild.
15. The Classical Oration: — The Poetic Character of the early Roman Annals.
Ambrose P. S. Stuart.
16. The Philosophical Oration: — The Academy of Plato. - George P. Fisher.
17. The Scepticism of Men of Science: — An Oration; with the Valedictory Addresses, - - - - - - Francis W. Weston.

Parts for Commencement were also assigned to the following members of the Class, who were excused from speaking, viz.: —

1. A Dissertation. - - - - - - - Henry S. Baker.
2. A Dissertation. - - - - - - - Albert H. Campbell.
3. A Dissertation. - - - - - - - Benjamin Thomas.
4. An Essay. - - - - - - - - James W. Lathrop.

1848.

1. Salutatory Oration in Latin. - - - - James E. Leach.
2. The Relation of the Author to his Age: — An Intermediate Oration.
Thomas B. Barnaby.
3. The Social and Moral Results of the increased Facilities of Communication: — An Essay. - - - - - - Joseph H. Bourn.
4. The Mission of St. Patrick to Ireland: — An Oration of the Second Class.
Samuel B. Vernon.
5. Architecture as an Exponent of a Nation's Character: — A Dissertation.
Augustus Hoppin.

COMMENCEMENT EXERCISES. 409

6. The New Netherlanders and their Descendants : — A Dissertation.
George Wolford.
7. Civil Freedom dependent upon pure Christianity : — A Dissertation.
James W. Smith.
8. The Treatment of the Insane : — A Dissertation. - - - George S. Taft.
9. The Remote Connections of Events : — An Oration of the Second Class.
Nehemiah A. Leonard.
10. Florence in the Middle Ages : — An Intermediate Oration. Pendleton Murrah.
11. The Classical Oration : — The Elysium of the Ancient Mythology.
Lafayette Burr.
12. The Ideal and the Real in the Life of the Scholar : — An Oration.
James E. Leach.

Parts for Commencement were also assigned to the following members of the Class, who were excused from speaking, viz. : —

1. An Oration of the Second Class. - - - - - Samuel Breck.
2. The Valedictory. - - - - - - - Jeremiah O. Carr.
3. A Dissertation. - - - - - - - Joseph B. Clark.
4. An Essay. - - - - - - - - Warren B. Clapp.
5. A Dissertation. - - - - - - - George G. Curtiss.
6. An Essay. - - - - - - - - - Miner Frink.
7. An Intermediate Oration. - - - - - Onslow Hemenway.
8. An Oration of the Second Class. - - - - - Jonathan Mabbitt.
9. The Philosophical Oration. - - - - - Alfred F. Wilder.

1849.

1. Salutatory Oration in Latin. - - - - - William E. Tolman.
2. Faith in Social Progress : — An Intermediate Oration. William H. Mills.
3. The Congress of 1774 : — An Intermediate Oration. William H. Alden.
4. Religion as an Element of Poetry : — An Oration of the Second Class.
Horatio Gray.
5. The English Race in America : — An Oration of the Second Class.
James H. Duncan.
6. The Historical Dramas of Shakspeare : — An Oration of the Second Class.
Julian Hartridge.
7. The Prospects of Italian Freedom : — An Oration of the Second Class.
Thomas D. Robinson.
8. The Uses of the Imagination in Philosophy : — An Oration of the Second Class.
Rowland Hazard.

9. Socialism : — An Intermediate Oration. - - - - Lloyd Morton.
10. The Saxons in the Reign of Henry II : — An Intermediate Oration.
   William R. Brownell.
11. The Christians of the High Alps : — An Intermediate Oration.
   Heman L. Wayland.
12. The Scholar in the Fourteenth and in the Nineteenth Century : — An Oration of the First Class. - - - - - - Benjamin F. Thurston.
13. The Philosophical Oration : — The Relations of Speculative Philosophy to Active Life. - - - - - - - - Adin B. Underwood.
14. The Classical Oration : — Roman Pride of Country as exhibited in Roman Literature. - - - - - - - - James Tillinghast.
15. Modern Ideas of Genius : — An Oration ; with the Valedictory Addresses.
   James B. Angell.

Parts for Commencement were also assigned to the following members of the Class, who were excused from speaking, viz. : —

1. An Oration of the First Class. - - - - - John M. Francis.
2. A Dissertation. - - - - - - - - Luther R. Long.
3. A Dissertation. - - - - - - - - John G. Loring.
4. An Oration of the Second Class. - - - - Isaac N. Tourtellott.
5. An Essay. - - - - - - - - Cæsar A. Updike.

1850.

1. The Salutatory Oration in Latin. - - - - George E. Allen.
2. Logic and Wit : — An Intermediate Oration. - - Erastus Worthington.
3. Brahminism : — A Dissertation. - - - - - Stephen W. Price.
4. The Revolutionary Leader : — An Intermediate Oration. Edward L. Pierce.
5. The Office of Poet-Laureate : — An Intermediate Oration. John W. Kennady.
6. The Early Legislation of New England : — An Intermediate Oration.
   James Brown.
7. Hallowed Ground : — An Oration of the First Class. - Charles E. Aaron.
8. Fidelity to the Constitution in Public Men : — An Intermediate Oration.
   Henry C. Rice.
9. The Newspaper Press : — An Oration of the First Class. Alvah W. Godding.
10. The Prometheus of the Grecian Drama : — The Classical Oration.
    Henry F. Lane.
11. Humility in the Character of the Philosopher : — The Philosophical Oration.
    George N. Anthony.

12. The Monastic Scholar:— An Oration; with the Valedictory Addresses.
James O. Murray.

Parts for Commencement were also assigned to the following members of the Class, who were excused from speaking, viz.:—

1. An Intermediate Oration. - - - - - - John Morris.
2. An Intermediate Oration. - - - - - - Jesse H. Buck.
3. An Oration of the Second Class. - - - - Samuel A. Simpson.

1851.

1. The Salutatory Oration in Latin. - - - - Hamilton B. Staples.
2. Diversities in the Estimation of Character:— An Oration. Emmons P. Bond.
3. The Loyalists of the American Revolution:— An Oration. John S. Brayton.
4. The Culture of the Sensibilities as a Part of Education:— An Oration.
Brainard W. Barrows.
5. The Literary Characters of Carlyle and Macaulay:— An Oration.
James B. Simmons.
6. Physics and Metaphysics:— An Oration. - - - Uriah Thomas.
7. The Taste for Politics among the American People:— An Oration.
Frederic Mott.
8. The Claims of Common Sense:— An Oration. - - Edwin H. Heard.
9. The Taste for the Beautiful:— An Oration. - - Asa M. Williams.
10. Passion — An Element of Genius:— An Oration. - Simeon B. Durfee.
11. The Perils of American Civilization:— An Oration. Daniel J. Glazier.
12. The Living Principle of Literature:— The Classical Oration. Jeremiah L. Diman.
13. Philosophical Views of History:— The Philosophical Oration. Alfred Lawton.
14. The true Fruits of Scholarship:— An Oration; with the Valedictory Addresses.
Richard Metcalf.

This was the first Commencement after the introduction of the so called "New System." It was held July 9, and the following year it was held July 14, after which the time was restored to the "first Wednesday in September."

1852.

1. The Salutatory Oration in Latin. - - - - Nathan W. Moore.
2. The Influence of Climate on Mental Development:— An Oration.
Joseph C. Wightman.

3. The Utilitarian Philosophy of the Times : — An Oration. Johnson A. Gardner.
4. The Gladiatorial Shows of Rome : — An Oration. Charles E. Stephens.
5. The Permanent Element of National Prosperity : — An Oration.
   William H. Watson.
6. The Republic of San Marino : — An Oration. - - Frederick O. Barstow.
7. English Travellers in America : — An Oration. - - Allen I. Ormsbee.
8. The Dignity of Agricultural Pursuits : — An Oration. Miles J. Fletcher.
9. Sincerity in Great Men : — An Oration. - - - Clarendon Waite.
10. The Buried Cities of the East : — An Oration. - Thomas F. Richardson.
11. Jerusalem and its Associations : — An Oration. - Edward S. Atwood.
12. The Influence of the Supernatural : — An Oration. George D. Boardman.
13. Virtue an essential Element of true Patriotism : — An Oration.
    William H. Dickinson.
14. The Tendencies of Grecian Mythology : — The Classical Oration.
    Alexander Farnum.
15. The Unity of History : — The Philosophical Oration. Samuel Brooks.
16. Humanity in Literature : — An Oration ; with the Valedictory Addresses.
    Lucius W. Bancroft.

Parts for Commencement were also assigned to the following members of the Class, who were excused from speaking, viz. : —

1. An Oration. - - - - - - George A. Allen.
2. An Oration. - - - - - - - William M. Brooke.
3. An Oration. - - - - - - Ebenezer W. Bloom.
4. An Oration. - - - - - - - Charles H. Parkhurst.
5. An Oration. - - - - - - - Alfred B. Satterlee.
6. An Oration. - - - - - - - Grenville S. Stevens.

1853.

1. The Salutatory Oration in Latin. - - - - Edward T. Caswell.
2. The Popular Patronage of Literature : — An Oration of the Second Class.
   Eaton W. Maxcy, Jr.
3. The Historical Associations of the Tower of London : — An Oration of the First Class. - - - - - - - Lewis F. Smith.
4. The Anglo-Saxon Monasteries : — An Oration of the Second Class.
   DeWitt C. Brown.
5. Written and Spoken Oratory : — An Oration of the Second Class.
   Asa Arnold.

COMMENCEMENT EXERCISES. 413

6. Will — the True Destiny : — An Oration of the Second Class.
Samuel D. Cozzens.
7. The Language of Emblems : — An Oration of the Second Class.
George D. Henderson.
8. The Prospects of Chinese Civilization : — An Oration of the First Class.
Howard M. Jones.
9. The Intellectual Benefits of Scientific Studies : — An Oration of the First Class.
Henry Westcott.
10. The Natural Motors : — An Oration of the Second Class.   Alexander L. Holley.
11. The Conflicts of Popular Opinion : — An Oration of the First Class.
Jared M. Heard.
12. The Supernatural Characters of Shakespeare : — An Oration of the First Class.
Osborn E. Bright.
13. The Commercial Spirit of the Age : — An Oration of the First Class.
John Sanderson, Jr.
14. The Claims of a True Philosophy : — The Philosophical Oration.
William H. Kingsbury.
15. The Extinction of Classical Paganism : — The Classical Oration.
Francis M. McAllister.
16. The Power of Personal Character : — An English Oration; with the Valedictory Addresses. - - - - - - - - Frank S. Bradford.

Parts for Commencement were also assigned to the following members of the Class, who were excused from speaking, viz. : —

1. An Oration of the First Class. - - - - Henry H. Durrington.
2. An Oration of the First Class. - - - - George F. Kilton.
3. An Oration of the First Class. - - - - - Charles T. Miller.
4. An Oration of the First Class. - - - - Isaac M. Murdock.
5. An Oration of the Second Class. - - - - Leonard B. Pratt.
6. An Oration of the First Class. - - - - George H. Woods.

1854.

1. The Salutatory Oration in Latin. - - - - Edward P. Taft.
2. The Civil Code of Napoleon : — An Oration of the First Class.
Everett A. Carpenter.
3. The Aggressive Policy of Russia : — An Oration of the Second Class.
Alexander M. Higgins.
4. Commerce — A Pledge of International Peace : — An Oration of the First Class. - - - - - - - - Charles H. Thompson.

5. The Ideal of the American Drama:—An Oration of the Second Class.
John Goforth.
6. The Last Days of Schiller:—An Oration of the First Class.   Edward L. Davis.
7. The Exile of the French Acadians:—An Oration of the First Class.
Harris R. Greene.
8. The Romance of King Arthur:—An Oration of the Second Class.
Henry C. Parsons.
9. American Forensic Tastes:—An Oration of the Second Class.
George P. Upton.
10. The Genius of Richard Baxter:—An Oration of the First Class.
Bartlett Mayhew, Jr.
11. The Power of Devotion to Principle:—An Oration of the First Class.
John W. Vernon.
12. The Popular Element of Christianity:—An Oration of the First Class.
Thomas Vernon.
13. American Loyalty:—An Oration of the First Class   -   Walter Hillman, Jr.
14. The Martyr Spirit:—An Oration of the First Class.   -   Julius E. Johnson.
15. The Prophetic Power of Historical Philosophy:—The Philosophical Oration.
Horatio N. Slater, Jr.
16. Classical Scholarship—An Element of the Power of the Orator:—The Classical Oration.   -   -   -   -   -   -   William B. Carpenter.
17. The Contemplative Scholar:—An English Oration; with the Valedictory Addresses.   -   -   -   -   -   -   -   Benjamin Braman.

Parts for Commencement were also assigned to the following members of the Class, who were excused from speaking, viz.:—

1.	An Oration of the Second Class.	George B. Cargill.
2.	An Oration of the Second Class.	Alexander W. Couper.
3.	An Oration of the First Class.	Dormer L. Hicock.
4.	An Oration of the First Class.	Henry W. Johnston.
5.	An Oration of the Second Class.	Enos Munger.
6.	An Oration of the First Class.	Nathaniel Pool, Jr.
7.	An Oration of the First Class.	Samuel A. Read.
8.	An Oration of the First Class.	John H. Rogers.
9.	An Oration of the Second Class.	Amos D. Smith, Jr.
10.	An Oration of the Second Class.	Thomas H. Tucker.
11.	An Oration of the Second Class.	Albert G. Utley.
12.	An Oration of the Second Class.	Jared I. Williams.
13.	An Oration of the First Class.	Charles H. Zug.

COMMENCEMENT EXERCISES. 415

After this year the names of those who were excused from speaking are omitted in the original PROGRAMMES.

1855.

1. The Salutatory Oration in Latin. - - - - William G. Dearth.
2. The Daimonion of Socrates: — An Oration of the First Class.
   Richard F. Putnam.
3. The last Days of Copernicus: — An Oration of the First Class.
   Charles F. Holbrook.
4. The Use of the Imagination in Geological Studies: — An Oration of the First Class. - - - - - - - - Theodore D. Warren.
5. The Uses and the Abuses of Biography: — An Oration of the Second Class.
   James W. Brooks.
6. Literature — A Solace in Sorrow: — An Oration of the Second Class.
   Morris B. Morgan.
7. Failures in Science: — An Oration of the Second Class. Cortland Hoppin.
8. Theodore Körner, the Hero-Poet: — An Oration of the First Class.
   Horatio Rogers, Jr.
9. The Power of Names: — An Oration of the First Class. Charles Turner.
10. The Turkish Power in Europe: — An Oration of the First Class.
    Henry D. Williams.
11. The Fiction of Lethe: — An Oration of the First Class. Thomas Simons, Jr.
12. Professional Enthusiasm, an Element of Success: — An Oration of the First Class. - - - - - - Charles Phelps.
13. Young America: — A Poem. - - - - - Marcus Waterman.
14. Comte's Law of Progress in Philosophy: — An Oration of the First Class.
    Albert H. Plumb.
15. The Literary Influence of the English Bible: — An Oration of the First Class.
    George B. Paine.
16. Misanthropy of Byron: — An Oration of the First Class. John F. Tobey.
17. Ecclesiastical Architecture and Religious Faith: — An Oration of the First Class. - - - - - - - - Joseph D. Long.
18. Aristotle and the Schoolmen: — The Philosophical Oration. William J. Batt.
19. The Civilizing Influence of the Olympic Games: — The Classical Oration.
    William H. Pabodie.
20. The Political Obligations of Educated Men: — An English Oration; with the Valedictory Addresses. - - - - - Joseph W. Congdon.

This is the last Commencement at which Dr. Wayland presided. At the close of the exercises Chancellor Tobey, in behalf of the Corporation, addressed the alumni and friends of the University, and also the retiring President, reviewing his long and faithful services, and stating the action of the Corporation in in regard to his resignation.

1856.

1. The Salutatory Oration in Latin. - - - - George L. Stedman.
2. The Influence of Physical Causes on New England Character.
   Charles H. Wood.
3. The Fitness of Military Commanders for Civil Office. - Charles Blake.
4. The Reverses of Lamartine. - - - - - Oliver S. Westcott.
5. The Modern Spirit of Intolerance. - - - Samuel L. Crocker, Jr.
6. The Literary Associations of the Mediterranean. - - John E. Tourtellotte.
7. Cooper's American Novels. - - - - - - Henry C. Ford.
8. Commerce and Civilization. - - - - Nicholas B. Bolles.
9. The Mutual Relations of Spain and America. - William B. Crocker.
10. Ancient and Modern Methods of Philosophical Investigation. Charles H. Alden.
11. The Moral Influence of Æsthetic Culture. - - - Benjamin L. Ray.
12. The Personal Responsibilities of the American Citizen. James M. Cutts, Jr.
13. Milton — The Advocate of Intellectual Freedom. - Ezra H. Heywood.
14. The Educating Power of Physical Science. - - Nathaniel G. Bonney.
15. Franklin before the House of Commons in 1766. - Francis W. White.
16. Patriotism in Literature : — The Philosophical Oration. - Richard Olney.
17. The Form and the Spirit of sound Literary Culture : — An English Oration ; with the Valedictory Addresses. - - - - Charles B. Goff.

This is the first Commencement at which Dr. Sears presided.

1857.

1. The Salutatory Oration in Latin. - - - - - George Tanner.
2. The Fairy Mythology of England : — An Oration. - George W. Carr.
3. Modern Scientific Defenders of Christianity : — An Oration. George H. Marston.
4. Pascal at Port Royal : — An Oration. - - - Elisha S. Aldrich.
5. The Reality of Fiction : — An Oration. - - Alexander T. Britton.
6. The Moorish Conquerors of Granada : — An Oration. - Frederick Paine.

7. The Social Condition of France : — An Oration. - - Thomas Dean.
8. Heathen Prophecies of Christianity : — An Oration. - Aaron C. Lyon.
9. The Sacred Places of New England : — An Oration. - Samuel C. Eastman.
10. The True Aim of Art : — An Oration. - - - Robert H. Ives. Jr.
11. The Development of Milton's Genius : — An Oration. - John B. Brackett.
12. The Classical Oration in Greek. - - - - Edward W. Clarke.
13. The Historic Imagination : — The Philosophical Oration. - Daniel Goodwin.
14. The Scholar's Sympathy with his Age : — An Oration ; with the Valedictory Addresses. - - - - - - - - Edward H. Cutler.

1858.

1. The Salutatory Oration in Latin. - - - - - Arnold Green.
2. True Success : — An Oration of the First Class. Leander C. Manchester.
3. The Pleasures of Mathematical Studies : — An Oration of the First Class.
   Samuel G. Silliman.
4. The Last Gladiatorial Show of Rome : — An Oration of the First Class.
   John L. Snow.
5. Monumental History : — An Oration of the First Class. Aaron H. Nelson.
6. Literary Labors in Old Age : — An Oration of the First Class.
   Henry G. Safford.
7. Chemistry,—A Detector of Crime : — An Oration of the First Class.
   Alfred North.
8. The Madonna,—A Subject for the Painter : — An Oration of the First Class.
   Edward M. Gushee.
9. The Conversion of Constantine : — An Oration of the First Class.
   Robert Millar.
10. The Worship of the Nile : — An Oration of the Second Class. Walter B. Noyes.
11. William the Conqueror, and William the Deliverer : — An Oration of the First Class. - - - - - - - - Howard M. Emerson.
12. The Recreations of Professional Life : — An Oration of the First Class.
    Samuel W. Abbott.
13. The Permanence of Literature : — An Oration of the First Class.
    Francis Mansfield.
14. The Imagination of the North American Indian : — An Oration of the First Class. - - - - - - - - Moses Lyman, Jr.
15. The Claims of Eloquence on the American Scholar : — An Oration of the First Class. - - - - - - - - Charles L. Colby.
16. Art,—A Religious Teacher : — An Oration of the First Class.
    Solon W. Stevens.

17. The Nobility of Intellect :—An Oration of the First Class. Robert B. Chapman.
18. Faust,—The Reflection of Goethe's Character : — An Oration of the First Class.
William B. Phillips.
19. The Dionysia :—The Classical Oration, in Greek. - - Eliab W. Coy.
20. The Philosophy of Spinoza : —The Philosophical Oration. Samuel Thurber.
21. The Unrecognized Power of Character :—An Oration ; with the Valedictory Addresses. - - - - - - - Joseph H. Gilmore.

1859.

1. Latin Salutatory. - - - - - - - Walter M. Potter.
2. Excessive Tendencies to Association : — An Oration of the First Class.
Albert K. Potter.
3. The Shrine of Canterbury : — An Oration of the Second Class.
Charles H. Perry.
4. The Versatility of Sir Walter Raleigh : — An Oration of the First Class.
Adoniram B. Judson.
5. The Illustrative Arts : — An Oration of the Second Class. Lucius S. Bolles.
6. The Tower of London : — An Oration of the First Class. Silas P. Holbrook.
7. The Venetian Dominion of the Sea : — An Oration of the Second Class.
William D. King.
8. The Social Satire of Thackeray : — An Oration of the Second Class.
George L. Porter.
9. The Victories of Peace : — An Oration of the First Class. Charles M. Smith.
10. A Knowledge of History necessary to the Reformer :— An Oration of the Second Class. - - - - - - - - Frederick D. Ely.
11. The Friendship of Goethe and Schiller : — An Oration of the First Class.
Elnathan Judson.
12. The Position of Power :— An Oration of the First Class. Timothy W. Bancroft.
13. The Future of the Slavic Race : — An Oration of the First Class.
Charles H. Brown.
14. The Melancholy of Cowper : — An Oration of the First Class.
Samuel T. Poinier.
15. Latin — The Language of Scholars : — An Oration of the First Class.
David Weston.
16. The Decline of Imagination in Old Age : — The Philosophical Oration.
Thomas F. Tobey.
17. The Scholar's Sentiment of Veneration for the Past :— An Oration ; with the Valedictory Addresses. - - - - - William W. Keen, Jr.

The valedictory honors of the Class were awarded by the Faculty to Edward Lawton Barker, of Newport, who declined them for the same reason that the class of 1835 refused to become candidates for degrees.

1860.

1. The Salutatory Oration in Latin. - - - - Horace S. Bradford.
2. The Eloquence of Political Revolutions: — An Oration of the First Class.
   Granville S. Abbott.
3. The Author's Dependence on the Public: — An Oration of the First Class.
   Benjamin F. Pabodie.
4. The Youth of Milton: — An Oration of the First Class. William Grosvenor, Jr.
5. New England Character developed by Local Causes: — An Oration of the First Class. - - - - - - - - Robert G. Johnson.
6. Arabian Fiction: — An Oration of the First Class. - George W. Hall.
7. Monumental Testimony to the Historic Truth of the Scriptures: — An Oration of the First Class. - - - - - - - - Wayland Hoyt.
8. The Battle Fields of the Po: — An Oration of the Second Class.
   Henry J. Spooner.
9. The Creative Power of Writers of Fiction: — An Oration of the First Class.
   Francis M. Pond.
10. The Law of Intellectual Sacrifice: — An Oration of the First Class.
    Henry K. Porter.
11. The Organizing Power of a Principle. — An Oration of the First Class.
    Adoniram J. Gordon.
12. The Social Discipline of College Life: — An Oration of the First Class.
    Howard M. Rice.
13. The Classical Oration in Greek. - - - - James D. Perry, Jr.
14. Healthy Scepticism: — The Philosophical Oration. - Samuel W. Duncan.
15. The Philosophic Method of Study: — An Oration; with the Valedictory Addresses. - - - - - - Franklin B. Gamwell.

Parts for Commencement were also assigned to the following members of the Class, who were excused from speaking, viz.:—

1. An Oration of the First Class. - - - - Martin Bennett, Jr.
2. An Oration of the Second Class. - - - Joseph G. Chapman.
3. An Oration of the First Class. - - - - George W. Ketcham.

BROWN UNIVERSITY.

4. An Oration of the First Class. - - - - - John S. Larwill.
5. An Oration of the First Class. - - - - William M. Ledwith.
6. An Oration of the First Class. - - - - - Horace G. Miller.
7. An Oration of the Second Class. - - - - Frederick A. Mitchel.
8. An Oration of the Second Class. - - - - John Whipple, Jr.

The practice adopted in 1855, of omitting from the PROGRAMMES the names of those who are excused from speaking, seems to have been departed from this year, and also the two years immediately following.

1861.

1. The Salutatory Oration in Latin. - - - - Albert N. Drown.
2. The Immortality of Literature : — An Oration of the First Class.
George M. Daniels.
3. Heroic Ignorance : — An Oration of the First Class. George A. Holbrook.
4. Truth of Manner in Literature : — An Oration of the First Class,
Elisha C. Mowry.
5. The Oratory of Henry Clay : — An Oration of the First Class. John J. Ely.
6. The Justifiableness of War : — An Oration of the First Class.
Charles F. Hosmer.
7. Charles Dickens, — A Reformer of Legal Abuses : — An Oration of the First Class. - - - - - - - Henry M. Lovering.
8. The Poetry of the Legends of King Arthur : — An Oration of the First Class.
Charles H. Lincoln.
9. The Dignity of the Mechanic Arts : — An Oration of the Second Class.
Stephen A. Cooke, Jr.
10. Sir Walter Scott,—The Painter of Chivalry : — An Oration of the First Class.
Frank H. Carpenter.
11. Naval Supremacy : — An Oration of the First Class. John K. Bucklyn.
12. The Brahmin Caste of New England : — An Oration of the First Class.
Henry S. Burrage.
13. The Love of Old Books :—An Oration of the First Class. Sumner U. Shearman.
14. The Confessions of Augustine and of Rousseau : — An Oration of the First Class. - - - - - - - William W. Douglas
15. Patriotic Scholarship : — An Oration of the First Class. Charles M. Stead.
16. The Purity of the Ideal of Christianity,—An Evidence of its Divine Origin : — The Philosophical Oration. - - - - Edward O. Stevens.

17. The Tragic Element in Greek Thought : — The Classical Oration
William H. Randall.
18. The Evils of Self-Consciousness :—An Oration ; with the Valedictory Addresses.
Isaac B Barker

Parts for Commencement were also assigned to the following members of the Class, who were excused from speaking, viz. :—

1. An Oration of the First Class. - - - - - Charles D. Cady.
2. An Oration of the First Class. - - - - - Charles H. Chapman.
3. An Oration of the Second Class. - - - - Thomas H. Edsall.
4. An Oration of the Second Class. - - - Charles H. Hidden.
5. An Oration of the Second Class. - - - - George O. Hopkins.
6. An Oration of the First Class. - - - - - Charles Matteson.
7. An Oration of the First Class. - - - - Alfred D. Thomas.
8. An Oration of the First Class. - - - - Washington B. Trull.
9. An Oration of the First Class. - - - - James C. Williams.

At the time of the final examinations and the assignment of parts, the following members of the Class were absent from College serving as volunteers in the army of the United States; they were therefore not appointed to speak :—

James A. DeWolf,   *Leland D. Jenckes,   Frederick M. Sackett.
William W. Hoppin, Jr.,   John W. Rogers,

1862.

1. Salutatory Oration in Latin. - - - - - Henry F. Colby.
2. National Policy determined by Commercial Interest : — An Oration of the First Class. - - - - - - - - Josiah R. Goddard.
3. Modern Lay Preachers : — An Oration of the First Class. † Frank W. Draper.
4. The Originality of Shakspeare : — An Oration of the First Class.
Isaac H. Saunders.
5. The Ministry of Science to Human Life : — An Oration of the First Class.
John D. Thurston.
6. The Conflict of Opinion and Interest : — An Oration of the First Class.
Henry C. Carr.
7. The Poetry of Popery : — An Oration of the First Class.   † George T. Woodward.

* Wounded and taken prisoner at Manassas.
† Enlisted in the army after preparing his Oration.

8. The Patriotic Influence of National Monuments: — An Oration of the First Class. - - - - - - - - - William D. Martin.
9. De Gasparin's Sympathy with the United States: — An Oration of the First Class - - - - - - - - Lucius H. Niles.
10. The Artistic Aspirations of Raphael: — An Oration of the First Class.
    John E. Lester.
11. The Physical Conditions of Poetical Productiveness: — An Oration of the First Class. - - - - - - - - *William I. Brown.
12. The Rewards of Authorship: — An Oration of the First Class.
    Thomas L. Angell.
13. The Perpetuated Growths of Early Years: — An Oration of the First Class.
    Francis A. Daniels.
14. The Sanctuaries of Decaying Language: — An Oration of the First Class.
    Josiah N. Cushing.
15. The Spontaneous Nature of Morality: — The Philosophical Oration.
    Thomas B. Stockwell.
16. The Origin of the Classic Myths: — The Classical Oration. Frederic Sherman.
17. The Scholar's Relations to Humanity: — An Oration; with the Valedictory Addresses. - - - - - - - James H. Remington.

Parts for Commencement were also assigned to the following members of the Class, who were excused from speaking, viz.: —

1. An Oration of the First Class. - - - - William M. Bailey, Jr.
2. An Oration of the First Class. - - - - - David S. H. Smith.
3. An Oration of the First Class. - - - - - Jason B. Kelly.

At the time of the final examinations and the assignment of parts, the following members of the Class were absent from College, serving as volunteers in the army of the United States; they were therefore not appointed to speak: —

Joshua M. Addeman,   Joshua Mellen,   Addison Parker, Jr.

1863.

1. The Salutatory Oration in Latin. - - - - Charles C. Cragin.
2. Absolute Truth — The Life of Literature: — An Oration of the First Class.
   Samuel R. Dorrance.

* Enlisted in the army after preparing his Oration.

3. Esprit de Corps: — An Oration of the Second Class. Frederick B. Sears.
4. Polish Nationality: — An Oration of the First Class. Samuel H. Pratt.
5. The Gothic Army-Bible: — An Oration of the First Class. Charles F. Taylor.
6. Spectrum-Analysis: — An Oration of the First Class. John H. Appleton.
7. The Accountability of Writers of Fiction:—An Oration of the First Class.
   Orville B. Seagrave.
8. Oratory in a Republic: — An Oration of the First Class. Daniel J. Holbrook.
9. The Labors of Erasmus: — An Oration of the First Class. Frank D. Douglass.
10. The Coliseum and St. Peter's — Each a Type of the Rome of its Day: — An Oration of the First Class. - - - - - Oscar B. Mowry.
11. The Office of the Semitic Tongues in Human Culture: — An Oration of the First Class. - - - - - - George H. Greene.
12. The Prospects of American Literature in case of Disunion: — An Oration of the First Class. - - - - - - George W. Calkins.
13. Character — A Power: — An Oration of the First Class. Forrest F. Emerson.
14. The Bible in Modern Poetry: — An Oration of the First Class.
    George H. Miner.
15. The Dignity of Trifles: — An Oration of the First Class. Benjamin F. Clarke.
16. The Platonic View of Mathematics: — The Philosophical Oration.
    Henry S. Latham, Jr.
17. The Greek Temple — A Representative of Greek Life: — The Classical Oration.
    Denham Arnold.
18. The Perpetuation of College Discipline in after Life: — An Oration; with the Valedictory Addresses. - - - - - Charles P. Robinson.

1864.

1. The Salutatory Oration in Latin. - - - - Henry B. Miner.
2. Diversity in the Forms of the State: — An Oration of the First Class.
   Frank W. Love.
3. Morality in the Development of Genius: — An Oration of the First Class.
   John S. Holmes.
4. The French and the English Revolutionary Spirit: — An Oration of the First Class. - - - - - - - *Francis M. Tyler.
5. The Puritan Spirit of New England: — An Oration of the First Class.
   George B. Barrows.
6. Competitive Examinations for Public Place: — An Oration of the First Class.
   Henry B. Whitman.

* Absent on account of enlistment for one hundred days.

7. Leadership — An Oration of the First Class. - - - Luther White.
8. St. Bartholomew's Day : — An Oration of the First Class. Henry C. Bowen.
9. Swiss Liberty : — An Oration of the First Class. - - Ratcliffe Hicks.
10. The Democratic Tendencies of Commerce : — An Oration of the First Class.
   David Fales.
11. The Providence of God in History : — An Oration of the First Class.
   Lewis F. Raymond.
12. Individuality essential to Success : — An Oration of the First Class.
   Joshua F. Ober.
13. Literary Dissipation : — An Oration of the First Class. - Benjamin C. Dean.
14. The Norman Element in English Civilization : — An Oration of the First Class.
   Amos Robinson.
15. Hawthorne's Delineation of Early New England Society : — An Oration of the First Class. - - - - - - - George F. Jelly.
16. The Significance of Preparation : — An Oration of the First Class.
   George H. Hurlbert.
17. The Argument of Success : — An Oration of the First Class.
   George M. Carpenter, Jr.
18. The Laws of a Nation — an Exponent of its Religion : — An Oration of the First Class. - - - - - - Frank T. Hazlewood.
19. The Utility of Scientific Research : — An Oration of the First Class.
   Samuel F. Hancock.
20. The Scotch Covenanters as presented in " Old Mortality: " — An Oration of the First Class. - - - - - - James W. Colwell.
21. The Faust Legend : — An Oration of the First Class. - Charles E Willard.
22. The Uses of the Imagination in Scientific Investigation : — The Philosophical Oration. - - - - - - Seth J. Axtell, Jr.
23. The Ideal Man of Socrates : — The Classical Oration. - Charles T. Lazell.
24. The True Glory of a College : — An Oration ; with the Valedictory Addresses.
   John Tetlow, Jr.

This will be remembered as the Commencement immediately succeeding the celebration of the one hundredth anniversary of the founding of the University. President Sears's discourse upon this occasion, with an appendix and an account of the Centennial Dinner, was published by S. S. Rider & Brother. It makes an octavo volume of one hundred and seventy-eight pages.

1865.

1. The Salutatory Oration in Latin. - - - - Minor R. Deming.
2. The Consecration of Hildebrand: — An Oration of the First Class.
   Charles H. Spaulding.
3. The Rome of Juvenal: — An Oration of the First Class. Reuben M. Streeter.
4. The Compensations of War: — An Oration of the First Class. Caleb E. Thayer.
5. Instability of British Sentiment towards the United States: — An Oration of the First Class. - - - - - - Jared W. Finney.
6. Specific Aims in Education: — An Oration of the First Class. George W. Gile.
7. Napoleon's Life of Cæsar: — An Oration of the Second Class.
   James K. Lawrence.
8. The Condition of the British Miner: — An Oration of the First Class.
   Joseph W. Rees.
9. The Saracens in Europe: — An Oration of the First Class. Oliver H. Arnold.
10. The Novelist as a Teacher: — An Oration of the First Class.
    William D. U. Shearman.
11. Training for Political Life: — An Oration of the First Class.
    Charles F. Easton.
12. The Modern Spirit of Persecution: — An Oration of the First Class.
    Mark D. Shea.
13. The Romantic Element in Early American History: — An Oration of the First Class. - - - - - - - Joseph E. Spink.
14. Greece — the Home of True Philosophy: — An Oration of the First Class.
    Richard M. Atwater.
15. The Economy of Mental Growth: — An Oration of the First Class.
    William H. Williams.
16. The Historic Preparations for Christianity: — An Oration of the First Class.
    George W. Shaw.
17. American Influence in Europe: — An Oration of the First Class. Joseph Ward.
18. The Prophetic Pledge of Unrealized Ideals: — An Oration of the First Class.
    Edward W. Pride.
19. The Myth of Prometheus Vinctus: — The Classical Oration. Edward Judson.
20. The Law of Self-Sacrifice: — An Oration; with the Valedictory Addresses.
    Warren R. Perce.

1866.

1. The Salutatory Oration in Latin. - - - - Arnold B. Chace.
2. The Slow Development of Correct Political Principles. - Nelson N. Glazier.
3. The Sentiment of Disgust. - - - - - LaRoy F. Griffin.

4. The Secret of Popularity. - - - - - - Lorin M. Cook.
5. The Influence of the New England Town-System on the Character and Condition of the American People. - - - - - - George O. King.
6. Dies Iræ. - - - - - - - - Reginald H. Howe.
7. Literary Inconstancy. - - - - - - Alexander D. Chapin.
8. The Influence of Ocean Life. - - - - - John B. Mustin.
9. The Evils of Living in Small Places. - - - James W. Blackwood.
10. A Knowledge of Men — Essential to Success. - - Cyrus B. Peckham.
11. The Socratic Method. - - - - - - - John J. Archer.
12. Heroic Doubt. - - - - - - - William H. Spencer.
13. The Attractiveness of Pantheism. - - - - John B. Peck.
14. The Decline of British Political Influence. - - Herbert C. Bullard.
15. The Influence of French Philosophy on American Institutions.
    Samuel H. Albro.
16. Organic Development — The Universal Law. - - Preston Gurney.
17. Unconscious Inheritances. - - - - - Francis A. Gaskill.
18. The Poet of "The Christian Year." - - - Emery H. Porter.
19. Dimly Seen Characters of History. - - - Laban E. Warren.
20. The Advantages of Liberal Culture to Non-Professional Men. Henry H. Earl.
21. The Poetical Element of Philosophy : — The Philosophical Oration.
    Charles A. G. Thurston.
22. Aristotle and Alexander — Teacher and Pupil : — The Classical Oration.
    Cornelius S. Sweetland, Jr.
23. The Thought of the Future, — An Incentive to Effort : — An Oration ; with the Valedictory Addresses. - - - - - - John B. G. Pidge.

APPENDIX.

RESIGNATION OF PRESIDENT SEARS.

WHILE these sheets are passing through the press, we learn with heartfelt sorrow, that Dr. Sears has resigned the Presidency of the University, having been appointed the General Agent of the Board of Trustees of the PEABODY EDUCATIONAL FUND. A special meeting of the Corporation, called to act upon his resignation and to choose a successor, was held on Wednesday, April 17, 1867. Forty-three members were present, constituting the largest meeting ever held. Of the FELLOWS who were absent, Mr. Alexander Duncan was in Europe, and the Hon. Isaac Davis, of Worcester, was detained at home in consequence of indisposition. Three only of the TRUSTEES were absent, viz.: the Hon. Edward Mellen, of Worcester, Mr. Stephen A. Chase, of Salem, and Mr. Richard J. Arnold, who was in Georgia. The following account of the proceedings of this meeting, together with the resolutions adopted, we copy from the PROVIDENCE JOURNAL:—

After President Sears retired, the Hon. James H. Duncan, the senior member of the Board of Fellows, took the chair.

The resignation of President Sears having been accepted, the Hon. William S. Patten offered the following resolutions, which were unanimously adopted:—

WHEREAS, The Reverend Barnas Sears, President of the University, having been appointed General Agent of the Board of Trustees of the Peabody Educational Fund for the benefit of the South and Southwestern States, recently instituted by George Peabody, Esq., which office requires entire devotion to its duties, and considering the magnitude and importance of its claims to be paramount, has tendered his resignation of the Presidency of this University, to take effect on the day after the next succeeding Commencement, September 5th : —

RESOLVED, That the Corporation of Brown University accept the resignation of President Sears with the sincerest regret.

RESOLVED, That while they release the President from the charge of this University with profound sorrow, they cannot but admit the preëminence of the claims involved in this new appointment, and of his qualifications to fulfill them.

RESOLVED, That our experience of those qualifications during his twelve years administration of the Presidency, manifested by his piety, learning and suavity, by his watchfulness over the interests of the University, his general ability and his great success, demands our commendation and receives our gratitude.

RESOLVED, That we congratulate the Trustees of the Peabody Educational Fund, and its noble and munificent founder, that in initiating their grand design to disseminate universal knowledge and patriotism, they have secured so adequate an agent and coadjutor.

RESOLVED, That this Corporation, rejoicing and sympathizing with them, in that design, heartily bid them "God speed;" and deeply as we feel the sacrifice we are called to make, we make it as our contribution to the same cause to which, on a scope less ample, our own "catholic, comprehensive and liberal Institution" has been consecrated for more than a century, to wit, in the words and spirit of our Charter, that of "forming the rising generation to virtue, knowledge, and useful literature ; and thus preserving in the community a succession of men duly qualified for discharging the offices of life with usefulness and reputation."

RESOLVED, As a memorial of our affection and respect for President Sears, and of our interest in the great purpose which he is called from us to promote, that these resolutions be entered upon our records; that a copy of them, signed by the Chancellor and Secretary of the University, be presented to him; and that a similar copy be communicated to George Peabody, Esq.

It was voted that a committee of three Fellows and five Trustees be appointed to report a nomination for President. This committee, after full deliberation, unanimously reported the name of Martin B. Anderson, LL. D., President of Rochester University, New York. The vote was then taken, and resulted in the unanimous choice of Dr. Anderson.

APPENDIX. 429

Whereupon the Rev. Dr. Woods offered the following resolution: —

RESOLVED, That Rev. Baron Stow, D. D., Rev. Edwards A. Park, D. D., and S. S. Bradford, Esq., with such other three persons, from the Trustees, as may be nominated by the Chancellor, be a committee to wait personally on the President elect, Dr. M. B. Anderson, and urgently solicit his acceptance of the Presidency of Brown University, to which he has been elected with entire unanimity, and that he be requested to enter upon the duties of his office September 5th, 1867.

The President elect was born in Bath, Maine. He graduated at Waterville College, now Colby University, in 1840, and after having pursued, for a time, studies in divinity at Newton Theological Institution, was elected to the Professorship of Rhetoric at Waterville, which office he filled for seven years. He afterwards edited with marked ability the NEW YORK RECORDER, the organ of the Baptist denomination at the time in the city of New York. In 1853, he was called to the Presidency of Rochester University, which office he has continued to fill, with rare ability and with remarkable success. Twenty-one years of his life have thus been devoted to the labors of collegiate education, so that he is eminently qualified by long experience, for the important office to which he has been so unanimously elected.

Before taking our leave of President Sears, we may be allowed to express the universal regret that is manifest at his resignation, especially on the part of his pupils, by whom he is everywhere regarded with almost filial love and veneration. In leaving an office which he has filled with such distinguished honor and usefulness for the past twelve years, it is pleasant to record the unanimity with which he has been appointed to a new and more important position by men of the highest eminence from all parts of the land, and to reflect that while the University, and the community around it, for the time being, lose by this sacrifice, the country at large gains. It is pleasant also to observe the cordial endorsement which this appointment receives from the

PRESS. The BOSTON TRANSCRIPT, in illustration, thus happily remarks:—

Thus by a combination of sagacity and good fortune on the part of those having the management of the fund, the right man has been found for the right place. Dr. Sears, indeed, unites qualities for the position which, rare in their separate excellence, are rarer still in their harmonious combination. He is a scholar of large accomplishments and vigorous talents, and at the same time a master of the practical methods of education. One of the most indefatigable of students, he has none of the bigotry, pedantry and exclusiveness which sometimes accompany exceptional acquirements, but possesses his learning instead of being possessed by it. As Secretary of the Massachusetts Board of Education, he amply proved his capacity to comprehend the wants of the common school system, and as President of Brown University he has shown no less facility in directing the studies of a college. A man of the highest moral and religious character, keen in the perception and resolute in the performance of duty, honest, manly and intrepid, he is still so dispassionate and unostentatious in his conscientiousness, and so simply bent on addressing the intellect and moral sense of those he desires to influence, that he never stings their passions into opposition to his teachings, nor rouses their willfulness to resist the reception of his views. He has, in short, all the reality of force, without any of its arrogance.

INDEX OF BENEFACTORS.

NOTE. The following is simply an index of the NAMES of those persons, whose BENEFACTIONS are recorded upon the pages of our work. For the "Commencement Exercises" no index is required, the TRIENNIAL CATALOGUE giving the names of all graduates of the College, with the year of their graduation. The necessity for a general index of subjects is obviated by the full table of contents at the beginning, and by the peculiar arrangement of the book.

ABELL, Joseph,	154	ALLEN, Bradford,	328
AHORN, Benjamin,	273	ALLEN, Crawford,	328
AHORN, Burrows,	257	ALLEN, John, of Dublin,	155
AHORN, Samuel,	258	ALLEN, John, of London,	159
ABRAM, John,	224	ALLEN, Paul,	239
ADAMS, Martha,	158	ALLEN, Philip,	258, 326
ADAMS, Seth,	258	ALLEN, Philip, Jr.	102, 326
ADAMS, Seth, Jr.	94, 273, 301, 326, 335	ALLEN, Philip & Son,	273, 289
		ALLEN, Samuel,	160
ADAMS & LOTHROP	257	ALLEN, Samuel P.	258
ADIE, Alexander,	258	ALLEN, Stephen G.	333
ADIE, A. F.	328	ALLEN, Zachariah,	273, 326
ADLAM, Thomas,	160	ALLIN, Francis,	154
AGITT, Joseph,	154	ALMY, Benjamin R.	327
AICKIN, James,	154	ALMY, William,	258
AIGOIN, David,	155	AMES, Asa,	257, 258
AIGOIN, Miss,	155	AMES, Ellis,	328
ALEXANDER, Robert,	156	AMES, James B.	328
ALLARD, Thomas,	160	AMES, Samuel,	257
ALLEN, Benjamin,	240	ANDREWS, Benjamin,	222

ANDREWS, James,	239
ANDREWS, Zephaniah,	240
ANGELL, Francis M.	222
ANGELL, Philip M.	222
ANGELL, Abraham,	240
ANGELL, Charles,	240
ANGELL, Nathan,	239
ANTHONY, Henry,	327, 335
ANTHONY, Henry B.	274, 334
ANTHONY, Hezekiah,	327
APLIN, John,	240
APPLETON, Nathan,	327
APPLETON, Samuel,	327
APPLETON, William,	91, 327
ARMSTRONG, John,	155
ARMSTRONG, Robert,	155
ARMSTRONG, Samuel T.	155
ARNOLD, Christopher,	239
ARNOLD, Frances R.	86, 94, 311
ARNOLD, James,	85, 240, 326

BROWN UNIVERSITY.

Arnold, James, Jr.	240	Beckman, Nicholas,	158	Bowles, John,	158
Arnold, Jonathan,	239	Beckwith, Truman,	273, 335	Box, Philip,	222
Arnold, Joseph,	239	Bedgegood, Nicholas,	223	Boyce, James P.	327
Arnold, Nathan,	239	Bee, William,	222	Boyd, John,	221
Arnold, Richard J.		Bell, Charles,	156	Brading, Elizabeth,	155
86, 273, 327		Bell, Henry,	156	Bradley, Charles S.	94, 327
Arnold, Salmon,	257	Bell, John,	156	Bradford, S. S.	311
Arnold, Samuel G.	80, 257	Bell, Thomas, of Antrim,	156	Bradford, Solomon,	240
Arnold, Samuel G.		Bell, Thomas, of London,	158	Brailsford & Muncreeff,	
94, 326, 332		Belknap, Abraham,	239		221
Arnold, Thomas,	257	Belknap, Jacob,	239	Branch, Sanford,	257
Arnold, Welcome,	239	Belknap, Jeremy,	73	Branford, Ezekiel,	222
Ashton, Thomas,	157	Bellamy, Clement,	158	Brayton, Isaac,	239
Atchison, John,	156	Benn, Elizabeth,	155	Brennon, James,	157
Atkins, Charles,	222	Bennet, Job,	238, 318, 319	Bridgham, Samuel W.	
Atkinson, John,	155	Bennet, Thomas,	240	86, 258, 273	
Atwell, Ichabod,	221	Benson, George,	76	Brimble, John,	160
Atwell, Moses M.	258	Bewfey, Nehemiah,	161	Brine, Mary,	159
Axson, William,	223	Bible, Thomas, of Cork,	154	Brisbane, James,	222
Babbitt Jacob,	328	Bible, Thomas, of Dublin,	155	Bristol Education Society,	
Babcock, Joshua,	318	Billings, Ethelbert R.	293		71, 72
Babcock & Moss,	327	Binney, Amos,	86	Brittain, William,	159
Bacon, Elijah,	239	Bird, Francis W.	328	Brock, Benjamin,	160
Backus, Isaac,	77, 319, 337	Bishop, Nathan,	327	Brocks, Samuel,	319
Baddeley, Susanna,	223	Blackley, John,	156	Brooks, B. F.	334
Bagnal, Timothy,	156	Blake, Ezekiel,	334	Brooks, Mrs. S. E.	313
Bagnal, Timothy, Jr.	156	Blake, M.	160	Brown, Avis,	75
Bailey, William M.	335	Blake, William,	327	Brown, Benjamin F.	334
Balch, Joseph, Jr.	274	Bland, Lancelot,	222	Brown, Chad,	240
Balch, J. P. & Son,	280, 335	Bland, Richard,	222	Brown, Dexter,	240
Baldwin, Thomas,	76	Blight, Caleb,	160	Brown, Elizabeth,	154
Ball, Judith,	221	Blodget, William,	257	Brown, Elizabeth & Rebecca,	
Ballantine, Susanna,	222	Blood, Caleb,	322		160
Ballou, C. A.	274	Bolles, James G.	332	Brown, George,	239
Banett, John,	159	Bolles, Lucius,	80, 86, 258	Brown, Gideon,	240
Banister, J.	159	Bolles, Matthew,	334	Brown, Isaac,	274, 327
Barclay, D. & J.	158	Bond, Thomas,	155	Brown, James,	86, 257
Barker, Peleg,	319	Boon, Benjamin,	161	Brown, Jeremiah,	240
Barlow, Robert,	158	Boorom, Isaac,	257	Brown, John,	68, 240, 242
Barnes, David L.	258	Booth, James,	155		320, 335
Barrow, John,	155	Booth, Thos., of Dublin,	155	Brown, John, of Bristol,	160
Barry, James,	240	Booth, Thomas, of West-		Brown, J., of Canterbury,	161
Barstow, Amos C.	327, 335	meath,	157	Brown, J., of Waterford,	154
Barstow, John,	86, 273, 327	Borden, Jefferson,	332, 333	Brown, John Carter,	45, 80
Bartlett, John R.	285-294	Boswood, Samuel,	222	91, 92, 94, 95-98, 101, 102	
Bartol, Elizabeth H.	81	Bosworth, Alfred,	328	268, 270, 276, 280, 286, 288	
Bartol, George M.	328	Bosworth, A. & S.	258	292, 300-302, 326, 332	
Barton, Charles,	159	Bosworth, Lewis,	240	Brown & Ives,	80, 258, 286
Baskerville, George,	158	Boulton, William,	155	Brown, Joseph,	222, 240
Batchellor, Richard,	161	Bowdlear, N. G.	334	Brown, Mary,	238
Batty, Ephraim,	239	Bowen, Ephraim,	257	Brown, Molly,	239
Baylies, William,		Bowen, Jabez, Jr.	239	Brown, Moses,	69, 240
86, 94, 327, 337		Bowen, John,	85	Brown, Nicholas,	
Beal, John,	222	Bowen, Oliver,	241	240, 275, 318	
Beal, Othniel,	221	Bowen, Tully D.	327, 334	Brown, Hon. Nicholas, 26, 27	
Beale, Caleb,	154	Bowen, William,	258	46, 47, 71, 76, 85, 87, 257	
Beale, Samuel,	154	Bowers, John,	257	261-270, 273, 300-302, 308-	
Beath, William,	156	Bowles, Carrington,	159	310, 323, 328, 335, 337, 338	

INDEX OF BENEFACTORS. 433

Brown, Obadiah,	258	Carlile, John,	258	Cobb, Martin,	223
Brown, Phineas,	239	Carlile, John S.	257	Cobb, Nathaniel R.	85
Brown, Richard,	240	Carlile, Thomas,	77	Codd, John,	157
Brown, Sarah,	159	Carlton, George,	327	Coffin, Timothy G.	86
Brown, Thomas,	328	Carlton, Mr.	159	Colby, Gardner, 311, 332, 333	
Brown, William,	240	Carpenter, Joseph,	327	Colby, H. G. O.	86
Bryan, Guy,	159	Carpenter, Lydia,	314–316	Cole, Andrew,	240
Bryan, Jonathan,	222	Carpenter, Thomas F.		Cole, John,	160
Bryant, Caleb,	160		86, 274	Colgate, George,	86
Bryson, James,	155	Carrington, Edward, 80, 326		Colgate, William,	86
Buckland, Mary,	160	Carter, John,	75	Collier, Richard,	240
Bucknell, Margaret C.	312	Carver, Robert,	238	Collins, Francis,	160
Buckley, Charles,	158	Caswell, Alexis, 86, 273, 327		Coleman, Robert,	160
Bull, Frederick,	158	Cattle, Robert & Sarah,	222	Coles, Thomas,	258
Bull, Isaac M.	326	Chace, George I. 86, 273, 327		Colvin, Stephen,	240
Bull, J. & F.	159	Champe, Bean,	155	Combes, Mr.	159
Bull, Thomas,	222	Champion, J.	159	Comstock, Jesse,	258
Bull, William.	221	Champion & Dickason,	158	Conder, John,	158
Bulline, John,	222	Chandle, B.	160	Cone, Spencer H.	86
Bulline, William,	222	Chandler, Benjamin T.	258	Congdon, Gilbert,	328
Bulliott, Mr.	221	Chandler, Isaac,	222	Connor, Rachel,	155
Bullock, Israel,	258	Chapin, Amory,	94, 273	Converse, Benjamin B.	334
Bullock, Julia, 280, 292, 326		Chapin, Henry,	328	Converse, James W. 327, 334	
Bullock, Richmond,	257	Chapin, John F.	280, 334	Converse, Joseph H.	334
Bullock, William P. 274, 326		Chapin, Josiah.	273, 327	Cooke, George,	221
Burch, Joseph,	158	Chapin, Royal,	327	Cooke, James W.	328
Burden, Francis,	156	Chapin, W. & G.	327	Cooke, Nicholas,	239
Burdock, Sarah,	160	Chase, Hezekiah S.		Coon, Elizabeth,	221
Burges, Tristam,	80, 258		311, 327, 334	Cooper, John,	159
Burges, Walter S.	274, 327	Chase, J. G.	334	Cords, Samuel,	221
Burgess, Ebenezer,	86	Cherry, David,	160	Corliss, John,	257
Burgess, J. D.	328	Chickley, William,	239	Cornish, Edward,	161
Burgess, Thomas,		Child, John T.	258	Cornwall, Alexander,	157
86, 94, 273, 327		Childs, Charles H.	328	Cornwall, John,	157
Burgess, Thomas M.	273	Chilson, Gardner,	334	Cottle, Robert,	160
Burhloe, Richard,	222	Chisnut, John,	223	Cowles, William,	160
Burnside, Ambrose E.		Chrisholme, John,	222	Cox, Leader,	150
292, 334		Church, William,	257	Cox, Manuel,	223
Burnside Rifle Co.	292	Church of Ashford,	161	Cox, Thomas,	159
Burnside, John,	159	Church of Folkstone,	161	Coy, Samuel,	240
Burrill, James,	240	Church of Hythe,	161	Cozzens, Benjamin W.	94
Burrill, James, Jr.	258	Church of Smardin,	161	Cranston, Robert B.	328
Burrough, James,	240	Churches of Providence,		Crawley, T.	159
Burrows, William,	221		103–104	Creighton, Joseph,	223
Bushell, S.	155	Clarke, John,	161	Creighton, William,	221
Butler, Elizabeth,	158	Clarke, Nicholas,	239	Crocker, Nathan B. 109, 258	
Butler, Henry,	292	Clarke, Robert,	221	Crocker, Samuel L.	86
Butler, Joseph,	161	Clarke, T. P.	258	Crocker, William A.	86
Butler, Samuel,	240	Clarke, William,	158	Crocker & Brothers,	326
Cahael, James,	159	Clarke & Nightingale,	239	Cromwell, Oliver,	221
Caldwell, S. A.	334	Clarkson, William,	221	Crosby, William B.	86
Caldwell, William,	156	Class of 1821,	103	Cross, Ann,	161
Cambridge, Peter,	154	Cleaveland, Ira,	328	Cross, William J.	327
Canty, John,	223	Clifford, Benjamin,	257	Crouch, Charles,	221
Carfly, John,	160	Clifford, John H.	86	Crowly, Humphry,	154
Carey Av. Bap. Church,	334	Clunie, Alexander,	159	Cummings, George,	326
Cargill, Magnus,	223	Coates, Benjamin,	240	Cushing, Benjamin,	240
Carlton, Francis,	154	Coates, William,	155	Cushing, D. C.	258

55

Cushing, T. P.	327	Duncan, James,	156	Fairly, John,	156
Cuthbert, James,	222	Duncan, James H.	273, 311	Fairly, Robert,	156
Cuttins, William,	222	Dunn, James,	155	Fales, Lothrop & Co.	327
Daniel, Edward,	160	Dunnell, Jacob,	332, 335	Fales, William,	328
Dansford, Samuel,	160	Dunnell, Jacob & Co.	326	Falkiner, Riggs,	154
Darby, George,	158	Dunnell, Thomas L.	94	Farley, Sarah,	160
Davies, John,	228	Dwight, Gamaliel L.	274	Farnum, John,	327
Davis, Evan,	159	Dwight, Capt. Gamaliel L.		Farwell, Levi,	86
Davis, Isaac,	86, 94, 311, 326		312	Farr, Thomas,	221
	332, 333	Dwyer, Matthew O.	154	Fawcett, John,	155
Davis, Isaac, of Boston,	87	Dyer, Benjamin and Charles,		Fawconer, Elizabeth,	159
Davis, John,	159		257	Fearing, Joseph W.	327
Davis, John C.	334	Dyer, Elisha,	86, 274, 289	Fearing & Hall,	327
Davis, Prudence,	158		292, 335	Fehrman, Gerard,	154
Davis, Samuel,	333	Earl, Caleb,	257	Fenner, John,	239
Dawson, Thomas,	161	Earle, George,	258	Ferguson, Frederic,	156
Day, Albert,	312	Earle, Henry,	274	Ferguson, Susanna,	156
Deane, John R.	334	Earle, Oliver,	258	Field Barnum,	328
Deaves, James,	157	Earle, William,	239	Field, James,	239
Dempsey, Edward,	221	Earle & Branch,	258	Field John,	238
Dendy, Stephen,	158	Easton, Nicholas,	319	Finch, Benjamin,	327
Dennis, John,	154	Edes, Henry,	258	First Baptist Church,	287
Devall, Stephen,	221	Eddy, Ezek,	238	Fisher, John D.	86
Devereaux, James,	222	Eddy, Moses,	257	Fitch, William,	223
Devroux, John,	154	Eddy, Richard,	240	Fitch, William, Jr.	223
Dewett, Charles,	228	Eddy, Samuel,	257	Fitz, E. C.	334
Dewett, William,	222	Eddy, Zachariah,	86	Fletcher, E. W.	327
Dewitt, Alexander,	327	Edmunds, George D.	334	Fletcher, Richard,	86, 327
Dewitt, William,	223	Edwards, Abel,	223	Fletcher, Thomas,	328
DeWolf, James F.	328	Edwards, E.	154	Flight, John,	158
DeWolf, John,	80	Edwards, James,	154	Flight, Joseph,	158
DeWolf, William B.	328	Edwards, John,	159	Flight, Thomas,	158
Dexter, Edward,	258	Edwards, Morgan,	147-171	Flight, Mrs.	158
Dexter, Knight,	239	Edwards, Samuel,	155	Flight, Miss,	158
Dexter, Samuel,	258	Edwards, Thomas,	223	Flight, Mr.	158
Dexter Stephen,	258	Edwards, William,	221	Foot, William,	159
Dickey, John,	222	Edwards, William, of Bristol,		Ford, D. S.	334
Dike, A. B.	327		160	Forsitt, Benjamin,	159
Dillon, Hugh,	223	Edye, John,	160	Foster, Benjamin,	73
Diman, Byron,	327	Elam, Samuel,	275	Foster, Samuel,	94, 335
Dixon, Phil.	157	Eldridge, Mr.	159	Foster, William,	94
Dixon, William,	154	Elliott, Barnard,	221	Fothergill, John,	158
Dobbin, William,	154	Elliott, John,	154	Foulce, Thomas,	157
Dodge, Nehemiah,	257	Elliott, Lemuel H.	274	Fowke, Joseph,	154
Dorr, Sullivan,	80, 86, 257	Ellis, James,	154	Fox, Joseph	77
Dorrance, John,	258	Elton, Romeo,	312	Fox, Mary,	161
Dorrance, William T.		Emerson, James,	154	Fox, Samuel,	161
	86, 94, 274, 327, 335	Emerson, William,	154	Francis, John,	73
Douglas, William,	328	Emly, Rev. Mr.	221	Francis, John B.	86, 327
Dow, William F.	328	Eustace, Thomas,	221	Francis, John W.	86
Down, James,	155	Evans, Caleb,	71, 159	Frampton, William,	160
Dozer, James,	223	Evans, Hugh,	159	Franklin, Benjamin,	158
Drennan, Thomas,	155	Evans, Thomas,	223	Franklin, Henry P.	258, 274
Drowne, Christopher R.	292	Evans, Thos., o. Bristol,	160	Franklin Society,	81
Drowne, George R.	292	Evans, Thomas E.	334	Freeman, Joseph,	161
Drowne, Henry B.	292	Eveleigh, George,	154	French, William S.	328
Drowne, Henry T.	292	Everard, John,	159	Frewen, Thomas,	161
Drowne, Thomas S.	292	Eyres, Thomas,	241	Frieze, Henry S.	328
Duncan, Alexander,	326	Fairbrother, Mrs. L.	312	Frink, Samuel,	222

INDEX OF BENEFACTORS. 335

Fritton, John,	240	Green, Cornelia E.	94, 312	Hart, Oliver,	317
Fullarton, John,	221	Green, John,	87, 327	Hartwell, John B.	322
Fuller, Abraham,	154	Green, Joseph,	160	Harvey, David,	156
Fuller, Joseph,	161	Green, Samuel,	222	Haslett, Charles,	156
Fuller, Major,	221	Greene, Caleb,	239	Hathaway, Elnathan P.	86
Fuller, Nathaniel,	223	Greene & Carter,	258	Hattersley, John,	159
Fuller, Oliver,	239	Greene, James,	240	Haughton, John,	155
Fury, John,	155	Greene, Nathanael,	239	Hawes, William T.	86
Gadsen, Christopher,	221	Greene, Richard W.	86, 273	Hawkins, Edward,	239
Gair, Thomas,	322	Greene, Simon H.	292	Hawksworth, A. R.	159
Gallup, A. S.	335	Greene, Thomas,	239	Hazard, I. P., R. G. & R.	327
Galt, John,	156	Greene, Timothy R.	86	Hazard, Thomas R,	327
Galt, William,	156	Griggs, Thomas,	334	Hazle, William,	160
Gammell, Asa M.	328	Grimball, Charles,	221	Hazard, William,	222
Gammell, William,	274, 327	Grimball, William,	222	Heath, Job,	159
Gano, John,	241, 317, 319	Grimes, Joseph,	160	Henderson, Anthony,	160
Gardner, Johnson,	328	Grinnell, Peter,	257	Hewetson, Hester,	155
Garner, Nathaniel,	155	Grinnell, Peter & Sons,		Heyward, Daniel,	222
Garner, Thomas,	155		273, 327	Hicks, George,	222
Garnsay, William,	160	Grinnell, William T.	86	Hidden, H. A.	335
General Assembly,	303–307	Grosvenor, William,	292	Higinbothom, Robert,	156
Gibbon, Rebecka,	155	Groth, A. H.	160	Hill, John,	156
Gibbons, Thomas,	158	Grubb, William,	155	Hill, Nathaniel P.	280
Gibbons, William,	222	Guertz, Miss,	159	Hill, Robert,	159
Gibbs, John,	240	Gully, William,	240	Hill, Samuel,	86
Gibson, George,	155	Gutter, Francis,	221	Hill, Thomas J.	327
Gibson, Gideon,	224	Guy, David,	160	Hillis, Timothy,	158
Gibson, William,	155	Habersham, James,	221	Hinds, James,	222
Gifford, Andrew,	158	Hacker, Joshua,	239	Hinds, Patrick,	221
Gilbert, Timothy,	87	Hadfield, Samuel,	156	Hincks, Edward,	155
Gill, John,	66, 158, 336	Haffield, Thomas,	155	Hitchcock, Enos,	78
Gilmore, John,	156	Hague, Jenkins,	161	Hitchcock, John,	224
Gladding, Timothy,	239	Hall, Edwin,	334	Hodsden, John,	221
Glenny, George,	156	Hall, Levi,	240	Hogg, William,	156
Glezen, E. K.	335	Hallett, George W.	326	Holden, Jonathan,	240
Glover, Henry R.	334	Hallowell, George A.	257	Holford, Thomas,	159
Goddard, Charlotte R.		Halsey, Elizabeth,	158	Hollis, Isaac,	159
	83, 289, 292, 326	Halsey, Thomas L.		Hollis, Thomas,	159
Goddard, T. P. I.	292		80, 94, 257, 273, 327	Holmany, John,	334
Goddard, William,	292	Hamill, James,	156	Holmes, George B.	327
Goddard, William G.		Hamman, John,	158	Holmes, John,	160
	86, 273, 335	Hamman, Jonathan,	240	Holmes, Joseph,	87
Godfrey, Richard,	240	Hammond, William,	154	Holmes, Rebekah,	221
Goodman, James,	155	Hancock, Jacob,	156	Holroyd, William,	257, 322
Goodwin, George C.	334	Hanna, John,	334	Homer, Jonathan,	81
Gough, Samuel,	155	Hardin, Eleazer & Son,	239	Hood, John,	156
Gowrlay, John,	222	Harford & Powell,	158	Hoope, Thomas,	156
Grace, Lawrence,	156	Harmon, Joshua,	154	Hopkins, John B.	239
Grace, William,	159	Harrington, William,	154	Hopkins, Rufus,	240
Graeme, David,	221	Harris, C. F.	292	Hoppin, Benjamin,	86, 257
Granger, Ann B.	313	Harris, David,	239		273, 289, 327
Granger, James N.	104, 327	Harris, Edward,	327, 332	Hoppin, George W.	258
Granger, Mr.	158	Harris, George,	160	Hoppin, John,	239
Grant, Luke,	154	Harris, John,	159	Hoppin, Thomas C.	258, 274
Graves, John,	66	Harris, Thomas,	240	Hoppin, Thomas F.	292
Grayson, Anthony,	155	Harrison, John,	222	Horton, Amos,	240
Great Britain,	81	Harrison, Richard,	160	Howard, Ezra W.	274, 327
Greggs & Cunningham,	155	Hart, Arthur,	223	Howard, Joseph,	223
Gregory, John,	222	Hart, Benjamin,	228	Howard, Robert,	161

Howarth, Robert,	221	Jenckes, Thomas A.		Ladson, I.		222
Howe, Mark A. D.	86, 328		292, 328, 335	Lahoe, John De,		221
Howell, Nicholas,	154	Jenkins, John,	222, 240	Lamboll, Thomas,		221
Howland, George,	326, 332	Jenkins, Joseph,	158	Lane, Abraham,		154
Howldy, Elizabeth,	160	Jenkins, Moses B,	292, 327	Lane, Samuel & Fraser,		158
Hoyle, James,	239	Jerman, Peter,	161	Lang, James,		155
Hoyt, Edwin,	327	Johnson, Dominick,	222	Langton, David,		158
Hughes, John L.	274	Johnson, James,	221	Larned, Daniel,		239
Humston, Hugh,	159	Johnson, William,	160	Larned, Samuel,		273
Hunt, George,	328	Jolleff, Dorcas,	160	Latham, John,		159
Hunt, Samuel,	94	Jones, Alexander,	257	Laughton, John,		221
Hunt, William,	155	Jones, Ann,	160	Laurens, Henry,		221
Hunter, Henry,	223	Jones, Daniel,	154	Lamb, Nathaniel,		154
Hunter, John,	156	Jones, David,	160	Lawrence, Abbott,		94
Huslet, Mrs.	159	Jones, Jenkin,	158	Lawrence, Alexander,		156
Hutchins, Shubael,	327	Jones, John B.	85	Lawrence, Amos,		327
Hutchinson, Matthias,	221	Jones, Noble W.	222	Lawrence, Samuel,		327
Ingraham, Samuel,	239	Jones, Thomas,	154, 222	Lawrence, Trimble & Co.		
Ives, Anne Allen,	83	Jones, William,	257			327
Ives, Harriet B.	83	Joseph, Israel,	221	Lawton, George,		312
Ives, Hope,	73, 83, 273, 326	Keach, W. W.	328	Lawton, William,		154
Ives, Moses B.	80, 85, 99	Keen, Robert,	158	Lazarus, Michael,		221
	100, 268, 273, 288, 323, 326	Keene, Henry,	159	Legacies & Bequests,		336
	331, 335	Keith, George,	158	Legare, Solomon,		222
Ives, Robert H.	80, 85, 268	Kelly, J. W. & Co.	86	Leger & Co.		221
	273, 276, 280, 288, 292, 312	Kelly, Mrs. Luke,	155	Legg, Alexander,		156
	326, 331, 333, 335	Kendall, Charles S.	333	Leiky, Thomas,		156
Ives, Thomas P.	80, 85, 94	Kendall, Henry L.	327	Leland, Ebenezer,		240
	257, 276, 326	Kendall, H. R.	327	Lemmon, John,		157
Ives, Capt. Thomas P.		Kent, Henry P.	312	Lemmon, Joseph,		156
	280, 292, 312, 332	Kershaw, Ely,	222	Lessene, Sarah,		221
Jacobs, Hiram,	87	Kershaw, Joseph,	223	Lewis, John Clarke,		156
Jacobs, Wilson,	238	Killingworth, Grantham,		Lewis, Michael,		157
Jackson, Daniel,	239		158	Lewis, Thomas,		160
Jackson, George,	257	Kimball, Amos,	240	Lide, Robert.		223
Jackson, Henry,	335, 336	Kimborough, John,	223	Lide, Thomas,		222
Jackson, Richard, Jr.	257	King, Abraham,	159	Lincoln, Heman,		86
Jackson, R.	158	King, Benjamin,	160	Lindo, Moses,		223
Jackson, Ward,	86	King, Charles,	289	Lindsey, Thos. & Benj.		239
Jackson, William,	155	King, Charles B.	288	Lippitt, Christopher,		240
Jaffray, Robert,	155	King, Edward,	327	Lippitt, Henry,		292
James, Benjamin,	223	King, George G.	327	Lippitt, H. & R.		328
James, Charles T.	327	King, Josiah,	240	Lippitt, Moses,	257,	258
James, Howell,	223	King, Thomas,	155	Little, Mrs. C. C.		293
James, Sarah,	222	Kingsbury, John, 86, 274, 327		Llewelyn, Thomas,		158
James, Thomas,	223	Kinlock, Mrs.	221	Lockwood, Moses B.		327
James, William,	223	Kinnicutt, Thomas, 86, 328		Logan, William,		238
Jeffries, Benjamin,	160	Kirkland, Joseph,	223	Longfray, Mr.		322
Jeffries, Ebenezer,	160	Kirkpatrick, James,	160	Loring, Prudence,		328
Jeffries, Edward,	158	Kitchen, Thomas,	159	Lothrop, Cyrus,		86
Jeffries, John,	87	Knap, Seth,	240	Loud, Jacob H.	87,	328
Jeffries, Joseph,	158, 160	Knight, Jabez C.	292, 332	Love, Horace T.		331
Jemmett, Isaac,	159	Knight, Nehemiah,	328	Lovett, James,		240
Jenckes, Christopher,	240	Knight, Richard,	238	Low, Charles,		258
Jenckes, Henry,	240	Knightly, Jane,	159	Lowdell, Stephen,		158
Jenckes, John,	238, 240	Knowland, Mrs.	156	Ludlow, Abraham,		159
Jenckes, Doct. John,	238	Knox, John,	156	Ludlow, Mrs. James,		293
Jenckes, Jonathan, Jr.	238	Kyle, Arthur,	156	Ludlow, Thomas,		159

INDEX OF BENEFACTORS. 437

LUDLOW, William,	159	McDOWELL, Samuel,	156	NORTH, James,	157
LUNNELL, William,	159	McGILVERY, Lachlan,	222	NORTH, Thurgood,	157
LYLE, Hugh,	156	McGOWAN, William,	155	NORTON, James,	160
LYNDON, Josias,	318, 319	McGREGOR, Robert,	155	NOYES, Samuel M.	328, 332
LYON, John,	154	M'INTIRE, A.	86	NUN, Benjamin,	155
LYON, Merrick,	328	McKACHAN, Alexander,	156	NUN, Joseph,	155
MABBS, J.	158	McKEAN, William,	156	OLDFIELD, John,	327
MACE, William,	158	McMASTER, Mary,	155	OLMSTEAD, J. W.	334
MACKAY, Nathaniel,	155	MEEK, John,	156	OLNEY, James,	239
MACKINTOSH, Alexander,	222	MEEK, William,	156	OLNEY, Jonathan & C.	239
MACKINTOSH, John,	223	MERRILL, J. Warren,	333	OLNEY, Nathaniel G.	258
MACKMERDS, Mrs.	158	MESSER, Asa,	250	ORR, Gilbert,	155
MACLAY, A.	86	METCALF, Nathaniel,	248	OSGOOD, Samuel,	103
MACOMBER, Ichabod,	86	METCALF, Theron,	81-83, 86	OSBURN, John,	154
MACTEN, William,	156	METCALF, Whiting,	328	OTWAY, Grace,	157
MAKEPEACE, George,	239	MIDDLETON, Nicholas,	157	OVERBURY, Jane,	161
MAN, Samuel F.	273	MILDRED & ROBERTS,	158	OVERBURY, John,	161
MANIGAULT, Gabriel,	221	MILLAR, William,	221	OVERBURY, Nathaniel,	161
MANIGAULT, Peter,	221	MILLER, Ann Eliza,	311	OVERBURY, William,	161
MANN, Benjamin,	239	MILLER, Pardon,	328	OWEN, Ezekiel,	328
MANN, James,	76	MILLS, John,	158	OWEN, George,	328
MANN, N. P., & Co.	334	MILLS, Stephen,	154	OWEN, Smith,	328
MANN, Percival,	159	MITCHELL, William,	156	PACKARD, Nathaniel,	240
MANNING, James,	319	MONTGOMERY, Hugh,	328	PADELFORD, Seth,	280, 292
MANNING, Robert,	160	MONTGOMERY, Robert,	155		327, 335
MANTON, Amasa,	94, 273, 326	MOODY, James,	156	PAGE, Benjamin,	155
MANTON, Daniel,	240	MOORE, John,	159	PAGE, George W.	257
MANYPENNY, James,	155	MOORE, Robert,	155	PAGE, John,	159, 160
MAQUAY, George,	155	MORGAN, John,	160	PAGE, Miss,	159
MARCHANT, Henry,	94	MORGAN, William,	223	PAINE, Daniel,	327
MARCY, William L.	86	MORRIS, John,	222	PAINE, Walter,	258
MARRION, Joseph,	223	MORRIS, William,	240	PARKER, John A.	326
MARSH, BOOTH & Co.	328	MOSSMAN, James,	222	PARKS, William,	154
MARTIN, James,	155	MOWRY, Elisha,	238	PARMENTER, Benjamin,	222
MARTIN, Joseph,	258	MUGGERIDGE, John,	159	PARMENTER, Isaac,	222
MARTIN, Joseph S.	258	MULLETT, Thomas,	70	PARMENTER, John,	222
MARTIN, Silvanus G.	328	MURRAY, James,	155	PARMESTER, Philemon,	222
MARTIN, Simeon,	258	MURPHY, Mary,	154	PARSLOW, John,	160
MARTIN, Wheeler,	258	NASH, Thomas,	158	PARSONS, Usher,	335
MASON, Amasa,	80, 86	NEAL, Jacob,	222	PARSONS, U. & C. W.	328
MASON, Earl P.	47, 280, 292	NEALE, Samuel,	154	PATRICK, Alexander,	156
	311, 326, 333, 334	NEEDHAM, John,	159	PATTEN, William,	258
MASON, James B.	257	NEWCOMEN, Thomas,	160	PATTEN, William S.	87
MASON, John H.	328	NEWELL, William,	155	PAYTON & HAWKINS,	328
MASON, John M.	335	NEWENHAM, George,	154	PEABODY, Ephraim,	239
MASON, Joseph,	159	NEWMAN, James,	160	PEARCE, Benoni,	238
MASON, Owen,	94, 328	NEWTH, Mary,	154	PEARCE, Edward,	327
MASON, William H.	258	NEWTON, Henry,	156	PEARCE, Nathaniel,	258
MATHEWS, James,	223	NEWTON, James,	159	PEARCE, William,	240
MAUNDER, Mary,	160	NIGHTINGALE, George C.	327	PEARSON, James,	158
MAURAN, Joseph,	86, 274, 328	NIGHTINGALE, Samuel, Jr.	239	PEASE, Simon,	319
MAXSON, John,	318, 319	NICHOLS, Thomas,	159	PECK, Allen,	240
MAXWELL, Richard,	155	NICHOLS, William,	87	PECK, Allen O.	274
MAYOR, Mrs.	159	NICHOLSON, Francis,	221	PECK, John,	239
McBURNEY, Alexander,	156	NOBLE, Ann,	159	PECK, Solomon,	86
McCALL, Charles,	223	NOBLE, Daniel,	158	PECKHAM, Sam'l W.	274, 328
McCARTHY, Francis,	154	NOBLE, Mrs.	160	PEGUES, Claudius,	222
McCORMICK, Samuel,	156	NORRIS, John,	328	PEGUES, William,	222

55†

438   BROWN UNIVERSITY.

Pelot, Francis,	317	Ramsey, Hugh,	154	Russell, George R.	326	
Pendarvis, Josiah,	222	Randall, George,	154	Russell, Jonathan,	257	
Penn, Thomas,	158	Randall Job,	239	Russell, Joseph D.	66	
Perkin, Lewis,	223	Randall, Peter,	240	Rutt, Henry,	159	
Perronneau, Alexander,	221	Ransford, Edward,	160	Ryland, John,	319	
Perry, Abel,	239	Ray, Isaac,	328	Sabin, James,	240	
Perry, Ann,	158	Read, Thomas,	155	Sabin, Thomas,	239	
Perry, Joseph,	158	Reeve, William,	159	Sackett, Davis & Potter,		328
Perry, Joseph, Jr.	158	Reily, Charles,	221			
Pervear, G. R. & H. A.	334	Reily, John,	155	Sampson, Joseph,	87	
Petty, John,	239	Remington, Joseph,	240	Sargeant, Joseph,	159	
Pewtress, Thomas,	158	Reynolds, William B.	86	Sargeant, Robert,	159	
Phillips, James,	221	Reynolds, William H.		Saurin, James,	155	
Philophysian Society,	81		47, 292, 295. 333	Savage, Daniel,	222	
Piety, Thomas,	161	Rhode Island,	303–307	Savage, John,	223	
Pike, Benjamin,	154	Rhodes, Christopher,	258	Sawyer, Joseph,	333	
Pike, Ebenezer,	154	Rhodes, James, 80, 257. 273		Sayles, Sylvanus,	240	
Pike, Jonathan,	327	Rhodes, Jas. T. 292, 327, 332		Scofield, T.	159	
Pilson, Susanna,	154	Rhodes, William,	157	Scott, Alexander,	158	
Pitcher, John,	239	Rice, Robert,	156	Scott, George,	156	
Pitman, Isaac,	258	Rich, Meredeth,	222	Scott, Jeremiah,	241	
Pitman, John,	86	Richard, Richard ap-	156	Scott, Thomas,	222	
Plater, Thomas,	161	Richards, James,	221	Scott, William,	156	
Plater, William,	161	Richards, Walter,	154	Screven, John,	223	
Pledger, Philip,	222	Richards. Wm. 78–80, 337		Screven, Thomas,	221	
Plimpton, Robert,	159	Richards, William C.	313	Seagrave, Jacob T.	335	
Poinsett, Elisha,	221	Richardson, Thomas,	326	Seamans, Young,	258	
Pollock, James,	156	Richmond, Sam'l N. 258, 274		Searle, Nathaniel, 80, 258		
Pollock, John,	156	Ridout, Jeremiah,	159	Searle, Nathaniel, Jr.	258	
Pomeroy, Bartholomew,	158	Riky, Robert,	155	Sears, Barnas, 310, 332, 333		
Pond, Joseph A.	334	Rippon, John,	75	Sears, David,	327	
Pond, Moses,	86	Ritto, Peter,	240	Sessions, Thomas,	258	
Poole, Mary,	160	Rivers, Isaac,	222	Sevier, Joseph,	160	
Pope, Joseph,	160	Rivers, John,	222	Shapland, Joseph,	160	
Pope, Richard,	154	Rivers, Thomas, Jr.	222	Sharp, Granville,	70	
Pope, Thomas,	160	Roach, Matthew,	222	Shaw, Francis v.	328	
Porter, Josiah,	154	Robarts, Edward,	158	Shaw, Robert G.	326	
Potter, Charles, 86, 327		Robarts, Joseph,	158	Shaw, Quincy A.	328	
Potter, E. R & J. B. M.	327	Robbins, Josiah,	87	Shaw, Thomas,	156	
Potter, William H.	327	Roberts, John,	160	Shearwood, J.	158	
Potts, John,	158	Roberts, Nathaniel,	161	Sheldon, Christopher,	211	
Pouney, Anthony,	223	Robinson, Luther,	328	Shenstone, John,	159	
Power, Nicholas, 238, 240, 258		Roffey, Samuel,	158	Shepard, Michael, 86, 91, 326		
Powell, Samuel,	155	Rogers, Benjamin,	222	Shepard, Thomas, 280, 327		
Pratt, Horatio,	86	Rogers, Daniel,	157	Shepard, Thomas & Co.	292	
Pratt, John C.	334	Rogers, Eliza B.	311, 327	Shepard, Abraham,	160	
Pratt, Peter, 86, 273		Rogers, Eliza J.	293	Sherman, George J.	313	
Presbyterian Churches,		Rogers, Henry A.	274, 327	Sherman, Robert,	221	
	155, 156	Rogers, John,	257	Shipley, S. G.	328	
Price, Hopkin,	221	Rogers, Robert,	258, 327	Shortt, James,	157	
Price, Thomas,	154	Rogers, Susanna,	160	Shortt, William,	157	
Prince, John,	75	Rolt, John,	154	Shurtleff, Benjamin,	86	
Providence Journal,	327	Rooke, Archibald,	161	Simon, Henry,	328	
Pugh, Evan,	223	Rose, Philip,	160	Simon, Isaac,	155	
Purser, Thomas,	86	Ross, Isaac,	223	Simmons, James F.	274	
Quested, George,	161	Rust, Richard,	159	Simmons, Martin,	239	
Rae, John,	222	Russel, Samuel,	223	Simmons & Co.	221	
Raines, Richard,	222	Russel, Mr.	161	Simpson, John K.	86	
Rains, James,	154	Russell, Charles,	86	Simpson, John K., Jr.	86	

INDEX OF BENEFACTORS.

Slater, Esther,	327
Slater, Horatio N.	47, 94, 273, 280, 289, 311, 326, 332, 333
Slater, Sarah J.	273
Slater, William S.	47, 333
Smith, Ann,	161
Smith, Amos D.	288, 292
Smith, A. D. & J. Y	280, 327
Smith, Amos D. & Co.	335
Smith, Henry,	222
Smith, Hezekiah,	211, 226, 318, 319, 322
Smith, J., of Barre,	328
Smith, James,	158
Smith, James Y.	260, 289, 292, 311, 327
Smith, Jehu,	240
Smith, Job,	289
Smith, John,	222, 241
Smith, John, Jr.	239
Smith, Joseph,	157
Smith, Josiah,	223
Smith, Samuel,	161
Smith, Simon,	239
Smith, William,	156
Snow, Lucy,	328
Snow, William,	258
Soesman, Jacob,	257
Spaulding, Edward,	239
Spence, John,	86
Spencer, William,	222, 240
Spooner, Joshua,	238
Sprague, A. & W.	292, 326, 332
Sprague, William,	94, 273
Sprague, William,	47, 292, 333, 335
Stakes, Nathaniel,	155
Stead, Thomas J.	273
Stead, William,	158
Stelle, Benjamin,	240
Stennett, Samuel,	67, 158
Stephens, Daniel,	223
Sterling, Henry,	240
Stery, Robert,	238
Stevens, John,	158
Stevelly, Robert,	154
Stewart, John,	155
Stewart, Thomas,	156
Stewart & Taylor,	239
Stiles, Mrs.	159
Stillman, Augustine,	223
Stillman, Samuel,	318
Stinton, Samuel,	158
Stirk, Benjamin,	222
Stirk, John,	222
Stites, John,	322
Stock, John,	159
Stocker, Charles S.	221
Stokes, Mary,	159
Stoll, Justinus,	221
Stone, William,	161
Stone, William L.	86
Stonehouse, Rev. Dr.	159
Stopkins, John,	222
Stout, Doctor,	221
Stower, Caleb,	161
Strapham, William,	159
Strettell, Thomas,	154
Strong, Richard,	160
Stych, John,	160
Subscriptions for the College,	337
Sullivan, John,	86
Sumter, Thomas,	223
Swint, John,	223
Taft, Cyrus,	280, 335
Taft, E. P.	334
Taft, Orray,	327
Taft, Royal C.	280, 335
Taft & Waterman,	258
Talbot, Charles N.	327
Talbot, Ephraim,	257
Tallmadge, James,	107, 337
Tallman, Benjamin,	241
Tanner, John,	70, 319
Tarrall, William,	223
Taylor, Gustavus,	257
Taylor, J. E.	334
Taylor, William,	158, 257
Tew, Paul,	241
Thayer, Abner,	239
Thayer, John E.	327
Thayer, James,	257
Theus, Jeremiah,	221
Thomas, Benjamin F.	020, 004
Thomas, John,	159
Thomas, Mary,	155
Thomas & Martin,	328
Thompson, Ebenezer,	240
Thompson, James,	156
Thompson, John,	156
Thompson, Sally,	328
Thompson, Thomas,	156
Thomson, Ebenezer,	258
Thomson, James,	156, 223
Thomson, Robert,	223
Thomson, Thomas,	257
Thornton, Daniel,	239
Thornton, John,	158
Thresher, Ebenezer,	86
Thurber, Charles,	312, 328
Thurber, Isaac,	328
Thurber, Samuel	239
Thurber & Cahoon,	239
Thurston, Gardner,	318, 319
Tiffany, Lyman,	273, 333
Tillinghast, John,	318, 319
Tillinghast, Joseph L.	86
Tillinghast, P.	328
Tillinghast, Stephen,	257
Tillinghast, Thomas,	258
Tinkham, H. N.	334
Tobey, Samuel B.	273, 327, 332
Tompkins, Benjamin,	161
Tompkins, William	161
Toomer, Henry,	222
Torrans, Paug, & Co.	223
Torrens, John,	156
Totterdale, Mrs.	160
Toulmin, Joshua,	160
Towle, Thomas,	158
Townsend, Stephen,	221
Trayer, Thomas R.	154
Treadway, T.	159
Tubbs, Rebeckah,	222
Tucker, Thomas,	221
Tuckerman, Edward,	86
Tufts, Otis,	328
Turner, David,	161
Twining, Thomas,	160
Tyndall, Samuel,	155
United States,	245
Upton, James,	333
Urmeneta, Don Geronimo,	108–109
Valentine, William,	258
Vance, Thomas,	155
Vanhorn, William,	322
Vaughan, Mr.	158
Vere, James,	158
Vickers, Jeremiah,	155
Vickers, Thomas,	155
Voysuy, John,	161
Wade, Thomas,	222
Walcutt, Abraham,	222
Walker, Ephraim,	239
Walker, John,	155
Walker, Susanna,	221
Wallace, Hans,	154
Wallin, Benjamin,	66, 322, 336
Wane, Isaac,	158
Wannell, Henry,	154
Wanton, Joseph,	238, 318, 319
Wanton, Joseph, Jr.	319
Ward, Elizabeth,	86
Ward, Hannah,	322, 336
Ward, John,	86, 160
Ward, Richard R.	86
Ward, Samuel,	85, 319
Ward, Samuel & Bro.	273
Warley, Milchar,	221
Warner & Tillinghast,	238
Waring, Benjamin,	221

WARREN, Charles H.	86
WARREN, George,	159
WARREN, Jonah G.	334
WASHBURN, Charles,	328
WASHBURN, Henry S.	328
WATCHMAN & REFLECTOR,	334
WATERFORD, Samuel,	160
WATERMAN, Andrew,	239
WATERMAN, Elizabeth,	274, 328
WATERMAN, Benjamin,	239
WATERMAN, John,	239
WATERMAN, Nathan,	241
WATERMAN, Resolved,	328
WATERMAN, Richard,	273, 327
WATERMAN, Rufus,	335
WATERMAN, Stephen,	328
WATERS, Ann E.	312
WATKINS, Lewis,	160
WATKINS, Nathaniel,	160
WATSON, Elisha,	328
WATSON, Matthew,	273, 327
WATSON, Thomas,	158
WATT, James,	156
WATTS, Jonathan,	159
WAVEL, Henry,	161
WAYLAND, Francis,	47, 85, 94, 273, 327
WAYLAND, Hepsey S.	81
WEARE, William,	158
WEBB, Thomas H.	103
WEBB, Thomas S.	258
WEEDEN, William B.	335
WELLS, John,	159
WELLING, Charles H.	328
WELSH, James,	222
WELTON, Samuel,	160
WEST, Benjamin,	158
WESTCOTT, John,	160
WESTON, Plowden,	222
WESTON, Thomas,	158
WEYMOUTH, Samuel,	160
WEYMOUTH, Master & Miss,	160
WHEATON, Comfort,	241
WHEATON, Ephraim,	239
WHEATON, James,	311
WHEATON, Martha B.	293
WHEATON, Samuel,	258
WHEATON, William,	238, 239
WHITE, Richard,	155
WHITE, Shuma,	156
WHITE & WATERMAN,	239
WHITEHEAD, Thomas,	161
WHIPPLE, Benjamin.	239, 240
WHIPPLE, Daniel,	240
WHIPPLE, David,	241
WHIPPLE, Jeremiah,	241
WHIPPLE, John,	273
WHIPPLE, Oliver,	238
WHIPPLE, Otis,	241
WHIPPLE, Phebe,	311
WHIPPLE, Stephen,	239
WHITMAN, Jacob,	240
WHITTUCK, Charles,	160
WHITTUCK, Joseph,	169
WIGGINS, Sarah,	159
WIGGINS, Thomas,	223
WILDER, Nahum,	241
WILKINS, William,	161
WILKINSON, Abraham,	155
WILKINSON, Anna,	157
WILKINSON, Elizabeth,	158
WILKINSON, George,	158
WILKINSON, Mary,	155
WILKINSON, Peter,	155
WILKINSON, William,	75, 257
WILLIAMS, Christopher,	239
WILLIAMS, David,	221
WILLIAMS, Henry,	159
WILLIAMS, John,	222
WILLIAMS, John,	159
WILLIAMS, Joshua,	160
WILLIAMS, Richard,	161
WILLIAMS, Samuel,	158
WILLIAMS, S.	159
WILLIAMS, Samuel K.	328
WILLIAMS, Simon,	67
WILLIAMS, Stephen,	158
WILLIAMS, Thomas,	222
WILLIAMSON, William,	156
WILSON, David,	156
WILSON, George,	155
WINSOR, Abraham,	240
WINSOR, Olney,	257
WINTHROP, John,	238
WINWOOD, John,	160
WISH, Benjamin,	221
WITTER, Matthew,	222
WOLLASTON, John,	158
WOOD, Joshua B.	258
WOOD, Margaret,	333
WOODROOF, Isaac,	241
WOODS, Alvah,	94, 311, 327
WOODS, Marshall,	326, 332, 336
WRAGG, Samuel,	222
WRAXALL, Nathaniel,	160
WRIGHT, James,	221
YEOMAN, Thomas,	159
YOUNG, Barnard,	221
YOUNG, George,	156
YOUNG, James,	155
YOUNG, John,	159
YOUNG, Mary,	239
YOUNG, Samuel,	239
YOUNG, Thomas,	221
ZUBLY, John J.	221

FINIS.

CORRIGENDA.

Page 42, line 2, note, for "Maxcy" read "Messer."
Page 100, line 18, for "Illustration" read "Illustrations."
Page 120, line 4, for "possibly" read "possible."
Page 278, lines 1 and 2, for "George" read "College."
Page 313, lines 4 and 5, for "L." read "J."
Page 313, line 12, for "his" read "hers."

SUBSCRIBERS.

LARGE PAPER.

JOHN R. BARTLETT, Providence.
JOHN C. BROWN, "
R. B. CHAMBERS, "
ALEXANDER FARNUM, "
DESMOND FITZGERALD, "

FRANCIS S. HOFFMAN, New York, N. Y.
A. V. JENCKES, Providence.
JAMES LENOX, New York, N. Y.
J. J. MEADER, Providence.
GEORGE T. PAINE, "

SMALL PAPER.

SETH ADAMS, Providence.
ETHAN ALLEN, New York, N. Y.
ZACHARIAH ALLEN, Providence.
HENRY B. ANTHONY, "
PROFESSOR APPLETON, Brown University.
SAMUEL G. ARNOLD, Providence.
RUFUS BABCOCK, New York, N. Y.
ORVILLE A. BARKER, Taunton, Mass.
S. B. BARTHOLOMEW, Worcester, Mass.
SAMUEL P. BATES, Harrisburg, Pa.
AMOS N. BECKWITH, Providence.
ETHELBERT R. BILLINGS, "
FRANCIS W. BIRD, East Walpole, Mass.
GEORGE D. BOARDMAN, Philadelphia, Pa.
JAMES G. BOLLES, Hartford, Ct.
TULLY D. BOWEN, Providence.
JAMES P. BOYCE, Greenville, S. C.
SHADRACH S. BRADFORD, Providence.
LEWIS H. BRADFORD, Fitchburg, Mass.
CHARLES S. BRADLEY, 3 copies, Providence.

JOHN S. BRAYTON, Fall River, Mass.
SAMUEL W. BRIDGHAM, New York, N. Y.
CHARLES H. BROWN, Philadelphia, Pa.
JOHN C. BROWN, Providence.
JOHN C. BROWN, 2d, "
EBENEZER BURGESS, Dedham, Mass.
AMBROSE E. BURNSIDE, Providence.
HENRY H. BURRINGTON, "
LYDIA CARPENTER, Pawtucket.
PROFESSOR CHACE, Brown University.
SAMUEL O. CHACE, Valley Falls.
ALEXANDER D. CHAPIN, Providence.
CHARLES H. CHILD, "
GEORGE W. CHIPMAN, Boston, Mass.
GEORGE L. CLAFLIN, Providence.
JOHN H. CLIFFORD, New Bedford, Mass.
GEORGE L. COLLINS, Providence.
EDWARD H. CUTLER, "
GEORGE W. CURTIS, New York, N. Y.
JOHN DAGGETT, Attleborough, Mass.

www.ingramcontent.com/pod-product-compliance
Lightning Source LLC
Chambersburg PA
CBHW022106300426
44117CB00007B/608